THE
SOCIAL WORK
DICTIONARY

The Social Work Dictionary

3rd Edition

by
Robert L. Barker

NASW PRESS

National Association of Social Workers
Washington, DC

Ann A. Abbott, PhD, ACSW, *President*
Sheldon R. Goldstein, ACSW, LISW, *Executive Director*

Linda Beebe, Executive Editor
Nancy Winchester, Director of Editorial Services
Christina A. Davis, Production Editor
Elizabeth Mitchell and Marina Rota, Copy Editors
Lynn Gemmell, Elizabeth Mitchell, and Catherine Siskos, Proofreaders

Library of Congress Cataloging-in-Publication Data

Barker, Robert L.
    The social work dictionary / by Robert L. Barker.—3rd ed.
      p.   cm.
    ISBN 0-87101-253-7 (acid-free paper)
    1. Social service—Dictionaries.   2. Social service—United States. I. Title.
    HV12.B37   1995
    361.3'03—dc20 95-3857

Printed in the United States of America

CONTENTS

EDITORIAL REVIEW BOARD

FOREWORD

One of the hallmarks of a profession is a unique body of knowledge, and most professions develop a distinctive vocabulary to describe the scope of their work and the knowledge they acquire. Social work has a particularly rich language. As a profession, we are concerned with individual people and the environmental factors, the societal supports and impediments that affect the quality of each individual's life. Consequently, our language is as complex and diverse as the people we serve.

Robert Barker has created the lexicon of social work, and it is a remarkable reference. Since the first edition was published in 1987, *The Social Work Dictionary* has become one of the most well-used, perhaps *the* most frequently used, reference work in social work. It is an essential reference for students not only because it gives them concise, accurate answers to specific questions, but also because it demonstrates the breadth and scope of the profession. Practitioners studying for licensing and credentialing exams find the dictionary a most useful text, and seasoned professionals use it as a reference to work outside their own specialties. Although the dictionary was created for social workers, we have found that other human services professionals and support personnel find it extraordinarily useful.

The third edition, which is double the size of the first, reflects the ongoing evolution of the professional language we use to describe our work, as well as the expansion of the boundaries of the practice of social work. Dr. Barker has added terms that are common to new arenas in social work, such as managed care, and he has built on the extensive list of international terms that appeared in previous editions. The reader will find definitions for terms that are new to the 4th edition of the *Diagnostic and Statistical Manual of Mental Disorders*. Besides refining and adding terms, Dr. Barker has included two new components in this third edition of *The Social Work Dictionary*. First, as a complement to the "Milestones," those major events that had relevance for social work, he has added brief biographies of people who had a major impact on the profession during their lifetimes. Second, he has incorporated knowledge from other cultures and professions that will enrich social work practice, but that social workers may not have easy access to in other references.

NASW is very pleased to publish this third edition. Once again we salute Dr. Barker for his exceptional scholarship and painstaking research. I hope that each reader finds the reference useful and stimulating.

Sheldon R. Goldstein, ACSW, LISW
Executive Director

PREFACE

The language of social work, like the profession itself, is growing and becoming more complex and refined. This is a positive trend, the result of both increased social work knowledge and the profession's desire to communicate with greater precision. It is also the product of closer relationships with other professions and segments of society, each of which has its own jargon and terminology.

Although the trend is positive, it presents a formidable challenge to social workers. To express themselves effectively and to comprehend the words of their colleagues and members of other professions, they have to be familiar with a growing and divergent body of complex terms. They also are expected to have ready access to a variety of resources, organizations, and services that can help meet the needs of their clients.

Another challenge to clear communication arises from the divergent specialties and conceptual orientations within the profession itself. For example, social workers who are policymakers or social advocates do not usually share identical vocabularies with their colleagues in clinical work. Even within a single social work practice specialty, there is risk of misunderstanding because of the many different theoretical perspectives in current use. Clinical social workers with psychodynamic orientations, for example, may have considerable difficulty interpreting the words used by their colleagues with behaviorist, psychosocial, systems, existential, or cognitive perspectives, and vice versa.

Although these trends increase the potential for communication problems, social workers face mounting pressure to minimize such difficulties. Legal actions and professional sanctions against professionals who misinterpret or improperly disseminate information are becoming more frequent. Society is more insistent in demanding that professionals prove they are competent and current. More than ever, this proof occurs through licensing and certification exams; to a great extent, passing these exams requires that the social worker understand the terms and concepts used in the profession.

It is in this context that *The Social Work Dictionary* was developed. Its aim is to give the social worker an abbreviated interpretation of the words, concepts, organizations, historical events, and values that are relevant to the profession. As such, it is designed to provide a concise overview of social work's terminology, not encyclopedic detail.

The terms defined here are used in social work administration, research, policy development, and planning; community organization; human growth and development; health and mental health; macro and micro social work; and clinical theory and practice. They are the terms that relate to social work's values and ethics and to its historical development. The terms are those that have developed within the profession as well as those that social workers have adopted for their own use from sociology, anthropology, medicine, law, psychology, and economics. The symptoms and diagnostic labels for various forms of mental disorders are defined as they are understood by social workers, psychiatrists, psychologists, and other mental health professionals. All the diagnostic terms and criteria found here are consistent with those in the *Diagnostic and Statistical Manual of Mental Disorders*, 4th ed.; the *International Classification of Diseases*, 10th ed.; and the *Person-In-Environment (PIE) System*. Many terms are derived from the theoretical orientations of psychodynamic, cognitive, behavioral, and existential, as well as systemic and linear, approaches. Also included are concepts in social work practice with individuals, groups, families, and communities.

The definitions include descriptions of some of the organizations, trends, people, philosophies, and legislation that have played major roles in the development of social work and social welfare. The appendix contains a chronology of the milestones in social work and social welfare, reproduces the *NASW Code of Ethics*, and delineates NASW chapter offices and state regulatory boards.

Some readers may find that one or more of their favorite terms have been excluded; others might question why some terms have been included. Sometimes a reader may have a different interpretation of the meaning of a term than that offered here. Naturally, it is hoped that any omissions, discrepancies, and errors are minimal. But in a dynamic field, populated by intelligent professionals with divergent views and experiences, it is inevitable that some discrepancies will occur. This dictionary does not purport to present all the words a social worker could ever use, nor does it provide "official" definitions of terms. The development of new knowledge and changing perspectives will necessitate commensurate revisions of *The Social Work Dictionary*.

As the author of this work, I assume full responsibility for the words that have been included and excluded, as well as for the way they are defined. I chose what terms to include by compiling a list of entries that have appeared in the indexes of the major social work journals and textbooks of the past two decades. The textbooks and journals I used were those in most general use in graduate and undergraduate schools of social work and in the larger social agencies. I also went through the indexes of the most important textbooks, journals, and manuals of disciplines that are related to social work. I presented the list to and received suggestions for additional terms from hundreds of my colleagues, students, members of related professions, and members of the editorial review board of this dictionary.

To define the terms, it was necessary to review how each word was used by several writers. As often as not there were slight differences in their interpretations of a given word. I tried to provide a definition that was closest to the majority view and to the mainstream of social work thinking. I also tried to make each definition original for this dictionary. No definitions have been deliberately quoted from any copyrighted sources.

Once my definitions were completed, they were examined by several hundred colleagues and students, mostly at The Catholic University of America in Washington, DC. Then they were submitted to the members of the dictionary's editorial review board, whose names and affiliations are on page vii. The members of this board were chosen for their considerable expertise in at least one area of social work knowledge or a related field such as medicine, law, administration, or economics. Members reviewed 50 to 100 of the definitions within their realm of expertise for accuracy, clarity, conciseness, and relevance of examples, and made many helpful suggestions.

The experts did not always agree with one another on how a term should be defined or on what parts of it should be emphasized, so compromises had to be made. Some reviewers believed certain words were offensive or outdated and recommended their exclusion. However, I chose to retain most of those terms that are still in common (if improper) use and to indicate why they are considered improper for use by competent professionals. This reflects my view that the purpose of a dictionary is to explain the meaning of terms, not judge whether people should use the terms or pretend they do not exist.

The first edition of *The Social Work Dictionary* was published early in 1987 and the second edition in 1991. Both editions were extremely well received. Colleagues from around the world expressed approval and indicated where the dictionary was being used—in schools of social work, in social agency libraries, in licensing exam preparation centers, and in the offices of experienced and novice social work practitioners.

As before, this third edition of *The Social Work Dictionary* uses the standard format for professional dictionaries and glossaries. The terms are listed in strict alphabetical order. Many terms are cross-referenced, and the words that appear in italics within definitions are themselves defined elsewhere in the dictionary.

The NASW Press and I plan to produce subsequent editions of *The Social Work Dictionary* every few years. Beginning with this edition, *The Social Work Dictionary* will be available in CD-ROM as well as in printed book form. Anyone who has suggestions, recommended changes, additions, deletions, or corrections is invited to write to me, in care of NASW. In this way the dictionary will remain a living, ever-improving document—the product of input from the widest possible range of social workers and members of related professions. I hope that this edition of *The Social Work Dictionary* will continue to be a useful tool for social workers in their efforts to communicate clearly and reach better professional understanding.

January 1995   Robert L. Barker

ACKNOWLEDGMENTS

Many people have made significant contributions to the development of *The Social Work Dictionary*. The members of the editorial review board were always supportive, generous in sharing their ideas and expertise, and prompt in responding to specific questions. The many baccalaureate, master's, and doctoral students at several schools of social work and universities reviewed terms to ensure that the definitions were clear and relevant to their needs. Staff members of the libraries at the National Association of Social Workers, Washington, DC; The Catholic University of America, Washington, DC; the University of Washington School of Social Work, Seattle; the National Library of Medicine, Bethesda, MD; and the Library of Congress, Washington, DC, were especially helpful. So too was staff at the National Association of Social Workers and the NASW Press. Jacqueline M. Atkins, Linda Beebe, Nancy A. Winchester, and Christina A. Davis managed the production of subsequent editions with remarkable competence. Susan H. Llewellyn, Laurel J. Rumpl, Marina Rota, and Elizabeth Mitchell were highly capable and diligent in their editing of the definitions. To all, I extend my deepest thanks.

— R. L. B.

A

AA   See *Alcoholics Anonymous (AA)*.

AAA   See *Area Agencies on Aging (AAA)*.

AAGW   See *American Association of Group Workers (AAGW)*.

AAHSW   See *American Association of Hospital Social Workers (AAHSW)*.

AAISW   See *American Association of Industrial Social Workers (AAISW)*.

AAMFT   See *American Association for Marriage and Family Therapy (AAMFT)*.

AAMR   See *American Association on Mental Retardation (AAMR)*.

AAMSW   American Association of Medical Social Workers. See *American Association of Hospital Social Workers (AAHSW)*.

AAPSW   See *American Association of Psychiatric Social Workers (AAPSW)*.

AARP   See *American Association of Retired Persons (AARP)*.

AASECT   See *American Association of Sex Educators, Counselors, and Therapists (AASECT)*.

AASSW   See *American Association of Schools of Social Work (AASSW)*.

AASSWB   See *American Association of State Social Work Boards (AASSWB)*.

AASW   1. See *American Association of Social Workers (AASW)*. 2. See *Asian American Social Workers (AASW)*.

AASWG   See *Association for the Advancement of Social Work with Groups (AASWG)*.

AB   See *Aid to the Blind (AB)*.

abandonment   Voluntarily giving up one's possessions, rights, or obligations with no intention of subsequently reclaiming them. In most jurisdictions, abandonment enables others to claim the surrendered property or rights. Abandonment of one's *family*, in most states, can be used as grounds for *divorce* or loss of *custody of children*, or both.

Abbott, Edith (1876–1957)   A pioneer in *social work education* and an advocate for *social justice* and *child welfare* programs. She was dean of the School of Social Service Administration at the University of Chicago, 1924–1942, a founder of *Social Service Review*, and author of several seminal social work texts. She also helped draft the *Social Security Act*.

Abbott, Grace (1878–1939)   A social work advocate for *child labor* laws and long-term director of the *Children's Bureau*, she organized one of the first *White House conferences* on children and was an adviser to President Woodrow Wilson.

abduct   To transport someone against that person's will often by force or *coercion*, or, if the person is a child, without the consent of the parent or legal guardian.

ABE   1. See *American Board of Examiners in Clinical Social Work (ABE)*. 2. See *Adult Basic Education program (ABE)*.

abet   To encourage someone to commit a *crime*. To "aid and abet" means that an individual encourages and actively facilitates the commission of a crime.

able-ism   Stereotyping and negative generalizing about people with disabilities.

abnormal   A term denoting atypical functioning that usually is seen as *maladaptive*. In social work, the term usually refers to *behavior* rather than a person. There is rarely a clear and consistent demarcation between *normal* and abnormal, but rather a continuum. In assessing whether a behavior is abnormal, social workers apply objective criteria such as those found in *DSM-IV* or the *Person-in-Environment System (PIE System)*. In a *pluralistic society,* behaviors of people in minority groups are more often defined as abnormal than those of the majority.

abortion   Termination of *pregnancy* before the *fetus* has developed enough to survive outside the woman's body. The term usually refers to a deliberate procedure to end the pregnancy. However, many pregnancies also are lost through natural or spontaneous abortions (miscarriages) in which the woman's body rejects the fetus. See also *Roe v. Wade, prochoice movement,* and *right-to-life movement.*

ABPN   See *American Board of Psychiatry and Neurology (ABPN).*

absolute confidentiality   A position held by some social workers and other professionals that no information about a client shall be disclosed to others, regardless of circumstances. The social worker who practices this position would not put the information obtained from a client into any written form—for example, a *case record* or a computer file—or discuss it with colleagues or supervisors. Most social workers believe that absolute confidentiality is impractical and that *relative confidentiality* is ethical and more productive.

absolute poverty   The possession of scant income and assets such that one cannot maintain a *subsistence level* of income. This is compared to *relative poverty,* in which one's standard of living is well beneath those of the mainstream community but still higher than the subsistence level.

abstinence   Voluntary *avoidance* of such physical activities as eating, consuming alcohol, taking drugs, or engaging in sexual intercourse.

abstract   A summary of a scholarly article. It usually appears immediately before the text in published articles and is often included in indexing and abstracting services (such as Social Work Abstracts and Psychological Abstracts) and in on-line databases (such as DIALOG and PsycINFO). Abstracts usually consist of a single paragraph of fewer than 200 words that outlines what the article is about, its key concepts, the method used to study the problem, and the conclusion reached.

abuse   Improper behavior intended to cause physical, psychological, or financial harm to an individual or group. See also *child abuse, drug abuse, elder abuse, spouse abuse,* and *substance abuse.*

academic skills disorder   The term formerly used by professionals for *learning disorder.*

academic underachievement   A longstanding pattern of poor performance in school, including substandard grades and minimal classroom participation relative to the student's intellectual and social skills. If the pattern is formally diagnosed, it is usually called *learning disorder.*

Academy of Certified Baccalaureate Social Workers (ACBSW)   A program established by the *National Association of Social Workers (NASW)* in 1991 to evaluate and certify the practice *competence* of baccalaureate social workers. Baccalaureate social workers are eligible for ACBSW if they obtain *BSW* degrees from accredited schools of social work, complete two years of fulltime or 3,000 hours of part-time postgraduate social work employment, agree to adhere to the *NASW Code of Ethics,* and complete a *certification* process that includes a written examination, supervisory evaluations, and professional references. NASW membership is not required for ACBSW certification.

Academy of Certified Social Workers (ACSW)   A program established by the

National Association of Social Workers (NASW) in 1962 to evaluate and certify the practice *competence* of individual social workers with advanced degrees. Social workers are eligible for ACSW membership if they have obtained an *MSW* or *DSW* or PhD (see *doctoral programs*) from an accredited school, have two years of supervised full-time or 3,000 hours of part-time practice experience, provide three professional references, and successfully pass the ACSW examination.

ACBSW See *Academy of Certified Baccalaureate Social Workers (ACBSW).*

acceptance Recognition of a person's positive worth as a human being without necessarily condoning the person's actions. In social work, it is considered one of the fundamental elements in the helping *relationship.* See also *unconditional positive regard.*

accessibility of service The relative opportunity for people in need to obtain relevant services. For example, a social agency with greater accessibility is located near its natural clientele; is open at convenient hours; maintains shorter waiting lists; has affordable fees; and has personnel, resources, settings, and policies that make clients feel welcome. Also, appropriate ramps and doors to permit entrance by people with disabilities are essential to an agency's accessibility.

accessory to a crime One who assists, advises, or commands another to commit an offense. An "accessory after the fact" is one who conceals or otherwise helps an offender avoid arrest or trial. An "accessory before the fact" is one who aids in the commission of a *crime* but is not present at the time of the act.

access provision The actions and procedures of a social program or service provider organization to ensure that its services are available to its target clientele. Three of these procedures are (1) educating the public about the existence of the service, its functions, and eligibility requirements; (2) establishing clear and convenient refer-

ral procedures; and (3) obtaining legal or *ombudsperson* services to overcome obstacles to getting the service. See also *information and referral service.*

"accident prone" A term applied to individuals who tend to become injured because of supposedly chance occurrences. Being accident prone is thought to be the result of personality factors.

acclimatization Biological and psychosocial adjustment to living in a new environment.

accommodation 1. In *community organization,* the ability of one group to modify aspects of its culture to deal better with other groups or aspects of the environment. 2. In *health care* and *geriatrics,* a property of visual perception in which the lens of the eye is able to change its shape to permit focusing on objects at different distances from the observer. 3. In developmental and *Piagetian theory,* a person's growing ability to modify current thought structure to deal with new or newly perceived features of the environment.

accountability 1. The state of being answerable to the community, to consumers of a product or service, or to supervisory groups such as a *board of directors.* 2. An obligation of a profession to reveal clearly what its functions and methods are and to provide assurances to clients that its practitioners meet specific standards of competence. See also *quality assurance.*

accreditation The acknowledgment and verification that an organization (such as an educational institution, social agency, hospital, or skilled-nursing facility) fulfills explicit specified standards. For example, schools of social work in the United States are evaluated periodically by the *Council on Social Work Education (CSWE)* and accredited if they meet CSWE standards.

accrual accounting In administration and management in the social services and other fields, an alternative to the cash accounting system. Each expenditure is recorded and considered a liability when the obligation is established rather than when the cash has been disbursed. Each item of revenue is recorded and considered an asset when the obligation has been incurred rather than when the actual cash has been received.

acculturation 1. The adoption by one cultural group or individual of the *culture* of another. 2. The process of *conditioning* an individual or group to the social patterns, *behavior, values,* and *mores* of others. See also *socialization.*

acetylcholine A biochemical that transmits information between nerve cells.

ACF See *Administration for Children and Families (ACF).*

achievement age A term used by psychologists, educators, and specialists in test scoring that refers to a student's acquired level of academic proficiency as indicated on educational *achievement tests.* Thus, a 14-year-old eighth grader who scores well on all parts of an achievement test might have an achievement age of 16, which corresponds to the 10th grade.

achievement tests Formal examinations that attempt to measure what one has learned. See also *aptitude tests.*

acid rain Precipitation in which the water is fouled by noxious chemicals, primarily sulfur dioxide and nitrogen oxides, mostly from automobiles and factories that burn *fossil fuels.* This rain pollutes lakes and rivers and damages buildings, crops, and forests, often far from the source of the chemicals. Efforts to minimize the problem emphasize cleaner and more-efficient fuel burning and chemically neutralizing the acid after it has entered the lakes and soil.

ACLU See *American Civil Liberties Union (ACLU).*

ACOAs See *adult children of alcoholics (ACOAs).*

ACORN See *Association of Community Organizations for Reform Now (ACORN).*

ACOSA See *Association of Community Organization and Social Administration (ACOSA).*

acquaintance rape Forced or coerced sexual intercourse by someone who is known to the victim. Typically, the victim is in some social encounter with the perpetrator such as a date or private meeting and is then manipulated into sexual intercourse through physical violence, restraint, threats, or power. The perpetrator ignores protests or interprets them as subtle encouragement. Often victims do not report the event, and frequently they or their assailants do not identify it as *rape.*

acquired immune deficiency syndrome (AIDS) A disease thought to always be fatal, caused by infection with *human immunodeficiency virus (HIV).* Many researchers now refer to this disease as *HIV disease* rather than AIDS. Following infection, symptoms include fever, night sweats, and swollen lymph nodes. This brief *acute* phase precedes the development of antibody responses (seroconversion), which usually takes place six to 12 weeks after infection. In the interval between infection and antibody response ("*window period*"), the individual is infectious, but the infection is not detected on antibody tests. Following the acute phase, there are four stages of the HIV disease continuum. Stage 1 lasts from a few months to many years, during which the infected person is mostly asymptomatic but infectious. Stage 2 symptoms include a range of mild infections, weight loss, and fatigue. Stage 3, formerly called "*AIDS-related complex*" *(ARC),* symptoms may include episodic occurrences of pulmonary tuberculosis, pneumonia, *Kaposi's sarcoma,* persistent fever, excessive weight loss, and other symptoms. In stage 4 the diagnosis of AIDS is made. The immune system is so severely suppressed that the body cannot defend against infection. Some drugs may play a role in slowing infection or in bolstering the immune system, but there is no cure for AIDS, and the body ultimately loses the capacity to defend itself against one or more fatal infections or conditions. People with AIDS often face *discrimination* and need health and social services ranging from pretest and posttest counseling, through assistance in applying for insurance or *social security* benefits, to *hospice care.*

acquittal The setting free or discharging from further legal prosecution for a charge of criminal misconduct. In a trial, the accused person is acquitted when the judge or jury renders a "not guilty" verdict.

acrophobia The pathological *fear* of high places or of being in the air.

ACSW See *Academy of Certified Social Workers (ACSW).*

acting out Expressing strong emotions through *overt behaviors* rather than words. When an individual's outward response to inner feelings is expressed in a disguised way to cover the emotion that cannot be revealed directly, the behavior is often destructive or *maladaptive.*

ACTION The federal government program established in 1971 as an umbrella organization that includes the *Peace Corps, Volunteers in Service to America (VISTA),* and *Foster Grandparents* programs and the *Office of Volunteer Action.*

action research In *social planning* and *community organization,* the linking of the data-gathering process with the development of a program designed to alleviate the problem that has been identified. *Mobilization for Youth* is one example.

action system The people and *resources* in the *community* with whom the social worker deals to achieve desired changes. For example, the action system for a client who is being evicted might include the other residents of the apartment building, local housing officials, and the media contacted by a social worker in an effort to change a landlord's policies.

action theory The group of concepts used by social scientists to understand social and personality systems by analyzing "acts" and the individuals who perform them, that is, the "actors." In assessing an act, the investigator considers the actor's values and goals in carrying out the act, as well as *overt*

behaviors. Action theory differs from classical *behaviorism* in that it emphasizes the value-motivated behavior of individuals and the subjective meanings attached to an action. *Behavior* is seen as occurring within culturally defined situations and relationships and includes the actor's internalized values and expectations of the reactions of others.

action therapy Treatment procedures and intervention strategies based on direct alterations of behaviors or of obstacles to change. Such therapies include *behavior modification,* some *cognitive therapy* methods, and *experiential therapy.* The term "action therapy" is often used to make a distinction from so-called *informational therapy,* which is oriented toward helping clients gain insight and other forms of self-awareness that foster changes indirectly.

activism Planned behavior designed to achieve social or political objectives through such activities as *consciousness-raising,* developing a *coalition,* leading *voter registration drives* and political campaigns, producing *propaganda* and publicity, and taking other actions to influence *social change.* See also *political activism.*

activist An individual who works to bring about *social change.*

activist role In social work, a rejection of the so-called objective, neutral, or passive stance in favor of taking specific actions in behalf of the *client system.* These actions may include engaging in overt *side-taking,* making specific recommendations to clients, leading campaigns to change a *social institution,* or exerting an influence on client *values.*

activities of daily living (ADL) The performance of basic self- and family-care responsibilities necessary for *independent living.* Such activities include meal preparation, bathing, dressing, shopping, cleaning, handling financial matters, light home maintenance, and household chores. The degree of ADL performance is considered by social workers in determining the type of *needs* clients have.

activity catharsis A psychotherapeutic procedure in which the client portrays *anxiety* and the effects of *unconscious* material through actions rather than words. The procedure is used primarily in *group psychotherapy.*

activity group A form of *group* involvement, which may or may not have a specifically designed therapeutic purpose, in which the participants work on programs of mutual interest. The members engage in activities as diverse as cooking, folksinging, carpentry, or crafts. Historically, activity groups were prevalent in early *social group work,* especially in *settlement houses* and *youth services organizations.* Their primary orientation was not therapeutic per se but was a means for learning *social skills,* engaging in democratic decision making, and developing effective relationship capacities. More recently, activity groups are found in nursing homes, mental hospitals, and recreation centers.

acute 1. Intense conditions or disturbances of relatively short duration. For example, a *mental disorder* lasting fewer than six months often is considered to be acute, and that lasting more than six months is considered *chronic.* 2. The relatively sudden onset of a condition.

acute brain syndrome A state of confusion, known as *delirium,* often accompanied by *delusion, anxiety,* and *emotional lability.* The disorder lasts fewer than six months, usually is reversible, and is caused by changes in cerebral metabolism typically induced by *drug abuse, shock,* or fever. The term is now rarely used.

acute care A set of health, personal, or *social services* delivered to individuals who require short-term assistance. Such care usually is provided in the community in hospitals or social agencies in which the extended treatment that exists in *long-term care* is not expected.

acute paranoid disorder One of the types of *paranoid disorders* in which symptoms have occurred for fewer than six months. The condition is most common in people who suddenly encounter severe crises and usually subsides after a period of *adaptation.* See also *delusional (paranoid) disorder.*

acute stress disorder An *anxiety disorder* that occurs within a month of encountering a distressing situation and results in recurrent thoughts, dreams, flashbacks, and upset when reminded of the *stressor.* The person develops *anxiety symptoms* (such as sleeplessness, poor concentration, restlessness, exaggerated startle response) and *dissociative symptoms* (such as numbing and emotional detachment, feeling dazed, *depersonalization, derealization,* and inability to remember aspects of the trauma). If the symptoms persist, the diagnosis becomes *posttraumatic stress disorder (PTSD).*

ACYF See *Administration on Children, Youth, and Families (ACYF).*

adaptation The active efforts of individuals and species over their life spans to survive, develop, and reproduce by achieving *goodness of fit* with their environments. Adaptation is also a reciprocal process between the individual and the environment, often involving changing the *environment* or being changed by it. Social workers oriented to *systems theories* consider that helping people move through stressful life transitions by strengthening or supporting their adaptive capacities is a central part of their *intervention* strategies. See also *environmental treatment, direct treatment,* and *indirect treatment.*

adaptedness A relationship between an organism and its environment in which the *goodness of fit* supports the needs of both. Adaptedness is a state, and *adaptation* is a process by which adaptedness is achieved.

adaptive spiral In *social group work* and *group psychotherapy,* the successfully integrated, healthy progression of the client from interpersonal distortions and its resulting anxiety and social inhibition to the formation of rewarding relationships within the group and then outside. As the client's interpersonal relationships on the outside become healthier, the relationships within the group become healthier, too.

Addams, Jane (1860–1935) Considered one of the founders of *social work*, she was a community organizer, peace *activist*, and leader of the *settlement house* movement. With *Ellen Gates Starr*, she founded *Hull House* in Chicago, which became a prototype for other such facilities. She advocated for honest government, world peace, U.S. membership in the League of Nations and the World Court, and was co-recipient of the Nobel Peace Prize in 1931. She and *Lillian Wald* are the two social workers to be named to the Hall of Fame of Great Americans.

addiction Physiological and psychological dependence on a chemical that results in increased *tolerance* and in *withdrawal symptoms* when the substance is unavailable. Addictive substances include alcohol, tobacco, *narcotics*, and many *sedatives*. Most professionals now use the term *substance dependence*.

additive effect The impact on a substance abuser of two or more drugs, which taken simultaneously result in greater or different responses than if taken separately.

additive empathy The interviewer's process of drawing out the inner and more-hidden feelings of the client with some mild to moderate *interpretation* and questions about underlying emotions and experiences (for example, "Perhaps you're feeling this way because. . . ."). According to Dean H. Hepworth and Jo Ann Larsen (*Direct Social Work Practice: Theory and Skills*, 2nd ed., Chicago: Dorsey Press, 1990, p. 461), additive empathy should be used sparingly until a sound social worker–client *relationship* is established, and only when clients are engaged in self-exploration. Additive empathy responses should be made only in relation to the client's current awareness and experience and should be presented tentatively rather than authoritatively. To minimize client resistance, the social work interviewer should avoid making several additive empathic responses in succession and should be

ready to retreat or acknowledge error if the client indicates a need to avoid the information.

ADEA See *Age Discrimination in Employment Act (ADEA)*.

ADHD See *attention-deficit hyperactivity disorder (ADHD)*.

adhesion Physiologically, the attachment or growth together of body tissues or other substances, sometimes causing organs to be abnormally connected.

ad hoc coalition An alliance of individuals and ideological groups to achieve a specific goal or address a single issue or social problem. The group is expected to disband once the goals are reached.

adhocracy A type of administrative organization characterized by minimization of personnel hierarchies, theoretically designed to achieve greater program flexibility; in social agencies, an alternative to *bureaucracy*.

adjudication 1. In law, a court decision and the process of reaching that decision through a trial or legal hearing. 2. In a professional organization, the process of determining whether a professional action is in violation of the *code of ethics* or *personnel standards*.

adjustment The activities exerted by an individual to satisfy a need or overcome an obstacle to return to a harmonious fit with the environment. These activities may become habitual responses. Successful adjustment results in *adaptation;* unsuccessful adaptation is called *maladjustment*.

ADL See *activities of daily living (ADL)*.

Adlerian theory The concepts about human personality characteristics and *psychosocial therapy* developed by Austrian psychiatrist Alfred Adler (1870–1937). He hypothesized that humans have an inherent drive for power and strive from feeling inferior toward superiority and perfection. The individual does this through one's lifestyle. People achieve goals by developing their social interests, and healthy people ultimately learn to place the good of society over immediate personal gain.

Administration for Children and Families (ACF) An organization within the U.S. *Department of Health and Human Services (HHS)*, created in 1986 through a consolidation of federal programs to aid low-income families. The six major programs included in ACF are *Aid to Families with Dependent Children (AFDC)*, the *Work Incentive program (WIN)*, the *Community Services Block Grant Program*, the Low-Income Home Energy Assistance program, the *Refugee Assistance program*, and the U.S. *Office of Child Support Enforcement*. ACF is one of the major units of HHS, which also includes the *Health Care Financing Administration (HCFA)*, the *Office of Human Development Services (OHDS)*, the U.S. *Public Health Service*, and the *Social Security Administration (SSA)*.

Administration for Native Americans The organization within the *Office of Human Development Services (OHDS)* of the U.S. *Department of Health and Human Services (HHS)* whose responsibilities are to ensure that *American Indians* and *Alaska Natives* have the same access to the nation's health care and welfare provisions as do all other Americans and that their unique needs are addressed. The functions of the administration complement those of the *Bureau of Indian Affairs (BIA)* within the U.S. *Department of the Interior*.

administration in social work Methods used by those who have administrative responsibility to determine organizational goals for a *social agency* or other unit; acquire resources and allocate them to carry out a program; coordinate activities toward achieving selected goals; and monitor, assess, and make necessary changes in processes and structure to improve effectiveness and efficiency. In social work, the term is often used synonomously with management. For social work administrators, implementation of administrative methods is informed by professional values and ethics with the expectation that these methods will enable so-

cial workers to provide effective and humane services to clients. The term also applies to the activities performed in a *social agency* that contribute to transforming *social policy* into *social services*. See also *management tasks*.

Administration on Aging The organization within the *Office of Human Development Services (OHDS)* of the U.S. *Department of Health and Human Services (HHS)* that oversees and facilitates the nation's programs for *older people*. The organization monitors the overall condition of older Americans, facilitates research, helps develop legislation, disseminates relevant information, and coordinates programs designed to foster the well-being of older Americans. See also *Older Americans Act*.

Administration on Children, Youth, and Families (ACYF) The federal organization within the *Office of Human Development Services (OHDS)* of the U.S. *Department of Health and Human Services (HHS)* that facilitates programs that provide social services to families, including *day care, adoption,* and *foster care* for children, particularly young *special-needs clients*.

admissions The department or unit of a health, mental health, or *social services* agency responsible for administering the procedures by which patients or clients enter the program.

admissions procedures The explicit rules and modes of action for bringing an individual under the care of an organization, *social agency,* or *health care facility*. Such procedures often include getting consent from the client (or those responsible for the client) to provide the appropriate care; obtaining pertinent background information about the client from a variety of sources (that is, interviews with the client or client's family, medical records, social histories, and medical and psychological tests); contracting with the client or third parties to provide financing for the care; advising the client about when to go to the appropriate place; and coordinating the initial information exchanges between the client and those concerned about the client. Admissions procedures often include criteria for screening applicants for the service.

adolescence The *life cycle* period between *childhood* and *adulthood*, beginning at *puberty* and ending with young adulthood. Adolescents struggle to find self-identity, and this struggle is often accompanied by erratic behavior.

adoption Taking a person, usually an infant or child, permanently into one's home and treating the child as though born into the *family*. A legal as well as a *child welfare* function and process, adoption includes changes in court records to show the legal transfer of the individual from the *birth parents* to the adopting parents. Adoption usually gives the individual the same rights of inheritance as birth children, and the adoptive parents the same responsibilities and rights of control as birth parents. See also *subsidized adoption, independent adoption, gray-market adoption, black-market adoption,* and *intercountry adoption.*

adrenaline A hormone secreted by the adrenal glands that mobilizes the body to meet perceived emergency or stressful situations. Adrenaline acts to release sugars from the liver and increase blood volume in the muscles to increase strength, stimulate the heart beat, increase mental alertness, and generally prepare the body for extraordinary activity.

ADS See *alternative delivery systems (ADS).*

adult An individual who has reached the legal age of maturity; in most nations and states this age is 18.

adult antisocial behavior An enduring pattern of criminal conduct and other acts that are counterproductive to social *norms* in a person whose behavior cannot be attributed to a specific and diagnosable *mental disorder.* This label is often applied to professional thieves, drug dealers, organized crime figures, and white-collar criminals.

Adult Basic Education program (ABE) Tutoring and classroom teaching programs for adults with educational deficiencies, sponsored by the U.S. *Department of Education;* also referred to as ABE–OE programs.

adult children of alcoholics (ACOAs) People who have been raised in the stressful environments created by parents who abused alcohol or other substances. Many ACOAs share similar emotional disorders, including *anxiety, depression,* low *self-esteem, anger,* and their own predisposition toward *alcohol abuse* and *substance abuse.* Many ACOAs have found comfort in *self-help groups* or a *support group* that exists for them. See also *support system* and *codependency.*

adult day care Programs that provide personal, social, and homemaker services to adults who are unable to care for themselves when their primary guardians are unavailable. Those most likely to require such care are people with physical and mental disabilities whose caregivers must be away every day for extended periods. Such care may be provided in private homes, nursing homes, and other facilities.

adult day center Publicly or sometimes privately funded facilities in which seniors or other adults gather to participate in recreational, social, educational, and developmental programs. Such facilities often are used by independently functioning seniors as well as by the clients of *adult day care.*

adult development Normal changes that occur in the individual from maturity to *death.* These include the physical, cognitive, social, emotional, and personality changes that occur after *adolescence.*

adult education The process—with people who are beyond the age of general public education—of acquiring and imparting knowledge, skills, and values. Adult education programs have been used to eliminate *illiteracy,* improve vocational and economic opportunities, and enhance human potential. The Adult Education Association of the United States sponsors research, issues publications, and maintains standards for those who provide such services.

adult foster care Residential care programs in the private homes of nonrelatives provided for *adults* who cannot live independently, including some people with a *mental disorder,* or *mental retardation,* and *frail elderly* people. Caregivers usually provide room and board and assistance in *activities of daily living (ADL)* in family-like environments, in exchange for a monthly payment, under the supervision of human services professionals. The professionals, who are employed by such organizations as the U.S. Department of Veterans Affairs or local social services agencies, find these homes, match them with appropriate adults in need, and provide ongoing counseling and needed health and community resources.

adulthood The *life cycle* stage in *human development* that begins at maturity and ends at *death.* Social scientists often divide adulthood into several periods, such as early adulthood (18 to 44 years); middle adulthood (45 to 64 years); and late adulthood (65 years to death). In legal terms, in most jurisdictions, adulthood is generally considered to begin at age 18.

adultified child A youth who, because of the family's *relationship* patterns, *psychopathology,* or socioeconomic circumstances, is compelled to assume roles and responsibilities normally reserved for older people. An example is a child who is a primary *caregiver* for younger siblings as well as meal preparer, housekeeper, and major emotional source of support for a single, working parent.

adult learner model An educational ideology that recognizes students as being responsible, self-directing, and motivated to learn and share from their accumulated life experiences. This model views adult learning as being more effective when students experience direct and relevant application of their developing problem-solving skills. This is the model of education in professional schools of social work. See also *andragogy.*

adult protective services (APS) *Human services* often including social, medical, legal, residential, and *custodial care* that may be provided for adults who are unable to provide such care for themselves or who do not have a *significant other* who might provide it. Such people often are incapable of acting judiciously on their own behalf and, thus, are vulnerable to being harmed by or to inflicting harm on others. In such situations, and typically after a legal decision has been made, the *social agency* or other care facility provides the relevant service until it is no longer deemed necessary. The 1975 *Title XX* legislation mandated that APS be provided without regard to a person's financial or residency eligibility.

advance directive A properly witnessed and documented statement that describes in detail the medical measures a person would or would not want used to prolong life when one is no longer able to make such measures known. The document may also name someone who could make such decisions for the individual. See also *living will.*

adventitious disability A condition acquired later in life, such as those caused by accident or disease rather than *congenital abnormalities* or *developmental disabilities.* A major cause of adventitious disabilities is *child abuse,* and hearing impairment is one of the more-common permanent disabilities resulting from child abuse.

adversarial process A procedure for reaching decisions by hearing and evaluating the presentation of opposing viewpoints. The adversarial process is most notably seen in courts of *law,* in which opposing attorneys present evidence and arguments in support of their respective views or clients. See also *arbitration* and *mediation.*

advice giving An *intervention* in social work in which the social worker helps the client to recognize and understand the existence of a problem or goal and to consider the various responses that might be made to deal with it. The social worker then recommends the best strategies to accomplish the objectives.

advisory board A committee that provides needed information, *expert opinion,* and recommendations about how to achieve an organization's goals, often according to predetermined criteria. Members of the advisory board are consulted for their expertise as a group or as individuals. Members may be elected, hired, or recruited as volunteers and may or may not include the organization's *board of directors.*

advocacy 1. The act of directly representing or defending others. 2. In social work, championing the rights of individuals or communities through direct intervention or through *empowerment.* According to the *NASW Code of Ethics,* it is a basic obligation of the profession and its members.

advocacy research Systematic investigation of specific social problems and objective measurement of their extent, progression, and response to corrective actions. This type of research also heightens public awareness of the social problems and recommends possible solutions.

AFDC See *Aid to Families with Dependent Children (AFDC).*

AFDC–EA programs The emergency assistance provision of the *Aid to Families with Dependent Children (AFDC)* program, designed to help such families meet their costs of temporary, unexpected needs such as natural disasters, extraordinary home-heating costs, and utility cutoffs. The programs are 50 percent funded by the federal government and the balance by state and local governments. Most counties that administer these funds give AFDC–EA recipients vouchers rather than cash or pay the vendors directly.

AFDC–UP See *Unemployed Parent Program of AFDC (AFDC–UP).*

affect An individual's expression of *mood, temperament,* and feelings; an individual's overt emotional state.

affective congruency Feelings that are consistent with those of most other people about the same thing. For example, a social worker who is distressed at seeing an abused child has affective congruency with most other people.

affective disorder Emotional disturbances characterized primarily by chronic or episodic changes of *mood,* such as *depression, euphoria,* or *mania.* This term has been replaced by the term *mood disorder.*

affiliation 1. An ongoing explicit relationship or association. 2. A coping strategy of dealing with emotional conflict or stress by turning to others for help and support and mutual problem solving.

affirmative action 1. Positive steps taken by an organization to remedy imbalances in the employment of people of color and women, promotions, and other opportunities. 2. Measures designed to change the employee ratio in an organization of people of color to white people and women to men.

AFGE See *American Federation of Government Employees (AFGE).*

AFL–CIO See *American Federation of Labor–Congress of Industrial Organizations (AFL–CIO).*

African American A term used by some people in referring to black residents of the United States who came from, or whose ancestors came from, Africa. This term is generally preferred over the term "Afro American." See also *black people.*

AFSCME See *American Federation of State, County, and Municipal Employees (AFSCME).*

AFTA See *American Family Therapy Association (AFTA).*

aftercare The continuing treatment, physical maintenance, and social support of formerly hospitalized or institutionalized clients during extended convalescence or social transition back to the community. See also *halfway houses* and *quarterway houses.*

aftercare, juvenile In judicial terminology, the status of a juvenile who has been conditionally released from incarceration as a result of delinquency and placed in a supervised treatment or rehabilitation program while living at home, in foster placement, or in a transitional living facility. The system is also known as *juvenile parole.*

age at onset The point in one's life when a specific disorder or problem started.

aged One term for older people. In the United States, this term is generally applied to people who have reached at least age 65. Developmental psychologists identify three groups of the aged population: (1) the "young old" (age 60 to 64), (2) the "middle old" (age 65 to 74), and (3) the "old old" (older than age 74).

age discrimination Unfair treatment of people on the basis of their ages. When these people are employees, the employer is breaking U.S. federal law (the *Age Discrimination in Employment Act [ADEA] of 1967*).

Age Discrimination in Employment Act (ADEA) of 1967 A U.S. federal law that prohibits employers with 20 or more employees from discriminating against people older than age 40. The law is enforced by the *Equal Employment Opportunity Commission (EEOC)* and explicitly forbids *age discrimination* in hiring, discharge, pay, promotions, and other aspects of employment. See also *mandatory retirement.*

age integration Bringing together people of different generations. The current trend is toward de facto *age segregation,* manifested in communities—for example, residential buildings, neighborhoods, and even cities that are restricted to people older than a certain age. There have been many negative consequences of this, for young as well as older people. Thus, some programs, facilities, and social causes are designed to combine the needs of people of all ages to encourage their interaction and mutual benefit.

ageism Stereotyping and generalizing about people on the basis of their ages; commonly, a form of *discrimination* against older people. This term is also spelled "agism." See also *gerontophobia.*

agency See *social agency.*

Agency for International Development (AID) The U.S. government program, created in 1961 by a consolidation of other international *relief* organizations, that administers and coordinates economic and *social welfare* assistance to other nations.

Agent Orange A herbicide used most notably in the Vietnam War to defoliate areas where enemy troops were thought to be hiding. Some veterans have claimed that their exposure to this dioxin resulted in their subsequent contracting of various diseases, including *cancer.*

age of consent The legal age, established by statute in the relevant jurisdiction, at which time an individual is permitted to marry without parental approval, enter into business contracts, or engage in sexual relations of his or her own volition. Engaging in sexual relations with one who is younger than the age of consent can result in criminal charges and conviction of the older person for *statutory rape.* An erroneous belief that the younger person was of the age of consent usually is not a sustainable defense against these charges.

age-related cognitive decline The diminished capacities in thought processes, such as memory and problem solving, within the normal limits of aging.

age segregation Isolating people from one another based on their ages. This may occur as a result of *ageism,* personal preferences, social convenience, or the necessity of providing different services to people with different needs and lifestyles. Examples occur in *gray ghettos,* in public elementary schools, and in retirement. When a community or society discourages this type of segregation, it is seeking a high degree of *age integration.*

aggravated assault A severe or intensified form of *assault* involving an attack or threat with a dangerous weapon.

aggression *Behavior* characterized by forceful contact and communication with other people. Human aggression is most directly observable in such expressions as verbal or physical attacks and indirectly through competition, athletic endeavors, and similar activities. Aggression may be appropriate and used for self-defense or self-enhancement, or it may be destructive to oneself and others. Some social scientists use the term "aggression" to refer only to harmful behaviors and the term *assertiveness* for behavior that is not intended to harm others.

"aging out"   The informal term used for status changes among young people who outgrow their qualification as dependents while in the responsibility of the health care and welfare system, such as foster care, juvenile detention facilities, or educational facilities. Often when such youngsters are *runaway* children or kidnap victims or are moving from one foster care facility to another, they "age out" and get lost. They still exist but are no longer counted, sought, or served when located and are extremely vulnerable to exploitation.

agitation   The organized effort to produce discomfort with the status quo to win popular support for some *social change*.

agitator   In *community organization*, a role in which an individual or group confronts and challenges existing social structures by such means as publicity, public debate, and *voter registration drives* and by organizing active and *passive resistance* campaigns. The goal of the agitator is usually to create new institutions or to change the ways in which established ones operate.

agnosia   The inability to comprehend familiar objects that are being perceived by the sense organs. This may be a partial or total inability to attach meaning to the input from one or more of the five senses. For example, in visual agnosia, the individual takes in all the normal light sensations in the visual field but cannot decipher or process this information to recognize or interpret what is being seen. This condition is often the result of brain damage, especially to the cortex, often the result of *stroke*.

agoraphobia   An irrational and persistent *fear* of being in unfamiliar places or of leaving one's home. Most people with this condition make special efforts to avoid crowded rooms, public transportation facilities, tunnels, and other environments from which escape seems difficult and where help is unavailable. Agoraphobia often accompanies *panic disorder*.

agraphia   See *dysgraphia*.

AHA   See *American Hospital Association (AHA)*.

AICP   See *Association for Improving the Condition of the Poor (AICP)*.

AID   See *Agency for International Development (AID)*.

AIDS   See *acquired immune deficiency syndrome (AIDS)*.

AIDS dementia complex   Impairment of cognitive functioning due to infections of the *central nervous system (CNS)* related to the *human immunodeficiency virus (HIV)*. As with other CNS disorders, the symptoms vary from day to day but at worst includes *grandiosity*, poor impulse control, aimless wandering, memory loss, and disorientation.

"AIDS-related complex" (ARC)   An imprecise term referring to the signs and symptoms that occur during the progression from *human immunodeficiency virus (HIV)* infection to *acquired immune deficiency syndrome (AIDS)*. These symptoms include diarrhea, weight loss, fever, headaches, bruising, bleeding, oral thrush, stomachache, fatigue, disease of the lymph glands, and neurological changes. According to Gary A. Lloyd ("AIDS and HIV: The Syndrome and the Virus," in *Encyclopedia of Social Work*, 18th ed., 1990 Supplement, Silver Spring, MD: NASW Press, 1990, p. 27), the progression from infection to the final stages of AIDS may take from a few months to many years, and the symptoms attributed to ARC appear during that time. Thus, although ARC once was thought to be a discrete stage in the progression of AIDS, researchers now think that it is not a useful concept and one that may even interfere with the accurate understanding of AIDS and HIV.

Aid to Families with Dependent Children (AFDC)   A *public assistance* program, originating in the *Social Security Act* as Aid to Dependent Children, funded by the federal and state governments to provide financial aid for needy children who are deprived of parental support because of death, incapacitation, or absence. AFDC is administered on the state and local levels, usually through county departments of *public welfare* (or human or *social services*). At the national level, it is administered by the *Administration for Children and Families (ACF)* of the U.S. *Department of Health and Human Services (HHS)*. Eligibility is determined by a *means test*. Many states provide benefits when the father is home but unemployed. See also *Unemployed Parent Program of AFDC (AFDC–UP)*.

Aid to the Blind (AB)   A *categorical program* for needy blind people, originating in the *Social Security Act*. The program was administered at the state and local levels before 1972, when it was consolidated with *Old Age Assistance (OAA)* and *Aid to the Permanently and Totally Disabled (APTD)* programs into the *Supplemental Security Income (SSI)* program.

Aid to the Permanently and Totally Disabled (APTD)   A program that was established by a 1950 amendment to the *Social Security Act* to provide financial assistance to needy people with serious and permanent physical or mental *disabilities*. In 1972, with passage of the federal *Supplemental Security Income (SSI)* program, the program was consolidated with the *Old Age Assistance (OAA)* and *Aid to the Blind (AB)* programs.

AIM   See *American Indian Movement (AIM)*.

AIME   See *Average Income Monthly Earnings (AIME)*.

akathisia   A sustained pattern of fidgety movements, such as swinging of the legs, rocking, tapping the feet or hands, pacing, and being unable to remain in a position for long. This pattern can be a symptom of *anxiety, psychosis, substance abuse,* or a *medication-induced movement disorder*.

Al-Anon   A voluntary *self-help organization* comprising primarily the relatives of alcoholics who meet regularly to give each other *mutual help* and to discuss ways to help solve common problems. Al-Anon is a national organization with chapters in most communities in the United States. See also *support system*.

alarmist   One who excites popular fear; often this is a term of derision made by political or administrative leaders against people seeking social change. See also *agitator*.

Alaska Natives   The *ethnic group* of American citizens, many of whom are commonly known as Eskimos and Aleuts, whose ancestors lived in the area now known as Alaska before Europeans explored and settled the Western Hemisphere.

alcohol abuse   Consumption of alcohol in such a way as to harm or endanger the well-being of the user or those with whom the user comes in contact. Such consumption often leads the abuser to cause accidents, to become physically assaultive and less productive, or to deteriorate physically.

alcohol dependence   A pattern of alcohol use that results in *impaired social functioning*. The behavior pattern typically includes a daily need or wish for alcohol, inconsistent attempts to control drinking, physical disorders aggravated by use of alcohol, occasional binges, absences or ineffectiveness at work, violence, and social relationship problems. Because it is rare for people with alcohol dependency to have all these symptoms, they sometimes rationalize that they do not suffer from *alcoholism*.

alcohol hallucinosis   Imaginary perceptions that occur after a person with an *alcohol dependence* problem has stopped or reduced the consumption of alcohol. The most common type of *hallucination* is auditory. The disorder most frequently lasts a few hours or days and rarely more than a week.

Alcoholics Anonymous (AA) A voluntary *self-help organization* of people who have experienced problems related to *alcohol dependence*. Founded in 1935 by two alcoholics, the organization functions through 1,000 local groups. None of these groups has formal officers, constitutions, or dues, and all groups are open to anyone with a drinking problem.

alcoholism Physical or psychological dependence on alcohol consumption. Alcoholism can lead to social, mental, or physical impairment. See also *primary alcoholism, secondary alcoholism,* and *reactive alcoholism.*

alcohol withdrawal Symptoms in one who suffers *alcohol dependence* following cessation or reduction in drinking, including some, but not necessarily all of the following: *tremor* ("the shakes"), nausea, *depression* and *anxiety,* irritability, hypersensitivity to environmental stimuli, weakness, *tachycardia,* sweating, agitated behavior, *delusion,* and *withdrawal delirium* (delirium tremens [DTs]). See also *withdrawal symptoms.*

alexia A reading disability that begins during adulthood and is usually brought about by head injury, *stroke,* or some other abnormality in the *central nervous system (CNS).*

algophobia The pathological *fear* of pain.

alien One who resides in a country but is not a citizen or national of that country. See also *undocumented alien.*

alienation The feeling of apartness or strangeness experienced in cultural or social settings that seem unfamiliar, unacceptable, or unpredictable.

Alien Labor Certification Division A division of the U.S. *Department of Labor* that authorizes workers from foreign nations to remain in the United States for a specified time to help meet labor demand. See also *green card.*

Alien Registration Recipient U.S. Government Form I-551, which is issued to citizens of other nations who become permanent U.S. residents. The form is more commonly known as the *green card.*

alimony Money paid by one former spouse to the other to provide for separate *maintenance* according to domestic law. Alimony payments are most commonly made by husbands to their former wives, although increasingly, wives are required to make such payments to their former husbands. Alimony is distinct from the obligation of child support payments. The term now preferred is *maintenance.* See also *palimony.*

Alinksy, Saul (1909–1972) A community organizer based in Chicago, he developed many innovative tactics and methods for effectively mobilizing a community. Author of the influential book *Reveille for Radicals* (1946), he advocated realistic goal setting and personalizing social problems by identifying scapegoats or "villains."

Alliance for Progress The program established in the Kennedy administration in 1961 to aid Latin American nations that agreed to begin democratic reforms.

allied health professionals The generic name for the *professional* personnel of hospitals and other health care facilities other than physicians and nurses. Social workers, including those specializing in *medical social work,* are usually included in this designation. Others include audiologists, optometrists, physical and occupational therapists, pharmacists, psychologists, registered dietitians, speech pathologists, radiology technicians, and respiratory therapists.

alloplasty In *psychoanalytic theory,* the psychic process in which the *libido* is directed away from the *self* and onto other people or objects in the environment. See also *autoplasty.*

allotment A financial grant or portion of a budget set aside to accomplish some purpose or manage some program. For example, the *United Way* has an annual allotment for the local family service agency.

almoner One who distributes money or needed goods to poor people. Many social workers were called "almoners" before the 20th century.

alms Money or goods to be given charitably by individuals to poor people. This term has been rarely used since 1900. See also *philanthropy.*

almshouse A home for poor people; a form of *indoor relief* prevalent before the 20th century, in which shelters funded by *philanthropy* were provided for destitute families and individuals. In recent decades, almshouses have largely been replaced by *outdoor relief* programs in which needy people are provided with money, goods, and services while living in their own homes. See also *relief* and *workhouse.*

alogia Poverty of thinking as manifested by restricted speech consisting mostly of short, concrete, repetitive, and stereotyped replies lacking in spontaneity or information.

alternative delivery systems (ADS) A combined *health care* and financing program. Unlike the traditional method of paying the physician or hospital directly or through *third-party payment* arrangements, the ADS consumer pays a fixed premium in advance and receives services at nominal or no charge. ADS programs include the *health maintenance organization (HMO), independent practice associations (IPAs),* health care alliances, *preferred provider organizations (PPOs),* and primary- care networks. See also *managed health care program.*

Altmeyer, Arthur J. (1891–1972) A principal designer of the legislation that became the *Social Security Act* in 1935. As a federal administrator he helped design the merit system for the U.S. *Civil Service* and state personnel programs. He was also a leading proponent and conceptualizer of *national health insurance.*

altruism Unselfish regard for the well-being of others, accompanied by motivation to give money, goods, services, or companionship. See also *philanthropy.*

Alzheimer's disease An organic *mental disorder* occurring most often in older people. Alzheimer's disease is characterized by confusion, forgetfulness, *mood swings,* impaired *cognition* to learn, disorientation, and *dementia.* It is thought to be the result of diffuse brain *atrophy,* especially in the frontal lobes. The cause is unknown.

ambiguous mandate Expectations and requirements made of a social welfare administrator or other official by the relevant constituency that are unclear and not sufficiently specific. Effective administrators often see ambiguous mandates not as frustrating obstacles but as opportunity for creative leadership and innovation.

ambisexual The possession of male and female sexual traits or role behaviors in approximately equal degrees such that neither sex seems predominant in the individual. The term is similar to *androgyny,* but emphasizes physical more than set *role behavior* characteristics.

ambivalence Contradictory emotions, such as love and hate, that occur simultaneously within an individual. In its extreme form, the term is related to indecisiveness and rapidly shifting emotional attitudes toward someone or some idea.

ambivert In the psychoanalytic theories of Carl Jung (1875–1961), an individual whose personality contains nearly equal characteristics of an *introvert* and an *extrovert.*

ambulatory care Medical treatment and health care in outpatient clinics, dispensaries, and in offices of physicians—that is, noninstitutional health care.

American Association for Marriage and Family Therapy (AAMFT) An interdisciplinary professional association founded in 1942 (as the American Association of Marriage Counselors). Its functions and goals include the enhancement of the well-being of families and couples in the United States and professional development of its members through conferences, accredited educational and training programs, and publications.

American Association for Organizing Family Social Work See *Family Service America (FSA)*.

American Association of Group Workers (AAGW) An organization of professional social workers who specialized in working with small groups. AAGW was formed in 1936 and discontinued as an autonomous entity in 1955 when it merged into the then newly created *National Association of Social Workers (NASW)*.

American Association of Hospital Social Workers (AAHSW) The organization, established in 1918, comprising social workers employed in medical facilities and hospital social work departments. In 1934 it was renamed the American Association of Medical Social Workers (AAMSW) to reflect its growing membership of workers employed in nonhospital medical facilities. In 1955 it merged with six other professional groups to form the *National Association of Social Workers (NASW)*.

American Association of Industrial Social Workers (AAISW) The organization of professional social workers who provide occupational social work services through employment with business organizations or through *employee assistance programs (EAPs)*. It develops and maintains standards of *quality assurance* and encourages the effective use of industrial social workers.

American Association of Medical Social Workers (AAMSW) See *American Association of Hospital Social Workers (AAHSW)*.

American Association of Psychiatric Social Workers (AAPSW) The membership association, founded in 1926, comprising social workers who specialized in clinical work with people with a *mental disorder* or who worked with a *mental health team*.

AAPSW merged with six other social work membership organizations in 1955 to form the *National Association of Social Workers (NASW)*.

American Association of Retired Persons (AARP) The largest senior citizens' group in the United States, founded in 1958 to influence legislation and provide social, economic, and recreational services to people older than 50 (retired or not).

American Association of Schools of Social Work (AASSW) The organization founded in 1985 to enhance the quality and focus of social work education and the educational institutions that provide it. Formerly an organization of deans of social work schools, the association comprises deans, faculty, and other concerned professionals. An earlier organization by the same name, established in 1919, was a forerunner of the *Council on Social Work Education (CSWE)*.

American Association of Sex Educators, Counselors, and Therapists (AASECT) The multidisciplinary professional organization founded in 1967 that advocates for greater public knowledge about and healthy expressions of human sexuality. The association, which publishes the *Journal of Sex Education and Therapy*, educates the general public and professionals about aspects of sexuality and treatment of its problems. It also defines and maintains standards for professionals who provide sex education in public schools, churches, and private institutions. Its major focus is on setting standards for therapists and counselors who treat *sexual dysfunction* and help people achieve sexual fulfillment.

American Association of Social Workers (AASW) A membership organization of professional social workers founded in 1921 and merged into the *National Association of Social Workers (NASW)* in 1955.

American Association of State Social Work Boards (AASSWB) An organization formed in 1979 comprising social workers and those public members who serve as members of the boards of state licensing bodies in those states that regulate social work. Usually, board membership is achieved by gubernatorial appointment. AASSWB enables those who serve on such boards to communicate with their counterparts in other states about such matters as developing competency tests, continuing education requirements, recertification policies, reciprocity, and other mutual concerns.

American Association on Mental Retardation (AAMR) The interdisciplinary professional organization, established in 1876, comprising professionals who study and work with those affected by *mental retardation.*

American Board of Examiners in Clinical Social Work (ABE) An organization established in 1987 as an independent certification authority for clinical *social workers.* ABE was formed through a collaboration of the *National Association of Social Workers (NASW)* and the National Registry of Health Care Providers in Clinical Social Work (now the *National Institute for Clinical Social Work Advancement* [*NICSWA*]). Its goals include enhancing professional standards by establishing practice guidelines for clinical social work, developing and administering written competency exams, and awarding board-certified *Diplomate in Clinical Social Work* credentials to qualified senior practitioners.

American Board of Psychiatry and Neurology (ABPN) An organization of physicians established in 1934 that examines and certifies diplomates in psychiatry, neurology, and related fields of medical practice. A "board-certified" *psychiatrist* or *neurologist* is credentialed by this group.

American Civil Liberties Union (ACLU) A *civil rights group* formed in 1920 and dedicated to the restraint of governmental interference with individuals' personal freedom. See also *civil rights.*

American Family Therapy Association (AFTA) A professional organization whose members treat couples and families who are experiencing relationship problems.

American Federation of Government Employees (AFGE) A labor organization, founded in 1932 with headquarters in Washington, DC, and local chapters throughout the nation, whose members are employed by the government of the United States. Many AFGE members are social workers employed as administrators, researchers, supervisors, and providers of direct social services.

American Federation of Labor–Congress of Industrial Organizations (AFL–CIO) The oldest and largest *labor union* in the United States. AFL was founded in 1886 to help assure workers of fairer and more-stable working conditions. In 1935 several AFL unions—unhappy with the emphasis on skilled craftspeople—broke away and formed the CIO to give greater voice to industrial workers. The two groups merged in 1955 and now include nearly 100 distinct unions, including the *American Federation of Government Employees (AFGE)* and the *American Federation of State, County, and Municipal Employees (AFSCME)*, with which many social workers are affiliated.

American Federation of State, County, and Municipal Employees (AFSCME) A labor organization founded in 1936, with headquarters in Washington, DC, and chapters throughout the nation, whose members are employed by nonfederal governments. Many of its members include state and county public assistance workers, child welfare workers, and other social services personnel. Other membership groups include police personnel, firefighters, and public agency administrators.

American Hospital Association (AHA) An organization founded in 1899 comprising more than 5,500 hospitals and other patient care institutions in the United States. AHA establishes and sanctions standards and guidelines to maintain *quality assurance.* One of its many affiliated membership groups is the *Society for Social Work Administrators in Health Care (SSWAHC).*

American Indian Movement (AIM) A *civil rights group,* founded in 1968 with headquarters in Minneapolis, Minnesota, whose purposes include encouraging self-determination among *American Indians* and gaining recognition of their treaty rights. AIM also conducts research, maintains historical archives, and sponsors educational programs.

American Indians Also known as *Native Americans,* the ethnic–racial–cultural groups of American citizens whose ancestors lived in the Western Hemisphere before its exploration and settlement by the Europeans.

American Public Health Association (APHA) An organization founded in 1872 to advocate for societal rather than individual responses to disease and health care. Members of APHA led the movement to prevent epidemics and to enhance the nation's sanitation, nutrition, health education, and government health programs.

American Public Welfare Association (APWA) A voluntary association of individuals and social agencies interested in maintaining effective administration and improved delivery of publicly funded human services. Founded in 1930, it includes more than 1,200 local, state, and federal public welfare organizations.

American Sign Language (ASL) Also known as "AmesLan," a language with a unique grammatical structure, vocabulary, and system of communication. Communication takes place not by vocalization, but by specific movements and shapes of hands, arms, eyes, face, head, and body that correspond to the words of spoken language. It is primarily used by people with hearing impairments.

Americorps A U.S. government program of the Clinton administration established in 1994 to help administer, finance, and train volunteers to provide health, education, vocational, economic development, or social services for designated groups. Most of the work occurs in poor urban or rural areas, American Indian reservations, and institutions. Americorps volunteers may recieve educational and other benefits.

AmesLan See *American Sign Language (ASL).*

amicus curiae brief A suit filed by a third party, generally a professional individual or organization, who is not a party to the litigation. Professionals in human services have used amicus curiae briefs to advocate for clients or for social causes. The term literally means "friend of the court."

amnesia Inability to recall some or all past experience as a result of emotional or organic factors, or combinations of both. See *retrograde amnesia* and *anterograde amnesia.* See also *psychogenic amnesia.*

amnestic disorder Impaired memory resulting from some specific organic impairment within an individual who otherwise has a clear consciousness (that is, no conditions such as *delirium* or *intoxication)* and no loss of major intellectual ability. The memory loss may be short term, which results in inability to retain newly acquired information, or long term, which results in inability to remember information that was known in the past. If memory loss occurs where no organic impairment is known to exist, the condition is known as *psychogenic amnesia.*

amnesty An excuse granted to individuals or groups to free them from being tried or punished for alleged criminal offenses. It may occur even before a trial or conviction. Amnesty is usually granted by a nation's chief executive or ruler in response to political pressure or public demand, rather than for legal reasons. Amnesty is usually granted to groups or classes of people, such as Vietnam War draft evaders, whereas the term *pardon* applies to individuals. See also *clemency.*

amniocentesis A test to determine the presence of some specific defect in a developing *fetus* by extracting and examining a sample of the amniotic fluid. See also *chorionic villa sampling (CVS).*

19

amok A *culture-bound syndrome,* found originally in Malaysia, characterized by a person's period of brooding, followed by violent or homicidal outbursts. It is found mostly in males and often follows perceived insults. It is often accompanied by *delusions of persecution, amnesia,* and exhaustion.

amotivational syndrome A pattern of behavior often found in patients who have exhibited extensive *substance dependence* in which there seems to be cooperation and little resistance to the intervention process but also little effort or interest expended toward resolution of either *substance abuse* or other social and emotional problems. Some social workers say clients who have been long-term, heavy users of *marijuana* often exhibit this behavior while in treatment.

amphetamine A drug that stimulates the cerebral cortex, tends to temporarily increase one's mental alertness, produces a sense of *euphoria* and well-being, and reduces fatigue; sometimes used clinically by physicians in treating children's *hyperkinesis* and used in weight control. Commonly known as "bennies," "*uppers,*" and "*speed,*" amphetamines are addictive and usually require increasingly large doses as *tolerance* develops. *Addiction* can and frequently does result in *psychosis* or *death* from overexhaustion or cardiac arrest.

anabolic steroids See *steroids.*

anaclitic A form of dependency, such as that experienced by an infant for its *caregiver.* A typical characteristic of young children, it indicates *pathology* when excessive in adults. It is most commonly seen as a form of *depression* that one experiences when fearing the possible loss of an important source of *nurturance.*

anal character See *"anal personality."*

"anal personality" A descriptive term from *psychoanalytic theory,* referring to an individual who is excessively fastidious, miserly, rigid, and compulsively obsessed with orderliness; also known as "anal character."

anal phase The second stage in *psychosexual development theory,* which occurs between the ages of two and three. During this stage of personality development, the child becomes oriented to the functions of the anus and learns to have more control over the environment by giving or withholding feces.

analysand One who is being psychoanalyzed.

analysis A systematic consideration of anything in its respective parts and their relationship to one another. The term is commonly used to indicate *psychoanalysis.*

analysis of variance (ANOVA) A statistical procedure commonly used in social work *research* for determining the extent to which two or more groups differ significantly when one is exposed to a *dependent variable.*

analyst See *psychoanalyst.*

anancastic A behavior pattern in which the individual is compulsive—that is, obsessed with rules, is emotionally constricted and intolerant, and a perfectionist. See also *compulsive personality disorder* or *obsessive–compulsive disorder.*

anarchism A doctrine and *social movement* that espouses the abolition of formal government and freedom from controls on individual actions.

andragogy The practice of helping adults to learn. The concept is important in *social work education,* which usually seeks to use the *adult learner model* in teaching social work students.

androgyny A *sexual orientation* in which mannerisms, appearance, and behaviors that are usually considered either male or female are both incorporated into one's behavioral repertoire. The term is similar to *ambisexual* but emphasizes *sex role* behavior more than physical characteristics.

anemia A disorder in which the blood is deficient in red cells or hemoglobin. The most apparent initial symptom is a feeling of tiredness resulting from the blood's inability to transport enough oxygen through the body.

aneurysm A permanent dilation of a weakened artery. Major causes of the weakening are infection, injury, *hypertension, arteriosclerosis,* or *congenital abnormalities.* The most serious and life threatening of these are the aortic aneurysm, which can result in loss of blood from the heart to the body cavities, or brain aneurysm in which the blood flow to parts of the brain can be interrupted.

"angel dust" A slang term for the psychedelic or hallucinogenic drug *PCP* (phencyclidine). This drug, one of the *drugs of abuse,* is smoked, snorted, or ingested orally and often produces distortion of the senses and symptoms of *psychosis.* It has a high incidence of psychological *dependency.*

anger A common and usually normal *emotion* that occurs in response to an indi-vidual's perception of being threatened or harmed. Its manifestations often include irritability, physical or verbal attacks, increased heart rate and respiratory activity, and rage and negativism. Anger may be continuous or intermittent, directed inward or outward, intense or mild, and according to some psychologists, conscious or unconscious. It is considered *maladaptive* or pathological when it is relatively continuous or occurs even when there is no immediate catalyst.

angina pectoris Sharp pains in the chest that occur when the heart muscle receives insufficient blood. Caused by sudden closure of the coronary arteries, often brought on by excitement or physical exertion, angina often is treated with drugs that dilate the blood vessels as well as with surgical procedures to remove obstructions.

anhedonia An emotional state in which the individual lacks the full capacity to experience pleasure in situations that seem pleasurable to most others. It is a symptom frequently seen in clients with *depression.*

anima In the *psychoanalytic theory* of Carl Jung (1875–1961), the feminine aspect of a male's personality. The male inherits this feminine *archetype* from the accumulated experiences of men as they have related to women through the ages.

animus In the *psychoanalytic theory* of Carl Jung (1875-1961), the masculine as-pect of a female's personality. The female inherits this masculine *archetype* from the accumulated experiences of women as they have related to men through the ages.

annona civica An institutionalized tradition in ancient Rome, established before 100 B.C., requiring patrician families to donate and distribute free or low-cost grain and other food to needy people.

annulment A religious or legal declaration that an agreement, contract, covenant, or relationship such as marriage does not and never has existed.

anomie Normlessness or the elimination or reduction of social and personal *values, mores, norms,* and codes of conduct; also, the inability of an individual or group to recognize the values, mores, or codes of conduct of another group with whom it must relate. Anomie frequently occurs in rapidly changing societies and communities or groups subject to catastrophic stress. In such circumstances, individuals often become alienated, apathetic, and devoid of previously valued goals.

anorexia nervosa An *eating disorder* most often encountered in girls and young women whose extended refusal to eat leads to severe weight loss, *malnutrition,* and cessation of menstruation. The usual medical criteria for this diagnosis include the loss of 15 percent or more of one's body weight. This life-threatening condition is related to a disturbed body image and an exaggerated fear of becoming obese. The word "anorexia" literally means loss of appetite, although the person in this condition has not lost appetite. See also *bulimia nervosa.*

ANOVA See *analysis of variance (ANOVA).*

anoxia Insufficient oxygen in body tissues.

ANS See *autonomic nervous system (ANS).*

Antabuse A drug that induces nausea when in the bloodstream of an individual who ingests alcohol. It is used to facilitate *aversion therapy* in the treatment of *alcoholism.*

antecedent In *behavior modification* and *social learning theory,* an event *(stimulus)* that precedes a behavior *(response)* and is thought to influence it.

antenuptial agreement See *prenuptial agreement.*

anterograde amnesia The inability to recall experiences that have occurred after a certain time, usually after some physical injury or psychic stress. See also *retrograde amnesia.*

anthropocentrism The view that the environment centers around and exists primarily for humans.

antianxiety drugs See *tranquilizer.*

anticathexis In *Freudian theory,* the psychic energy the individual uses to keep repressed material in the *unconscious.* This term is not synonymous with *decathexis.*

Anti-Defamation League of B'nai B'rith *A civil rights group* founded in 1913, the Anti-Defamation League works to end *anti-Semitism,* improve *intergroup relations,* and promote the democratic process. The league's headquarters are in New York City, with branches in 28 areas of the United States and the world.

antidepressant medication *Psychotropic drugs* used by psychiatrists and other physicians to help patients achieve relief from the symptoms of *depression.* Some of the major drugs of this type are known by the trade names Elavil, Vivactil, Tofranil, Pertofrane, Sinequan, Marplan, Parnate, Prozac, and Nardil. Relief through antidepressant medication is not usually apparent until several days after it has been taken in compliance with prescription.

antimanic medication *Psychotropic drugs* prescribed by physicians to counter the symptoms of *mood disorder, manic episode,* and some forms of *bipolar disorder.* The most popular of these drugs, *lithium carbonate,* is sold under such trade names as Eskalith and Lithane. See also *major affective disorder.*

antipoverty programs The generic term for public and private associations and ac-

tivities devoted to the eradication of *poverty.* As well as direct help to poor individuals, such activities include research into the causes and consequences of poverty and actions that may eliminate economic inequality and instability.

antipsychotic medication The group of *psychotropic drugs* prescribed by physicians to control certain symptoms seen in *schizophrenia* and other psychoses. These drugs include those sold under the trade names Compazine, Haldol, Mellaril, Navane, Prolixin, Serentil, Stelazine, Thorazine, and Trilafon.

anti-Semitism Negative attitudes and behaviors about Jewish people manifested in *discrimination, bias,* and the attempt to prejudicially attribute to them some of the problems of society. The term "Semitic" actually refers to a group of languages of the Middle East, including Arabic and Hebrew. Thus, technically, anti-Semitism also suggests bias against Arabs.

antisocial behavior A pattern of actions that results in an individual's isolation from other people or frequent conflict with others and social institutions.

antisocial personality disorder One of the 11 types of *personality disorders* characterized by irresponsibility, inability to feel guilt or remorse for actions that harm others, frequent conflicts with people and social institutions, the tendency to blame others and not to learn from mistakes, low frustration tolerance, and other behaviors that indicate a deficiency in *socialization.* Less-precise labels *psychopathic personality, psychopath,* and *sociopath* are often used as synonyms.

anxiety A feeling of uneasiness, tension, and sense of imminent danger. When such a feeling occurs within a person with no specific cause in the environment, it is known as *free-floating anxiety.* When it recurs frequently and interferes with effective living or a sense of well-being or is otherwise *maladaptive,* it is known as *anxiety disorder.*

anxiety disorder A chronic or recurring state of tension, worry, fear, and uneasiness arising from unknown or unrecognized perceptions of danger or conflict. The major types of anxiety disorders include *generalized anxiety disorder; acute stress disorder; obsessive–compulsive disorder; posttraumatic stress disorder (PTSD); panic disorder,* with and without *agoraphobia; social phobia; specific phobia;* and *substance-induced anxiety disorder.*

anxiety disorder of childhood   An emotional or mental disturbance found in youngsters from infancy through adolescence characterized by excessive fear; apprehension; nervousness; and often such symptoms as trembling, faints, nausea, choking, headaches, and overall tension. These symptoms occur even though there is no directly related cause or threat in the environment. Specific types of anxiety disorders in childhood or adolescence include *separation anxiety disorder of childhood, avoidant disorder of childhood,* and *overanxious disorder of childhood.* This term is no longer used as an official diagnosis.

anxiety hysteria   A psychoanalytic term referring to *psychoneurosis* that includes intense anxiety-induced dramatic behavior, *free-floating anxiety,* and *phobia.* Analytically oriented therapists consider this condition to be the result of repressed sexual conflict.

anxiety neurosis   See *generalized anxiety disorder* and *panic disorder.*

anxiety symptoms   The psychophysiological responses one experiences as a result of *anxiety.* The most common of these include nervousness, sweating, irritability, sleeplessness, motor agitation, fidgetiness, muscular tension, fear, uneasiness, compulsive behavior, obsessive thoughts, trembling, pain, apprehension, forgetfulness, poor concentration, depression, confusion, and general discomfort.

anxiolytic   Pertaining to substances or procedures for reducing *anxiety.*

APA citation system   The format and style by which references are indicated in the texts of academic books and scholarly journal articles as developed by the American Psychological Association. The system is now preferred by most social science publications, including the social work literature. In this style the references are "cited in the text using the author's last name, and date of publication" (Beebe, 1993, p. 181) with the full reference at the end of the article, with all the other articles referred to, and placed in alphabetical order by author's last name, for example, as in: Beebe, L. (Ed.). (1993). *Professional writing for the human services.* Washington, DC: NASW Press.

apartheid   A term in the Afrikaans language meaning "separate development" that refers to the policy of racial separation once maintained by the white-controlled South African government. The policy ended with South Africa's 1994 national elections giving people of all races the right to vote. However, apartheid has left an institutional legacy of differential education, sanitation, health services, infant and maternal mortality, housing, employment, and land distribution that may take generations to overcome.

apathy   Indifference; lack of interest in or desire for anything. Apathy is often a symptom of such mental disorders as *depression* or a response to social conditions such as oppression, restricted opportunities, or limited education.

Apgar rating   A score, devised by Dr. Virginia Apgar in 1954, to indicate the relative health of a baby at birth. This measure is now commonly used in neonatal care facilities. Five factors are each assigned the values 0, 1, or 2, so that a baby in ideal health would achieve an Apgar rating of 10. The criteria are heart rate (absent = 0, slow or irregular = 1, rapid = 2), respiratory effort (absent = 0, slow or irregular = 1, good, crying = 2), reflex irritability (absent = 0, grimace = 1, cough, sneeze = 2), color (blue = 0, body pink, extremities blue = 1, completely pink = 2), and muscle tone (flaccid = 0, weak = 1, strong = 2).

APHA   See *American Public Health Association (APHA).*

aphasia The inability to use previously possessed language skills. Specific types of aphasia may include loss of ability to utter words, loss of ability to understand written or spoken words, inability to put words and phrases together properly, or various combinations of these. See also *developmental expressive language disorder*.

aphephobia The abnormal *fear* of being touched.

aphonia Loss of ability to speak normally as a result of physiological or emotional disorders.

aplastic anemia Failure of the bone marrow to produce sufficient blood elements, especially red cells, often occurring as a result of overexposure to antibiotic drugs, X-rays, or toxic substances.

APM Annual Program Meeting, the name social work educators use to refer to the *Council on Social Work Education (CSWE)*–sponsored conference that meets in a different U.S. city every March.

apnea A disturbance in the respiratory mechanism, usually resulting in temporary cessation of breathing. In some infants, the disturbance may be related to *crib death*. See also *sudden infant death syndrome (SIDS)* and *sleep disorder*. Clinicians use the term *breathing-related sleep disorder*.

apparatchik An administrative functionary. The term is the Russian for "bureaucrat" but, as used in English, implies a public official who mindlessly follows rules even if those rules keep the official and others from reaching the organization's goal. See also *technocrat*.

appeal In legal terms, a request of a higher court to review and reverse a lower court decision or grant a new trial.

appellate court A judicial institution and procedure that determines if the judgments made in lower courts were in accordance with *law*. Appellate courts only scrutinize previously adjudicated cases, not by reviewing new testimony or evidence, but by reviewing written briefs and oral arguments about how the previous judgment was made.

applied research Systematic investigations to acquire facts that can be used to solve or prevent problems, enhance lifestyles, advance technologies, or increase income. This is contrasted to *basic research*. Most of social work research is considered applied research because it pertains mostly to the interactions between people and their environment, social problems, and methods for helping.

appointment 1. The designation of a specified period during which the social worker, or other professional, and the client have agreed to meet. It commonly lasts 50 to 60 minutes for individuals and couples, 90 to 120 minutes for groups, and longer for home visits. 2. The designation of a person to fill a position. For example, a social worker is appointed chief administrator of an agency.

apportioned tax A tax collected by one level of government whose proceeds are shared with other governmental entities. For example, a city or county government distributes some of the funds collected from property taxes to the state or to school and park districts. Or money from a state gasoline tax is apportioned to local governments for city street construction. See also *revenue sharing*.

apprenticing Putting one person under the care and tutelage of another, ostensibly for the purpose of learning certain skills. This process is historically significant in *child welfare* in that it was widely practiced in the United States in the 18th and 19th centuries as a way to care for homeless youths. As such, it was a major precedent for the subsequent system of *foster care*.

appropriate technology (AT) Methods for handling environmental problems or developing resources that are suitable and efficient for people of the area given their stage of economic and social progression. For example, building a small windmill to pump water in a primitive village might be a more appropriate technology than installing a hydroelectric dam or irrigation system.

appropriation An allocation of funds, usually made by a government legislative body, to an organization or program empowered by that body to accomplish a specific goal.

apraxia The inability to perform purposeful movements, which usually is related to lesions in the motor area of the cortex rather than paralysis or dysfunctioning senses.

APS See *adult protective services (APS)*.

APTD See *Aid to the Permanently and Totally Disabled (APTD)*.

aptitude tests Formal examinations that attempt to determine an individual's innate ability and potential for a future undertaking, such as success in an educational or workplace setting. See also *achievement tests*.

APWA See *American Public Welfare Association (APWA)*.

aquaphobia The pathological *fear* of water.

arbitration A decision-making mechanism used when two or more opposing factions cannot reach agreement or continue working toward complementary goals. The disputing parties agree to appoint a neutral person and to abide by that person's decision following a hearing on the issues at which the parties have had an opportunity to present their case. See also *mediation*.

ARC See *"AIDS-related complex" (ARC)*.

archetype In the theories of Carl Jung (1875–1961), the inherited structural component of the *collective unconscious*. It is a deep, unconscious representation of a group of experiences that have been accumulating within each new generation of humans. This collection of experiences remains part of the individual's personality in the *unconscious* and influences the thought and behavior patterns of each individual to varying

degrees. Archetypes are also referred to as primordial images or *imagos,* and the major archetypes are the *anima* and the *animus*. See also *nativism*.

Area Agencies on Aging (AAA) A national network of federally funded agencies established in 1965 to advocate and provide human services for older people.

arousal 1. A state of becoming excited into action. Social workers involved in community organization sometimes seek to provoke arousal in client groups by making them aware of a relevant problem and its potential solution. 2. In human sexuality, the term refers to physiological and psychological changes in response to stimulation and leading to preparation for sexual intercourse. Sexologists William Masters and Virginia Johnson described arousal as occurring primarily in the first of the four stages of sexual response (excitement, plateau, orgasm, and resolution). They indicated that arousal begins in the excitement phase, in which vasocongestion (swelling of the blood vessels) commences, the heart and pulse rates increase, and the skin becomes flushed.

arteriosclerosis Hardening of the arteries or loss of elasticity of arterial wall, a condition that makes it difficult for the blood to circulate. This can result in *hypertension, stroke, aneurism,* and brain cell destruction, with consequent loss of memory, confusion, and inattention.

arthritis Painful inflammation of the joints of the body. Causes include dysfunction of the endocrine glands, nerve impairment, or degeneration as a result of infections and old age. The major types include rheumatoid arthritis, osteoarthritis, and gout.

articulation disorder A speech problem characterized by the inability to pronounce certain sounds clearly. The individual may have difficulty pronouncing one or more sounds or sound blends such as r, sh, th, f, z, l, or ch, often making substitutions for these sounds and giving the impression of "baby talk." Most professionals now prefer the term *phonological disorder*.

artificial insemination The joining of sperm and ovum for the purpose of reproduction by means other than sexual intercourse or natural *conception*. Using surgical instruments, the physician implants semen taken from the woman's husband, or sometimes from an anonymous donor, into a fallopian tube or into the uterus, where sperm can form a union with the ovum. See also *in vitro fertilization, reproductive technology,* and *surrogacy*.

art therapy The use of paintings, sculpture, and other creative expressions in the treatment of people with emotional problems. Art therapy is often used in *social group work* and in *group psychotherapy*. Often used with institutionalized people or inpatients, it is also considered to be effective with healthy people who wish to share art as a means of enhancing personal growth and development. In some forms of art therapy, clients create their own works and discuss the results with the therapist or with other members of an art therapy group. In other forms, the clients are exposed to works of art by a variety of artists and asked to assess how the works affect their own feelings and understandings. See also *bibliotherapy*.

asceticism A lifestyle involving rigid self-discipline and self-denial, abandonment of worldly goods, and social isolation, usually to improve one's spiritual or moral state.

ASCO See *Association for the Study of Community Organization (ASCO)*.

Asian Americans Residents or citizens of the United States whose racial background and sometimes ethnic identification is with the peoples of Pacific–Asian areas, including Chinese, Japanese, Vietnamese, Koreans, Filipinos, migrants from the Indian subcontinent, and others.

Asian American Social Workers (AASW) The national professional association established in California in 1968 by social workers of Pacific–Asian background. The purpose of AASW is to develop and promote social welfare programs that benefit and protect the rights of *Asian Americans* as well as to enhance its members' professional development.

as-if assumptions A technique used in *psychotherapy,* especially with small groups, in which the therapist seeks to help the client understand the reasons for resisting or fearing change. The therapist suggests the client is behaving "as-if" change would lead to specified problems. The client and group then look more objectively at the anticipated consequences and come to fear them less.

ASL See *American Sign Language (ASL)*.

Asociación Nacional por Personas Mayores The association for Hispanic senior citizens that provides information to its members (individuals and organizations) about the opportunities, benefits, and problems of older people of Spanish-speaking heritage and represents these people to lawmakers, policy makers, and other organizations.

asocial behavior Behavior characterized by indifference to people or social norms.

Asperger's disorder One of the *pervasive developmental disorders* characterized by severe and sustained impairment in social interaction and the development of restricted, repetitive patterns of behavior, interests, and activities, causing impairment in most areas of functioning. Similar to *autistic disorder* but with a later onset, the individual with the disorder usually has difficulties in social interactions throughout life.

assault An attempt or threat to physically harm or intimidate an individual through the use of unlawful force. Assault may be found even where no physical injury occurs if the victim has been subjected to a reasonable fear of harm.

assertiveness Behavior characterized by self-confident communication of one's rights and values.

assertiveness training A program designed to teach individuals to express their feelings, needs, and demands directly and effectively.

assessment The process of determining the nature, cause, progression, and prognosis of a problem and the personalities and situations involved therein; the social work function of acquiring an understanding of a problem, what causes it, and what can be changed to minimize or resolve it. See also *diagnosis*.

assimilation 1. The social integration or adoption of one group's *values, norms,* and *folkways* by another group. For example, a group of immigrants may eventually integrate with or adopt many aspects of the culture of their new society. 2. In *Piagetian theory,* the individual's act of incorporating an aspect of his or her environment into an existing thought structure. See also *culture shock*.

assisted suicide The intentional act of providing someone with the means and information needed to commit *suicide*. When this is done by a physician or other medical professional, it is known as *medically assisted suicide*. See also *right to die*.

Association for Improving the Condition of the Poor (AICP) An organization founded in New York by *Robert M. Hartley* in 1843 to combat poverty primarily through "character-building" activities. Volunteers tried to get poor people to abstain from alcohol, become more self-disciplined, and acquire the work ethic. Many of the methods and goals of AICP were later adopted by some *Charity Organization Societies* (COS) and by *friendly visitors*.

Association for the Advancement of Social Work with Groups (AASWG) A professional organization founded in 1982 to encourage the social work profession's interest in working with groups.

Association for the Study of Community Organization (ASCO) An organization established in 1946 by social workers specializing in or interested in *community organization*. In 1955 it was merged into the newly established *National Association of Social Workers (NASW)*.

Association of American Indian Social Workers (AAISW) See *National Indian Social Workers Association (NISWA)*.

Association of Community Organization and Social Administration (ACOSA) An independent organization of social work educators oriented to training students in the macro aspects of the curriculum, including *planning, policy, community organization, advocacy,* and adminstration. ACOSA often works with the *Council on Social Work Education (CSWE)*.

Association of Community Organizations for Reform Now (ACORN) A federation of *community organization* groups founded in 1970 in association with the *National Welfare Rights Organization (NWRO)* and located in many larger cities of the United States. ACORN uses *community organization* principles to advocate for stronger local and neighborhood voices in and power over economic, social, and political institutions that influence the lives of low- and moderate-income families.

Association of Women in Social Work (AWSW) A professional association founded in 1984 that advocates equal opportunities, rights, and benefits for female social workers. The association also brings together social workers to consider the special needs and concerns of women social workers and their clients.

asthenia Lack of strength or musculature.

asthma One of the *pulmonary disorders,* in which the muscles in the walls of the bronchi contract, causing the individual to have difficulty breathing.

asylum 1. A refuge or sanctuary. 2. An institution for the care of people suffering from mental disorders, certain physical illnesses, or economic destitution.

AT See *appropriate technology (AT)*.

ataque de nervios A *culture-bound syndrome* found most commonly among Latin American and Latin Mediterranean groups in which individuals experience a wide range of panic and anxiety symptoms, including fainting, attacks of crying, shouting, aggressive behavior, suicide gestures, and dissociative experiences, usually following a stressful life event.

ataxia Loss of ability to control all or some voluntary muscle movement.

atherosclerosis Artery wall congestion caused by accumulation of fats, cholesterol, and calcium salts and resulting in increased risk of *hypertension,* impaired circulation, and *stroke.*

at-risk population Those members of a group who are vulnerable to, or likely to be harmed by, a specific medical, social, or environmental circumstance. For example, overweight people or smokers are an at-risk population because they are more likely to have heart attacks or cardiovascular problems. Infants born to women who drank alcohol heavily while pregnant constitute a population at risk for birth defects. This term is roughly synonymous with *vulnerable populations.*

atrophy Wasting away of body tissues.

attachment 1. An emotional bond between individuals, based on attraction and dependence, which develops during critical periods of life and may disappear when one individual has no further opportunity to relate to the other. 2. In legal terms, the seizure of property by legal processes while a court action is pending.

attachment theory A group of concepts developed in the 1970s by developmental researchers C. Ainsworth, N. Bowlby, and others about the stages through which young children progress in their development of social relationships and the influence of this development on personality characteristics in later life. In four sequential stages toward social attachment, the healthy young child exhibits characteristic behaviors: at birth to age three months, the infant main-

tains closeness with the *caregiver* through sucking, grasping, visual tracking, and cuddling. From age three to six months, the infant becomes more responsive to familiar people and discomforted by others *(stranger anxiety).* At age six months to toddler age, the infant seeks contact and closeness with the object of *attachment* and experiences discomfort *(separation anxiety disorder of childhood)* when the object is missing. Beyond toddler age, the child uses an increasing variety of behaviors to influence the actions of the object of attachment to meet the child's needs for closeness. In this development, three general patterns of attachment occur: *secure attachment, avoidant attachment,* and *resistant attachment.*

attendant care A *home health care service,* sponsored by local departments of human services, health care facilities, senior centers, or private organizations, in which individuals trained in nontechnical nursing, home care, and other activities make regular, usually daily, visits to assist homebound people. Attendants often help in light housekeeping, meal preparation, hygiene, and health care monitoring.

attending In social work and other professional *interviews,* maintaining attentiveness expressed through appropriate verbal following, eye contact, mindful but relaxed posture, and disciplined attention. A nonattending interviewer might be staring out a window or glancing at a clock, yawning, or generally showing lack of focus on the *relationship* process. See also *following responses.*

attention-deficit hyperactivity disorder (ADHD) A disorder that starts in infancy, childhood, or adolescence, characterized by impulsive behavior, inattentiveness, excessive motor activity, and short attention span. Subtypes of this disorder include "predominately inattentive type," "predominately hyperactive–impulsive type," and the "combined type." The term ADHD is now used in place of several less-accurate and less-precise terms, including *hyperactive child syndrome, minimal brain dysfunction, hyperkinetic reaction of childhood,* and "attention deficit disorder, hyperactive type." Apparently, in most cases, it is the result of one or more factors, including *anxiety, stress,* physiological disorder, *neurological disorder,* and some *organic mental disorders.*

attitude   A mental predisposition or inclination to act or react in a certain way. It is often used as a synonym for *mood* or opinion, and in a current slang usage, it is a synonym for "defiance."

audio feedback   A procedure in social work and other professional interventions to show clients how they sound to others, by playing back tape recordings and systematically analyzing the results. The procedure has been used with particular effectiveness in working with clients who have substance abuse problems or communications problems with family members or peers. See also *video feedback.*

audit   An inspection of the accounting records or procedures of an individual or organization to verify their accuracy and completeness. For example, the records of social agency might be audited annually by representatives of funding sources. Auditing also can involve inspecting the work done by staff, determining compliance with regulations, and completing inventories.

auditory hallucination   An imagined perception of a sound; hearing something that does not exist outside subjective experience.

authoritarian   Pertaining to a system in social organizations and administration characterized by the relative absence of democratic decision making and implementation processes and the requirement of submitting to higher-ranking members of the organization. Punishments or sanctions are often imposed on those members of the organization who do not comply, and rewards are given to those who do.

authoritarian management   An administrative style sometimes used in social welfare organizations by leaders who tend to make most of the decisions unilaterally and to use their power to demand that the members of the organization accept and support these decisions.

authority   Expertise or power.

autistic disorder   A *pervasive developmental disorder* in which the individual appears to have little interest in the external world or capacity to relate effectively to people or objects and is presumed to be devoting full attention to inner wishes and sensations. Other symptoms may include deficient communication and social skills, abnormal interpersonal skills, and unusual responses to stimuli. This condition is most commonly seen in young children and infants.

autonomic   Functioning automatically and without willful or conscious intent. See *autonomic nervous system (ANS).*

autonomic conversion symptoms   Psychogenic physical symptoms that suggest *autonomic nervous system (ANS)* responses, such as *tachycardia* and vomiting.

autonomic nervous system (ANS)   That part of the nervous system that regulates the nonvolitional bodily responses such as digestion, breathing, and the rate of heartbeat and glandular secretions. See also *central nervous system (CNS)* and *peripheral nervous system (PNS).*

autonomous practice   Professional activity and decision making that occurs in relative independence of social agency auspices, supervision, and organizational requirements. The practitioner sets the standards of performance and self-monitors the work done. This is a relative concept, in that all professions and professional activities are regulated and influenced to some extent by social, ethical, legal, political, and economic forces. Some social workers use this term to indicate *private practice.*

autonomy   1. An individual's sense of being capable of independent action; the ability to provide for one's own needs. 2. Independence from the control of others.

autonomy versus shame and doubt   The basic conflict found in the second stage of the *psychosocial development theory* of Erik Erikson (1902–1994), occurring approximately between ages two and four.

During this stage, the toddler may come to feel more in control of the environment and exhibit growing independence of actions or may be overcome with feelings of guilt if independent actions are inconsistently tolerated by others.

autoplasty In *psychoanalytic theory,* the psychic process in which the *libido* is directed toward the *self* and away from other people or objects in the environment. See also *alloplasty.*

Average Income Monthly Earnings (AIME) A measure used by the *Social Security Administration (SSA)* to determine *Old Age, Survivors, Disability, and Health Insurance (OASDHI)* benefits. AIME is calculated on the basis of earnings made in covered employment during the worker's lifetime, minus five years of low earnings. Earnings are indexed to account for changes in average wages over the years. See also *social insurance.*

aversion stimulus In *behavior modification,* an object or situation that the subject identifies as being painful or unpleasant and attempts to avoid whenever possible. See also *aversion therapy* and *social learning theory.*

aversion therapy A procedure commonly used in *behavior therapy* designed to eliminate a maladaptive behavior, such as overeating or *substance abuse,* by associating the behavior with some real or imagined *aversion stimulus.*

avoidance 1. In *behavior modification* procedures, an individual's response that postpones or averts presentation of an aversive event. 2. In *psychodynamic theory,* an ego *defense mechanism* resembling *denial,* involving refusal to face certain situations or objects because they present unconscious impulses or punishments for those impulses.

avoidant attachment A form of *insecure attachment* first observed in children who show less distress than other children when left alone but seem as anxious when in the presence of their *caregiver* as with others. Such children avoid contact with parents and other caregivers or ignore their efforts to interact. See also *attachment theory, secure attachment,* and *resistant attachment.*

avoidant disorder of childhood A childhood disorder characterized by intense efforts to avoid strangers. The child with this disorder wants relationships with familiar people but has difficulty in peer relationships and new contacts. The child may act embarrassed, relatively immature, self-conscious, and inarticulate when compelled to confront strangers. These symptoms are similar to the normal developmental behavior known as *stranger anxiety,* which disappears in healthy children younger than age two to three. The *DSM-IV* no longer uses this as a diagnosis. See also *social phobia.*

avoidant personality disorder One of the *personality disorders* in which the individual is hypersensitive to potential rejection, has low self-esteem, is socially withdrawn, and is generally unwilling to enter social relationships unless there is assurance of uncritical acceptance.

avolition Loss of willingness or ability to pursue goals.

AWSW See *Association of Women in Social Work (AWSW).*

Axis II disorder In the multiaxial assessment system of *DSM-IV* (Washington, DC: American Psychiatric Association, 1994), the *personality disorders* and *mental retardation.* Listing these conditions on a separate axis is to ensure that their possible presence is not overlooked when attention is focused on the more-florid disorder of Axis I. DSM-IV moved several disorders from Axis II, where they appeared in *DSM-III,* to Axis I, including *pervasive developmental disorders, learning disorders, motor skills disorder,* and *communication disorders.*

B

Babinski reflex An automatic response in infants in which the toes extend and spread out when the sole of the foot is gently stroked. As the infant's nervous system matures, the same type of stroke tends to result in the toes curling downward.

baby boom generation The men and women in the United States who were born in the two decades immediately following World War II. Demographers indicate that many more than the usual number of births occurred during these years because many people had postponed having children during the war. This "bulge" in the population necessitates many adjustments in social and economic planning as the baby boomers move through the *life cycle*. When this group reaches retirement age in the years 2010 to 2020, it is anticipated that the *social security* system will be severely strained. See also *Generation X*.

backlash A reaction by one group when it comes to believe a social change to benefit another group has negative consequences. The term is usually used with an adjective that identifies the group with the reaction, as in "white backlash," "conservative backlash," or "smokers' backlash." For example, white backlash was said to have begun shortly after *civil rights* and *affirmative action* legislation was passed, when for the first time, white workers had to compete with *African Americans* for jobs.

"bag lady" A term often applied to impoverished, homeless women, many of whom are mentally ill and carry their possessions in shopping bags.

bail A monetary or other form of security posted by or for someone accused of a *crime*. The purpose is to ensure that the accused person will appear at subsequent legal proceedings, to enable the accused to avoid imprisonment while awaiting trial, and to relieve the authorities of the cost of incarcerating the accused during this period.

BAL See *blood alcohol level (BAL)*.

balance of payments The money value of all economic transactions between a nation and all other nations during a stated time. A balance of trade deficit occurs when a nation buys more goods and services from other countries than it sells to them. This situation causes the nation to borrow, devalue its currency compared with other nations, or pay back from its stock of gold and foreign currencies.

Balch, Emily Greene (1867–1961) Educator in social work and economics, social reformer, and antiwar activist, she founded the Women's International Peace Commission in 1915 and was a winner of the 1946 Nobel Peace Prize.

balkanization Division of a nation or organization into smaller units whose members are often at odds. The term derives from the Balkan peninsula in East Europe, which was divided into several small countries.

bankrupt Financial insolvency resulting in the legal process of fairly distributing the remaining property among the creditors, except for those properties that the debtor is permitted to retain to meet *basic needs* and to achieve fiscal rehabilitation.

barbiturates Drugs that act as *central nervous system (CNS)* depressants. Physicians often use them clinically to facilitate their patients' sleep and to control convulsive disorders. In slang, they are known as *"downers."*

Barclay Report The 1980 British government-sponsored study about the need for and delivery of social services. The report also evaluated and delineated the role of social workers in providing social services. The report recommended increased involvement in *counseling, social planning*, promoting *community decision networks, negotiation,* and social *advocacy.*

bargaining The negotiating of agreements between various factions so that the parties can compromise and make equitable exchanges. A plan to bring together the parties in such a *negotiation* is called a "bargaining strategy." Bargaining is an important component of labor–management relations and in *community organization* and *planning.*

bar graph A depiction of data in which parallel strips are drawn from a common base. Each strip represents a quantity of something being studied, and the strips' respective lengths illustrate their comparative values. For example, a state public-assistance office wants to show that all its white client–families receive twice as much money as black families and four times as much as Hispanic families. A graph with three strips of appropriately varying lengths represents the three groups.

Barnett, Samuel A. (1844–1913) Founder of the original *settlement houses,* he worked with *Octavia Hill* in the development of the original *Charity Organization Societies (COS)* in England. He used his church for a type of discussion group that became a model for many *social group work* methods. A community organizer and activist for improved housing and treatment of mental illness, in 1884 he founded *Toynbee Hall,* the first settlement house, and named it after one of his recently deceased volunteer workers. Later he came to the United States and worked with *Jane Addams* and *Ellen Gates Starr* in establishing *Hull House.*

Barrett, Janie Porter (1865–1948) Leader in the *settlement houses* movement and proponent of education for African American women. She founded one of the first settlement houses for African Americans (the Locust Street Social Settlement) and the influential rehabilitation facility, the Virginia Industrial School for Colored Girls.

barrio In Spanish, a neighborhood. In the United States the term often connotes a residential area inhabited primarily by peoples of Spanish-speaking backgrounds of low or moderate incomes.

Barton, Clara (1821–1912) Founder of the American Red Cross and its long-time leader, she supervised *relief* work for *disaster* victims of war, famine, and epidemics in various nations. She also led the movement of the International Red Cross to provide relief in disaster situations other than war.

basal metabolism rate (BMR) The amount of energy used by an individual at rest.

baseline The frequency with which a specific behavior or event occurs in a natural state, measured before any attempts are made to influence it.

basic needs In *social planning,* those items considered to be essential for the maintenance of human well-being, including adequate food, shelter, clothing, heating fuel, clean water, and security from bodily harm.

basic research A systematic knowledge-building inquiry whose product has no known practical or commercial use—that is, seeking "truths" for their intrinsic worth. This is contrasted with *applied research.* Social work research is infrequently basic because it is oriented to solving social problems.

basic skills training Structured educational programs to help students acquire rudimentary proficiency in reading, writing, and arithmetic; also, sometimes improving attention span, memory, and the ability to transfer and generalize recently acquired knowledge.

BASW   See *British Association of Social Workers (BASW)*.

battered child   A youngster who has been physically abused or injured. The injury is usually inflicted on the child by a parent, other adult *caregiver*, or older sibling and may occur intentionally or impulsively in episodes of uncontrolled *anger*. See also *child abuse*.

battered spouse   A wife, or sometimes a husband, who has been physically injured by the other. Battering is a physically violent form of *spouse abuse*.

Batterers Anonymous   A national *self-help organization* with chapters in most larger communities, whose members (most of whom have been wife abusers) help one another to end abusive behavior. They have regular meetings to provide support and encouragement, and they maintain a "buddy system" and telephone hot lines.

battery   A form of illegal *abuse* that involves physical force or injury.

BEAM   See *Brain Electrical Activity Mapping (BEAM)*.

bedlam   Chaotic behavior of a group who seem to be acting irrationally and without reference to one another. The term derives from the London asylum for people with mental disabilities, officially named Priory of St. Mary of Bethlehem (Bedlam) when it opened in 1247. Bedlam became a synonym for *mental hospitals* for several centuries.

bed-wetting   *Enuresis*, the involuntary discharge of urine, usually by a child who had formerly achieved bladder control, during sleep or bed rest.

Beers, Clifford W. (1876–1943)   Leader of the *mental hygiene* movement in the United States. After spending three years in a mental hospital, in 1908 he wrote the influential book *A Mind That Found Itself* and told the world about the inhumane conditions in the treatment of people with mental disorders. He helped create various organizations for the improvement in treat-

ing mental illness. See also *Mental Health Association (MHA)*.

behavior   Any action or response by an individual, including observable activity, measurable physiological changes, cognitive images, fantasies, and emotions. Some scientists consider even subjective experiences to be behaviors.

behavioral assessment   In *behavior modification* and *social learning theory*, the delineation of undesired behavior patterns and their controlling conditions. The description of these patterns is based on direct observation rather than on *inference* about underlying pathology based on surface cues. See also *psychosocial assessment*.

behavioral family therapy (BFT)   The use of *social learning theory* and the therapeutic techniques of *behavior modification* to help families achieve specific goals. In behaviorally oriented *family therapy*, the social worker helps the client–family members define their problems clearly in terms of *overt behaviors* and develop problem-solving behaviors to which all agree. Homework assignments, quantifying specific actions, and maintaining certain communications activities are frequently part of this form of *intervention*.

behavioral rehearsal   The technique used by social workers and other helping professionals, especially those with behaviorist orientations, in which the professional suggests or demonstrates desired behavior to a client and then encourages the client, through description, *role playing*, and other demonstrations, to behave similarly. With practice, feedback, and repetition of the behavior in the relatively "safe" environment of the professional's office, the client is more likely to be successful in achieving the desired behavior at the appropriate time.

behaviorism   The school of psychology and related sciences, founded by Ivan Pavlov (1849–1936), J. B. Watson (1878–1958), B. F. Skinner (1904–1990), and others, which seeks to explain *behavior* in terms of observable and measurable responses. Basic tenets of the orientation are that *maladaptive* behavior patterns are learned and can be unlearned and that *introspection* and the *unconscious* are unscientific hypotheses. Behaviorism has led to theoretical concepts and therapeutic methods such as *behavior modification* and *social learning theory*.

behavior modification A method of assessing and altering *behavior* based on the methods of applied behavior analysis, the principles of *operant conditioning*, *classical conditioning*, and *social learning theory* (for example, *positive reinforcement*, *extinction*, and *modeling*).

behavior therapy Application of *behavior modification* principles in clinical settings to assess and alter undesired behaviors such as *fear*, *anxiety*, *depression*, *sexual disorder*, and other problems using techniques based on empirical research.

Bell's Palsy Muscle paralysis on one side of the face, resulting from temporary damage to the facial nerve. Most patients recover completely, many without treatment.

Bender gestalt test A test used in diagnosing certain psychological and neurological disorders. After the subject has copied several designs, the results are analyzed, usually by a trained psychologist or neurologist, for spatial errors that help locate and determine the type of disturbance.

benefactor One who provides financial or other support for some aspect of the public good.

benefit reduction rate (BRR) In social welfare programs, the amount of money that is withheld from a *public assistance* payment for each additional dollar of household income beyond a specified amount. For example, in *Aid to Families with Dependent Children (AFDC)*, the *Food Stamp program*, and *housing programs*, benefits vary depending on the other sources of client income. Thus, when a client becomes employed, the AFDC benefits are reduced by 100 percent of the amount earned, and food stamp benefits are reduced by 30 percent of the amount earned. However, the major practical alternative leads to the *cliff effect*, which is also a *disincentive*.

benefits 1. Cash benefits are payments in the form of money or redeemable vouchers. 2. In-kind benefits are services or goods rather than money—for example, food baskets, agricultural surpluses, housing, and personal counseling.

benign neglect A policy of leaving a situation, organization, or class of people alone, with the expectation that by doing so the situation, organization, or class of people will be able to improve on its own merits.

benzodiazepines A group of *psychoactive drugs* that act as *central nervous system (CNS)* depressants. Popularly referred to as tranquilizers, benzodiazepines are prescribed by physicians to help patients reduce *anxiety* and pain and to sleep. Trade names include Valium and Librium. Some substance abusers use these drugs nonmedically to produce a state of alcohol-like *intoxication*.

bereavement The emotional and physical reaction to loss of a loved one. See also *grief* and *uncomplicated bereavement*.

beriberi A nutritional disease caused by an insufficiency of vitamin B.

Besant, Annie (1847–1933) An English community organizer, she helped organize unions for poor working women and published and distributed information about *birth control* to poor families. She helped found and lead the British Malthusian Society to promote *contraception*.

Bethune, Mary McLeod (1875–1955) Leader in the movement for the education and social development of African Americans, she founded what is now Bethune–Cookman College in Daytona, Florida, and organized and led several *civil rights* groups. She was also influential in the administration of Franklin D. Roosevelt, especially in assuring that *New Deal* programs included African Americans.

Better Business Bureau A voluntary association found in most cities and towns comprising business owners and managers who define fair and ethical practices in the conduct of business. These bureaus often accept complaints from the public about businesses who violate their standards and exercise persuasion to encourage their compliance.

Beveridge Report   A 1942 report, by economist *William Henry Beveridge* (1879–1963), that proposed a plan providing for *"cradle-to-grave"* economic protections. The report formed the basis for much of the current British social security and health care system.

Beveridge, William Henry (1879–1963) Founder of the British welfare state. Before World War II, he planned and wrote major social legislation to help poor people, laborers, and children. An early *settlement house* leader and social worker, Beveridge served as director of *Toynbee Hall*. His 1942 *Beveridge Report* was implemented after the war and is the basis for Great Britain's current social security and health care system. It has also been used as a model by many other nations, especially former British colonies.

BFT   See *behavioral family therapy (BFT)*.

BHP   See *Bureau of Health Professions (BHP)*.

BIA   See *Bureau of Indian Affairs (BIA)*.

bias   1. An *attitude* that can influence feelings, usually resulting in an individual's having positive or negative predispositions about a particular group, individual, idea, or object. 2. In *research*, a tendency for the results to lean in one or another direction because of improper *sampling*, misuse of statistical or research tools, or other improper methods.

biased writing   See *unbiased writing*.

bibliotherapy   The use of literature and poetry in the treatment of people with emotional problems or *mental illness*. Bibliotherapy is often used in *social group work* and *group therapy* and is reported to be effective with people of all ages, with people in institutions as well as outpatients,

and with healthy people who wish to share literature as a means of personal growth and development. See also *art therapy* and *poetry therapy*.

bigamy   The illegal offense of having more than one wife or husband at the same time. In the United States, bigamous marriages have no legal validity in any state. See also *polygamy*.

Big Brothers/Big Sisters of America   *Voluntary associations* whose work under professional supervision, usually by social workers, provides individual guidance and companionship to boys and girls deprived of a parent. Big Brothers was founded in 1946, especially to provide role models for fatherless boys. Big Sisters was formed in 1971, primarily to provide role models and positive female images for girls and boys. The two groups were merged in 1977.

bilingual special education   An educational alternative for Limited English Proficiency students with disabilities. The *Education for All Handicapped Children Act* (P.L. 94-142) specifies that children with disabilities must be given the same educational opportunities as other children and that these opportunities are not precluded by poor command of English.

bilis   A *culture-bound syndrome* found especially among Latino groups in which the individual experiences nervous tension, trembling, screaming, and various *somatic complaints*, said to be the result of feeling intense anger or rage. This syndrome is also known as *muina*.

bimodal   In frequency distributions, two categories whose values occur most frequently. For example, in a city where the delinquency rate peaked every January and July, there would be a bimodal distribution of delinquency.

binge eating disorder   The rapid consumption of unusually large amounts of food in a short time without necessarily being hungry. Individuals often feel embarrassed, guilty, or depressed about the lack of control over it. In this proposed diagnosis of the *DSM-IV,* the behavior is not associated with compensatory behaviors (such as purging, fasting, or excessive exercise seen in *bulimia nervosa).*

biodegradability The capability of decaying (being broken down into component elements, usually including water, carbon dioxide, and other simple, small molecule substances), caused by the actions of living things such as bacteria and molds. Biodegradability is an important environmental concern because it is a natural recycling process; all new life and the substances necessary to sustain life use the products of biodegration. Because synthetic materials are not biodegradable, their disposition after use is not a resource but an environmental problem.

bioethical decision making The system and procedures for establishing the type and degree to which medical services will be provided to a patient. These patients are most frequently newborns with birth defects or very old persons suffering from serious mental or physical dysfunctions. Although modern medical technology can maintain at least a diminished quality of life for people with extremely debilitating health problems, the health care professionals must use carefully specified criteria in deciding whether to use these procedures. Moreover, their work must be overseen by representatives from the public.

bioethics Also known as biomedical ethics, the analysis and study of legal, moral, social, and ethical considerations involving the biological and medical sciences. Issues of particular interest include *genetic engineering, reproductive technology, surrogacy,* organ transplantation, use and withdrawal of medical and mental health treatment, *suicide,* and *patients' rights.*

biofeedback A method of training people to modify their own internal physiological processes, such as heart rate, muscle tension, blood pressure, and brain wave activity, through self-monitoring. Usually, this is done by using mechanical instruments to provide information about variations in one or more of a subject's physiological processes. The resulting information is displayed to the subject *(feedback),* which helps the individual to control these processes even though he or she may be unable to articulate how the learning was achieved.

biogenic Originating physiologically or biologically rather than psychologically.

biomedical ethics See *bioethics.*

biometry The study of all the factors that determine an individual's probable life span.

Bion group See *Tavistock group.*

biopsy Removal and examination of body tissue samples to detect the presence of *cancer* and other diseases.

biopsychosocial A term applied to phenomena that consist of biological, psychological, and social elements, such as *stress.*

bipolar disorder A category of mental illnesses in which *mood* and *affect* are *maladaptive.* Formerly known as *manic–depressive illness,* the category may be subcategorized as *manic* type (symptoms often include *hyperactivity, euphoria,* distractibility, pressured speech, and *grandiosity),* depressed type (symptoms often include deep sadness, *apathy,* sleep disturbance, poor appetite, low *self-esteem,* and slowed thinking), and mixed type (frequently alternating patterns of manic and then depressed traits). The diagnosis of this condition distinguishes between *bipolar I disorder* (predominately manic) and *bipolar II disorder* (predominately depressive).

bipolar I disorder The bipolar *mood disorder* characterized by a single *manic episode* or much more commonly by recurrent *manic episodes* or *hypomanic episodes* often immediately preceded or followed by a major depressive episode. In formal diagnoses the clinician also indicates the type of most recent episode, as in "bipolar I disorder, most recent episode hypomanic" (or manic, depressed, mixed, or *NOS).*

bipolar II disorder The bipolar *mood disorder* characterized by one or more major depressive episodes and at least one *hypomanic eposide*. By definition there has never been a manic or mixed episode (in which case the diagnosis becomes *bipolar I disorder*). In formal diagnoses the clinician also indicates the type of episode, as in "bipolar II disorder, most recent episode hypomanic" (or depressed).

birth cohort All the people who were born within a specific year or other time frame.

birth control Limiting or preventing reproduction by various means. These include contraceptive (antipregnancy) devices such as *condoms,* contraceptive pills, diaphragms, intrauterine devices (IUDs), and spermicides. Another type of birth control occurs through the more-or-less permanent surgical *sterilization* of men (as in *vasectomy)* or women (as in *tubal ligation)*. Among the more-common efforts to control *conception* is "natural *family planning,*" in which there is awareness of the *fertility* cycle and sexual intercourse occurs only during those times in the cycle believed to be less likely to result in *pregnancy. Abstinence* from sexual intercourse and *abortion* are other methods used in birth control. See also *contraception* and *reproductive technology.*

birth defects See *congenital abnormalities.*

birth-order theories Hypotheses to explain apparent differences among *siblings* depending on whether they are oldest, middle, or youngest *children*. Some theorists suggest that the personalities of the first born are influenced by the fact that more is usually expected of them, so they tend to become achievers but also tend to have more feelings of insecurity and failure. On the other hand, middle children are often made to feel inferior to their older siblings, so they may try harder to catch up or display traits of inadequacy feelings or anger in interacting with others. Youngest children, according to many of these theorists, may refine attention-getting skills and narcissistic traits. The research on such hypotheses is still inconclusive and somewhat contradictory.

birth parents An individual's genetic mother and father. Adopted children and adoptions workers prefer this term over such words as "real parents."

birthrate The ratio of the number of births in a given population and period of time to the total *population,* usually expressed in terms of the number of births per 1,000 or 100,000 of the population.

bisexuality 1. Erotic attraction to males and females. 2. The coexistence in an individual of *homosexuality* and *heterosexuality.*

bivariate analysis Statistical analysis focusing on the simultaneous relationship between two variables. One example is *cross-tabulation.*

blacklist A file containing the names of those people deemed ineligible to participate in some activity or privilege because of their alleged behaviors or adherence to certain ideologies. For example, a group of business leaders might share the names of people who are considered potential union organizers and agree not to hire them.

Black Lung program A federally regulated *workers' compensation* program for coal miners disabled by tubercular-type illness associated with working in underground mines. The program is financed primarily through a tax on mine owners.

blackmail The *crime* of unlawfully taking money or property from a person or forcing that person to commit a crime by using fear, *coercion,* or threats. Typically, the coercion involves disclosing information the victim wants to keep concealed. See also *extortion.*

black-market adoption The *adoption* of children by couples or individuals who are unable to adopt through legitimate public or *private adoption agencies*. Typically, the party who wants a child contracts with an intermediary to obtain a child and makes monetary payments to the intermediary and indirectly to the child's legal guardian. See also *gray-market adoption* and *independent adoption.*

"blackout"   Lay term for the loss from memory of experiences, thoughts, or perceptions that occur during the state of alcohol or other substance *intoxication.*

black people   The term often used for people of color who come from, or whose ancestors came from, middle and southern Africa. Some people prefer the term *African American;* however, this designation excludes black people who are not Americans.

black power   The *social movement* whose goal is the achievement of greater racial *equity* in economic, political, and social influence. A basic premise of the movement is that black influence will grow as more black people gain positions of leadership in elective office, government, and business and acquire enough money to use in seeking legal rights and educational opportunities. The movement seeks to get black people who achieve these positions to work together in pursuit of these goals rather than dilute such efforts by working in disparate directions.

blamer role   A recurrent pattern of interpersonal communication characterized by acting superior, finding fault, behaving dictatorially, and attributing one's problems to others. The role was delineated by *Virginia Satir (Peoplemaking,* Palo Alto, CA: Science and Behavior Books, 1972, p. 66), who described the blamer as a person who conceals inner feelings of loneliness and failure by making persistent accusations. Other roles are the *computer role,* the *distracter role,* and the *placater role.*

blaming the victim   Attributing self-responsibility to individuals who are poor, socially or educationally deficient, victims of rape or other crimes, mentally or physically ill, or in some other ways casualties of unforeseen circumstances. This practice (for example, "if they had worked harder or saved their money, they wouldn't be poor"; "if she hadn't worn those clothes, she wouldn't have been raped or harassed") is often used by opponents of pro-grams to prevent victimization or to help victims.

blanket group   In *social group work* or *group psychotherapy,* the type of group that has no criterion for membership or orderly procedures. It is the opposite of *structured group.* Groups that are totally unstructured are rare, because group leaders usually have some plan for the composition of its membership.

"bleeding heart"   A pejorative expression, often applied to social workers and others who compassionately show concern for the disadvantaged or who attempt the *consciousness-raising* of more-advantaged people about disadvantaged people.

blended family   1. A family that is formed when separate families are united by marriage or other circumstance; a *stepfamily.* 2. Various kinship or nonkinship groups whose members reside together and assume traditional family roles. See also *reconstituted family.*

blighted area   A land area, region, or urban center damaged by economic depression, toxic chemicals, or social changes.

bloc   A *group* or *coalition* of groups with a common interest in advocating, promoting, or obstructing an ideology, cause, or legislation. Such groups often achieve power far above their individual numbers by voting uniformly, as in the case of Southern conservative legislators or the African American electorate.

block grant   A system of disbursing funds to meet a locality's health, education, and social welfare needs while permitting the recipient organizations to determine how best to distribute the money. Used mostly by the federal and sometimes state governments, the system is designed to consolidate budget itemization and eliminate the necessity of earmarking funds for every individual and *categorical program.* The system was a major provision of the *Omnibus Budget Reconciliation Act (OBRA)* of 1981 (P.L. 97-35). Proponents say it increases efficiency and local control, and opponents suggest that it is a covert way of reducing expenditures for social welfare needs.

blocking A temporary failure of memory, interrupting one's flow of speech or thought.

block organizations Formal or informal social groups who live in physical proximity to one another (as in a city block); have shared values, problems, and vulnerabilities; and meet to achieve their mutual goals.

block placement In *social work education,* an alternative to the traditional *concurrent placement* in *field instruction.* In the traditional model of *field placement,* the student alternates classroom experiences with work in a *social agency* on different days of each week. In block placements, the student attends classes only for several months and then works virtually full-time in a social agency under academic and professional supervision for several months. The amount of time spent in the agency during a block placement is the same as in concurrent placement, and students must meet the same academic requirements.

blood alcohol level (BAL) The amount of alcohol in a person's bloodstream expressed as a percentage of the total blood volume. For example, if the level is 0.05 percent, then five parts alcohol per 10,000 parts of blood exist. The amount may be determined by direct chemical analysis of the extracted blood or by a *Breathalyzer.* After alcohol is consumed, much of it enters the bloodstream until it is processed (that is, oxidized). The liver oxidizes alcohol at the rate of about one-half ounce per hour.

BLS See *Bureau of Labor Statistics (BLS).*

blue collar Members of a wage-earning *socioeconomic class.* The term originally applied to people who worked in factories or manual labor settings in which blue or dark clothes were worn and was used to distinguish these workers from those employed in offices or retail stores (white-collar workers).

blunted effect A dulling or deintensifying of the expression of *mood* or *emotion,* of-

ten noted as an important symptom in *schizophrenia.*

BMR See *basal metabolism rate (BMR).*

board of directors A group of people empowered to establish an organization's objectives and policies and to oversee the activities of the personnel responsible for day-to-day implementation of those policies. The boards of social agencies often comprise volunteers who are influential in the community and reflect the views prevalent in the community.

boat people Refugees who flee their homelands in barely seaworthy vessels to find more hospitable environments in other nations. Many of these people have faced great risks, including capture by their governments, piracy, malnutrition, and possible exploitation at the sites of their new locations. People from Southeast Asia, Haiti, and Cuba are recent examples.

body dysmorphic disorder A type of *somatoform disorder* characterized by excessive preoccupation about some imagined defect in appearance by someone who is of normal appearance. See also *dysmorphophobia* and *anorexia nervosa.*

body language See *kinesics.*

bonding The development by one person of *attachment* for another. The process begins when the individual has needs that are regularly fulfilled by the other, and his or her identity is partially shaped by the interrelationship.

"boondoggle" A negative term applied to allegedly wasteful or seemingly unproductive public works projects. The term first became prominent during the 1930s *New Deal* programs, which seemed to some to be more concerned with putting people back to work than with producing any goods or services of value.

Booth, Charles (1840–1916) A British pioneer in methods of surveying social problems, he wrote one of the first treatises on the conditions and causes of poverty and the working classes. He developed a classification of the types of poor people, used in early social work literature, and advocated many of the old-age and survivors insurance programs that were implemented in Great Britain.

bootleg To unlawfully make, carry, or sell alcohol or other illegal products.

borderline A descriptive term applied to a premorbid condition or any phenomenon located between two categories. Social workers and mental health workers often use the term informally in describing individuals who are at or near the dividing line between psychosis and nonpsychosis or normalcy and mental illness; not to be confused with *borderline personality disorder.*

borderline intellectual functioning *Intelligence* abilities that measure on *intelligence quotient (IQ)* tests at the 71 to 84 range (just below what psychologists refer to as *dull-normal* and just above the highest level of *mental retardation).*

borderline personality disorder One of the 11 *personality disorders* characterized by some of the following symptoms and traits: deeply ingrained and maladaptive patterns of relating to others, impulsive and unpredictable behavior that is often self-destructive, lack of control of anger, intense mood shifts, identity disturbance and inconsistent self-concept, manipulation of others for short-term gain, and chronic feelings of boredom and emptiness.

borderline schizophrenia A descriptive term applied to individuals who, to some clinicians, seem to be at or near a conceptualized line between *schizophrenia* and a *normal* state. In such people, some of the symptoms seen in schizophrenia are observed or inferred, but the severity, duration, and progression of those symptoms are inconsistent or do not meet all the diagnostic criteria. The term has been confused with or considered synonymous with *latent schizophrenia* or *simple schizophrenia.* Because it is so imprecise, the term is now rarely used by skilled diagnosticians.

Many who were once diagnosed as people with borderline schizophrenia are now given the diagnosis of *schizotypal personality disorder.*

Borstal system British penal program for young offenders (ages 15 to 23) in closed or open prisons that emphasize education, training, and rehabilitation. The system has undergone many changes and is now merging with the British corrections system for adult and youthful offenders. See also *reformatory.*

botulism A serious type of food poisoning caused by a bacteria found in improperly canned or refrigerated foods. The toxin attacks the *central nervous system (CNS)* causing headaches, weakness, constipation, and paralysis.

boufée délirante A *culture-bound syndrome* found mostly in West Africa and Haiti in which the individual experiences a sudden outburst of excitement, aggressive behavior, confusion, and sometimes paranoid thoughts and hallucinations.

boundaries Regions separating two psychological or social systems. A central concept in *family system theories,* pertaining to the implicit rules that determine how the family members or subsystems are expected to relate to one another and to nonfamily members. Analogous to the membranes of living cells, a function of boundaries is to differentiate systems and their subsystems and to permit the development of *identity.* Healthy family functioning largely entails clear boundaries; less-healthy functioning is seen where boundary subsystems are either inappropriately rigid or not consistently clear (that is, in a *disengaged family* or an *enmeshed family).* See also *family rules.*

bounded rationality In *social planning* theory, the recognition that rationality (specifying all the alternative strategies toward goal achievement, determining all their consequences, and evaluating these consequences) is the most efficient means toward action, but that such complete listings and evaluations are ultimately impractical.

Given that the obtainable information will be incomplete and somewhat inconsistent, the social planner instead decides on an action that is good enough to meet minimal criteria. See also *satisficing*.

boycott An organized refusal to maintain certain relationships with a person, organization, or government body. For example, a community organizer might convince all residents of a neighborhood to stop patronizing a store that discriminates against minorities.

Brace, Charles Loring (1826–1890) Founder of the *Children's Aid Society* in 1853, the private organization that provided shelter, education, and family *placing out* for homeless and destitute children, more than 50,000 of whom were sent on *orphan trains* to be adopted by Western farmers. His studies of the conditions of poor people in New York were widely reported and gained public awareness. His work greatly influenced modern *child welfare* programs and the *foster care* system.

Bracero program The transportation of Mexican farm laborers (braceros) to and from U.S. farms for seasonal work. This federal program was created during World War II primarily to alleviate shortages of farm workers, and it ended in 1964 because of opposition by organized labor. An informal and unlawful bracero program still exists on many U.S. farms with illegal aliens from Mexico.

Brady Bill *Gun control* legislation signed into law in 1993 that requires a five-day waiting period before certain handguns can be purchased and requires gun sellers to check applicants to ensure they comply with laws. The law was named after President Ronald Reagan's Press Secretary James S. Brady, who was shot during an assassination attempt against the president.

brain damage A lay term referring to extragenetic influences that impair or stop the normal growth, development, or function of brain tissue. The term "brain damage" is vague, however, because professionals would need to know what part of the brain has been damaged, when, how, and to what extent. A damaged brain does not necessarily impair learning, and impaired learning is not always caused by brain damage.

brain drain A nation's or institution's loss of scientific, technical, or leadership talent when these people relocate. This is an especially serious problem in *developing countries,* which use their limited resources to educate citizens, only to see them migrate to other nations that can offer higher salaries or other desirable conditions.

Brain Electrical Activity Mapping (BEAM) A computerized diagnostic tool for assessing *central nervous system (CNS)* functioning by turning signals from an electroencephalograph into colored maps depicting blood flow and other electrochemical processes in the brain.

brain fag Short for "brain fatigue," a *culture-bound syndrome* most frequently identified among peoples of West Africa in which the individual, usually a high school or university student, feels anxious, depressed, tired, and tense with pain around the eyes, head, and neck, attributed to intense mental exercise.

brainstorming In social work administration, a method of stimulating the development of ideas by assembling certain staff and board members and encouraging open discussion, while postponing criticism or analysis of the ideas proposed. See also *electronic brainstorming*.

brain trust A group of expert advisers to a public official, political candidate, or planning organization.

breach of promise Failure to wed after both parties have made a serious and specific agreement to marry and then one party unilaterally decides not to go through with it. In legal terms, "breach" refers to any failure to fulfill an agreed-on act or duty owed to an individual or to society, as in "breach of contract" or "breach of the peace."

bread line A procedure for distributing to assembled, needy people those bakery products, groceries, agricultural commodities, and surplus items that typically cannot be sold on the open market because they usually do not meet optimal quality or freshness standards. See also *soup kitchen.*

Breathalyzer   Trademark for a test device used to determine if a person is intoxicated. Most commonly administered by a trained police officer on those people operating motor vehicles, the test chemically analyzes the *blood alcohol level (BAL)* as indicated by a breath test. Most states require that applicants for driver's licenses consent in advance to taking the test when requested, and failure to take or pass the test is admissible in court.

breathing-related sleep disorder   A synonym for *apnea,* a *sleep disorder* involving disruption of sleep patterns caused by abnormalities of ventilation. This usually results in sleepiness, irritability, and less effectiveness in carrying out *activities of daily living (ADL).* Typically it results in loud snoring, gasps, and body movements likely to disturb the individual or bed partner.

Breckinridge, Sophonisba (1866–1948) Developer of *social work education* within universities, she was a founder of the School of Social Work at the University of Chicago where she established much of the graduate school curriculum for social workers. She introduced the *case method system* of teaching and was a founder of the *American Association of Schools of Social Work (AASSW),* now known as the *Council on Social Work Education (CSWE).*

bribery   The *crime* of offering or giving to a person, especially an official such as a police officer or legislator, money or something of value to influence that person's actions.

bridge housing   1. A *transitional living facility* for people who move from institutional settings to relatively autonomous homes, as in *halfway houses* or *quarterway houses.* 2. Temporary shelters for those people who have left their homes because of natural disasters, war, or economic problems but who lack the resources, opportunity, or replacement shelters for more permanent residence.

brief psychotic disorder   The sudden onset of psychotic symptoms such as *delusion, hallucination,* disorganized speech or behavior, or *catatonia,* lasting at least one day and less than one month. This condition is not caused by medical conditions, substance abuse, or other mental disorders. The disorder may be the result of a marked *stressor* (such as loss of a loved one or other psychological trauma) or occur without marked stressors or within four weeks postpartum. This disorder, when the result of marked stressors, was formerly known as *brief reactive psychosis.*

brief reactive psychosis   A term formerly used for *brief psychotic disorder* caused by marked stressors.

brief therapy   Any form of *psychotherapy* or *clinical social work* intervention in which specific goals and the number of sessions are predetermined. Brief therapy is usually goal oriented, circumscribed, active, focused, and directed toward specific problems or symptoms.

Briquet's syndrome   A rarely used diagnostic term for *somatization disorder.*

British Association of Social Workers (BASW)   The major professional association of social workers in the United Kingdom, headquartered in Birmingham. BASW publishes *Social Work Today.*

British National Insurance Act   The 1911 *social security* legislation in Great Britain devised by Lloyd George that provided old-age insurance; *unemployment compensation;* sickness insurance; and, in 1925, survivors insurance for most workers. Many of the features of the National Insurance Act were emulated in the U.S. *Social Security Act.* The National Insurance Act was replaced by the post–World War II social security system recommended in the *Beveridge Report.*

brittle bone disease   See *osteogenesis imperfecta.*

broken home   A family in which at least one parent is absent because of *divorce, death,* or *desertion*. Social workers now generally prefer the term *single-parent family*.

broker role   A function of social workers and community organizers in which clients (individuals, groups, organizations, or communities) are helped to identify, locate, and link available community resources; and various segments of the community are put in touch with one another to enhance their mutual interests.

Brown v. Board of Education   The 1954 U.S. Supreme Court ruling that the "separate but equal" interpretation of the 14th Amendment was unconstitutional and that racial *segregation* of public schools was illegal. See also *Plessy v. Ferguson*.

BRR   See *benefit reduction rate (BRR)*.

Bruno, Frank J. (1874–1955)   One of the first developers of a theory base in the new field of social work, he led the George Warren Brown School of Social Work at Washington University in St. Louis for many years. A *civil rights* activist, he worked to achieve opportunities for minorities in *social work education*. He wrote some of the most influential early social work texts, including *The Theory of Social Work* in 1936.

BSW   A bachelor's degree awarded to qualified students who major in social work in an undergraduate college accredited by the *Council on Social Work Education (CSWE)*.

budget   An itemized list of the amount of all estimated revenues a *social agency* or organization anticipates receiving, and the delineation of the amount of all estimated costs and expenses necessary to operate the organization; a statement of probable revenues and expenditures during a specified period.

Buell, Bradley (1893–1976)   A developer of the *community organization* and *social planning* fields in social work, he helped found the *American Association of Social Workers (AASW)* and published numerous books, including the influential *Community Planning for Human Services* in 1952.

bulimarexic   One who has *bulimia nervosa*.

bulimia nervosa   One of the *eating disorders* in which a pathologically excessive appetite with episodic eating binges is sometimes followed by purging. The purging may occur through such means as self-induced vomiting or the abuse of laxatives, diet pills, or diuretics. Bulimia usually starts as a means of dieting. Its subtypes include the purging and nonpurging type (using other inappropriate compensatory behaviors such as fasting or excessive exercise).

bumping   In bureaucratic organizations, the practice under which a senior employee, whose job has been eliminated, is allowed to take over the job of a junior employee.

bureaucracy   A form of social organization whose distinctive characteristics include a task-specific division of labor; a vertical hierarchy with power centered at the top; clearly defined rules; formalized channels of communication; and selection, promotion, compensation, and retention based on technical competence. See also *technocrat*, *apparatchik*, and *adhocracy*.

bureaucratization   The trend in social institutions and organizations toward more centralized control and enforced conformity to rigidly prescribed rules and channels of communication.

Bureau of Health Professions (BHP)   The bureau within the U.S. *Public Health Service* whose function is to facilitate the training and coordinate the distribution of people in the health care professions.

Bureau of Indian Affairs (BIA)   A federal organization, now within the U.S. *Department of the Interior*, created in 1824 to provide social services, health care, and educational programs; agricultural and economic assistance; and *civil rights* protections to *American Indians* and *Alaska Natives*.

Bureau of Labor Statistics (BLS)   A research agency of the U.S. *Department of*

Labor that compiles and publishes statistics about many variables of interest to social workers and social planners, including employment and unemployment rates, consumer prices, and wage rates.

Bureau of the Census, U.S. The bureau functioning within the U.S. Department of Commerce that carries out the constitutional requirement that all the people in the nation be counted every decade. The bureau, centered in Suitland, Maryland, conducts surveys and analyzes and disseminates resulting data about individuals, population groups, and social trends.

bureaus of public assistance State and county organizations that administer programs to provide economic and social services to needy families; funded from local, state, and federal revenues, these bureaus often help administer such programs as *Aid to Families with Dependent Children (AFDC)* and *general assistance (GA)*. In some jurisdictions, these bureaus are known as the department of welfare, the department of social services, or the bureau of health and human services.

burglary The *crime* of breaking and entering into someone's home, office, or other place with the intention of stealing property therein.

burnout A nontechnical term to describe workers who feel apathy or *anger* as a result of on-the-job *stress* and frustration. Burnout is found among *social workers* and other workers who have more responsibility than control.

Burns, Eveline M. (1900–1985) Educator at Columbia University School of Social Work and consultant to government planners on economic security programs, she helped write the *Social Security Act* and drafted plans for public assistance and work programs. She wrote the influential text *Social Security and Public Policy* (1956).

busing The transporting of students across school district boundaries, usually court ordered, to facilitate more equitable racial balance.

buying pool A group practice in which people join to purchase larger quantities of a given commodity than they could buy separately, thus benefiting from lower costs. Buying pools have often been organized by or in behalf of poor people's groups or homeless organizations.

C

Cabot, Richard C. (1865–1939) A physician and medical educator whose work with the *Children's Aid Society* led him to appreciate the part social work plays in the treatment process. Cabot established the nation's first *medical social work* department at Massachusetts General Hospital in 1905.

cachexia A weakened, emaciated, rundown (cachectic) condition caused by chronic disease.

caffeine withdrawal Symptoms of *withdrawal* (headache, marked fatigue, drowsiness, anxiety, depression, nausea, or vomiting) caused by abrupt cessation or reduction in use of caffeine (coffee, tea, cocoa, cola, chocolate). This is proposed as an official diagnostic category of the *DSM-IV*.

CAI program Computer-assisted instructional program. See also *IVD program*.

campaign An organized, intensive effort to achieve a goal, such as raise funds, win an election, gain publicity, or increase membership of an organization. See also *negative campaigning*.

Canadian Association of Schools of Social Work (CASSW) The organization whose membership comprises the professional schools of social work in Canada and whose purpose is to facilitate communication among schools and to maintain standards through accreditation reviews.

Canadian Association of Social Workers (CASW) The *professional association* of qualified Canadian social workers. Its purposes include professional development of its membership through educational programs, conferences, and publications, and the development and enforcement of ethical standards. CASW was founded in 1926; its headquarters are in Ottawa.

cancer A malignant tumor; uncontrolled growth of abnormal cells. Unlike normal body cells, cancer cells do not stop growing when in contact with other cells and thus may spread in the body. The cells spread either by invading surrounding tissue or by *metastasis*. Cancer cells compete with normal tissue for nutrients and eventually kill normal cells by depriving them of needed nutrition. Causes, specific symptoms, prognosis, and treatment vary considerably. See also *carcinoma, sarcoma, leukemia,* and *lymphoma*.

cannabis See *marijuana*.

cannabis abuse Continued use of psychoactive substances derived from or based on the cannabis plant such as *marijuana, hashish,* or purified tetrahydrocannabinol *(THC)*, despite the related health, socioeconomic, or vocational difficulties. Except when cannabis is used legally for medical purposes, all other use is considered abusive.

cannabis organic mental disorder *Intoxication, delusion,* or both, occurring after *marijuana, hashish,* or tetrahydrocannabinol *(THC)* use. Symptoms of cannabis intoxication include *euphoria, tachycardia,* the feeling of intensified perceptions, increased appetite, *paranoid ideation, panic attack, depression,* and *impaired social functioning*. When these symptoms occur with severe persecutory delusions, marked *anxiety, depersonalization,* and *amnesia,* it is called "cannabis delusion disorder." The usual duration of cannabis intoxication and delusional disorder is less than several hours.

Cannon, Ida M. (1877–1960) Medical social work conceptualizer and developer, she advocated for the establishment of social work departments in the nation's hospitals and published influential works for the field, including *Social Work in Hospitals* in 1923. She was a founder of the American Association of Hospital Social Workers, which was renamed the *American Association of Medical Social Workers (AAMSW)*.

canvass To make a systematic inquiry of specified groups of people (such as potential consumers, registered voters of a city, or members of a legislature) to determine their intentions or to influence their actions.

CAP See *Community Action Program (CAP)*.

capitalism An economic system in which the production and distribution of goods and services for consumers are controlled through private ownership and open competition.

capital offense A *crime* punishable by death.

capital punishment Government-sanctioned implementation of the death penalty, imposed on some criminals convicted of a *capital offense*, which may include murder, *rape*, or treason.

capitation A set amount of money per person. Managed care companies generally express capitation in terms of revenue or cost per member per month.

carcinogen A substance that causes *cancer*.

carcinogenic *Cancer* causing.

carcinoma One of the four major types of *cancer* (including *sarcoma, leukemia,* and *lymphoma*), characterized by the clawlike spread of the disease over the skin and membranes of internal organs.

cardiovascular disease Disease of the heart or blood vessels, responsible for nearly 50 percent of all deaths in the United States. Those at greatest risk are smokers and men with elevated blood pressure and serum cholesterol levels. Other risk factors are *heredity, obesity, stress,* and physical inactivity.

CARE See *Cooperative for American Relief Everywhere (CARE)*.

care-and-protection proceedings The legal *intervention* on behalf of a dependent whose parents or guardians no longer seem willing or able to provide for the dependent's needs.

career counseling The procedure used by social workers, personnel, and guidance advisers, educational specialists, and other professionals to provide information, advice, support, and *linkage* of *resources* to people who are deciding about future vocations or to workers who seek to maximize their vocational potential. Career counseling is most commonly offered to students in high schools or colleges to help them learn about existing opportunities and to help them recognize their assets and limitations.

caregiver One who provides for the physical, emotional, and social needs of another person, who often is dependent and cannot provide for his or her own needs. The term most often applies to parents or parent surrogates, day care and nursery workers, health care specialists, and relatives caring for older people. The term is also applied to all people who provide nurturance and emotional support to others including spouses, clergy, and social workers.

caregiver support group A support group comprising individuals who have in common the responsibility of managing the lives and providing for the needs of those unable to do so independently. Typically, such groups are made up of people who care for *frail elderly* parents, children with a *disease* or *disability, special-needs clients,* or family members with a *mental disorder.* The stress of caring for these people is often relieved through the mutual support the members provide one another. The groups may be led by social workers, other professionals, or the members themselves; the degree of structure varies widely.

caries Decay of the bones or teeth.

carnal knowledge   A legal term for sexual intercourse.

cartel   An association of businesses in the same or related industries that seeks to stabilize the supplies or conditions of production and thus influence prices.

case aide   In social work, a *paraprofessional* who helps the social worker, as a member of a *social work team,* to provide specified services for the client. Frequently, the aide has developed expertise in a set of specific functions and is called on to fulfill those functions when they are deemed important by the social worker in charge of the case. For example, the aide might be asked to telephone members of the client's family to obtain additional information or accompany a client to a clinic. Most case aides are paid employees of the social worker's agency, but some are volunteers or part of the *natural helping network.* See also *social work associates.*

case conference   A procedure often used in social agencies and other organizations to bring together members of a professional staff and others to discuss a client's problem, objectives, intervention plans, and prognoses. The participants in the conference may include the social workers who are providing the direct service to the client or client system and the professional supervisor of these social workers. Additional participants might include other agency workers who have special expertise or experience with similar problems or populations, members of other professional groups or disciplines who can provide more information and recommendations, and sometimes personal associates or relatives of the client who may be asked to provide information or helping resources. Some agencies schedule conferences on all ongoing cases; others review cases of special interest or concern. Case conferences are intended to improve communication, generate new ideas, and improve services.

case finding   Searching out and identifying those individuals or groups who are vulnerable to or experiencing problems for which the social worker or social agency has responsibility to provide needed help and service. See also *child find* and *outreach.*

case integration   Coordination of the activities of social workers and service providers from other relevant auspices who are simultaneously serving the needs of a client. This coordination means that the respective providers' services are consistent, additive, nonduplicative, and directed purposefully toward achieving the same goals. Case integration occurs both within and between organizations. See also *case management.*

caseload   All the clients for whom a given social worker is responsible.

case management   A procedure to plan, seek, and monitor services from different social agencies and staff on behalf of a client. Usually one agency takes primary responsibility for the client and assigns a case manager, who coordinates services, advocates for the client, and sometimes controls resources and purchases services for the client. The procedure makes it possible for many social workers in the agency, or different agencies, to coordinate their efforts to serve a given client through professional teamwork, thus expanding the range of needed services offered. Case management may involve monitoring the progress of a client whose needs require the services of several professionals, agencies, health care facilities, and human services programs. It typically involves *case finding,* comprehensive multidimensional *assessment*, and frequent reassessment. Case management can occur within a single, large organization or within a community program that coordinates services among agencies. Federal legislation enacted in 1981 allows states to pay for case management for *Medicaid* recipients under waiver of the usual rules. Social workers and nurses are the professional groups most often called on to fulfill this function. Case management is seen as an increasingly important way of limiting problems arising from fragmentation of services, staff turnover, and inadequate coordination among providers. See also *case integration.*

case method system In professional education, the procedure in which students review, discuss, and propose solutions to detailed descriptions of a representative hypothetical or actual problem. Social work education has made extensive use of this procedure since it was first advocated by *Sophonisba Breckenridge*.

case-mix reimbursement A system in which government or third-party organizations pay an institution, such as a nursing home or hospital, for its expected services to a group over a specified period. Typically, the amount paid to the institution depends not on the individual's specific health care requirements but on the variety of services likely to be required for the group for which care is provided. The system of *diagnosis-related groups (DRGs)* is one form of case-mix reimbursement.

case record Information about the client situation and the service transaction that is documented by the social worker during the intervention process and retained in the files of the social agency or social worker. Case records are an important source of information about clients, services, goals, intervention strategies, and outcomes. They are used in *case management* and interprofessional communication on *quality assurance*. According to Jill Doner Kagle (*Social Work Records*, 2nd ed., Belmont, CA: Wadsworth, 1991), case records also exist to demonstrate *accountability*, justify funding, and support supervision and research. See also *problem-oriented record (POR)* and *SOAP charting method*.

case study A method of evaluation by examining systematically many characteristics of one individual, group, family, or community, usually over an extended period.

casework See *social casework*.

cash benefits See *benefits*.

cash out Providing a welfare benefit in money rather than coupons, vouchers, or in-kind service. For example, some states provide food stamp benefits in cash rather than coupons with cost reductions and greater convenience to clients, social workers, and storekeepers.

cash vouchers A certificate permitting the recipient to purchase up to a specified amount from a designated supplier. Such vouchers are provided in various government programs to provide for needy individuals and stimulate the business of the supplier.

CASSW See *Canadian Association of Schools of Social Work (CASSW)*.

caste A highly restrictive *social class*. In some societies people are born into their castes, which thereafter limits their choices of level and type of education, occupations, associations, and marital partners.

castration theory A theory held by some psychoanalysts and others that boys fear harm to their genitals usually by their fathers once the boys become sexually attracted to their mothers. According to this theory, girls fear they already have been castrated. See also *penis envy theory*.

casual laborer An individual who seeks employment and works periodically, often based on current economic need or availability of desired jobs.

CASW See *Canadian Association of Social Workers (CASW)*.

Catalog of Federal Domestic Assistance A publication of the U.S. General Services Administration, printed and distributed bimonthly by the U.S. Government Printing Office, describing the programs that provide financial, technical, and in-kind assistance for all service groups in the United States.

catalyst role The intervention process whereby the social worker creates a climate of introspection and self-assessment for the client or community and facilitates communication, stimulates awareness of problems, and encourages belief in the possibility of change.

cataract Cloudiness in the lens of an eye resulting in impaired vision. Surgical treatment for cataracts has become relatively convenient and inexpensive.

Catastrophic Care Coverage A *social insurance* plan to reimburse eligible people for expenses incurred as a result of *catastrophic illness.* In 1988 the U.S. Congress passed a catastrophic care coverage legislation to protect *Medicare* recipients against these costs, but the bill was repealed in less than a year because of public dissatisfaction with its funding provisions.

catastrophic illness A physical or mental disorder that represents a sudden and very serious change in the victim's lifestyle. The term is defined more narrowly by the *Social Security Administration (SSA)* and *Medicare* as prolonged and disruptive illness requiring long hospital stays and expensive treatment.

catatonia The state of a person with a *mental disorder* who seems detached from reality and oblivious to environmental stimuli. Typically, catatonic people move very slowly and rigidly or may be stiff and statuelike. On some occasions and with no apparent provocation, their movements may become active and uncontrolled, and their moods may become excited. This is usually followed by a return to the more-characteristic state of stupor. See also *waxy flexibility.*

catatonic schizophrenia Technically known as "schizophrenia, catatonic type," one of the five major subtypes (also including *paranoid, disorganized, undifferentiated,* and *residual*) of *schizophrenia,* characterized by marked psychomotor disturbance that may involve immovability or excessive movement, *echolalia, echopraxia,* inappropriate postures, extreme negativism, and *mutism.*

catchment area The geographic region in which all potential clients are served by a given *social agency.*

catecholamines Biochemicals that transmit information between nerve cells. Some researchers hypothesize that deviations in these *neurotransmitters* may sometimes lead to *depression, mood disorder,* and *schizophrenia.* See also *dopamine hypothesis.*

categorical assistance *Welfare* programs for specific groups of people identified in the *Social Security Act.* Originally, the programs were *Old Age Assistance (OAA), Aid to the Blind (AB),* Aid to Dependent Children, and *Aid to the Totally and Permanently Disabled (ATPD).* Needy people in these categories could receive financial assistance from their respective states, supplemented by federal grants. In 1974 responsibility for the three adult categories was assumed by the federal *Supplemental Security Income (SSI)* program.

categorical grant Payment of funds or transfer of goods made by an organization, *social agency,* or individual (grantor) to a recipient (grantee) for agreeing to accomplish some specified objective. For example, *public assistance* programs such as *Aid to Families with Dependent Children (AFDC)* are funded by categorical grants made by the federal government to state governments in considering state governments' distribution of funds to needy families in a prescribed way. See also *grant* and *block grant.*

categorically needy People who are automatically eligible for certain welfare benefits, without a *means test,* because they fit some predetermined criteria. For example, some needy categories of people eligible for *Medicaid* include recipients of *Aid to Families with Dependent Children (AFDC)* and *Supplemental Security Income (SSI).* See also *joint processing.*

categorical program The provision of social services and other benefits to people who belong to specifically designated groups that are particularly at risk, such as older people, parentless children, and blind and disabled people.

catharsis Verbalization and other expression of ideas, fears, past significant events, and associations, the expected result of which is a release of *anxiety* or tension, resulting in improved functioning; also called *ventilation.*

cathexis The concentration of emotional energy and feelings onto a person, idea, object, or oneself. See also *decathexis.*

Catholic Charities USA An organization founded in 1910 to coordinate the 3,000

Roman Catholic Church–related local organizations and individuals who provide voluntary *social services* such as *family therapy, child welfare,* vocational and financial *counseling,* and recreational and educational services. The organization was formerly known as the National Conference of Catholic Charities.

Catholic Relief Services (CRS) The international organization founded and sponsored by the Roman Catholic Church to raise funds and distribute needed resources and provisions to those *populations* victimized by *poverty* and disasters, including *famine, epidemics,* floods, hurricanes, droughts, earthquakes, war, and *civil disorder.* CRS coordinates many of its activities with the *United Nations Disaster Relief Organization (UNDRO)* and, through the *Steering Committee for International Relief,* other church organizations and *private relief groups.*

Catholic Worker Movement The sociopolitical movement that began in the 1930s under the leadership of *Dorothy Day* (1897–1980) to promote *social justice* and social welfare for all, particularly immigrants to the United States, unemployed and marginally employed breadwinners, and people of color. The movement has been influential in advocacy for *pacifism, equal rights* for women and African Americans, and organized *labor unions.*

CAT scan Computerized axial tomography, a medical diagnostic tool for taking pictures of the interior of the head and body of the patient.

caucus A meeting, usually closed or semiprivate, comprising the leaders of an organization, to establish its agenda or platform, or to nominate candidates.

cause-oriented organization A formal or informal group comprising individuals who are united by shared *values* and goals and devoted to achieving specific social change or solving certain problems.

cause-versus-function issue The controversial historical dichotomy in social work between *social reform* activities and *social casework.* Some early social workers, such as *Jane Addams* (1860–1935), advocated a cause orientation, emphasizing social change through political action and community organization. Others, such as *Mary Richmond* (1861–1928), stressed the function of individual betterment through the technical skills of the social worker, such as interviewing and advice giving. The current view among most social workers is that the field must include both cause and function orientations.

CBO See *Congressional Budget Office (CBO).*

CCC 1. See *Civilian Conservation Corps (CCC).* 2. See *Commodity Credit Corporation (CCC).*

CCETSW See *Central Council for Education and Training in Social Work (CCETSW).*

CCRC See *continuing-care retirement communities (CCRC).*

CD See *community development (CD).*

CDCP See *Centers for Disease Control and Prevention (CDCP).*

CDF See *Children's Defense Fund (CDF).*

CDR See *Continuing Disability Review (CDR).*

cease-and-desist order A statement issued by a judicial authority and court of law prohibiting a person or organization from commencing or continuing a specified activity, such as tearing down a historic building, clearing a forest, or removing a child from one city to another. These orders are generally issued after the court is shown that the activity will likely be found to be unlawful.

Center for Health Statistics See *Department of Health and Human Services, U.S. (HHS).*

Center for Social Development and Humanitarian Affairs (CSDHA) The United Nations organization oriented to the world's development of social welfare and cultural development programs. The organization provides member nations with technical assistance, research, and information in their efforts to enhance their human services programs.

Centers for Disease Control and Prevention (CDCP)   An organization, which is part of the U.S. *Department of Health and Human Services (HHS)* and based in Atlanta, that coordinates efforts throughout the nation to prevent and minimize the spread of *disease*. The center acquires, analyzes, and disseminates data about the incidence of disease and its etiology, progression, and elimination.

centers for independent living   See *independent living, centers for.*

Central Council for Education and Training in Social Work (CCETSW)   The major accrediting body for *social work education* in Great Britain. CCETSW monitors the curriculum offered by British schools of social work at all levels and issues certificates that qualify social workers for professional practice. See also *Certificate of Qualification in Social Work (CQSW).*

centralization   The concentration of administrative power within a group, organization, or political entity. For example, public assistance programs that had been managed primarily at the state and local levels became more centralized with the passage of the *Social Security Act* and later the *Supplemental Security Income (SSI)* program.

central nervous system (CNS)   The brain and spinal cord. The CNS supervises and coordinates the activity of the entire nervous system. See also *autonomic nervous system (ANS)* and *peripheral nervous system.*

centration   A tendency to focus attention on one part of an object, situation, or aspect of a relationship while ignoring others that may be equally significant. See also *decenter.*

centrifugal family structure   In *family systems theory,* the pattern of relationship among family members in which there is little cohesiveness or attachment, and each member feels compelled to seek emotional support from outside the family.

centripetal family structure   In *family systems theory,* the pattern of relationship among family members in which each person is bound into the family and relatively isolated from outsiders. For example, the children remain at home even after reaching adulthood, and all family members encourage each other to remain highly interdependent.

centrist   One who holds an ideological position between the extremes; a moderate or "middle of the roader." See also *leftist* and *right wing.*

cerebral palsy   A disability of muscle control and coordination caused by brain damage that occurred before or during birth. The degree of severity depends on the extent of the brain damage. Although no cure exists, appliances such as braces and treatment involving physical, occupational, speech, and psychosocial therapy are often effective in minimizing disability.

cerebrovascular   Pertaining to the brain or the blood vessels that supply it.

cerebrovascular accident (CVA)   See *stroke.*

certificate of need (CON)   A permission grant to developers permitting them to build new hospitals or health facilities only when properly justified. The purpose of CON legislation is to distribute and control the number of hospitals and medical resources equitably to help keep down health care costs. The national network of health systems agencies reviews, plans, and recommends certification.

Certificate of Qualification in Social Work (CQSW)   The credential for the practice of professional social work throughout Great Britain. The certificate is awarded to applicants by the *Central Council for Education and Training in Social Work (CCETSW)* based on successful completion of specified levels of education at CCETSW–accredited educational institutions.

certification   An official assurance that someone or something possesses the attributes he, she, or it claims to have. Legal certification of a profession is the warranting by a state that the people certified have attained a specified level of knowledge and skill. *Professional certification* is such warranting by a *professional association*. Certification typically does not prohibit uncertified people from engaging in the specified activity (as does a license), but it prevents their use of the title "certified." Certification is usually considered to be a stronger form of regulation than *registration of social workers* but weaker than the license. See also *legal regulation, Academy of Certified Social Workers (ACSW),* and *Licensed Clinical Social Worker (LCSW).*

certified social worker A social work practitioner who is warranted by a professional association or legal body to have attained a specified level of education, knowledge, and skills; the title "certified social worker" is protected by statute in some jurisdictions and by professional associations in others, so that its use is restricted to those who qualify. See also *Academy of Certified Social Workers (ACSW)* and *legal regulation.*

CETA The Comprehensive Employment and Training Act (P.L. 93-203), a federal program begun in 1973 to retrain and place long-term unemployed, underemployed, or disadvantaged people in more-suitable jobs and jobs with future potential. The *JOBS program,* sponsored by CETA, was replaced in 1982 by the *Job Training Partnership Act,* which encouraged more private-sector, local, and state involvement in training programs. See also *employment programs,* the *Job Corps,* and *Neighborhood Youth Corps.*

CEUs Continuing education units, a specific amount and type of formal education required by certain professional associations, state licensing authorities, and employers to demonstrate that the professional is keeping current in relevant knowledge. For example, attending a three-hour workshop at a professional conference that is recognized or accredited by the authority might "earn" a social worker three CEUs to be counted toward continuing education requirements.

CFD See *Concern for the Dying (CFD).*

CFIDS See *chronic fatigue immune dysfunction syndrome (CFIDS).*

Chadwick, Edwin (1800–1890) Controversial social reformer and newspaper writer who pioneered in methods of inquiry about social problems. His writings about the sanitary conditions in London slums led to cleanup, renewal, and public health programs. Oriented to *blaming the victim,* he was the major author of the *Poor Law of 1834.*

chaining In *behavior modification,* a specific and complex series of connected or associated stimulus–response units that terminate with the delivery of a reinforcer. Social workers using behavioral techniques also use "backward chaining" in which the last stimulus–response unit of a chain is established first, and the other units are then added in reverse order until the desired chain is complete.

Chalmers, Thomas (1780–1847) Scottish theologian and professor of moral philosophy, he developed a system of private philanthropies to help Glasgow's poor. He organized volunteer workers and contributors to meet regularly with disadvantaged people to give them encouragement and training as well as material aid. Many of his extensive writings were used as guides for later efforts to help the poor. See also *Joseph Tuckerman.*

CHAMPUS The Civilian Health and Medical Program of the Uniformed Services, a federally funded health insurance program for the dependents of active duty and retired U.S. military personnel. CHAMPUS pays a significant proportion of the health care costs for the beneficiary in the private health care service–delivery system when such care is unavailable or inaccessible in military medical facilities. In certain circumstances, qualified social workers are directly reimbursed by CHAMPUS for providing their professional services in the care of people with mental disorders. See also *military social work.*

change agent A social worker or other helping professional or a group of helpers whose purpose is to facilitate improvement.

change agent system The organizations, social agencies, and community institutions that provide the auspices and additional resources through which the social worker *(change agent)* provides service.

change residue In the planned changes that community organizers help to bring about, the side effects that occur after the newly implemented structures are in place. The residue may be intended or unintended, desired or not, tangible or elusive. Because side effects are inevitable, organizers find it necessary to build ways of dealing with them into the plan.

channeling An administrative procedure in *case management* in which social agency workers are aware of resources in the community and often direct their clients to relevant programs for additional or supplementary service during the ongoing helping process. See also *linkage*.

character The most deeply ingrained aspects of personality and the resulting habitual modes of response.

character building Efforts to improve one's behavior, habits, and effectiveness in dealing with the biopsychosocial and physical environment, particularly through study and education, hard work, experience in relevant activities, and moral and spiritual training. Sometimes this term is used by unsympathetic authority figures to justify imposing difficult conditions such as excessive work demands or deprivation on others.

character disorder A *maladaptive* personality pattern involving inflexibility in thinking, perceiving, and reacting; also known as "character neurosis." Individuals with this dysfunction are often obsessively meticulous, pedantic, and cruel in an intellectual way. Psychoanalytically oriented professionals also describe certain specific maladaptive character traits such as the *oral character, anal character*, and *genital character*.

charette A technique used by community organizers and *disaster relief* planners to stimulate *citizen participation* during *crisis planning*. Professionals and community members (especially those most likely to be affected

by the crisis) work together intensively to plan a means of coping with the situation. See also *community reorganization*.

charismatic leader An individual whose influence is derived primarily from force of personality rather than legal authority or official title. Often the leader or founder of a social movement is charismatic (such as Martin Luther King, Jr., Mohandas K. Gandhi, and *Jane Addams*), but their successors often base their leadership on legal or official sanction.

charitable gambling Organized legal playing of games of chance to raise money for educational, religious, or public service uses. The games are usually conducted by churches, service clubs, civic associations, and similar organizations and include such activities as bingo, raffles, card games, and casino games. In many areas, especially those in rural or economically depressed towns, gambling has become a major source of funding for many human services programs. Many contend that this type of fundraising is the only way these service programs can survive, whereas others argue that gambling undermines society, moral values, and the very programs it helps to fund.

charity 1. Literally, love for one's fellow humans. 2. The donation of goods and services to those in need.

Charity Organization Societies (COS) Privately administered and philanthropically funded organizations that were the essential forerunners of modern social services agencies. The first COS was established in London in 1869. The first American COS was in Buffalo, New York, in 1877 and was duplicated in most larger eastern cities soon thereafter. COSs were staffed by volunteer workers who provided direct services to clients and coordinated community efforts to deal with social problems. As more COS workers, sometimes known as *friendly visitors,* gradually became professionalized, they were called *social workers*. By the 1930s, as government assumed more responsibility for people's economic and social security, the original COS goal was reached; thus, most of the organizations became or merged with family agencies united in the Family Service Association of America, which was later named the *Family Service America (FSA)*.

Chartist Movement   The reform campaign conducted by English workers (1838–1848) demanding universal male suffrage, voting by secret ballot, proportionally divided electoral districts, and the abolition of property qualifications for members of the House of Commons. The people were reacting to a period of low wages, high prices, and the recently enacted *Poor Law of 1834*.

checkbook activism   Donation of funds to public-interest organizations because the contributor lacks the time or opportunity for personal involvement.

check-in   A structure exercise often used in social work with groups or families in which each of the members is asked, at the beginning of the session, to indicate what they are specifically concerned about or would like to discuss. Check-ins are used to assure that all members of the session are heard from and become the focus of some attention. When the procedure occurs at the end of a group session, it is known as the "check-out." Check-in is the most common of the group procedures known as *go-round*.

"cheeking"   A practice used by many supervised patients to avoid taking their prescribed medications by concealing the pills inside their cheeks rather than swallowing them. The patients save the pills for later inappropriate use, or they discard the pills when unobserved. The practice is widespread because many patients dislike the effect or side effects of medications or wish to create their own side effects.

chemotherapy   The treatment of a disease, such as *cancer,* with chemicals.

Chicano   A term sometimes used to describe American citizens of Mexican birth or ethnic heritage.

child abuse   The recurrent infliction of physical or emotional injury on a depen-

dent minor, through intentional beatings, uncontrolled *corporal punishment,* persistent ridicule and degradation, or *sexual abuse,* usually committed by parents or guardians. State laws require social workers and other professionals to report instances of suspected child abuse to the appropriate authorities. See also *child neglect.*

child advocacy   Championing the rights of children to be free from *abuse* or exploitation by others and to have opportunities to develop toward their full potential. Since the beginning of their existence, social workers have led in this effort by fighting for *child labor* laws; calling public attention to inadequate care facilities and *orphanages*; and working to set up juvenile justice programs, to expand *foster care* and *adoption* care, and to eradicate *child snatching, kidnapping,* and *child abuse.*

child care   Nurturance and management of the day-to-day requirements to sustain the successful development of children. Although the term can apply to any activity in which a youngster's needs are provided for by a parent or guardian, it is specifically applied to children in institutions or 24-hour group-living situations. In this context, child care activities include physical care (such as feeding and clothing), habit development (such as personal hygiene and socialization), self-management (discipline), therapeutic care (counseling), tutoring, and first aid. These activities also include running the living group as a cohesive unit and managing the institutional program.

child care worker   A *professional* or *paraprofessional* who is responsible for the daily care and nurturance of a group of youngsters who reside in an institution. Such workers are often known as houseparents, residential workers, or group-living counselors. They fulfill the activities of institutional *child care* and are employed primarily in residential-care facilities for emotionally disturbed and dependent children and for people who are mentally retarded, in corrections facilities, in institutions for people with disabilities, and in homes for unwed mothers.

child custody   See *custody of children*.

child find   Diagnostic programs in many public schools in which children between the ages of three and five are screened to determine the existence of any physical or *developmental disorder* and when appropriate, then placed in early-intervention preschool programs.

child find organizations   Social agencies and programs oriented to locating *runaways* or *thrownaway children* and changing the conditions that contribute to such problems. These programs often are staffed by volunteers and funded by voluntary contributions and sometimes supported by public monies. The organizations work closely with local law enforcement organizations, child find organizations in other regions, and the *National Center for Missing and Exploited Children (NCMEC)*.

child guidance   The process of helping youths make optimal life decisions, develop decision-making skills, channel behaviors appropriately, and solve their problems. The guidance counselor, usually a person with a specialized background in education, provides youths with necessary information or access to that information. Special focus is on educational planning, academic and relationship problems, scholarships, and family problems. Counseling and testing (especially in terms of aptitude, vocational, and personality factors) are major activities. See also *achievement tests*.

Child Health and Human Development, National Institute of   The organization within the *National Institutes of Health (NIH)* that provides information and expertise on such factors as *sudden infant death syndrome (SIDS)*, *congenital abnormalities*, *developmental disabilities*, and human reproduction and fertility.

childhood   The early stage in the human *life cycle* characterized by rapid physical growth and efforts to model adult roles and responsibilities, mostly through play and formal education. Many developmental psychologists say this stage occurs after infancy and lasts until *puberty* (that is, from about 18 to 24 months to 12 to 14 years) or until *adulthood* (18 to 21 years). This stage is sometimes divided into early childhood (from the end of infancy to about age six) and middle or late childhood (from age six to, or through, *adolescence*).

childhood disintegrative disorder   A *developmental disorder* characterized by a marked regression in the child's development after more than two years of apparently normal development. After age two and before age 10, the child loses previously acquired communication skills, social relationships, and adaptive behavior and exhibits behavior generally observed in autistic disorders. The loss of skills eventually reaches a plateau and minimal improvement may occur; however, the difficulties remain relatively constant throughout life.

childhood schizophrenia   A chronic *psychosis* involving disturbances in thought, *perception*, *affect*, and *behavior* that appears in an individual before *puberty*. A youngster typically shows extreme *withdrawal*, gross immaturity, and failure to develop much *autonomy* or *identity* separate from parents or surrogate parents. Because this term is imprecise, professionals now rarely use it.

child labor   Paid or forced employment of children who are younger than a legally defined age. The minimum age for employment may vary from ages 14 to 18 depending on the nature of the work and the child labor standards of the country in which it takes place. The *International Labor Organization (ILO)* and the U.N. Convention on the Rights of the Child consider child labor to be exploitative when the work or conditions are harmful to the child's health or physical, mental, spiritual, moral, and social development. In the United States, child labor standards were established in 1938 by the *Fair Labor Standards Act*. Social worker *Grace Abbott*, as director of the *Children's Bureau*, led the fight for such standards. See also *apprenticing* and *Rights of the Child Convention*.

child molestation 1. Forcing a child to participate in some sexual acts that can include *rape, incest,* and erotic fondling. 2. Compelling a child to behave in a way that erotically stimulates the perpetrator.

child neglect The failure of those responsible for the care of a minor to provide the resources needed for healthy physical, emotional, and social development. Examples of neglect include inadequate nutrition, improper supervision, or no provisions for educational or health care requirements. Child neglect is seen as an act of omission by caregivers because of limited abilities or resources or other circumstances; it is differentiated from *child abuse,* which is seen as more willful.

child protective services (CPS) Human services, often including social, medical, legal, residential, and custodial care, which are provided to children whose *caregiver* is not providing for their needs. Social workers who work in units of government agencies often help legal authorities with investigations to determine if children are in need of such services, help children get services when needed, and may provide such services themselves. Social workers investigate alleged abuse and neglect and make assessments and recommendations to legal or social welfare authorities. CPS also include the related shelter services and community supervisor services. See also *adult protective services (APS).*

child psychoanalysis The use of *psychoanalytic theory* and methods in helping children overcome psychic conflicts and emotional disturbances that impede their healthy development. Practitioners of this discipline, which also is known as child analysis, are psychiatrists, psychologists, and social workers with education in *psychoanalysis* and added training for work with children.

child psychotherapy Treatment by trained professionals of youngsters for mental illness, emotional conflict, impaired psychological development, or behavioral maladaptations. *Psychotherapy* with children includes all the theory and method applied to other psycho-

therapies but may emphasize *play therapy, small-group therapy,* and supportive and reeducative therapies. Professionals who provide child psychotherapy services include specially trained psychiatrists, social workers, psychologists, educational specialists, mental health nurses, and other mental health professionals.

children Youngsters who are younger than the legal age of responsibility or emancipation; in most states and nations, this age is 18 years.

Children's Aid Society The private organization founded by *Charles Loring Brace* (1826–1890) in 1853 in New York to provide shelter, education, care, and family placement for homeless and destitute children. The society's methods greatly influenced modern *child welfare* programs and the *foster care* system.

children's allowances See *family allowance.*

Children's Bureau The U.S. government organization, created in 1912 and now part of the *Administration on Children, Youth, and Families (ACYF)* of the U.S. *Department of Health and Human Services (HHS),* that plans, integrates, and advocates national programs on behalf of children.

Children's Defense Fund (CDF) An advocacy and lobbying organization on behalf of the nation's children that scrutinizes regulations and legislation affecting children and also proposes new and modified programs. It strives to create and enforce *child welfare* laws and to support organizations that serve the special needs of children.

child sexual abuse A form of *child abuse* in which a dependent child is compelled, by manipulation or force, to fulfill the sexual demands of an older person, often a family member. See also *child molestation.*

child snatching The illegal act of removing a dependent child from the legal care and authority of the parent or guardian, usually by another of the child's relatives. Most typically, child snatching occurs among families that are dissolving, as in divorces or foster care placements, and one of the former caregivers does not accept the legal ruling granting custody to another person or group. The unauthorized person takes the child and often conceals the child's whereabouts or otherwise keeps moving so that the authorities have difficulty returning the child to the rightful custodian. See also *custody of children* and *stolen children*.

Child Support Enforcement, Office of The organization within the *Administration for Children and Families (ACF)* of the U.S. *Department of Health and Human Services (HHS)* that helps states and local jurisdictions compel parents to meet their obligations to their children. The office helps plan and manage programs to locate absent parents, establish paternity, coordinate activities among states, and bring to justice parents who do not fulfill their obligations.

child welfare That part of *human services* and *social welfare* programs and ideologies oriented toward the protection, care, and healthy development of children. Child welfare measures are found in national, state, and local programs and are also designed to prevent conditions that interfere with children's positive development.

Child Welfare League of America (CWLA) The major national voluntary association for promoting the interests of children. Founded in 1920, it is a federation of accredited *child welfare* agencies that provides standard setting, accreditation, technical leadership to local governments, and advocacy for children.

CHINS Children in need of supervison. See *persons in need of supervision (PINS)*.

"chiseler" A slang expression referring to one who gets money and goods by cheating, begging, or "sponging off" others. The term often has been applied disparagingly to welfare recipients who are said to have misrepresented their needs and resources to increase benefits.

chlamydia One of the *sexually transmitted diseases (STDs)* caused by nongonococcal (not gonorrhea) organisms. Symptoms are similar to those of *gonorrhea* and are equally severe in women but usually less severe in men. In women, symptoms include inflammation in the pelvic region, scarring of tissue, and sometimes sterility; in men, they include inflammation in the urethra and prostate gland. Babies born to infected women can develop pneumonia and eye infections. Often no symptoms are evident until the disease has advanced to more-serious levels. Early treatment of the infected person and partner with antibiotics is usually successful.

chlorpromazine See *antipsychotic medication*.

Choice in Dying A national, not-for-profit organization dedicated to advocating for the rights of people to make their own decisions about medical care and to receive compassionate and dignified care at the end of life. The organization educates the public, health care providers, and policymakers about the needs of dying patients and their loved ones, and it provides free *advance directives* and counseling. Choice in Dying was created in 1991 by the merger of *Concern for the Dying (CFD)* and *Society for the Right to Die*. The society, under the aegis of the Euthanasia Society and the Euthanasia Educational Fund, pioneered the *living will* in 1967.

cholera An epidemic disease spread through polluted water resulting in such symptoms as diarrhea, vomiting, thirst, and cramps.

choreiform movements Irregular, nonrepetitive, dancelike movements, often symptomatic of mental or physical disorders.

chore service A home maintenance program, in which unskilled or semiskilled tasks that would usually be done by family members, such as washing walls and windows and removing trash, are provided by public departments of human services and social agencies for needy, homebound people. These services exclude skilled housing repairs or regular cleaning that is necessary if the person is to be able to remain at home. See also *homemaker services*.

chorionic villa sampling (CVS) A medical procedure for detecting chromosomal abnormalities and inherited metabolic disease in the *fetus* by removing and examining a small amount of placental tissue. See also *amniocentesis*.

Christian Democracy   A political movement and philosophy that espouses traditional Judeo–Christian religious values in combination with the social values of *capitalism*. The philosophy is the foundation of the Christian Democrat parties that are particularly influential in Germany and Italy.

chromosomal disorders   A type of *genetic disorder* resulting from faulty structure or incorrect numbers of chromosomes. These chromosome aberrations can cause miscarriage, stillbirths, neonatal death, *congenital abnormalities*, and *Down's syndrome*. Women younger than 15 and older than 35 have greater chances of giving birth to children with chromosomal disorders.

chronic   Pertaining to problems, abnormal behaviors, and medical conditions that have developed and persisted over a long period. Many helping professionals consider problems that have lasted more than six months to be chronic and those that last fewer than six months to be *acute*.

chronic fatigue immune dysfunction syndrome (CFIDS)   The name preferred by patient advocacy groups for what has been called *chronic fatigue syndrome*, to emphasize the organic nature of the disease.

chronic fatigue syndrome   A physical disorder characterized by excessive and prolonged lethargy, low energy, sleepiness, and apathy, often accompanied by psycho-social problems such as *depression, anxiety,* vocational difficulties, and family conflict. See also *chronic fatigue immune dysfunction syndrome (CFIDS)*.

chronic motor or vocal tic disorder   A persistent pattern of involuntary rapid muscle movements and vocalizations that have lasted for more than one year. A condition of this type that has lasted less than one year is known as a *transient tic disorder*.

CIDES   See *Inter-American Social Development Center (CIDES)*.

CIO   See *American Federation of Labor–Congress of Industrial Organizations (AFL–CIO)*.

CIP   See *Council of International Programs (CIP)*.

circadian rhythm sleep disorder   A *dysomnia* type of *sleep disorder,* formerly called *sleep–wake schedule disorder,* in which the individual's routine sleep pattern is mismatched with daily demands regarding the timing and duration of sleep. This disorder occurs often in nightshift workers, people on watches where sleep is taken at short intervals, and those experiencing "jet lag."

circuit-breaker tax relief   State or local tax laws that reduce the property tax rates on the homes of needy residents. The provision occurs when the home escalates in value to a point where the homeowner can no longer afford to pay all the property taxes.

circular causality   The concept, particularly in *systems theories,* that describes the cause of an event, behavior, problem, or pattern as being part of a complex sequence of reciprocally influential interactions. Behavior in one component of an organized system affects behavior in another component, which affects behavior in the first, and so on, in a recurring circular fashion. In this view, the *linear causality* concept is an error in *epistemology*.

circumflex model   A model for viewing and understanding human relationships that assumes a curvilinear relationship between variables. For example, community representatives sit around a circular table, with those most similar to one another sitting on either side and others who are progressively less similar sitting farther removed, until those with no similarities sit opposite.

cirrhosis   The scarring of body tissue, most commonly the liver. Those most susceptible to cirrhosis are middle-age men with a nutritional (protein) deficiency brought about by *alcoholism*. The damage to the liver may result in such symptoms as *emaciation,* jaundice, gastrointestinal disturbances, *hepatitis,* enlargement of the liver and spleen, and distension of the veins. Treatment usually includes a diet with adequate protein, vitamin supplements, and sometimes blood transfusions and excess fluid removal.

cisvestism Dressing inappropriately in the clothes of one's own gender (for example, adult as a child, civilian as a firefighter). See also *transvestism*.

citizen participation Involvement of members of the general public who are likely to be affected by a changed *social policy*, law, or circumstance in the process of planning and implementing that change. Community organizers usually attempt to facilitate citizen participation in change efforts. Many laws dealing with the public welfare (such as *Title XX* of the *Social Security Act*) require citizen participation in the development and implementation of certain social services plans. Some social workers identify various types of citizen participation, including agencies or bureaucracies that initiate the involvement and those in which citizen groups and individuals themselves initiate the involvement.

citizens committee A supposedly nonpartisan organization established to bring about social change or elect a candidate. Often such committees develop in response to a specific problem, stay focused only on that problem, and disband when that problem is solved. Many citizens committees are set up by political parties or permanent social cause groups to organize otherwise independent voters or residents of a specific jurisdiction. See also *voter registration drives, Common Cause,* and *rainbow coalition*.

city planning Systematic efforts to order urban development; establish priorities; and implement goals pertaining to the overall well-being of a city, town, neighborhood, or metropolitan region. City planners were originally oriented toward the physical development of a city, including development of its infrastructure and aesthetic amenities. Later, their objectives expanded to include developing sound land-use patterns, improving governmental procedures, and enhancing the quality of life and welfare of citizens.

civic associations Private *voluntary associations* whose members meet regularly to socialize and to plan and implement activities for the benefit of the community. These associations vary considerably in their goals, methods, and membership requirements. Some of these associations, which have chapters in most communities, include the Rotary, Lions, Jaycees, Junior League, and Business and Professional Women's clubs.

civil contempt A form of *contempt of court* that occurs when an individual fails to follow a court order, such as not making regular child support payments or not appearing for scheduled meetings with a social worker for court-ordered therapy.

civil defense Procedures, structures, plans, and systems designed to protect the lives and property of the civilian population from enemy attack or natural disaster.

civil disobedience Noncompliance with a government's laws or demands, usually to call attention to those laws that are considered unfair and to bring about changes or concessions in them. Civil disobedience often takes the form of group actions such as marches and assemblies, deliberate nonpayment of taxes, and the obstruction of the free movement of others. See also *passive resistance* and *freedom riders*.

civil disorder A public disturbance in which a group is involved in violent activity causing danger, injury, or property damage to others.

Civilian Conservation Corps (CCC) A federal program established in 1933 to conserve and develop U.S. *natural resources* and create jobs for unemployed young men. The program, abolished in 1942, was used in part as a model for the 1964 *Job Corps* program.

civil liberties Certain freedoms that may not arbitrarily be taken away or denied by society or external authority. The freedom to act according to one's own conscience; to worship, speak, and travel without restriction; and to choose one's own profession or associates are examples of civil liberties.

civil rights Rights of citizens to be protected against *discrimination* or arbitrary treatment by government or individuals and to engage in certain behaviors as long as they do not infringe on the rights of others. In the United States, these rights include those guaranteed in the Constitution's Bill of Rights (such as freedom of speech, religion, and the press) and others instituted since the adoption of the Bill of Rights (such as due process and equal protection under the law). Several civil rights acts and constitutional amendments have sought to bestow specific protections on *African Americans* and other racial and ethnic groups. This legislation includes such acts as the *Civil Rights Act of 1964*, the Voting Rights Act of 1965, and the 1968 housing acts designed to eliminate discrimination in housing and real estate. See also *civil liberties.*

Civil Rights Act of 1964   The comprehensive federal legislation (P.L. 88-352) prohibiting *discrimination* for reasons of race, religion, or national origin in schools, employment, and places of public accommodation including restaurants, theaters, and hotels.

civil rights group   A *cause-oriented organization* whose members share the goal of achieving equal opportunity for all people including racial and ethnic groups, people with a *disability,* and women. Civil rights groups seek changes in the sociopolitical system that fosters *discrimination, ethnic stereotyping*, and inequitable treatment in legal institutions. Some of the major national civil rights groups include the *National Association for the Advancement of Colored People (NAACP), National Urban League, American Civil Liberties Union (ACLU), American Indian Movement (AIM), Anti-Defamation League of B'nai-B'rith, National Organization for Women (NOW), Congress of Racial Equality (CORE), Operation PUSH, Southern Christian Leadership Conference (SCLC),* and *Concern for the Dying,* as well as the *National Abortion Rights Action League (NARAL)* and *National Right-to-Life Committee (NRLC).* Many state and federal organizations, including the U.S. *Commission on Civil Rights,* are concerned with the enforcement of *civil rights* laws.

civil servants   Government employees below elected or policymaking ranks whose employment is based on the specified and needed skills and performance of certain duties. See also *Office of Personnel Management (OPM).*

Civil Service, U.S.   The federal organization responsible for managing most of the nonelected, nonappointed civilian employees of the U.S. government.

Civil Works Administration (CWA)   A federal program established in 1933 to provide employment for millions of citizens in public works projects and to stimulate depressed industries such as construction. The program was abolished at the beginning of World War II. See also *Public Works Administration (PWA).*

clang association   A mental process in which the sound of one word reminds an individual of a similar-sounding expression. Often this process leads the person to think of the meaning in the new expression or to other similar-sounding words. Frequent fixation on clang associations is sometimes symptomatic of mental disorders such as *schizophrenia* and *obsessive–compulsive disorder.*

class action social work   Collaborative litigation with the goal of obtaining a favorable court ruling that will benefit the social welfare of a group of socioeconomically disadvantaged people. For example, in class actions in mental illness prevention, social workers and attorneys seek court rulings that have positive psychological effects for people who were at risk of developing mental disorders (Armando Morales and Bradford W. Sheafor, *Social Work: A Profession of Many Faces,* 5th ed., Boston: Allyn & Bacon, 1989).

class action suit   A civil legal action taken by or on behalf of a group, community, or members of a social entity against an alleged perpetrator of harm to that group or some of its members.

classical conditioning See *respondent conditioning.*

classical conservatism   The sociopolitical *ideology* that tends to prefer the status quo or only minimal, incremental changes in social institutions. The British philosopher Edmund Burke (1729–1797), who in 1790 wrote *Reflections on the Revolution in*

France, was among the first thinkers to systematically delineate the tenets of this ideology by advocating that society should conserve the best institutions of the past and slowly blend them into the needs of the present, rather than destroy and replace them with untested social innovations. This ideology is not synonymous with *neoconservatism.*

classical liberalism   The sociopolitical *ideology* that originally promoted personal freedom and limited government control, a *free-enterprise system,* and a belief in *human rights* that are inherent and independent of the state. This philosophy was developing during the time of the Magna Carta in 1215 and was further delineated by political philosophers such as John Locke (1632–1704) and Thomas Jefferson (1743–1826). Classical liberalism influenced many national revolutions, especially during the period 1688 to 1789, and the establishment of many governments that had detailed bills of rights. The liberal view that "government that governs least governs best" began to change at the beginning of the 20th century. The emerging view, now most commonly called *neoliberalism,* was that individual freedom is mitigated by poverty and inequal opportunity and that government is the suitable vehicle to overcome these wrongs.

classification   The process of organizing information into categories or classes so that the data can be more readily analyzed and understood. For example, a social worker might plan for the needs of potential clients in the agency's *catchment area* by categorizing the area's population by age, gender, economic well-being, recent hospital intakes, and incidence and type of mental illness.

class polarization   The tendency in some societies for the socioeconomic gap to widen between the wealthy and the poor populations with a corresponding decrease in the number of people who belong in the middle class.

claustrophobia   The pathological *fear* of closed spaces.

clearing house   A central site used by people and organizations with mutual interests to store, process, analyze, and retrieve information. For example, in the United States the *National Institutes of Health (NIH)* maintains many clearing houses, each for designated diseases, for the use of health care providers and patients.

cleft palate   A congenital abnormality in which a groove in the roof of the mouth occurs because the palate bones fail to fuse. Often accompanying this birth defect is the cleft lip, a split between the nostril to the margin of the lip.

clemency   An official grant issued by a nation's chief executive that forgives an individual for any liability or punishment for specified criminal acts. Clemency differs from *amnesty* in that it applies to specific crimes and people rather than classes of people. See also *pardon.*

client   The individual, group, family, or community that seeks or is provided with professional services.

client-centered therapy   A form of *psychotherapy* originated by psychologist Carl Rogers in the 1940s. Its central hypothesis is that clients are inherently motivated to develop and maximize their capacities (that is, to self-actualize) and can resolve their own problems provided that the therapist establishes a caring, warm, empathic, permissive, and nonjudgmental atmosphere. The client-centered therapist assumes a nondirective stance and usually does not advise, interpret, or challenge, except to encourage the client or to restate the client's remarks to clarify them. See also *nondirective therapy.*

"client dumping"   A term used to depict the unethical practice by some social workers and other professionals of discontinuing services to clients who are still in need. *Premature termination* of service occurs most commonly because the client's financial resources or insurance benefits have diminished. The three principal ways professionals terminate services without revealing to the client or others their motivation for termination include (1) telling the client that goals have been reached; (2) referring the client to another service provider on the premise that only the other has the skills necessary to meet the client's need; or (3) making unreasonable demands, changes, or recommendations and then ending treatment when the client does not comply.

client self-monitoring   A procedure used by social workers in direct practice and research to measure *client behavior* and behavioral changes by having clients note their own behaviors outside the interviews using systematic procedures and assessment tools. Typically, the social worker has the client maintain a diary, checklist, or log to check the frequency of specified behaviors. Client self-monitoring seems most effective when used in conjunction with *collateral monitoring*.

client system   The *client* and those in the client's environment who are potentially influential in contributing to a resolution of the client's problems. For example, a social worker may see a *nuclear family* as the client and the *extended family* and neighbors, teachers, and employers as making up part of the client system.

cliff effect   The abrupt termination of eligibility of some social *benefits* once the client's earnings have reached a certain point. Making one more dollar causes loss of all benefits. This often results in clients striving to keep any income below that point. Many public-assistance administrators point out that people become trapped in the public assistance cycle by fear of losing all their economic and medical benefits under this system and thus recommend more gradual reductions. However, other administrators claim the alternative is the *benefit rate reduction (BRR),* which also has *disincentives*.

Clinical Federation   The designation informally given to the *National Federation of Societies for Clinical Social Work (NFSCSW).* Another informal name for the organization is the *Clinical Society.*

clinical gerontology   The professional practice of helping older people with psycho-social, physical, and lifestyle problems and with the coping tasks unique to them.

clinical picture   The overall impression of a client or case based on the observed symptoms, *presenting problems*, test results, data input from all available sources, and client self-assessment.

clinical social work   A specialized form of direct *social work practice* with individuals, groups, and families. The *National Association of Social Workers (NASW)* has defined clinical social work as the professional application of social work theory and methods to the treatment and prevention of psychosocial dysfunction, disability, or impairment, including emotional and mental disorders. Some professional social workers use the term as a synonym for *social casework* or *psychiatric social work,* although others believe that each of these terms has a somewhat different meaning. Most professional social workers agree that clinical social work practice includes emphasis on the *person-in-environment perspective*. See also *methods in social work.*

Clinical Society   The designation informally given to the *National Federation of Societies for Clinical Social Work (NFSCSW).* Another informal name for the organization is the *Clinical Federation.*

clinician   A professional, working directly with clients, whose practice occurs primarily in an office, hospital, clinic, or other controlled environment. In such settings, the practitioner studies the problem, assesses and diagnoses the client situation, and directly treats or helps the client to achieve prescribed goals. The social work clinician is generally one who provides direct treatment to the client (individual, family, or group), usually in the social worker's office.

clique   A small group of associates who try to maintain some prestige by being exclusionary.

closed-ended questions   Questioning designed to encourage the client to reveal specific information concisely and factually, without opinion, embellishment, or detail.

Such questions are usually posed by the social worker to keep the client from digressing, evading, or providing irrelevant information when interview time is limited. Such questions are frequently answered "yes" or "no" or with one-word responses. Examples of closed-ended questions are "Did you go to school every day this week?" and "When did you lose your job?" See also *open-ended questions*.

closed family   A family structure whose members maintain highly interdependent relationships, providing little opportunity for relationships with non–family members. See also *centripetal family structure*.

closed group   In *social group work* or *group psychotherapy*, a group in which no new members are added once it has begun. Usually in such groups, all the members remain with the group until a predetermined time has been reached, at which time all the members terminate. The more-common group intervention model is the *open group*.

closed system   In *systems theories*, a self-contained system with rigid *boundaries* that is organized to resist change and maintain the status quo. For example, a closed family system is relatively uninvolved with non–family members, less tolerant of ideas that differ from the *family myths*, and structured to maintain its interrelationships with minimal outside interference. See also *open system*.

clouding   A symptom noted by clinicians in which the conscious awareness of the client seems disoriented, ill-focused, inattentive, or confused.

cluttering   A speech disorder involving an abnormally rapid rate or erratic rhythm of speech or dramatic changes of vocal pitch that impedes the listener's ability to comprehend what is being communicated. See also *stuttering*.

CNS   See *central nervous system (CNS)*.

CNSW   See *Council of Nephrology Social Workers (CNSW)*.

coaching   In interviews, an intervention procedure in which the social worker tells the client how to do something and follows with suggestions for improving the activity until optimal performance is reached. This procedure is used primarily with people who are poorly functioning, undersocialized, lacking in currently needed social skills, or with people who have not responded to nondirective interventions.

coalition   An alliance of various factions or ideological groups in a society brought together to achieve a goal. In *community organization*, social workers often attempt to form such alliances among influential groups or among less-powerful groups to increase their influence. Coalitions may be ad hoc (organized to address a specific goal or single issue and expected to disband when it is achieved), semipermanent (more formally organized around broader and longer-range goals), or permanent (such as political parties). See *ad hoc coalition*.

COBRA   The Consolidated Omnibus Budget Reconciliation Act (P. L. 99-272) passed in 1985 which, among other things, requires all hospitals participating in *Medicare* in the United States to provide appropriate medical screening examinations and treatment to all individuals in their care who have medical conditions, regardless of their economic status or insurance benefits.

cocaine   A *drug of abuse* derived from the leaves of the coca plant that gives the user feelings of *euphoria*, energy, alertness, confidence, and heightened sensitivity. Sometimes known as "coke" or "snow," the drug is usually taken through the nostrils ("snorting") and sometimes injected in combination with other drugs such as *heroin* ("speedballing") or chemically converted and smoked ("freebasing"). Cocaine has a particularly strong reinforcing capability. For example, when allowed to freely self-administer cocaine rapidly, animals escalate their dosage and prefer taking it to meeting their biological and psychological needs. Repeated use can produce marked deterioration of the nervous system and general physical deterioration, destruction of the mucous membranes, *paranoia, depression,* and *hallucination.* See also *"crack."*

codeine A narcotic analgesic (pain-relieving drug) found in some prescription medications, and, in certain states, in over-the-counter medications such as some cough syrups. Like all *narcotics,* codeine is addictive when used with some degree of frequency.

code of ethics An explicit statement of the *values,* principles, and rules of a *profession,* regulating the conduct of its members. See also *NASW Code of Ethics.*

codependency A relationship between two or more people who rely on each other to meet and provide for reciprocal needs, particularly unhealthy emotional ones. For example, a widow and her adult daughter both lack self-esteem and are consequently fearful about contacts with others, so they meet most of their social needs by being virtually inseparable. This pattern is considered similar to but not as seriously pathological as *conjugal paranoia, shared paranoid disorder, folie à deux,* or *induced psychotic disorder.* See also *adult children of alcoholics (ACOAs).*

code words Phrases or expressions made primarily by political office seekers and others under public scrutiny to reveal adherence to an ideology without addressing it directly. For example, a political candidate might espouse "equal rights for the unborn" as a code for opposition to *abortion.*

coding The *social research* procedure in which numbers or other symbols are assigned for each *variable* or category of answer in a survey or other study. For example, a "1" may be assigned for every "yes" response and a "0" for every "no."

coercion Forcing or compelling an individual or group to perform (or stop performing) some activity. This may occur through legal actions, government interventions, social influence, or political pressure, as well as through threats of violent harm. An important role of social workers, especially those in community organization, is to bring people together so that they can resist the attempts of others to coerce them into actions they do not want to take.

coexistence An *ideology* that advocates and seeks to enable nations and organizations of different values and interests to maintain their territorial integrity, *self-determination,* and sovereignty.

COG See *Council of Governments (COG).*

cognition The mental process of recognizing, understanding, remembering, and evaluating relevant information.

cognitive–behavioral therapies Approaches to treatment using selected concepts and techniques from *behaviorism, social learning theory, action therapy, functional school in social work, task-centered treatment,* and therapies based on *cognitive models.* These forms of therapy are contrasted with those known as *insight therapies* and tend to be comparatively short term, focused on the present, and fairly limited and specific in goals. The therapist with a cognitive–behavioral orientation tends to be fairly directive and focused on the client's *presenting problem.*

cognitive development The process by which individuals acquire the intellectual capacity to perceive, evaluate, and understand information. Jean Piaget (1896–1980) formulated one of the most complete cognitive development theories to date. He divided *human development* into four typical stages (1) the *sensorimotor stage* (birth to age two); (2) the *preoperational stage* (ages two to seven); (3) the *concrete operations stage* (ages seven to 11); and (4) the *formal operations stage* (age 11 to adulthood). See also *Piagetian theory.*

cognitive dissonance The mental state in which a person experiences two or more incompatible beliefs or cognitions simultaneously. In the healthy individual, this state usually leads to psychological discomfort that remains until the person acts to clarify the discrepancy.

cognitive dysfunction Any temporary or permanent decrease in the ability to think, remember, comprehend, or process information.

cognitive map An individual's image or perceptual picture of the environment.

cognitive models Representations of the ways by which people come to know, perceive, or understand phenomena. Such models can be used to envision or describe how humans develop their abilities to organize knowledge and understand their worlds, as in *Piagetian theory*. Such models can also be used to describe certain treatment approaches, such as *rational–emotive therapy* (Albert Ellis), *reality therapy* (William Glasser), *individual psychology* (Alfred Adler), and *rational casework* (Robert Sunley and Harold D. Werner).

cognitive style An individual's preferred way of organizing and processing information. There are individual differences in how people perceive, remember, understand, and solve problems that influence the way information is organized and processed. For example, some people are more analytical and others have more-global approaches to their environments.

cognitive theory A group of concepts pertaining to the way individuals develop the intellectual capacity for receiving, processing, and acting on information. Cognitive concepts emphasize that behavior is determined by thinking and goal determination, rather than primarily resulting from instinctive drives or unconscious motivations.

cognitive therapy Clinical *intervention* using *cognitive theory* concepts that focus on the client's conscious thinking processes, motivations, and reasons for certain behaviors. Alfred Adler (1870–1937) is said to have been a major originator of cognitive therapy. Current forms of this approach include *rational–emotive therapy, reality therapy, existential social work,* and *rational casework*. The psychosocial orientation of early, "pre-Freudian" social workers was considered to have much in common with the cognitive approach.

cohabitation The term that is commonly applied to a man and woman residing together in husband–wife roles without for-mal marriage; however, it also applies to others such as *gay* men and *lesbians* and to more than two people living together.

Cohen, Wilbur (1913–1987) Social work educator and administrator who became Secretary of the U.S. *Department of Health, Education and Welfare (HEW)* during the Johnson administration and implemented many of the programs of the *Great Society*.

cohort In *demography* research studies, a group of subjects who were born during a specific time or who share another characteristic that is related to the subject being investigated. For example, when life expectancies are being calculated, one cohort might be a group of 100,000 people who were born in the same month.

cohort sequential analysis A *research* method that systematically evaluates selected age groups of people over a staggered period. This method helps correct any bias inherent in a *longitudinal study*.

Coit, Stanton (1857–1944) Founder of the *settlement house* movement in the United States and leader in the Ethical Culture movement. He developed programs for poor youths in New York; and using his former experience at *Toynbee Hall* in London as his model, he developed settlements for them and others. He also advocated for public works jobs for unemployed people, developed the "mutual aid" model, and in 1891 published the book *Neighborhood Guilds* that described settlements.

coitus Sexual intercourse.

COLA See *cost-of-living adjustment (COLA)*.

Cold War The nonmilitary conflict and political competition for world power and influence over other nations waged between the United States and its allies and the former Soviet Union and its allies from 1945 to 1990.

coleadership In *group psychotherapy* and *social group work,* the use of two or more professionals, each fulfilling distinct roles, to facilitate group processes. Although the procedure is generally more costly and complex, the use of coleaders for groups has four advantages: (1) they may observe different aspects of the group processes, (2) together they might bring out behaviors in members that would not occur with a single leader, (3) they can play different roles and provide *role modeling* opportunities for members, and (4) they can expand the range of knowledge and *values* available to the group.

colic 1. A behavior pattern in infants manifested by continual crying for as long as 12 to 14 hours daily. Causes are unknown but usually not symptomatic of life-threatening diseases. For most, the worst consequence is distress to the parents and interference with good family relationships. Usually the behavior resolves itself within a few months. 2. Pain in the stomach or intestines.

colitis Inflammation of the large intestine.

collaboration The procedure in which two or more professionals work together to serve a given *client* (individual, family, group, community, or population). The professionals may work relatively independently of one another but communicate and coordinate their respective efforts to avoid duplication of services, or they may work as members of a single helping team. Collaboration also takes place among social agencies and other organizations on a variety of projects. See also *interdisciplinary teaming, interprofessional team, linkage,* and *interorganizational collaboration.*

collaborative avoidance In *social group work* and *group psychotherapy,* the phenomenon in which group members consciously or unconsciously agree to not discuss certain topics.

collaborative therapy A treatment format in which two or more social workers or other professionals each treat a single member of a family and, to some extent, coordinate their efforts. For example, a husband might be seen by one social worker and the wife by another, or a disturbed child might be seen by a child psychoanalyst and the parents treated conjointly by a social worker.

collateral monitoring A procedure social workers in direct practice and research use to measure client behavior and behavioral changes by having others observe and record the client's actions. Typically, the social worker has the client's spouse or other family members, friend, co-worker, or teacher do this monitoring using checklists, diaries, and logs in which the frequency of some behavior is counted. Collateral monitoring is usually used in conjunction with *client self-monitoring,* and it may be done overtly or unobtrusively, but it should be done only with the client's *informed consent.*

collective action A *social movement* to seek political, economic, or cultural changes. Many people prefer this term to "protest" or "rebellion" because the use of such words often prejudices uncommitted people toward the side of those in power.

collective bargaining A coordinated activity undertaken by a group of people who share a common interest or objective to influence change in some policy, law, or business arrangement. The term most commonly applies to the efforts of an organized *labor union* in negotiating a contract.

collective preconscious Simultaneous or similar responses to a *stimulus* perceived on a *preconscious* psychological level among members of a group or society. Preconscious refers to thoughts that are *unconscious* at a particular moment but are not repressed or unacceptable impulses or ideas rendered unconscious. The collective preconscious is based on beliefs, *norms, mores,* and *values* acquired through the *acculturation* process of informal and formal education.

collective responsibility Assignment of obligation, trust, or blame to more than one person or organization. For example, all the "smokestack industries" of a region may be considered responsible for *acid rain,* and special taxes might be levied on them to be used for cleaning up the problem.

collective unconscious In *Jungian theory,* that part of the *unconscious* that contains the inherited psychic functions or brain structure of the human species. In this theory, some information, value orientations, and behavioral patterns for meeting needs are shared by all humans through genetic transmission. In the Jungian theory, the other part of the unconscious is the *personal unconscious.*

Colonial Development and Welfare Acts   A body of legislation enacted by the British Parliament, primarily in the first half of the 20th century, to establish, organize, finance, and administer the *social welfare* and economic programs of the British colonies. As most of the colonies became independent nations, they have tended to continue using the structure of these programs as the basis of their current social welfare systems.

colostomy   Surgery to create an artificial anus in the abdominal wall.

coma   A medical condition characterized by unconsciousness with complete absence of all voluntary activity.

combined therapy   A model of *intervention* in which a client participates in group therapy concurrently with individual therapy.

"coming out"   The process of self-identification as a *lesbian* or a *gay* man, followed by revelation of one's *sexual orientation* to others. See also *outing* and *"passing."*

Commission on Civil Rights, U.S.   The independent federal body whose mission is to advance the cause of *equal rights* and investigate alleged denials of *civil rights* because of race, color, religion, gender bias, age discrimination, disability, national origin, or the administration of justice. The commission does fact-finding on voting rights and equality of opportunity in education, employment, and housing.

Commission on Recognition of Post-Secondary Accreditation (CORPA)   The accrediting body for university and graduate school education in the United States, including social work, that was established in 1994. CORPA includes many regional and specialized accrediting bodies, including the *Council on Social Work Education*

(CSWE). CORPA provides for the public review of the accrediting process and helps member organizations maintain appropriate standards for evaluating graduate schools. CORPA took over most of the functions of the *Council on Post-Secondary Accreditation (COPA),* which suspended operations in 1993.

commitment   1. The act of consigning an individual to a hospital or prison, usually after undergoing *due process of law.* 2. A pledge or obligation. For example, social work students, to fund their educations, sometimes accept "commitment scholarships," in which a *social agency* or organization provides financial support in exchange for agreement to work for that organization for a predetermined period after graduation.

Committee for the Advancement of Social Work with Groups   See *Association for the Advancement of Social Work with Groups (AASWG).*

committee on inquiry   Permanent and ad hoc groups of professionals and others brought together to determine if any wrongdoing has been committed by or to a peer. Of particular interest to such committees are alleged violations of professional *codes of ethics,* illegal activities, or other disputes among professionals or between professionals and clients. These committees also exist to raise the public consciousness about mistreatment of peers by governments or political organizations. Such groups are often sponsored by *professional associations,* third-party organizations, or alliances of consumers. For example, the *National Association of Social Workers (NASW)* has a national committee for dealing with violations of the *NASW Code of Ethics* and personnel standards, and association standards require that each chapter maintain a committee on inquiry. See also *peer review organization (PRO)* and *accountability.*

Commodity Credit Corporation (CCC)   A U.S. agency that loans money to farmers, using the crop as collateral. At harvest time, if the market price falls below the previously established *price supports,* the farmer may turn the crop over to the CCC and keep the loaned money. If the market price is higher than the price supports, the farmer may sell the crop and repay the loan. Over the years this system stabilizes farm prices and farmer incomes and builds huge crop stockpiles. Critics say this system artificially inflates farm prices, discourages foreign buyers, and runs counter to tariff and trade agreements with other nations.

Commodity Supplemental Food Program (CSFP) A federally funded *food assistance program* that provides monthly packages of food to women of low-to-moderate income who have children younger than age six.

Common Cause A *voluntary association* founded in 1970 and known as the "citizens' lobby." Its primary goal is to represent the interests of the public and to counterbalance special-interest lobbies. Its role is to inform the public about legislation and act as a *watchdog group* over the lawmaking process and its implementation.

common-law marriage *Cohabitation* by a man and a woman who consider themselves, and are generally considered by others, to be married but who have not had a civil or religious marriage ceremony. In some jurisdictions, this marriage is recognized by law for some purposes.

communicable disease A disease that is transmissible from one person to another.

communication The verbal and nonverbal exchange of information, including all the ways in which knowledge is transmitted and received.

communication disorders A group of disorders classified in the *DSM-IV* (Washington, DC: American Psychiatric Association, 1994) as "disorders usually first diagnosed in infancy, childhood, or adolescence" and pertaining to limitations in the ability to impart information to others. The disorders that comprise this group include *expressive language disorder, mixed receptive–expressive language disorder, phonological disorder,* and *stuttering.*

communication leakage In social work and other professions, the transmission of information that the sender did not intend to convey. For example, a social worker blushes when asking about the client's sexuality or the client looks contemptuous when referring to a "loved one."

Communications Workers of America (CWA) A labor organization founded in 1938 whose members are employed in telecommunications, printing and news media, public service, health care, television, electronics, construction, and utilities. With headquarters in Washington, DC, and local chapters throughout the United States and Canada, CWA represents many social workers.

communication theory The body of concepts and hypotheses that pertains to the way people exchange information. Some major elements of communication theory are *content analysis, cybernetics, decoding, feedback, kinesics, metamessage, paralinguistics,* and *proxemics.*

communism 1. An *ideology* that advocates a classless society based on need rather than productivity. 2. Theoretically, a society in which workers are not exploited by employers. When most people casually use the term "communism," they actually are referring to *Marxism.*

community A group of individuals or families that share certain values, services, institutions, interests, or geographic proximity.

Community Action Program (CAP) The neighborhood organizations established in 1965 under the *Office of Economic Opportunity (OEO).* The goal of the program and its agencies was to develop the social and economic resources in poor communities and to help find alternative ways to attack the forces that perpetuate poverty. CAP originally was responsible for the *Head Start* program, the *Legal Services Corporation (LSC),* and other programs that have since been transferred to other government agencies or have disbanded. To develop a variegated series of innovations, each community action agency was at first somewhat independent of local and federal control. Subsequently, the agencies were led by elected officials with only a minority of poor people in leadership positions. CAP established about 3,000 neighborhood service centers in poor communities to provide counseling, employment placement, legal advice, and, in some, health care and child care facilities.

Community Chest An organization working for or on behalf of *private social agencies* in various geographic areas to raise and distribute funds through unified campaigns. The name originated in 1918, and the organization has since been renamed *United Way*.

community decision network The aggregate of key organizations and individuals who have the formal or informal power to determine courses of action to be taken by a community. The decision network may include political leaders and legislative bodies, industrial leaders, religious groups, and civic associations. Its composition varies depending on the specific issue or community.

community development (CD) Efforts made by professionals and community residents to enhance the social bonds among members of the community, motivate the citizens for self-help, develop responsible local leadership, and create or revitalize local institutions. Community development workers have been active in *Third World* nations at least since the 1920s, especially in *consciousness-raising,* helping community residents to achieve greater collective participation, and developing local leadership. In the United States, CD workers have worked especially in underdeveloped rural settings and poor urban neighborhoods to to facilitate the residents' collaboration in increasing influence, self-sufficiency, and economic and educational opportunities.

community mental health center A local organization, partly funded and regulated by the federal government, that provides a range of psychiatric and social services to people residing in the area. These include inpatient, outpatient, partial hospitaliza-

tion, emergency, and transitional services; programs for older people and for children; screening and follow-up care; and programs that deal with *alcohol abuse* and *substance abuse.*

community organization An *intervention* process used by social workers and other professionals to help individuals, groups, and collectives of people with common interests or from the same geographic areas to deal with *social problems* and to enhance social well-being through planned *collective action*. Methods include identifying problem areas, analyzing causes, formulating plans, developing strategies, mobilizing necessary resources, identifying and recruiting community leaders, and encouraging interrelationships among them to facilitate their efforts.

community organizers Facilitators of planned efforts to achieve specified goals in the development of a group, neighborhood, constituency, or other community. Community organizers may be indigenous community leaders, political office holders, or government bureaucrats, but more often they are professionals with backgrounds in social work, political science, planning, interpersonal relations, public relations, sociology, or community development. They work as consultants, planners, grant developers, or active leaders, and they usually seek to help community members achieve social justice, economic or social development, or other improvements.

Community Planning and Development Office The federal organization within the U.S. *Department of Housing and Urban Development (HUD)* responsible for stimulating growth, rehabilitation, and new development in urban areas, especially those that are economically distressed. The office seeks to provide adequate housing and suitable environments, especially for people of low or moderate incomes. Grants and loans are provided through state agencies.

community property The material possessions acquired by a husband and wife during the years of their marriage. Community property usually excludes all property owned by each party before the marriage or property acquired after the marriage through inheritance or gifts, but includes salaries, investments, and unearned income that each partner has received while married.

community psychology The specialty within psychology that emphasizes prevention of mental illness, education about good mental health practices, and early diagnosis and treatment of mental disorders.

Community Reinvestment Act of 1977 A U.S. law (P.L. 95-128) forbidding the practice of *redlining*. The act obliges banks and other insured mortgage lenders to meet the reasonable credit needs of people in low-income communities.

community self-help The process of involving volunteers and other citizens in a community in decision making, social services planning, and coordination with professionals and agency employees. This process includes decentralization of responsibility and control from national, state, or local agencies to individuals and community groups.

community service Efforts by volunteers, paid indigenous workers, and professionals to meet the educational, recreational, health, legal, political, vocational, and social welfare needs of people at the local level. This term is used widely to refer to activities for neighborhood improvements made by *civic associations*, churches, social groups, and fraternal organizations. Typical community service activities include drug prevention education, recreation for people with disabilities, physical fitness programs for older people, and neighborhood cleanup drives.

Community Services Block Grant Program A program of the *Administration for Children and Families (ACF), U.S. Department of Health and Human Services (HHS)* that helps fund and operate a wide variety of antipoverty activities. These include the coordinating of local programs and providing nutrition services, emergency services, and employment services. Grantees of the block grant also seek funds from other sources to help operate such programs as *Head Start,* weatherization and low-income energy assistance, emergency food and shelter programs, employment and training, and legal services. This program was originally part of the *Office of Economic Opportunity (OEO).* In 1969 OEO was dismantled, and many of its programs were discontinued or transferred to other government agencies. The Community Services Block Grant Program became part of the Family Services Administration (now ACF) in 1986. See also *block grant.*

community service sentence A punishment ordered by a court that requires some specified work to improve a relevant community by an individual convicted of a *crime.* The convict is obliged to perform the service for a specified amount of time in lieu of incarceration for an equal amount of time. The work required includes such activities as serving food in homeless shelters, taking parentless children on outings, giving antidrug talks at schools, and doing volunteer work in hospitals. See also *work release program.*

Community Work Experience Program (CWEP) A federally sponsored training program designed to help recipients of *Aid to Families with Dependent Children (AFDC)* acquire workplace *coping skills* (such as coming to work on time, relating to other employees responsibly, or communicating with customers appropriately), as well as gain self-confidence and motivation for work, so they can enter the workforce and save taxpayer dollars. CWEP requires clients to work a specified number of hours monthly (based on the amount of the AFDC benefit divided by the minimum wage) at public or nonprofit organizations. See also *workfare, learnfare,* and *JOBS program.*

commutation In legal terms, a change from a greater to a lesser sentence or punishment, as in changing a death sentence to life imprisonment.

compadrazgo In Spanish-speaking cultures, those people who are tied to a *family* not through a kinship network, but through historical ties. They are considered companion parents who help with the raising of the family's children. See also *padrino* and *hijos de crianza*.

comparable worth The concept that payment or salary is to be based solely on the value of the work performed instead of on such considerations as the employee's gender, minority status, or need; also known as *pay equity*.

comparative social welfare Analysis of the alternatives for providing the social services, economic, educational, and health care needs of a nation or social group by reviewing how different societies have addressed the same objectives. See also *international social work*.

compensation 1. A mental mechanism in which one tries to make up for imaginary or real characteristics that are considered undesirable. When this occurs unconsciously, it is considered a *defense mechanism*. 2. Payment for services rendered.

compensatory education Special school programs for children or adults who previously have been deprived of educational opportunities. These programs often are used for children in poor neighborhoods to raise their levels of educational readiness. The most prominent of these programs is *Head Start*.

competence 1. The ability to fulfill the requirements of a job or other obligation. Competence in social work includes possession of all relevant educational and experiential requirements, demonstrated ability through passing licensing and certification exams, and the ability to carry out work assignments and achieve social work goals while adhering to the *values* and the *code of ethics* of the profession. 2. In the legal system, the capacity to understand and act reasonably.

competency-based practice In social work, the demonstrated ability to fulfill the professional obligations to the client, the community, the society, and the profession. This demonstration occurs through acquisition of *certification* and *licensing*, keeping up with the *knowledge base* by fulfilling *continuing education* requirements, and participating in agency *supervision* and *inservice training*.

competent evidence In the legal justice system, the facts about a case that are admissible in courts of law, as well as convincing, reliable, and valid. Such information is to be distinguished from the opinions, guesses, or secondhand data offered by a professional *expert witness*. For example, an assessment by a social worker that an infant's bruises were probably the result of child abuse owing to a past history of similar events in the family would not be considered competent evidence. Eyewitness testimony by a competent observer of an act of child abuse would be considered competent evidence.

competing mandate The legitimate requirements made of an organization to fulfill two or more functions even though no clear priorities are set and resources permit support for only one. For example, in combating the drug problem, various public constituencies have competing demands for better law enforcement and imprisonment, more-effective controls against smuggling, preventative education, and treatment for drug abuse. However, public monies cannot fund all these programs; thus, choices must be made. Effective administrators cope with competing mandates by finding ways to increase resources and by establishing better systems for ordering priorities and long-range planning. See also *conflicting mandate* and *ambiguous mandate*.

complementarity 1. The fit of two or more roles within an individual. 2. The way certain roles of one individual fit with the roles of a *relevant other*. For example, the social worker–client roles are usually complementary because the behaviors expected of each are compatible. See also *role discomplementarity*.

complementary therapy An additional type of *intervention* that the social worker or other psychotherapist provides for certain clients, occurring along with individual therapy. Most commonly this is group therapy or family therapy. It is important that the two forms of therapy are well integrated so that the goals of the different procedures are consistent.

complex   As used by psychologists and clinical social workers, an interrelated group of ideas and experiences that are partially or entirely repressed but which compel the client to think, feel, and behave in a pattern. Carl Jung (1875–1961), who first used the term, said complexes were fundamental psychic conflicts that were dealt with by habitual types of attitude, responses, or acts. Some of the better known of these are the *Oedipus complex, Electra complex,* authority complex, castration complex, femininity complex, and *inferiority complex.*

Comprehensive Employment and Training Act   See *CETA.*

comprehensive planning   Efforts by policy-makers to coordinate knowledge, influence, and resources on a broad (rather than piecemeal) scale to achieve overall goals. This includes looking for the underlying causes rather than the overt symptoms of human problems. Comprehensive planning also considers and seeks to facilitate the reaching of human potential rather than confining itself to eliminating problems. To achieve this, comprehensive planning seeks to coordinate program resources not according to the specialized functions of existing social agencies and professions, but across organizational lines of responsibility.

compulsion   1. A strong and repetitive urge to act in a certain way. It is frequently a means of relieving *anxiety* that results from conflicting ideas and wishes that cannot be directly expressed. 2. Forcing a person to act according to the wishes of another.

compulsive personality disorder   A type of *personality disorder* that has all or many of the following characteristics: perfectionist behavior, insistence on having others submit to a certain way of doing things, limited ability to express warm feelings or tenderness, preoccupation with trivial details and rules, stinginess, stiff formality in relationships, and poor ability to prioritize and

make decisions. This disorder is also known as *obsessive–compulsive disorder.*

computerized databases   Electronic storage of information, especially from the academic, scientific, legal, medical, and business professional literature. Social workers have access to these databases using a computer, modem, and an on-line database such as NASW's Social Work Abstracts, which covers social work journal literature abstracts from 1977. Another useful database is the American Psychological Association's Psyc INFO, which covers psychology, psychiatry, and social work literature since 1967. The National Library of Medicine covers the medical literature since 1966. Hundreds of other databases can be found in public and academic libraries. Most of the on-line database information is also available on CD-ROM disks.

computer role   A recurrent pattern of communication in relating to others, characterized by very correct and proper behavior and calmness without apparent feeling. This role was delineated by *Virginia Satir* (*Peoplemaking,* Palo Alto, CA: Science and Behavior Books, 1972, p. 68), who described the person playing this role as one who feels vulnerable and responds to the perceived threat by pretending it is harmless and by hiding inadequacy feelings through the use of big words. See also *blamer role, distracter role,* and *placater role.*

Computer Use in the Social Services (CUSS)   An organization whose members are oriented to communicating by computer technology about innovations and techniques in the use of computers, videodisks, and software packages that facilitate the provision of social services.

CON   See *certificate of need (CON).*

con artist   One who skillfully but unlawfully takes money or property from others by winning their confidences and promising that their "contributions" will be rewarded. See also *confidence crimes* and *extortion.*

conation   That part of the mental function involving will or volition.

concentrations The term used by social work educators for clusters of courses, parts of courses, or other formal learning experiences that provide the social work student with deeper and more-focused knowledge and skill in certain areas of professional concern. After students have acquired formal education in basic areas of social work knowledge, they are often required, as part of their education, to select one or more concentrations that reflect their own interests and professional directions. Schools of social work have different concentrations and ways of defining their concentrations. In most schools of social work, concentrations are defined according to specific *methods in social work, fields of practice, special populations*, and special problems. Methods concentrations may include *social casework, social group work, community organization, research* evaluation, direct clinical practice, administration–policy–planning combination, family–marital treatment, and *generic social work* practice combining a *macro orientation* and a *micro orientation*. Fields-of-practice concentrations include *child welfare, mental health, health care, school social work*, criminal justice, *gerontology, rural social work, industrial social work*, family and *child welfare* services, and various combinations. Special problems concentrations include *substance abuse* and *poverty*, and *special populations* concentrations include such groups as people of color and women.

conception The uniting of a sperm cell and an egg, resulting in an embryo.

Concern for the Dying (CFD) A national organization, founded in 1975, focused on educating the public about their right to make end-of-life medical decisions. Fomerly the Euthanasia Education Fund, CFD merged with *Society for the Right to Die* in 1991 to become *Choice in Dying*.

conciliation A mediation process in which two or more parties seek to minimize or eliminate their differences. The role of the social worker in such instances is usually to advise, referee, and arbitrate. See also *mediator role, mediation*, and *divorce*.

concrete operations stage The phase of *cognitive development* that, according to *Piagetian theory*, occurs between ages seven and 11, in which the individual learns to apply logic to observable and manipulable physical relationships.

concrete services The type of direct social services in which clients are provided with tangible resources needed to resolve specific problems or attain a normative standard of well-being, such as food, housing, transportation, clothing, or access thereto. These social services are compared with those in which the social worker provides important but intangible services, such as reassurance, knowledge, psychotherapy, and relationship-building skills.

concretization A thought pattern that overemphasizes "hard data," detail, immediate experience, and objective phenomena and avoids locus on subtleties and subjective experience. Concretization is often symptomatic of such mental disorders as *paranoia, personality disorders*, and some types of *schizophrenia*.

concurrent placement In *social work education*, the format for *field placement* in which the student alternates classroom experiences with work in a *social agency* on different days of each week. This provides the student with opportunities for discussion and questions in the classroom about field experiences as well as opportunities in the agency to apply what is learned in class. See also *block placement*.

concurrent therapy The treatment format in which the social worker or other helping professional sees different members of a family or *client system* separately in individual sessions. This format has been used most commonly in *marital therapy* to maintain *confidentiality* and to encourage the participants to reveal their thoughts and behaviors when they might not feel able to do so in the presence of their spouses. This format is the opposite of *conjoint therapy*.

condemnation A legal process of acquiring privately held property for more public use through the power of *eminent domain*.

For a condemnation to be successful, the purpose must clearly be to benefit the public and the owner must be given just compensation.

conditioned inhibition In *behavior modification*, the pattern in which the subject is taught not to respond to a *stimulus* that previously elicited a *response*.

conditioned response (CR) In *behaviorism*, a classically conditioned response that has been learned after being associated repeatedly with a *conditioned stimulus (CS)*. For example, an abused child develops anxiety (CR) whenever in the presence of the abuser (CS).

conditioned stimulus (CS) A previously neutral event in the environment that begins to elicit a learned or *conditioned response (CR)* when paired with an *unconditioned stimulus (US)*. For example, seeing a dog does not elicit fear in all individuals, but if an individual associates dogs with being bitten, the sight of a dog can elicit fear.

conditioning A process through which behavior is learned. The two major types of conditioning, *respondent conditioning* (also known as classical) and *operant conditioning*, are differentiated by the sequence in which the *stimulus* is presented. See also *conditioned stimulus (CS), unconditioned stimulus (US),* and *respondent behavior.*

condom A thin sheath of rubber, latex, polyurethane, or similar material that fits tightly over the penis and is used for *contraception* and the prevention of *sexually transmitted diseases (STDs)* such as *acquired immune deficiency syndrome (AIDS), syphilis, gonorrhea,* and genital *herpes.* Condoms for females are being tested and marketed.

conduct disorder A repetitive and persistent pattern of behavior in which the rights of others are violated as are age-appropriate norms and social rules. This condition, which is noted primarily in children and youths, is of four types: (1) aggressive conduct (causes or threatens physical harm to others), (2) nonaggressive conduct (causes property loss), (3) deceitfulness or theft, (4) and serious violations of rules. The disorder is classified as "childhood onset type" if it seems to begin before age 10, and "adolescent-onset type" if it occurs after age 10. See also *oppositional defiant disorder.*

confabulation The act of making up for gaps in memory by fabricating stories or details.

confidence crimes Unlawfully cheating people out of their money or property by winning their trust and falsely claiming that their money will be put to some beneficial use. Such an act is also referred to as a "con game." See also *con artist.*

confidence level A *research* term referring to the degree to which an inference is reliable. This is expressed quantitatively as a percentage. Thus, when a conclusion is stated as being at the .05 level of confidence, the statement is likely to be wrong only 5 percent of the time. The lower the percentage (for example, .01 or .001), the higher the degree of confidence in the statement.

confidentiality A principle of *ethics* according to which the social worker or other professional may not disclose information about a client without the client's consent. This information includes the identity of the client, content of overt verbalizations, professional opinions about the client, and material from records. In specific circumstances, social workers and other professionals may be compelled by law to reveal to designated authorities some information (such as threats of violence, commission of crimes, and suspected child abuse) that would be relevant to legal judgments. See also *Tarasoff, absolute confidentiality,* and *relative confidentiality.*

confiscation 1. Legal seizing of private property, often as a penalty or restitution for criminal conduct. 2. The taking of private property during times of military takeover or disaster emergencies.

conflict 1. In groups or communities, the striving by two or more parties to achieve opposing or mutually exclusive goals. 2. In psychological terms, the mental struggle of two or more mutually exclusive impulses, motives, drives, or social demands.

conflict induction   The technique used especially by social workers in *community organization* and *family therapy* in which divergent issues and values are introduced to force members of the group into active confrontation, debate, and new coalition building. The families and citizens' groups with whom this is effective tend to be those that habitually avoid conflict and social discomfort, thus maintaining a stalemate that is unhealthy for some or all of their members.

conflicting mandate   The legitimate requirements made of an organization to fulfill a variety of functions that are inherently contradictory or opposed to one another. For example, the citizens of one city want the administration to get its homeless population off the streets but also to end overcrowding in its homeless shelters. See also *competing mandate* and *ambiguous mandate*.

conflict management   The ongoing and constructive process of dealing with *conflict* between members of an organization. Conflict is inevitable and serves positive functions such as identifying important problems and providing an impetus for change. It involves four basic steps: (1) recognizing the conflict or potential conflict, (2) assessing the conflict situation, (3) selecting appropriate strategy, and (4) intervening.

conflict resolution   The process of eliminating or minimizing the problems that result when different parties or groups compete with one another for the same limited objectives. This process most commonly occurs by facilitating compromises, achieving *accommodation,* or sometimes by the total surrender of one group to the other. Social workers often engage in this process when they help clarify, educate, mediate, and propose compromises or alternative solutions to clients or client systems who are contesting some mutual objectives.

conflict theories   Explanations about the nature, progress, and consequences of social conflict. The most prominent theories have been developed by Karl Marx, George Simmel, Lewis Coser, and others. Marx hypothesized that conflict would eventually lead to an overthrow of the power group, leading to a classless, conflict-free society. Simmel and Coser suggested that conflict is not inherently bad and that it serves such important functions as solidifying the in-group, increasing group cohesiveness, and mobilizing the energies of group members.

conformity   *Behavior* that is consistent with the *norms* and expectations of the relevant social group.

confrontation   The act of bringing together opposing ideas, impulses, or groups for the purpose of systematic examination or comparison.

congenital   Existing since *conception*. The term is applied to a disorder or condition that originated before birth.

congenital abnormalities   Diseases or disorders present at birth, such as *cleft palate, hemophilia*, and *spina bifida*.

congregate housing   *Residential facilities* for those who benefit from group living but do not require institutional care such as in a nursing home. Congregate housing provides individuals with the amenities, security, and economies of a family-style home even through the residents are not necessarily related. Although most are privately owned, for-profit facilities, social workers and housing specialists have established such facilities especially for older people or people with disabilities.

Congressional Budget Office (CBO)   The organization within the legislative branch of the U.S. government that provides Congress with basic budget data and analysis of alternative fiscal and policy issues. CBO prepares an annual budget report to Congress that includes a discussion of alternative spending and revenue levels and allocations. CBO monitors the results of congressional action on individual authorizations and appropriations and provides five-year projections of the costs of continuing current policies on taxes and expenditures. See also *Office of Management and Budget (OMB)*.

Congress of Racial Equality (CORE) The *civil rights* organization founded in 1942 to ensure fair application of the law to all races and to promote opportunities for people of color.

conjoint therapy A type of *intervention* in which a therapist or team of therapists treats a family by meeting with the members together for regular sessions; also, a type of intervention in which a husband and wife are treated as a unit and seen together by the marital therapist or therapy team. See also *family therapy* and *marital therapy*.

conjugal paranoia A form of *jealousy* in which one spouse suspects the other of infidelity without good reason.

conjugal rights A legal term for the obligations and opportunities of husbands and wives to be together socially, sexually, spiritually, and regularly.

conjugal visitation Private meetings in prisons and jails between inmates and their spouses or significant others to engage in sexual intercourse.

conscience A person's system of moral *values*, standards of *behavior*, and sense of right and wrong. See also *superego*.

conscientious objector One who is opposed to participation in war and military activity because of religious beliefs. A conscientious objector may be exempted from a combat role but not from public service duties such as military or civilian hospital work. One need not be a member of an established religious organization to become a conscientious objector, but the objection to war must be based on religious rather than social or political beliefs.

conscientization A term coined by educator Paulo Freire referring to the process of helping clients and others become aware of and feel concern about a problem, objective, or value.

conscious Mental awareness; that part of the mind that is aware of the immediate environment and of feelings and thoughts.

consciousness-raising The process of helping an individual or group become aware of and more sensitive to a social condition, cause, or idea that had been of little prior interest.

consensual validation The use of mutual agreement as the criterion for the truth or reality of a phenomenon; often used in *community organization* and in *clinical social work* as the objective or goal and to demonstrate progress toward that goal.

consensus The process in which individuals and groups achieve general agreement about goals of mutual interest and the means to achieve them. Consensus is often facilitated by the community organizer by focusing first on goals and methods of high acceptability, by emphasizing common values, and by mediating and circumventing conflicts.

consequence In *behaviorism*, an event that follows a behavior and that may increase or decrease the probability of that behavior's recurrence. A consequence may also have no effect on the behavior.

conservation 1. The planned use, preservation, and protection of the natural environment. 2. In *cognitive theory*, the ability to remember or retain relevant information and also to ignore irrelevant cues. For example, conservation was seen in Jean Piaget's experiments when young children began to retain the idea that water does not change when it is poured into pitchers of different shapes.

conservatism An ideological orientation that tends to oppose change from previously established social *values, mores,* and structures. Many conservatives justify their *ideology* by presuming that traditional mores and structures are based on accumulated wisdom and are more effective than other options.

conservator   A court-appointed *guardian* or custodian of the assets or property belonging to someone who is judged unable to manage them properly. The conservator may be an individual or, in some jurisdictions, a public or private agency.

conspiracy   Collaborative activities by two or more persons to commit a *crime.*

constellation   An arrangement or grouping of ideas, symptoms, or causes of problems.

constituency   A group of supporters, customers, voters, or clients whose interests are served by someone with the authority to represent them in seeking to meet their collective needs and interests. If the individual is an elected officeholder, the constituents are the voters, supporters from the relevant jurisdiction. See also *interest groups.*

constraint   In *social planning* and policy development, any general limitation on the level of rights. For example, zoning laws accompanied by fines, jail terms, and other penalties limit the rights of landowners.

constricted affect   Diminished variability and intensity with which emotions are expressed.

construct validity   In *social research*, a complex method for assessing the *validity* of an instrument. The instrument is regarded as valid to the extent that it is correlated with variables that compose a theoretical framework that is relevant to that instrument.

consultant   One with a special expertise or access to those with the needed expertise whose skills are sought by professionals or organizations. Consultants advise or educate about the nature of the problem or possible solutions or find better ways to achieve the organization's goals. Social workers are often sought as consultants to social agencies, law courts, political groups, activist organizations, and clinicians or to clients who need to know how to deal with specific social institutions.

consultation   An interpersonal relationship between an individual or organization possessing special expertise and someone who needs that expertise to solve a specific problem. Social work consultation is a problem-solving process in which advice and other helping activity from the consultant is offered to an individual, group, organization, or community that is faced with a job-related problem. Unlike *supervision*, which is relatively continuous and encompasses many areas of concern, consultation occurs more on an ad hoc, or temporary, basis and has a specific goal and focus. Unlike the supervisor, the consultant has no special administrative authority over those to whom advice is given.

consumer boycott   An organized refusal by a group to purchase goods or services from a firm or industry to change its methods of doing business. The goal is usually to lower prices, recognize a *labor union*, or put economic pressure on government to change it policies.

consumer-centered social work   An orientation by social work practitioners that places a high value on the self-determination of the client and emphasizes those intervention strategies that encourage client independence, self-advocacy, and self-judgment in negotiating the social services or welfare system. According to Kristine D. Tower ("Client-Centered Social Work Practice: Restoring Client Self-Determination," *Social Work,* 39[March 1994], pp. 191–196), thinking of the client as a consumer and one who is capable of deciding what is best helps move away from paternalism.

consumerism   A *social movement* and orientation designed to advocate for and protect the interests of people in their roles as users of services or commodities and to scrutinize the activities, skills, training, effectiveness, outcomes, and products of those who provide these goods or services.

Consumer Price Index (CPI)   A measure of the *cost of living* issued monthly by the *Bureau of Labor Statistics (BLS).* It shows changes in the expenses for goods and services purchased by moderate-income families.

Consumers League, National   See *National Consumers League (NCL)*.

consumption-versus-investment concept   See *investment-versus-consumption concept*.

Contact Family Program   In Sweden, a national program to recruit and modestly reimburse families who agree to provide specified supports for other families in need. Most recipient families consist of single mothers with younger children and minimal economic or social resources. The contact family often gives weekend respite care for the children, additional family supports and structure (for example, playing the "grandparent" role), helping in chore services, and providing transportation. The contact families are not especially trained and may see members of the recipient family once a month or more often if they all desire.

containment   Efforts to maintain boundaries and reduce movement beyond them; a method of *social control* in which a group of people who are separated from their peers are given special benefits so that they have less incentive to challenge their separation.

contempt of court   Behavior that interferes with the administration of justice or shows disrespect for the dignity and authority of the court. Such behavior may occur within the courtroom during a trial ("direct contempt") or outside ("constructive contempt"). See also *civil contempt*.

content analysis   In *communication theory*, the systematic study of some group interaction, written document, or other exchange of information primarily by evaluating the frequency with which certain ideas, reactions, or expressions occur.

content-and-process issue   A historic debate in social work about the degree of emphasis the profession places on its knowledge versus skill components. Social work content is the "what" of professional practice and includes substantive knowledge about entities such as diagnostic criteria, resources, special populations, the nature of social problems, and the like. Social work process is the "how" of professional practice and includes interviewing skills, evaluation research, relationship-building qualities, and effective intervention techniques.

content validity   In *social research*, a method for assessing the *validity* of an instrument or a scale. Items that actually exist on a scale are compared with items that could have been used.

contextual theory   The *family systems* concept, originated by Ivan Boszormenyi-Nagy in the 1970s, that seeks to understand family interactions, conflicts, and loyalties in terms of the legacy of accumulated obligations, debts, and hurts that occur in a family system through several generations.

contingency   1. In *social research* and statistics, a term connoting an association or correlation between variables, as in contingency tables. 2. In *behaviorism,* the consequences that are expected to follow behaviors.

contingency analysis   An approach to *social work practice* based on principles of *behaviorism,* including four propositions that (1) individuals, families, groups, communities, and societies behave; (2) all behavior is followed by consequences; (3) the consequences of a given behavior largely influence the future occurrence of that behavior; and (4) empirical analysis of these contingencies can be used effectively in understanding and treating all strata of social work clients. According to Bruce A. Thyer ("Contingency Analysis: Toward a Unified Theory for Social Work Practice," *Social Work, 32*[March–April 1987], pp. 150–157), contingency analysis can form the basis of a unified theory for all levels of social work practice.

contingency contracting   In *behavior therapy,* a technique in which an agreement is made specifying the behaviors to be performed for a certain consequence to follow. The technique is used particularly in behavioral family therapy to help family members carry out "if–then statements."

continuing-care retirement communities (CCRC)   Villages usually designed for about 300–500 older people, most of whom enter when older than age 75 and relatively healthy. The facilities are in campuslike settings with apartments, townhouses, and group recreation centers; close monitoring and easy access to health care are provided. CCRCs are usually for-profit real estate ventures and cater to affluent older people by requiring significant entry payments (depending on health care options chosen) and monthly maintenance fees.

Continuing Disability Review (CDR) The legally required periodic evaluation of one who receives social security disability benefits to determine if that person continues to be disabled. The time between reviews depends on the beneficiary's age, type and severity of disability, and the chances of improvement. CDR requires a full medical review by the *Disability Determination Service (DDS)* and possibly a consultative medical exam.

continuing education Training taken by social workers and other professionals who have already completed the formal education required to enter their field. Most professions require their members to keep up with the current knowledge base by participating in specified additional training within certain time limits. For example, state licensing boards for social workers may require them to obtain a specific number of *CEUs* (continuing education units) by successfully completing qualified academic or professional courses.

continuity of care Coordination of the efforts made by different organizations or divisions within one organization to provide for the needs of a client with a minimum of duplication or gaps in service. See also *case integration.*

continuous reinforcement In *behavior modification,* a *schedule of reinforcement* in which a *target behavior* is reinforced each time it occurs (compared with the less-frequent *intermittent reinforcement*). See also *reinforcement.*

continuum A phenomenon that has variability even though no discrete gaps or separate parts are evident.

contraception Any action or device used to prevent *pregnancy.* This includes abstinence; limiting *coitus* to nonfertile periods in the woman's cycle; or using devices such as a *condom,* intrauterine device (IUD), diaphragm, contraceptive pills, and *sterilization.*

contract A written, oral, or implied agreement between the client and the social worker as to the goals, methods, timetables, and mutual obligations to be fulfilled during the intervention process.

contracting The therapeutic procedure of discussing with the client the goals, methods, and mutual obligations of *treatment* to obtain a clear verbal understanding or to establish a formal agreement about them.

contract model An orientation in *social work practice* in which the social worker and client identify goals at the beginning of the *relationship* and formally establish a working agreement about how to reach them. The agreement includes a specification of terms, the timetables, and other procedures. The contract may be written or oral, and unlike a legal contract, may easily be renegotiated during the course of the intervention process. See also *covenant model.*

contraindication A symptom, condition, or circumstance that warns against taking some course of action. For example, bruises and cuts found on a hospitalized foster child would be a contraindication for returning the child to that foster home.

contributing to the delinquency of a minor A criminal action by parents or guardians who through *neglect, coercion,* example, or outright encouragement foster unlawful behavior by their children. These actions may include permitting the child to avoid school, to stay out late at night, to consume alcohol and other drugs, and to be exposed to unlawful activities by the parents.

control 1. To regulate. 2. To exercise direction or restraint over another. 3. In *social research,* a standard for comparison. 4. In *social welfare* management, a procedure for regulating the flow of information and activity so that efforts to achieve goals are coordinated.

control group In *research*, a group of subjects who are equivalent in every possible respect with an *experimental group*, except that they are not exposed to the variable being tested.

controlled emotional involvement An ethical principle in social work in which feelings, support, and empathy for the client are felt and expressed but only to the extent that such reactions are effective, helpful, and part of the intervention plan. The skilled practitioner learns to show and conceal emotional reactions to the client, finding the optimal response somewhere between apathy and overidentification. Controlled emotional involvement is one of the major factors in the helping *relationship*.

controlled substances Drugs that, because of their potential for abuse or addiction, have limited availability and are strictly regulated or outlawed. These substances include *marijuana, narcotics* (*opiates* such as *opium, heroin, morphine,* and *codeine* and nonopiates such as *methadone*), *stimulants* (such as *cocaine* and *amphetamines),* *depressants* (such as *barbiturates* and *tranquilizers),* and *hallucinogens* (such as *LSD,* mescaline, and peyote).

controlled-substances categories The delineation in the U.S. Controlled Substances Act (P.L. 91-513) of five schedules or types of *psychoactive drugs*, rated according to their perceived degree of potential harmfulness, abuse potential, and accepted medical use. The higher categories have greater potential for medical use and less abuse potential. Category 1 includes *heroin, LSD, marijuana,* and most addictive drugs of abuse. Category 2 substances include *morphine, methadone, amphetamines,* and other drugs that have accepted medical use but high potential for abuse.

control variable A variable introduced by a researcher to check the apparent relationship between an *independent variable* and a *dependent variable.*

convalescent home A private or public *health care facility* for patients who no longer need to be hospitalized but who require greater care than would be available in their homes.

conventional morality The second of the three stages delineated in *Kohlberg moral development theory* that usually occurs in young people between ages nine and 20. In this phase, the youth obeys rules to gain approval and avoid rejection and later begins to appreciate the need for social rules and feel guilty in wrongdoing. See also *preconventional morality* (up to age nine) and *postconventional morality* (older than age 20).

conversion A *defense mechanism* in which *anxiety* or emotional conflict is transformed into overt physical manifestations or symptoms such as pain, loss of feeling, or paralysis.

conversion disorder One of the *somatoform disorders*. The condition generally includes symptoms suggesting neurological disease, such as paralysis, coordination disturbance, anesthesia, blindness, or seizures. The psychological purpose of the disorder is primarily to achieve some *primary gain* or *secondary gain*. See also *hysteria* and *anxiety hysteria.*

conversion symptoms *Somatic complaints* that are *psychogenic*. The term derives from *psychodynamic* theories that hypothesized that unconscious and intolerable thoughts or drives are converted into physical manifestations, most commonly involving the nervous system (for example, paralysis and blindness).

Cooperative for American Relief Everywhere (CARE) A *voluntary organization* founded in 1945 through which gift parcels are sent from the United States to needy people in other nations. Its original name was Cooperative for American Remittances to Europe.

co-optation A strategy for minimizing anticipated opposition by absorbing or including the opponent in the group's membership. Once a member of the group, the opponent has less ability to criticize the program in public. Opposition within the organization is also less effective because the person is in the minority. The term is also used to indicate any election of a person or group into another group's membership.

COPA See *Council on Post-Secondary Accreditation (COPA)*.

"cop a plea" An expression used by some people charged with *crime* as well as by their lawyers, when requesting a *plea-bargaining* arrangement.

copayment A provision in some insurance programs that requires the policyholder to share the cost of any loss or claim. In many health insurance programs, the beneficiary is required to pay a percentage of the provider's bill before reimbursement is made for the rest. The major purpose of this arrangement is to discourage inappropriate use of resources and to encourage responsible participation. See also *third party* and *third-party payment*.

coping index One of several rating systems that social workers and other professionals use to consistently rank and describe the degree of *coping skills* or resources a client can call on to address the problem. Several indexes are in current use. A typical coping index is found in the *Person-in-Environment (PIE) System* whose rating scores range from no coping skills through outstanding coping skills.

coping mechanisms The behavioral and personality patterns used to adjust or adapt to environmental pressures without altering goals or purposes.

coping skills Effective *behavior* an individual uses in responding to or avoiding sources of *stress*. Typical coping skills include obtaining new needed information, preplanning, maintaining control over one's emotions and impulses, delaying gratification, and seeking more-appropriate alternative ways to achieve goals.

co-practice In *social group work*, the format in which two equally ranked professionals or leaders share responsibilities for the group.

coprolalia The frequent use of obscene or otherwise offensive language, often in an impulsive way.

Coram, Thomas (1668–1751) English philanthropist and colonist who assisted poor people and artists to live in the New World. He established England's first *foundling hospital* for abandoned babies in 1739 and developed it into a model for such facilities and for early *indoor relief* programs.

CORE See *Congress of Racial Equality (CORE)*.

CORPA See *Commission on Recognition of Post-Secondary Accreditation (CORPA)*.

corporal punishment Inflicting physical pain for the purpose of punishment, as in spanking a misbehaving child.

corporate elder care The provision of facilities and *caregivers* in the workplace for older relatives of employees. This program, which is currently offered by few employers, is equivalent to child day care or nurseries in business and government organizations. The elder care program is usually a short-term arrangement to enable employees to continue working while responsible for seniors who cannot be left alone.

corporate welfare Providing services, financial assistance, subsidies, or other benefits to organizations to help them maintain their viability or profitability. For example, a national government might reduce the tax rates or subsidize part of the expenses of a labor-intensive industry because it supposedly provides many jobs. To enhance the local economy, a municipal government might offer to give land at low or no cost to companies that relocate to the area. Some who are most strongly opposed to governmental welfare benefits for individuals favor corporate welfare programs for businesses.

corrections The legal specialty that seeks to change and improve the behaviors of convicted law offenders through *incarceration, parole, probation*, and ideally educational programs and *social services*. See also *penology*.

corrective feedback In social work administration and supervision, the communication of a discrepancy between existing and desired goals and behaviors. This feedback may be positive as well as negative and should occur privately, without blame, and with emphasis on desired behaviors. See also *supportive feedback*.

correlation In *research*, a mutual relation; a pattern of variation between two phenomena in which change in one is associated with change in the other. High correlations are not necessarily indicative of causality.

correlation coefficient A numerical index of the extent to which two variables are related. When the score is positive (+0.1 to +1.0), it indicates that the frequency of one phenomenon is associated with the frequency of the other. When the score is negative (−0.1 to −1.0), it indicates that a high frequency of one phenomenon is associated with a low frequency of the other. Perfect agreement between two variables is expressed as +1.0. Perfect inverse relationships are expressed as −1.0. A correlation coefficient of 0.0 indicates no apparent relationship.

corruption In political and public service administration, the abuse of office for personal gain, usually through *bribery, extortion, influence peddling*, and special treatment given to some citizens and not to others.

COS See *Charity Organization Societies (COS)*.

COSH Groups Committees on Occupational Health and Safety, private, nonprofit organizations, located in most of the larger states in the nation, whose goal is to help prevent worker injury, disease, and death. The groups maintain *hot lines* and provide information about such things as identifying and controlling toxic substances, and they refer callers to emergency health care providers and attorneys. See also *Occupational Safety and Health Administration (OSHA)*.

cost–benefit analysis An administration and management procedure in which various goals of the organization are evaluated systematically along with the expenses and resources required to achieve them.

costing Estimating the total expenditure of a program or plan that would be necessary to reach a specified goal. Costing is also referred to as "costing out."

cost of living The amount of money required to purchase the goods and services needed to live adequately in a given society.

cost-of-living adjustment (COLA) An increase or decrease in *benefits* based on changes in the relative purchasing power of money (*inflation* or *deflation*).

cost-of-living allowance Increased cash or *in-kind benefits* based on the amount of money deemed necessary to live according to a specified economic standard. For example, members of such groups as retired military personnel, federal employees, and social security recipients are sometimes paid a sum in excess of their originally contracted income to take into account the increased amount of money required to maintain their living standard.

cost-of-living index A measure to determine the relative purchasing power of money at a given time in a given society. In the United States, the index is calculated by weighting the average prices of 296 commodities that are considered important or representative of people's overall needs.

cost sharing A budgeting and administrative procedure that occurs when two or more governments or other organizations divide certain financial obligations. Each participating organization agrees to pay a portion of the total outlay—the amount usually depending on its own needs, resources, and expected benefits from the expenditure. For example, the federal government and a state government agree to share the costs of public-assistance payments to eligible recipients in that state. In another example, two social agencies that provide similar services in the same area agree to employ one consulting firm to provide both agencies with information about the area's demographic characteristics. See also *revenue sharing*.

cotherapy   Psychosocial *intervention* on behalf of a client conducted by two or more professionals working in *collaboration*.

Council of Economic Advisers   An agency within the executive branch of the U.S. government established in 1946 to inform the president about its analysis of the economy; to evaluate the effect of proposed and existing government programs on the economy; and to help formulate national economic policies, including those pertaining to health care and welfare.

Council of Governments (COG)   Comprehensive planning organizations comprising representatives of several local governments that are usually in geographic proximity (that is, several towns, cities, and counties in an area). COG members meet periodically to consider the mutual needs of the people in the area and ways of combining resources to meet those needs. Their purposes include planning, coordinating, and integrating their respective efforts and achieving more influence with their state governments and at the national level than could be achieved through their isolated efforts. Typical service-planning activities include transportation, water and sewage treatment, and services to older people.

Council of International Programs (CIP)   The international social work organization, founded in 1956 and headquartered in Arlington, Virginia, to facilitate educational and cultural programs for professionals in human services fields. CIP helps social work practitioners, students, and administrators develop their knowledge and skills through sponsored work study exchanges in other countries. It is funded by contributions from foundations, corporations, and more than 120 participating nations.

Council of Nephrology Social Workers (CNSW)   A professional association of social workers that is an advisory unit and integral part of the National Kidney Foundation. Founded in 1973, CNSW comprises primarily medical and health care social workers who are concerned about social services for people with kidney disease, urinary system disorders, diabetes, collagen disease, and related disorders. See also *medical social work*.

Council on Post-Secondary Accreditation (COPA)   An accrediting body for university and graduate school education in the United States, including social work, that was established in 1949 and ceased operations in 1993. Many of its functions have been taken over by the *Commission on Recognition of Post-Secondary Accreditation (CORPA)*.

Council on Social Work Education (CSWE)   An independent organization comprising social work educators, professional organizations, social agencies, and academic institutions for the purpose of establishing and maintaining standards in *social work education*. A predecessor organization of CSWE was established in 1919 and later became known as the *American Association of Schools of Social Work (AASSW)*. Another group, the National Association of Schools of Social Administration (NASSA), was founded in 1936. In 1952 AASSW merged with NASSA to form CSWE. The organization is the primary body for accrediting schools of social work in the United States. CSWE also sponsors an annual program meeting every March in different cities and publishes books, pamphlets, and the *Journal of Social Work Education*. See also *curriculum policy statement*.

counseling   A procedure often used in *clinical social work* and other professions to guide individuals, families, groups, and communities by such activities as giving advice, delineating alternatives, helping to articulate goals, and providing needed information.

counselor   Anyone who provides counseling. The term is often applied to highly trained mental health, education, or legal professionals, but it is also used for volunteers with minimal training and for paid workers who provide guidance and structure in group settings (as in camp and dorm hall counselors).

counterdependents In *group psychotherapy,* a name given to those members who persistently communicate disagreement with and disparagement for the group leader's advice, suggestions, or efforts to facilitate the group process. These members are so designated because of their opposite counterpart, "dependents" who unquestioningly follow the leader's every word or suggestion.

countertransference A set of *conscious* or *unconscious* emotional reactions to a client experienced by the social worker or other professional, usually in a clinical setting. According to *psychodynamic* theory, these feelings originate in the social worker's own developmental conflicts and are projected onto the client. Countertransference is identical to *transference* except that it applies to the feelings, wishes, and defensive operations of the social worker or therapist toward the client. Like transference, it must be constantly monitored and understood.

couples group therapy A *family therapy* strategy and *group psychotherapy* format in which several couples meet on a regular basis with a therapist to work systematically on resolving marital and family problems.

covenant model An orientation in the social work *relationship* in which the social worker implicitly or explicitly promises a commitment to empathetically serve the whole client inclusively and to work toward meeting the client's maximum needs, whether or not the needs are known or specified in advance. This model is in contrast to the *contract model,* which limits the goals, more narrowly defines client needs, and explicates the procedures for meeting them. According to Pamela Miller ("Covenant Model for Professional Relationships," *Social Work, 35*[March 1990], pp. 121–125), the covenant model emphasizes the social worker's role as teacher and companion to the client and commitment to a life of service to society.

covert reinforcement 1. In *behavior therapy,* the strengthening of the likelihood of desirable behavior by remembering a pleasant event when a given act occurs. 2. The surreptitious presentation of a reward when the subject has acted in the desired way.

Coyle, Grace L. (1892–1962) Developer of the scientific approach to *social group work,* she wrote many textbooks and articles on the subject and, as president of various social work organizations, assured that group work would be an integral part of the profession.

CPI See *Consumer Price Index (CPI).*

CPS See *child protective services (CPS).*

CPT See *Current Procedural Terminology (CPT).*

CQSW See *Certificate of Qualification in Social Work (CQSW).*

CR See *conditioned response (CR).*

"crack" A highly addictive form of *cocaine* made by mixing small amounts of it with baking soda and water. When dry, the substance is broken or cracked into small pebbles and usually smoked in special pipes. Crack is relatively inexpensive, highly potent, and can be lethal. Users tend to become obsessed about getting additional supplies. Effects may include agitation; confusion; *anxiety;* and sometimes convulsion, *tremor,* and *heart attack.*

"cradle to grave" The phrase used, often pejoratively, in describing the socioeconomic security available to people in an idealized *welfare state.* The expression "womb to tomb" has the same connotation.

"crank" A highly addictive methamphetamine that is injected to produce a period of intense *euphoria* that lasts up to 24 hours. Cheaply made and far less expensive than other *drugs of abuse,* crank often produces symptoms of acute *depression* and *psychosis* after the euphoria ends. When this substance is smoked, it is known as *"ice."*

creaming 1. The use of social services and programs, presumably available to all, by people who are most likely to succeed with the help of a given intervention program. 2. The process in which such programs are most often used by the more knowledgeable, sophisticated, and less needy, so that they are less accessible to others.

"creeping socialism" A derisive term, uttered mostly by people who espouse minimal government, referring to the gradual increase of health and welfare programs funded and maintained by government.

Creutzfeldt–Jakob disease A *central nervous system (CNS)* viral disease, resulting in *dementia* and involuntary jerky movements.

crib death See *sudden infant death syndrome (SIDS)*.

crime Any behavior that violates a law. Some social scientists extend this definition to include any behavior that is contrary to the society's moral codes for which there are formalized group sanctions, whether or not they are institutionalized as laws.

criminal justice policy Society's guidelines and established procedures to be considered when deciding how to cope with illegal conduct. Elements of current U.S. criminal justice policy include the right to trial by jury, the right to competent counsel, rights of appeal and *habeas corpus*, determinant sentencing, *probation* rather than *incarceration* for less-serious crimes with no prior conviction, and *parole* for appropriate conduct during incarceration.

criminal justice system The programs, policies, sociopolitical and legal institutions, and physical infrastructure designed to help prevent and control crime and to adjudicate, incarcerate, and rehabilitate people engaged in illegal behavior.

criminally insane A legal term referring to one who has committed a crime while under the influence of a *psychosis* or other *mental disorder* that inhibits the knowledge that such an act was wrong or the ability to refrain from doing it. An institution for the criminally insane would ideally combine the confinement of a prison with the therapy of a mental hospital.

crisis A term used by social workers in two ways: (1) an internal experience of emotional change and distress and (2) a social event in which a disastrous event disrupts some essential functions of existing social institutions. When seen as a period of emotional distress, it is considered to be precipitated by a perceived life problem or to pose an obstacle to an important goal resulting in internal discord because the individual's typical coping strategies are inadequate. The outcome of the crisis can be positive if the individual eventually finds new *coping mechanisms* to deal with the unfamiliar event, thus adding to the repertoire of effective adaptive responses.

crisis bargaining Actions taken by people during times of upset or duress to improve the situation or minimize the conflict. The concept is delineated in the *Kübler-Ross death stages* theory. In this theory, bargaining is the third crisis stage in responses to impending death. After the individual typically goes through a period of *denial* and then *anger*, he or she attempts to avoid or delay death by making promises or "deals" or by conforming to different standards.

crisis care centers Facilities in *social agencies* and health care organizations oriented toward providing short-term emergency assistance and helping individuals and groups return to precrisis functioning. These centers provide such services as *disaster relief*, *suicide* prevention, emergency food and shelter, counseling for victims of *rape* or other crimes, shelter to victims of *spouse abuse* or *child abuse*, detoxification for substance abusers, and many other activities. See also *emergency financial assistance*.

crisis hot line See *hot line*.

crisis intervention The therapeutic practice used in helping clients in *crisis* to promote effective coping that can lead to positive growth and change by acknowledging the problem, recognizing its impact, and learning new or more-effective behaviors for coping with similar predictable experiences.

crisis planning   Systematic preparation for the inevitable changes that will occur at unpredictable times in the life of an individual or community. Crisis planning ranges from *disaster relief* planning for communities to helping individuals prepare for deaths or disabilities of family members.

crisis sequence   A series of five predictable changes experienced by the person in *crisis:* (1) hazardous event (a *stressor* that may be a single catastrophic event or a series of mishaps that have a cumulative effect), (2) vulnerable state (heightened tension and *anxiety* caused by the hazardous event, intensified as the individual uses the entire repertoire of coping techniques before seeing that they do not work in this new situation), (3) precipitating factor (the "last straw," often seen as the *presenting problem* or event that brings tension to a peak), (4) active crisis state (disequilibrium has set in and is manifested by psychological and physical turmoil, aimless activity, disturbances in mood and intellectual functioning, and painful preoccupation with events leading to the crisis event), and (5) reintegration (the individual adjusts or accepts and learns new and effective coping techniques, a phase that may be adaptive or maladaptive). See also *coping index.*

crisis theory   A group of related concepts pertaining to people's reactions when confronted with new and unfamiliar experiences. These experiences may come in the form of natural disasters, significant loss, changes in social status, and life-cycle changes. This theory suggests that when people experience crises, they tend to follow predictable patterns of response. See also *crisis sequence* and *crisis intervention.*

cross-dressing   Wearing clothing that is considered more appropriate to members of the opposite sex. See also *transvestism.*

cross-racial treatment   Intervention by a professional who is of a different racial background than the client. Social workers debate whether this can be as effective as interventions within racial and ethnic boundaries but existing empirical studies, rather than advocacy statements, are inconclusive. According to Larry E. Davis and Joe Gelsomino ("An Assessment of Practitioner Cross-Racial Treatment Experiences," *Social Work,* 39[January 1994], pp. 116–123), there are five potential problem areas: (1) racism may exist, (2) worker–client rapport may not exist, (3) the intervention may be inappropriate, (4) clients may believe the worker lacks understanding about the relevant racial group, and (5) clients may believe workers lack sufficient skills because of their race.

cross-sectional research   1. A research design whereby the researcher collects data on the phenomenon under investigation at one point in time, as in a one-time survey. 2. A comparison of subjects who represent different aspects of a single variable, such as "upper class," "middle class," and "lower class."

cross-tabulation   A method for assessing the joint relationship between two variables by using tabular methods.

cross tolerance   The condition in which use of one drug leads to *tolerance* in the use of one or more other drugs.

CRS   See *Catholic Relief Services (CRS).*

crystallized intelligence   The mental skills and abilities accumulated through *socialization,* cultural contact, and other aquired information, and the ability to use these skills appropriately and effectively. Unlike *fluid intelligence* (nonculturally related problem-solving abilities), which is thought to decline in later adulthood, crystallized intelligence continues to increase with age as experience and exposure to new knowledge accumulates. See also *multiple intelligences.*

CS   See *conditioned stimulus (CS).*

CSDHA   See *Center for Social Development and Humanitarian Affairs (CSDHA).*

CSFP   See *Commodity Supplemental Food Program (CSFP).*

CSWE See *Council on Social Work Education (CSWE).*

CSWE Curriculum Policy Statement See *curriculum policy statement.*

cult 1. A group whose members hold strong beliefs associated with the teachings of a leader. 2. A body of beliefs and rites practiced by a group that usually attributes religious, mystical, or magical powers to its leader.

cultural deprivation The absence of certain *socialization* experiences that an individual may need to cope effectively in new social situations. One who has been deprived in this way often lacks the social skills, values, or motivations necessary to deal with the relevant environment. See also *anomie.*

cultural lag The retention of customs, habits, and technologies even though they have become obsolete or irrelevant to the new standards set by the prevailing culture.

culturally biased tests Examinations designed to determine an individual's intelligence, aptitude, or anticipated success in a given endeavor but that are inherently disadvantageous to members of some groups. For example, a test item asks something about European history, a disadvantage to children from Asian backgrounds. An effect of such tests is to justify placement of culturally disadvantaged people into limited opportunity situations.

culturally sensitive practice In social work, the process of professional intervention while being knowledgeable, perceptive, empathic, and skillful about the unique as well as common characteristics of clients who possess racial, ethnic, religious, gender, age, sexual orientation, or socioeconomic differences. Theoretically, all professional social work practice is culturally sensitive practice. The term is synonymous with *ethnic-sensitive practice.*

cultural pluralism The existence within a society of various racial, religious, and ethnic groups, as well as other distinct groups, each of which have different values and lifestyles.

cultural racism The belief in the inherent inferiority of a particular cultural group's language, music, art, interests, lifestyles, and values.

cultural relativism The view that specific norms or rituals can be understood accurately only in the context of a culture's goals, social history, and environmental demands.

culture The customs, habits, skills, technology, arts, values, ideology, science, and religious and political behavior of a group of people in a specific time period.

culture-bound syndrome A pattern of nonnormative (aberrant) behavior whose unique symptoms and progression tend to be specific to a particular geographic, ethnic, or cultural group. The *DSM-IV* (Washington, DC: American Psychiatric Association, 1994, pp. 845–849) describes 25 of the best studied of these syndromes, including *ataque de nervios, mal de ojo, spells,* and *zar.*

culture of poverty A premise according to which poor people are impoverished because their *values, norms,* and motivations prevent them from taking advantage of widespread opportunities to achieve economic independence.

culture shock The experience of temporary confusion, *depression,* and *anxiety* when an individual enters another cultural or subculture group environment and is uncertain about the expected roles and norms. When these symptoms become chronic, the problems are called *disorders of change.* See also *anomie.*

curandero In the cultures of some Hispanic groups, a person without formal medical training who is consulted about cures for various physical, emotional, or spiritual problems.

curfew A time deadline after which certain groups of people (such as children in some jurisdictions or racial groups in some countries) are not permitted to be outside designated areas.

Current Procedural Terminology (CPT) A physician's manual that systematically lists and codes the services and procedures performed by physicians. CPT, first published in 1966, is periodically revised. The part of CPT that lists and codes the services and procedures commonly used by psychiatrists is also published separately as *Procedural Terminology for Psychiatrists (PTP)*. CPT or PTP codes do not include, and should not be used to report, services of nonphysicians.

curriculum The defined program of study in an educational institution. In schools of social work, the curriculum includes a prescribed number and variety of required and elective courses, field placement, and other educational experiences.

curriculum policy statement A document that formally and officially describes the educational objectives, standards, and required outcomes of affiliated institutions. In social work in the past 50 years, many curriculum policy statements have been issued by various *social work education* groups. Currently, most social work educators use this term when referring to the curriculum policy statement adopted by the *Council on Social Work Education (CSWE)* in 1982. This document delineates the official criteria for accrediting *MSW* and *BSW* social work programs. The statement does not prescribe any particular curriculum but does specify certain content areas to be covered and how they are to be related to each other; the purpose and values of social work; and the mission, resources, and educational content of each professional program. The curriculum policy statement is revised and updated periodically (it was last updated in 1992). See also *Hollis–Taylor Report*.

CUSS See *Computer Use in the Social Services (CUSS)*.

custodial care The provision of shelter, food, and basic physical needs without amenities. Social workers also use this term to refer to assistance that does not require medical training—that is, help with *activities of daily living (ADL)*. Most health care insurance programs, including *Medicare*, do not cover these services.

custodial parent A mother or father who, after *divorce,* is granted by legal authority the responsibility for care and control of minors. This parent is considered by the court to be the most likely one to promote the child's best interests. See also *joint custody* and *Mothers Without Custody*.

custody A legal right and obligation of a person or group to possess, control, protect, or maintain guardianship over some designated property or over another person who is unable to function autonomously (for example, children and certain adults with disabilities). See also *guardian*.

custody of children A legal determination in *divorce* cases specifying which parent or other *guardian* will be in charge of the children. This determination is based on what is considered to be in the best interests of the children. In some circumstances, *joint custody* is awarded so that responsibility is shared between both parents. Typically, in joint custody the child lives with each parent for fixed periods. See also *custodial parent*.

cutback Reduction in service, funding, budget, or allocation of resources usually related to a decline in demand, cessation or reduction of former sources of revenue, inaccessibility of personnel, or discontinued support.

cutback strategies In *social welfare* administration, the planned activities for reducing or eliminating programs, which are necessitated by financial constraints, new priorities, ineffectiveness of programs, or achievement of goals. These activities include instituting administrative and labor efficiencies (through increased workloads, reduced support services, contracting out services and hiring lower-paid workers), reducing services (by eliminating programs and reducing the *accessibility of service*), and *cost sharing* and mergers with other organizations.

CVA Cerebrovascular accident. See *stroke*.

CVS See *chorionic villa sampling (CVS)*.

CWA 1. See *Communications Workers of America (CWA)*. 2. See *Civil Works Administration (CWA)*.

CWEP See *Community Work Experience Program (CWEP).*

CWLA See *Child Welfare League of America (CWLA).*

cybernetics The study of the processes that regulate or control systems, especially the flow of information. See also *communication theory.*

cycle of abuse The perpetuation of abusive behavior patterns that occur when an individual who has been abused acts similarly toward others. Studies confirm that people who commit *child abuse, spouse abuse,* or *elder abuse* are far more likely to have been abused themselves. The cycle is likely to continue in the succeeding generation when the abused children of such parents become parents and spouses themselves.

cycle of poverty The condition of *poverty* that exists within one family from one generation to the next. Because the children of impoverished parents are more likely to be deprived of quality education, healthy lifestyles, vocational opportunities, self-esteem, financial backing to pursue opportunities, and nurturing family support, they are more likely to remain poor and to raise their own children to be poor.

cyclical unemployment Loss of jobs caused by periodic downward trends in the business cycle. Usually this type of *unemployment* affects more workers for longer periods than the other types of unemployment *(frictional unemployment, seasonal unemployment,* and *structural unemployment).*

cyclothymia See *cyclothymic disorder.*

cyclothymic disorder A chronic fluctuating mood disturbance that has lasted more than two years (one year in children or adolescents) and includes numerous depressive symptoms and *hypomanic episodes.* The condition is similar to *bipolar disorder* except that the symptoms are not as severe (that is, no major depressive, manic, or mixed episodes). The symptoms are not due to physiological or medical problems but cause clinically significant distress or *impaired social functioning.* This disorder was formerly called cyclothymia.

cystic fibrosis A hereditary disease of the endocrine glands that causes them to produce abnormally thick and sticky secretions that form cysts and often cause obstructions in the pancreas, liver, and lungs. Symptoms vary according to the severity of the condition and the organs particularly involved, but they most often include nutritional deficiency, diarrhea-distended abdomen, and respiratory infections.

D

database A large pool of organized information available to users of *on-line* computer systems. Because each user seeks only portions of the data, the computer program extracts only that data sought. For example, a social agency might request from the NASW on-line system information about all the articles published on the topic of AIDS in the past three years. See also *computerized databases.*

date rape See *acquaintance rape.*

day care Facilities and programs that care for children or other dependents when their parents or guardians are unavailable for their care. The term also applies to physical and health care programs for people of all ages who return to their homes each evening. These facilities include *adult day care, day hospitals,* medical day care, mental health day care, and social adult day care.

Day, Dorothy (1897–1980) Founder of the *Catholic Worker Movement* and *social activist,* especially for immigrants to the United States and unemployed minorities.

day hospitals Facilities primarily for older people and people with disabilities who sleep in their own homes but receive medical and social services in hospital-like settings during the day.

DDS See *Disability Determination Service (DDS).*

DEA See *Drug Enforcement Administration, U.S. (DEA).*

death The total and permanent cessation of vital functions; currently, in humans, the determining factor is the absence of measurable brain waves.

death control Actions taken by a nation, society, or organization to decrease the *death rate,* usually through programs in hygiene, nutrition, safety, disease prevention, environmental initiatives, and avoidance of war. See also *Centers for Disease Control and Prevention (CDCP), preventative health programs,* and U.S. *Public Health Service.*

death rate The ratio of the number of deaths in a specific period to the total population or to an identified segment of that population; it is usually expressed in terms of the number of deaths per 1,000 or 100,000 people. It is also known as *mortality rate.*

death wish A person's behavior or thought patterns that become self-destructive, physically harmful, and oriented toward one's own *death.* According to some psychoanalytic theories, every individual has a certain degree of unconscious desire to die that may be consciously manifested in *masochism,* masochistic tendencies, or *self-defeating personality disorder.*

decathexis The mental process of reducing and eliminating emotional energy and feelings an individual has held for another person, idea, object, or oneself. Thus, a client might decathect from a social worker as part of the *termination* process. See also *cathexis* and *anticathexis.*

decenter Getting clients to focus their attention on aspects of their situation other than the one of most immediate concern. See also *centration*.

decentralization Diffusion of responsibility, planning, and implementation of change from the highest levels of an organization's authority toward those closer to the problem or area of action. An example is the federal government's *revenue sharing* with states and municipalities.

decertification The process of removing the title and commensurate responsibility and privileges from an identified individual or group because they have not complied with predetermined qualifications or criteria or because they no longer want the designation.

decile In research and testing, when ranked scores are distributed, a division of one-tenth of the cases.

decision support systems (DSS) In management and administration, the use of computer systems to gather and categorize data and to help administrators decide from among specified choices. The computer program uses a predefined set of facts in conjunction with decision rules to recommend optimal choices. The administrator can then concur with or reject the recommendation.

decision theory A mathematical approach to decision making using such devices as *gaming, modeling,* and simulation.

declassification A personnel policy used by public and private employers, often as a means of reducing personnel expenditures, to eliminate educational and experience requirements for holding a job and performing its functions. For example, some professional social work positions were declassified when agencies no longer required that specific jobs had to be done only by social workers with *MSW* degrees.

decoding In *communication theory,* the process of translating verbal and nonverbal cues, body gestures, and other signals into messages that are comprehensible to the recipient.

decompensation The progressive loss of normal mental functioning, *defense mecha-*

nisms, or coherent thought processes, often culminating in a form of *psychosis*.

decriminalization The repeal or adoption of legislation, the result of which is that an action formerly considered to be a *crime* is no longer so regarded and legal punishments can no longer be imposed.

deductible A provision in health and other insurance coverage in which a beneficiary is required to contribute a specified sum for each claim in a given period before the insurer pays the remaining amount of the claim.

deductive reasoning The process by which particular conclusions are reached by starting with general principles believed or shown to be true. For example, a social worker believes that all rape victims subsequently suffer some degree of emotional distress. The social worker sees a client who was raped and deduces that she is experiencing some distress even without her saying so. See also *inductive reasoning*.

de facto In actual fact, regardless of legal or normative standards. For example, de facto *segregation* occurs when a neighborhood is underrepresented by ethnic minorities even though it has no legal provision to exclude them. See also *de jure*.

default judgment In the judicial system, a decision made against a defendant who fails to appear for a court hearing after due notice has been given and the statutory delays have elapsed.

defense levels Related groups of *defense mechanisms* and coping styles that may indicate the degree to which one is adapting to stressors, used in the *Defensive Functioning Scale*. According to the *DSM-IV* (Washington, DC: American Psychiatric Association, 1994, p. 752) individuals functioning at optimal adaptive levels use coping styles such as anticipation, *affiliation, altruism,* humor, self-assertion, self-observation, *sublimation,* and *suppression*. The defensive level at the midpoint of this scale is the disavowal level, characterized by keeping unpleasant stressors, impulses, or ideas out of awareness by using such defenses as *denial, projection,* and *rationalization.* The poorest level of defensive functioning is *defensive dysregulation.*

defense mechanism A mental process that protects the personality from *anxiety, guilt* feelings, or unacceptable thoughts. Psychoanalytic theories consider such mechanisms to be *unconscious.* Some of the best-known defense mechanisms include *denial, displacement, idealization, substitution, compensation, overcompensation, conversion, sublimation, reaction formation, projection, rationalization,* and *intellectualization.*

defensive dysregulation The poorest level of defensive functioning and a coping style in which the individual cannot deal with stressors, which leads to psychosis or other breaks with objective reality. See also *Defensive Functioning Scale.*

Defensive Functioning Scale An assessment tool in development by the American Psychiatric Association (included in the *DSM-IV*) to assist in the clinician's evaluation of the degree to which an individual's *defense mechanisms* or coping styles are providing protection against anxiety and stressors. The clinician lists up to seven defenses or coping styles to rank the *defense levels* achieved by the individual.

defensiveness 1. Excessive sensitivity to actual or potential criticism or disapproval. 2. Behavior that attempts to avert criticism or embarrassment.

deficit The excess of expenditures and liabilities over income and assets during a budgetary period.

deficit spending The government economic action of spending more than it receives in taxes and other revenues. When this happens, as it has in the United States every year since 1960, the government must print new money, which leads to inflation, or borrow the difference, which further increases the national debt. To balance the budget would require raising taxes to pay for the desired expenditures or reducing the level of spending commensurate with revenues.

deflation A reduction in the *cost of living* and general price levels of an economy.

DeForest, Robert Weeks (1848–1931) Philanthropist and social reformer who helped develop the nation's first school of social work, the New York School of Philanthropy (now Columbia University School of Social Work), as well as the *Russell Sage Foundation* and many of the early programs for improving the conditions of poor people.

defrauding Criminally depriving a person of his or her rightful property through deception or misrepresentation.

deinstitutionalization The process of releasing patients, inmates, or people who are dependent for their physical and mental care from *residential care facilities,* presumably with the understanding that they no longer need such care or can receive it through community-based services.

de jure According to law or by statute. For example, de jure *segregation* refers to the legally enforced separation of groups of people (by race, sex, age, and so on). This condition existed in U.S. public schools before the 1954 Supreme Court decision *(Brown v. Board of Education)* and through *apartheid* in South Africa until 1994. See also *de facto.*

delay of gratification An ability to postpone receiving pleasure or reward. This is an important factor in maturity and in accomplishments that take time to achieve, such as academic degrees or success in helping multiproblem families. Lack of ability to delay gratification is seen in young children, narcissistic adults, immature people, and some people with chronic mental disorders.

delinquency 1. The failure to fulfill one's duties or obligations. 2. The actions of youngsters who violate laws or fail to conform to the reasonable demands of the caregiver and other authorities.

delinquent 1. In the *criminal justice system,* an offender who is considered to be a minor (in most states, younger than age 18, in some, up to age 22) by the jurisdiction of residence or where the offense is committed. Some acts, which are not crimes for adults, are forbidden by law for children (such as *curfew* violations, drinking alcohol, smoking, and *truancy*). 2. A debt that has not been paid when due or an agreement that has not been fulfilled.

delirium A state of confusion, often accompanied by *hallucination, delusion, emotional lability,* and *anxiety.* It is usually the result of changes in cerebral metabolism typically induced by alcohol or *drug intoxication, shock* or fever, general medical conditions, or multiple etiologies. See also *substance intoxication delirium* and *withdrawal delirium.*

delirium tremens (DTs) A form of *delirium* resulting from withdrawal from excessive consumption of alcohol. The victim often develops such symptoms as fever, convulsions, *tremor,* and *hallucination,* generally occurring between one and four days after the drinking has stopped. The preferred professional term is *withdrawal delirium.*

Delphi method A procedure, especially in *social planning* and *community organization,* that uses a highly structured, multistage questionnaire with a group of experts or panelists so that they can make focused assessments about the desirability, value, and feasibility of a proposed plan or policy, including *feedback* about results.

delusion An inaccurate but strongly held belief retained despite objective evidence to the contrary and despite cultural norms that do not support such beliefs. It is often a characteristic of *psychosis* or *paranoid ideation.* Major types include *delusions of grandeur* and *delusions of persecution.*

delusional disorder A *mental disorder* characterized by the existence of certain nonbizarre delusions (those involving situations that occur in life such as being followed, being deceived by a spouse or lover, or having a disease). The delusions persist more than one month and, apart from the impact of the delusions, psychosocial func-

tioning is not severely impaired. Specific subtribes of delusional disorder include *erotomanic type, grandiose type, jealous type, persecutory type, somatic type,* and mixed delusions. The *DSM-IV* (Washington, DC: American Psychiatric Association, 1994, pp. 296–302) has replaced delusional (paranoid) disorder and *paranoid disorder* with this label.

delusional (paranoid) disorder See *delusional disorder.*

delusions of grandeur An exaggerated sense of self-importance. Delusions of this type may be symptoms of *psychosis, narcisstic personality disorder, paranoid ideation,* or *overcompensation* for excessive *inadequacy feelings.*

delusions of persecution The inaccurate but strongly held and persistent belief that one is being threatened or harmed by others. It is often a symptom of *psychosis, delusional disorder, paranoid ideation,* or excessive *inadequacy feelings.*

demagogue A political or organizational leader who wins support by appealing to *fear,* hatred, or greed, often using effective oratory, charisma, and lies. See also *charismatic leader.*

demand subsidy The concept of providing *cash vouchers* or *tax incentives* so that consumers can purchase needed services or products through the existing marketplace. This is in contrast to the concept of *supply subsidy,* in which funding is provided to organizations so that they may provide their services. The *Food Stamp program* and *Medicaid* use the demand subsidy principle, whereas *community mental health centers* and public hospitals are examples of supply subsidy.

dementia Deterioration of the mental processes, usually characterized by memory loss, personality change, and impaired judgment and ability to think abstractly or systematically. Dementia is caused by physiological changes, the result of *stroke, Alzheimer's disease, substance abuse,* medical conditions, or multiple etiologies. Some of the medical conditions related to dementia include *head injury, HIV disease, Parkinson's disease, Huntington's disease, Pick's disease,* and *Creutzfeldt–Jakob disease.*

dementia of the Alzheimer's type See *Alzheimer's disease.*

democratic socialism *Socialism* in a nation whose citizens have freely elected to have that form of political and socioeconomic system.

demogrant A benefit provided to those in specified population categories (for example, children, mothers, older people, or citizens) without regard to need. Rare in the United States, this type of benefit is a common form of income redistribution in many other nations. See also *income distribution, maternity benefits,* and *Medicare.*

demographics A depiction of the frequencies with which specified social characteristics occur within a designated population. These characteristics may include such factors as gender, *race, ethnic group,* educational level, *socioeconomic class,* and religious affiliation.

demography The systematic study of population variables and characteristics. See also *psychographics.*

demonstration 1. In *social change* efforts, a group action designed to call public or political attention to a problem or issue of interest to the participants. This typically takes the form of massing or marching together in highly visible setting or picketing the entrances of buildings where the behavior that the demonstrators find objectionable is believed to be taking place. 2. In *direct practice,* behaviors intended to show how something can be done effectively, such as when a social worker shows a client how to communicate better with others by *role playing.*

demonstration programs Service delivery programs that are usually limited by time and geographic range but are designed to test whether measures proposed for solving specific problems are desirable and effective. When these programs use rigorous controlled research, they are also known as experimental programs. In theory, programs that are demonstrated as effective can then be made permanent and expanded for a larger population. Examples of demonstration programs are *Mobilization for Youth* in New York City and the Mental Health Manpower studies of the *National Association of Social Workers (NASW).*

demonstrative A term applied to behavior that is outwardly expressive of emotions and to people who exhibit such behavior.

demosclerosis A government's decreasing ability to adapt or respond to social conditions or the needs of its people. According to Ronald E. Dear ("Social Welfare Policy;" in Richard L. Edwards [Ed.-in-Chief], *Encyclopedia of Social Work,* 19th ed., Washington: NASW Press, 1995), its causes include public opposition to increased taxation, distrust of government, indifference by political leaders, disagreement about goals, bureaucratic entrenchment and unresponsiveness, and the power and effort of interest groups and their political action committees to prevent change.

dendrites The branched fibers off the *neuron* cell that carry impulses from other nerve cells into the cell body.

denial The *defense mechanism* that protects the personality from *anxiety* or *guilt* by disavowing or ignoring unacceptable thoughts, emotions, or wishes.

deontology The philosophy of moral duty and obligation.

Department of Agriculture, U.S. (USDA) The federal agency created in 1862 to administer the nation's farm programs, meat and dairy inspection, food production, and distribution; to conserve farmland and related resources; and to provide education and information to farmers. This department also administers many food assistance programs, including the *Food Stamp program,* the *School Lunch program,* and the *WIC program.*

Department of Education, U.S. The federal agency, created in 1979 by separation from the U.S. *Department of Health, Education, and Welfare (HEW)*, that administers programs to provide and promote the nation's educational opportunities and to supplement state and local educational efforts. It sponsors research on teaching methods and educational programs; provides financial aid for elementary through college education; provides educational programs for disabled, disadvantaged, and gifted students; and supervises numerous educational functions including *school social work* programs.

Department of Health and Human Services, U.S. (HHS) The federal agency formed in 1979 when the U.S. *Department of Health, Education, and Welfare (HEW)* was divided into two federal-level agencies. The principal components of the department now include the *Administration for Children and Families (ACF)*, the *Social Security Administration (SSA)*, the *Health Care Financing Administration (HCFA)* (including *Medicare* and *Medicaid*), and the U.S. *Public Health Service*, under which falls the National Institute of Child Health and Human Development.

Department of Health, Education, and Welfare, U.S. (HEW) A federal agency formed in 1953, replacing the Federal Security Agency, to administer, develop, and improve the national programs for social welfare, health, and education. When the autonomous U.S. *Department of Education* was created in 1979, the remaining components of the agency became known as the U.S. *Department of Health and Human Services (HHS)*.

Department of Housing and Urban Development, U.S. (HUD) The federal agency formed in 1965 to administer, develop, and improve the national *housing programs*, including *urban renewal* and *community development*. Its major divisions include the *Office of Fair Housing and Equal Opportunity*, the *Office of Community Planning and Development*, and the *Government National Mortgage Association (GNMA)*.

Department of Justice, U.S. The federal agency established in 1870 and headed by the Attorney General, whose primary mission is to enforce all federal laws, administer the nation's law enforcement and investigation system, advise the president in legal matters, argue suits involving the U.S. government in the Supreme Court, and supervise federal penal institutions. This department includes the *Drug Enforcement Administration (DEA)*, the *Immigration and Naturalization Service (INS)*, the Federal Bureau of Investigation, and the U.S. Parole Commission.

Department of Labor, U.S. The federal agency created in 1913 to improve working conditions and worker safety and welfare, to secure employee benefits, to enhance employment opportunities, and to acquire and disseminate information about social conditions affecting employment. Its major offices and organizations include the *Occupational Safety and Health Administration (OSHA)*, the *Labor Management Programs Services Administration*, the *Employment and Training Administration*, and the *Bureau of Labor Statistics (BLS)*.

Department of Social Services (DSS) The name used by many states and municipalities for their agencies that provide *human services*, *public assistance*, and other *welfare* services. See also *Human Resources Administration (HRA)*.

Department of the Interior, U.S. The federal agency established in 1849 whose primary mission is to conserve and develop the nation's natural resources, including its fish and wildlife, minerals and land management, national parks, government and public buildings, and many other programs. The department manages the *Bureau of Indian Affairs (BIA)*, including its health and social service programs. At various times in its history, this agency was also in charge of the nation's educational system, hospitals, and interstate commerce as well as the U.S. *Bureau of the Census*, which is currently under the U.S. Department of Commerce.

de Paul, Vincent (1581–1660) Catholic priest and advocate for the poor people of France, he established seminaries, and poor relief organizations including the Daughters of Charity to provide relief and assistance to the needy. He was canonized in 1737. See also *Ozanum, Antoine Frederic.*

dependency A state of reliance on other people or things for existence or support; a tendency to rely on others to provide nurturance, make decisions, and provide protection, security, and shelter. When reliance becomes excessive, it is a symptom of *neurosis, regression,* or emotional *insecurity.*

dependent personality disorder One of the 11 *personality disorders,* in which the individual is generally passive in most relationships, allows others to assume responsibilities, lacks self-confidence, feels helpless, and tends to tolerate abusiveness from others. See also *passive–dependent.*

dependent variable In systematic *research,* the phenomenon or reaction to be tested or measured when a new stimulus, condition, or treatment is introduced. The factor that is introduced is the *independent variable.*

depersonalization A feeling of being in an unreal situation or a sense that one's self or body is detached from the immediate environment. This experience is often found in individuals who are subjected to inordinate *stress* or are in *crisis,* as well as individuals with specific mental disorders such as *neurosis* and *psychosis.*

depersonalization disorder A type of *dissociative disorder* in which the individual copes with internal *conflict* and *anxiety* through psychological detachment or by experiencing the feeling of being in an unreal situation. *Depersonalization* and *derealization* are the major symptoms, and some individuals also concurrently experience *depression* and *hypochondriasis.*

deposition Legal testimony of a witness under oath taken outside a courtroom.

depressants A group of drugs that induce in their users a state of deep relaxation, apathy, lethargy, and emotional depression by inhibiting the responses and actions of the *central nervous system (CNS).* The drugs most common within this class are *barbiturates* and *tranquilizers.* See also *"downers."*

depression A group of emotional reactions frequently characterized by sadness, discouragement, despair, pessimism about the future, reduced activity and productivity, sleep disturbance or excessive fatigue, and feelings of inadequacy, self-effacement, and hopelessness. In some individuals, such traits may be mild, intermittent, and undetectable by observers, but in others they may be constant and intense. In its more-severe forms, pathology may be a manifestation of a *major affective disorder, bipolar disorder,* or *cyclothymic disorder.* See also *exogenous depression* and *endogenous depression.*

depression, economic A socioeconomic condition in which business activity is reduced for a prolonged time, unemployment rates are high, and purchasing power is greatly diminished. See also *stagflation* and *recession.*

depressive reaction A term indicating sadness, pessimism, and lowered activity often precipitated by an actual or perceived severe loss. The term is now replaced by *bipolar disorder, major depression, dysthymic disorder,* or *cyclothymic disorder,* depending on other symptoms.

depressive neurosis See *dysthymic disorder.*

deprivation A state of unfulfilled, unmet, or incompletely met physical, social, or emotional *needs.*

derailment A speech pattern in which the individual repeatedly changes the subject and moves from topic to topic, even within the same sentence.

derealization A *dissociative symptom* in which one experiences the external world as strange or unreal. The individual may see others as being unfamiliar or robotlike and perceive alterations in the size or shape of viewed objects. Derealization is often a symptom of *panic attack* and *depersonalization disorder.*

deregulation The reduction or cessation of government control over the operations of various industrial, governmental, professional, or other organizations. The policy of deregulation in the 1980s led to significant changes in the airline industry, railroads and trucking, and financial institutions.

derelict 1. A person who is experiencing *homelessness* and *unemployment.* 2. Property, such as a car, that has been abandoned by its owner.

derepression Therapy designed to bring back to conscious awareness the thoughts and feelings that the *client* had unconsciously pushed to the unconsciousness. Much of psychoanalysis may be said to engage primarily in this activity. See also *psychodynamic.*

desegregation The act of abolishing *segregation,* whether *de facto* or *de jure,* that has been imposed on certain *minority* groups.

desensitization The elimination or minimization of physical or psychological reactions to stimuli. Behaviorally oriented social workers use a form of this, known as *systematic desensitization,* especially to help some clients overcome certain fears or ineffective behavior patterns.

desertion 1. The act of abandoning a person or position to whom or to which one has certain obligations. 2. In *marriage,* desertion occurs when one spouse leaves the other without the other's consent and has no intention of returning. Desertion may or may not be accompanied by *nonsupport.* Desertion is usually grounds for *divorce.*

DeShaney decision The 1988 U.S. Supreme Court ruling (*DeShaney v. Winnebago County Department of Social Services*) that the social workers and their social agency could not be held liable for damages for failure to protect a child who

had been abused by the father. The ruling does not, however, mean that social workers employed in *child protective services (CPS)* are free from the risk of lawsuits at the state court level; moreover, they may still be at risk at the federal level.

designer drugs Compounds that differ slightly from the chemical structures of illegal drugs, usually made by "street chemists." Until recently, these drugs were technically legal but still had all the properties of their illegal counterparts. Now they are illegal.

destitution A state of *poverty* in which one lacks sufficient resources even for food or shelter.

detention The act of restraining a person, usually in an institution (a jail or other holding facility), for some legal purpose. This term usually implies a short-term holding while awaiting trial. See also *incarceration.*

deterrence In the judicial system, a policy that uses fear of restraint and punishment to attempt to discourage crime.

detoxification The process of removing drugs or other harmful substances from the body for a sufficient length of time to restore adequate physiological and psychological functioning. This is achieved by withholding the substance from the individual while providing rest, proper diet, health care, medication, psychological support, and social services.

devaluation Attributing exaggerated negative qualities to one's self or others, usually as a way to deal with emotional conflict, stressors, or inadequacy feelings. See also *idealization* and *halo effect.*

developing countries Nations with low per capita incomes and relatively small financial reserves that have worked to develop their natural resources, develop numbers of skilled and educated citizens, and aspire to economic and political parity with developed countries. Often called *Third World* countries, this category includes India, Brazil, Egypt, Nigeria, and Indonesia; not usually included are *underdeveloped countries* such as Bangladesh, Ethiopia, and Chad. See also *Fourth World.*

developmental approach In *direct practice,* an orientation toward or focus on the predictable changes that occur throughout the human *life cycle,* including physical, mental, social, and environmental changes.

developmental arithmetic disorder The inability to acquire arithmetic skills that is not a result of poor education and socialization or intelligence deficits. The preferred term for this is *mathematics disorder.*

developmental coordination disorder Inhibited motor skill development so that the child or adult seems poorly coordinated, clumsy, and awkward; the child falls behind peers in ability to tie shoelaces, play ball, or write. This disorder is not due to physical disability or mental retardation. The preferred term for this is *motor skills disorder.*

developmental disabilities A condition that produces functional impairment, as a result of disease, genetic disorder, or impaired growth pattern manifested before adulthood, likely to continue indefinitely, and require specific and lifelong or extended care. Some of the conditions classified as developmental disabilities include *cerebral palsy, Down's syndrome, epilepsy, mental retardation,* and *autism.*

Developmental Disabilities, Administration on An agency within the U.S. *Department of Health and Human Services (HHS)* that provides information and coordinates expertise about the causes, prevention, and treatment of human *developmental disorders* such as *mental retardation, autism, seizure disorders,* and *cerebral palsy.*

developmental disorder A classification of physical and mental dysfunctions that appear before the individual reaches maturity. *Pervasive developmental disorders* include *autistic disorder, Rett's disorder, childhood disintegrative disorder,* and *Asperger's disorder.*

developmental research Analysis, design, development, and evaluation of human services innovations. Developmental research in social work studies assessment methods, intervention methods, service programs and systems, policy analysis and development, and the physical and infrastructure aspects of providing for human services needs.

developmental social welfare An approach to *social welfare* that encourages and plans for indigenous and culturally appropriate models of social services delivery, according to the unique demands and resources of the *Third World.*

developmental stages The progression of physical and mental changes occurring over time and that result in clusters of identifiable and predictable characteristics tending to occur during specific periods.

deviance The act of differing sharply from normal *behavior* or maintaining standards of conduct, *norms,* and *values* that are in marked contrast to accepted standards. The term was formerly used to indicate sexual *perversion.* See also *maladaptive* and *maladjustment.*

Devine, Edward T. (1867–1948) As a contributor to *social work education,* he helped found the New York School of Philanthropy in 1898 and guided it toward its development as the Columbia University School of Social Work. He also founded the leading social work journal of the time, *The Survey,* and wrote several texts about the history of social work and social welfare, including *Misery and its Causes* (1909), *Social Work* (1928), and *When Social Work Was Young* (1939).

dhat A *culture-bound syndrome* found most commonly in India in which the individual experiences anxiety and fear of bodily dysfunctions because of the discharge of semen or the discoloration of urine. See also *shenkui.*

DI See *disability insurance (DI).*

diabetes A disease, caused by a disorder in the islet of Langerhans in the pancreas,

99

in which an insufficient amount of insulin is produced or secreted so that the body cannot process sugars properly.

diabetes mellitus   A serious, chronic deficiency in the body's ability to produce insulin, resulting in excessive sugar in the blood and urine.

diagnosis   The process of identifying a problem (social and mental, as well as medical) and its underlying causes and formulating a solution. In early social work delineations, it was one of the three major processes, along with social study and *treatment*. Currently, many social workers prefer to call this process *assessment* because of the medical connotation that often accompanies the term "diagnosis." Other social workers think of diagnosis as the process of seeking underlying causes and assessment as having more to do with the analysis of the relevant information.

"diagnosis of convenience"   A term used by some providers of mental health services to refer to an inaccurate description of the condition of the client on an insurance form. This is sometimes done by providers because most insurance companies will reimburse only for diagnosable conditions. For example, the professional provides marital therapy, which is not usually reimbursable, but indicates depression as the diagnosis of convenience. This is a fraudulent as well as unethical practice, and it is also detrimental to the therapeutic relationship because it fosters an improper collusion between the provider and client.

diagnosis-related groups (DRGs)   The name applied to a federally mandated prospective payment mechanism designed to control the costs of medical and hospital care for *Medicare* recipients. The system is administered by the *Health Care Financing Administration (HFCA)*. Payments made to the hospitals caring for Medicare patients are determined in advance, based on which one of 467 discrete categories of disorder—or DRG—the patient has at the time of admission, as well as on the patient's age; whether surgery is necessary; and in some cases, the presence of complications.

Each category, with relevant additional factors, is equated with a flat sum. If costs for care exceed the predetermined amount, the hospital is expected to bear the excess; if they are lower than the predetermined amount, however, the hospital may keep the difference. This is supposed to encourage shorter hospital stays, a less-extensive mix of services during hospitalization, and the diminished likelihood of rehospitalization.

Diagnostic and Statistical Manual of Mental Disorders   See *DSM-III, DSM-III-R,* and *DSM-IV.*

diagnostic school in social work   The name given to the orientation in social work that emphasized *psychodynamic* and *social change* theories and *insight therapies*. The term was first used to distinguish this group of social workers from colleagues who were identified with the *functional school in social work.*

dialysis   Treatment for kidney disease. The various types of dialysis include *hemodialysis, peritoneal dialysis,* and chronic ambulatory peritoneal dialysis. Dialysis can be performed in hospitals, special outpatient centers, and in some cases, in the home of the patient. Dialysis has no curative value but substitutes for the function of the kidneys.

diathesis   Genetic predisposition toward certain diseases. For example, the *dopamine hypothesis* suggests that certain people are "diathetic" toward *schizophrenia.*

diathetic–stress theory   See *stress–diathesis theory.*

dichos   Proverbs or folk sayings commonly used in Spanish-speaking cultures. Dichos are usually brief and spoken spontaneously, often in rhymes, and are used as guidelines in the development of attitudes, moral values, and social behavior. Social workers who serve Hispanic clients sometimes use these *metaphors* as tools to facilitate the working *relationship* and overcome *resistance*. Maria E. Zuniga ("Using Metaphors in Therapy: Dichos and Latino Clients," *Social Work,* 37[January 1992], pp. 55–60) suggests that non-Spanish–speaking clinicians use such dichos only when guided by Latino clinicians.

didactic analysis *Psychoanalysis* whose primary goal is instruction rather than therapy; otherwise, the procedure is identical with all other forms of psychoanalysis.

differential acculturation The process of adapting to new cultures (that is, to language, lifestyle, norms, and so forth) as experienced by people with different demographic characteristics. For example, individuals and families who emigrate to new countries adapt at different rates of speed and success, depending on factors such as age and developmental stage, educational level, prior experience or knowledge of the new culture, level of sophistication and self-esteem, and degree of available emotional support and nurturance.

differential diagnosis The process of distinguishing between similar mental disorders or social problems on the basis of their compared and unique characteristics.

differential life expectancy The probable life span of people based on distinct classifications such as gender, *socioeconomic class, race,* and current age. Life expectancy is influenced by the degree to which people have access to economic benefits.

differential response In *behaviorism* and *social learning theory,* a response that is elicited by a particular *stimulus* among many possible different stimuli. For example, a child may learn to smile when a parent smiles and frown when the parent frowns.

differentiation In *family systems theories,* the ability of family members to distinguish or separate their identities, thoughts, and emotions from those of other family members. See also *fusion.*

differentiation phase The fourth of five *group development phases* in which group members develop a greater sense of their own unique problems and ability to solve them within themselves and among the other group members. This phase follows the *intimacy phase* in which the member becomes such an integral part of the group-

as-a-whole that individuality is somewhat subordinated to the needs of the group. These two stages in the group progression follow the *preaffiliation phase* and the *power-and-control phase* and precede the *separation phase.* Many other typologies have also been proposed to describe the different phases in the typical life of a groupwork or therapy group.

dioxin A chemical compound often used as a herbicide. These toxic substances are long lasting and labeled by the U.S. *Environmental Protection Agency (EPA)* to be, under certain circumstances, a *carcinogen.* See also *Agent Orange.*

diphtheria A contagious disease that occurs mostly in preschool children and is transmitted by droplets of moisture exhaled by infected individuals. The bacteria that cause the disease lodge in the mucous membranes of the throat, producing tissue-destroying toxins. Diphtheria deaths are caused by tissue damage, particularly in the heart. The disease was once common in the United States and elsewhere, but inoculations of diphtheria *toxoids* routinely given to infants have minimized its incidence rate.

Diplomate in Clinical Social Work A credential to distinguish advanced-level, professional clinical social workers who meet the qualifications of the sponsoring organization (such as *American Board of Examiners in Clinical Social Work [ABE]* or the *National Association of Social Workers [NASW]).* Qualifications typically include many or all of the following: a graduate degree from a *Council on Social Work Education* (CSWE)–accredited school, postgraduate supervision, direct practice experience (usually more than 7,500 hours within five years), fulfillment of requirements for state licensing, and the passing of an advanced examination.

dipsomania An abnormal or insatiable desire to drink alcohol. This has become a rarely used term.

direct cost The amount paid by a recipient of any goods or services—a sum that may only partially cover the expense of producing them. See also *indirect cost.*

direct influence An *intervention* in *social casework* or *clinical social work* in which the social worker attempts to promote a specific type of behavior in the client. It is done systematically and cautiously, often by offering suggestions and advice about how best to reach the client's own goals.

directive therapy An approach in counseling in which the social worker or other mental health care provider offers advice, suggestions, information about resources, and prescriptions for more-effective behavior.

direct practice The term used by social workers to indicate their range of professional activities on behalf of clients in which goals are reached through personal contact and immediate influence with those seeking social services. It is to be distinguished from *indirect practice*.

direct practice skills The ability to put social work knowledge into effective intervention activities with individuals, families, groups, and communities. According to Ruth R. Middleman and Gail Goldberg Wood (*Skills for Direct Practice in Social Work*, New York: Columbia University Press, 1990), these skills are inner (perception and cognition), interactional (setting the stage, dealing with feelings and information), and strategic (dealing with behavior and coping with conflict). Additional skills for working with groups include building groups, facilitating the work of groups, working with groups that do not verbalize readily, and providing nontalking times with groups. See also *social work skills*.

direct treatment A group of *intervention* procedures used in *social casework* or *clinical social work* in which the social worker seeks to implement specific changes or improvement through personal contact with the client. The term was first used by *Mary Richmond* (1861–1928) to designate a social worker's face-to-face interactions with individual clients, as distinguished from *indirect treatment* or problem solving and from developmental work in the environment.

disability Temporary or permanent inability to perform "normal" activities, usually as a result of a physical or mental condition or infirmity. See also *International Classification of Impairment, Disability, and Handicapped (ICIDH)*; *impairment*; and *handicap*.

disability benefit The provision of cash, goods, or services to one who is not capable of performing certain activities because of a physical or mental condition; a form of *categorical assistance* based on incapacity. In the United States, the *Disability Insurance (DI)* program for disabled people and the *Supplemental Security Income (SSI)* program for needy disabled people are currently the most extensive examples of this type of program. See also *temporary disability insurance*.

Disability Determination Service (DDS) A program within the *Social Security Administration (SSA)* for applicants for disability or *Supplemental Security Income (SSI)*. When a claim is about to be denied, the applicant can request reconsideration by means of a face-to-face meeting with a DDS examiner.

Disability Insurance (DI) The U.S. *Social Security Administration (SSA)* program to provide for the economic needs of those who can no longer earn an income because of chronic incapacity. To be eligible clients must be no longer able to do the work for which they were trained and experienced or other suitable kinds of employment. The disability must be expected to last for at least a year or to result in death. Others who may be eligible under certain circumstances include disabled children (such as those with *mental retardation* or various childhood conditions), disabled former spouses (older than age 50 if the marriage lasted 10 years or longer), and people with *human immunodeficiency virus (HIV)* infection.

disabled A term used to describe an individual whose specific physical or mental condition or infirmity limits his or her ability to carry out certain responsibilities. The condition may be temporary or permanent; it may be partial or total. In the United States, the *Social Security Administration (SSA)* considers a person disabled if he or she is unable to do any kind of appropriate work because of a disability that is expected to last for at least one year.

disadvantaged   A term used to describe an individual who is deprived of needed material resources, mental capacities, emotional and social development, or opportunities to acquire them.

disarmament   The intentional decisions and actions that bring about a reduction in or elimination of the weapons possessed by a nation or group. Many social workers have been active in the peace movement, in which nations are encouraged to lay down their arms or discontinue supplying arms to others. See also *peace dividend.*

disassociation   See *dissociation.*

disaster   An extraordinary event, either natural or human-made, concentrated in time and space, that often results in damage to property and harm to human life or health and that is disruptive of the ability of some social institutions to continue fulfilling their essential functions.

disaster relief   Efforts and activities to provide immediate refuge and security from the continuing physical and emotional risks encountered in the *disaster* and also work toward restoring the social and physical structures that had existed to meet essential needs. See also *emergency basic-needs services.*

disaster relief planner   One who predicts the probabilities, consequences, and locations of a potential *disaster;* organizes people and structures to provide *disaster relief;* and educates the populace about how to respond and minimize a disaster's consequences. Many communities have offices of emergency management in which this function is performed. The U.S. *Federal Emergency Management Agency (FEMA)* fulfills some of these functions nationally. See also *emergency basic-needs services.*

disaster syndrome   The psychological and social relationship problems typically experienced by victims of a crisis or calamity.

Social workers who specialize in *disaster relief* identify several phases of the syndrome: preimpact (apprehension and anxiety accompanying the threat or warning); impact (the hazard strikes and the community organizes its relief effort); postimpact (often characterized as a "honeymoon" phase of high energy for coping and mutual cooperation); and disillusionment (when people encounter the long-term obstacles brought about by the disaster).

discharge planning   A social service in hospitals and other institutions that is designed to help the patient or client make a timely and healthy adjustment from care within the facility to alternative sources of care or to self-care when the need for service has passed. When practiced by skilled social workers, discharge planning helps the client and relevant others understand the nature of the problem and its impact, facilitates their adaptations to their new roles, and helps arrange for postdischarge care. See also *channeling* and *premature termination.*

discretionary funds   The money available after purchase of necessities; also referred to as disposable income. In budgeting, the term also refers to funds allocated outside rigid *categorical grants.* The use of these funds is generally determined by those empowered to choose how to spend them.

discrimination   1. The prejudgment and negative treatment of people based on identifiable characteristics such as *race*, gender, religion, or *ethnicity.* 2. In general terms, also the process of distinguishing between two objects, ideas, situations, or stimuli. See also *separatism* and *apartheid.*

disease   A condition in which a system (including all or part of a living organism) is not functioning properly; a *disorder.*

disease patterns   In epidemiology studies of diseases, the incidence of a *disease* in a community and the frequency from one population group to another. Rates of disease are calculated by dividing the number of people who have the disease by the number at risk. See also *morbidity rate.*

disease risk factor Phenomena in the environment or within the individual that are known to be associated with increased chances of developing a particular *disease*. A risk factor may or may not be the cause of the disease, but identifying it is important in prevention.

disengaged family A family whose individual members and subsystems have overly rigid *boundaries* that result in restricted interaction and psychological isolation from one another. Some disengaged families may also have diffuse boundaries. See also *enmeshed family*.

disengagement theory The perspective held by some experts on the process of aging that says that as some older people slow down they gradually become more self-preoccupied, lessen emotional ties with others, have less interest in world affairs, and slowly withdraw from society. The theory also holds that society disengages from the older individual. The resulting mutual disengagement results in a decrease in life satisfaction. This theory is controversial, and some researchers point out that many older people maintain very active lives in late adulthood and show no decrease in life satisfaction.

disincentive A factor that discourages an individual or group from doing something. For example, reducing welfare or Medicaid benefits to people who have low-paying jobs sometimes discourages efforts to become economically independent. See also *cliff effect*.

disorder A *disease* or ailment; a condition in which a system (including all or part of a living organism) is not functioning properly.

disorderly conduct The *crime* of violating the public peace or safety. Charged with this crime often are homeless people, those intoxicated in public places, social *activists* or *agitators*, and labor picketers.

disorder of written expression A type of *learning disorder* in which a student is below the norm in writing skills and the understanding of numbers concepts as that expected of others of similar ages, intellectual levels, and educational levels without physical and neurological problems. For the condition to be diagnosable, it must significantly interfere with the student's academic achievement or activities that require writing. Many educators call this disorder *dysgraphia* or *agraphia*. The other major types of learning disorder are *reading disorder* and *mathematics disorder*.

disorders of change Psychosocial problems an individual develops as a consequence of having to adapt to unfamiliar social environments or developmental experiences. These disorders may be permanent but generally are overcome in healthy people with good *coping skills*. See also *culture shock*.

disorganized schizophrenia Technically known as schizophrenia, disorganized type (formerly known as *hebephrenic schizophrenia*), this disease is distinguished from other forms of *schizophrenia* by such symptoms as wild excitement, giggling, silly behavior, and rapid mood shifts.

displaced homemaker A person who becomes widowed or divorced after spending years as a family's *caregiver* and who usually has not developed other marketable skills to facilitate economic independence.

displaced populations Groups of people who are uprooted from their established locations and lifestyles, including *refugees, immigrants, undocumented aliens, migrant laborers*, and *seasonal workers*. According to Fariyal Ross-Sheriff ("Displaced Populations," in Leon Ginsberg et al. [Eds.], *Encyclopedia of Social Work*, 18th ed., 1990 supplement, Washington, DC: NASW Press, pp. 78–93), these groups tend to adapt to their new locations in one of four general ways: (1) assimilation (giving up one's former culture and its values to acquire those of the host society), (2) integration (maintaining a significant part of the cultural identity of the past while participating in the larger society), (3) separation (establishing a separate set of institutions or interactions), or (4) marginalization (loss of cultural identity resulting in confusion, alienation, and striking out against the larger society).

displacement   A *defense mechanism* used to reduce *anxiety* that accompanies certain thoughts, feelings, or wishes by transferring them to another thought, feeling, or wish that is more acceptable or tolerable.

disposition   The arrangement made on behalf of a client or patient by the provider of health care or a social service to conclude the intervention. This may include referral to a more-appropriate resource, follow-up care, or successful achievement of goals so that help is no longer needed. In many types of *case record*, professionals conclude entries by writing "Disposition" (or "Disp."), followed by the course of action recommended for the ongoing care of the client.

disruptive behavior disorder   A group of *developmental disorders* in which the individual's behavior persistently interferes with the social activities of those nearby. The specific types of disruptive behavior disorder include *attention-deficit hyperactivity disorder (ADHD), oppositional defiant disorder,* and *conduct disorder.*

disruptive tactics   Actions that interfere with the normal operations of social institutions to bring about changes in laws, norms, or social structures. These activities are undertaken and coordinated, especially by *social activists* and *community organizers,* to call public attention to problems and injustices and to put pressure for change on an organization. Examples include *sitdown strikes, sit-ins* in the offices of corporate executives, picket lines on roads leading to nuclear reactors, organized heckling of political candidates during their speeches, and *greenlining.*

dissident   An individual who disagrees with the policy of a government or other organization and refuses to participate therein.

dissociation   A *defense mechanism* in which the individual has thoughts or feelings that are inappropriate to the current situation. For example, a client attending a funeral has thoughts about being at a party and begins to laugh. The mechanism is also known as "disassociation."

dissociative amnesia   A *dissociative disorder* characterized by an inability to remember important (usually stressful or traumatic) personal information. The condition is not the result of *general medical conditions, substance abuse,* or *age-related cognitive decline.* Several types of memory disturbance include localized amnesia (inability to remember anything occurring during a specific time), selective amnesia (inability to remember parts of an experience within a specific time), continuous amnesia (inability to recall personal experiences after a certain point in one's life, and generalized amnesia (inability to recall any personal life experience). This term replaces *psychogenic amnesia.*

dissociative disorder   A type of *mental disorder* characterized by a sudden, temporary change in the normally integrative functions of consciousness, identity, and memory. Specific forms of the disorder include *dissociative amnesia* (which may be selective or generalized, continuous or intermittent), *dissociative fugue, dissociative identity disorder,* and *depersonalization disorder.*

dissociative fugue   A *dissociative disorder* characterized by an individual's sudden travel away from familiar places, inability to recall past events, and sometimes by the assumption of a new identity. The condition is not the result of *general medical conditions, substance abuse, age-related cognitive decline,* or *malingering.* This term replaces *psychogenic fugue.*

dissociative identity disorder   Formerly called *multiple personality disorder,* a form of *dissociative disorder* in which an individual has two or more distinct personalities. The individual may not be aware of the existence of these other personalities; alternative identities are experienced as taking control, supplanting the previous identity, or being in conflict with one another. The change in identity usually happens within seconds but in some cases occurs more gradually. The number of identities ranges from two to 100, with women averaging 15 and men averaging eight.

dissociative symptoms Psychophysiological reactions to *stress* by voluntarily or involuntarily changing one's functions and focus of consciousness, memory, identity, or perception of the environment. These symptoms include numbing, detachment, absence of emotional responsiveness, reduced awareness of one's surroundings, *derealization, depersonaliation, amnesia, fugue, identity disorders, poor concentration,* and *preoccupation.*

dissociative trance disorder Involuntary entry into an apparent state of trance or possession in a way that is outside one's sociocultural or religious norms and causes distress and *impaired social functioning.* This is a proposed official diagnosis of the *DSM-IV.*

dissonance theory of groups The view that some discomfort and tension among group therapy members are important motivators and catalysts for growth. Those who hold this view seek a state of imbalance or *heterogeneous group* membership.

distracter role A recurrent pattern of communication in relating to others, especially family members, characterized by evasiveness, diverting attention, bringing in irrelevant statements, changing the subject, and moving in such a way that the focus of attention is changed. The role was delineated by *Virginia Satir* (*Peoplemaking,* Palo Alto, CA: Science and Behavior Books, 1972, p. 70), who described the distracter as a person who fears the threat of close relationships and obstructs them through these diversionary tactics. Other roles are the *blamer role,* the *computer role,* and the *placater role.*

distribution In *research,* the frequency with which a given variable or demographic factor appears in an identified category, geographic area, map, or graph.

divorce The legal dissolution of a *marriage.* Each state establishes its own laws determining the criteria (grounds) for dissolution. Adultery, incompatibility, and living apart for specified periods of time are the grounds most commonly accepted. Many marriages are also dissolved through *no-fault divorce.*

divorce mediation See *mediation, divorce.*

divorce therapy A type of clinical *intervention* designed to help couples who have decided to dissolve their unions. Divorce therapy includes helping the couple consider alternatives to divorce, minimize adjustment problems, consider the needs and best interests of the children, review fair property dissolution, and discuss rationally how to disengage in the healthiest way possible. This therapy also deals with practical and legal aspects of the dissolution, such as *custody of children* and property decisions; it also helps people learn to manage relationships with their former spouses and to adjust to new lifestyles.

Dix, Dorothea (1802–1887) *Social activist* and advocate for the humane treatment of prisoners and especially for mentally ill people. Her lobbying activities led to the establishment of many public and private *mental hospitals.*

DNA Deoxyribonucleic acid, a complex molecule found in living cells. Its components are arranged in particular sequences, the pattern of which determines the genetic information carried by the chromosomes.

DO doctor of osteopathy, the name used by graduates of colleges of osteopathy. The DO, or *osteopath,* has training, leisure, and health care responsibilities that are equivalent to physicians with MD (medical doctor) degrees, but DOs are usually more oriented toward treatment that is natural and holistic.

doctoral programs In *social work education,* the professional and academic training that culminates in the PhD or *DSW* degree. Doctoral education in social work has tended to emphasize development of the student's research and knowledge-building skills and advanced practice competence. The DSW and PhD degrees are equivalent and have virtually the same requirements. It was sometimes erroneously believed that DSWs would be for those seeking increased professional practice competence and PhDs for those more involved in research and building of theory or the knowledge base. However, the differences are more related to the preferences of the particular degree-granting institution than to different requirements. See also *Group for the Advancement of Doctoral Education in Social Work (GADE)*.

"do-gooder" A term of derision often applied to social workers and other people whose professions or consciences require them to do what is necessary to uphold the laws and ethics of a society and to protect the disadvantaged from exploitation by the privileged.

"dole" A pejorative term once commonly applied to *public assistance* payments.

domestic partners In some jurisdictions a legal designation for those who register as cohabitating unmarried adults who intend to maintain permanent relationships. The designation was established primarily for (but is not exclusively used by) *gay* and *lesbian* partners to provide them with the same legal supports and mutual obligations that exist for married couples (such as access to rent-controlled apartments, survivors' benefits, and family health insurance programs).

"Domestic Peace Corps" See *Volunteers in Service to America (VISTA)*.

domestic relations court A court of law that handles cases involving *divorce, spouse abuse, child abuse, relatives' responsibility,* and family disputes.

domestic violence 1. Abuse of children, older people, spouses, and others in the home, usually by other members of the family or other residents. 2. The social problem in which one's property, health, or life

are endangered or harmed as a result of the intentional behavior of another family member.

domicile A person's legal and permanent home, rather than residence (which may be temporary).

domiciliary care services Programs usually conducted by local and state departments of human services designed to assist people to remain in their own homes even if they are having problems that preclude basic self-care. Such programs include *homemaker services,* home-delivered meals, *chore service, home health services, respite care,* and attendant care. This is also called *home care service.* Some human services agencies use "domiciliary care" to refer to programs that help needy people with the physical maintenance of their homes, and "home care" to refer to homemaker services.

donor constituency The contributors of funds and resources to a social agency or other organization. These people and groups may exert an implicit or formal influence on the priorities, values, and programs of the organization.

dopamine hypothesis In research on the biochemistry of the *central nervous system (CNS),* the possibility that the excessive amount of dopamine (a neurotransmitting chemical) found in *schizophrenia* causes some of its symptoms. See also *catecholamines*.

double bind 1. In *communication theory,* a form of paradoxical communication in which one person expresses a message that can be interpreted in two or more contradictory or mutually exclusive ways, and the recipient of the message is prevented from escaping the consequences or commenting on the contradiction. 2. Competing demands to which a person must respond.

double blind In *research*, a technique in which neither the subject nor the experimenter knows whether a real change was actually introduced. For example, in researching the effects of drugs, the experimenter and the subjects do not know whether inert drugs (*placebo*) or active drugs are being administered.

double-entry bookkeeping   An accounting procedure used in most social agency budget records, in which every transaction is recorded twice and the resulting increase or decrease in one account is reflected by a decrease or increase in another account.

double jeopardy   Being subjected to prosecution and trial a second time for the same offense. Freedom from double jeopardy is guaranteed to people in the United States by the U.S. Constitution in its *Fifth Amendment rights*.

"downers"   A slang term referring to *barbiturates, tranquilizers,* or other *depressants* of the *central nervous system (CNS)* often used by certain drug abusers to induce a state of deep relaxation. Some abusers become highly dependent on these substances, often leading to increased *tolerance.*

downsizing   A reduction in work force and program. In the mid- to late 1980s, social work management—like its counterpart in corporations—was faced with the need to manage declining *resources.* According to Richard L. Edwards and John A. Yankey ("Managing Organizational Decline," in Richard L. Edwards and John A. Yankey [Eds.], *Developing Managerial Skills for the Human Services,* Washington, DC: NASW Press, 1992), this reduction in staff and funding represents a dramatic change after nearly 50 years of uninterrupted growth in the human services.

Down's syndrome   A congenital form of *mental retardation,* often characterized by a flattened face, widely spaced and slanted eyes, a smaller head, and lax joints. Genetically determined by the presence of an extra chromosome, the disorder was formerly known as "mongolism."

downward mobility   Socioeconomic declines by individuals, groups, or nations. In nations, this decline is due to poor economic conditions resulting in unemployment and underemployment, lower wages, inflation, diminution of natural resources,

and political changes. In individuals, it is also common among *dropouts* and may be the result of health problems, poor planning, relocation, and other idiosyncratic factors. See also *upward mobility.*

dream analysis   A technique used in *psychoanalysis* and some other forms of *psychotherapy* and *counseling* in which the analyst interprets the dream content of his or her clients. Many analysts, beginning in 1900 when Sigmund Freud (1856–1939) published *The Interpretation of Dreams,* believed that access to the *unconscious* was made possible by dream analysis. The people, situations, and context in the dreams are viewed as symbols for deeper, more-underlying mental constructs. See also *psychoanalytic theory.*

dream anxiety disorder   A *sleep disorder,* paraphilia type, characterized by repeated awakening from sleep with detailed recall of frightening dreams. Clinicians refer to this condition as *nightmare disorder.* See also *sleep terror disorder.*

Dred Scott decision   The controversial 1857 ruling by the U.S. Supreme Court that a slave was considered property and not a U.S. citizen. Dred Scott was a slave who lived for a time with his master in a "free" state.

DRGs   See *diagnosis-related groups (DRGs).*

drive   In *psychoanalytic theory,* a basic impulse or urge that motivates *overt behavior.*

dropout   One who withdraws from and terminates continued participation in some social activity where there is an implied or explicit responsibility to continue. Such activities include attending school until graduation, continuing in therapy until goals are reached, or contributing to society as a taxpaying citizen.

drug abuse   The inappropriate use of a chemical substance in ways that are detrimental to one's physical or mental well-being. See also *substance abuse.*

drug abuse detection   Efforts, usually by those with certain types of authority over others (for example, parents and employers), to assess the possibility that illegal or *controlled substances* are being used. Such efforts include urine sampling, confinement to observe the presence of *withdrawal symptoms,* covert investigation, and many other activities. Experts suggest that the presence of several of the following indicators can be clues to *substance abuse* in youths: long- or short-term forgetfulness; aggressiveness and irritability; school tardiness, truancy, or declining grades; difficulty concentrating; reduced energy and self-discipline; uncaring or sullen behavior; constant disputes with family members; disappearance of money and valuables; unhealthy appearance, including bloodshot eyes; changes in and evasiveness about friendships; and trouble with the authorities.

drug addiction The abuse of chemical substances that results in a physiological dependence in which the body tissues require the substance to function comfortably. In the absence of the substance, the individual experiences *withdrawal symptoms.* See also *substance dependence.*

drug dependence The misuse of and reliance on chemical substances, resulting in *drug addiction* or *drug habituation.*

Drug Enforcement Administration, U.S. (DEA) A unit of the U.S. *Department of Justice* charged with enforcing the regulations that apply to *controlled substances.* DEA is responsible for overseeing and managing the legal production and use of *narcotics, amphetamines,* and *barbiturates* handled by pharmacists, physicians, and hospitals.

drug-free zone An area designated by police, public officials, residents, or concerned citizens as being off limits for any drug use, sales, purchases, marketing, or recruiting of dealers. These areas are most commonly located on school grounds or adjacent properties; in or near recreation centers and parks; and in some residential neighborhoods, especially where drug problems have existed previously. Enforcement occurs through extra police and citizen vigilance.

drug habituation The pathological craving for or abuse of chemical substances that

results in psychological rather than physical dependence. The abuser who is habituated experiences psychological discomfort that may or may not be as severe as in *withdrawal symptoms.*

drug intoxication *Maladaptive* behavior and other symptoms specific to the particular psychoactive substance recently taken. These symptoms may include impaired judgment, belligerence, *impaired social functioning,* occupational problems, *depression, euphoria, coma,* and *death.*

drug of choice The specific type of drug or chemical that a substance abuser settles on and prefers to use over all the other drugs with which the individual has experimented.

drugs of abuse *Psychoactive substances* that typically are used to produce, in the user, some sense of immediate pleasure or gratification, followed by long-term deleterious consequences. Most of these drugs are illegal, and all of them lead to *habituation* and *withdrawal symptoms.* The illegal drugs of abuse include opioids (including *heroin), cocaine, amphetamines* or similarly acting sympathomimetics, phencyclidine hydrochloride *(PCP)* or similarly acting arylcyclohexylamines, *hallucinogens* such as *LSD,* and cannabis *(marijuana).* Other psychoactive substances that are not illegal but have led to widespread abuse include alcohol, sedatives, nicotine, caffeine, and gluelike substances that are inhaled. See also *opioid abuse.*

drug testing The systematic procedure for determining an individual's abuse of *illicit drugs. Urinalysis* is the most common procedure used, although analyzing samples of hair, blood, and saliva can also reveal drug use. These tests can detect the use of *cocaine, PCP, amphetamines, barbiturates,* and *heroin* taken within the past two to seven days. *Marijuana* can be detected over longer periods, up to 21 days. Because the tests are often inaccurate, the standard procedure for most employers is to conduct a second test on those employees whose first tests are positive. The second test, using a more-reliable procedure, is nearly always accurate. Drug testing is part of most drug treatment programs, designed to help motivate and strengthen the determination of the patient. Drug testing is increasingly required in the workplace, especially in those settings where impairment by workers can jeopardize others.

drug tolerance   See *tolerance*.

DSM-III   The third edition of the American Psychiatric Association's *Diagnostic and Statistical Manual of Mental Disorders*. This version of psychiatry's official classification of mental disorders and their symptoms was published in 1980 and was the first to use the *multiaxial assessment system*.

DSM-IIIR   The 1987 revision of the *DSM-III*, officially replaced by the *DSM-IV*, in 1994.

DSM-IV   The fourth and current edition of psychiatry's official classification of mental disorders and the symptoms and characteristics found in each. Published by the American Psychiatric Association in 1994, the DSM-IV labels each disorder and provides a numerical code and systematic criteria for distinguishing it from other mental disorders. DSM-IV calls for the subject to be evaluated on each of five levels or axes. Axis I disorders include clinical syndromes as well as certain conditions that are not caused by mental illness but are the focus of attention or treatment. Axis II disorders are the *personality disorders* and *mental retardation*. Axis III is used for the subject's relevant physical diseases and conditions. Axis IV is for the subject's psychosocial and environmental problems, and in Axis V the clinician uses a *Global Assessment of Functioning (GAF) Scale*. The DSM-IV also describes *culture-bound syndromes*, lists proposed classifications of mental disorders, and has a section coordinating its coding of mental disorders with those listed in the *International Classification of Diseases (ICD)*. Definitions of mental disorders in this dictionary are consistent with those in DSM-IV.

DSS   1. See *decision support systems (DSS)*. 2. See *Department of Social Services (DSS)*.

DSW   doctor of social work (or doctor of social welfare), an advanced professional degree in *social work education*. The DSW degree requirements typically include several years of previous experience in social work practice, acquisition of required preliminary degrees such as the *MSW*, successful completion of prescribed doctoral-level course work in a qualified school of social work, passing written and oral comprehensive examinations, and successful completion and defense of a dissertation. Most DSW programs are affiliated with professional schools of social work that are part of accredited colleges and universities. See also *doctoral programs* and *Group for the Advancement of Doctoral Education in Social Work (GADE)*.

DTs   See *delirium tremens (DTs)* and *withdrawal delirium*.

dual diagnosis   The identification of co-existent diseases within an individual. Often the disease or its treatment influences the other disease or its treatment, especially if not identified. The use of this term is most commonly associated with a problem with drugs or alcohol and another, usually psychiatric, disorder.

dual eligible   The term used by the *Social Security Administration (SSA)* for people who are eligible for both *Medicaid* and *Medicare*. Many *Departments of Social Services (DSS)* also apply the term to people who meet the criteria to benefit from two or more assistance programs simultaneously.

dual relationships   In *clinical social work*, the unethical practice of assuming a second role with the client, in addition to professional helper, such as friend, business associate, family member, or sex partner. According to Jill Doner Kagle and Pam N. Giebelhausen ("Dual Relationships and Professional Boundaries," *Social Work*, 39 [March 1994], pp. 213–220), dual relationships tend to exploit *clients* or have long-term negative consequences for them. Workers who engage in these relationships are liable to legal as well as professional sanctions and probably should seek help. The *NASW Code of Ethics* has explicitly forbidden sexual relationships since the 1979 revisions; the explicit prohibition against other dual relationships was included in the 1994 code revisions. The prohibition against dual relationships has been in the *code of ethics* of the *National Federation of Societies for Clinical Social Work (NFSCSW)* since 1988.

due process of law   Adherence to all the rules, procedures, protections, and opportunities legally available when a person accused of a *crime* is brought to trial and risks possible deprivation of life, liberty, or property.

dull-normal   A term sometimes used by educators and educational psychologists in describing an individual whose *intelligence quotient (IQ)* scores are between 70 and 90 or an individual with slightly limited intellectual capacity but not of such deficiency as to require extensive care and protection by others.

Dunham, Arthur (1893–1980)   Social work educator who developed the profession's systematic conception of *community organization*. He wrote the influential texts *Community Welfare Organization* (1958) and *Community Organization in Action* (1959).

durable power of attorney   A legal document authorizing another person to take action and make decisions on one's behalf, within certain conditions and guidelines, even when one suffers from *incapacitation* or is *incompetent*. The one given power of attorney may make all decisions or be limited only to such things as selling one's house. Whereas an ordinary power of attorney becomes nullified if the signer becomes incapacitated or incompetent, durable power keeps it in effect in such circumstances. See also *living will*.

durable power of attorney for health care   A legal document by which an individual appoints someone trusted to make decisions about the individual's medical care in case he or she should be unable to make them. Also known as a "health care proxy" or "appointment of a health care agent," this document becomes effective when an individual is temporarily incapacitated or irreversably ill. State-specific documents are available through *Choice in Dying*.

duration index   A rating scale used in the *Person-in-Environment (PIE) System* to indicate how long or how recently the problem of the client has persisted. The scale ranges from two weeks or less to more than five years.

Durham rule   The 1954 court decision declaring that if a person's unlawful act was the product of mental disease or defect, then the accused is not criminally responsible. This is a modification of the *McNaughten rule*, but is not in effect in many jurisdictions.

duty to warn   See *Tarasoff*.

dyad   Two people or objects in a relationship or interacting system.

dynamic   1. In theories of human *personality*, an orientation that emphasizes intrapsychic influences, conscious and unconscious thought processes, and nonobservable mental phenomena such as *drive, conflict, motivation,* and *defense mechanisms*. 2. In field theory, the forces that act on a psychological field. 3. In *systems theories* and in *general systems theory,* the process of striving for and maintaining *homeostasis*.

dysarthria   Speech and articulation problems caused by disturbances of muscular control.

dyscalculia   A *learning disorder* in which the student demonstrates mathematics skills significantly below average. The term more commonly used by social workers is *mathematics disorder*.

dysentery   An intestinal disease whose symptoms include inflammation, pain, and diarrhea. The disease is caused by bacteria or viruses and is most commonly transmitted by contact with water or food that has been contaminated by human waste.

dysfunction   A deficiency in a system that precludes its optimal performance; synonymous with "malfunction."

dysgraphia A *communication disorder* involving the partial or total inability to write letters, words, or phrases, by a person who once possessed such abilities. This condition is also known less commonly as *agraphia*. See also *disorder of written expression.*

dyskinesia A dysfunction of the involuntary muscle activities resulting in tics, spasms, and stereotyped movements. See also *tardive dyskinesia (TD).*

dyslexia An impairment of reading and writing skills, often with the tendency to reverse letters or words while reading or writing them or not noticing certain letters or words.

dyslogia Difficulty in speaking or communicating ideas because of mental disorder or mental deficiency. This is not synonymous with developmental *expressive language disorder.*

dysmnesia A defect in *memory.*

dysmorphophobia Excessive preoccupation and *fear* of appearing to be ugly or defective. This term is outdated and is replaced by the term *body dysmorphic disorder.*

dyspareunia The experience of pain during the act of sexual intercourse, which occurs more commonly in women. See also *vaginismus.*

dysphagia Impaired ability to swallow resulting from nonorganic causes such as anxiety-related spasms of the throat muscles.

dysphoria A condition of general unhappiness, dissatisfaction, pessimism, restlessness, and a pervasive feeling of discomfort.

dyspnea Breathing difficulty.

dyspraxia Inability to perform skilled or specific movements; impaired coordination.

dyssocial A term pertaining to an individual who behaves according to the norms of the immediate peer group or subculture but contrary to the norms of the larger society, or to one who engages repeatedly in criminal and destructive activities. This term is now used by professionals to replace the term "sociopath."

dyssomnia A primary *sleep disorder* of the amount, timing, and quality of sleep, including *insomnia, hypersomnia, narcolepsy, breathing-related sleep disorder (apnea),* and *circadian rhythm sleep disorder.*

dysthymia See *dysthmic disorder.*

dysthymic disorder One of the *mood disorders* characterized by sadness, pessimism, *dyssomnia,* poor appetite or overeating, irritability (especially in children), fatigue, low self-esteem, and indecisiveness, symptoms that occur most of each day, most days, for at least two years. This disorder differs from *major depressive disorder* in that its symptoms are usually less severe but exist almost continuously for years. Also, in major depressive disorders, discrete major depressive episodes can be distinguished from the individual's usual functioning.

dystonia Sustained abnormal postures or muscle spasms, symptomatic of mental disorders (such as *catatonic schizophrenia*), *neurological disorders,* or a *medication-induced movement disorder.*

E

EAPs See *employee assistance programs (EAPs)*.

earmarked taxes Income, whose purpose has been designated in advance, received by a government body from citizens and corporations. For example, gasoline sales taxes are largely designated for highway maintenance and construction, and a *payroll tax* is often earmarked for *unemployment compensation*.

earned income The amount of money one receives from work in the form of wages and salaries. All other sources of income—from interest, gains on capital investments, rent, dividends, inherited money—are *unearned income*. Social Security revenues come from earned income collected from employees, their employers, and people who are self-employed. However, the amount of earned income received by retired persons reduces their Social Security benefits, whereas their unearned income does not.

Earned Income Tax Credit (EITC) A provision in the U.S. Internal Revenue tax code to give *cash vouchers* to working parents whose incomes are very low. The parent or parents file federal income tax statements, and if their taxable earnings are below a specified amount, they receive a check for a percentage of earnings up to a specified low amount. The earned income tax credit is reduced as the income increases and reaches zero when income reaches a specified amount.

Earth Day An annual observance by people in many nations to celebrate the natural *environment* and to raise the pub-

lic consciousness through parades, teach-ins, demonstrations, and intensified lobbying activities about the need to protect and conserve the environment. Social workers have been among the leaders of the movement since its initial celebration on April 22, 1970.

Earthwatch A program sponsored by the United Nations of worldwide coordination to monitor, analyze, and report trends in the *environment*. Earthwatch was created in 1972 by the United Nations Declaration on the Human Environment and is coordinated by the *United Nations Environmental Program*.

Easter Seal Society The organization, founded in 1919, that coordinates fund-raising and disbursements made in the United States on behalf of children and adults with *disabilities*.

eating disorders *Maladaptive* or unhealthy patterns of eating and ingestion. Major types include *anorexia nervosa* and *bulimia nervosa*. Eating disorders first diagnosed during infancy or early childhood include *pica* and *rumination disorder*.

EBT system See *electronic benefit transfer (EBT) system*.

ECF See *extended-care facilities (ECF)*.

ECHO housing Elder cottage housing opportunity, also known as a *granny flat*, which is a self-contained mobile-system home built for temporary use on the property of an existing residence, usually the older person's relatives. The utilities hookups are connected to the main house. This provides low-cost private housing for senior citizens with convenient access to their offspring but requires approval by local zoning laws.

echolalia Repetitive imitation of the speech of another. This is a normal phase of language development in the nine- to 12-month-old infant. Later, it is seen as *maladaptive*. It is often seen in adults with certain types of *schizophrenia*.

echopraxia Repetitive imitation of the movements or behavior of others, often a symptom of *schizophrenia* or other *mental disorder*.

eclampsia Recurrent convulsions occurring primarily during *pregnancy* or childbirth.

eclectic A collection of certain aspects of various theories or practice methods that appear to be most useful for practice interventions.

ECOA See *Equal Credit Opportunity Act (ECOA)*.

ecological overstress The application of more demands on an *environment* than it can meet, ultimately reducing its restorative functions and making it permanently unproductive or less productive. This phenomenon is notable in sub-Saharan Africa, the flood plains of the Indian subcontinent, and the areas adjacent to the South American rain forest. It is the consequence of the combined effects of population growth, overgrazing, deforestation, air and water pollution, and soil erosion.

ecological perspective An orientation in social work and other professions that emphasizes understanding people and their *environment* and the nature of their transactions. Important concepts include *adaptation, transactions, goodness of fit* between people and their environments, *reciprocity,* and *mutuality*. In professional interventions, the *unit of attention* is considered to be the interface between the individual (or *group, family,* or *community*) and the relevant environment. See also *life model*.

ecology The study of relationships between *environment* and organisms.

ecomap A diagram of family relationships created by Ann Hartman and used by social workers, family therapists, and other professionals to depict a variety of reciprocal influences between the client and those people related to the client, relevant social institutions, and environmental influences.

econometrics Statistical analysis of economic trends and problems.

Economic Opportunity Act of 1964 The major legislation (P.L. 88-452) of President Lyndon B. Johnson's *War on Poverty*. Enacted in 1964, it established the *Office of Economic Opportunity (OEO)* and helped create such programs as *Volunteers in Service to America (VISTA)*, the *Job Corps, Head Start, Upward Bound*, the *Neighborhood Youth Corps,* and the *Community Action Program (CAP)*. Many of these programs were subsequently dismantled.

economies of scale A tendency for some costs of providing services to increase less than proportionately with increased output. For example, in certain circumstances, a social agency might be able to triple its service output while only doubling its budget.

ECOSOC See *United Nations Economic and Social Council (ECOSOC)*.

ecosystem A concept in the biological science of ecology pertaining to the physical and biological *environment* and the interaction between every component thereof.

ecosystems perspective A conceptual lens through which the social worker can note the systemic relatedness of case variables. The ecosystems perspective offers no prescription for intervention but as a metatheory attempts to depict phenomena in their connectedness and complexity. This perspective permits multiple practice theories, approaches, and practitioner roles.

ecotage Ecological sabotage; planned action that obstructs, damages, or destroys facilities and equipment thought to be harmful to the *environment*.

ECP practitioner A social worker or other helping professional oriented to an empirical clinical practice that is said to use scientific methods of inquiry for data gathering and interpreting.

"ecstasy" Street name for an illicit *designer drug* that combines methamphetamine and hallucinogenic chemicals to make a compound called "MDMA." The combination of a stimulant and *hallucinogen* has a powerful effect with many negative side effects.

ECT Electroconvulsive therapy. See *electroshock therapy (EST)*.

ectopic pregnancy *Pregnancy* in which the fertilized egg develops outside the uterus, usually in the fallopian tubes.

edema Accumulation of fluid in the body tissues and cavities leading to swelling. Edema may be a symptom of a variety of disorders, including heart failure, kidney disease, pneumonia, and infection.

EDL See *equitable distribution law (EDL)*.

educable Having potential for learning, especially for formal education and basic survival skills. Professionals often use the term in referring to mentally retarded individuals whose retardation does not preclude learning certain social or academic skills.

Educational Legislative Action Network (ELAN) A program within the *National Association of Social Workers (NASW)* that was established in 1971 to coordinate efforts to inform national and state legislators about issues of concern to social workers. NASW chapters have continued to use the term ELAN to refer to their legislative networks. See also *legislative advocacy* and *legislative advocacy tactics*.

educationally disadvantaged Children whose educational attainments are below age-appropriate levels not because of intellectual deficits but because of factors such as growing up in a home where education is not valued.

Educational Resources Information Center (ERIC) U.S. *Department of Education* centers in more than 500 locations across the United States that provide data about the nation's educational programs and facilities. Information covers such topics as resources for exceptional children, disabled people, people unable to speak English, and people seeking to become teachers.

Education for All Handicapped Children Act The federal law (P.L. 94-142) enacted in 1975 that distributes funds for public schools so that they may provide equal educational opportunities and free special services for all children with learning and other disabilities. Such services may include special testing, remedial lessons, counseling, and tutoring.

Education of the Handicapped Amendments of 1986 This federal law (P.L. 99-457) amended the *Education for All Handicapped Children Act* (P.L. 94-142). A key component of the amendments is Part H, which mandates early intervention for children from birth until their third birthday if they are developmentally delayed or at risk of substantial developmental delay. Services may include psychological services, parent and family training, counseling, and transition services to preschool programs.

Education of the Handicapped Amendments of 1990 Improvements in this federal law (P.L. 101-476) aimed at increasing access for students and their families to needed services include the addition of social work services to the definition of "related services" and to the definition of "early intervention services." The law also established an *ombudsperson* program to help resolve problems that create barriers for students.

Education, U.S. Department of See *Department of Education, U.S.*

educator role In social work, the responsibility to teach clients necessary adaptive skills. This is done by providing relevant information in a way that is understandable to the client, offering advice and suggestions, identifying alternatives and their probable consequences, modeling behaviors, teaching problem-solving techniques, and clarifying perceptions. Other social work roles are identified as the *facilitator role*, the *enabler role*, and the *mobilizer role*.

EEOC   See *Equal Employment Opportunity Commission (EEOC)*.

efficacy   1. The degree to which desired goals or projected outcomes are achieved. 2. In social work, the capacity to help the client achieve, in a reasonable time period, the goals of a given intervention.

egalitarianism   A social value; a belief in human equality leading one to treat others as peers or equals and to espouse equal access to goods and resources.

ego   The self; the part of the mind that mediates between the demands of the body and the realities of the *environment*, consisting of *cognition, perception, defense mechanism*, memory, and motor control. In *psychodynamic* theory, one of the three major spheres of the *psyche*, along with the *id* and the *superego*. The healthy ego finds ways to compromise between these competing pressures and enables the person to cope with the demands of the environment.

ego alien   A synonym for *ego dystonic*.

ego boundary   Limits set by the *ego* between the self and the environment.

egocentrism   1. Excessive preoccupation with oneself. 2. An exaggerated view of one's importance. 3. In *Piagetian theory*, the normal state of the child younger than age six who has not yet learned to take into account another person's perspective.

ego defense   See *defense mechanism*.

ego disintegration   1. Breakdown of the ability of the *ego* to carry out its functions, such as defending against *stressors*, distinguishing between reality and *fantasy*, delaying gratification, and mediating between the demands of the body and the environment. 2. In *psychoanalytic theory*, the ego's loss of ability to continue in its function of mediating between the competing demands of the *id* and the *superego*.

ego dystonic   Traits of personality, behavior, thought, or orientation considered to be unacceptable, repugnant, or inconsistent with the individual's *perceptions*—*conscious* or *unconscious*—of himself or herself; a synonym for *ego alien*. The term "ego dystonic homosexual" is no longer considered a diagnosable category. See also *ego syntonic*.

ego functioning   The manner in which the *ego* deals with the demands of society and mediates between internal psychological conflicts and psychosocial realities.

ego ideal   1. An individual's goals, positive standards, and highest aspirations. 2. One or more *significant others* in a person's life who are emulated.

ego integration   Achievement of inner harmony and compatibility of the various aspects of one's personality as a unified whole.

ego-oriented social work   Clinical social work that incorporates the principles of *ego psychology* into professional practice.

ego psychology   Psychosocially oriented concepts that build on *Freudian theory* but emphasize the individual's adult development and ability to solve problems and deal with social realities. See also *defense mechanism*.

ego strengths   1. In *psychodynamic* theory, the degree of *psychic energy* available to the individual for problem solving, resolving internal conflicts, and defending against mental and environmental distress. 2. The individual's capacity for logical thinking, *intelligence*, perceptiveness, and *self-control* over impulses to achieve immediate gratification.

ego syntonic   Traits of personality, thought, *behavior*, and *values* that are incorporated by the individual, who considers them acceptable and consistent with his or her overall "true" self. See also *ego dystonic*.

eidetic memory   The ability to bring to consciousness a mental picture of such clarity and vividness that most of the details therein are retained; a "photographic memory."

EITC See *Earned Income Tax Credit (EITC)*.

ejaculatory inhibition A *sexual disorder* in which a man can become sexually aroused and erect but has difficulty ejaculating intravaginally.

ELAN See *Educational Legislative Action Network (ELAN)*.

elder abuse Mistreatment of older people and relatively dependent people. According to Toshio Tatora ("Elder Abuse," in Richard L. Edwards [Ed.-in-Chief], *Encyclopedia of Social Work*, 19th ed., Washington, DC: NASW Press, 1995), elder abuse includes physical battering, neglect, exploitation, and psychological harm. Abuse may be inflicted by the older person's adult children or other relatives, legal custodians, or other care providers.

elderly Advanced in age. This term is commonly used to designate people older than 65. The term *pre-elderly* is used for people who have not yet reached age 65. Most social workers prefer the adjective "older" instead of "elderly." See also *frail elderly*.

elective mutism The refusal to talk in almost all social situations even though the ability to speak and comprehend language exists and there is no *organic* or physical cause for the refusal. This condition is most commonly found in younger children during the time they are compelled to participate in social situations such as school.

elective surgery Surgery considered nonessential because the related condition is not life-threatening, urgent, or physically incapacitating. Patients usually choose to undergo this surgery for psychosocial reasons. Cosmetic surgery to improve an individual's appearance is an example. These medical procedures are often not reimbursable as a *third-party payment*.

Electra complex The term used in early *Freudian theory* for the *unconscious* sexual attraction girls, especially from ages three to seven, have for their fathers. The term is roughly analogous to the *Oedipus complex* for boys.

electronic benefit transfer (EBT) system The use of an encoded card, similar to an automated teller machine card, to replace the *Food Stamp program*. The client runs the card through the terminal at a store's checkout counter after entering the identification number. The value of the food purchases is deducted from the client's monthly allotment. This system helps remove the stigma of using food coupons and makes it more difficult for clients to misuse the coupons.

electroshock therapy (EST) Treatments administered by physicians, primarily neurologists and psychiatrists, in which convulsions are induced in patients by applying small amounts of electrical currents to the brain. Its purpose is to treat patients who suffer certain types of *mental disorder*, including some severe *depression*, *mood disorder*, and *psychosis*, when medications and other treatments have not been helpful. Although its use has been significantly curtailed because of the increased use and development of *psychotropic drugs*, EST (or ECT, for electroconvulsive therapy) is reported to be effective with certain patients, especially some with mood disorders.

Elementary and Secondary School Improvement Amendments of 1988 The federal law (P.L. 100-297) that amended the Elementary and Secondary Education Act of 1965. Officially titled the Augustus F. Hawkins–Robert T. Stafford Elementary and Secondary School Improvement Amendments of 1988, the law significantly increased funding ceilings for programs and added more than a dozen programs. The amendments gathered many educational programs under a single legislative umbrella and offered new opportunities for school social workers.

eligibility 1. The meeting of specific qualifications to receive certain benefits. 2. The criteria used in welfare and social services systems to determine which people may receive help. For example, to be eligible for the *Food Stamp program,* a person must meet certain income requirements, and to be eligible for *Medicare* a person must be older than a certain age.

eligibility workers   Employees in *public welfare* offices who determine whether an applicant meets the criteria for *public assistance*. This function once was served by social workers until state and federal laws separated the provision of *social services* from *income maintenance*. Thus, eligibility workers have freed social workers to do more technical and professional work with clients on public assistance. In many jurisdictions, however, eligibility workers are given little training in interviewing or interpersonal skills and are frustrated with the clerical emphasis of their work.

elimination disorder   Inability to control elimination of body-waste products, not as a result of a specific physiological disorder. The two types of elimination disorder are *encopresis* and *enuresis*. See also *functional encopresis* and *functional enuresis*.

Elizabethan Poor Laws   The statutes, codified in England in 1601 during the reign of Queen Elizabeth I, that established many of the principles that are still influential in dealing with economically disadvantaged people. Among their provisions were local rather than national responsibility for the care of poor people, the distinction between the *"worthy poor"* and the *"unworthy poor,"* punitive measures for those refusing to work, standards of responsibility for relatives, and the *means test* to determine need for assistance.

elopement   1. Running away. The term is often applied to patients in mental hospitals or other institutions who leave precipitously without authority. 2. The act of couples going away suddenly to marry.

emaciation   Extreme thinness as a result of starvation or *disease*.

emancipation   Freeing an individual or members of a social group from the control of another or others. For example, a minor child may become emancipated from parental control (and from the right to parental support or *maintenance*) on getting married.

emasculate   1. To castrate, literally or symbolically. 2. To act toward a man in such a way that his male *sexual identity* is supposedly diminished.

embezzlement   The *crime* of willfully appropriating money or property that is in one's control but belongs to another. The embezzler has possession of the property by virtue of a business relationship or through some office, employment, or position of trust with the owner. For example, if the treasurer of a social agency uses funds that were donated to the agency to pay personal expenses, that individual is guilty of embezzlement.

emergency basic-needs services   Programs often found in state and local departments of *public welfare* or *human services* designed to provide immediate food, shelter, clothing, and fuel for individuals and families in crisis. These programs are thought of as "one-time" services, in effect only until needy people can obtain a more-permanent means of providing for their *basic needs*.

emergency financial assistance   Programs often found in state and local departments of *public welfare* or *human services* designed to immediately provide cash or credit for individuals and families in crisis. These funds usually are granted on a "one-time" basis to prevent evictions, hunger, or deprivation of some *basic needs* until more-permanent means of income provision occurs.

emergency medical technicians (EMTs)   Health care workers who assist the more highly trained *paramedics* and physicians in administering critical and life-saving treatment.

Emergency Relief Administration   See *Federal Emergency Relief Administration (FERA)*.

emetic   An agent used to cause vomiting, often as an immediate antidote to the ingestion of toxic substances.

eminent domain   The legal right of the government, under certain conditions, to take ownership of private property to be used for public purposes. The procedure is to pay the owner fairly after a *condemnation* of the property.

emit To respond or behave. See *operant conditioning.*

emotion 1. A feeling, *mood,* or *affect.* 2. A state of mind usually accompanied by concurrent physiological and behavioral changes and based on the *perception* of some internal or external object.

emotional divorce A distancing between members of a *dyad,* usually a married couple, because they have experienced considerable *pain, anxiety, anger,* or other similar reactions in their previous encounters. Typically, the resulting behavior includes avoidance of one another's physical presence, avoidance of discussions about certain emotionally charged events, or refusal to provide needed emotional support.

emotional lability A tendency to change *moods* rapidly and frequently. This is a commonly encountered symptom of *affective disorder* and of immaturity.

empathy The act of perceiving, understanding, experiencing, and responding to the emotional state and ideas of another person.

emphysema A chronic disease of the lungs, characterized by extreme shortness of breath owing to stretching or rupturing of the lung's air sacs. In many instances, emphysema is a *lifestyle-associated disorder,* often occurring among heavy smokers, coal miners, and people who live in air-polluted environments.

empirical Based on direct observation or experience.

empirically based practice A type of *intervention* in which the professional social worker uses research as a practice and problem-solving tool; collects data systematically to monitor the intervention; specifies problems, techniques, and outcomes in measurable terms; and systematically evaluates the effectiveness of the intervention used.

employable A term applied to those in the population who are potentially able to work.

Economic planners sometimes identify this group as being within certain age parameters and without incapacitating infirmities.

employee assistance programs (EAPs) Services offered by employers to their employees to help them overcome problems that may negatively affect job satisfaction or productivity. Services may be provided on-site or contracted through outside providers. They include *counseling* for *alcohol dependence* and *drug dependence, marital therapy* or *family therapy, career counseling,* and referrals for dependent care services. See also *industrial social work.*

employment The state of working in exchange for money.

Employment and Training Administration A branch of the U.S. *Department of Labor* that focuses on programs to increase employment, help unemployed workers, facilitate access to jobs, enhance the quality and opportunity for vocational and on-the-job training, and encourage employers to hire workers. It includes the U.S. Employment Service, the Unemployment Insurance Service, the Bureau of Apprenticeship and Training, and the *Work Incentive (WIN) program.*

employment policy The principles, guidelines, goals, and regulations pertaining to the way a nation or an organization deals with its actual and potential *work force.* Aspects of an employment policy include hiring and firing rules and procedures, salary and benefits structure, occupational safety and health provisions, and economic programs to stimulate the creation of more jobs. In the United States, organizations affiliated with the U.S. *Department of Labor* that shape employment policy include the *Occupational Safety and Health Administrators (OSHA),* the National Commission for Employment Policy, the National Occupational Information Coordinating Committee, and the President's Committee on Employment of People with Disabilities.

employment programs Programs at the federal, state, and local government levels and in private industry designed to secure more jobs for more people and to ensure that those jobs include decent wages and benefits and equal opportunities. In the United States, in addition to the *Unemployment Insurance* program, these programs have included the provisions of the *Job Training Partnership Act,* the *Job Corps,* and the *Neighborhood Youth Corps.* See also *Equal Employment Opportunity Commission (EEOC).*

Employment Retirement Income Security Act See *ERISA.*

empowerment In *social work practice,* the process of helping individuals, families, groups, and communities to increase their personal, interpersonal, socioeconomic, and political strength and to develop influence toward improving their circumstances.

"empty nest" A term applied to the *nuclear family* after the children have matured and left the home.

EMTs See *emergency medical technicians (EMTs).*

enabler 1. An individual who makes something possible. 2. In social work, the orientation of the social worker toward enhancing the ability of the client to solve problems and achieve goals by providing information and access to resources, strengthening *coping skills,* and changing socioenvironmental conditions that impede progress.

enabler role In social work, the responsibility to help the client become capable of coping with situational or transitional stress. Specific skills used in achieving this objective include conveying hope, reducing *resistance* and *ambivalence,* recognizing and managing feelings, identifying and supporting personal strengths and social assets, breaking down problems into parts that can be solved more readily, and maintaining a focus on goals and the means of achieving them. Other primary social work roles are identified as the *facilitator role,* the *educator role,* and the *mobilizer role.*

enabling state A version of the modern *welfare state* that emphasizes the private production of welfare benefits. According to Neil Gilbert and Barbara Gilbert (*The Enabling State: Modern Welfare Capitalism in America,* New York: Oxford University Press, 1989), the enabling state also emphasizes *transfer payments* in the form of cash rather than *in-kind benefits* through tax expenditures, regulatory measures, and credit subsidies, as well as direct public expenditures.

enactment 1. The process of institutionalizing an action that has great impact or influence on individuals or groups, as in the establishment of law or party. 2. In *psychoanalytic theory,* the symbolic interactions between the client and psychoanalyst that have unconscious meanings to both.

encephalitis Inflammation of the brain or its covering. Usually this is an acute condition but may lead to personality or organic changes that continue after the inflammation.

encopresis The repeated passage of feces into inappropriate places at least once per month over a period of three consecutive months. By definition the condition is not due to constipation and overflow or *incontinence.*

encounter group Intense, short-term *group therapy*—using principles and techniques that include *gestalt therapy, group psychotherapy,* and *humanistic orientation* principles and techniques—designed to promote the personal growth of the participants. The emphasis is not on correcting disorders, but rather on increasing the emotional and sensory aspects of being and on increasing open communication and self-awareness.

endemic A term applied to a phenomenon, social problem, or disease that is peculiar to a given *population, group, culture,* or geographical area. See also *pandemic.*

endogamy The practice of confining *marriage* to members of one's own *social class* or *ethnic group.*

endogenous Something that originates in the body. See also *exogenous.*

endogenous depression *Depression* apparently resulting from internal mental or physical processes. This term often is used to describe depression that arises without any particular *stressor* or unhappy event in the person's life.

endowment   1. A permanent fund held by an educational *institution, social agency,* or other organization. Usually the fund comes from special donations rather than regular sources of revenue, and usually only the fund's interest proceeds are spent. 2. The inherited or inherent qualities of a person, nation, or people.

end-stage renal disease (ESRD)   Irreversible loss of kidney function, caused by genetic or metabolic factors or by external factors such as *trauma* or infection. ESRD patients require artificial *dialysis* treatment or kidney transplants to survive.

enmeshed family   A concept used in the *structural family therapy* orientation to designate an unhealthy family relationship pattern in which the *role boundaries* between various family members are so vague or diffuse that there is little opportunity for independent functioning. This condition is contrasted with the *disengaged family,* in which the role boundaries of the various members are so rigid and inflexible that members withdraw from the relationship.

enneagram   A star-shaped diagram in which personality types are depicted on a nine-point scale ("ennea" is nine in Greek). The personality types are perfectionist, giver, performer, romantic, observer, questioner, epicure, boss, and mediator. The *typology* is widely used in government, business, and *self-help organizations.*

entitlement   Services, goods, or money due to an individual by virtue of a specific *status.*

entitlement programs   Government-sponsored benefits of cash, goods, or services that are due all people who belong to a specified class. Examples include the *social security* programs such as *Old Age, Survivors, Disability, and Health Insurance (OASDHI)* and *Medicare* in the United States and *family allowance* in many European nations.

entrapment   A law authority's act of inducing an individual to commit a *crime* not previously contemplated, usually to prosecute that person.

entrepreneurial practice   In social work, the activities involved in the provision of human services and social services for profit. Such activities include private *clinical social work,* providing consultations to social agencies and community organizations for fees, and establishing for-profit social services facilities such as private schools for disturbed children, employment agencies for unemployed social workers, training facilities for business organizations, and homes for at-risk population groups such as the frail elderly, unwed mothers-to-be, and children requiring foster care.

entropy   A concept used in *systems theories* pertaining to the winding down, dissolution, or deorganization of a system. It is hypothesized that without intervention, systems are always going through this process in their movement toward and away from *equilibrium.*

enuresis   The involuntary discharge of urine. In the diagnosis "enuresis (not due to a general medical condition)," the discharge must occur at least twice weekly for more than three consecutive months. Three subtypes are nocturnal only, diurnal only, and both.

environment   All the influences, conditions, and natural surroundings that affect the growth and development of living things.

environmentalist   One who works toward resolving the problems of the *environment,* especially the *ecosystem,* pollution, wildlife habitats, and the natural world. Many social workers have been leaders among environmentalist movements.

environmental modification   See *environmental treatment.*

environmental movement   Social activism by concerned citizens and groups directed toward protecting the natural world from civilization's destructive effects. The movement is not heterogenous. Actions of environmentalist groups and individuals range from lobbying, public education, and financing research to litigation, protesting, and sometimes sabotaging enterprises that are considered environmentally harmful. See also *ecosystems, ecotage, social activist, ozone layer, Environmental Protection Agency (EPA), toxic waste sites, greenhouse effect, Earth Day,* and *Earthwatch.*

Environmental Protection Agency (EPA) The federal organization established in 1970 to develop and enforce standards for controlling water, air, and noise pollution and to promote those activities that result in a healthy habitat for wildlife and human well-being.

environmental treatment The *social casework* concept that recognizes the effect of forces outside the individual and strives to modify these effects through techniques such as providing or locating specific resources, interpreting the needs of the client to others, *advocacy,* and *mediation.* Some social workers call this activity *indirect treatment* or "environmental modification."

envy A group of uncomfortable emotions pertaining to the wish to have something that others possess. See also *jealousy.*

EOS See *episode of service (EOS).*

EPA See *Environmental Protection Agency (EPA).*

epidemic The occurrence of a *disease, disorder,* or *social problem* that spreads rapidly and affects many people in a community within a relatively short period. See also *disease patterns.*

epidemiology The study of the frequency and distribution of a specified phenomenon, such as a *disease,* that occurs in a *population* group during a given period. Usually this is expressed in terms of an *incidence rate* and *prevalence rate.* Other commonly used terms in epidemiology are *point prevalence, period prevalence,* and *morbidity risk.* See also *morbidity rate.*

epidermis The outer layer of the skin.

epigenesis 1. Emergence. 2. The perceived original occurrence of a phenomenon.

epilepsy A disorder characterized by recurrent, involuntary episodes of altered states of consciousness, frequently but not always accompanied by convulsive body movements. Most professionals now refer to this condition as *seizure disorders.*

episiotomy Surgical incision in the vaginal wall to prevent its tearing during childbirth.

episode of service (EOS) A specific social services goal and all the alternative means used by a *social work team* and their client to achieve it. The team members first assess the client's need and then, often with the client, translate this into specific and realistic goals. The team then discusses the variety of techniques and resources that might be used and selects those that are most feasible.

epistemology 1. The study of the nature, methods, and limits of knowledge. 2. For many social workers and family therapists, the term means how we know what we know.

Equal Credit Opportunity Act (ECOA) The federal legislation (P.L. 93-495) enacted in 1974 that requires retail firms and lending institutions to use the same criteria for everyone in deciding whether to grant credit, regardless of gender, marital status, or minority- or ethnic-group background. To protect the economic rights of women, the act gives wives as well as husbands the right to have credit records in their own names.

Equal Employment Opportunity Commission (EEOC) The five-member federal panel that administers Title VII of the *Civil Rights Act of 1964,* prohibiting *discrimination* by employers, labor unions, or employment agencies and striving to promote fair practices in the *workplace.*

equality The principle that individuals should have equal access to services, resources, and opportunities and be treated the same by all social, educational, and welfare institutions; a fundamental social work value.

equal rights   The obligations of a society or organization to provide the same opportunities and access to all, regardless of status.

equifinality   1. The property of living systems that permits them to reach identical points, although by different routes. 2. A concept in *systems theories* stating that different behaviors by living organisms can lead to the same or "equal final" results. The opposite of equifinality is *equipotentiality* or *multifinality*.

equilibrium   1. A concept in *systems theories* in which opposing forces and elements achieve balance. 2. A state or condition that is never truly reached because each variable continues to change, requiring some offsetting or equivalent change in another variable. See also *goodness of fit*.

equipotentiality   The property of living systems in which subsystems may have identical origins or beginnings but achieve different outcomes. This is the opposite and corollary principle to *equifinality*.

equitable distribution law (EDL)   Distribution of real and personal property between interested parties in a way that is fair and just. In *divorce* cases, this law requires that all the property acquired during the marriage is divided equally or according to criteria that assure fairness. For example, if a wife works to put her husband through medical school and is then divorced, the degree may be considered marital property, and she may be entitled to part of his future earnings as a physician.

equity   The state of fairness or impartiality, including any systems (for example, the *criminal justice system* and the *social welfare* system) that determine how one's rights and claims are fulfilled.

equity planning   An orientation in *social planning* that gives the most attention to problem solving for populations that are most in need with the fewest resources.

erectile disorder   A *sexual disorder* in which a man is unable to achieve or maintain penis rigidity sufficient for completion of sexual intercourse. Clinicians use the diagnostic term *male erectile disorder*.

ergonomics   The analysis of working conditions, employee relations, tools, and working patterns to fit the person with the job and the job with the person.

ERIC   See *Educational Resources Information Centers (ERIC)*.

Eriksonian theory   In human *psychosocial development theory*, the eight stages of life as proposed by German-born psychologist Erik Erikson (1902–1994). The stages are *trust versus mistrust* (occurring at about ages one to two), *autonomy versus shame and doubt* (about ages two to four), *initiative versus guilt* (ages three to six), *industry versus inferiority* (ages six to 12), *identity versus role confusion* (ages 12 to 18), *intimacy versus isolation* (ages 18 to 24), *generativity versus stagnation* (ages 24 to 54), and *integrity versus despair* (older than age 54).

ERISA   The Employee Retirement Income Security Act of 1974 (P.L. 93-406), a federal program administered by the U.S. *Department of Labor* and other agencies, which protects the interests of workers who participate in private pension plans.

erogenous zone   Any area of the body whose stimulation leads to sexual *arousal*.

erotic orientation   The orientation individuals have as to their objects of sexual desires. For example, an individual may be oriented for sexual gratification to a member of the opposite or the same sex, groups, objects, children, or various combinations. According to Harvey L. Gochros ("Sexual Distress," in Richard L. Edwards [Ed.-in-Chief], *Encyclopedia of Social Work*, 19th ed., Washington, DC: NASW Press, 1995), an individual's erotic orientation may change over time and in different circumstances.

erotomanic delusion   A *delusional disorder* in which the individual develops a sense of idealized *love* or sexual attraction for another who is not reciprocating. Usually, the object of this *delusion* is an unapproachable person, for example, a movie or athletic star or political leader.

erotomanic-type delusional disorder   A disorder characterized by nonbizarre delusions, particularly the intense belief that one is the object of another person's secret or overt desires and love.

ESRD   See *end-stage renal disease (ESRD).*

essential hypertension   Chronic high blood pressure, not resulting from immediate reactions to threat, vigorous physical activity, or a temporary stress or crisis situation.

EST   1. See *electroshock therapy (EST).* 2. The initials are also used, often not capitalized, for the psychoeducational group experience founded by Werner Erhardt and originally called Erhardt Seminar Training.

estrangement   The loss of contact with or antagonism toward one's relatives or associates because of apathy or active disagreement.

ethical conduct   Behavior that meets a community's positive moral standards—distinguishing right from wrong and adhering to the right. For professional social workers ethical conduct is also following the profession's *code of ethics,* providing the highest and most skillful level of service to clients as possible and relating to colleagues, other professionals, all people, and society in an honorable manner.

ethical will   A spiritual document prepared by one to be read after death that expresses wishes and advice for loved ones and attempts to summarize what has been learned in life. This information is usually comforting to survivors and helps minimize controversy when such thoughts are not included in a last will and testament.

ethics   A system of moral principles and perceptions about right versus wrong and the resulting philosophy of conduct that is practiced by an individual, *group, profession,* or *culture.* See also *code of ethics.*

ethics committees   Formal panels established by a service organization to provide practitioners opportunities to consult with one another about ethical issues. *Institutional ethics committees (IECs)* and *institutional review boards (IRBs)* are located in hospitals, universities, federal agencies, and many public and private organizations. Their functions include education of practitioners and their clients, formulating agency policies on ethical issues, providing case consultation, and reviewing existing cases involving possible ethical dilemmas. The composition of the committees depends on the nature of the host agency, but often includes interdisciplinary staffs or staff members from only one discipline and sometimes outside representatives such as clients, community leaders, lawyers, and independent experts on ethics. See also *committee on inquiry.*

"ethnic cleansing"   The term used for achieving racial, religious, or cultural homogeneity in a nation or area through policies that eliminate or force the permanent evacuation of minority group members and their sympathizers. See also *holocaust* and *genocide.*

ethnic group   A distinct group of people who share a common language, set of customs, history, *culture, race,* religion, or origin.

ethnic intimidation   A *hate crime* in which an individual or group threatens other individuals or groups who belong to ethnic minorities with words, gestures, or actions.

ethnicity   1. An orientation toward the shared national origin, religion, *race,* or language of a people. 2. A person's ethnic affiliation, by virtue of one or more of these characteristics and traditions. Ethnicity is a powerful determinant of an individual's patterns of feeling, thinking, and behaving.

ethnic-sensitive practice   Professional social work that emphasizes and values the special capabilities, distinctive cultural histories, and unique needs of people of various *ethnic groups.* Social work *values* and *ethics* emphasize ethnic-sensitive practice.

ethnic stereotyping Preconceived, usually negative, ideas about the behaviors of a racial, religious, or geographic group.

ethnocentrism An orientation or set of beliefs that holds that one's own *culture*, racial or *ethnic group*, or nation is inherently superior to others.

ethnology The scientific study of humanity's division into *races* and the history, characteristics, and *culture* of these racial groups.

ethnoviolence A purposeful act to harm someone or some organization identified with an *ethnic group*. Such activities include assaults, property destruction, harassment, firebombings, and distribution of hate propaganda. See also *hate crime.*

ethology The scientific study of the formation of human character and animal behavior by assessing the genetic, physiological, and evolutionary development and adaptation to the environment of living organisms.

ethos The moral beliefs or ethical character of a people or *culture.*

etiology 1. The underlying causes of a problem or disorder. 2. The study of such causes.

ET programs Employment training programs, used in many states to help recipients of *public assistance* become economically independent by training them to get and keep jobs and to help them learn marketable skills. In most states in which ET programs exist, the children of the recipients are provided with *health care* and *day care* services while the parent is in the training program. See also *GAIN programs.*

eugenics The science of "improving" human qualities genetically or minimizing genetic disorders. The practice may be negative (discouraging or preventing parenthood among those who are considered biologically deficient) or positive (encouraging reproduction among healthy people).

euphoria A *perception* of extreme well-being, excessive optimism, and increased motor activity. It is often pathological and indicative of such conditions as *bipolar disorder, mania, organic mental disorders,* and *drug intoxication.* See also *dysphoria.*

euthanasia 1. Elective *death.* 2. Putting to *death* or permitting the death of a person with *terminal illness,* also known as *mercy killing.* See also *"assisted suicide."*

euthenics The study and movement oriented to improving lifestyles and environments to improve humans and other species.

evaluation research Systematic investigation to determine the success of a specific program. For example, a social work researcher might conduct a study of the incidence rate of nutritional deficiency in an Appalachian town before and after its citizens are made eligible for an antipoverty program.

eviction Forcing an individual, family, or business to discontinue its occupancy of housing, land, or other real property, usually by *due process of law.*

exceptional children A designation applied to dependent youths who, because of unusual mental, physical, or social abilities or limitations, require extraordinary forms of education, social experience, or treatment. These children include mentally retarded youngsters who can benefit from educational training facilities designed to help them reach their potential. Other such children may be those with physical *disabilities* and deformities, *mental disorders,* special talents, very high *intelligence,* or unusual physical abilities. See also *gifted child.*

exceptional eligibility A social welfare policy in which services or benefits are established for people who constitute a special group even though they may not have unique or special needs and although others outside the group may have the same needs or be in the same circumstances. Such programs are often developed because of strong political pressure or public sympathy for the group. Some veterans' programs are a notable example.

exchange model In social work administration, the concept of interorganizational linkages whereby similar agencies (for example, those agencies with the same mandates, constituencies, supervising organizations, or sources of funds) sometimes transfer or trade their resources (such as personnel, clients, or information) according to specified criteria.

exclusion allowance A portion of some benefit that may not be counted as taxable income. Examples include certain tax-deferred retirement annuity plans and some *social security* benefits.

"ex-con" Slang for a person who once served time in a penal institution, that is, a former convict.

exhibitionism 1. The tendency to show off one's real or imagined traits and talents to gain the attention of others. 2. Frequently, the display of one's genitals or sexual characteristics in socially unacceptable circumstances. See also *"flasher."*

existential social work A philosophical perspective in social work that accepts and emphasizes the individual's fundamental *autonomy,* freedom of choice, disillusionment with prevailing social *mores,* a sense of meaning derived from suffering, the need for dialogue, and the social worker's commitment to the concept of client *self-determination.*

ex officio member Someone who belongs to a group or board by virtue of holding another office or status. For example, an ex officio member of the board of a sectarian social agency might be the highest-ranking local clergy of that denomination.

exogenous Something that affects an individual emotionally or physically but originates outside the body or self.

exogenous depression *Depression* apparently due to some external life event that is stressful or unhappy. The term is often used to imply acute depression in an individual who has healthy *affect* but who is currently experiencing sorrow or dejection, as in *bereavement* or failure to achieve an important goal.

expatriation The process of leaving one's native country and living elsewhere, usually permanently.

expenditure A payment, or obligation to pay, for some goods or services received. For example, a social agency budgets for specific anticipated operating expenses. Capital expenditures are those the social agency makes to acquire or improve a relatively permanent asset, such as the building where the agency's activities take place. Revenue expenditures are those the agency makes from its operating budget for such purposes as expendable supplies.

experience rating 1. A measure of a corporation's employee retention–layoff rate. Employers with high ratings—that is, those who lay off fewer employees than their competitors in similar industries—may be rewarded with payroll tax benefits. 2. In the insurance industry, a measure used to indicate the probability of risk to a specified group.

experiential therapy A form of psychosocial *intervention* or clinical treatment that emphasizes activity, acting out of conflicts and situations, *role playing, confrontation,* and simulating situations that are similar to the frequent life experiences of the client. Experiential therapies focus on the "here and now" and discourage the client from relying solely on a description of past circumstances. Experiential therapies often occur in *group therapy* or *family therapy* settings.

experiment A systematic project to test a *hypothesis.*

experimental group In *research*, a collection of subjects who are matched and compared with a *control group* in all relevant respects, except that they are also subject to a specific *variable* being tested.

experimental programs See *demonstration programs.*

expert opinion The presentation of pertinent knowledge, thoughtful speculation, or demonstration of needed skills by a *professional* or an authority to a committee or organization that needs the information to make a decision with an effective means of implementing a plan it has developed. This information tends toward "educated guesses" and providing reasonable prognoses about the future consequences of an act the group is thinking about implementing. For example, a social worker may be asked by a court of law to provide information about the possible long-term harm and emotional consequence to a victim of child abuse.

expert witness One who testifies before a lawmaking group or in a court of law, based on special knowledge of the subject in question, enabling the decision makers to better assess the evidence or merits of the issue. Social workers are often called as expert witnesses before legislative bodies that seek to draft legislation to enhance the public welfare. Social workers are also frequently asked to testify as expert witnesses in court hearings, especially in disputes over *custody of children, child neglect, welfare rights*, marital dissolution, landlord–tenant controversies, and care for people with mental and physical *disabilities*. See also *forensic social work*.

explosive disorder An *impulse control disorder* characterized by an individual's loss of control of aggressive impulses and fits of rage out of proportion to any *stressor*. The individual may have numerous repeated episodes of this aggressivity (called *intermittent explosive disorder*) or have a single discrete episode (called "isolated explosive disorder"). Isolated explosive disorder is not included in *DSM-IV* because of potential misdiagnosis based on one episode.

exponential growth Expansion of a system in which the amount being added is proportional to the amount already present, so that the bigger the system the faster it increases. This term is often applied to uncontrolled growth in social phenomena such as urban sprawl, population, taxes, and waste products.

ex post facto experiment In *research*, an *experiment* conducted after the event being tested has already occurred. Thus, the experimenter cannot introduce the experimental stimulus but attempts to control, sometimes statistically, all extraneous factors.

expressed need An indication of the degree to which *needs* exist and the number of people who perceive themselves to have the need as revealed by specific factors. These factors might include the number of people who wait in lines to ask for a service, the amount of money most people seem willing to pay, or the obstacles clients need to overcome to acquire the services.

expressive language disorder A *communication disorder* characterized by markedly limited vocabulary and amount of speech, difficulty producing sentences of appropriate length and complexity, errors in tense, and general difficulty expressing ideas. The language difficulties interfere with academic or occupational achievement or with social communication. This disorder may be developmental or acquired (as a result of medical conditions such as head trauma). If *mental retardation*, motor or sensory deficits, or sociocultural deprivation is present, the language difficulties are greater than usually found in those problems. See also *mixed receptive–expressive language disorder, phonological disorder,* and *stuttering*.

expunge A legal procedure in which certain records about an individual are destroyed. In many jurisdictions, some juveniles may have records pertaining to delinquent acts expunged on reaching *adulthood;* also, people who have been arrested unlawfully or not convicted may apply to have their arrest records expunged.

extended-care facilities (ECF) Nursing homes for patients who need to remain in a *residential care facility* for extended periods, up to 100 days. To receive the ECF designation and thus be eligible for *Medicare* reimbursement, the facility must meet special federal and state certification standards. It must have staffs that usually include a medical director; registered nurse, nursing director, nursing supervisor, and skilled nursing staff; dietician; physical therapist; occupational therapist; and a director of social services. ECFs are subject to *utilization review* by government bodies and *third parties*. See also *skilled-nursing facility*.

extended family   A kinship group comprising relatives of a *nuclear family,* such as grandparents, uncles, aunts, and second cousins.

externality   The concept in s*ocial group work* in which the members apply what they have learned from their experiences in the group to their worlds outside the group and use their newly acquired skills to relate more effectively with their families and their communities.

externalization   1. The projecting of one's own thoughts or values onto some aspect of the environment. 2. The distinction young children make between themselves and their environments.

extinction   In *behavior modification,* the elimination or weakening of a *conditioned response (CR)* by discontinuing *reinforcement* after the response occurs *(operant conditioning)*. In *respondent conditioning,* this occurs through repeated presentations of a *conditioned stimulus (CS)* without the *unconditioned stimulus (US)*.

extortion   The *crime* of illegally taking money or other property from another person by using *fear, coercion,* or threats. Extortion is generally synonymous with *blackmail*; it differs from *robbery* in that the immediate personal and physical safety of the victim is not at risk.

extradition   The legal process of bringing a person accused or convicted of a *crime* from one nation, state, or jurisdiction to another.

extrapolation   Making inferential estimations based on, but beyond the scope of, available data. For example, a social worker might conclude that a client is not really as ill as claimed solely because the *case record* indicates a tendency toward *hypochondriasis*.

extrinsic anxiety   The client's unnecessary *anxiety* that occurs in the individual or group therapy situation and derives primarily from the uncertainty about the goals of the therapy and the methods by which the therapist or group will seek to reach them. This is contrasted with *intrinsic anxiety.*

extrovert   An individual who tends to be outgoing and directs attention to others. Carl Jung (1875–1961) spelled this "extravert." The opposite of an *introvert.*

F

face sheet   A page, usually in the front of a client's *case record* or in front of a *questionnaire,* on which specific identifying data about the subject are recorded, such as age, gender, income, family members, and prior contacts with the agency.

face validity   A simple method for assessing the *validity* of a scale or instrument, in which the researcher using his or her professional judgment alone accepts the instrument as valid if it looks or sounds valid.

facilitation   An approach to social work *intervention* in which the social worker stimulates and mediates linkages between client systems, helps develop new systems, or helps strengthen existing ones. The social worker acts as an *enabler,* supporter, mediator, and broker for the client, paving the way for the client to reach desired goals. Facilitation activities include eliciting information and opinions, encouraging the expression of feelings, interpreting behavior, discussing alternative courses of action, clarifying situations, providing encouragement and reassurance, practicing logical reasoning, and recruiting members, usually within the context of a collaborative or bargaining relationship.

facilitator   One who serves as a leader for some *group* experience.

facilitator role   In social work, the responsibility to expedite the change effort by bringing together people and lines of communication, *channeling* their activities and resources, and providing them with access to expertise. Other primary social work roles are identified as the *enabler role,* the *educator role,* and the *mobilizer role.*

fact-gathering interview   An interview in which the social worker seeks predetermined and specific data from the client. The social worker asks specific questions and records relevant answers, often on a *face sheet* or forms. Its purpose is not primarily therapeutic and thus gives relatively little opportunity for the client to ventilate feelings or work through problems.

factitious disorder   *Behavior* that appears to be *abnormal* or a symptom of *mental illness* but is probably under the subject's voluntary control. It is similar to *malingering,* except that in factitious disorder there is no apparent benefit to be gained from the problem.

factitious disorder by proxy   The deliberate feigning of mental or physical symptoms of someone under the individual's care. This most commonly occurs when a parent or guardian of a child reports and induces symptomatic behavior. Motivation is not for economic or other external gain but for the caregiver to assume a role in the illness or its treatment. This is a proposed official diagnostic category of the *DSM-IV.*

failure to thrive   See *marasmus.*

Fair Debt Collection Practices Act   Federal legislation, passed in 1977 (P.L. 95-109), to control abusive behavior made by debt collectors such as late-evening telephoning, warnings about loss of reputation, and threats of job loss.

Fair Employment Practices Committee (FEPC)   The first federal program to monitor and eliminate *discrimination* in the U.S. labor force, created in 1941 by executive order of President Franklin D. Roosevelt. The program was opposed by Congress and finally abolished in 1945.

Fair Housing and Equal Opportunity Office   An organization within the U.S. *Department of Housing and Urban Development (HUD)* responsible for enforcing the laws that require home sellers and landlords to give all potential tenants or purchasers equal access.

Fair Labor Standards Act   Federal legislation originally enacted in 1938 (52 Stat. 1060) and amended periodically and administered by the U.S. *Department of Labor* that sets minimum wages, payment of time-and-a-half for work beyond 40 hours in a week, provisions of equal pay for equal work, and *child labor* standards.

faith healing   The use of prayer and belief in divine intervention to alleviate symptoms of physical or mental disorders.

falling out   A *culture-bound syndrome* occurring primarily among people in the southern United States and Caribbean islands in which the individual suddenly collapses; "blacks out"; feels dizzy; and even though he or she usually hears and understands what is going on nearby, feels powerless to move or respond.

false-memory syndrome   *Confabulation,* the act of filling gaps in memory by fabricating and reporting these thoughts. Some clients with this syndrome come to believe they remember an event that did not happen. Others who have used *repression* or *suppression* to help avoid the distress of painful experiences eventually remember but distort all or parts of the experiences. The many others who eventually remember and accurately report what truly happened are not, of course, experiencing a false-memory syndrome. This is often used as a legal defense by accused child molesters. See also *memory recovery therapy.*

familial   Characteristics or traits that seem prevalent among closely related people.

family   A *primary group* whose members assume certain obligations for each other and generally share common residences. The National Association of Social Workers (NASW) Commission on Families (*Promoting Family Supports Statement,* 1990) defines a *family* as two or more people who consider themselves family and who assume obligations, functions, and responsibilities generally essential to healthy family life. *Child care* and child *socialization,* income support, *long-term care (LTC),* and other caregiving are among the functions of family life.

family allowance   A *demogrant* form of benefit in many nations, not including the United States, in which every eligible family, regardless of financial need, is allocated a specified sum of money. There are many variations to this system depending on the nation's social policy goals. These variations include making higher payments for families with more children, reducing payments if families have more than a prescribed number of children, and requiring families whose income exceeds a certain amount to pay back the family allowance at tax time. In some nations, these programs are known as *children's allowances* or *maternity benefits*.

Family and Medical Leave Act   The federal law (P.L. 103-3) enacted in 1993 that requires U.S. companies with more than 50 employees to offer up to 12 weeks each year of job-protected, unpaid leave with their health care coverage intact so they can care for any sick family member, newborn, or newly adopted or foster child.

Family Assistance Plan (FAP)   A proposal to reform part of the U.S. *social welfare* system by providing every employed American family a *guaranteed annual income* above a specified low amount. The proposed legislation was developed in 1969 by the Nixon administration but was not passed by Congress.

family care   The placement of institutionalized persons into the homes of relatives or unrelated *guardians* where they are permitted to participate as family members. Family care is often recommended for patients in mental hospitals, incarcerated juveniles, and frail elderly residents of nursing homes.

family court A court of law that hears cases pertaining to conflicts among family members, such as *divorce, domestic violence, custody,* and *maintenance.* In many jurisdictions, family courts also include *juvenile court* functions.

Family Credit in U.K. The welfare system of supplementing the income of low-wage working families in the United Kingdom. This program was started in 1988 to replace the Family Income Supplement program.

family-driven support system A program usually sponsored by state and local departments of public welfare and human services to help families provide at-home care for their mentally retarded members. The system provides funds to the family to be used in purchasing services or goods.

family, extended See *extended family.*

family map A pictorial representation of the way a family is structured around a specific problem or concern. Each member of the family is represented by circles or squares, and the type of relationship that tends to exist between them is illustrated by drawing various types of lines.

family myths A *family therapy* concept pertaining to a set of beliefs, based on distortions of facts or history, shared by members of a family. These beliefs serve to enforce the *family rules* that influence the way the members interact and ensure cohesiveness and stability in the family. (For example, one family might believe and communicate the view that its male members are less assertive than its female members.) The family members may be aware that these ideologies are inaccurate, but they are allowed to go unchallenged to preserve the existing family structure.

family, nuclear See *nuclear family.*

family of orientation A kinship group united not necessarily by blood but by such factors as common residence, shared experiences and backgrounds, mutual affection, and economic dependency.

family of origin A kinship group united by blood or genetic similarity.

family of procreation A kinship group created by an adult couple.

family planning Making deliberate and voluntary decisions about reproduction. A couple practicing family planning decides on the number and timing of *pregnancies* after considering economic circumstances, life goals, the nature of the reproductive process, and *contraception* methods. See also *reproductive technology* and *birth control.*

family policy A nation's principles and planned procedures that are intended to influence or alter existing patterns of family life. Technically, all of a nation's *social policy* concerns (such as income maintenance, housing, education, and defense) affect families. Thus, the term family policy generally focuses more on issues such as fertility rates and family size, child care for working parents, care of older people, foster care programs, and income maintenance programs for families, as in *family allowance.* A nation's family policy may be explicit or implicit.

family preservation Planned efforts to provide the knowledge, resources, supports, health care, relationship skills, and structures that help families stay intact and maintain their mutual roles and responsibilities. Government family preservation programs have been developed in many nations to help keep families from losing their children, especially through foster placement, abandonment, runaway, and juvenile incarceration. Some of these programs also help empower fathers and mothers so they can maintain traditional roles.

family projection process A *family therapy* concept developed by Murray Bowen (1914–1990) that refers to the way some members of a family, especially parents, attribute sources of conflict to other members of the family, especially children. This process frequently results in one or more of the children in a family becoming the bearers of the symptoms of the family's ills.

family rules A *family therapy* term that refers to repetitive patterns of behavior and mutual expectations regulating that behavior in a family. One family, for example, might maintain a mutual expectation that none of its members is to express outwardly any feelings of affection for one another. Another family might have a rule that every dispute is to result in threatened or actual physical violence.

family sculpting An evaluation and intervention technique in some forms of *family therapy* in which family members are asked to position and choreograph the movements of other family members and to form a living tableau of people that reflects the communication and relationship patterns in the family unit.

family secrets A *family therapy* concept pertaining to shared but concealed beliefs and perceptions that some or all of the family members may hold but hide from one another to achieve certain family interactions.

Family Service America (FSA) The national organization comprising privately funded, local family service organizations in most larger communities in the United States, plus professionals and private citizens interested in social services for families. Formerly known as the Family Service Association of America, FSA was established as an outgrowth of the National Association of Societies for Organizing Charities in 1911 and took its present name in 1983. Its member agencies provide *family therapy* and *marital therapy,* guidance and educational programs, and social services to the community. The national organization sets standards for member agencies, provides public relations and educational programs, and sponsors research and publications. Its board helps set policy and advise lawmakers about family needs.

family service organizations *Social agencies* that provide a variety of human services, especially to couples, families, and extended family units. These organizations are most often funded through grants and private donations and follow policies established by independently elected or appointed boards of directors. Services include *family therapy* and *marital therapy,* family life education, and community activities to enhance healthy family development. Many of these agencies are affiliated with national organizations.

Family Services Administration See *Administration for Children and Families (ACF)*.

Family Support Act (FSA) of 1988 The welfare reform program (P.L. 100-485) that attempted to reduce the number of welfare recipients by encouraging vocational training while providing child care and maintaining *Aid to Families with Dependent Children (AFDC)* eligibility and *Medicaid* benefits. Major features of the act were the *JOBS program* and provisions to maintain AFDC benefits and pay for child care for those in need for up to 12 months.

family system theories The application of *systems theories* (those that emphasize reciprocal relationships and mutual influences between the individual components and the whole and vice versa). Virtually all current *family therapy* approaches and theoretical orientations that focus on understanding or treating families use a systems theory; however, there are many variations and differences in emphases in these theories.

family therapy *Intervention* by a professional social worker or other family therapist with a group of family members who are considered to be a single *unit of attention*. Typically, the approach focuses on the whole system of individuals and interpersonal and communication patterns. It seeks to clarify roles and reciprocal obligations and to encourage more-adaptable behaviors among the family members. The therapist concentrates on verbal and nonverbal communications and on the "here and now" rather than on family history. Variations in family therapy techniques are practiced by proponents of psychosocial, behavioral, systems, and other orientations. Some of the more-influential family therapy "schools" have been influenced by Salvador Minuchin *(structural family therapy)*, Jay Haley *(strategic family therapy)*, *Virginia Satir* and the Palo Alto Group, Murray Bowen, Carl Whittaker, Henry V. Dicks, Mara Selvini-Palazzoli, and Peggy Papp.

Family Unification Program A program of the U.S. *Department of Housing and Urban Development (HUD)* established in 1992 to provide rental housing assistance to families whose children are at risk of being placed in foster care because of the family's potential for homelessness.

family violence Aggressive and hostile behaviors between members of a family that result in injury, harm, humiliation, and sometimes death. These behaviors may include physical *abuse, rape,* destruction of property, and deprivation of *basic needs.*

family welfare One of professional social work's first designated *fields of practice.* The activities include *marriage counseling, parent training,* and *child protective services (CPS),* as well as helping clients get access to financial assistance, health care, educational provisions, and employment. Family welfare work takes place in public and private agencies such as departments of *public assistance* and *family service organizations.*

famine A widespread and severe scarcity of vital needs, especially food.

fantasy The mental picturing of events, objects, or other forms of symbolic thought in daydreams or while sleeping. Normally, fantasy is a healthy outlet for an individual's adjustment and creative needs but when excessive can be a symptom of *mental disorder.*

FAO See *Food and Agricultural Organization (FAO).*

FAP See *Family Assistance Plan (FAP).*

fascism A political *ideology* and party that advocates a totalitarian structure of governance, extreme nationalism under a charismatic dictator, high favor for private capitalism, a regimented populace devoted to social productivity, and sanctions against individuals who are considered less economically productive or responsible for economic problems. Benito Mussolini and Adolf Hitler espoused this ideology.

Fauri, Fedele F. (1909–1981) Public welfare expert and social work educator, Fauri was long-time dean at the University of Michigan School of Social Work after serving as the state's director of social welfare. He helped develop doctoral programs for social work and presided over many national social welfare organizations.

FDA See *Food and Drug Administration (FDA).*

FDIC See *Federal Deposit Insurance Corporation (FDIC).*

fear The emotional and physical reaction to an identifiable or perceived source of danger.

feasibility study A systematic assessment of the *resources* needed to accomplish a specified objective and concurrent evaluation of an organization's existing and anticipated capabilities for providing those resources.

featherbedding Requiring an employer to hire workers who are not needed. For example, a union contract might require that 10 workers are hired even though the job needs only five. The Labor–Management Relations Act (Taft–Hartley Act) of 1947 forbids the practice, but it is easily circumvented.

fecundity A given *population* group's potential for reproduction, determined by counting the number of fertile women of childbearing age.

Federal Crime Insurance Program A program established in 1971 and administered by the U.S. *Department of Housing and Urban Development (HUD)* that underwrites insurance against the risks of *crime* when it is unavailable from commercial insurance companies. It is used primarily by small businesses located in high-crime neighborhoods.

Federal Deposit Insurance Corporation (FDIC) A government corporation that insures people's deposits in national and some state banks that are members of the Federal Reserve System. Depositors are assured that their funds, up to an amount specified in advance, will be returned to them in the event that the bank fails or has insufficient resources to meet all its obligations.

Federal Emergency Management Agency (FEMA) An independent agency of the U.S. government designed to organize and coordinate the nation's emergency preparedness. It oversees *civil defense* programs, urban riot response, and *disaster relief.*

Federal Emergency Relief Administration (FERA) The government organization established during the Roosevelt administration in 1933 and directed by *Harry Hopkins* (1890–1946), a social worker. The program distributed federal funds to the states for emergency unemployment relief and required every local administration to have at least one experienced social worker on its staff. FERA and other *New Deal* programs were terminated as World War II began.

Federal Employee Health Benefits Program (FEHBP) A program that provides health benefits for employees of the federal government. In 1986, the program was amended by the Federal Employees Benefits Improvement Act (P.L. 99-251); one of the provisions eliminated the requirement for physician supervision as a condition for reimbursing clinical social workers.

Federal Housing Administration (FHA) The national program implemented in 1938 to encourage home ownership. Its most important feature has been to guarantee loans to finance individual homes, permitting homeowners to make lower down payments (5 and 10 percent) and to take longer to pay the balance (30 and sometimes 40 years).

Federal Insurance Contributions Act (FICA) The federal law that authorizes the government to levy payroll taxes on employers and employees. The revenues are earmarked to finance *Old Age, Survivors, Disability, and Health Insurance (OASDHI)*. See also *Self-Employment Contributions Act (SECA) of 1954.*

Federal Register The U.S. government publication in which all executive orders, proclamations, proposed rules and legislation, and notices of all government agencies are printed and distributed to the public.

Federations of Social Agencies Organizations comprising private welfare agencies in a given community that combine some of their resources and efforts for fundraising, public relations, lobbying, and educational activities.

feedback Transmitting information about the results of an action to the individual who performed that action. This permits a more-objective evaluation of the action's effectiveness. It also permits modifications in the ongoing action to increase the likelihood of success. In social work administration, feedback is often used in supervision, personnel evaluations, client reports, and objective *outcome evaluations* to help social workers achieve desired improvements or to give them positive indicators when they are performing well.

feeding disorder of infancy or early childhood Persistent failure to eat adequately resulting in weight loss or failure to gain weight. The onset of this disorder is in the first year but occasionally occurs after ages two or three. The disorder is not the result of gastrointestinal, endocrinological, or neurological conditons or lack of food. See also *eating disorders, rumination disorder,* and *pica.*

fee for service A charge made to clients or their *fiscal intermediaries* for a specified service (such as an hour of counseling) provided by a social worker.

fee schedule A listing of the maximum fee that a health plan will pay for any service based on *Current Procedural Terminology (CPT)* codes.

FEHBP See *Federal Employee Health Benefits Program (FEHBP)*.

Feingold diet A treatment modality designed for children who have *attention-deficit hyperactivity disorder (ADHD)*. B. F. Feingold claimed that children with behavioral and learning problems have a natural toxic reaction to flavorings, preservatives, and coloring in food, and he proposed a nutritious diet free of such additives. The hypothesis is empirically unsubstantiated but has a wide following.

felony A *crime* that is more serious than a *misdemeanor*. Felonies include *burglary* and some categories of *larceny, homicide, rape,* and *assault.*

FEMA See *Federal Emergency Management Agency (FEMA)*.

female orgasmic disorder A *sexual disorder* in women characterized by the persistent or recurrent delay or absence of orgasm following a normal sexual excitement phase. This condition has also been known as "inhibited female orgasm" or as "orgasmic impairment." See also *male orgasmic disorder.*

female sexual arousal disorder A *sexual disorder* in women characterized by a persistent or recurrent inability to attain or maintain a satisfactory lubrication and swelling response of sexual excitement (when sexual stimulation is adequate in focus, intensity, and duration) leading to distress or interpersonal difficulties. When using this term as a diagnosis, sex therapists and other clinicians specify whether the condition is lifelong or acquired, genealized or situational, and due to psychological or combined factors. See also *male erectile disorder.*

feminism The social movement and doctrine advocating legal and socioeconomic equality for women. The movement originated in Great Britain in the 18th century. See also *women's liberation movement.*

feminist social work The integration of the *values, skills,* and knowledge of social work with a feminist orientation to help individuals and society overcome the emotional and social problems that result from *sex discrimination.*

feminist therapy A psychosocial treatment orientation in which the professional (usually a woman) helps the client (usually a woman) in individual or group settings to overcome the psychological and social problems largely encountered as a result of *sex discrimination* and *sex role stereotyping.* Feminist therapists help clients maximize potential, especially through *consciousness-raising,* eliminating sex stereotyping, and helping them become aware of the commonalities shared by all women.

feminization of poverty concept The fact that women, especially those raising children without husbands or significant others, are far more vulnerable to being poor. The high rate of *divorce,* unwed motherhood, family breakdowns, and the burden of child care tending to fall on the mothers, many of whom have not had good employment experience, result in gender-skewed poverty rates.

fence One who receives stolen property and sells it for a profit.

FEPC See *Fair Employment Practices Committee (FEPC)*.

FERA See *Federal Emergency Relief Administration (FERA)*.

Fernandis, Sarah (1863–1951) Founder of the first black social *settlement house* in the United States, she received her *MSW* degree from New York University before beginning her work as organizer for improved health and sanitation in black neighborhoods.

fertility The biological capacity to reproduce.

fertility rate A demographic characteristic indicating the number of live births that occur in a *population* group during a specific time span.

fertilization in vitro See *in vitro fertilization.*

fetal alcohol syndrome Various forms of damage to a *fetus* as a result of heavy maternal alcohol consumption. Potential problems include retarded growth, *mental retardation,* and sometimes craniofacial and limb abnormalities.

fetishism   A *sexual disorder* of the *paraphilia* class involving erotic attraction to an inanimate object or specific body part, especially clothing, shoes, and hair. See also *erotic orientation.*

fetology   The science and medical specialty that deals with the study, care, and treatment of the *fetus* during prenatal development.

fetus   An unborn infant; usually the term is applied to developing human organisms from the third month after conception until birth. Development from the ninth week consists primarily of the refinements of existing organ systems and increases in size.

feudalism   The socioeconomic and political system in medieval Europe in which people of high social rank were given land grants (fiefs) by people of even higher rank in exchange for tax payments and the military services of those who managed and worked the land.

FFA   See *force field analysis (FFA).*

FHA   See *Federal Housing Administration (FHA).*

FICA   See *Federal Insurance Contributions Act (FICA).*

fidgetiness   Restless movements and increased motor activity, often seen in people experiencing anxiety, hyperactivity, anger, or impatience. It also occurs in *tics* and gross motor disturbances.

field instruction   In *social work education,* an integral part of the *BSW* and *MSW* educational curricula, providing students with supervised opportunities to engage in direct social work practice with individuals, families, groups, communities, and organizations. Students are helped to refine professional skills, acquire and solidify social work values, and integrate the knowledge acquired in the academic setting with that obtained in the field.

field placement   A part of the social work student's formal educational requirement, consisting of ongoing work in a community social agency. The *MSW* student typically is given a work assignment (of 16 to 20 hours weekly) in one agency during the first training year and assigned to another agency with about the same time requirements during the second year. The student receives close supervision by agency personnel and has the opportunity to integrate, use, and apply classroom content to practical experiences. Field placements also exist in undergraduate *(BSW)* social work programs and in some doctoral programs. See also *concurrent placement* and *block placement.*

fields of practice   The social work term pertaining to the profession's various practice settings and the special competence needed to work in those settings. Fields of practice were established by the 1920s when it became apparent that social work practice itself was so far-reaching that it was becoming difficult for individuals to encompass. The first fields of practice included *family welfare, child welfare, psychiatric social work, medical social work,* and *school social work.* These fields have, to some extent, subsequently changed their names and their focus (for example, from *psychiatric social work* to "social work in mental health," and from *medical social work* to "social work in health care"), and new ones have emerged. They now also include *occupational social work, gerontological social work, rural social work, police social work,* and *forensic social work.*

field study   A *social research* method of investigating subjects in their natural environments instead of in a laboratory or clinician's office. For example, a social worker doing research in a *ghetto* would stay in that neighborhood making systematic observations for an extended period.

Fifth Amendment rights   Protections under the Fifth Amendment of the U.S. Constitution guaranteeing that no citizen may be compelled to give self-incriminating testimony for a court or congressional committee. This amendment also protects the individual from being tried a second time for the same *crime (double jeopardy)* or being deprived of life, liberty, or property without *due process of law.* See also *self-incrimination.*

filial responsibility See *relatives' responsibility.*

filial therapy The use of parents in a structured *intervention* for children with mental, social, or behavioral disorders. The therapist meets with small groups (six to eight parents) in didactic and information-gathering sessions. The parents then rehearse treatment techniques in the group before using them at home with their children. They discuss the ongoing results with the group.

financial management The planning, control, and direction of one's income and expenditures. This includes appropriate recording and bookkeeping, establishing and implementing consistent priorities and timing for purchasing decisions, minimizing waste, and budgeting. Social work administrators are concerned with financial management as an integral part of their managerial responsibilities. Social workers in *direct practice* often teach or help some of their clients plan and control their finances. See also *administration in social work.*

fine motor skills The ability of muscles to make small movements, increments, and adjustments to achieve delicate manipulations such as threading a needle, putting a golf ball, or tying a shoelace. See also *gross motor skills.*

First Amendment rights Protections under the First Amendment of the U.S. Constitution guaranteeing that government will not abridge the rights of free speech and press, worship, and peaceable assembly, or of petitioning the government for redress of grievances.

first-order change In *systems theories,* a temporary or superficial change in a system and the way it functions. See also *second-order change.*

fiscal intermediaries Organizations that provide third-party and fourth-party financial services between recipients and providers of a benefit. For example, whereas a government organization *(third party)* provides funds for *Medicaid* health care providers, a private insurance company such as Blue Cross–Blue Shield *(fourth party)* may provide the related administrative support.

fiscal policy A nation's economic goals and the manipulation of its finances to reach those goals, usually through raising or lowering taxes, spending levels, and interest rates.

fiscal year A 12-month accounting period used by governments, business organizations, and social agencies that often does not coincide with the calendar year. The fiscal year of the U.S. government begins October 1 and ends September 30.

501(c) organizations A type of nonprofit public interest or public service organization, such as a lobbying group, social welfare group, or charitable foundation, identified by the U.S. Internal Revenue Service to indicate its tax status. Lobbying organizations are 501(c) (4) groups and not exempt from paying taxes. Contributors to political action committees (PACs), which are 501(c) (5) groups, cannot deduct from their taxes. Charitable foundations are 501(c) (3) groups and are tax exempt. To take advantage of tax laws, many 501(c) organizations form foundations outside of their functions. For example, the Sierra Club comprises several organizations, including a PAC that is a 501(c) (5) organization and a foundation that is a 501 (c) (3) organization.

fixation 1. A continuing mode of behavior, persistent thought, or enduring emotional attachment that has become inappropriate for one's present circumstances or age. 2. In *psychodynamic* theory, the partial or complete arrest of personality development at one of the psychosexual stages.

fixed assets An organization's or social agency's financial holdings, such as land, buildings, and properties, that are not readily negotiable. Fixed assets exclude such values as accessible cash, expertise of personnel, and the agency's reputation or goodwill factors.

fixed-interval schedule   A procedure used in *behavior modification* in which a *reinforcement* is delivered when a specified period has elapsed after a response has occurred. For example, a child may be given a reward 10 minutes after completing a homework assignment.

Fizdale, Ruth (1908–1994)   A social work practitioner, administrator, and scholar, Fizdale developed the fee-for-service system now used in public and private social agencies and by private practitioners. She encouraged efforts to provide social work services to more-affluent clients and led the profession's movement toward more accountability, licensing, peer review, and competence certification.

flashback   A mental sensation of a sudden recurrence of a previous experience or perception. See also *hallucinogen persisting-perception disorder*.

"flasher"   Slang for a certain type of exhibitionist who suddenly opens and closes articles of clothing, such as an overcoat, to reveal flashing glimpses of genitals. See also *exhibitionism*.

flat affect   The appearance of *apathy* in *mood*. For example, an individual may show no emotion when told of bad news or take good news with indifference. It is sometimes a symptom of *schizophrenia* or *depression*.

flat-rate fee   A predetermined amount of money charged by a social worker or other professional for providing a particular service. The amount assessed is related to the service itself rather than to the client's unique economic circumstances. See also *sliding fee scale*.

Flexner, Abraham (1866–1959)   Educational reformer whose study about medical education led to changes in the curricula of medical schools; his *Flexner Report* (1915) stimulated social work to develop changes that led to its becoming a profession.

Flexner Report   An influential paper delivered to social workers in 1915 by *Abraham*

Flexner (1866–1959) that declared that social work was not yet a *profession* because it lacked a unique technology, specific educational programs, a professional literature, and practice skills. Although it was controversial, the report stimulated social work to make the changes that eventually resulted in the fulfillment of Flexner's criteria of *professionalism*.

flight into health   A phenomenon commonly seen in clinical social work and other psychotherapies in which the client's symptoms or problems suddenly seem to cease without intervention. At that point, the client wants to terminate treatment or change the focus of attention in the treatment. The major reason this occurs is that the client fears some material or emotions that the therapy is uncovering and hopes to avoid the revelation by ending the work. Other causes are that the client is being pressured by financial or family constraints to end treatment.

flight into illness   A phenomenon commonly seen in clinical social work and other psychotherapies in which the client whose therapy is coming to an end suddenly exhibits new symptoms of the *presenting problem*. It is considered a manifestation by the client of overdependency on the social worker, a *transference* experience, or fear of *abandonment*.

flight of ideas   Rapid skipping from one thought or mental association to another without much basis for connection. It is sometimes a symptom of *hyperkinesis*, *bipolar disorder* (manic type), and drug-induced *euphoria*.

flooding   A procedure used in *behavior therapy* in which stimuli that elicit anxiety are presented, either in reality or imagery, with such regularity or intensity that the subject eventually stops responding with anxiety. See also *implosive therapy*.

"flophouse"   A derisive term sometimes applied to cheap transient hotels, mission homes, and *shelters* for homeless people.

Florence Crittenden Association   An organization of private social agencies throughout the United States that originated to provide residential treatment and social services for unwed mothers and to facilitate *adoption* of children. The association has expanded its range of services to include education, pregnancy prevention, and counseling. See also *maternity homes*.

fluid intelligence The mental skills and abilities that pertain to problem solving, adaptability, and integration of ideas. Unlike *crystallized intelligence*, which continues to develop throughout life, fluid intelligence tends to decline in later adulthood. See also *multiple intelligences*.

focus group A group typically of six to 12 people convened to discuss a specific issue or single topic, often with the aid of questionnaires and a moderator who actively keeps the conversation oriented to that topic. Such groups are often established to acquire information and generate ideas that would not be as accessible through individual interviews. Focus groups are frequently used in *social group work* and *community organization* and may include the *nominal group technique*, the *Delphi method*, and *brainstorming*.

folie à deux The sharing of delusions by two people. For example, a husband and wife may come to believe and help reinforce one another's conviction that they are being ridiculed secretly by their neighbors. This phenomenon is also known as *shared psychotic disorder*. See also *codependency* and *conjugal paranoia*.

folklore The traditions, legends, beliefs, and sayings of a group of people (such as an *ethnic group*, a tribe, a nation, a regional group, or an *extended family*).

Folks, Homer (1867–1963) A *child welfare* reformer, he worked at the *Children's Aid Society* in New York but disagreed with their methods. He became an advocate of home placement of orphans and juvenile delinquents and urged an end to child dumping in *orphanages* and *almshouses* and unsupervised placing-out programs. In 1904 he wrote the influential text *Care of Destitute, Neglected, and Delinquent Children*.

folkways Informal, traditional, and not strongly enforced patterns of *behavior* and standards of conduct in a *culture*.

Follett, Mary Parker (1868–1933) Social activist in the *vocational guidance* movement, she also developed many of the principles used in *administration in social work* and wrote the posthumously published text *Dynamic Administration* (1941).

following responses In the social work *interview*, the process of giving clients immediate *feedback* that their messages have been heard and understood. The social worker does this not by asking questions or directing discussion but by *paraphrasing* the client's words, conveying *empathy*, and showing attentiveness through such verbalizations as "I see," "I understand," or "You did?".

Food and Agricultural Organization (FAO) An agency of the United Nations established in 1945 to improve the world's agricultural production and distribution and to enhance the nutritional level of all peoples. It devises plans for improving yields in agriculture, oceans, and forests and also supervises research to improve seeds and hybrid crops and to develop fertilizers and pesticides.

Food and Drug Administration (FDA) A federal program, established in 1931 and now part of the U.S. *Department of Health and Human Services (HHS)*, that maintains standards and conducts research on the safety, reliability, and value of food and drug products available for human consumption.

food assistance programs *Social welfare* benefits for eligible people to assure that their nutritional requirements are met. The major food assistance programs in the United States are managed by the U.S. *Department of Agriculture (USDA)* and include the *Food Stamp program*, the school breakfast and *School Lunch program*, and the *WIC program*. USDA also arranges the donation of surplus agricultural products to some charitable institutions and nonprofit summer camps.

Food Stamp program A federal *food assistance program*, enacted in 1964 and administered by the U.S. *Department of*

Agriculture (USDA) through state welfare departments. Coupons are distributed to needy eligible individuals and families to be used like cash in participating stores to purchase most foods, plants, seeds, and sometimes *meals-on-wheels*, but not alcohol or tobacco products. The objective is to improve the diets of low-income households by supplementing their food-purchasing ability.

force field analysis (FFA) A problem-solving tool often used in social welfare planning, administration, and *community organization* for assessing the degree of resistance or receptivity to a proposed change. FFA includes listing the social forces that push for change (such as high costs of the existing program or ineffectiveness in reaching stated goals) and then listing those forces expected to obstruct change (such as the existing personnel's fear of losing job security or authority). FFA then delineates actions that can be taken to increase or decrease certain forces so as to facilitate movement toward the desired goal.

foreclosure The legal termination of the right to a specified property, usually as a consequence of nonpayment of the obligation.

Foreign Equivalency Determination Service A program of the *Council on Social Work Education (CSWE)* that evaluates the academic credentials of people educated in nations other than the United States to determine their equivalency to CSWE-accredited education programs. These evaluations are used to establish qualifications for *certification, licensing, employment,* graduate school admission, and membership in social work–related *professional associations.*

forensic social work The practice specialty in social work that focuses on the law and educating law professionals about social welfare issues and social workers about the legal aspects of their objectives. The activity also includes being an *expert witness* (or preparing other social workers to provide such testimony) in courts of law on such disputes as *custody of children, divorce, juvenile delinquency, nonsupport, relatives' responsibility,* and *welfare rights.*

forgery Counterfeiting or fabricating an object of value, such as a signature, document, or work of art, with the intent to commit *fraud.*

formal operations stage In *Piagetian theory,* the developmental stage that occurs during *adolescence* and that is characterized by greater flexibility in thought, increasing ability to use logic and *deductive reasoning,* the ability to consider complex issues from several viewpoints, and a reduction of *egocentrism.*

fossil fuels Burnable products, including oil, natural gas, and coal, formed from ancient living organisms extracted from the earth.

foster care The provision of physical care and family environments for children who are unable to live with their natural parents or legal guardians. Foster care is typically administered by county social services departments. Their social workers evaluate children and their families to help legal authorities determine the need for placement, evaluate potential foster homes as to their appropriateness for placing the particular child, monitor the foster home during the placement, and help the legal authorities and family members determine when it is appropriate to return the child to the natural family. The precedent for foster care in the United States originated largely with *apprenticing* and *indenture,* procedures in which homeless youths were placed in the care of a merchant or craftsperson for instruction and lodging in exchange for work. The term "foster care" also applies to full-time residential care for older, developmentally disabled, or mentally ill adults. See also *adult foster care.*

Foster Grandparents A federal program, administered by *ACTION,* that employs low-income senior citizens to provide care and emotional support for children who are socioeconomically disadvantaged, mentally retarded, or neglected.

foundations Institutions through which private funds are distributed for public purposes such as education, international relations, health, welfare, research, the humanities, and religion.

foundling hospitals Institutions that receive and care for abandoned children. Traditionally, the hospitals have been financed by *philanthropy* and by local taxpayers. The first foundling hospital was established in Milan, Italy, in 787. *Thomas Coram* established the first one in England in 1739. St. Vincent's Infant Asylum was established in 1856 as the first such facility in the United States. For the most part, they have been replaced by *foster care* programs.

four freedoms President Franklin D. Roosevelt's proposed goal for the peoples of all the world and the major objective for the forthcoming United Nations. The four freedoms were freedom of speech, freedom of religion, freedom from want, and freedom from fear.

4-H club An international organization for young people interested or involved in agriculture or homemaking through the development of one's head, heart, hands, and health.

fourth force The name given to a *transpersonal psychology* orientation toward understanding people and providing psychosocial services. It refers to the major orientations of psychological thought and therapy. The first force was the psychodynamic or analytical orientation that grew in the psychologically repressive Victorian era and focused on the psychopathology of inner-directed humans. The second force was the behaviorist orientation that focused on outer-directed human action and responses to the stresses faced in the environment. The third force was the humanistic, experiential, existential approach to therapy whose goal was *self-actualization*. The transpersonal fourth force goes beyond self-actualization toward a "trans-human" orientation centered in the connection of the soul and morality with the cosmos.

fourth party A fiscal intermediary between the provider of a health care or social service, the consumer of that service, and the organization that pays for the service. The fourth party does not provide the cash to cover the charges but provides administrative services for the cash provider *(third party)*. For example, the U.S. government is the third party for the *CHAMPUS* program, which pays health care providers for their treatment of dependents of military personnel. But in most locales, CHAMPUS contracts with a private insurance company, such as Blue Cross–Blue Shield (the fourth party), to process the administrative details.

Fourth World The underdeveloped nations, colonies, and protectorates that have extremely low per-capita incomes and rates of literacy, few natural resources, and low financial reserves. Countries including Bangladesh, Sudan, Ethiopia, and Chad are called "Fourth World" to distinguish them from nonaligned *(Third World)* countries, which do have resources and aspirations and are working toward more economic sufficiency.

frail elderly Older men and women who suffer from or are vulnerable to physical or emotional impairments and require some care because they have limited ability or opportunity to provide entirely for their own needs. See also *elderly* and *old old*.

franchising The process by which one organization grants another organization, group, or individual the right and obligation to fulfill one of its customary functions. For example, a state government might contract with a private company to provide penal facilities and services to some of its convict criminal population. Or a county government might engage a group of private social work practitioners to conduct all the investigations for *foster care* placements.

Francis of Assisi (1181–1226) Founder of the Franciscan Order whose members lived in poverty while serving poor and ill people. Although many members of his order or its branches became priests and nuns, he remained a layman. The Roman Catholic Church declared him to be a saint after his death.

fraud Intentionally deceiving someone who thereby is injured.

fraudulent contract   1. An explicit or implied agreement between two closely related people that is repeatedly violated by one person, forcing the other to adopt new behaviors to accommodate. 2. In *law*, the term refers to a written document, to which both parties agree, that contains deceptive statements or information.

free association   A therapeutic procedure, most commonly used in *psychoanalysis* and other *insight therapies*, in which the professional encourages the client to express whatever thoughts or emotions come to mind. The client verbalizes at length, and the therapist gives no distracting external cues that could influence the material being presented. See also *catharsis* and *Freudian theory.*

Freedmen's Bureau   Originally known as the Bureau of Refugees, Freedmen, and Abandoned Lands, this U.S. War Department organization was established in 1865 and was the nation's first federal welfare agency. Its major purpose was to assist former slaves in the transition to freedom by distributing food rations to the needy, finding employment opportunities, developing educational and medical institutions, and providing legal assistance. The bureau was eliminated in 1872.

Freedom of Information Act   Federal legislation enacted in 1966 (P.L. 89-487) to establish the right of citizens to know (with specific exceptions) what information the government and some other organizations are keeping about them. For example, under certain circumstances, the act gives clients of federally administered health and welfare agencies the right of access to their *case records.* See also *relative confidentiality* and *absolute confidentiality.*

freedom riders   *Civil rights* activists who rode buses into the American South in the 1960s to challenge racial *segregation* laws and practices.

free-enterprise system   An economic orientation of a nation or community that permits open competition for customers with minimal government regulation or involvement in the economy. This is a relative concept, because any social system except anarchy must have some public regulation or controls.

free-floating anxiety   Pervasive tension not attached to specific threats, situations, or ideas.

freestanding social services   Social services agencies and programs that operate independently of other service provider organizations and usually offer a wide range of *personal social services.* Examples include *child welfare* and *family service organizations.* Freestanding social services are contrasted with those provided within "host" organizations, such as the social services departments of hospitals, schools, industrial organizations, and the military.

Freudian slip   See *parapraxis.*

Freudian theory   An integrated set of principles about human *behavior* and the treatment of *personality disorders* based on the ideas of Viennese neurologist Sigmund Freud (1856–1939) and his followers. Central concepts about personality development include the growing organization of drives (*instincts, libido, pleasure principle,* and *reality principle*), personality structure (*unconscious, preconscious,* and *conscious*), personality dynamics (*id, ego,* and *superego*), and the stages of psychosexual development (the *oral phase,* the *anal phase,* and the *phallic phase*). Treatment concepts include *free association, catharsis, transference,* and *countertransference.* See also *psychoanalytic theory* and *psychosexual development theory.*

frictional unemployment   One of the four kinds of unemployment (the others being *seasonal unemployment, cyclical unemployment,* and *structural unemployment*) that occurs when people are moving geographically or occupationally from one job to another with only slight intervals of time with no work.

friendly visitors   Volunteers and, later, paid employees of the *Charity Organization Societies (COS)* who eventually became known as *social workers*. Their primary job was to investigate the homes of needy people, determine the causes of problems, provide guidance for solving problems, and—as a last resort—provide material assistance to those clients deemed "worthy." Friendly visiting was supplanted by *casework* as the "visitors" developed greater *professionalism*, more-thorough training, and better understanding of the causes of problems. This term is used currently in some social services organizations to refer to a professional practice of systematically going to the houses of clients, usually shut-ins.

"frigidity" An early term used to describe sexual disorders of women who do not experience sexual arousal or orgasms. Whereas the terms now used to describe these problems include *sexual aversion disorder, dyspareunia,* and *vaginismus,* the preferred term is *female sexual arousal disorder.*

frotteurism A *sexual disorder* characterized by strong and recurring sexual urges and erotic fantasies involving touching and rubbing against a nonconsenting person. The individual usually acts on these urges (commits frottage) in crowds where the behavior is less noticeable—except to the victim.

frustration A state of tension that occurs as a result of some goal-directed behavior being thwarted or postponed.

frustration tolerance The capacity to endure having a goal thwarted or postponed.

FSA 1. See *Family Service America (FSA).* 2. See *Family Support Act (FSA) of 1988.*

FTE Full-time equivalent, determined by the number of hours that staff work measured against the hours in a work-week. For example, if an agency's work-week is 40 hours and a program employs one staffperson 40 hours a week and another 28 hours a week, the program employs 1.7 FTEs.

fugue Amnesic flight; a *psychogenic* condition in which individuals, usually after experiencing intolerable internal or external *stress,* develop *amnesia* and abandon their homes, jobs, or familiar environments.

The more-appropriate term is *psychogenic fugue.*

functional assessment Systematic procedures and criteria used by social workers and other professionals, especially in health care and institutional settings, to determine the capacity of clients to provide for their own care and well-being. The client is evaluated as to his or her ability to carry out needed *activities of daily living (ADL)* and possession of the tools needed to fulfill those activities.

functional community A class of people or organizations that have common purposes, goals, or orientations toward their achievement. Examples are the education, military, business, religious, or medical communities. Social workers and others belong to the welfare or human services functional community.

functional dyspareunia Painful sexual intercourse resulting from *psychogenic* rather than *organic* factors. The term currently preferred by professionals is *dyspareunia.*

functional encopresis Uncontrolled bowel movements resulting from *psychogenic* rather than *organic* factors.

functional enuresis Involuntary urination resulting from *psychogenic* rather than *organic* factors.

functional illiteracy See *illiteracy, functional* and *literacy volunteer programs.*

functional impairment The inability of an individual to meet certain expectations or responsibilities because of temporary or permanent physical or mental incapacitation. The term is used by some social workers to refer to a situation in which an individual is only partially disabled and can effectively carry out most, but not all, normal functions.

"functional mental illness" A term that pertains to psychological disorders for which there is no apparent physical or *organic* basis. With increased recognition of the importance of physiological factors in mental processes, this term is becoming obsolete.

143

functional requisites   In *social policy* development, the delineation of anticipated program activities and services, identification of service targets, and specification of anticipated types of intervention to be used.

functional school in social work   A theoretical and practice orientation in social work based partly on the "will" concept of Otto Rank and the ideas of *Virginia Robinson* (1883–1977) and *Jessie Taft* (1882–1960). It is also known as the *Rankian School* and the *Pennsylvania School* to distinguish it from the *diagnostic school in social work*. Most influential from 1930 to 1950, the approach deemphasized diagnostic inquiry, history taking, and *Freudian theory*; instead, it stressed a strategy that was time-limited and focused on those issues that came within the function of the *agency*.

functional vaginismus   A sexual pain in women in which continuing involuntary spasms of the musculature of the outer third of the vagina interfere with *coitus*. This term is now replaced by the term *vaginismus*.

function-versus-cause issue   See *cause-versus-function issue*.

fundamentalist movements   The religious-based political and social cause activities of people with strong religious convictions who espouse their faiths to be the basic and only truthful tenets and who work toward convincing others likewise. These movements tend to be politically conservative and often are led by charismatic clergy who cite the holy writings of their faiths to justify and advocate for social change.

funding   Allocation of a specific amount of money to be used in carrying out an organization's program for a certain amount of time.

fundraising   The process of soliciting and acquiring income through *philanthropy* and other private donations, grants, fee for service, investment, and other means.

furthering responses   The interview strategy of encouraging clients to communicate with more clarity, depth, and focus and to enhance the working *relationship*. These activities are based on attentive listening and stimulating the client's verbalization. Furthering responses include minimal prompts ("I see" and "And then . . . ?") and accent responses (repeating a word or phrase from the client's verbalization to encourage further elaboration). See also *following responses*.

fusion   In *family systems theory*, the obscuring of separate identities between the family members. See also *differentiation*.

G

GA See *general assistance (GA)*.

GADE See *Group for the Advancement of Doctoral Education in Social Work (GADE)*.

GAF Scale See *Global Assessment of Function (GAF) Scale*.

gag order Instructions from some authority to refrain from disclosing, discussing, or advocating specified information. The order is sometimes issued by judges to witnesses or jurors during a trial, military officers to their troops, and social agency administrators to their staffs during budget hearings with legislators.

Gaia The earth and its ecosystem seen as a single, living creative system (named after the Greek goddess of the earth). The hypothesis is that the earth is a living organism, or superorganism, that adjusts and regulates itself. Whereas proponents maintain that some parts of the earth (tropical rain forests, oceans, ozone layer) are equivalent to vital organs, opponents argue that the Gaia analogy does not conform to the usual definitions of life, including the ability to reproduce itself.

GAIN programs Greater Avenues to Independence, a series of state public welfare programs originating in California, in which *public assistance* recipients are provided with training, education, job counseling, and job placement. If the programs are not successful in getting an eligible *Aid to Families with Dependent Children (AFDC)* family head into the *work force,* the recipient is provided with up to one year of employment in relevant public service positions. See also *ET programs*.

Gamblers Anonymous A *self-help organization* for compulsive gamblers and all people who experience problems as a result of gambling. Patterned to some extent after the *Alcoholics Anonymous (AA)* program, the organization was founded in 1957 and now has chapters in major cities throughout the United States.

gambling, compulsive A behavior disorder in which the individual becomes preoccupied with wagers and develops a progressively worsening urge to bet money. The urge often becomes uncontrollable and occurs even when funds for making bets are unavailable.

gaming A process in which participants are *role playing* potential or actual life simulations in which problems must be resolved. The term "simulation" refers to an analogy to some process in the real world, however it is perceived. Unlike other role-playing situations, gaming has specified rules that are used to govern actions. There are "move rules" (which specify who can do what, with or to whom, and with what resources) and "termination rules" (which define who has won and when the game is over). Games and simulations, as herein defined, are social, as contrasted to such physical simulations as wind tunnels in aircraft-design centers.

gang In sociological terms, a group that originally forms spontaneously and whose members maintain a relationship because they share certain attributes. These attributes include age, *ethnicity,* residence in a neighborhood, or common *values* that lead to mutual bonding. Social workers and legal authorities often use the term to refer to a fairly cohesive group of adolescents who support one another in various antisocial pursuits.

Ganser's syndrome   A pattern of behavior in which the client gives silly or absurd and irrelevant answers to questions. The behavior is sometimes seen in defiant or shy youngsters and prison inmates. Sometimes it is a symptom of severe *anxiety, depression,* or *schizophrenia.*

GANTT chart   A scheduling technique commonly used in *social work* and *social planning* to show graphically each of the activities of an organization and the time taken to complete each of them. For each activity, there is a horizontal line drawn under calendar dates, and a horizontal bar is drawn to show the duration of time spent on the task. Because the GANTT chart does not show interconnections between activities, the *Program Evaluation and Review Technique (PERT)* chart tends to be used for more-complex planning.

GAO   See *General Accounting Office (GAO), U.S.*

GARF Scale   See *Global Assessment of Relational Functioning (GARF) Scale.*

garnishment   A legal process by which a creditor may have a judgment against a debtor's money or other property (such as wages, salary, or savings) in the possession or control of a third party. Under state law, the court may order the employer, banker, or other holder of the property to remit such funds to an agent of the court or to the creditor until the obligation has been fulfilled. For example, an employer may be required to withhold a portion of an employee's salary and remit it to the court to meet the employee's child support obligation.

gastroenterology   The medical specialty that focuses on diseases of the digestive system, stomach, and intestines.

gatekeeper   1. One who facilitates or obstructs movement from one status to another or communication between one group and another. 2. In *community organization,* the term refers to an indigenous member of a community who permits or precludes real access by the organizers to those in the target population. In this sense, gatekeepers are typically the natural leaders of a community, or they work in key positions that permit them to know what and who is influential. These people may be playground workers, traffic patrol people, gang leaders, bartenders, or neighborhood "busybodies." 3. In *social work education,* it refers to the role of the faculty person who is instrumental in including or excluding certain students as members of the profession. 4. The gatekeeper role is also performed by formal organizations and social agencies that evaluate potential clients for certain eligibilities.

Gault decision   The 1967 judgment rendered by the U.S. Supreme Court *(In re Gault)* that affirmed the right of *juveniles* to the same legal protections as adults in criminal court proceedings. This decision gave juveniles the right to proper advance notification of the charges, the right to counsel, freedom from *self-incrimination,* and the opportunity to have their counsel confront witnesses. Before the Gault decision, juvenile proceedings were regarded as civil, not criminal, and the state was supposedly acting in the interest of the child. The decision strengthened the role of law enforcement personnel and formalized court procedures. It decreased the influence of social workers and required new modes of operation by social work personnel.

gay   The term preferred by many homosexuals, primarily males, in describing themselves and their sexual orientation. Female homosexuals usually prefer the term *lesbian.* See also *homosexuality.*

GED certificate   General Equivalency Diploma, a program by which people who did not obtain high school degrees can demonstrate to prospective employers, college admission boards, and others that they have achieved an equivalent level of education. In some educational institutions, the "GED" refers to Graduate Equivalency Diploma.

gender bias An attitude or predisposition, usually negative, about all males or all females. See also *sex discrimination* and *sex role stereotyping.*

gender dysphoria An aversion to the physical or social characteristics associated with one's own sex.

gender equity A fair and appropriately balanced distribution of resources and responsibilities between the sexes. In many nations and cultures, gender equity is unrealized in that vocational and educational opportunities are heavily weighted in favor of males. Gender inequities may be explicit, as a part of national policy, or implicit, as in the existence of the *"glass ceiling."* See also *Title IX.*

gender gap A nonspecific term referring to disparities between men and women in employment and promotion opportunities, pay, and sex-based discrimination.

gender identity The relative degree to which an individual patterns himself or herself after members of the same sex. See *sexual identity.* See also *sex roles.*

gender identity disorder A strong and persistent self-identification with members of the opposite sex and feelings of discomfort and denial about one's ascribed *sex role.* In gender identity disorders of childhood, children often "cross-dress" and may become convinced they will grow up to be members of the opposite sex. They tend to maintain their preoccupations with the stereotypical activities of the opposite sex despite pressure against this behavior from parents, peers, teachers, and professionals. In adults, *transsexualism* is the most common of these disorders.

gender roles The behaviors and personality characteristics that are attached, often inaccurately, to people because of their sex. For example, men often are expected to be more competitive and aggressive, and women often are expected to be more emotional and nurturing. These gender role distinctions are criticized by feminists and others, but many in society use them to define what is considered "socially appropriate" male and female behavior. Gender role is used, for example, in identifying the mental disorder called *gender identity disorder.*

gene pool The totality of genetic information within any species, people, or other biological group.

General Accounting Office (GAO), U.S. The independent federal agency within the legislative branch of government that assists the Congress in determining whether public funds are efficiently and economically administered and spent and in evaluating the results of existing government programs and activities. As such, GAO has general rights of access to and examination of any records of the federal departments and agencies for which Congress has allocated funds.

general assistance (GA) A residual or emergency *welfare* program operated under state and local auspices to provide means-tested financial and other aid to individuals who are ineligible for any *categorical program,* such as *social security; Old Age, Survivors, Disability,* and *Health Insurance (OASDHI); Aid to Families with Dependent Children (AFDC);* or *Supplemental Security Income (SSI).* Local departments of *public welfare* (also called departments of *human services* or *social services* in some counties) determine *eligibility* and help coordinate the distribution of these funds. See also *emergency basic-needs services.*

General Equivalency Diploma See *GED certificate.*

generalist A social work practitioner whose knowledge and skills encompass a broad spectrum and who assesses problems and their solutions comprehensively. The generalist often coordinates the efforts of specialists by facilitating communication between them, thereby fostering *continuity of care.* See also *generic social work.*

generalization 1. The process of forming an idea, judgment, or abstraction about a class of people, things, or events based on limited or particular experiences. 2. In *psy-*

chotherapy, an act or pattern of behavior in which an individual avoids discussing personal problems by characterizing them as being universal. For example, a client may say, "Every couple fights," to conceal current marital conflicts. 3. Generalizations are also used in social work practice to connect or clarify a client's experiences with others. For example, the social worker might say, "Everyone feels depressed at times."

generalization, behavioral In *behaviorism* or *social learning theory*, the tendency of a *response* to occur in the presence of a *stimulus* that is similar to one that was present when the response was learned.

generalized anxiety disorder One type of *anxiety neurosis* (or anxiety state). This disorder is characterized by such symptoms as *motor tension*, apprehension (fear and worry), autonomic hyperactivity (sweating, clammy hands, dizziness, light-headedness, upset stomach, flushing, and increased pulse and respiration rate), inability to concentrate, insomnia, irritability, and general impatience.

general medical condition The relative health and presence of one or more diseases in a client. The term is used by psychiatrists and other physicians in diagnosing mental disorders that are the direct result of specific organic and physiological disorders, for example, "dementia, due to (the general medical condition of) Parkinson's disease."

general practitioners Nonspecialist licensed *physicians*. In the United States, nearly all new physicians qualify in one of the 23 medical specialties. Primary care, or initial contact *health care,* is now provided by doctors who specialize in internal medicine or family practice. Other aspects of the general practitioner's role have been taken over by *registered nurses (RNs), physician's assistants (PAs), paramedics,* and other *allied health professionals.*

general systems theory A conceptual orientation that attempts to explain holistically the behavior of people and societies by identifying the interacting components of the system and the controls that keep these components *(subsystems)* stable and in a state of *equilibrium.* It is concerned with the *boundaries, roles, relationships,* and flow of information between people. General systems theory is a subset of *systems theories* that focuses on living entities, from microorganisms to societies. See also *ecological perspective* and *life model.*

general welfare clause Part of the U.S. Constitution, in Article I, Section 8, which authorizes Congress and the government to "provide for the common defense and general welfare of the United States." Social workers traditionally have cited this clause to justify improvements in the nation's welfare programs.

generational equity A fair and appropriately balanced distribution of resources and responsibilities between age groups. Where such equity does not exist, for example, younger people might be unfairly burdened with high taxes and future national indebtedness to provide a standard of living for older people that is higher than what they can expect when they become old. Conversely, in a "pay-as-you-go" economy, older people could be required to pay high taxes for the education and infrastructure used by the young without a commensurate assurance that their own economic needs will be met in their older years.

Generation X People born in the years 1962 to 1978, identified as unique because of the claim that although they are less well-prepared educationally to cope with future realities, they are expected to assume a disproportionate burden of repaying the national debt, to pay the social security entitlements for prior generations, and to deal with decaying infrastructure and international competition. The members of this generation are the children of the *baby boom generation.*

generativity An orientation and activity involving some contribution to the quality of life for future generations. According to *Eriksonian theory,* this orientation develops as a normal stage of life in healthy people and most commonly occurs toward the end of middle *adulthood.*

generativity versus stagnation According to the *psychosocial development theory* of Erik Erikson (1902–1994), the longest stage of a person's psychosocial development, occurring roughly from ages 24 to 54. In it, the individual tries to reconcile conflicts between egocentric desires and the need to contribute to the well-being of future generations. See also *Ericksonian theory.*

generic drug A medical compound that possesses no proprietary or brand name. The active ingredients of the drug are chemically identical to the brand name medicine but are less expensive because the consumer does not pay for advertising or promotion.

generic social work The social work orientation that emphasizes a common core of knowledge and skills associated with social service delivery. A generic social worker possesses basic knowledge that may span several *methods in social work.* Such a social worker would not necessarily be a specialist in a single *field of practice* or professional technique but would be capable of providing and managing a wider range of needed client services and intervening in a greater variety of systems.

generic–specific controversy A debate among social workers that has existed since at least the 1920s. One faction sees the profession as comprising a group of different *specialists,* each with a unique body of knowledge and highly refined professional skills that require considerable training and practice to master and that are applied to a specific and defined area of social welfare needs. The other faction sees professional social work as being made up of *generalists* who have a *macro orientation* and who can be useful by developing and integrating services and *channeling* people to them. The generalist faction also believes that social work skills are sufficiently similar from one specialty to another so that a social worker can be effective in a variety of settings. Since the 1929 *Milford Confer-*

ence was convened to attempt to resolve the controversy, most social workers have taken positions that fall somewhere between these extremes. See also *content-and-process issue.*

genetic counseling The specialty in medicine and related fields that helps people who have, or risk having, physical problems as a result of inherited defects. Such problems include *Down's syndrome, cystic fibrosis, diabetes, sickle-cell anemia, hemophilia,* and *Huntington's disease.* Counseling includes prevention of new problems by advising individuals about their reproductive risks and alternatives.

genetic disorder Diseases or dysfunctions that have resulted from defective genes, genomes (constellations of genes), or chromosomes. There are four categories of genetic disorder. First are the single-gene disorders in which a defective gene results in such diseases as *cystic fibrosis, sickle-cell anemia, Tay–Sachs disease, Huntington's disease, Marfan's syndrome, hemophilia,* neurofibromatosis, and Duchenne's *muscular dystrophy.* Second are the multifactorial inheritance disorders in which several genes and environmental factors interact to sometimes result in such disorders as *cleft palate, spina bifida,* congenital heart disease, and some cases of *mental retardation.* Third are the *chromosomal disorders,* resulting from the faulty structures or incorrect numbers of chromosomes, which can cause miscarriage, stillbirths, neonatal death, *congenital abnormalities,* and *Down's syndrome.* Fourth are environmentally induced genetic disorders in which factors potentially damaging to an embryo or fetus, such as alcohol, infections, drugs, tobacco, and some prescription medicines, harm fetal development.

genetic engineering The planned modification of genes or genetic material in living organisms to produce desirable traits and eliminate undesirable ones.

genital personality A descriptive term originating in *psychoanalytic theory* referring to one who is excessively preoccupied and concerned about *sexuality;* the term is also known as the *oedipal personality* or genital character. The individual is seen as having personality problems involving self-image, *sexual identity,* and *sexual orientation,* and sometimes a *paraphilia.* See also *anal personality* and *oral personality.*

genital stage   In *psychodynamic* theory, the last significant phase of psychosexual development, that begins with *puberty* and continues for several years thereafter. Sigmund Freud (1856–1939) postulated that, with the onset of adultlike sexual feelings, the individual has an opportunity to resolve the *Oedipus complex,* sever erotic attachments to parents of the opposite sex, and transfer sexual drives to peers of the opposite sex.

genius   A nonspecific lay term that refers to a person of one or more extremely superior traits, especially intellectually and creatively. Professionals are more likely to use somewhat more-specific descriptions of such persons. For example, educators sometimes describe such a child as gifted in a specific trait.

genocide   The systematic elimination of racial, religious, ethnic, or cultural groups, usually through mass extermination by the government of the nation in which they reside. See also *Holocaust* and *"ethnic cleansing."*

genogram   A diagram used in *family therapy* to depict family relationships extended over at least three generations. The diagram uses circles to represent females and squares for males, with horizontal lines indicating marriages. Vertical lines are drawn from the marriage lines to other circles and squares to depict the children. The diagram may contain other symbols or written explanations to indicate critical events, such as death, divorce, and remarriage, and to reveal recurrent patterns of behavior.

genophobia   The *fear* of sexual intercourse. The term preferred by professionals is *sexual aversion disorder.*

genotype   The inherited traits common to a biological group.

gentrification   The social phenomenon in which homes in formerly poor, overcrowded ghettos are purchased and privately rehabilitated by more-affluent families for their personal dwellings or for investment. This has the effect of raising the property values, rents, and property tax rates of all the homes in the neighborhood, forcing the removal of the remaining less-affluent people and their replacement by those who can afford to live there. The gentrified neighborhood may seem more desirable, but the people who are displaced have to crowd into other neighborhoods, and the resulting overcrowding causes those neighborhoods to decline. See also *urban homesteading* and *redlining.*

genuineness   Sincerity and honesty; one of the important qualities in developing an effective therapeutic *relationship.* Genuineness includes being unpretentious with clients, speaking honestly rather than only for effect, acknowledging one's limitations, and providing only sincere reassurances.

geragogics   The education and training of gerontologists and others who provide professional *health care* and *social services* to older people. This term is used mostly in Britain and Northern Europe. See also *gerontology* and *gerontological social work.*

geriatricians   Board-certified *physicians* who specialize in treating older people, especially *frail elderly* people with complex age-related medical problems.

geriatric mental status interview   A systematic procedure for assessing the possibility and type of mental deterioration in an older person. The procedure is nearly the same as in any other *mental status exam,* except that the interviewer tends to use shorter, more-frequent sessions, a more formal and gentle manner, and is careful to assure the older person about why such questions are being asked.

geriatrics   A branch of the medical profession that specializes in the prevention and treatment of diseases of old age. Physicians practicing geriatrics are known as *geriatricians.*

geriopharmacotherapy The prescription and administration of *medications* to prolong the physical and emotional health of older persons. This process includes monitoring, *counseling,* and educating the older person about health factors and the use of the medicine.

gerontological social work An orientation and specialization in social work concerned with the psychosocial treatment of older people—the development and management of needed social services and programs for older individuals.

gerontology The multidisciplinary study of the biological, psychological, and social aspects of aging.

gerontophobia *Fear* or loathing of older people.

Gerry, Elbridge Thomas (1837–1927) Founder of the *Societies for the Prevention of Cruelty to Children (SPCC)* in 1885. As a practicing lawyer, he worked in cases of *child abuse* and discovered the only laws and programs were those protecting animals. He modeled the society, also called "Gerry Societies," after the Society for the Prevention of Cruelty to Animals. Later he fought against national child protection laws and structures such as the U.S. *Children's Bureau,* saying that local controls and administrations would be more effective.

gerrymandering The creation of political boundaries of unusual or unnatural shape so that some groups are politically under- or overrepresented. For example, a city might divide its legislative districts so that residents of an inner-city *ghetto* are divided among five other districts, making them minorities in each new district.

gestalt psychology A group of theories that emphasizes the whole of an organism or environment rather than its parts and focuses on the interrelationships in mental perceptions. It is a school of psychology influenced by Kurt Lewin and Wolfgang Kohler in the 1920s and 1930s. Gestalt psychology has influenced, but is not synonymous with, *gestalt therapy.*

gestalt therapy A form of psychotherapeutic intervention developed and popularized by Frederick S. Perls and others in the 1960s. The approach seeks to help individuals integrate their thoughts, emotions, and behaviors and orient themselves more realistically toward their current perceptions and experiences. Emphasis is placed on becoming aware of and taking responsibility for one's own actions, on spontaneously expressing emotions and perception, and on recognizing the existence of gaps and distortions in one's own thinking.

gestation The period from *conception* to birth. For humans, the healthy gestation period is between 266 and 294 days, with 280 the average.

ghetto A geographic and usually poor section of a city, inhabited predominantly by *ethnic groups* or people of color. Usually, those who reside in such areas do not do so by choice. Ghettos originated in Spain in the late 14th century to segregate Jewish people, often behind guarded walls, to minimize their influence on Christian people. Ghettos for Jewish people continued to exist in various European cities until after World War II.

ghost sickness A *culture-bound syndrome* sometimes related to witchcraft, found most commonly among some Native American tribes whose individuals experience anxiety, hallucinations, loss of consciousness, feelings of futility, fainting, and sleep problems.

GI Bill The common name for the group of laws and programs starting in 1944 that provide educational, housing, insurance, medical, and vocational training opportunities for U.S. military veterans. These programs originated to help the veterans returning from World War II integrate into society and to upgrade the American *work force.*

GIDAANT *Gender identity disorder* of *adolescence* or *adulthood,* nontranssexual type.

Gideon v. Wainwright The 1963 U.S. Supreme Court ruling that all indigent defendants in criminal cases have the right to free legal counsel.

gifted child A child who possesses one or more talents, exceptional skills, or high *intelligence*. This designation has come to be preferred by parents of such children over the former designation, *exceptional children,* which also included children with disabilities or below-normal intellectual functioning.

Gilbert Act The 1782 English welfare reform laws that classified needy people into groups including the elderly, infirm, children, and the "idle." The legislation repealed the right of *overseers of the poor* to contract them out to private caretakers. Overseers were to find jobs for employable people or maintain them in the *community* rather than the *workhouse.*

Ginnie Mae See *Government National Mortgage Association (GNMA).*

Girls Clubs of America See *youth services organizations.*

"glasnost" The Russian term, roughly implying "openness" and "public relations." Government officials and social agency administrators in many nations increasingly use the term to describe their own organization's intent to be more candid and forthright about policies and activities.

"glass ceiling" A popular term referring to barriers to advancement in industry and government leadership positions that tend to restrict women and minorities. The term implies that the barrier cannot actually be seen and is not part of the organization's official policy but is manifested in women and minorities of equal or greater competence being passed over for promotions. See also *gender equity.*

glaucoma An eye disease in which fluid builds up between the cornea and the iris, and the resulting pressure on the eyeball injures certain nerve cells.

Global Assessment of Function (GAF) Scale A tool used by mental health professionals to rate the relative degree to which a client is able to function psychologically, socially, and occupationally, not due to physical or environmental limita-

tions. The practitioner rates the client's functioning on a rating scale with a continuum from 100 (superior functioning in a wide range of activities and no symptoms) to under 10 (persistent danger of severely hurting self or others or persistent inability to maintain minimal personal hygiene, or serious suicidal act with clear expectation of death). The GAF checklist was developed by L. Luborski ("Clinicians Judgments of Mental Health," *Archives of General Psychiatry,* 7[1962], pp. 407–417) and subsequently modified for use with the *DSM-IV.* It is used in the Axis V part of DSM-IV in completing a clinical *assessment.* See also *Global Assessment of Relational Functioning (GARF) Scale* and the *Defensive Functioning Scale.*

Global Assessment of Relational Functioning (GARF) Scale A 100-point scale in development by the American Psychiatric Association to assist in the clinician's evaluation of the degree to which a relational unit (such as a family or other ongoing relationship group) meets the affectional or instrumental needs of its members. Those relational units that function most satisfactorily (from self-reports and perspectives of observers) score highest (81–100), whereas those that become too dysfunctional to maintain attachment and contact score lowest (1–20).

GNMA See *Government National Mortgage Association (GNMA).*

GNP See *gross national product (GNP).*

goal-directed behavior Any activity that is directed toward conscious or explicitly defined objectives.

goal-setting A strategy used by social workers and other professionals to help clients clarify and define the objectives they hope to achieve in the helping relationship and then to establish the steps that must be taken and the time needed to reach those objectives. The community organizer–social worker uses goal-setting by helping key members of the target population or client community define their objectives and spell out the goals they want their people to achieve.

go-between role The process of *mediation* that occurs when a social worker or other professional intervenes between conflicting parties (such as husband and wife, parent and child, buyer and seller, landlord and tenant, or two members of a therapy group) and seeks to enhance mutual understanding and reduce tensions.

"goldbricking" A pejorative term indicating that an individual is only appearing to be working on a job but is actually loafing.

gold coast An affluent *neighborhood,* often where a city's most-influential families live.

gonorrhea One of the *sexually transmitted diseases (STDs)* that causes inflammation of the genitals and may eventually lead to sterility. The gonococcus organisms are highly vulnerable to most antibiotics. The disease was once a major cause of blindness among newborn children whose mothers were infected, but the routine use of silver nitrate solution in babies' eyes at birth has largely overcome the problem. See also *chlamydia.*

good-faith bargaining The requirement that both parties in a dispute, such as a couple or members of a family or community, discuss issues with open minds and make the possibility of discussion equal for all participants.

goodness of fit The degree of congruence between people's needs, capacities, and goals and the properties of their social and physical environments. See also *adaptation, ecological perspective,* and *life model.*

good works A term formerly used to describe activities to help disadvantaged people through *philanthropy, charity, volunteerism,* and personal examples of moral behavior. These activities were viewed by religious and political leaders and social philosophers as moral obligations to God and society, a view that motivated many of the social welfare activities that preceded government-funded welfare programs.

go-round The procedure used in some social work groups in which each member is specifically asked, in turn, to discuss a particular topic or respond to a specific stimulus. Often the go-round is a structured exercise or technique aimed at helping members get acquainted and keep oriented to one another. It is also used to get a group started or establish the topics for the session's agenda. See also *check-in.*

government The established institutions and formal processes by which a society or organized group determines, implements, administers, and evaluates its decisions.

Government National Mortgage Association (GNMA) An agency of the U.S. *Department of Housing and Urban Development (HUD)* that finances or ensures financing for the purchase of low-cost housing or of homes in areas where conventional loans are difficult to obtain. Mortgages issued by the association are informally known as "Ginnie Maes."

grace period A time after a decision or agreement is reached and before its terms must be implemented.

graduated tax See *progressive tax.*

Graduate Equivalency Diploma See *GED certificate.*

graft Misappropriation of public money by one or more public officials.

Gramm–Rudman–Hollings Act The budget reduction legislation (Balanced Budget and Emergency Deficit Control Act of 1985, P.L. 101-508) requiring progressively lower deficits in the federal budget in each fiscal year from 1986 through 1991. The act's deficit-lowering goals were not reached.

grandiose-type delusional disorder A subtype of *delusional disorder* characterized by nonbizarre delusions, particularly an exaggerated sense of self-importance and the conviction of having some great mission, talent, insight, or potential.

grandiosity An exaggerated sense of self-importance; in its more extreme forms, it is equivalent to *delusions of grandeur.*

grand jury A group of citizens selected by the justice system of a jurisdiction to decide together whether there is enough evidence to justify accusing a person of a *crime* (which would result in a trial before a *petit jury*). Most grand juries have 23 members.

grand larceny *Larceny* that involves property valued in excess of a certain amount. Each jurisdiction legislates the cutoff amount at which a larceny becomes grand larceny (in most U.S. states it is between $50 and $500).

grandparenting clause Also known as a "grandfather clause," an exemption to a new agreement, rule, or requirement so that those who were already engaged in the relevant activity before a certain time need not fulfill the new requirements. For example, social workers who were members of the *National Association of Social Workers (NASW)* and who met certain practice and supervision requirements before 1973 could become members of the *Academy of Certified Social Workers (ACSW)* without having to pass the qualifying examination that was required of later applicants. See also *recertification.*

Granger, Lester (1896–1976) Social and *civil rights* activist and proponent of equal opportunity for *African Americans,* he was a long-time leader of the *National Urban League;* he also helped the U.S. Armed Forces become racially integrated and served as president of national and international social work organizations.

granny flats The informal name for *ECHO housing,* they are temporary, mobile-home–style living units for one or two people usually installed on the grounds of their offspring and connected to the utilities of the main house. These facilities are designed to give older people privacy and security while enabling them to be close to their children or others who care about them.

grant A transfer of funds or assets from one government, organization, or individual to another for fulfilling some broadly specified function or purpose (usually to enhance knowledge or otherwise provide for the well-being of people and their cultural institutions). See also *block grant* and *categorical grant.*

grants-in-aid Payments made by one organization, such as a government agency, to another to achieve a specified purpose. For example, the federal government might grant payments to states or states might make such payments to cities to help fund and ensure the existence of the local organization's *public assistance* programs. See also *block grant.*

grantsmanship In social administration, the ability to develop proposals for special project funding. The ability includes skills in research design, verbal communication, sales, writing, needs assessment, innovation of new techniques for problem solving, coordination of plans, and political and administrative activity, as well as knowledge about the appropriate sources of project funds.

grass roots The public, especially the voters, and those who provide the basic support for a political movement or social cause. See also *political activism.*

grass-roots organizing The *community organization* strategy of helping at the local level the members of a neighborhood or geographic region to develop stronger relationships, common goals, and an organization that will help them achieve those goals. The focus is on organizing the people who will be affected by change, rather than on organizing only the community leaders. This involves educating and mobilizing people for action toward agreed-on goals. See also *political activism.*

gray ghettos 1. *Neighborhoods* or housing projects, often in older, decaying areas of inner cities, whose residents are primarily poor and *elderly.* 2. Private retirement villages and communities zoned for the exclusive use of people older than a certain age.

gray-market adoption The *adoption* of dependent children outside the legitimate social agencies and legal institutions. Such adoptions are often arranged by physicians, lawyers, or other professionals who personally know the couples who seek to adopt and the birth mothers who choose to give up their children for adoption. See also *private adoption.*

Gray Panthers An intergenerational advocacy group founded by Maggie Kuhn in 1970 to work on behalf of the social and economic needs of elderly people. The group's major focus is on state and national legislation affecting older people and on issues affecting all ages. It also acts as watchdog in implementing legislation.

Great Depression The severe and extended economic crisis that occurred in the United States and many other nations during the 1930s, ending with reindustrialization in preparation for World War II. In 1933, 16 million people were unemployed (nearly one-third of the U.S. *work force*). Largely in response to the resulting hardship, President Franklin D. Roosevelt's administration established the *New Deal* programs, which redefined the role of the federal government in helping individuals and assuring the general welfare.

Great Society The name given by President Lyndon B. Johnson to *social welfare* goals and programs established as a *War on Poverty* during his administration. Some of these efforts included the *Model Cities program, Head Start,* the *Office of Economic Opportunity (OEO), Medicaid,* and *Medicare.*

green card The name commonly used for the registration card issued by the U.S. government that identifies the holder as a permanent U.S. resident who is a citizen of another nation. The card (no longer green), which is issued by the U.S. *Immigration and Naturalization Service (INS),* is officially U.S. Government Form 1-551, *"Alien Registration Recipient."*

greenhouse effect The heating of the *environment* as a result of the burning of fossil fuels (such as coal and oil). Burning these fuels results in an atmospheric gain in carbon dioxide molecules. The excess carbon dioxide in the atmosphere does not prevent the sun's rays from reaching the earth's surface but prevents the escape of heat radiating from the ground. Some scientists believe that unless there is a drastic reduction in the use of fossil fuels the earth's weather and heat level is likely to increase by five degrees in the next 30 to 100 years, an increase that could significantly change the earth's climatic patterns.

greenlining A tactic used by community organizers in which residents of a neighborhood are mobilized to withdraw their funds from banks that are not equal opportunity lenders or that practice *redlining.* See also *Equal Credit Opportunity Act (ECOA).*

Greenpeace An international *social activist* organization devoted to preserving the *environment* and wildlife habitats through education, lobbying, political campaigning, and overt obstruction of those activities that it considers environmentally destructive.

green politics A *social movement* initially concerned with pursuing environmental goals through political action. Its major goal is protecting the *environment* and enhancing its declining mechanisms, as well as fighting organizations whose actions and products are considered harmful to the environment. This ideology has led to formation of several political parties, especially in Germany, Italy, France, United Kingdom, Belgium, and New Zealand.

green revolution The movement throughout the world to increase food production, especially in *developing countries,* by using high-yield hybrid seeds, plants that are resistant to destruction, crop rotations, fertilizers, and biotechnology.

gregariousness A tendency to be with and interact with other people.

"greystocking" A term applied, somewhat derisively, to social workers and other helping professionals and volunteers in Great Britain and some other English-speaking nations. The term was originally applied to welfare investigators who supposedly made unexpected visits to the homes of welfare recipients, but were usually identified by their neighbors in advance because of their predictable attire. The most similar term in the United States has been *"lady bountiful."*

grief Intense and acute sorrow resulting from *loss*. It has many of the same symptoms as physical or mental illness, although it tends to diminish with time. However, like all illnesses, grief can end in complete or partial recovery.

grief reaction Experiencing deep sadness as the result of an important *loss*. This emotional response is normal and in healthy people will gradually subside in a limited time.

grief work A series of emotional stages or phases following an important *loss*, which gradually permit adjustment and recovery. The individual typically reminisces, expresses emotions, accepts, adjusts to the new situation, and forms new relationships.

grievance A formal complaint about some procedure or regulation that is not being followed and that has resulted in some harm to the complainant.

grievance committee A formal group established to evaluate whether an organization's policies and activities have resulted in harm to a complainant, to recommend changes in the policy or activity that has been deemed harmful, and to recommend ways to make amends for those harmed. Grievance committees usually comprise members of the organization.

grippe Influenza, or sometimes colds. The term is used by older people and people from nations in the former British commonwealth.

Griscom, John (1774–1852) Founder in 1817 and long-time leader of the Society for the Prevention of Pauperism, the most influential of the early efforts to understand, resolve, and prevent problems of poverty.

gross motor skills The ability to cause effective movement of the body's large muscle groups.

gross national product (GNP) The total value of a nation's annual output of services and goods.

group A collection of people, brought together by mutual interests, who are capable of consistent and uniform action. Major types of groups include the *primary group* and the *secondary group*.

"group balance" A term used in *social group work* or by group therapists for achieving the optimal mix of group members to achieve the group's goals. For example, if the group consists of so many socially withdrawn people that its norm is silence, more outgoing members are added to give it better balance.

group climate The social–emotional atmosphere of a group, also called the "group mood." Group leaders often describe the group in terms of its climate: angry, depressed, celebrative, serious, flighty, suspicious, caring, and so forth. Leaders often try to influence climate or use it to influence individual members in desirable ways. The group achieves its climate when the attitudes, ideas, and feelings of one or more members of the group become those of the other members by their association. See also *reciprocal interactions*.

group cohesiveness The degree of mutual attraction or reciprocal benefit experienced or anticipated by individuals in relation to a social collective with which they identify. See also *reciprocal interactions*.

group contagion The process of association and interconnectedness among members of a group that leads to the *group climate* or group mood. See also *reciprocal interactions*.

group development Changes through time in a group's internal structures, norms, processes, and culture.

group development phases In *social group work*, the stages through which the group grows in its normal life cycle. Various group work theorists have identified five phases: (1) the *preaffiliation phase*, (2) the *power-and-control phase*, (3) the *intimacy phase*, (4) the *differentiation phase*, and (5) the *separation phase*.

group dynamics The flow of information and shifts of power influence among members of a social collective. These exchanges can be modified by group leaders or helping professionals and used to achieve certain predetermined objectives that may benefit the members.

group eligibility Being qualified for benefits or obligations as the result of membership in some association or occupation of a defined social *status*. For example, everyone who reaches a certain age may become qualified for specified social insurance benefits.

Group for the Advancement of Doctoral Education in Social Work (GADE) The association of social work educators in the nation's *doctoral programs*. These educators began meeting in 1974 to synchronize their efforts to coordinate and standardize doctoral requirements. The organization became official in 1977, and its members now have annual meetings, conduct workshops, and prepare materials to assist doctoral programs in schools of social work.

group goals model A concept about different types of group work and therapy groups based on the overall objectives of the group. The delineation was originated by Catherine Papell and Beulah Rothman ("Social Group Work Models: Possession and Heritage," *Journal of Education for Social Work*, 1966, pp. 66–77) and emphasized three major types: *social goals model, remedial goals model*, and *reciprocal goals model*.

group health insurance A plan for insuring against the cost of illness all members and dependents of an established group who want to enroll (for example, all employees of a company, all government workers, all members of the *National Association of Social Workers [NASW]*).

group identity The degree to which an individual affiliates with, feels part of, and emulates the characteristics of a social collective.

group leader An individual who facilitates group processes. The leader can be an indigenous member (for example, one of the students in a class) who, through charisma, skill, or other attributes, influences the others. The leader also can be external (for example, a group therapist) whose position or expertise usually results in some influence over the group. Each group has a leader (whether or not the group recognizes it as such), but the leader may change from one meeting to the next or from one minute to the next.

group leadership roles Activities that an indigenous or professional *group leader* uses to accomplish the group's goals include giving and seeking information and opinions, proposing tasks and goals, summarizing, coordinating, diagnosing, energizing, testing reality, and evaluating whether goals have been accomplished. Activities that leaders use to maintain the group's social and emotional bonds include encouraging participation, compromising, relieving tension, helping members communicate, setting standards, listening actively, and building a climate of trust for others to emulate.

group psychotherapy A form of *psychotherapy* that treats individuals simultaneously for emotional and behavioral disorders by emphasizing interactions and mutuality. Most professionals consider the term to be synonymous with *group therapy*. Some writers, however, make a distinction between *group psychotherapy, group therapy,* and *social group work*; they consider group psychotherapy to be only one type of group therapy. Whereas group psychotherapy uses group treatment techniques to help individuals resolve emotional problems, group therapy uses a wider range of intervention strategies to help individuals deal with both social maladjustment and emotional disorders. Social group work, although sharing some of these objectives and techniques, is not limited to treating disorders and problems but includes education support groups and positive group experiences that help healthy individuals achieve greater personal fulfillment and change conditions in the environment and society.

group, structured   A purposeful bringing together of clients, who meet some predetermined criteria, for *social group work* or *group therapy* membership. Because effectiveness is achieved largely by the characteristics each member brings to the group, the social worker or therapist may seek the right balance or structure. For example, the structured group might include at least one outgoing and talkative person, one who is quiet, one who is tense, and one who is relaxed. The opposite of a structured group is not an *open group* but a *blanket group*.

group support systems   Computer-based technologies designed to assist groups that are convened to accomplish specific tasks. For example, the group support system known as "electronic brainstorming" asks the group participants to interact in idea formation and development, using integrated computers and programs that often hasten the process and give equal credence to those who may be reluctant to discuss ideas or suggestions in face-to-face encounters.

group therapy   An *intervention* strategy for helping individuals who have emotional disorders or social maladjustment problems by bringing together two or more individuals under the direction of a social worker or other professional therapist. The individuals are asked to share their problems with other members of the group, discuss ways to resolve their problems, exchange information and views about resources and techniques for solving the problem, and share emotional experiences in a controlled (by the professional) setting that enables the members to work through their difficulties. A typical format in group therapy is to have six to eight members meet with a professional therapist in a facility provided by the therapist for 90 minutes once each week. Among the many variations of group therapy are *closed group* and *open group*. Group therapy is a format used by practitioners of many orientations, including *behaviorism, transactional analysis (TA),* *family therapy, gestalt therapy,* and *psychoanalysis.* See also *sensitivity group* and *marathon group.*

group, transitional   See *transitional group.*

group-type conduct disorder   One of the three types of *conduct disorder,* in which the maladaptive behavior occurs as part of a gang or group of peers. The other types are *solitary aggressive–conduct disorder* and "undifferentiated type."

group work   See *social group work.*

GROW mutual help group   A *mutual help* organization founded in Australia in 1957, now with thousands of groups throughout the world to provide reciprocal support for people who have shared the experience of emotional or *mental disorder.* In communities where it exists, it is a vital part of the mental health care system and usually maintains 24-hour support, long-term availability, regular group meetings, and social activities. See also *support system.*

guaranteed annual income   A proposal made by some social policy experts to eliminate the *means test.* Rather than evaluate each person's resources and needs as the basis for assistance, every individual or family would receive a specified amount of money or service each year from the relevant government agency, regardless of need. See also *negative income tax.*

guardian   A person (or entity) who has the legal responsibility for the care and management of another person, usually a child or an adult who has been declared in court to be incapable of acting for himself or herself.

guardian ad litem   A court-appointed representative designated to preserve and manage the affairs and property of another person who is considered incapable of managing his or her own affairs in the course of *litigation.* The guardian ad litem has no permanent control over the person's property and is considered an officer of the court.

guerrilla warfare   Military operations within an area controlled by the opposition, often in the form of surprise raids and harassment of the people and facilities protected by the controlling force. The strategy is to patiently wear down the ruler force and replace it after it has lost its power to rule. "Guerrilla" is a Spanish term for "small war."

guidance counselor A professional who is knowledgeable and skilled in delineating alternatives, articulating goals, providing information and advice, and facilitating client self-awareness. Guidance counselors are frequently employed in educational institutions and personnel offices of business organizations to provide guidance in vocation opportunities, work and study habits, and problem resolution.

guilt An emotional reaction to the perception of having done something wrong, having failed to do something, or violating important social *norms*. The reaction is often a loss of *self-esteem* and a desire to make *restitution*. In *psychodynamic* theory, this reaction can be *unconscious* and be based not on any actual wrongdoing but on concealed drives and motives that are contrary to the prohibitions established by the *superego*.

Gulf War syndrome A series of symptoms, including vision loss, headaches, skin rashes, and joint pain, found in a significant number of soldiers who served in the Kuwait–Iraq military action in 1990–1991.

gun control Laws and other efforts by governments and citizens to regulate the acquisition and use of firearms. Most nations have stringent gun controls that make it difficult to possess firearms; firearm use for those who get permission is strictly monitored. The United States is an exception. The Second Amendment of the U.S. Constitution states, "A well-regulated militia, being necessary to the security of a free state, the right of the people to keep and bear arms, shall not be infringed." Although gun control advocates interpret this amendment to refer to the military, opponents say the amendment gives citizens the right to possess and carry guns with only limited, if any, controls. See also *Brady Bill*.

gustatory hallucination An imagined perception of taste; tasting something that does not exist outside subjective experience.

gynecology The branch of medicine specializing in female reproductive health.

H

habeas corpus A court requirement that the custodian of a prisoner (or otherwise institutionalized individual) bring the person before the judge. The court may then determine whether the party is being held in violation of his or her constitutional rights to *due process of law*. See also *Fifth Amendment rights*.

habilitation A practice orientation of the social worker that views the client as a competent and coequal problem solver who is empowered through education, newly developed *coping skills*, and resources. This view is in contrast to the *rehabilitation* orientation in which the social worker sees clients as dysfunctional or dependent recipients of treatment.

habituation 1. A type of *adaptation* in which an individual has learned to eliminate responses to repeated and distracting stimuli. For example, an abused child might appear to become indifferent to continued physical punishment. 2. Some social workers and other professionals also use the term to refer to a form of *drug dependence* in which the individual has more of a psychological craving than a physical addiction (manifested by *withdrawal symptoms*).

halfway houses Transitional residences for individuals who require some professional *supervision*, support, or protection but not full-time institutionalization. Such facilities are used primarily by formerly hospitalized mental patients and those under *parole* or who have problems with *alcohol dependence* and *drug dependence*. Other transitional residences are *quarterway houses* and three-quarterway houses, which offer more or fewer services, according to need.

hallucination An imagined *perception* of some object or phenomenon that is not really present. Often a symptom of a *psychosis*, it may involve hearing nonexistent voices *(auditory hallucination)*, seeing objects that are not there *(visual hallucination)*, smelling *(olfactory hallucination)*, tasting *(gustatory hallucination)*, and touching *(haptic hallucination)*.

hallucinogen A drug or chemical that when ingested results in *hallucination*. Examples are *LSD* and *mescaline*.

hallucinogen abuse Ingestion, usually orally, of an *illicit drug* that is known to result in *hallucination*. Such drugs include *LSD* (lysergic acid diethylamine, dimethyltryptamine (DMT), and *mescaline*. The resulting *hallucinosis* is accompanied by other symptoms such as intensification of *perceptions; depersonalization;* and sometimes *tremor, tachycardia*, sweating, blurred vision, and poor coordination.

hallucinogen affective disorder A depressive or manic mood disturbance and accompanying recurrent hallucinations, all occurring as a result of *hallucinogen abuse* but lasting longer than the period of direct effect.

hallucinogen persisting-perception disorder A substance-related disorder characterized by a *flashback* reminiscent of the experiences (hallucinations) during earlier *intoxication* by a *hallucinogen*.

hallucinosis Disorders characterized by *hallucination* either resulting from a *substance abuse*, psychotic disorder, or *general medical condition*.

halo effect   The tendency to evaluate individuals either too favorably or too negatively on the basis of one or a few notable traits. See also *devaluation* and *idealization.*

Hamilton, Gordon (1892–1967)   Social work educator and writer who advanced *social casework* in the profession. As an educator, she helped develop doctoral training in social work, and as a writer, she produced the classic social work text *Theory and Practice of Social Casework* (1940, revised in 1951), used by countless social work students. She was also the first editor of the journal *Social Work.*

handicap   A physical or mental disadvantage that prevents or limits an individual's ability to function as others do.

handicapism   Prejudicial behavior that promotes unequal or unjust treatment of people because of apparent or assumed physical or mental disability; a synonym for *able-ism.* The behavior most commonly occurs in speech ("he's a moron . . . a spastic"), behavior (avoiding contact with a disabled person), and policies (unequal access to facilities).

Handicapped Children Act of 1975   See *Education for All Handicapped Children Act of 1975.* See also *Education of the Handicapped Act Amendments of 1986* and *Education of the Handicapped Act Amendments of 1990.*

hangover   Physical aftereffects of consuming alcohol or other drugs, which often lead to such temporary symptoms as nausea, *tremor,* headache, dry mouth, *anxiety,* and *depression.* The symptoms of hangover are similar to but less severe than *alcohol withdrawal.*

haptic hallucination   An imagined perception of touching something or being touched by something that does not exist outside of subjective experience.

harassment   See *sexual harassment.*

harboring a fugitive   The illegal practice of concealing someone wanted by law enforcement authorities or providing a refuge or shelter for one who should be in police custody.

hard-core unemployment   The lack of job availability, even when ample *employment* opportunities exist, for those people who lack appropriate education or social skills or have a physical or *mental disorder.*

"hard sciences"   The name sometimes attached to empirically based bodies of knowledge, including such natural sciences as biology, chemistry, and physics. This is contrasted to what are called the *"soft sciences,"* including such social sciences as economics, psychology, and sociology. *Social work* is usually placed in the "soft science" category as an applied social science.

hard-to-reach clients   Individuals, families, and communities who need and are eligible for professional assistance and social work *intervention* but who are unaware of, unmotivated for, or fearful of the service offered.

hardware   In computer technology, the physical machinery—including the computer, keyboard, monitor, modem, and other equipment—designed for entering, storing, processing, analyzing, and transmitting data. See also *software.*

Hart, Hastings Hornell (1851–1932)   Prison reformer and leader of the child-saving movement, Hart helped develop the *juvenile court* system, championed defendant's rights, and established the federal parole system. He criticized then-current efforts to place out orphaned children as being too unsupervised to protect them. For many years he was consultant on child help, delinquency, and penology to the *Russell Sage Foundation.*

Hartley, Robert M. (1796–1881)   Founder of the Association for Improving the Condition of the Poor in 1843 and its long-time leader, Hartley believed the major causes of *poverty* were intemperance, improvidence, and extravagance and worked to correct these characteristics in individuals. His advocacy resulted in laws requiring school attendance and parental responsibility. He divided cities into sections and got volunteers to visit poor families within these neighborhoods.

hashish A resin produced in the tops of *marijuana* plants, which contains the most powerful concentration of tetrahydrocannabinol *(THC)*, the active ingredient in *marijuana.*

hate crime The illegal acts motivated by the wish to harm groups or individuals whose affiliations, values, or actions are intolerable to the perpetrator. Such crimes include vandalizing synagogues or black churches, killing physicians who administer abortions, and terrorizing or intimidating people who want to speak out on a certain political issue. See also *ethnoviolence.*

Hawthorne effect The phenomenon that often occurs in *social research* in which subjects behave differently from their norm because of their awareness of being observed. For example, a social worker who observes the interactions of the members of a psychiatric ward may not be seeing the same behaviors that occur when the ward is not being observed.

Haynes, George E. (1880–1960) Cofounder, with Ruth Standish Baldwin, of the *National Urban League,* Haynes was the first black graduate of the New York School of Philanthropy and was an authority on the effects of migration on *black people.*

hazardous substances Manufactured materials or their residue (or some products of nature) that can lead an exposed person to immediate or gradual illness or death. These substances are often associated with cancer, brain damage, respiratory diseases, birth defects, and reproductive damage. Exposure is usually through air or drinking water. Most toxic dumps are near population centers and directly above groundwater supplies. Exposure to some of these substances occurs in homes where asbestos, lead, and radon (a natural radioactive gas) are often found.

HCFA See *Health Care Financing Administration (HCFA).*

head injury A *trauma* that temporarily or permanently damages tissue in or near the cranium, possibly resulting in brain or nerve damage. Internal head injury may affect some cognitive or motor functions or result in some *functional impairment,* even though there may be no overt symptom of damage. Many victims of even severe head injuries can be treated by physicians and health care and social services personnel and can achieve virtually full return to healthy functioning.

head lice Skin parasites found in the scalp hair, especially among school-age children, and spread by direct contact and sharing combs, hats, pillows, and so forth. The tiny lice and lice eggs may be seen attached to hairs, and the major symptom is severe itching. Although the condition is mostly associated with children from poor and unhygienic environments, it is also seen in children from affluent families. Lice infestations are called "pediculosis." The disease *typhus* is transmitted by lice to humans.

"headshrinker" A slang expression applied to *psychiatrists, psychologists,* and clinical *social workers* who seek to develop insight and to bring about behavioral changes in their clients.

head of household A family member or other resident of a dwelling unit who is regarded by the other residents and relevant outsiders as the arbiter and ultimate decision maker for those belonging to the group. Usually, but not always, this person is the household's primary income producer or money manager.

Head Start The *Great Society* program established by the federal government in 1965 to provide preschool children of disadvantaged minority families with compensatory education to offset some of the effects of their social deprivation. *Project Follow Through* was established in 1967 to help children from low-income families receive additional compensatory education through the elementary years. See also *Upstream Head Start program* and *Migrant Head Start program.*

head tax   See *poll tax.*

health   According to the *World Health Organization (WHO),* not merely the absence of disease or infirmity, but the state of complete physical, mental, and social well-being.

Health and Human Services, U.S. Department of   See *Department of Health and Human Services, U.S. (HHS).*

health care   Activities designed to treat, prevent, and detect physical and mental disorders and to enhance people's physical and psychosocial well-being. The health care system includes personnel who provide the needed services (physicians, nurses, hospital attendants, medical social workers, and so on); facilities where such services are rendered (hospitals, medical centers, *nursing homes, hospices, outpatient* clinics); laboratories and institutions for detection, research, and planning; educational and environmental facilities that help people prevent disease; and myriad other organizations and people involved in helping people to become more healthy, stay healthy, return to health, or minimize the consequences of ill health.

health care facility   Organizations and structures in which the detection and treatment of physical and mental disorders take place, including hospitals, medical centers, *nursing homes, outpatient* clinics, and *hospice* centers.

Health Care Financing Administration (HCFA)   The organization within the U.S. *Department of Health and Human Services (HHS)* that assesses the nation's health care programs and their financing and oversees *Medicare* in cooperation with the *Social Security Administration (SSA)* and *Medicaid* in cooperation with state departments of *public assistance.* HCFA sets the standards that hospitals, skilled-nursing facilities, and hospices must meet to be certified to provide *Medicare* services.

health care workers   The generic name for all the professional, paraprofessional, technical, and general employees of a system or facility that provides for the diagnosis, treatment, and overall well-being of patients. Informally, this designation is more commonly used when referring to nonprofessional hospital staff. When referring to professionals other than physicians and nurses in such settings, the term most commonly used is *allied health professionals* or allied health workers. Those included in this designation are home health aides, medical records personnel, nurses aides, orderlies, and attendants.

Health, Education, and Welfare, U.S. Department of   See *Department of Health, Education, and Welfare, U.S. (HEW).*

health maintenance organization (HMO)   A comprehensive health care program and medical group that offers services for a fixed annual fee. In this alternative to the fee-for-service model, enrollees voluntarily prepay for their medical and health care, including treatment and prevention of physical and mental illness. HMOs usually have their own medical care facilities, staffed by physicians of all specialties as well as social workers and other health care providers. See also *managed health care program* and *independent practice associations (IPAs).*

health planning   Rational efforts to assure that people's physical care and mental health care needs are being met and that available health care resources are used as effectively as possible toward this end. Health planning is conducted in government organizations, private medical and research organizations, and educational institutions. It includes prevention and early-detection activities as well as treatment and follow-up care. Health planning also involves decision making about such matters as how many health care personnel will be needed in the future, how to finance and control health care costs, where to locate medical facilities, and what methods are most effective and cost-effective. It also involves environmental considerations such as proper sewage treatment, air quality, and the provision of nutritious food.

Health Resources Administration (HRA) The organization within the U.S. *Public Health Service* whose mission is to maintain and improve the utilization, quality, and cost-effectiveness of the nation's health care system. HRA helps fund the training of health care personnel, facilitates the appropriate distribution of health resources and personnel, stimulates the construction of needed health care facilities, and identifies anticipated health resource problems.

Health Services Administration (HSA) The organization within the U.S. *Public Health Service* that helps local communities find effective ways of meeting their present and future health needs. HSA provides health professionals to areas designated as having critical shortages of such personnel.

Hearn, Gordon (1914–1979) Social work educator and theoretician, Hearn developed theories about *social group work* and *general systems theory* into social work thought. He wrote *Theory Building in Social Work* in 1958.

hearsay evidence Statements made by witnesses in courts of law based not on their direct observation but on what they have heard others say. When social workers or other professionals testify as expert witnesses, they are sometimes challenged about the conclusions they have reached on the basis that it is hearsay.

heart attack Partial failure of the pumping action of the heart. Generally, an event in which the blood vessels that feed the heart become blocked and the heart muscle does not receive enough blood. Symptoms usually include severe chest pains, sweating, hot flashes, and nausea; moreover, permanent damage to the heart may occur. See also *myocardial infarction*.

heart disease A term for any of a variety of disorders affecting the heart muscle, adjacent tissue, and the circulatory system. Heart disease is the leading cause of death among men older than age 40. Those with increased risk include smokers, people with *diabetes*, people with high blood pressure, and individuals with high serum cholesterol.

hebephrenic schizophrenia A type of *psychosis* characterized by wild excitement, giggling, silly behavior, and rapid *mood* shifts. This disorder is known as "schizophrenia, disorganized type" in current diagnoses. See also *disorganized schizophrenia*.

hedonistic behavior Pleasure-seeking activity without much concern about the accompanying responsibilities or consequences.

helping network A *linkage* comprising various combinations of individuals, groups, families, organizations, government offices, or social agencies and so forth, all of which work together or autonomously to provide a person with the supports, resources, information, and access that is required for problem solving or meeting a need. Helping networks differ from *social networks* in that they are linked only with respect to the help they seek to provide, whereas social networks have far more bases for their existence. One form of helping network is the *natural helping network*. See also *collaboration*.

helplessness, learned See *learned helplessness*.

help line A telephone-based social service to provide contact between people in need of assistance and professionals or volunteers who provide encouragement and access to necessary services. Trained listeners are immediately available for callers, especially those at risk of *suicide* and *family violence* and *runaways* and those seeking information about how to get needed services. The term is often used interchangeably with *hot line*, although the latter may also emphasize communications such as *whistle blowing*, where the caller is not seeking help but providing information. See also *Nineline*.

help-rejecting complaining A pattern of complaining and appeals for help followed by explanations about why the offer of assistance was deficient. One who engages in this behavior is often dealing with emotional conflicts and seeks help to disguise unconscious feelings of hostility and self-pity. The pattern is often seen in *hypochondriasis* and *narcissistic personality disorder.*

hematophobia   The pathological *fear of* blood.

hemodialysis   The medical process of purifying the blood of patients who have had kidney failure. This process involves a machine through which the body's blood circulates past a semipermeable membrane. Waste products in the blood are absorbed through the membrane and discarded.

hemophilia   A *genetic disease* in which the blood has insufficient capacity for rapid clotting, often resulting in excessive bleeding when injuries occur.

Henrician Poor Law   The English legislation, enacted in 1536 during the reign of King Henry VIII, whose primary purpose was to organize the ways the nation would deal with its "able-bodied" poor population. Officially named "The Act for the Punishment of Sturdy Vagabonds and Beggars," it placed responsibility for the care of the poor with local officials who could collect taxes for the purpose. The officials furnished work for unemployed people and restricted begging to people with disabilities. Penalties for begging by the able-bodied included branding; enslavement; removal of their children; and for repeated offenses, execution.

hepatitis   A viral disease resulting in swelling and inflammation of the liver. Symptoms include nausea, fever, weakness, loss of appetite, and often jaundice. Treatment involves extensive bed rest and controlled diet. The virus is spread by contact with contaminated food or water (infectious hepatitis), injections of contaminated blood, or the use of contaminated needles (serum hepatitis). It also sometimes occurs as a complication of other diseases, such as *cirrhosis* of the liver, *mononucleosis*, and *dysentery.*

heredity   1. The transmission of characteristics from parents to offspring through chromosomes that bear the genes. 2. The tendency of an individual to manifest the traits of his or her progenitors. See also *chromosomal disorders* and *genetic disorder.*

heroin   A potent narcotic synthesized from *morphine.* It can be snorted or injected under the skin or into a vein *("mainlining").* Its effect on the user is *euphoria* or apathy, and for some, a "rush"—a sensation described as similar to an orgasm throughout the entire body. Once addicted, the user also seeks further doses to avoid the intensely discomforting experience of *withdrawal symptoms.* Heroin is highly addictive and, partly because of its high cost and nonexistent quality control, contributes to an increased death rate and to higher incidence of organized and street crime. Heroin use is illegal in most nations. See also *opioid abuse* and *methadone treatment.*

herpes   A viral infection resulting in blisterlike eruptions. Herpes simplex takes the form of recurring blisters filled with clear fluid, known as cold sores when they appear around the lips and as canker sores when in the mouth. Herpes genitalis is a viral infection in the genital area. Herpes zoster, also called shingles, is a painful viral infection of the nerves, most commonly appearing on the chest–abdomen area and sometimes following other nerve pathways.

heterogeneous   Possessing dissimilar traits.

heterogeneous groups   Groups whose memberships comprise people with different traits, such as a wide age range, different ethnic backgrounds, and divergent political orientations. Some group leaders who hold the *dissonance theory of groups* seek to have a disparate membership as a catalyst for more dynamic interactions. See also *homogeneous groups.*

heterosexism   Institutional and sociocultural arrangements that discriminate against people who are *homosexual.* These arrangements may be actively discriminatory, as in military regulations against homosexuals or court decisions about *lesbian* mothers and child custody. Or it may occur through omission of equal rights, such as the lack of marriage and inheritance rights for homosexual partners. Heterosexism is the equivalent in society to *homophobia* in individuals.

heterosexuality   Association with and orientation toward sexual activity with members of the opposite sex.

heterostasis   The tendency of a system or organism to become unstable.

HEW   See *Department of Health, Education, and Welfare, U.S. (HEW).*

HHS   See *Department of Health and Human Services, U.S. (HHS).*

hidden agenda   The underlying goals, expectations, and strategies of members within a group, as opposed to the overt purposes of the meeting.

hidden inflation   An economic situation in which costs for products or services apparently remain constant while the quality or quantity declines. For example, the price for a box of cereal stays the same, but the manufacturer puts less in each box.

hierarchy of needs   The view developed in 1954 by Abraham Maslow and other professionals with a *humanistic orientation* that people's needs occur in ascending order. One fulfills physiological needs first, followed by needs for safety, belonging, self-respect and self-worth, and finally *self-actualization* or achieving one's full potential. See also *motivation.*

high blood pressure   See *hypertension.*

high-rise slums   Groups of multifloored apartment houses, usually surrounded by bare earth or asphalt, in disrepair and crime-ridden, and most often part of *public housing* projects.

hijos de crianza   In Spanish-speaking cultures, "the children of upbringing," a term that refers to the traditional practice of everyone in a community assuming responsibility for helping to raise a child as one's own without the necessity of blood or even friendship ties. See also *compadrazgo* and *padrinos.*

"hillbilly"   A disparaging term referring to an individual who comes from mountainous regions or other nonmetropolitan areas.

Hill, Octavia (1838–1912)   Advocate for better housing for poor people in England, Hill developed principles for more equitable landlord–tenant relationships. She founded the London Society for the Prevention of Pauperism, a forerunner of the first of the *Charity Organization Societies (COS).*

Hispanic   Pertaining to the culture of Spanish- and Portuguese-speaking people. In the United States, the term is often applied to people of Latin American ethnic background and to aspects of the culture of Spanish-speaking people. Some people prefer the term "Latino." See also *Chicano.*

historical research   The systematic collection and evaluation of data about past events. It follows the procedures of all research (defining the problem to be studied, posing hypotheses, collecting data in a systematic way, analyzing the information obtained, and interpreting it within the limits of generalizability). Because the data that survive are so limited and the studied phenomena are not replicable, the potential for *bias* is great.

histrionic personality disorder   One of the 11 types of *personality disorders* with all or many of the following characteristics: overly dramatic behavior, overreaction to minor events, craving for attention and excitement, tantrums, appearance to others of shallowness and lack of genuineness, apparent helplessness and dependence, proneness to manipulative gestures, and threats of *suicide.* A person who has this disorder is commonly referred to as a "hysterical personality" or a *"hysteric."*

histrionics   Manipulative *behavior* that is overly dramatic, demanding, volatile, self-indulgent, and attention-seeking.

HIV See *human immunodeficiency virus (HIV)*.

HIV disease See *acquired immune deficiency syndrome (AIDS)*.

HIV negative A result of a blood test to detect antibodies to the *human immunodeficiency virus (HIV)* when no antibodies are found. Care must be taken to gather an accurate history of risk practices or behaviors to ensure that the antibody test was not given during the *"window period."*

HIV positive A result of a blood test that has determined the existence of antibodies to the *human immunodeficiency virus (HIV)*.

HMO See *health maintenance organization (HMO)*.

hoarding Acquiring and holding goods, such as food, water, gold, and money. Disaster planners have to contend with a tendency of some people in impending crises to buy up all available supplies leaving others without access to needed goods.

Hoey, Jane (1892–1968) A *public welfare* administrator influential in advances of the federal government in social welfare policy, Hoey was a social researcher for health and welfare organizations and served as president of the *National Conference on Social Welfare (NCSW)* and the *Council on Social Work Education (CSWE)*.

holistic Oriented toward the understanding and treatment of the whole person or phenomenon. In this view, an individual is seen as being more than the sum of separate parts, and problems are seen in a broader context rather than as specific symptoms. One who maintains a holistic philosophy seeks to integrate all the social, cultural, psychological, and physical influences on an individual.

holistic medicine An approach to health care that stresses treatment of the whole person, with emphasis on the interconnections of the various physical systems, including the mind. It encourages the active involvement of the patient in the treatment process through diet, exercise, pleasurable activities, and positive attitude.

Hollis–Taylor Report A 1951 study of *social work education* conducted by Ernest Hollis and Alice Taylor, demonstrating the profession's increasing specialization, fragmentation, and growing orientation toward the case-by-case treatment of problems. The report recommended social work education that emphasized a more-generic orientation and a greater concern for social issues and social action. Many of the recommendations were accepted by the profession and became a foundation for the current objectives of social work education.

Holocaust Great destruction of the lives and property of a people. Today, the term is most often applied to the planned efforts of the Nazis during World War II to eliminate the Jewish population of Europe. See also *genocide, pogrom,* and *"ethnic cleansing."*

home-alone children Children whose parents or guardians leave them without needed care and supervision. See also *latchkey child*.

home-based instructional services Programs designed to provide education for children or adults who are unable to attend schools or other training facilities, usually as a result of illness or severe physical disability.

homebound A term referring to a shut-in or one who because of illness or *disability* must remain bedridden or within the confines of the home, *institution,* or immediate *neighborhood*. See also *location bound*.

homebound employment Jobs that people who are *homebound* are paid to do in their homes. Typical jobs include babysitting and day care, telephone solicitation, direct mail marketing, secretarial work, and computer services.

home care The provision of health care, homemaker, and social services to clients in their homes.

home care services Programs usually conducted by local and state departments of human services to assist people who have problems that preclude basic self-care needed to remain in their own homes. Such programs include *homemaker services, meals-on-wheels, chore service, home health services, respite care,* and *attendant care*. Some social workers also call this *domiciliary care services*; others use the term "home care services" as a synonym for "homemaker services" and "domiciliary care services" as a synonym for programs to help needy people with the physical repairs and maintenance of their homes.

home detention   A *corrections* program in which as part of the sentence a convicted felon is confined to home or other restrictions outside of penal facilities. Many jurisdictions use electronic home-monitoring systems to ensure compliance. In these systems, convicts are fitted with small radio transmitters riveted on their ankles, which keep a central computer notified about the person's whereabouts.

home health aides   Health care workers who provide personal care and homemaker services and some nursing to patients who are disabled or recovering on discharge from health care facilities.

home health services   Programs that provide for medical, nursing, occupational therapy, physical therapy, speech therapy, and follow-up care of patients in their homes. Many of these services are provided in the private sector for a fee by health care personnel or by private nursing service care, financed in part by *third-party payment*. Public health care services in the patient's home are also available. This provides a system that often is more comfortable for the patient and more economical than hospitalization or *nursing home* care.

homelessness   The condition of being without a home. Generally, the homeless man or woman is impoverished and transient and often lacks the social skills or emotional stability needed to improve the situation unless help is provided.

homeless shelters   Private or publicly funded residential facilities for individuals and families who otherwise have no homes. The shelters typically offer beds, meals, and sometimes health and social services to as many needy people as possible, depending on available room, supplies, and demand. Some shelters have strict requirements about who is accepted, whereas others admit anyone on an as-available basis. Many shelters are highly dependent on private contributions of money, food, and volunteer workers.

homemaker   A person whose primary role and activity is to maintain a comfortable and secure living environment for his or her family.

homemaker services   A health or social services program to help clients remain in their own homes. Usually, one or more helpers visit the clients' homes on predetermined schedules to prepare meals, do laundry, clean house, and provide transportation and some nursing care. These homemakers are usually public employees or volunteers, and their services often help keep clients out of more-expensive hospitals or nursing homes. In many communities, the homemaker service program is oriented primarily to educating and training family members to do this work, and those in *chore service* do the work.

homeostasis   The tendency of a system or organism to maintain stability and, when disrupted, to adapt and strive to restore the stability previously achieved. See also *general systems theory*.

homeowner tax deferrals   State and local laws that allow property owners to postpone paying residential taxes until the homes are sold or the owners die. The program is designed to protect older people (whose property taxes have increased substantially because of the escalating value of their homes) from being forced by taxation to vacate. See also *circuit-breaker tax relief*.

home relief   A means-tested welfare program operated under state and local auspices to provide financial assistance to needy individuals and families who are not eligible for any other categorical program.

The term is synonymous with *general assistance (GA)* and is used in many larger cities in the eastern United States, including New York City.

Homestead Act   The 1862 federal legislation designed to redistribute the population, provide opportunities, and settle the open lands in the West. The law authorized any U.S. citizen to receive 160 acres of unoccupied government land free of charge by agreeing to live on it for five years.

homestead exemptions   State and local laws that give property tax breaks to qualified homeowners to permit them to remain in their homes or encourage people to live in certain neighborhoods. The law subtracts some of the home's value from the property assessment to lower its taxes. The law is designed mostly to protect older people from being forced out of their increasingly valuable homes because of tax increases. It is also used to encourage occupancy of vacant homes in transitional neighborhoods.

home visits   In social work, the act of going to clients' homes to provide professional social services. Home visits have been part of the social work repertoire since the days of *friendly visitors,* and they occur for many reasons. Some social workers make home visits because their clients have disabilities or otherwise are unable to come to the agency. Some do so because they believe the helping process can be more effective and efficient if conducted in an environment familiar to the client. Children and *frail elderly* people, for example, may benefit. Other home visits occur because the social worker seeks to mobilize a neighborhood or county toward a social cause. In some instances, social workers are required to make such visits unexpectedly to investigate the client's normal living conditions. This is occasionally done to find out if the client is as poor or as incapable of providing child care as has been claimed.

homicide   The killing of one human being by another.

homogeneous   Possessing the same or similar traits. See also *heterogeneous.*

homogeneous groups   Groups whose membership comprise people of similar traits; for example, members who are of the same age or sex or who share the same problem. Some group leaders believe homogeneity permits the members to focus on their core problem areas without having to deal so much with distracting side issues. See also *single-focus group, heterogeneous groups,* and *dissonance theory of groups.*

homophobia   The irrational *fear* or hatred of people oriented toward *homosexuality.* The term is often applied to people who have strong negative feelings about homosexuals and to people who support antihomosexual activities. See also *heterosexism.*

homosexuality   The sexual or *erotic orientation* by some men and women for members of their same sex. This orientation is not considered to be a mental disorder. The term is used for men and women. See also *gay* and *lesbian.*

homosexuality, latent   In *psychodynamic* theory, the presence of erotic impulses outside the individual's conscious awareness toward one or more members of the same sex. The individual might give behavioral clues about this orientation but does not engage in overt homosexual activity. Some theorists suggest that latent homosexuality, accompanied by efforts by the individual to conceal the orientation from oneself and others, can result in *homophobia.* See also *latent homosexual.*

homosexual panic   Severe distress related to an individual's fear or delusion of being thought to be homosexual by others or of being raped or seduced by someone of the same sex. It sometimes appears as an initial symptom of *schizophrenia* (especially paranoid type) or as a manifestation of *latent homosexuality.*

honor system   A principle followed by members of some organizations or associations based on mutual trust and the understanding that all members will fulfill their responsibilities without being monitored or coerced. This system is implicit in the *adult learner model* in *social work education.*

"Hooverville" A term of derision for the *shantytowns* and encampments of poor people that formed near various cities during the *Great Depression.* They were named for President Herbert Hoover who was president when the depression began.

Hopkins, Harry (1890–1946) Administrator of the *Federal Emergency Relief Administration (FERA),* President Franklin D. Roosevelt's adviser on *New Deal* programs, and director of the *Works Progress Administration (WPA).* After completing his social work training, he worked for the *Association for Improving the Condition of the Poor (AICP)* and as a relief worker. He also served Roosevelt as the U.S. Secretary of Commerce in 1938.

Horatio Alger story An expression referring to an individual's transition from poverty to affluence supposedly because of hard work, thrift, and honest character; based on the 19th-century "rags-to-riches" novels of the Reverend Horatio Alger, Jr.

horizontal career move Taking a new job that represents the same level of attainment as the old, such as similar pay and benefits, responsibilities, and prestige, usually to fulfill nonvocational objectives. See also *vertical career move.*

horizontal disclosure In *social group work,* the revelation by a member of a therapy group of some distressing information and the group's analysis of that information as it affects the relationship between the revealer and the other group members. This is the opposite of *vertical disclosure.*

hospice A philosophy of caring and an array of programs, services, and settings for people with *terminal illness.* Hospice services are usually offered in nonhospital facilities with homelike atmospheres where families, friends, and the significant other can be with the dying person.

hospice care The provision of health care and homemaker and social services in nonhospital, homelike facilities for people with a *terminal illness.*

hospital social work The provision of social services in hospitals and similar health care centers, most often within a facility's department of social services or social work. The services provided include prevention, rehabilitation, and follow-up activities, as well as discharge planning and information gathering and providing. Other services include assisting patients with the financial and social aspects of their care and counseling patients and their families.

host setting An organization within which another organization provides specialized services. For example, a host setting for a hospital social services department would be the hospital.

hot line A communications system that provides for immediate and direct telephone contact between certain people in times of emergency. Many communities have established such systems so that trained listeners are on hand to receive calls from people who experience emotional or social problems. There are also special-purpose hot lines such as those for *runaways, whistle-blowing, suicide* prevention, *family violence,* and other problems. See also *help line* and *Nineline.*

hot-seat technique In social work with groups and other *group therapy* approaches, a procedure in which the group leader and all members focus exclusively on one member for a long period of time.

household The U.S. *Bureau of the Census* term referring to all people, whether related or not, who live in the same dwelling unit. This includes individuals (single-person households) as well as groups of people.

house of corrections A jail or prison. Usually the term is applied to minimum-security facilities for incarcerating those convicted of minor offenses who have good potential for rehabilitation.

housing allowance Funds allocated and earmarked for payment of rent or mortgage on one's home, usually provided by an employer or human services agency.

Housing Benefit in U.K.   The welfare provision in the United Kingdom for low-income families and individuals that provides financial assistance to cover rent payments and reduces property taxes on the residences of needy people. See also *Family Credit in U.K.*

housing programs   Publicly funded and monitored programs designed to provide suitable homes, especially for those unable to find or pay for them themselves. In the United States, most of these programs are administered by the U.S. *Department of Housing and Urban Development (HUD)*. These programs include Low-Rent Public Housing, the Rent-Subsidy Program, Lower-Income Housing Assistance, Home Ownership Assistance for Low-Income Families, Rural Rental Housing Loans, Farm Labor Housing Loans, Indian Housing Improvement programs, and Housing Repair Assistance for Low-Income Families. In addition, the government sponsors a guaranteed mortgage loan program and housing assistance for veterans.

HPV   See *human papillomavirus (HPV)*.

HRA   See *Human Resources Administration (HRA)*.

HR-10 plan   See *Keogh Plan*.

HSA   See *Health Services Administration (HSA)*.

HUD   See *Department of Housing and Urban Development, U.S. (HUD)*.

Hull House   The most famous of the *settlement houses*, founded in Chicago in 1889 by *Jane Addams* and *Ellen Gates Starr*. Among the first of its kind, it was a community center for poor and disadvantaged people of the area and was the setting for initiating various *social reform* activities.

human capital   1. Expenditures to enhance the quality of a people, which increase their productivity. 2. Investment in

the citizens of a nation through public education, health and security programs, and job training, which ultimately contributes to a more economically healthy society. 3. An individual's overall *skills*, abilities, educational experience, and intellectual potential, which are brought to the labor market. See also *investment-versus-consumption concept.*

human development   The physical, mental, social, and experiential changes that occur over a person's *life cycle*. These changes are continuous, occur in fairly consistent sequences, and are cumulative with other changes. Human development occurs in a predictable manner, but the rate of change is unique to each individual.

human diversity   The range of differences between peoples in terms of *race, ethnicity,* age, geography, religion, *values, culture,* orientations, physical and mental health, and many other distinguishing characteristics.

human immunodeficiency virus (HIV)   The *acquired immune deficiency syndrome (AIDS)* virus, which attacks the body's immune system and thereby leaves the HIV-infected person vulnerable to a debilitating or fatal *opportunistic infection, cancer,* or neurological condition. Two types of HIV have been identified: HIV 1 is found worldwide and HIV 2 appears mainly in central Africa. The progression of infection is similar. Blood, semen, vaginal secretions, and breast milk have been implicated in transmission. HIV is transmitted by unprotected penetrative sexual intercourse with an infected person, by infected hypodermic needles, by medical transfusion of untreated blood, and from infected mother to child (in utero, during birth, or shortly after birth). HIV cannot be transmitted casually through, for example, touching an infected person or sharing a drinking glass. HIV infection and infectiousness are presumed to be lifelong.

humanistic orientation   A group of concepts, *values,* and techniques that emphasize people's potential rather than their dysfunctions. Social workers and other therapists with this orientation tend to help clients by developing the therapeutic *relationship* and by concentrating on the "here and now." See also *self-actualization*.

human papillomavirus (HPV) One of the *sexually transmitted diseases (STDs)* that causes genital warts, HPV is also known as venereal warts. HPV affects up to 40 million people in the United States.

human resources The knowledge and skill that some people can and do make available to others for the improvement and enrichment of their lives. See also *natural resources*.

Human Resources Administration (HRA) The title used in many state and municipal governments, such as New York City, for their departments of *social services, public welfare, social welfare*, or *human services*.

human rights The opportunity to be accorded the same prerogatives and obligations in social fulfillment as are accorded to all others without distinction as to race, sex, language, or religion. In 1948, the U.N. Commission on Human Rights spelled out these opportunities. They include the basic *civil rights* recognized in democratic constitutions such as life, liberty, and personal security; freedom from arbitrary arrest, detention, or exile; the right to fair and public hearings by impartial tribunals; freedom of thought, conscience, and religion; and freedom of peaceful association. They also include economic, social, and cultural rights such as the right to work, education, and social security; to participate in the cultural life of the community; and to share in the benefits of scientific advancement and the arts.

human SERVE Human Service Employees Registration and Voter Education Fund, an organization founded in 1983 to encourage people to vote and to make the voting process more accessible. The organization's supporters, most of whom have backgrounds in the social services, achieve their objectives through educating people about how to register; by bringing registration facilities to the potential voters; and by placing legal or political pressures against boards of elections that make it difficult for some groups, especially racial and ethnic groups, to register. See also *motor voter law* and *voter registration drives*.

human services Programs and activities designed to enhance people's development and well-being, including providing economic and social assistance for those unable to provide for their own needs. The term "human services" is roughly synonymous with the terms "social services" or "welfare services" and includes planning, organizing, developing, and administering programs for and providing direct social services to people. The term came into wider use in 1979 when the U.S. *Department of Health and Human Services (HHS)* was established to replace the U.S. *Department of Health, Education, and Welfare (HEW)*. It was thought that the term "welfare" had a negative connotation and that the organization would have more influence with the new name. Use of the term "human services" (and "human resources") instead of "social welfare services" is also part of the trend toward employing other professionals in addition to social workers in the services arena. Some social scientists identify the six basic human services as (1) personal social services, (2) health, (3) education, (4) housing, (5) income, and (6) justice and public safety.

hunger strike Refusal to eat, as a protest against unjust or unacceptable conditions. Social workers and other activists have called attention to existing conditions by going on such fasts themselves or by organizing groups to refuse food.

Huntington's disease A *genetic disorder* also known as Huntington's chorea. It is transmitted by a dominant gene and affects half the offspring of those who carry the genes. The symptoms, which include mental deterioration, such as *hallucination*, profound *mood swings, dementia*, and *choreiform movements*, do not appear until about age 30. *Genetic counseling* is important for those who have the disease and for their offspring.

"hustling" The term used by *"street people"* to describe any activities designed to extract money from those they encounter. Hustling may occur through prostitution, swindling, *panhandling*, "borrowing," gambling, stealing, and *extortion*.

hwa-byung A *culture-bound syndrome* most commonly found among Korean peoples in which the individual experiences insomnia, fatigue, panic, fear, and various somatic complaints said to be the result of suppressing anger.

hyperactive child syndrome A term formerly used for *attention-deficit hyperactivity disorder (ADHD)*.

hyperactivity Excessive muscular activity, usually with rapid movements, restlessness, and almost constant motion. Its causes may be a symptom of *anxiety, neurosis, organic mental disorders,* or physiological or *neurological disorders*. This term is still used informally, but has been replaced diagnostically by *attention-deficit hyperactivity disorder (ADHD)*.

hyperacusis Extreme and sometimes painful sensitivity to sounds.

hyperkinesis A childhood disorder characterized by excessive motor activity, reduced attention span, and accompanying difficulties in learning and perceiving accurately. Roughly synonymous with *hyperactivity,* the term now preferred by professionals is *attention-deficit hyperactivity disorder (ADHD)*. The syndrome has also been known as "hyperactive child syndrome," "hyperkinetic reaction of childhood," "minimal brain damage," "minimal brain dysfunction," and "minimal cerebral dysfunction."

hyperkinetic reaction of childhood A term formerly used for *attention-deficit hyperactivity disorder (ADHD)*.

hypersomnia One of the *sleep disorders* that involves excessive sleepiness and sleep attacks during all daytime and nighttime hours; the condition is the opposite of *insomnia*.

hypertension High pressure of blood pulsing against the walls of the blood vessels. This chronic disorder of the cardiovascular system, is a predominant risk factor in *stroke, heart attack, renal disease,* and eye diseases. A person with high blood pressure generally cannot feel any symptom, so it can only be detected reliably by using a blood pressure cuff (sphygmomanometer). Physicians are especially concerned when the systolic pressure (caused when the heart contracts) exceeds 140 or the diastolic pressure (caused when the heart relaxes) exceeds 90.

hypertonia Extreme muscle tension.

hyperventilation Taking in more air than can be processed by the body, which results in lowered levels of carbon dioxide in the blood stream. Usually the behavior is the result of *anxiety* and often causes the individual to feel dizzy, light-headed, and faint.

hypnosis The phenomenon of being in a mental state of aroused concentration so intense that everything else in the subject's consciousness is ignored. All hypnosis is *self-hypnosis,* and the role of the hypnotist is to offer suggestions for deepening the level of concentration. Generally, hypnotized subjects will not do anything contrary to their moral or ethical codes and can come out of trances at will. Forms of hypnosis are used successfully in therapeutic interventions, such as *hypnotherapy*. Subjects can be taught to use self-hypnosis to achieve specific goals such as weight loss, cessation of smoking, pain relief, and overcoming of a *phobia*.

hypnotherapy The use of *hypnosis* and *self-hypnosis* is an adjunct or central tool in the psychotherapy process. Hypnotherapy has been used in psychotherapy since Sigmund Freud's (1856–1939) earliest analytic cases and is now used especially in the treatments of *phobia*, pain relief, weight loss, cessation of smoking, and *anxiety*.

hypoactive Less active than what is considered *normal*.

hypoactive sexual desire disorder A *sexual disorder* in which the individual has little or no urge for sexual activity. In making this diagnosis, sex therapists and other clinicians specify whether the condition is lifelong or acquired, generalized or situational, and caused by psychological or combined psychological–physiological problems. See also *sexual arousal disorders.*

hypochondriasis Preoccupation with the details of one's bodily functions and excessive concern about the possibility of having a disease. It is generally believed to be caused by neurotic *anxiety.* Hypochondriacal individuals typically present physical symptoms but no actual disturbance in bodily function. These people often develop physical symptoms such as dizziness, sweating, and rapid pulse, arising from fears about their health. They often seek help from various medical specialists but are reluctant to accept reassurance of well-being. See also *neurosis* and *somatoform disorders.*

hypoglycemia Low level of sugar in the blood. Left untreated, it may cause the appearance of psychogenic symptoms that can lead to inappropriate treatment for emotional disorders. Because of the possibility of hypoglycemia, prudent social workers advise clients about to enter psychotherapy to get a physical exam first.

hypokinetic Fewer movements than what is considered *normal.*

hypomania Behavior that is similar to but less severe than that observed in individuals with *bipolar disorder,* manic type. The individual in this state seems euphoric, energetic, and creative but may also be impatient and grandiose and use poor judgment.

hypomanic episode A symptom found in some of the *mood disorders,* especially *bipolar disorder,* consisting of an abnormally and persistently elevated, expansive, or irritable mood lasting at least four days. This may include feelings of inflated self-esteem, *grandiosity,* pressured speech, *flight of ideas,* distractibility, and psychomotor agitation, all of which are a clear departure from the individual's usual mood and functioning. The symptoms are identical to those in a *manic episode* except they are not as severe and do not include the possibility of *delusion* or *hallucination* or other psychotic features.

hypothalamus The part of the brain that controls the *autonomic nervous system (ANS)* and many of the body's regulating systems such as hunger, thirst, and temperature. It is also thought to play a major role in *emotion* and *motivation.*

hypothesis A tentative proposition that describes a possible relationship among facts that can be observed and measured. The proposition is often stated in negative fashion as a *null hypothesis* (for example, "There is no difference between the work of MSWs and BSWs as measured by. . . . "). Social workers and other professionals also use the term informally to indicate a *theory* believed to account for what is not entirely understood.

hypotonia Minimal muscle tension; flaccidity.

hypoxia Less oxygen than is needed to maintain health.

hysteria A term originally used by Sigmund Freud (1856–1939) to describe patients with symptoms he believed to be the result of suppressed sexual and oedipal conflicts. Lay people tend to use this term for any intensely felt and dramatically expressed range of emotions. See also *conversion disorder* and *anxiety hysteria.*

"hysteric" A historical term still used informally and inappropriately by social workers and other professionals to describe a person with some or all of the following characteristics: overly dramatic behavior, overreaction to minor events, craving for attention and excitement, tantrums, appearance to others of shallowness and lack of genuineness, apparent helplessness and dependency, proneness to manipulative gestures, and suicide threats. In treatment, such a person would likely to be diagnosed as having a *histrionic personality disorder.*

hysterical neurosis, conversion type A *somatoform disorder* caused by *anxiety* and resulting in the appearance of some physical dysfunction that has no apparent physical cause. The individual is said to use the symptoms unconsciously to avoid some undesired activities or to get some support from others that might not otherwise be available. This *psychiatric label* is no longer used in official diagnoses. It is now called *conversion disorder.*

I

IASSW See *International Association of Schools of Social Work (IASSW)*.

IASWR See *Institute for the Advancement of Social Work Research (IASWR)*.

iatrogenic A term describing a physical or *mental disorder* originating in the *treatment* or *intervention* process. Technically, the term refers to the action of a physician or to medication that results in the patient's developing a new disease. However, the term has been broadened and now also includes the illnesses that individuals or groups develop as a result of intervention by helping professionals, including social workers. For example, some clients develop extreme dependency on their social workers and may become afraid to act independently, a syndrome that may be iatrogenic.

I–CAPP See *International Conference for the Advancement of Private Practice in Social Work (I–CAPP)*.

ICD-10 The tenth and current edition of the *International Classification of Diseases (ICD)*.

"ice" A highly addictive methamphetamine that is smoked to produce a period of *euphoria* that is more intense and much longer lasting than with *cocaine* or its derivative *"crack."* Far less expensive than other drugs of abuse, ice often produces symptoms of acute *depression* and *psychosis* after the euphoria ends. When this substance is injected, it is known as *"crank."*

ice breaking In *social group work,* the activities originated by group leaders in the *preaffiliation phase* of *group development*

to create a comforting and productive atmosphere and become usefully acquainted with one another. Structured exercises help achieve this. For example, the leader might ask the new members to describe their goals for the group or indicate what they would most like to know about or reveal to the others. Another exercise is for the leader to ask each member to describe to the group everything imaginable about another member of the group, without the subject indicating whether the speculation is accurate or simply a *projection* or *prejudice.*

ICFs See *intermediate-care facilities (ICFs)*.

ICIDH See *International Classification of Impairment, Disability and Handicapped (ICIDH)*.

ICSW See *International Council of Social Work (ICSW)*.

id In *psychoanalytic theory,* the part of the mind or *psyche* that harbors the individual's instinctive or biological *drive, libido,* or psychic energy. The id is completely *unconscious,* but id wishes are always being discharged. Its demands are centered on the body, and it is governed solely by the *pleasure principle.* It attempts to force the *ego,* which is generally governed by the *reality principle,* to meet its demands without regard to the long-term consequences.

idealization The overestimation of another person or of that person's specific attributes. See also *devaluation* and *halo effect.*

ideas of reference An inaccurate belief that the behaviors of others or environmental phenomena occur to have some effect on the individual. For example, a man encounters two strangers who are conversing and assumes they are talking about him. This is a form of *delusion* and sometimes appears as a symptom in *delusional disorder, schizophrenia,* and *histrionic personality disorder,* and in people who have profound *inadequacy feelings.*

ideation The process of developing a belief. For example, a person with *suicidal ideation* is one who starts thinking about *death,* about wanting to die, and about specific actions that will help to reach that goal.

identification A mental process in which a person forms a mental image of another person who is important and then thinks, acts, and feels in a way that resembles the other person's *behavior.* Identification often promotes *ego integration* and personal growth.

identification with the aggressor The phenomenon that sometimes occurs when the victims of *rape, kidnapping,* hostage-taking, and *assault* come to develop sympathy or approval for the perpetrators and their aggression. For example, the victim may take on attributes of the aggressor.

identified patient (or client) The member of a family or social group for whom *therapy,* help, or *social services* are ostensibly sought. This person has typically been viewed by *relevant others* as "sick" or "crazy," even though they may have just as many or more problems and may implicitly need and receive just as much help from the perceptive therapist or social worker.

identity An individual's sense of *self* and of uniqueness, as well as the basic *integration* and continuity of *values, behavior,* and thoughts that are maintained in varied circumstances.

identity crisis Confusion about one's role in life. The individual enters a period of doubt about being willing or capable of living up to the expectations of others and is uncertain about what kind of person to be if those expectations are not met.

identity disorder A *mental disorder* usually first observed in children and adolescents characterized by persistent and long-standing self-doubts. The individual experiences uncertainty about goals, moral values, sexual orientation, family, and friends. Symptoms of identity disorder are similar to the conflicts seen in *identity crisis,* except they have lasted longer and persist even when in supportive environments.

identity problem A general category (that is, not a formal diagnosis) used especially by counselors, therapists, educators, and social workers for clients dealing with issues relating to doubt, indecision, and personal confusion about goals, career choices, ethnic and group loyalties, moral values, *sexual orientation,* and *spirituality.*

identity versus role confusion According to the *psychosocial development theory* of Erik Erikson (1902–1994), the fifth stage of human development occurs at about ages 12 to 18. The conflict facing adolescents is to establish clear ideas about their values, vocational objectives, and role in life, or there may be a lack of clarity about how to fit into the social environment. This is the period in which there is greatest likelihood of an *identity crisis.*

ideologue An individual who is preoccupied with one or more ideas and tends to see much of the world in terms of those ideas. Many effective social reformers have been called ideologues.

ideology A system of ideas that is the product of one's values, experiences, political persuasion, level of moral development, and aspirations for humanity. For example, the ideology of a social worker is likely to include a concern for *equal rights* for all people and an interest in providing greater opportunities for less-privileged people.

idiopathic Having to do with diseases or disorders that arise entirely within an individual rather than originating in environmental influences such as viruses, social stress, or accidents.

idiosyncratic A term applied to a trait or characteristic that is unique to the subject or phenomenon being observed and unrepresentative of others of the same class.

idiosyncratic intoxication A significant change of behavior in an individual who recently has consumed alcohol or other drugs. Typically, the substance ingested is too little to account for the degree of change.

idiosyncratic life-cycle transitions Non-normative changes in an individual's phases of life. These transitions are considered unusual; thus, they are not marked by celebrations or rituals, and the person generally has even more difficulty coping with the new circumstance than the normal transitions. Examples include unexpected death, birth of a child with disabilities, imprisonment, homosexual marriage, and migration.

idiot An obsolete term once used to refer to a person with *mental retardation,* having an *intelligence quotient (IQ)* score of 25 or less. The term in current professional use for such conditions is *profoundly handicapped.*

idiot savant A designation sometimes given to individuals with *mental retardation* or a *mental disorder* who otherwise possess some highly specialized talent, such as playing a musical instrument or calculating mathematical equations.

IECs Institutional ethics committees. See *ethics committees.*

IEP See *individualized education plan (IEP).*

IFA See *International Federation on Aging (IFA).*

IFPS See *intensive family preservation services (IFPS).*

IFSW See *International Federation of Social Workers (IFSW).*

illegal A specific act that is contrary to the *law* and that can result in punishment imposed by the *justice system.*

illegal alien A citizen of one nation who has unlawfully taken up permanent residence in another nation.

illegitimate 1. An activity that is against the *law, norms,* or *values* of a society. 2. A term commonly applied to people born to parents who are not legally married to each other.

illicit drugs Chemical substances whose use is unlawful. In the United States, these include *cocaine, marijuana, opiates,* and *psychedelics.*

illiteracy Not knowing how to read or write.

illiteracy, functional Possessing some reading and writing skills but not of sufficient quality to permit their use in normal socioeconomic relationships. This term usually refers to those whose literacy deficits are the result of cultural factors rather than *mental retardation* or developmental expressive writing disorder.

ILO See *International Labor Organization (ILO).*

image 1. A consciously experienced mental picture arising from one's memory. 2. The overall judgmental reaction of relevant others to an individual, institution, organization, or nation.

imagery relaxation technique A self-help and therapeutic procedure to reduce *anxiety,* in which the subject concentrates on being in an environment that is his or her ideal place for relaxation. Thinking about the place and recreating its sounds, colors, smells, and pleasures for about five to 10 minutes helps the person become more relaxed.

image, social work The way people typically judge the profession and occupation of social work and its practitioners, regardless of whether this is an accurate view.

imago See *archetype.*

imbecile An obsolete term once used to refer to a person with *mental retardation,* an *intelligence quotient (IQ)* score between 25 and 50.

immigrant One who has moved to and intends to reside permanently in another country. See also *green card.*

immigration Moving to a new country or region, usually for the purpose of permanent settlement.

Immigration and Naturalization Service (INS), U.S. The federal government organization within the U.S. *Department of Justice* that is responsible for regulating and enforcing the laws pertaining to the entry into and residence in the United States of people from other nations. The McCarran–Walter Act of 1952 (Immigration and Nationality Act, P.L. 82-414) and its 1965 amendments (P.L. 89-326) have been the nation's major codification of procedures for *immigration* and *naturalization*. In 1986, these regulations were changed, permitting any *undocumented alien* who entered the United States before that time to remain but making it more difficult for others to enter the country.

immunity Exemption from a responsibility or from legal prosecution, usually granted because of some service. For example, some churches are granted immunity from paying taxes in lieu of other services they provide society. Some people charged with crimes are granted immunity because they agree to testify against other people.

immunization Preventive medical procedures that reduce susceptibility to certain diseases. Immunization occurs most frequently through *inoculation* or a vaccine—that is, injecting into the body certain viruses or bacteria to cause a mild and controllable form of the disease so that the body develops *resistance* to the more-serious forms.

impact analysis The assessment used by social policymakers in determining the effect of a new law or policy on the relevant community.

impaired professional An individual who is unable to fully carry out his or her professional responsibilities because of some physical or psychosocial disorder. The impairments may include *substance abuse, alcoholism, depression,* or *sexual disorder.*

impaired social functioning The inability or diminished ability to fulfill one's so-cial roles or responsibilities as a result of *disease, mental disorder, stress,* or preoccupation with personal concerns.

impaired social worker One who is unable to function adequately as a professional social worker and provide competent care to clients as a result of a physical or *mental disorder* or personal problems, or the inability or desire to adhere to the *code of ethics* of the profession. These problems most commonly include *alcoholism, substance abuse, mental illness, burnout, stress,* and relationship problems.

impairment A loss or abnormality in psychological, physiological, or anatomical structure or function, including blindness, loss of sight in one eye, deafness, paralysis of a limb, or mental retardation. See also *disability, handicap,* and *International Classification of Impairment, Disability, and Handicapped (ICIDH).*

impeach To accuse a public official of unlawful conduct before a legally constituted tribunal, such as a court of law or legislature.

implanted memory The unethical practice of influencing a client to "remember" events in the past that did not actually happen and to convince the client that the memory represents actual experience. This practice is often associated with clients who eventually claim to have recovered suppressed memories of such traumatic events as *incest, rape,* and *child abuse.* See also *recovered memory.*

implied consent An agreement to participate expressed by gestures, signs, actions, or statements that are interpreted as agreement, or by nonresisting silence or inaction. This is often used as a defense in *rape* trials in which the defendant claims to have acted in the belief that the victim consented to the defendant's advances. See also *informed consent.*

implosive therapy In *behavior therapy,* the technique in which the client is presented with images of anxiety-producing stimuli and is encouraged to experience as much *anxiety* as possible. Because the anxiety-producing images do not result in any harm, the anxiety responses are not reinforced, and the symptoms are more likely to be extinguished.

impotence A male *sexual disorder,* also known as *erectile disorder,* characterized by an inability to achieve or maintain an erection. See also *sexual aversion disorder* and *inhibited sexual excitement.*

impound To seize funds, records, or property by an officer of the law or court, usually until some matter that involves those items can be legally determined and adjudicated.

impounding The legal action of taking into the *custody* of a court or law enforcement officer any item of a person's possessions, including automobiles, funds, and financial records. This is done for the safekeeping of the item pending the outcome of a legal action.

impulse control disorder A diagnostic group of *mental disorders* characterized by the repeated inability to resist some temptation that is harmful to one's self or others. In most cases, the individual becomes increasingly tense before succumbing to the temptation, feels pleasure and emotional release on completing the act, and then experiences regret after the act is over. Types of impulse control disorders are *pathological gambling, kleptomania, pyromania, trichotillomania*, and *explosive disorder.*

impulsiveness The inclination to act suddenly, in response to inner urges, without thought and with little regard to the consequences of the action.

IMRAD An acronym used by editors and referees of social work and other scholarly journals to remind them of the order and formats that some journals require for research articles. IMRAD stands for "Introduction" (what is the article about?), "Method" (how was the problem studied?), "Results" (what were the findings?), and "Discussion" (what do the findings mean?).

inadequacy feelings An individual's *perception* of being inferior or of being incapable of fulfilling certain social expectations.

inalienable rights Rights that cannot be taken away or given away except by the person possessing them. Societies have varying concepts of these rights. In the United States, inalienable rights include the rights of life, liberty, the pursuit of happiness, the freedom of speech and worship, and the right of *due process of law.* See also *First Amendment rights* and *Fifth Amendment rights.*

inappropriate affect A lack of consistency between one's words or ideas and the mood or feeling that accompanies it. This is often symptomatic of serious mental disorders such as *schizophrenia* or *bipolar disorder.*

incapacitation Lack of ability to provide sufficient care for oneself or to demonstrate adequate judgment as a result of diminished physical or mental functioning.

incarceration Confinement in an institution, such as a prison or mental hospital. Usually this occurs for the purpose of punishment or protection of society from the individual or to impose treatment or protective custody on the individual. See also *detention.*

incentive A reward or object of value that produces in an individual the motivation to act in a way that will lead to its acquisition.

incentive contracting A systematic method often used by public organizations to improve the delivery and quality of goods or services. The provider (contractor) is guaranteed more compensation if the goods or services meet predetermined time and quality standards.

incest Sexual intercourse or *sexual abuse* between close relatives—that is, people who are too closely related to be permitted by law to marry.

incestuous desire An individual's urge, whether conscious or not, to engage in erotic activity with a close relative.

incidence rate In population and demographic reports, the number of new cases of a physical or mental disorder, crime, or social problem that develops in an identified population group within a specific time frame. See also *prevalence rate* and *epidemiology.*

inclusionary cultural model An experiential learning process, using group work methods as a supplement to the presentation of didactic material, designed to help participants develop awareness about behaviors and attitudes within themselves that are likely to be culturally influenced. The model is generally used with classes and training groups of 18 to 45 members, often in settings such as social agencies in which the workers serve identifiable cultural groups. The group members are led through discussions about behaviors they consider typical of various ethnic groups, followed by exercises in identifying *bias* and *stereotypes.* Participants then include themselves in subgroups with those characteristics they can identify, thus facilitating their opportunity to distinguish between objective data and culturally influenced "information."

incoherence Disconnected thoughts, often a symptom of *psychosis, bipolar disorder* in the manic phase, and severe *anxiety.* Incoherent behavior includes talking about many subjects almost simultaneously, *loose association,* and nonlogical reasoning.

income distribution The division of moneys and other resources among individuals or family units in an economy. Economists also apply this term to the division of income among functions in the economy, such as labor, capital, and real estate. Income distribution is a primary indicator of the economic well-being of various demographic groups in society (such as women, older people, black people, people who live in the South, and divorced people). The U.S. *Bureau of the Census,* the U.S. *Department of Labor,* and U.S. *Department of Health and Human Services (HHS)* compile income distribution statistics to determine the extent and location of poverty and affluence and to help in economic and social welfare planning. See also *Lorenz curve.*

income maintenance *Social welfare* programs designed to provide individuals with

enough money or goods and services to maintain a predetermined *standard of living.*

income strategy A *social welfare* policy of providing direct monetary aid, based on predetermined objective criteria, to those in need. This is distinguished from a *service strategy* policy, in which social workers evaluate each person's situation and provide *counseling* and *in-kind benefits.* For example, an income strategy would be to pay each needy family a certain amount for housing so that the family can make their own choices. In this example, the service strategy would be to provide public housing or advice about living more frugally.

income test A financial test of *eligibility* for welfare benefits that considers only income (usually that reported for income tax purposes), in contrast to the *means test,* which considers income, assets, and other resources.

income transfer payments See *transfer payments.*

incompetent 1. Without the ability to fulfill obligations. 2. A legal term that has several connotations, depending on the circumstances. These include inability to consent legally to make or execute a contract, insufficiency in knowledge needed to carry out some legal obligation, inability to stand trial because the person is unable to assist rationally in his or her own defense, or inability to understand the nature of the charge or the consequences of conviction.

incontinence 1. Lack of *self-control.* 2. The inability to control elimination of body waste.

incorporation In psychosocial theory, a primitive *defense mechanism* in which the individual imagines he or she is ingesting or absorbing another person, part of a person, or an object to whom or for which there is great *attachment.* In the first months of life, this may be a literal goal, but later it is an *unconscious* fantasy.

incorrigible Not amenable to correction. This term once was applied to habitual criminals, juvenile delinquents, and unmanageable youths but is now rarely used by professionals.

incrementalism Gradual change in policies, attitudes, and behaviors. Social welfare planners tend to use incrementalism because of public resistance to adopting comprehensive programs all at once. For example, the *Old Age, Survivors, Disability, and Health Insurance (OASDHI)* program has made incremental changes by gradually increasing benefits and eligibility over the past 50 years.

incremental social change Gradual adaptation and adjustment made by social institutions to reflect changes in the values, needs, and priorities of the people. Institutions retain their existence and basic character but modify their goals and means to accommodate to the demands of those served. This is the opposite of *structural social change.*

incubation In the progression of a disease, the time between the onset of infection until the first symptoms appear. See also *"window period."*

indemnification Protection or immunity from lawsuits or the penalties or liabilities stemming from an action, as in "hold harmless agreements," *malpractice insurance,* or payment for some damages to avoid incurring greater losses later.

indenture An obligation in which one person is required to serve or work for another for a specified length of time. In colonial America, indentured servitude was a common practice by which immigrants would receive transportation to their new homes in exchange for working for several years. Later, the practice was frequently applied to parentless children who were compelled to become indentured to a custodian. From this practice and that of *apprenticing* originated many of the principles of *foster care.* Indenture is still practiced, illegally or covertly, by some people who exploit the circumstances of an *immigrant* or *undocumented alien.*

independent adoptions The process of *adoption* outside of established social agen-

cies. There are many variations in this process. In family adoptions, the *birth parents* place the child with a relative. In stepparent adoptions, the most common type of independent adoption, a stepparent adopts a spouse's child. In nonprofit intermediate arrangements, an individual or organization acts as a go-between for birth parents and adoptive parents who do not know each other. In *intercountry adoption,* a child from one nation is adopted by parents in another, with arrangements monitored with varying degrees of formality by authorities and individuals in the child's original country. A final category, that of for-profit intermediate arrangements, is controversial. For-profit arrangement has been called *black-market adoption.* However, because the process is not "adoption" unless it is legal, it is a contradiction of terms. Thus, some child welfare specialists have used the term *gray-market adoption.*

independent living The capability of an individual to be self-governing and not dependent on others for care, well-being, or livelihood. To be capable of independent living is seen as being able to manage one's own finances and to perform the necessary *activities of daily living (ADL)* without the necessity of continued reliance on others. Programs to help people achieve independent living provide for the social and medical services and also for the modification of homes that permit people access to all rooms and facilities.

independent living, centers for Facilities and programs located in more than 200 communities in the United States and other nations to provide social and health care services for people with disabilities. The centers are staffed largely by people who themselves have disabilities and offer such services as peer counseling, legal assistance, financial guidance, job placement, mental health counseling, transportation, wheelchair repair, and referrals. The programs provide a peer support system and information for families and professionals.

independent practice associations (IPAs) A consortium of individual health care providers, mostly in *private practice*, that represents all specialties and that provides for the health care needs of groups of people who contract for the service in advance. IPAs in some regions are also known as "individual practice associations." IPAs developed mostly as a competitive response to the proliferation of the *health maintenance organization (HMO)*. See also *preferred provider organizations (PPOs)* and *managed health care program*.

independent social work The practice of social work outside the auspices of traditional social agencies or government organizations. In addition to private practitioners, those engaged in such social work include self-employed proprietary social workers who have autonomous consulting firms or who organize and manage private, for-profit institutional facilities or educational institutions. See also *private practice* and *proprietary practice*.

independent variable In systematic *research*, the factors that are thought to influence or cause a certain behavior, phenomenon, or reaction. The factor that is being influenced is the *dependent variable*.

indeterminant sentence In the *criminal justice system*, the *incarceration* of an individual for an unspecified amount of time. Thus, the decision to release is based on the prisoner's demonstrated ability and willingness to satisfy certain standards. Variations of this system have been tried in many nations. The *juvenile courts* in many U.S. jurisdictions once used some elements of the system.

indexing The automatic adjustments of salaries, welfare payments, *social security*, and other benefits based on *inflation* rates and the changing *cost of living*.

Index of Social Health An annual publication of the U.S. government that reports on a wide variety of factors pertaining to social well-being. The factors include such things as number of jobs held, *Average Income Monthly Earnings (AIME)*, housing, health factors, crime, education, and other *social indicators*. The *Index* quantifies each

of these factors and compares them with previous years, thus showing if the nation is progressing. The publication was first issued in 1987 to replace *Social Indicators*, which ceased publication in 1981.

Indian Health Service A U.S. program comprising a network of hospitals and health care facilities, clinics, and personnel to provide for the direct care of *American Indians* and *Alaska Natives*.

indictment A sworn written accusation submitted by a grand jury to a court charging an individual with a *crime*.

indigenous worker A member of a community who becomes active in helping professionals achieve some service goals for that community. Indigenous workers may be paid employees or volunteers, and their roles often include identifying sources of problems, educating residents as to the services being offered, linking clients with professional service providers, and counseling.

indigent Poor and needy.

indirect contact abuse A form of childhood *sexual abuse* in which the perpetrator derives erotic pleasure by involving a child in some sexualized activity other than touching. Examples include covertly or overtly watching the naked child or displaying one's genitals, sometimes while masturbating. Such behavior is abusive, because studies show that children are harmed as a result.

indirect cost Consequences, outcomes, or expenditures that are not immediately anticipated, apparent, or paid for by those who initiate an action. For example, although most of the *direct cost* of the U.S. drug problem is the funding that goes for law enforcement and treatment, an indirect cost is the lack of productivity on the part of the addicts.

indirect practice Those professional social work activities, such as administration, research, policy development, and education, that do not involve immediate or personal contact with the clients being served. Indirect practice makes *direct practice* possible and more efficient; as such, it is considered essential and of equal importance to the mission of the profession.

indirect treatment In *social casework,* the term used by some to describe work in the environment on behalf of the client. Such work includes *mediation,* education, *advocacy,* and locating resources. These activities are said to require virtually the same skills and techniques as are needed in *direct treatment.*

individualism The sociopolitical and philosophical concept that emphasizes the pursuit of people's own interests rather than the common or collective good. See also *rugged individualism.*

individualization The ethical value in social work and other helping professions for understanding the client as a unique person or group rather than as one whose characteristics are simply typical of a class. For example, a social worker adhering to this principle would treat a young unwed mother as though her background, needs, and values were hers alone and not necessarily the same as those of others in similar circumstances.

individualized education plan (IEP) A legal requirement, based on a provision in the *Education for All Handicapped Children Act of 1975* (P.L. 94-142) that each identified child with disabilities must be evaluated and that a plan to meet his or her unique needs must be developed before placement in any educational program.

individual practice associations (IPAs) See *independent practice associations (IPAs).*

individual psychology theory A school of thought about the development of personality and *psychopathology,* originated by psychiatrist Alfred Adler (1870–1937) that emphasizes a person's lifestyle and the individual's striving to overcome *inadequacy feelings.* This is also known as *Adlerian theory.*

individual racism The negative attitudes one person has about all members of a racial or ethnic group, often resulting in overt acts such as name-calling, social exclusion, or *violence.* See also *institutional racism* and *institutional discrimination.*

individuation The process by which individuals come to understand themselves as differentiated from others and the whole social system of which they are a part. The term is frequently used to describe the process by which toddlers and young children grow progressively independent from their mothers or other caregiver. See also *separation–individuation.*

indoor relief A historically important form of *social welfare* benefit in which the recipient was required to reside in an institution to maintain his or her *eligibility.* The *almshouse* and *poorhouse* were the most common types of indoor relief; they have been mostly discontinued in the United States. See also *relief* and *outdoor relief.*

induced psychotic disorder A delusional mental system that is brought about as part of a close relationship with one other person or many people. The term is roughly synonymous with *shared psychotic disorder* but is used by diagnosticians to imply some conscious intent by the other person to exacerbate the condition. See also *folie à deux* and *codependency.*

inductive reasoning The process by which theories and generalizations are evolved from a set of particular observations. Specific observations may be chosen to create explanations about a larger set of phenomena. See also *deductive reasoning.*

industrial policy A nation's plan and regulation of its entire means of production, marketing, and distribution of goods through laws, subsidies, tax incentives, disincentives, and access to privileges. Nations vary in the degree to which their industrial policies are comprehensive and controlled, ranging from planned economies (for example, in Japan, Taiwan, and Korea) to relative *laissez-faire* (for example, in the United States and Australia). See also *disincentive.*

185

industrial social work Professional social work practice, usually conducted under the auspices of employers or *labor unions,* or both, for the purpose of enhancing the employees' overall quality of life within and beyond the work setting. Many social workers use the term synonymously with *occupational social work.* See also *employee assistance programs (EAPs).*

industry versus inferiority According to the *psychosocial development theory* of Erik Erikson (1902–1994), the fourth stage of development occurring at about ages six to 12. The child may seek to acquire the basic social skills and competencies required for effective survival in the adult world or may come to feel unworthy and less able than peers to accomplish these tasks.

inequality Social disparity in power, opportunity, privilege, and justice. The term often implies the actual disparity of possessions, education, and health care.

inequity A disparity of power or opportunity to receive just treatment or equal rights. Social workers often apply this term to social conditions in which people face *institutional discrimination* or social barriers that impede their efforts to achieve the same goals available to others. The term usually differs from *inequality* in that inequity implies lack of opportunity for justice or privilege (such as fair court trials or opportunities to elect representative officials). See also *glass ceiling* and *generational equity.*

infanticide The killing of a baby.

infantile autism See *autistic disorder.*

infantilization Overtly or covertly encouraging a person to behave in a manner more appropriate to an infant or small child. This pattern is often seen in parents or spouses who are overprotective. Examples are speaking to the person in baby talk or not requiring the person to behave with appropriate maturity. The term is also used to indicate behavioral regression or to indicate that a person's behavior is appropriate to a much younger person.

infant mental health A multidisciplinary specialty to understand and improve the factors that influence the psychological well-being of infants. Social work is joined by pediatrics, nursing, special education, psychiatry, and developmental psychology to develop methods of preventing future mental illness and to assess and treat those psychological problems that are found in infants. The focus is usually on at-risk infants, especially those who are potentially at risk of *neglect, abuse,* or *deprivation* or whose parents have substance abuse or physical or mental illness.

infant mortality rate The demographic measure of the number of *neonatal* deaths that occur in proportion to the population as a whole or to the population of potential mothers (*fecundity* rate). The infant mortality rate is often used as a key factor in assessing the health and health care programs of a nation or community.

infectious disease A disease caused by the entrance of pathogenic microorganisms (bacteria or viruses). The disease may be contagious and enters the body through air, water, food, clothing, and insects. See also *opportunistic infection.*

inference Forming a conclusion based not on direct observation but on reasoning from something known. For example, a clinical social worker notes that a young child returns from a visit with a noncustodial parent covered with bruises and scars and laden with anxiety and fear. The social worker infers but has not seen child abuse.

inferiority complex An individual's persistent and extensive *inadequacy feelings* and a self-concept of being of a lower order than is expected.

infertility The inability to conceive. Infertility sometimes may result from a lack of sexual intercourse, the use of certain techniques in intercourse, effects of *contraception,* health factors, alcohol and drugs, radiation, and toxic substances. Infertility in men is attributed to problems related to testicular temperature, blockage of ducts, retrograde ejaculation, immunological problems, and *sexual disorders* such as *erectile disorder* or *premature ejaculation*. Infertility in women is attributed to such problems as blocked fallopian tubes, endometriosis, cervical conditions, hormonal problems, infectious disease, and sexual disorders including *vaginismus* and *inhibited sexual desire*.

inflation Increases in the *cost of living* in an economy and the resulting decrease in purchasing power.

influence peddling Facilitating access to policymakers for money or bribing public officials on behalf of third parties.

influence tactics See *tactics of influence*.

informational therapy Counseling and psychotherapy oriented to and emphasizing growth through the acquisition of conscious knowledge. This orientation is contrasted with *insight therapies*.

information and referral service A social agency or an office established within an agency that informs people about existing benefits and programs and the procedures for obtaining or using them and that helps people find other appropriate resources and sources of help. See also *access provision*.

information theory See *communication theory*.

informed consent The granting of permission by the client to the social worker and agency or other professional person to use specific *intervention*, including diagnosis, treatment, follow-up, and research. This permission must be based on full disclosure of the facts needed to make the decision intelligently. Informed consent must be based on knowledge of the risks and alternatives. One of the greatest risks in professional *malpractice* suits is failure to achieve informed consent. See also *implied consent*.

infrastructure The foundation facilities, buildings, and systems of a society, such as its highways, parks, public spaces, railroads, bridges, telephone lines, power plants, and water and sewage lines.

inhalant use disorder Abuse or dependence on the reaction resulting from inhaling vaporous substances such as gasoline, glue, paint thinners, spray paints, cleaners, spray-can propellants, or their combinations. Symptoms of *intoxication* include tremor; dizziness; psychomotor retardation; stupor or coma; sleep disturbances; nausea; irritability; fleeting illusions; and family, school, or vocational problems.

inhibited orgasm A *sexual disorder* in which the client is unable to achieve satisfactory orgasm following a period of sexual excitement. In women, orgasm is delayed or absent even though the sexual activity is considered adequate in focus, intensity, and duration. In men, ejaculation is delayed or absent even though there may be an erection and adequate sexual arousal. This disorder is not caused by *organic* disorders. Sex therapists and other clinicians have replaced this term in diagnosis with the terms *male orgasmic disorder* or *female orgasmic disorder*.

inhibited sexual desire A *sexual disorder* involving the persistent lack of interest in or abhorrence for participation in *coitus* or *sexual foreplay*.

inhibited sexual excitement A *sexual disorder* in which the partner in *coitus* or *sexual foreplay* is unable to maintain the physical characteristics of *arousal*. Once labeled as *impotence* in men, there is failure to achieve or maintain an erection through to completion of coitus. Once described as *frigidity* in women, there is failure to achieve or maintain the lubrication–swelling response through to completion of the sexual act.

inhibition 1. Hesitancy or restraint in action or behavior. 2. In *psychoanalytic theory*, the term refers to the restraining of some instinctual impulse by the *superego*. 3. In behavioral terms, it is any process in which a response is restrained.

initiative versus guilt According to the *psychosocial development theory* of Erik Erikson (1902–1994), the third of the eight stages occurring at about ages three to six. The child may be encouraged for actively seeking to learn, discover, and experiment. On the other hand, the child may develop a pattern of passivity because rejection, punishment, and restrictiveness lead to a sense of wrongdoing or "badness."

injunction A court process and legal order by which a party is forbidden to take or is made to refrain from taking a particular action (for example, entering another party's home, selling a contested property, or visiting an unwilling former spouse). The order may be of temporary, permanent, or indefinite duration.

inkblot test See *Rorschach test.*

in-kind benefits See *benefits.*

in loco parentis The legal expression referring to the circumstances in which an organization assumes the obligations of parenting a child or other person without a formal adoption. Most commonly, such relationships exist when a child is in a residential institution such as a *reformatory* or boarding school.

inmate One who is confined in a prison, hospital, or other institution; a prisoner or patient.

innate Traits, abilities, or characteristics that are present at birth.

inner city A term used in *urbanology* and other social sciences to describe an area within a city that is usually characterized by high population density, racial *ghettos,* and a decaying *infrastructure.*

inoculation The process of introducing, usually through injection or ingestion, a serum or *vaccine* into a living organism to create some *immunity* to disease. The process works by stimulating the organism's production of disease-resistant antibodies.

input–output analysis A tool used by economists and planners to chart the *linkages* between organizations. In social welfare, the chart is constructed by listing all the social agencies in a column and then listing them in the same order in a row across the top. Numbers are written in the resulting columns to indicate the frequency with which any two agencies are linked according to some criteria. This method graphically reveals which organizations are isolated, which are sharing responsibilities and resources, and so on.

inracial adoption *Adoption* of a child of one *race* by adoptive parents of that same race (for example, an African American child being adopted by African American parents). See also *transracial adoption.*

INS See *Immigration and Naturalization Service (INS), U.S.*

insanity A legal and lay term used to indicate the presence of a severe *mental disorder* in an individual. Used as a legal term, the mental disorder is considered to be so serious as to negate the individual's responsibility for certain acts such as criminal conduct. The person declared legally insane is thought to lack substantial capacity either to appreciate the wrongfulness of a crime or to act in conformity with the requirements of the law. Used as a lay term, insanity is roughly synonymous with "crazy" or "psychotic." The term is not used by mental health professionals in their diagnostic nomenclature. See also *McNaughten rule* and *Durham rule.*

insecure attachment In *attachment theory,* a pattern of attachment in which children are unable to comfortably explore their environments and interact with strangers even in the presence of their primary *caregiver.* Two forms of insecure attachment are *avoidant attachment* and *resistant attachment.*

insecurity A feeling of being unprotected or helpless owing to economic or social realities, emotional conflicts, or other problems.

in-service training An educational program provided by an employer and usually carried out by a supervisor or specialist to help an employee become more productive and effective in accomplishing a specific task or meeting the overall objectives of the organization. Usually, but not always, such training occurs on the job and for short periods. See also *staff development.*

insight 1. Self-understanding and awareness of one's feelings, motivations, and problems. 2. In several forms of *psychotherapy* and *clinical social work*, raising awareness of or illuminating the client's inner conflicts and their origins, areas that previously had not been well understood.

insight therapies Treatment approaches oriented to helping individuals achieve greater self-awareness and understanding of their own *conscious* and *unconscious* motivations, emotions, thought processes, and underlying reasons for their behaviors. These forms of therapy tend to be more long-term, broader, and more general in goals and focused on one's historical psychosocial development. They are contrasted with *cognitive therapy, behavior therapy, problem-solving casework,* and *task-centered treatment.* Some types of insight therapies include *psychoanalysis, existential social work,* and *client-centered therapy.*

insolvency An individual's or business's inability to pay debts when they come due, even if the party has assets that are sufficient but inaccessible.

insomnia Inability to sleep. The term is most commonly applied to chronic and persistent sleeplessness that interferes with social functioning and is a symptom of *anxiety, depression, pain,* or *organic* disorders. See also *hypersomnia.*

instincts Patterns of *behavior* that are characteristic of a given species and seem to derive from inherited rather than learned processes.

Institute for the Advancement of Social Work Research (IASWR) An independent social work organization to promote the profession's research capacity and provide technical assistance to social work researchers, provide research training, establish linking and networking opportunities for researchers, and develop a researcher database. IASWR was organized in 1993 through the efforts of several social work organizations, including the *National Association of Social Workers (NASW),* the *Council on Social Work Education (CSWE),* the Association of Baccalaureate Program Directors (ABPD), and the *Group for the Ad-*

vancement of Doctoral Education in Social Work (GADE).

institution 1. A fundamental custom or behavior pattern of a culture, such as marriage, justice, welfare, and religion. 2. An organization established for some public purpose and the physical facility in which its work occurs, such as a prison. See also *social institution.*

institutional discrimination Prejudicial treatment in organizations based on official policies, overt behaviors, or behaviors that may be covert but approved by those with power.

institutional ethics committees (IECs) See *ethics committees.*

institutional network The aggregate of human services agencies in a community that make up the service system.

institutional racism Those policies, practices, or procedures embedded in bureaucratic structures that systematically lead to unequal outcomes for people of color. See also *individual racism.*

institutional review boards (IRBs) See *ethics committees.*

institutional-versus-residual model See *residual-versus-institutional model.*

institutional welfare provision The conception of *social welfare* as a "mainline" function of society (equal to other *social institutions,* such as family, religion, economics, and politics) in which programs are permanent and provide for the overall security and emotional support of people.

instrumental conditioning See *operant conditioning.*

instrumental means The tools and facilities necessary to complete a task or fulfill a *role* successfully.

insurgency A nonbelligerant *social action* that attempts to depose and replace an existing government. The insurgents use political tactics, including *propaganda, demonstra-*

tion, strike, and *sabotage,* to seek legitimacy for some aspect of the political system that the ruling authority considers illegitimate.

insurrection An organized uprising against the established government or other authority.

intact reality testing The ability of an individual who is experiencing hallucinations to understand that they do not represent external reality. For example, this may occur with some substance abusers and people experiencing recurrent nightmares.

intake Procedures used by social agencies to make the initial contacts with the client productive and helpful. Generally, these procedures include informing the client about the services the agency offers; providing information about the conditions of service, such as fees and appointment times; obtaining pertinent data about the client; interviewing to get a preliminary impression of the nature of the problem; arriving at an agreement with the client about willingness to be served by the agency; and assigning the client to the social worker or social workers who are best suited to provide the needed services.

Integrated Child Services Development Scheme of India The *social welfare* program established in 1970 that provides nutritional, health care, educational, and social services to needy children in the nation of India. Social workers administer these programs at the community level using volunteers, with added support from health care professionals.

integrated method *Social work practice* that involves a high degree of professional knowledge and skill in bringing together the concepts and techniques used in serving individuals, families, groups, and communities. The social worker, using the integrated method, is considered to be more than a *generalist,* or one who simply combines knowledge and skills of some basic *casework, group work,* and *community organization.* See also *knowledge base.*

integration 1. The process of bringing together components into a unified whole. 2.

Psychologically, an individual's internal connection of values, ideas, ideals, knowledge, motor responses, and relevant social norms. 3. Sociologically, the process of bringing together diverse social or ethnic groups and achieving harmonious relations.

integrity versus despair The last of the eight stages in human psychosocial development, according to the *psychosocial development theory* of Erik Erikson (1902–1994), occurring from about age 54 to *death.* The individual may develop a sense of integration with humanity and of the unique meaning of his or her own life, or there may be a sense of regret about how that life has been lived and a fear of death.

intellectualization A *defense mechanism* and personality tendency in which the individual ignores feelings and emotions and analyzes problems or conflicts as objectively as possible but usually in a stylized or overly rational manner.

intelligence The ability to learn from experience and respond effectively to new situations, mentally store and retrieve information, solve problems, successfully manipulate the environment, and find ways of producing desired results. See also *multiple intelligences, fluid intelligence,* and *crystallized intelligence.*

intelligence quotient (IQ) An index of a person's relative level of *intelligence,* as determined by performance on a specialized test. The tests are designed to determine a person's abilities to use abstract concepts effectively, to grasp relationships, to acquire information about the relevant environment, and to meet and adapt to novel situations. The resulting IQ scores are said to indicate the individual's mental potential, and test subscores are sometimes used in psychiatric assessments. The mean IQ score is 100, and those with scores between 90 and 110 are considered "average." Those whose scores are below 70 are often considered to need special education. Major intelligence tests include the WAIS (Wechsler Adult Intelligence Scale) and the WIS (Wechsler Intelligence Scale for Children).

intensive family preservation services (IFPS) A program using a *multisystems orientation* to provide a holistic range of social services to families in crisis, usually through the involvement of *social work teams* and *social agencies* involved in *interorganizational collaboration.* Many social work intervention systems are determined less by the family's need than by the type of agency that has initial contact with the family. For example, when a *multiproblem family* enters the helping network through the juvenile court system, the intervention plan is likely to be different than if the family enters through the child welfare or mental health clinic routes. In the IFPS system, the same services are provided regardless of where the family enters. Several agencies are organized to collaborate when a given family enters any one of their systems and meets the appropriate criteria. The family is assigned to a social work team comprising workers from each participating agency.

interactional model A *holistic* orientation to *social group work* and other forms of *social work practice* developed by William Schwartz and Lawrence Shulman (*Social Work,* 38[January 1993], pp. 91–97) that emphasizes the reciprocal influences of each person and system involved in the helping process, including the worker, the client, the worker's supervisor and agency, the client's family, and relevant others as they are all engaged or acknowledged as participants in the service provided. The skill of the worker leads to the client's perception of the worker as a caring professional, which positively affects the *relationship* and the outcome of practice.

interactional problems A term used by social workers as a category for the difficulties clients are having in their relationships with others as a consequence of some acts of commission or omission. In the *Person-In-Environment (PIE) System,* nine types of interactional difficulties are indicated: power type, ambivalence type, responsibility type, dependency type, loss type, isolation type, victimization type, mixed, and other.

Inter-American Children's Institute An office within the *Organization of Ameri-*

can States (OAS) devoted to the social development and welfare of North and South American children, adolescents, and families. With headquarters in Montevideo, Uruguay, the organization sponsors the Pan American Child Conference every four years and helps coordinate the child welfare policies and activities of OAS–member nations.

Inter-American Commission on Women An office within the *Organization of American States (OAS)* that works toward educational and vocational opportunities for women, *consciousness-raising* about the problems of women, and the development of Women's Bureaus in member nations.

Inter-American Human Rights Commission The agency within the *Organization of American States (OAS)* that seeks to assure that the rights of the peoples of all its member nations are not abused.

Inter-American Indian Institute An office within the *Organization of American States (OAS)* that coordinates the policies and activities of Western Hemisphere nations pertaining to their Indian populations. The institute emphasizes education and *consciousness-raising* about the problems of Indians and helps Indian groups provide for their health, economic, health care, and social services needs.

Inter-American Social Development Center (CIDES) The principal educational and research facility of the *Organization of American States (OAS),* with headquarters in Buenos Aires, Argentina. CIDES sponsors national and regional instruction for social planners on effective social development activities and program evaluation.

intercountry adoption *Adoption* in which a child from one nation is placed with couples in another country. Subject to the laws of the country of the child's birth, arrangements are monitored with varying degrees of strictness by authorities and individuals in the child's original country. This is one of the most rapidly increasing forms of adoption in the United States. Most of these children come to the United States from Asia (especially

Korea and India) and Latin America (especially Colombia and El Salvador).

interdependence The sharing of responsibilities and benefits that are required for survival or well-being.

interdisciplinary teaming Team *intervention* or *collaboration* on behalf of a specific *client* or *client system*, which involves members of different professions or disciplines. For example, a social agency might call on a social worker, psychologist, clergy member, nurse, and physician to coordinate their respective specialties to help a *multiproblem family*. See also *social work team* and *interprofessional team*.

interest group A segment of the population or members of a formal or informal association who have common interests, goals, concerns, or desires that often lead to purposeful and united action; also known as a special-interest group. See also *constituencies*.

interface The point of contact or communication between different systems or organizations.

interferon Chemical substances produced naturally in the white blood cells that prevent the spread of viral infections. Interferon now is produced in laboratory cultures and has proved useful in the treatment of some cancers and *leukemia*. It also has been tested as treatment for immune deficiency diseases such as *acquired immune deficiency syndrome (AIDS)* or *human immunodeficiency virus (HIV)*.

intergenerational relations The degree to which members of different age groups engage with one another. See also *age segregation, gray ghettos, gerontophobia,* and *generational equity*.

intergroup relations Societal institutions and activities that involve and seek to enhance operation and mutual respect between various identifiable sectors in the population, especially ethnic, racial, religious, geographic, socioeconomic, and other kinds of groups. These activities are also known as "race relations," "interreligious relations," and "intercultural education." Social work specialists often engage in intergroup activities in which they seek to remove or reduce the barriers, different priorities, and misunderstandings that exist between groups. Among the national organizations involved in intergroup relations are the National Conference of Christians and Jews, American Friends Service Committee, and the *Southern Christian Leadership Conference (SCLC)*.

Interior Department See *Department of the Interior, U.S.*

interlocutory decree In law courts, an interim decision that does not determine the final outcome of the case.

intermarriage Legal wedlock between couples of different *races, ethnic groups,* religions, or *social classes*.

intermediate-care facilities (ICFs) Nursing residences for older people who are not fully capable of living alone but do not require full-time nursing home care. ICFs usually have medical and nursing care conveniently available and provide social programs and room and board, but the residents can usually handle *activities of daily living (ADL)*. See also *skilled-nursing facility* and *continuing-care retirement communities (CCRCs)*.

intermittent explosive disorder Numerous repeated episodes of a loss of control of aggressive impulses and fits of rage out of proportion to any *stressor*. See also *explosive disorder*.

intermittent reinforcement In *behavior modification*, a schedule of *reinforcement* in which one type of *response* is reinforced at some times but not at others.

internalization 1. The process of incorporating the *norms* of one's *culture*; taking in and accepting as one's own the *values*, attitudes, style, and social responses of one's primary group or other reference groups. 2. In *psychoanalytic theory*, this term refers to the taking in of attitudes, feelings, and traits of significant others and making them one's own.

International Association of Schools of Social Work (IASSW) An organization of social work schools and educators throughout the world whose mission is to improve training and ensure consistent standards for *social work education.* Founded in 1928 with headquarters in Vienna, Austria, IASSW is affiliated with the *International Council on Social Welfare (ICSW).*

International Bank for Reconstruction and Development See *World Bank.*

International Classification of Diseases **(ICD)** A statistical classification of all human diseases, including *mental disorders,* that is compiled by the *World Health Organization (WHO).* The publication, generally referred to as the ICD and followed by an edition number, is issued about every 10 years. The first edition, called the *International List of Causes of Death,* was completed in 1900. The current edition is the ICD-10.

International Classification of Impairment, Disability, and Handicapped (ICIDH) A codification and publication of the *World Health Organization (WHO),* similar to its *International Classification of Diseases (ICD),* to delineate the types and degrees of impairment. ICIDH has three classes of these problems: (1) *impairment,* (2) *disability,* and (3) *handicap.*

International Conference for the Advancement of Private Practice in Social Work (I–CAPP) The professional social work organization whose goals include promoting *private practice,* maintaining and improving standards for its members, providing members with learning and communication opportunities, developing the knowledge and skills of private practitioners, enhancing licensing and certification, and advocating for greater client access to private practice and social workers.

International Council of Social Work (ICSW) An organization with headquarters in Vienna, Austria, that fosters coop-

eration among nations in the development and maintenance of *social welfare* programs. ICSW coordinates welfare activities between nations, facilitates research, disseminates information, and sponsors conferences among social welfare leaders of different nations.

International Federation of Social Workers (IFSW) The professional association of social workers from nations in every geographical area of the world. Its purpose is to establish policy and actions designed to meet more of the human services and welfare needs and to establish better standards of service and related activities of interest to the membership. IFSW cosponsors, with other international organizations, various international meetings and symposia that foster opportunities for social workers to meet and exchange knowledge. Founded in 1928 with headquarters in Oslo, Norway, IFSW is also known by its French title Federation Internationale des Assistantes Sociales. IFSW publishes the influential journal *International Social Work.*

International Federation on Aging (IFA) The nongovernmental international organization comprising national associations of and for older people that provides advocacy and education and promotes social and economic well-being for the world's older populations. IFA works closely with other organizations, especially the *World Health Organization (WHO),* the *International Labor Organization (ILO),* and other United Nations organizations.

International Labor Organization (ILO) A specialized agency within the United Nations concerned about employment, economic security, and social services among people in the world's nations. ILO helps nations develop programs for economic development and social security, especially in old-age insurance, workers' compensation, unemployment programs, as well as health care and education benefits.

International Social Security Association (ISSA) A membership organization comprising government departments and national institutions responsible for the administration and development of *social security* programs. ISSA disseminates information about social security between nations and promotes, protects, and helps develop social programs in all nations. ISSA publishes the *International Social Security Review.*

international social work   A term loosely applied to (1) international organizations using social work methods or personnel, (2) social work cooperation between countries, and (3) transfer between countries of methods or knowledge about social work. Virtually every country has a national department responsible for some phase of social services and personnel to carry out the functions of those departments. International social work organizations emphasize efforts to educate workers to ensure that social services needs are met. Organizations that have been active in international social work include the *United Nations Children's Fund (UNICEF),* the *Organization of American States (OAS),* the *International Labor Organization (ILO),* the *International Social Security Association (ISSA),* and the *United Nations Educational, Scientific, and Cultural Organization (UNESCO).* Many voluntary organizations also have international social work aspects, including the *Red Cross* and *Red Crescent,* the *Young Men's Christian Association (YMCA),* the *Young Women's Christian Association (YWCA),* the *International Union for Child Welfare (IUCW),* and others. A major forum for international social work is the *International Federation of Social Workers (IFSW).* See also *comparative social welfare.*

International Society for Rehabilitation of the Disabled   A federation of voluntary organizations in more than 80 nations, whose goal is to improve *rehabilitation* services and provide education and knowledge about people with disabilities and their care and rehabilitation.

International Union for Child Welfare (IUCW)   An organization, with headquarters in Geneva, Switzerland, comprising government, public, and private organiza-

tions of many nations that are concerned about *child welfare.* The union facilitates research, provides training, and disseminates information that can benefit children.

internment   Confinement to *relocation camps,* prison, or other designated places during wartime of a group of people thought to be dangerous or potentially sympathetic to the enemy. Americans of Japanese ancestry experienced internment during World War II. See also *Nisei generation.*

interorganizational collaboration   A system whereby social workers and other professionals from different agencies work together to make decisions about and provide a more-extensive range of services for the same client than would be possible or efficient when one agency or one worker alone engages the client. The collaboration may be highly integrated (as in developing a single goal with a central mechanism to coordinate its attainment) to loose (as in agency professionals communicating to coordinate the attainment of their autonomous goals). This type of system is used for example, in *intensive family preservation services (IFPS).*

interpersonal skills   See *social skills.*

interpersonal theory   Concepts developed by American psychiatrist Harry Stack Sullivan (1892–1949) that emphasized conflicts between people as a primary factor in the development of psychopathology. Treatment uses systematic interventions by professionals, which symbolically reverse the development of the pathogenic conflicts.

interpretation   Explanations offered to the client by a social worker or psychotherapist to enhance understanding, make connections, and facilitate the development of *insight.*

interprofessional team   A small, organized group of people, each trained in different professional disciplines and possessing his or her own skills and orientations, working together to resolve a common problem or achieve a common goal. The team members contribute their special talents through continuous intercommunication, reexamination, and evaluation of individual efforts toward team objectives and with group responsibility for the final outcome. The interprofessional team may include but is not limited to the members of a *mental health team* (such as psychiatrists, psychologists, social workers, and psychiatric nurses). For example, a team that might be formed to provide a community with disaster relief could consist of social workers of various specializations as well as physicians, nurses, economists, architects, engineers, sanitation specialists, and political scientists. See also *social work team, interdisciplinary teaming,* and *collaboration.*

interrater reliability In systematic *research,* the degree to which different people give similar scores for the same observation. For example, a researcher might give all the social workers in an agency identical lists of a client's problems and then ask them to rank those problems according to which must be dealt with first. If the social workers identify the same problems for immediate attention, this would be described as "high interrater reliability."

intersectoral planning The attempt by social planners to look at problems or groups of people in a comprehensive fashion. This makes possible the coordination and integration of the efforts of single-issue organizations, which focus their efforts on one problem *(sectoral planning).* Intersectoral planning occurs, for example, in welfare councils and agencies of *Community Action Program (CAP)* and on human resources commissions. See also *social planning.*

Inter-University European Institute on Social Welfare A research and educational organization oriented to acquiring, developing, and disemminating information about European social welfare. The multidisciplinary organization, founded in 1970 and headquartered in Marcinelle, Belgium, comprises members from universities in most European nations and seeks a uniform European social welfare policy.

interval measurement In *research,* a level of measurement that includes the properties

of *nominal measurement* and *ordinal measurement* but also requires that there are equal intervals between the units of measurement. Most of the well-standardized psychological tests use interval measurement.

intervention 1. Interceding in or coming between groups of people, events, planning activities, or an individual's internal conflicts. 2. In social work, the term is analogous to the physician's term "treatment." Many social workers prefer using "intervention" because it includes "treatment" and also encompasses the other activities social workers use to solve or prevent problems or achieve goals for social betterment. Thus, it refers to *psychotherapy, advocacy, mediation, social planning, community organization,* finding and developing *resources,* and many other activities.

interview A meeting between people in which communication occurs for a specific and usually predetermined purpose. When the interview is between a social worker and client, the most typical purpose is some form of problem solving. To achieve that purpose, there are many types of social work interviews, including *directive therapy, nondirective therapy, fact-gathering interview,* and *intake.* Interviews may be of individuals, groups, families, and communities. Most interviews often combine different types in the same sequence of contacts.

interview schedule A tool used especially in fact-gathering conferences or surveys to guide the interviewer toward the information that is sought. For example, schedules may consist of specific yes–no or *closed-ended questions* that are to be read to the respondent, or they may consist of *open-ended questions* that stimulate the respondents to answer in their own words. The interviewer often reads the questions to the respondent and records the answers verbatim in the space provided.

intestate Not having a valid will. When a person dies intestate, the estate is generally settled by court-appointed administrators.

intestate death To die without a valid will. This means the state has control over the distribution of the assets according to its own rules.

intimacy phase The third of five *group development phases* in which group members tend to lose their mutual guardedness and struggle to establish their roles and power within the group and become genuinely concerned about the well-being of the other members. In most groups this is the longest phase and the time when most of the individual and group goals are reached. In this concept of the various stages through which groups progress, this one follows the *preaffiliation phase* and the *power-and-control phase* and precedes the *differentiation phase* and the *separation phase*. Many other typologies have also been proposed to describe the phases in the typical life of groupwork or a therapy group.

intimacy versus isolation According to the *psychosocial development theory* of Erik Erikson (1902–1994), the sixth of eight stages that occurs at about ages 18 to 24. The individual faces the challenge of developing one or more close and warm relationships or facing life alone.

intoxication The state of being inebriated as a result of ingesting *exogenous* substances. These substances include alcohol and drugs, and the resulting behavior ranges from temporary euphoria, slurred speech, and impaired motor functioning to maladaptive behaviors such as ineffective job performance, impaired judgment, and deteriorating social functioning. See also *substance intoxication*.

intrapsychic Occurring within one's personality or *psyche*.

intrinsic anxiety The *anxiety* of the client that derives from the necessary focus on unpleasant material that is uncovered, analyzed, and processed. This is contrasted with *extrinsic anxiety*.

introjection In *psychoanalytic theory*, a mental mechanism in which the individual derives feelings from another person or object and directs them internally to an imagined form of the person or object. For example, an individual may introject pa-

rental criticism, turning it into some type of self-criticism.

introspection Self-examination of thoughts, values, and feelings.

introvert One whose psychic energy, interests, thoughts, and feelings tend to be directed inward rather than toward the social and physical environment; the opposite of an *extrovert*.

intuition An informal, lay term referring to an individual's perceptiveness, awareness of characteristics and feelings within another person, and an accurate sense of what is going to happen.

Invalid Care Allowance A *social security* program in Great Britain that provides compensation for some people, other than wives, who care for their disabled family members at home.

inventory In *social research*, a type of *interview schedule* used to guide the researcher in assessing the presence or absence of specific phenomena, behaviors, or attitudes.

inverse relationship 1. An association between two phenomena in which a higher frequency in one variable accompanies a lower frequency in another. 2. In *social research*, it is sometimes called negative correlation.

investment-versus-consumption concept A controversy about the ultimate objectives of social services, often faced in *social planning*. The one view (investment) holds that social programs should exist as an economic and social investment by enabling recipients to become more economically productive and that social services programs that serve this purpose should have priority. The other view (consumption) holds that social programs should provide goods and services to disadvantaged people to improve their standard of living and that this is a worthwhile goal in itself. See also *human capital*.

invisible hand The premise of some economic theorists, beginning with Adam Smith in the 18th century, that unrestricted trade and the free economic market, in which people can pursue their self-interests, will ultimately (invisibly) lead to the general welfare.

invisible loyalties Alliances between family members that occur outside the *conscious* awareness of any of them. Most commonly this *family therapy* term refers to *unconscious* commitments that children acquire to support one or both parents or other family members.

in vitro fertilization Human *conception* by removing the woman's ovum surgically, placing it in a medium that preserves and nourishes it, introducing live sperm cells, maintaining the live cells until some growth and divisions occur, and then inserting the embryo in a woman's uterus.

in vivo assessment Evaluating client progress by directly observing the client in actual life situations. It is conducted either overtly or unobtrusively with the client's awareness and permission. For example, in overt in vivo assessment, a social worker may accompany a claustrophobic client into a crowded elevator. In unobtrusive in vivo assessment, the worker may enlist an associate to observe a passive client use newly learned assertiveness techniques in the marketplace. These assessments are used when situational assessments are difficult to create and *client self-monitoring* is unlikely to demonstrate client behavior accurately.

in vivo desensitization A *behavior therapy* procedure in which the subject gradually approaches a feared *stimulus* while in a relaxed state. The subject and worker make a list of situations that elicit fear and rank these items from least to most anxiety producing. The subject then enters a state of relaxation through *meditation*, deep-breathing relaxation, *imagery relaxation technique, muscle relaxation technique,* and so on. In this state, the subject is gradually desensitized to the feared stimuli.

involuntary client One who is compelled to partake of the services of a social work or other professional. For example, an individual may be required to seek a social

worker's services by a court decision, by the fact of *incarceration,* or by family or employer pressure.

IPAs See *independent practice associations (IPAs).*

IQ test See *intelligence quotient (IQ).*

IRBs See *institutional review boards (IRBs).*

irritation response theory The view, held by some economists and social planners, that people will strive harder to improve their circumstances if social welfare is punitive and minimal.

"isms" As used in social work, this suffix has become a term in itself and refers to the group of ideologies and prejudgments that most affect social work clients. Some social workers think of the "isms" only as negative belief systems and resulting behaviors (such as *racism, ageism, fascism,* or *speciesism*). However, there are many other "isms" that many people do not consider negative (such as heroism and *altruism*).

isolated explosive disorder See *explosive disorder.*

isolation 1. The condition of being separated and kept apart from others. 2. Psychologically, it is aversion to or fear of contact with others. 3. In *psychodynamic* theory, it is a *defense mechanism* in which memories are separated from the emotions that once accompanied them. For example, a client may have been terrified when subjected to child abuse, but when relating the incident to the social worker 20 years later, the client seems to feel indifferent to it.

isolationism The political view advocating the avoidance of relationships with foreign nations, especially military alliances and economic treaties.

ISSA See *International Social Security Association (ISSA).*

IST defendants In legal terminology, those people alleged to have committed crimes who are considered "incompetent to stand trial."

Such people may be held pending completion of the IST evaluation within 90 days or treated as an outpatient until the competency status is resolved. See also *NGRI patients.*

IUCW See *International Union for Child Welfare (IUCW).*

IVD program Interactive video program, a CD-ROM computer-assisted instruction program *(CAI program)* used by social workers and other professionals, especially in medicine, engineering, and the physical sciences. This program is used to simulate real situations and develop practice experiences under laboratory conditions. For example, social work students can try different interview techniques with simulated clients shown on a monitor and immediately see the consequences.

IV drug user An individual who ingests *controlled substances,* or sometimes legal drugs in an inappropriate way, through intravenous (IV) injections, usually self-administered. See also *needle exchange program.*

IWW The Industrial Workers of the World. See *"Wobblies."*

J

Jacobs, Frances Wisebart (1843–1892) A charity organizer and welfare worker, she developed and led Denver's movement to consolidate its charitable organizations. She formed the Denver Federation of Social Agencies, which became the model for the national *Community Chest* and *United Way* organizations.

jargon The special language that is used by various professional groups as a short-hand method of communicating complicated concepts, which usually seem obscure and confusing to those outside the group. Social work jargon includes many of the terms found in this dictionary.

Jarrett, Mary Cromwell (1876–1961) Developer of psychiatric social work. Based on her own work in *mental hospitals,* she developed a training course for social workers who worked in these facilities, which became part of the curriculum at the Smith College School for Social Work. In 1923, she founded the organization that became the *American Association of Psychiatric Social Workers (AAPSW).*

JCAHO See *Joint Commission on Accreditation of Healthcare Organizations (JCAHO).*

JCIA See *Joint Commission on Interprofessional Affairs (JCIA).*

jealous-type delusional disorder A subtype of *delusional disorder* characterized by non-bizarre delusions, particularly an intense belief that one's spouse or significant other is being secretly unfaithful. The delusion often leads one to exhibiting hypervigilant behavior, seeking evidence and threatening attacks.

jealousy A combination of uncomfortable emotions and reactions to the perceived threat of losing a possession to a perceived rival.

Jewish communal services A program of services provided by local and national Jewish welfare federation offices, including *social services, health care,* education, and *intergroup relations* activities. Most American communities with Jewish populations of more than 5,000 have Jewish welfare federation offices that raise funds for local and overseas allocations and provide planning and leadership development.

Jewish social agencies Private organizations originally established in larger cities to serve the unique *social welfare* needs of Jewish families and individuals. The organizations included Jewish Family Service Agencies, Hebrew Benevolent Associations, and Jewish Welfare Societies. Most of these agencies now provide services to members of all faiths and ethnic groups.

"Jim Crow" laws Statutes requiring or condoning racial *segregation* in the United States. Such laws have been ruled unconstitutional.

JINS Juveniles in need of supervision. See *persons in need of supervision (PINS).*

Job Corps The federal program established as part of the *Economic Opportunity Act of 1964,* designed to provide employment and work skills to school dropouts. Jobless youths between ages 16 and 21 work and study at training centers or in conservation camps. The Job Corps is managed by the U.S. *Department of Labor,* which contracts with local public and private agencies to establish the training centers. The program was partially modeled after the *Civilian Conservation Corps (CCC)* and similar *New Deal* programs.

job description Explicit obligations and specific tasks required of an employee as conditions of employment. Some job descriptions also state certain educational, experiential, and skill requirements expected of the incumbent.

Job Opportunities and Basic Skills Training (JOBS) program A federal program started with the *Family Support Act (FSA) of 1988* (P.L. 100-485) designed to educate and train mothers receiving *Aid to Families with Dependent Children (AFDC)* to improve their employability. The program provides these mothers, as an incentive, transitional assistance for *child care* and *health care* for up to one year after leaving AFDC. This program is not related to the federal jobs program that was part of the *Economic Opportunity Act of 1964* and largely supplanted by the *CETA* program in 1973.

JOBS program Job Opportunities in the Business Sector, one of the federally supported *employment* programs established in 1964 as part of the *Economic Opportunity Act of 1964*. Aimed at able-bodied but long-term unemployed individuals, the program was meant to encourage the private-sector employer, through tax incentives and direct wage subsidies, to hire unskilled workers. *CETA* largely supplanted this program in 1973.

Job Training Partnership Act The 1982 federal law (P.L. 97-300, P.L. 97-404) designed to replace some of the functions of the *CETA* program and to encourage more private-sector, local, and state involvement in *employment* training programs.

joining The *family therapy* process, described in 1974 by Salvador Minuchin and others, in which the *therapist* becomes a part of the family's interactional system to help change the dysfunctional parts of the system.

joint budgeting A form of interagency *linkage* in which two or more service providers share decisions about the financing of existing or new social services. For example, two organizations could decide to reduce their respective expenses by eliminating some of their duplicated services. See also *joint funding*.

Joint Commission on Accreditation of Healthcare Organizations (JCAHO) A private, not-for-profit organization dedicated to promoting high-quality health care through a voluntary accreditation process. Its mission is to enhance the quality of care and services provided in organized health care settings. JCAHO develops and continually refines its standards for accreditation, surveys facilities and programs to measure and encourage compliance with the standards, and accredits organizations that have demonstrated substantial compliance with the standards.

Joint Commission on Interprofessional Affairs (JCIA) An informal organization comprising elected leaders and staff of the American Nurses Association, the American Psychiatric Association, the American Psychological Association, and the *National Association of Social Workers (NASW)*. The commission meets three times a year to share relevant information and plan joint strategies to deal with a wide variety of mental health issues, ranging from relationships with the *National Institute of Mental Health (NIMH)* to encouraging and promoting interdisciplinary *collaboration* at the state and local levels.

Joint Commission on Mental Illness and Health The organization of health care and welfare agencies that in 1961 completed a five-year study of the nation's need for mental health services. The findings led to federal funding for *community mental health centers* and improvements in state mental hospital programs.

joint custody A legal decision involving a divorcing husband and wife and the respective responsibilities each of them will have for the care of their children. Typically, both parents maintain permanent homes for the children, and the children live with each for relatively equal amounts of time. Joint custody can also refer to an arrangement whereby the child lives with one parent most of the time, although the other parent has an equal say in important decisions regarding upbringing.

Joint Economic Committee A combined committee of the U.S. Senate and House of Representatives established in 1946 to obtain information and make recommendations to Congress on possible legislative action pertaining to the U.S. economy and the economic welfare of its citizens.

joint funding A form of interagency *linkage* in which two or more service providers or two or more *funding* services help to finance a project or ongoing service collaboratively. For example, agencies or foundations that might be unable to afford to establish their own *outreach* programs could establish one together. See also *joint budgeting.*

joint interview Variations of the *interview* format in which more than a single interviewer and interviewee meet. In one form, the social worker or other professional meets with the client and his or her *relevant other* (for example, teachers, guidance counselors, and classmates). In another form, the social worker meets simultaneously with several clients who may have no relationship with one another. In a third form, the client meets with two or more workers simultaneously.

"jointly and severally" A stipulation in legal agreements under which each of the signers becomes individually liable for payment of the remaining debt.

joint processing A procedure for welfare clients to apply for more than one program at a time, thus reducing the waste of resources, number of interviews, and paperwork. The procedure works best in *categorically needy* programs in which the eligibility criteria are the same.

"jump bail" A slang term referring to the actions of some defendants in failing to appear for their criminal trials after depositing significant funds with the court to

ensure that they will appear for their trials or will remain in the jurisdiction. If they fail to appear or leave the jurisdiction, they forfeit the deposit.

Jungian theory Concepts about the development of human personality and *psychopathology* formulated by Swiss psychiatrist Carl Gustav Jung (1875–1961). These concepts emphasize the *conscious* and *unconscious* influences on behavior. Important concepts include the *collective unconscious* (collection of human thoughts and experiences that have developed through many generations, called an *archetype*), *dream analysis,* introversion and extroversion, and *anima* and *animus.* See also *introvert* and *extrovert.*

junket Travel by government officials (especially legislators) at taxpayer expense, supposedly to conduct official investigations.

junior life skills The ability to carry out the *activities of daily living (ADL)* that are expected of young people before emancipation in preparation for independent living. These include such tangible *life skills* as housekeeping, financial management, hygiene, personal appearance, and the ability to access public transportation. Intangible junior life skills include knowing how to greet people, form and maintain friendships, and behave compatibly according to parental and educator expectations.

jurisprudence The philosophy and science of law in terms of its origins, nature, and structure.

justice of the peace A local magistrate or court official with the authority to try minor cases, administer oaths, and perform civil marriages.

justice system The social institutions, facilities, and people—including police, the prison and parole systems, the legal profession, the judiciary, and investigative organizations—that provide the means for enforcing and interpreting the *laws* of the land. In the United States, this system is coordinated and influenced, to a major extent, by the U.S. *Department of Justice,* which is headed by the Attorney General. This department oversees the Federal Bureau of Investigation (FBI), the Bureau of Prisons, the *Drug Enforcement Administration (DEA)*, the *Law Enforcement Assistance Administration (LEAA)*, the *Immigration and Naturalization Service (INS)*, the Parole Commission, and other agencies. The system also includes the judicial and court system, from the Supreme Court to the local *justice of the peace*. See also *criminal justice system* and *juvenile justice system*.

justifiable homicide   Taking the life of another human under circumstances that usually make it not a *crime*. Examples include killing in self-defense, executing an individual convicted of a *capital offense*, or military combat.

juvenile   For purposes of criminal law, a young person who has not yet attained the age at which he or she would be treated as an adult. The term is distinguished from *minor*, which is used to refer to legal capacity. The age differs from state to state, although the *Juvenile Justice and Delinquency Prevention Act of 1974* defines a "juvenile" as one who has not yet reached age 18.

juvenile court   A court of law that has jurisdiction over abused, delinquent, dependent, or neglected children and their parents or guardians. Generally, the court is also responsible for determining whether the alleged offense was committed by the accused juvenile and for overseeing the resulting rehabilitation or penalty process. See also *Gault decision*.

juvenile delinquency   In a jurisdiction, a pattern of *antisocial behavior* by juveniles that would be regarded as criminal in nature if committed by adults.

Juvenile Justice and Delinquency Prevention Act of 1974   The federal law (P.L. 93-415) whose purpose is to discourage the institutionalization of juveniles. It provides the federal *block grant* to states to achieve community-based alternatives to reformatories and to juvenile correctional institutions.

juvenile justice policy   A component of *criminal justice policy* involving guidelines and established procedures to be considered when deciding how to cope with the illegal conduct of minors. Elements of current U.S. juvenile justice policy include giving the juvenile the same legal rights to trial and counsel granted to adults, incarceration in facilities that are segregated from adult institutions, shorter sentences, clearing the record after a specified period of good behavior, and an orientation that tries to be more therapeutic than punitive. See also *Gault decision*.

juvenile justice system   That part of the *criminal justice system* that is oriented toward the control and prevention of illegal behavior by young people (those younger than age 22 in some jurisdictions and younger than age 16 or 18 in others) and toward the treatment of a *minor* engaged in such behavior. See also *Borstal system*, *juvenile court*, and *family court*.

juvenile offenders   Young people, usually under the age of legal responsibility (age 18 in most states) who have been convicted of legal violations, including *felony, misdemeanor*, and any other form of *delinquency*.

juvenile parole   In the judicial terminology, the status of a juvenile who has been conditionally released from incarceration as a result of delinquency and placed in a supervised treatment or rehabilitation program while living at home, in foster care, or in a transitional living facility. The system is also known as *aftercare*.

K

Kaposi's sarcoma A form of *cancer* in which tumors grow in the blood vessel walls. Symptoms include purple or brown lumpy spots appearing on the skin and mucous membranes of the mouth. The condition was once seen primarily in older men of Jewish or Mediterranean ancestry but now occurs as a major symptom of *human immunodeficiency virus (HIV)* infection or *acquired immune deficiency syndrome (AIDS)* in people of all ages and ancestry.

kapuna Native Hawaiian female elders, considered in the traditional Hawaiian culture to be the custodians of family history, the primary sources of wisdom, and the arbitrators of family disputes.

Kelley, Florence (1859–1932) Crusader for *child labor* laws and protections for workers, Kelley helped organize the *National Consumers League (NCL),* and with *Lillian Wald,* founded the *Children's Bureau.*

Kellogg, Paul Underwood (1879–1958) Founder and editor from 1909 to 1952 of *The Survey,* social work's unofficial and vastly influential journal. *The Survey* was one of the few national publications to give in-depth analyses of social problems and their solutions. Kellogg was also an active leader in the development of various social work organizations.

Keogh Plan A retirement pension system for self-employed people. Also known as the HR-10 plan, Keogh permits self-employed people, including social workers in *private practice,* to set aside a specified portion of their net earnings each year. No income taxes on these funds must be paid until retirement. Payouts begin between ages 59 1/2 and 70, at which time taxes on the income and interest are paid. The plan holder must keep the funds in a qualified financial institution (such as a bank, insurance company, or securities firm) set up for this purpose and permit all full-time employees to participate in the retirement plan. The plan holder must report Keogh activity to the Internal Revenue Service annually and cannot withdraw the funds until retirement without a financial penalty.

Kerner Commission The National Advisory Commission on Civil Disorders, a fact-finding group appointed by President Lyndon B. Johnson in 1967 and headed by Governor Otto Kerner of Illinois to determine the causes of and make recommendations on solutions to the *civil rights* protests and riots of that period. The commission report, issued in 1968, blamed white *racism* and the limited opportunities available to the African Americans who lived in ghettos. Few of its proposals were implemented.

Keynesian economics The theories of British economist John Maynard Keynes (1883–1946), including the recommendation that during economic slumps, government should increase public spending to stimulate commerce and create employment.

kibbutz A collective residential *community* in Israel. Residents own almost no personal property and work for the community not for a salary but for goods and services from other members. The needs of the residents, including food, housing, education, child care, and health care, are provided for by the combined resources of the community.

Kibei Japanese Americans who are born in the United States but travel to Japan for education or temporary or permanent residence. See also *Sansei generation.*

kidnapping The *crime* of taking persons by force or manipulation and holding them against their will or that of their legal guardian.

kidney dialysis See *hemodialysis.*

kinesalgia Vivid pain that is experienced only with movement.

kinesics *Nonverbal communication* through body motions. See also *communication theory.*

kinship A group of people bound by the same blood-line (genetic inheritance). Use of the term usually implies other characteristics shared by the *family,* such as similar behaviors, values, and talents.

KKK See *Ku Klux Klan (KKK).*

kleptomania 1. Compulsive stealing. 2. An *impulse control disorder* in which the person unlawfully takes property belonging to another. The theft act is motivated by emotional release, excitement, or gratification and not by need for the object or its material value. Explanations for this phenomenon vary, but most jurisdictions do not accept it by itself as justification or as a defense against punishment or other legal action.

"knee-jerk liberal" A disparaging term applied (mostly by conservatives) to people who, supposedly without thought, elect to raise taxes and mobilize resources to solve social problems. The term is similar to *"bleeding heart."*

knowledge base In social work, the aggregate of accumulated information, scientific findings, values, and skills and the methodology for acquiring, using, and evaluating what is known. The knowledge base is derived from the social worker's own research, theory building, and systematic study of relevant phenomena and from the direct and reported experiences of other social work practitioners. It is also derived from information made available by clients and members of other disciplines and professions and from the general knowledge of society as a whole.

Kohlberg moral development theory A set of related concepts proposed by Lawrence Kohlberg in the early 1970s to explain the way an individual's ethics and ideas about "right and wrong" change with age. Six stages or levels of development are delineated: (1) rules are obeyed to avoid punishment, (2) rules are obeyed to obtain rewards, (3) the individual obeys rules mostly to avoid being disliked and to be seen as being "good," (4) the individual develops an appreciation for society's need for rules and a conscience or sense of guilt at wrongdoing, (5) the individual understands that there are competing and contradictory values and that some impartial judgments are necessary, and (6) the individual appreciates the validity of universal moral principles and develops a commitment to them. Most individuals are believed to have completed the first two stages (preconventional level of moral development) by age nine. The next two stages (conventional level) are usually completed during early adolescence. Most people do not reach the last two (postconventional level) until after age 20, and many people never reach this level at all, according to Kohlberg.

Kohutian theory See *self-psychology.*

koro A *culture-bound syndrome,* found especially among peoples of Chinese and East Asian ancestry, in which a man experiences intense anxiety that his penis will recede into his body or in which a woman fears her vulva and nipples will recede into her body.

Korsikoff's disease *Amnesia* related to the prolonged heavy use of alcohol.

Kübler-Ross death stages The psychological reactions to impending *death* described by Elisabeth Kübler-Ross in 1969, based on her interviews with terminally ill patients. The five stages identified are (1) *denial* and *isolation,* (2) *anger,* (3) *bargaining,* (4) *depression,* and (5) *acceptance.* Some patients go through these stages in a different order, some go back and forth between some or all of the stages, and still others never go through any of them.

Ku Klux Klan (KKK)   A loose confederation of *white supremacist groups* and *secret societies* comprising people who oppose the advancement of minority groups, including Jews, Roman Catholics, immigrants from other nations, and especially African Americans. This opposition is expressed through attempted intimidation and terrorism. The KKK formed after the Civil War to keep African Americans from exercising their newly won rights. Through burning crosses, wearing hoods and robes, and committing murder and assaults, the KKK accomplished some of their goals until federal troops all but eliminated them in the 1970s. New KKK groups, mostly independent, have emerged and declined, especially from 1915 to 1930 and again in the 1960s. In recent years, there has been a modest KKK resurgence, especially in areas that have experienced a large influx of nonwhite immigrants.

kurtosis   In statistics, the degree of flatness or pointedness around the mode of a frequency curve. For example, a social agency plots on a graph the times during a one-year period that new clients are accepted and finds that most come during the summer. A frequency curve would show a peak during that period.

kwashiorkor   A disease of *malnutrition* caused by protein deficiency. It is found most commonly in *Third World* and *Fourth World* countries or impoverished areas where children receive too little milk or other protein foods. Growth retardation, anemia, abnormal distension of the abdomen, weakness, and apathy are major symptoms.

L

labeling The application of a name to a person or a person's problem based on observed traits or patterns of *behavior*. Some social workers view labels (for example, such psychiatric diagnostic terms as *passive–aggressive*) as a form of name-calling or generalization about people that leads toward stereotyping and away from *individualization*. Other social workers consider it a necessity to facilitate *research* and *communication* about a person's problem without having to include prolonged detailed descriptions. See also *psychiatric labels* and *DSM-IV*.

labeling theory The hypothesis that when people are assigned a label, such as *paranoid schizophrenia*, to indicate some kind of disorder or *deviance*, others tend to react to the subjects as though they were deviant. Also, the subjects may begin to act in a way that meets the others' expectations. This may be a type of *self-fulfilling prophecy* and an example of the *Hawthorne effect*.

la belle indifference An apparent form of *apathy* or lack of concern for existing or potential problems, noted as a symptom in people with certain mental disorders including *schizophrenia*.

labile Having the tendency toward emotional flexibility, freedom of movement, and abrupt changes in *mood* or *affect*. See also *emotional lability*.

labile affect Abrupt shifts and excessive variation in an individual's expression of *affect*.

labor force The segments of a society that can or do produce all its marketable goods and services. The U.S. *Bureau of the Census* includes in this definition employed and unemployed people. Those not in the labor force include some people who are retired, in school, raising families, disabled, "voluntarily idle," and others.

labor-force participation rate (LFPR) The U.S. *Bureau of the Census* designation for the number of people who produce marketable goods and services divided by the number of people eligible for *employment*.

labor intensive 1. Pertaining to those organizations in which the greatest outlay is for personnel. 2. Pertaining to corporations and agencies that require many workers to provide the service or manufacture the product and that do not or cannot replace personnel through automation. Social agencies and most other service provider organizations tend to be labor intensive.

Labor Management Services Administration A branch of the U.S. *Department of Labor* that administers laws affecting union activities and facilitates negotiations between worker groups and employer groups.

labor mobility The degree to which a society permits or encourages its workers to move from one job to another within the same employment organization, between organizations, and from one location to another. Economists generally believe that those societies with a relatively high level of labor mobility are likely to become more economically productive than those that are less flexible.

labor theory of value The concept suggested by Karl Marx (1818–1883) and other socialist theoreticians stating that the value of each product or service should be determined by the amount of labor required to produce it.

labor union An association, primarily of wage or salary earners and employees in a particular industry (such as government employees or automobile workers) or craft (plumbers or teachers), whose purpose is to advance the economic interests and working conditions of its members. Many social workers belong to labor unions such as the *American Federation of State, County, and Municipal Employees (AFSCME),* the *American Federation of Government Employees (AFGE),* and the *Communications Workers of America (CWA).*

labor welfare Programs in industrial organizations to provide personnel- and employment-related *social services.* This is a term used in some *Third World* nations where *social welfare* services for the general public are limited, thus compelling some industries to provide such services for their employees.

"lady bountiful" A term once frequently applied, somewhat derisively, to social workers and volunteer workers who provided goods and services to those in need. The term originated during the U.S. Civil War when upper-class women donated and personally delivered food, clothing, and advice to those in need. Many of these women subsequently began working as *friendly visitors,* the precursors to professional *social workers.* See also *"greystocking."*

laissez-faire 1. In *social policy,* the idea that government should not interfere with any aspect of the economy and that individuals will provide all services and fulfill all needs by means of financial incentives. This is a relative concept, but in its literal form, it is the classic capitalistic model of society. 2. In social administration, the term refers to the management practice of minimal involvement.

La Leche League An international advocacy and educational organization to encourage natural infant feeding and discourage widespread use of commercial baby formula.

Lamaze method Natural childbirth without the use of anesthetics or other medication but with the use of exercise, systematic breathing, and relaxation procedures.

lame duck An office holder or manager whose time of departure has been specified and announced. This announcement sometimes weakens the power of the incumbent among those who know they soon will be dealing with a different leader.

LAMM A chemical compound (L-alpha-acetylmethadol) used in the *maintenance therapy* of people addicted to an opiate drug. LAMM treatment is an alternative to *methadone treatment.* Because it is slower acting but longer lasting, the addicted person need not stay at or make daily trips to the methadone maintenance clinic.

Lane Report The study, conducted in 1939 by Robert P. Lane, analyzing the field of *community organization* and describing it as a professional entity. The report influenced the social work profession to incorporate *community organization* as one of its three major practice methods, along with *social group work* and *social casework.* The report drew on earlier conceptualizations, especially those of *Edward C. Lindeman* and Jesse F. Steiner.

language disorder An inability to use language to communicate satisfactorily, caused by developmental, cognitive, or physical impairment. The term does not apply to people who have communication problems in areas where the languages are not in their native tongue. Language disorders include never having acquired any language (usually the result of *mental retardation*) and acquired disorders resulting from physical problems such as *trauma,* hearing disabilities, *stroke, neurological disorder,* and developmental language disorder. Developmental language disorders are of the expressive or receptive types and, more frequently, combinations of both. See *expressive language disorder* and *mixed receptive–expressive language disorders.*

laparoscopy A surgical procedure that uses a laparoscope (a fiberoptic instrument) inserted in small incisions into the peritoneal cavity. The procedure, sometimes colloquially termed "band-aid" surgery, obviates the need for large abdominal incisions; it has been used for *in vitro fertilization,* female *sterilization,* and removal of gall bladders.

La Raza Unida The political movement and party, comprising mostly *Chicano* people and others of Spanish-speaking heritage, that advocates for policies and candidates favorable to the needs of *Hispanic* people.

larceny Stealing or theft; the unlawful taking of property that belongs to another person. See also *grand larceny* and *petit larceny.*

Lassalle, Beatriz (1882–1965) Social activist for *suffrage* and other rights for Puerto Ricans, she headed the Puerto Rico Emergency Reconstruction Administration during the *Great Depression* and led the successful campaign for Puerto Rico to be the first state or territory to have social work *licensing.*

last-hired/first-fired principle *Seniority* as the criterion in employment retention. This principle has been criticized, especially by women and people of color, as being discriminatory because it works against those who have more recently entered the *labor force.*

latah A *culture-bound syndrome* noted especially in Indonesia, Malaysia, Thailand, Japan, and the Philippines, in which the individual enters a trancelike state, imitates the speech and manner of others, and seems highly sensitive to fright.

latchkey child A youngster who comes home from school to spend part of the day unsupervised because the parents are still at work. See also *home-alone children.*

latency-age child A child who has passed about age six but has not yet reached *puberty.* Common in social work usage, the term refers to the *latency stage* in the *Freudian theory* of psychosexual development. The term was used originally to suggest that the individual's sexuality is latent or dormant, although this premise is now questioned.

latency stage In the *Freudian theory* of psychosexual development, the stage of personality development in the child that follows the *phallic* (oedipal) *phase* and precedes the *genital stage (adolescence).* Sigmund Freud (1856–1939) viewed this as a time in which no new conflicts are introduced, but the child consolidates previous progress. Other analytic theorists, such as Harry Stack Sullivan (1892–1949) and Erik Erikson (1902–1994), saw this stage as important for the child's developing *social skills* and *sexual identity.* See also *psychosexual development theory.*

latent homosexual A term sometimes applied to an individual who believes himself or herself to have a heterosexual orientation but who has *unconscious* desires for erotic gratification with members of the same sex. Latent homosexuals may be in deep conflict about their *sexual orientation* and expend great psychic energy in denying to themselves and others that such conflicts exist. Such denial might take the form of overt hostility toward homosexuals, avoidance of them, or avoidance of any behaviors that seem more appropriate to members of the opposite sex. See also *homosexuality, latent* and also *homosexuality* and *homophobia.*

latent schizophrenia An imprecise and obsolete term rather than a diagnostic entity, referring to early or mild signs of *schizophrenia* (sometimes *flat affect,* some *paranoid ideation,* and *thought disorders*) but no clear-cut psychotic episodes or gross breaking with reality. Other obsolete terms also in common use by professionals to describe this condition have been "borderline schizophrenia," "prepsychotic," or "incipient psychosis."

Lathrop, Julia C. (1858–1932) Advocate for *child welfare* and a leader in establishing the U.S. *juvenile court* system, Lathrop was the first director of the *Children's Bureau* and later became active in the *women's suffrage movement.*

law A system of rules and legislative pronouncements established and recognized by a state, nation, tribe, society, or community as binding to its members.

Law Enforcement Assistance Administration (LEAA) The federal program created by the Omnibus Crime Control and Safe Streets Act of 1968 (P. L. 90-351) that provides funds, often in matching arrangements with state governments, for rehabilitation of offenders, recruitment and training of corrections personnel, and improvement of correctional facilities. LEAA's functions have been taken over by many other federal and state justice and law enforcement offices.

Law of Settlement and Removal The historically significant English statute, enacted in 1662, that led to the widespread use of *residency laws* in determining eligibility for *public assistance.* Under this law, municipal employees were authorized to help only poor citizens and to expel from their jurisdictions anyone who might become dependent on assistance.

lay analysis *Psychoanalysis* as practiced by one who does not have a medical degree but who has acquired special training in its theory and technique. Social workers and others with this training and experience may be considered lay analysts.

layoff A temporary but indefinite separation from employment, not associated with job performance but with the employer's economic situation, supply shortages, or market declines.

LCSW See *Licensed Clinical Social Worker (LCSW).*

LD children Those with *learning disabilities.*

LDCs See *less-developed countries (LDCs).*

LDS Social Services The organization of social agencies affiliated with the Church of Jesus Christ of Latter-Day Saints, with branches in major communities throughout the United States, that provide family, *child welfare,* and gerontological services as well as other *social services* for all individuals in need. See also *sectarian services.*

LEAA See *Law Enforcement Assistance Administration (LEAA).*

lead poisoning The absorption of quantities of lead, sometimes resulting in brain damage, respiratory illness, other health problems, or *death* in the affected individual. The lead may come from such sources as lead-based paint or the exhaust of automobiles that burn leaded gas. The population at greatest risk for lead poisoning is young children who live in older buildings in which lead-based paints were used. They may ingest paint chips or breathe lead residue. Another *at-risk population* includes people in highly congested cities where automobile exhaust may contain high levels of lead.

League of Red Cross Societies An organization founded in 1919 comprising 60 national *Red Cross* societies to coordinate *disaster relief* activities by member societies, including raising funds, procuring emergency provisions, distributing resources to populations experiencing natural or human-made disasters, and training relief workers.

League of Women Voters A voluntary organization established in 1920 to educate citizens about the political process and to scrutinize and conduct research on the electoral process and government structure at the national, state, and local levels. An outgrowth of the Woman Suffrage Association, the league originally sought to educate women in the rational use of their newly acquired right to vote. The league, which opened its membership to men in 1974, has chapters in most cities in the United States. See also *suffrage* and *women's suffrage movement.*

learned helplessness A pattern of *behavior,* frequently seen in victims of *spouse abuse* and *child abuse,* in which the individual responds passively to risks of harm. The person may behave without obvious symptoms in every other way but has come to believe there is nothing that can be done and that no effective help is available. See also *self-defeating personality disorder.*

Learnfare A plan and program in various *public assistance* systems that ties the client's benefits to participation in specified educational programs. The idea is to encourage recipients to acquire additional education to enable them to achieve greater economic independence. The program is sometimes part of *workfare* welfare benefits.

learning curve A graphic representation of the amount and frequency with which skill or information is acquired; usually the horizontal axis indicates time and the vertical axis indicates the activity learned, the skill demonstrated, or the errors involved.

learning disability A descriptive term for children of normal or above-average *intelligence* who experience a specific difficulty in school, such as *dyslexia* (reading difficulty), *dysgraphia* (writing difficulty), or *dyscalculia* (math or calculation difficulty).

learning disorder A level of achievement in reading, writing, and mathematics that is substantially below that expected for age, education, and intelligence. The condition may be related to low self-esteem, discouragement, cultural factors, or other diagnosable mental disorders, especially *conduct disorder, oppositional defiant disorder, attention-deficit hyperactivity disorder (ADHD)*, major depressive disorder, or *dysthymic disorder*. Learning disorders were formerly called "academic skills disorder."

learning theory *Behaviorism* and *social learning theory,* the concepts that underlie *behavior therapy* and *behavior modification;* the concept that human behaviors result from finding success or failure with certain responses to various environmental stimuli.

least-developed countries A designation by the United Nations for countries with low economic growth, *literacy* rates, and per capita incomes, and few natural or *human resources* with which to progress. See also *Fourth World*.

"least-restrictive environment" (LRE) The term educators use for the legal requirement to place children with disabilities in learning situations that meet their special needs while most closely approximating that of the child without disabilities. Many educators think LRE is a synonym for *mainstreaming*. However, even though most children with disabilities under this provision are placed in normal classrooms, in some circumstances, some restrictions are required.

Leboyer method A system designed to minimize the infant's birth *trauma* by maintaining a quiet postdelivery environment in a dimly lit room and by placing the newborn on the mother's abdomen with the umbilical cord intact. Physicians do not spank or hold the infant upside down.

Lee, Porter (1879–1939) Social work educator and leader in curriculum development for schools of social work, Porter helped organize the *American Association of Schools of Social Work (AASSW)* in 1919 and advocated the integration of multidisciplinary knowledge into social work. He wrote and was coauthor of many early social work textbooks including *Mental Hygiene and Social Work* and *Social Work: Cause and Function*.

leftist An individual whose sociopolitical orientation is more liberal than those in the mainstream. The term originated in the British Parliament where liberals sat on the left of the aisle. The label also has been applied to anyone considered sympathetic to *Marxism*. See also *liberalism*.

legal adoption The legal process by which a parent–child relationship is created between people genetically unrelated. Those who are legally adopted become heir to all the privileges with the parents that natural children would have. Technically, because *adoption* is a legal process, this term should be redundant. However, it often is used by social workers, necessitated by the practice of *black-market adoption*.

legal aid The provision of free or reduced-fee legal counsel to a *litigant* who cannot afford a private attorney. Legal aid offices exist throughout the United States and many other nations and are sponsored by local bar associations, law schools, and government organizations. See also *Legal Services Corporation.*

legal defense fund Moneys collected and held to pay the expenses of individuals or groups who are or who may become involved in *litigation.* Those for whom such funds are established are usually unable to meet these expenses themselves.

legal regulation The control of certain activities, such as professional conduct, by government rule and enforcement. In social work, legal regulation occurs through *licensing, certification,* or *registration of social workers.* In each of these, the public is assured by the relevant legal jurisdiction that the social worker possesses the knowledge or qualifications required by law to receive that designation.

legal separation An agreement between a husband and wife, enforced by *law,* that permits them to live apart without being divorced.

Legal Services Corporation The federal agency, established in 1974, that provides funding for local programs that furnish legal services to eligible clients, especially poor people.

legislative advocacy The process of influencing the course or content of a bill or other legislative measure. This may be facilitated by individuals, agencies, organizations, or coalitions to protect or establish the rights and entitlements of their clients. Legislative advocacy may occur directly by using specific *legislative advocacy tactics* or indirectly by mobilizing community groups.

legislative advocacy tactics Procedures used to influence lawmakers and the legislative process and to modify, pass, or defeat legislation. Seven specific procedures have been delineated by Ronald B. Dear and Rino J. Patti ("Legislative Advocacy: Seven Effective Tactics," *Social Work,* 26[July 1981], pp. 289–296) to be used by advocates, staff, agencies, community groups, and lobbyists to influence state legislators: (1) introduce a bill as early as possible, pref-

erably before the legislative session; (2) obtain multiple sponsorships and avoid solo sponsorship; (3) obtain bipartisan sponsorship with the prime sponsor in the majority party; (4) seek an influential prime sponsor, such as a committee chair, but only if that person will use available power to promote the bill; (5) obtain the support or neutralize the opposition of relevant state agencies and the governor; (6) press for open hearings and organize effective testimony; and (7) be ready to compromise and support the amendatory process to obtain a favorable outcome. Other activities to enhance the chances of a bill's passage are to clearly define the problem that the bill addresses; fully assess the fiscal impact of the bill's passage; provide clear, concise, and relevant information to committee members and staff; support the sponsors to help move the bill through the legislative process; mobilize constituencies; and use the media to publicize the problem and the legislative remedy.

legitimation The acquisition of rights or authority to fulfill specified functions or pursue specified goals.

leisure class The socioeconomic group that has sufficient resources to enable the group to devote most of its time to recreational or hedonistic pursuits.

lending out a license The practice in which a licensed *professional* employs an assistant to perform functions that would lead a reasonable-thinking client to consider the assistant a licensed professional. Social workers sometimes practice dubious ethics by hiring unlicensed assistants to see some of their clients. It is more commonly done by psychiatrists who hire social workers to do *psychotherapy* with their clients while charging the client the higher physicians' rate. In such cases, the supervisor or employer may be liable for any damages even if that person has never seen the injured client.

LePlay, Pierre Guilluame Frederic (1806–1882) French political economist who may have been the first to address the problems of *poverty* using the scientific method of inquiry; in the 1850s and 1860s, he collected and analyzed the budgets of hundreds of French workers and wrote about how some of them became impoverished.

lesbian A woman whose sexual or *erotic orientation* is for other women. See also *gay* and *homosexuality.*

less-developed countries (LDCs) The poorest nations on earth, including those with fewest natural resources and lowest level of education among the population. See also *Fourth World.*

less-eligibility principle The premise that poor people should not be given financial assistance that raises them to a level exceeding that of the lowest-paid employed person in the community.

lethality The degree to which someone or something is capable of causing *death.* Social workers primarily apply the term to clients who are *suicide* or *homicide* risks. For example, a client might be said to have a high degree of suicidal lethality if symptoms include feelings of *depression* and hopelessness, the recent *loss* of loved ones, development of a suicide plan, failing health, and deprivation of a supportive family or friends.

leukemia *Cancer* of the blood-producing tissues—including bone marrow, lymphatics, liver, and spleen—resulting in increased production of white cells and a commensurate reduction of red cells and other blood elements. The onset of leukemia can occur at any age.

level of measurement In *research*, the range and degree of complexity with which data collected about a phenomenon are observed, processed, classified, and systematically evaluated. Levels of measurement include *nominal measurement, ordinal measurement,* and *interval measurement.*

LFPR See *labor-force participation rate (LFPR).*

liability A legal obligation to perform some duty, pay for some action, or refrain from doing something. Professional liability can take the form of paying clients who have been harmed by the *intervention,* and the liability can extend beyond the direct practitioner to that person's supervisor. See *"respondeat superior" doctrine.*

libel Writing and publishing a statement that is untrue, misleading, malicious, and damaging to the person being written about. To win a lawsuit against a libel charge, an individual must prove that the statements were either true or nonmalicious and undamaging. See also *slander.*

liberal arts education Undergraduate education designed to give students a foundation of knowledge that equips them to make free, informed choices about themselves and the world in which they live. Liberal arts education is distinguished from vocational training or professional or technical education. Originally, the liberal arts consisted of language, logic, rhetoric, arithmetic, geometry, astronomy, and harmony but now are studies of the natural sciences, social sciences, and humanities. One of the requirements for admission to accredited graduate schools in social work in the United States is a degree signifying liberal arts education.

liberalism The sociopolitical orientation that currently emphasizes the development of opportunities for all people, especially the disadvantaged, the poor, the elderly, children, and minorities through economic, educational, and social programs that are principally financed, regulated, and administered by the *government.* Use of this term, as well as that of *conservatism,* has accurate meaning only in the context and time frame in which it is used. This is because the orientation and goals of liberalism have changed through the centuries (see *classical liberalism*), have been associated with many political movements along the way (see *leftist*), and may be about to change once again (see *neoliberalism*).

libertarian A political movement and party that advocates minimal government outside of police and military forces, the cessation of all *welfare* programs, greater privatization of education and health care, and an unregulated economy. Libertarians also have advocated quarantines for patients with *HIV disease.*

liberty A people's freedom from arbitrary controls, slavery, ignorance, or government interference with private actions.

libido In *psychoanalytic theory,* sexual instinct (energy toward expression of pleasure and seeking a love-object as well as erotic gratification); a basic psychic energy.

licenciado The credential or license to practice professional social work awarded in many South American nations to those who have completed required university social work training. The term also applies to the credentials for other professions.

Licensed Clinical Social Worker (LCSW) A *professional* social worker who has been legally accredited by a state government to engage in *clinical social work* in that state. The acronym LCSW after a professional's name indicates possession of the license and the relevant qualifications. Qualifications for the license vary from state to state. Many states require an *MSW* degree from an accredited graduate school, several years of supervised professional experience, and successful completion of the state's social work licensing exam. According to Marilyn A. Biggerstaff ("Licensing, Regulation, and Certification," in Richard L. Edwards [Ed.-in-Chief], *Encyclopedia of Social Work,* 19th ed., Washington, DC: NASW Press, 1995), information about these requirements can usually be obtained from the relevant state's bureau of professional licensing or the state department of mental health.

Licensed Independent Clinical Social Worker (LICSW) A designation used by some state professional licensing bodies and some third-party financing institutions to indicate that the practitioner is qualified for independent practice. The designation is sometimes used for social workers who have been granted the status of an independent

vendor, requiring neither referral nor supervision as a condition of *third-party payment.* See also *independent social work.*

licensed practical nurse (LPN) See *practical nurse (PN).*

licensing Granting a formal governmental authorization to do something that cannot be done legally without that authorization. For example, many states license clinical social workers.

LICSW See *Licensed Independent Clinical Social Worker (LICSW).*

lie detector A machine used in police investigations designed to record physiological rates of change in pulse, blood pressure, skin moisture, and respiration. The subject answers questions, and the physiological rates of changes are recorded for expert analysis. Answering a question falsely is said to be emotionally charged for most people and stimulates the *autonomic nervous system (ANS)* over which one has no control. Because accuracy is possible in about 75 percent of those tested, the machine is used more to help in the investigation process than as evidence in courts of law.

lien A claim on some property placed there to secure payment of a debt. Until the lien is cleared, the property holder risks having the property sold to pay the debt if payment terms are not followed. Also, when such property is sold, the lien holder is usually entitled to debt repayment before any of the remaining funds goes to the property holder. Specific types of lien include tax liens (levied by states and federal governments against properties held by tax avoiders); landlords' liens (against furniture and other goods of tenants who damaged property or failed to pay rents); and mechanics' liens (against buildings, automobiles, or equipment as a security for work and materials performed thereon).

life cycle The age-related sequence of changes and systematic development undergone by an individual from birth to death. Although most people are said to go through similar changes in a fairly predictable order, the life cycle concept also includes individual and cultural differences.

life expectancy   The average length of time before death of people belonging to specified statuses, such as age group, occupation, gender, race, mental state, and health factors. For example, the life expectancy of newborn girls is several years longer than newborn boys who are similar in every other way.

life model   The social work practice approach that uses the *ecological perspective* as a metaphor for focusing on the interface between the client and the environment. The social worker who uses this approach views stressful problems in living (life transitions, interpersonal processes, environmental obstacles) as consequences of person–environment transactions. According to Carel B. Germain and Alex Gitterman (*The Life Model of Social Work Practice,* New York: Columbia University Press, 1980, p. 5), the approach uses an integrated method of practice with individuals and groups to release potential capacities, reduce environmental stressors, and restore growth-promoting transactions.

life review   The process of looking back over one's own life, analyzing it, uncovering the hidden themes, and understanding the meaning of the life. This occurs naturally among most older people, especially those approaching *death*. Conflicts that were unresolved during earlier years are addressed and dealt with. Reintegration occurs as conflicts are resolved. For some people, the life review process is effective and helpful when a therapist facilitates it through a systematic questioning and listening process. This life review therapy has been an important part of *existential social work.*

life script   A concept originated by psychiatrist Eric Berne in the 1970s to describe a person's lifelong pattern of *behavior,* predominant roles, orientation regarding choices, and the manner of interacting (transacting) with others. Life scripts have themes (such as martyr, victim, lover, failure, or nurturer), which the person tends to act out regularly. Four general life scripts that Berne-popularizer Thomas Harris identified as guides to transactions are as follows: (1) I'm OK—You're OK, (2) I'm OK—You're not OK, (3) I'm not OK—You're OK, and (4) I'm not OK—You're not OK.

life skills   The relative abilities to carry out *activities of daily living (ADL),* such as home management, budgeting, meal planning and preparation, home maintenance, personal hygiene, finding and maintaining appropriate educational and vocational opportunities, using the social system to obtain needed assistance, and maintaining positive social interactions. See also *junior life skills.*

life skills education   Individualized and classroom instruction, practical training, and guidance to help people correct deficits in their *life skills.* Such education often is provided under the auspices of local departments of social or human services.

life–space interview   The interview procedure designed to take place around the time and place of important symbolic events in the interviewee's life. The premise is that the effect of the meeting at such times and places is so powerful that it more than makes up for the time taken by the interviewer to be available at such times.

life–space social work   Professional social work *intervention* based on the concepts of the *life–space interview* that takes place outside the walls of the agency and in the environment of the client at times that are important to the client.

lifestyle-associated disorder   A health problem brought about by an individual's manner of living rather than a specific disease. Examples of such disorders may include *obesity* and physical weakness as a result of a lack of exercise.

limbic system   That part of the brain beneath the cortex that helps regulate long-term memory functions and emotions, especially rage, fear, and sexual arousal. The limbic system also is involved in the transmission of information between the brain and the body's peripheral sensory and motor systems.

"limousine liberal"   A term of disparagement applied to affluent citizens who advocate programs for poor and disadvantaged people but who do not tend to personally work or associate with them. It is similar to the term *checkbook activism*.

Lindeman, Edward C. (1885–1953)   Social work theorist and educator, at the New York School of Social Work from 1924 to 1950, he developed many of the conceptual foundations of *community organization* and *social group work*. He fought to keep the social context within social work during its movement toward intrapsychic concerns and sought to develop the integrated, holistic view of social work. He was also called the "father of adult education" in the United States. See also *Lane Report*.

linear causality   The idea that one event is the cause and another is the result or response. This notion has been questioned by many family systems theorists who suggest that it is too simplistic, at least where families are concerned. They say *circular causality* is a more-accurate depiction of the way people, especially families, influence one another—that is, not in a cause–effect relationship but through a series of repeating cycles and interacting loops.

linear perspective   The term used by family therapists with *systems theories* perspective to describe people who think in cause–effect terms. To have a linear perspective is to view *behavior* and events as resulting directly from specific causes rather than as being part of an endless cycle in a system. The linear perspective is said to be narrow and rigid because it does not consider the myriad influences and circularity of patterns that exist in social and environmental systems.

line-item budget   A financial statement listing each of the objects of expected expenditures for the forthcoming year, often presented by comparing the expenditures for each item with those of the previous year.

line of business   A *health maintenance organization (HMO), preferred provider organization (PPO),* or other health plan set up within a company, often an insurance company. A line of business is differentiated from a subsidiary or separate company.

linkage   In social work, the function of bringing together the resources of different agencies, personnel, voluntary groups, and relevant individuals and brokering or coordinating their efforts on behalf of a client or social objective. See also *collaboration*.

liquidation   Dismantling of an organization or estate by settling all its obligations and debts and distributing its remaining assets.

literacy   The ability to read and write.

literacy test   Examination of an individual's capacity for reading and writing. Often such exams have been used to keep some people of color, *ethnic groups,* and disadvantaged people from access to voting, jobs, education, or other opportunities.

literacy volunteer programs   National organizations of trained volunteers who provide, at no cost, individualized and peer-group tutorial services to people who need help with reading and writing skills and in cases of limited English proficiency, help in the English language. The largest of these are Literacy Volunteers of America and the Literacy Program of Laubach.

lithium carbonate   The chemical compound that in carbonated form is used by physicians in the treatment of a serious *affective disorder* such as the manic phase of *manic–depressive illness*. The most common trade names are Eskalith and Lithane.

litigant   An individual or organization that is actively involved in a lawsuit either as a plaintiff or defendant.

litigation   1. Civil and other disputes contested in courts of *law*. 2. The process of being involved in legal action.

litigious client A recipient of social work services who indicates a predisposition to initiate a lawsuit against the social worker or the agency. See also *malpractice*.

litigophobia The excessive *fear* of being sued or otherwise involved in legal actions.

little people The minority group comprising people who, as adults, are no taller than 4 feet 11 inches or who have disproportionately shorter limbs. The principal advocacy organization is Little People of America, which provides information to average-size parents of these children, raises funds for medical research, sponsors recreational activities, and advocates for equal opportunities for little people in jobs, housing, and civil rights. The organization also tries to get the public to call its members "little people" rather than "dwarfs" or "midgets."

live supervision A technique for enhancing *clinical social work* skills whereby the supervisor sits in on sessions or observes them in progress through one-way mirrors or closed-circuit television monitors and periodically points out various client dynamics and suggests different approaches or techniques.

living wage Income received by a worker that is enough to cover the costs of housing, food, health care, and other social and physical needs that are prevalent in that locality. What is generally considered a living wage tends to be much higher than a federally sanctioned *minimum wage*.

living will A formal statement made while the person is mentally competent that specifies an individual's wishes about the management of his or her own *death*. The statement is made particularly about the possibility of maintaining life, when viability and cognitive functions are impaired, by means of life support systems. State-specific documents are available from *Choice in Dying*.

loan shark A moneylender who exploits poor people by charging excessive interest for instant cash and sometimes recovers the money by taking the client's property or through threats or actual violence. See also *fence* and *usury*.

lobbyists The term used for *interest groups* and individuals who seek direct access to lawmakers to influence legislation and public policy. The term originated in the tendency of some of these people to frequent the lobbies of legislative houses to meet lawmakers. See also *legislative advocacy*.

localized amnesia See *psychogenic amnesia*.

location bound An individual who is constricted to living in a region or area because of social or health factors. Some reasons include a spouses' employment or preferences; the need to care for aging parents; the need for children to be near special-education facilities; and breathing disorders requiring residence in a clean, dry climate. Location-bound people are often disadvantaged in terms of vocational opportunities. See also *homebound*.

locura A term used by Spanish-speaking peoples to describe individuals who experience severe psychotic symptoms, including hallucinations, incoherence, unpredictability, and sometimes violent behavior.

logical positivism The orientation that accepts as meaningful only that which can be verified by empirical procedures or logic.

logorrhea Excessive and frequently incoherent verbalization, sometimes a symptom of *anxiety, paranoia,* and *schizophrenia*.

logotherapy The meaning-oriented philosophy and *treatment* method developed in 1967 by Victor Frankl and others and used by members of many disciplines to help people search for the humanistic and spiritual significance of their lives.

"log rolling" Legislators helping one another to get bills passed. For example, Senator A votes for Senator B's bill not because of the virtues of the bill but because Senator B has agreed to support Senator A's bill in turn.

longevity The length or duration of life.

longitudinal study Repeated testing of the same phenomenon or group of subjects over a significant period.

long-range planning Efforts to assess objectives and examine proposed programs, services, and resources to establish priorities for an extended period in the future. The long-range planner supplements the normal year-by-year decision-making process with a comprehensive overview of goals and the means needed to achieve them over periods often exceeding five or 10 years.

long-term care (LTC) A *system* of providing social, personal, and health care services over a sustained period to people who in some way suffer from *functional impairment* including a limited ability to perform the *activities of daily living (ADL)* such as dressing, eating, bathing, using the toilet, cooking, shopping, or taking medicine. LTC services are required mostly by older people, adults with developmental disabilities, people with *mental illness,* and people with *acquired immune deficiency syndrome (AIDS)*. It is provided by professionals, family members, and volunteers under public or private auspices in nursing homes, boarding houses, assisted-living centers, day care centers, and community-based facilities. In addition to health care and case management services, LTC services include transportation, escort, *homemaker services,* night sitting, recreation, *home health services,* home meals, and *ombudsperson* services. See also *long-term long-term care (LTLTC).*

long-term long-term care (LTLTC) A designation applied by health care providers to indicate *long-term care (LTC)* that lasts 90 days or more and to distinguish it from *short-term long-term care (STLTC),* which is fewer than 90 days.

long-term therapy *Psychotherapy* or other forms of *intervention* in which the professional and the client expect to meet regularly, longer than three months, often years. In this form of therapy, the goals are extensive and not specified or even precisely known in advance, and the issues dealt with in the sessions are not restricted. See also *short-term therapy.*

loose association The tendency to shift abruptly from one thought to another, with little, if any, apparent direct connection between the thoughts. Loose association is sometimes a symptom of severe *anxiety* or *depression* and in its more-severe forms can be a symptom of *psychotic* processes or *primary process thinking.*

loose coupling A concept administrators use to understand the nature of social welfare organizations and their environments. Although the organization is necessarily interdependent with the environment (coupled), its response can be flexible. Its self-modifications need not be immediate or extensive because environmental effects are usually unclear and incremental. See also *ambiguous mandate.*

Lorenz curve A graphic representation, developed by economist M. O. Lorenz, of a nation's existing degree of income inequality. The vertical axis of the graph represents the percentage of the nation's total family income. The horizontal axis indicates the percentage of families that receive a specified level of income. Thus, a nation with perfect income equality would be represented by a 45-degree line, because 10 percent of the nation's families receive 10 percent of total income, and so on. The amount of deviation from that line indicates the degree of inequality.

loss The state of being deprived of something that was once possessed, as a result of *death, divorce, disaster,* or *crime*. Social workers and other professionals consider loss to be the crucial element in *crisis* and a major precipitator of many forms of *depression*. Many social workers spend most of their time helping individuals, families, and communities adjust to loss by helping them to compensate or substitute for loss in the short and long term.

love A combination of biologically based, culturally modified perceptions, feelings, and actions signifying strong affection and attachment. Every person's experience of love and way of expressing it are unique. There is considerable variability between people and even within the same person from one time to the next. This is because each person's genetic makeup, physiology, stage of development, cultural background, and immediate stimuli, all of which contribute to the way love is experienced, vary. Thus, it is probable that when any two people profess love, they are not communicating about exactly the same thing; also what one person means when professing love one minute is probably not what that person means when using the term later. The context in which the term is used also influences its meaning. It is also commonly used to signify eroticism ("to make love"), strong interest ("to love music"), and *philanthropy* ("to love humanity").

Lowell, Josephine Shaw (1843–1905) A leader in the *scientific philanthropy* movement, which was the forerunner of professional social work. Lowell was a founder of the *Charity Organization Societies (COS)* in New York and, as an opponent of conditions facing women and children in the labor force, became a founder and first president of the *National Consumers League (NCL)*.

lower class According to sociologists, the *socioeconomic class* in which people tend to have the least amount of income and financial security, the poorest job prospects, minimal educational attainments, and orientations that often include apathy and hopelessness.

Low-Income Home Energy Assistance Program The federal program of the U.S. *Department of Health and Human Services (HHS)* that helps poor families pay their heating bills.

LPN Licensed practical nurse. See *practical nurse (PN)*.

LRE See *"least-restrictive environment."*

LSD Lysergic acid diethylamide, also known simply as "acid," a synthetic *hallu-cinogen* that produces changes in sensation and perception, sometimes resulting in *hallucination,* changes in the thought process, and *depression.* Prolonged heavy use of the drug may result in recurrence *(flashback)* of the effects of prior use of the drug weeks or even months after the last dose.

LTC See *long-term care (LTC).*

LTLTC See *long-term long-term care (LTLTC).*

lucidity The degree to which a person seems to experience clear perceptions and the ability to communicate about the experience.

"lumbago" A term, used mostly by older people, for lower back pain.

lunacy An obsolete term now used to ridicule people or ideas that seem unusual or unacceptable to others. The term once was used as a synonym for *psychosis* or *insanity* and is the basis for such words as "lunatic," "loony," and "looney tune." It derives from "lunar," because of the belief by some people that the full moon frequently brought out psychoses in people.

"lunatic fringe" A term of disparagement applied to people and groups who are extremely devoted to their political or social causes. To those less zealous about the issue, these people seem likely to commit unreasonable or illegal actions in support of their views.

lupus A disease in which the antibodies in the person's immune system attack the body's own substances. The disease ranges from mild to fatal and most often affects younger women. Symptoms include a butterfly-shaped rash on the face and tissue inflammation. Heart, joint, kidney, skin, and connective tissue disorders are also common.

Lutheran Social Services The organization of social agencies affiliated with the Lutheran Church, with branches in major communities throughout the United States, that provides family services, child welfare services, services for older people, and other *social services* for all families and individuals in need. See also *sectarian services*.

Lutheran World Federation (LWF) The international Lutheran Church–based organization that raises funds and provisions and distributes needed resources to those populations victimized by poverty and disasters, including famine, epidemics, floods, hurricanes, droughts, earthquakes, war, and civil disorder. LWF coordinates many of its activities with the *United Nations Disaster Relief Organization (UNDRO)* and through the *Steering Committee for International Relief*, other church organizations, and private relief groups.

LWF See *Lutheran World Federation (LWF)*.

lymphoma One of the four major types of *cancer* (including *carcinoma*, *sarcoma*, and *leukemia*) that involves the lymphatic system.

M

macroeconomics The study of production, distribution, and consumption of a nation, society, or the world, as influenced by long-term trends, ecological changes, international relations, and large-scale technological advances. See also *microeconomics.*

macro orientation In social work, an emphasis on the sociopolitical, historical, economic, and environmental forces that influence the overall human condition, cause problems for individuals, or provide opportunities for their fulfillment and equality. This perspective is contrasted with social work's *micro orientation.*

macro practice *Social work practice* aimed at bringing about improvements and changes in the general society. Such activities include some types of *political action, community organization,* public education campaigning, and the administration of broad-based *social services* agencies or public welfare departments.

MADD See *Mothers Against Drunk Driving (MADD).*

magical thinking The pattern of reasoning and mental imaging in which an individual attributes experiences and perceptions to unnatural phenomena. For example, a client might attribute winning a lottery bet to wearing a lucky hat. Magical thinking is often seen in young children and in those with *schizophrenia.* It is the idea that one's thoughts or desires influence the environment or cause events to occur. It is normal in children younger than age five and is also commonly seen among some uneducated people and in certain relatively isolated societies. Among mature people in modern society, it may be a symptom of certain mental disturbances such as *paranoia.* See also *ideas of reference.*

magnetic resonance imaging (MRI) A computer-based diagnostic tool physicians use to envision neurological activity and other physiological processes. MRI is replacing computerized axial tomography *(CAT scan),* because it provides cross-sectional two-dimensional images of higher resolution without exposing the patient to radiation.

magnet schools Also known as "alternative schools," these are established within public school districts to allow students to voluntarily participate in unique curricula and methods of instruction. Most magnet schools have well-defined educational goals and provide further education in such special areas of interest as science, the arts, business and technology, and vocational arts.

"mainlining" A slang expression to describe the injection of a narcotic drug, usually *heroin,* directly into the bloodstream through a vein.

mainstreaming Bringing people who have some exceptional characteristics into the living, working, or educational environments to which all others have access. In education, for example, a child with certain learning or physical disabilities is permitted to attend classes and activities available to "normal" children. Mainstreaming permits individuals to have greater opportunity for *socialization* and *integration.* However, it also subjects them to greater risks of social rejection and reduction of special care. See also *"least-restrictive environment"* (*LRE*).

maintenance Money paid to a former spouse by the other in accordance with legal requirements to provide for independent living arrangements. Maintenance is the current term for *alimony* and is distinct from the obligation of child support payments.

maintenance therapy In the treatment of persons with drug addictions, the use of substitute drugs, usually those that are less harmful and not illicit, to help wean the client from the original substance. Maintenance therapies ideally use the substitute drug along with professional intervention, peer support, and counseling. *Methadone treatment* for heroin users is the most well known of these therapies. *LAMM* and *naltrexone treatment* are similar programs.

major affective disorder See *mood disorders*.

major depression One of the *mood disorders* characterized by such symptoms as loss of interest in one's usual activities, irritability, poor appetite, sleeplessness or excessive sleeping, decreased sexual drive, fatigue, psychomotor agitation, feelings of hopelessness, inability to concentrate, and *suicidal ideation*. Major depression can be subdivided into two groups: the "single episode" (at least four symptoms present almost daily for more than two weeks) and the "recurrent episode" (the episodes come and go for intervals of at least two consecutive months). Someone with major depression may be distinguished from someone with a *bipolar disorder* by the fact that he or she has not had a *manic episode*. Major depression may be distinguished from *dysthymic disorder* in that its symptoms are more severe but occur in discrete episodes that can be distinguished from the person's usual functioning; in dysthymic disorders, the symptoms are almost continuous.

major tranquilizer An *antipsychotic medication* prescribed by physicians to reduce, in people with *schizophrenia* or other psychoses, symptoms of severe *anxiety* and *hallucination*. In the mid-1950s, these drugs were found to be successful in reducing psychotic symptoms but not in curing the *psychosis* itself. Side effects include dry mouth, drugged feeling, respiratory problems, weight gain, and *tardive dyskinesia (TD)*. Trade names for some major tranquilizers include the phenothiazine derivatives such as Thorazine, Mellaril, Compazine, Stelazine, Trilafon, Prolixin, Vesprin, Sparine, and Largactil. Other major tranquilizers with slightly different chemical composition include Haldol, Serpasil, Moderil, Harmonyl, Navane, Taractan, Raudixin, Moban, and Loxitane.

make-work Nonessential employment provided not to produce something but to give a needy person some activity that results in payment or benefit. Many government programs have been labeled (often inaccurately) as "made-work" or make-work programs, including the *Civilian Conservation Corps (CCC)*, the *Works Progress Administration (WPA)*, the *Job Corps,* and various *workfare* plans.

maladaptive Pertaining to behaviors or characteristics that prevent people from meeting the demands of the environment or achieving personal goals.

maladjustment The inability to develop or maintain the values, thoughts, and behaviors needed to succeed in the environment.

mal de ojo Spanish for "evil eye," a *culture-bound syndrome* in which the individual, most often a child, experiences fitful sleep, diarrhea, vomiting, fever, and crying without apparent cause.

male climacteric syndrome Often called the "male menopause," a time of adjustment for many men in their sixties and seventies when they are faced with declining physical energy and some diminution of sexual potency. The syndrome does not result from hormonal changes as in female *menopause.*

male erectile disorder A *sexual disorder* in which a man experiences a persistent or recurrent inability to achieve or maintain penis rigidity (tumescence) sufficient for completion of sexual intercourse, causing marked distress or interpersonal difficulty. By definition this disorder is not the result of a *general medical condition* or *substance abuse*. When using this term as a diagnosis, sexual therapists and other clinicians specify whether the condition is lifelong or acquired, generalized or situational, and due to psychological or combined factors. See also *female sexual arousal disorder*.

male orgasmic disorder A *sexual disorder* in which a man experiences persistent or recurrent delay or absence of orgasm following a normal sexual excitement phase. See also *female orgasmic disorder*.

malfeasance Wrongful or unlawful conduct committed intentionally, usually by someone holding a public office. See also *misfeasance*.

malingering The act of feigning disability or illness, usually to avoid some undesired obligations or to achieve some real or imagined personal benefit *(secondary gain)*. See also *factitious disorder*.

malnutrition A physical condition, usually but not necessarily evidenced by *emaciation*, due to an insufficiency of needed food elements. Primary malnutrition is caused by a deficiency in the quantity or quality of foods containing such essentials as protein, vitamins, and minerals. This may result from an overall scarcity of food, from the individual's economic inability to purchase food, or from poor eating habits. Secondary malnutrition is caused by the body's inability to use or absorb certain nutrients, as sometimes happens in diseases of the pancreas, liver, thyroid, kidneys, and gastrointestinal system. Some of the diseases of malnutrition are *rickets*, *scurvy*, *beriberi*, *pellagra*, *kwashiorkor*, and some forms of *anemia*.

malpractice Willful or negligent *behavior* by a professional person that violates the relevant *code of ethics* and professional standards of care that proves harmful to the client. Among a social worker's actions most likely to result in malpractice are inappropriate divulging of confidential information, unnecessarily prolonged services, improper termination of needed services, misrepresentation of one's knowledge or skills, providing social work treatment as a replacement for needed medical treatment, providing information to others that is libelous or that results in improper *incarceration*, financial exploitation of the client, sexual activity with a client, and physical injury to the client that may occur in the course of certain treatments (such as group encounters).

malpractice insurance An *indemnification* agreement in which a financial organization protects a professional from specified economic losses due to *malpractice* or accusations of malpractice. Usually the insurer agrees to reimburse the practitioner who is legally compelled to pay for harm done to the client up to a predetermined amount. In most coverages the insurer also helps cover costs of a legal defense.

Malthusian theory The theory proposed in the 19th century by English economist Thomas R. Malthus (1766–1834) stating that populations will increase in geometric ratio (2–4–8–16–32, and so on), whereas food supplies and other necessities can only increase in arithmetic ratios (2–3–4–5, and so on). According to the theory, this will lead to overpopulation problems unless populations are controlled by war, natural disasters, or sexual restraint. This theory was used, in part, to justify the sufferings of poor people, especially at the beginning of the Industrial Revolution.

managed care organizations (MCOs) Regulated groups of health care professionals, administrators, and ancillary staff who provide for employers a full range of health care services for their employees. The MCO organization offers the services to the employer at negotiated rates directly or by subcontracting with networks of institutional and individual providers. Thus, employers avoid the costs and inconveniences of providing health care insurance for employees. MCOs often provide services beyond those traditionally covered through health insurance programs, including prevention programs and nonmedical concerns, such as marital and family problems.

managed competition   A system in which vendors are free to develop the most desirable services or products at the best possible price to attract consumers, but within the rules and constraints established in advance by the competing organizations or overseers such as a government body. Use of the term originated in 1994 with an early Clinton administration plan to provide funding for health care by existing insurance programs within government rules. This term is not synonymous with *managed health care program.*

managed health care program   1. The systematic administration of *health care* delivery systems within the context of fiscal responsibility. 2. A formal network of health care personnel, third-party funding organizations, and other fiscal intermediaries who provide for virtually all the health and mental health care an individual or family might need in exchange for regular premium payments. Cost containment, effective marketing, and overseeing providers are emphasized in many of these programs. See also *preferred provider organizations (PPOs)* and *health maintenance organization (HMO).*

management   See *administration in social work.*

management by objectives (MBO)   The administrative procedure in which an organization's members reach *consensus* about group results to be achieved, the resources to be devoted to each result, and the deadline for reaching objectives. Inherent in this managerial approach is a clear and accessible *budget,* specified performance criteria, managers to assess the criteria, and monitoring procedures that encourage individual group members to assess progress.

management information systems (MISs)   An administrative method often used in social agencies to acquire, process, analyze, and disseminate data that are useful for carrying out the goals of the organization efficiently. MISs may be used to track staff activity and the services that are provided to clients.

management tasks   The principal activities of a social welfare administrator or manager. According to Rino Patti (*Social Welfare Administration,* Englewood Cliffs, NJ: Prentice Hall, 1983, pp. 34–35), there are six basic tasks: (1) planning and developing the program, (2) acquiring financial resources and support, (3) designing organizational structures and processes, (4) developing and maintaining staff capability, (5) assessing agency programs, and (6) changing agency programs.

mandate   The authority, expectations, and requirements to carry out some order or desire expressed by those to whom the administrator is responsible, such as the voters, the customers, or the government entity that pays the agency for the services to be rendered. See also *ambiguous mandate, competing mandate,* and *conflicting mandate.*

mandated benefits   Health care benefits that the law requires health care plans to provide. Mandated benefits vary widely from state to state.

mandatory retirement   The requirement that employees who have reached a previously specified age relinquish their jobs. With passage of the *Age Discrimination in Employment Act (ADEA) of 1967* and enforcement by the *Equal Employment Opportunity Commission (EEOC),* mandatory retirement is generally prohibited. However ADEA has some exceptions: company executives older than 65, tenured university professors older than 70, and law enforcement officials older than the state age of retirement may be retired under certain circumstances.

mania   1. An intense preoccupation with some kind of idea or activity, as in *kleptomania, nymphomania,* and *pyromania.* 2. A state of agitation, accelerated thinking, hyperactivity, and excessive elation seen in some major affective disorder (such as the *manic episode* in *manic–depressive illness)* and certain *organic mental disorders.* 3. A lay term used in describing *insanity* or "mental breakdowns" in which the individual seems violent or highly agitated.

manic–depressive illness   A disorder characterized by profound *mood swings* ranging from deep, prolonged *depression* to excited, euphoric, agitated *behavior.* Genetic and chemical studies are beginning to suggest an *organic* basis for this illness. The term has been replaced in the diagnostic nomenclature of mental health professionals by the label *bipolar disorder.*

manic episode A symptom found in some of the *mood disorders,* especially *bipolar disorder,* consisting of an abnormally and persistently elevated, expansive, or irritable mood lasting at least four days. This may include feelings of inflated self-esteem, *grandiosity,* pressured speech, *flight of ideas,* distractibility, and *psychomotor* agitation, all of which are a clear departure from the individual's usual mood and functioning. See also *hypo-manic episode.*

"man in the house" rule A provision, once common in many state welfare departments, in which the presence of a man, whether or not related to the family, was considered sufficient evidence that financial dependency did not exist, leading to curtailment of *public assistance* eligibility. Most states ended the practice in the 1960s through legislation and court rulings.

manipulative behavior Actions intended to control and often exploit the thoughts, feelings, or responses of others. The *behavior* may be intentional or *unconscious,* and it may be motivated by efforts to help the other person or to harmfully take advantage.

Mann Act The federal law ("White-Slave" Laws, 36 Stat. 263, 36 Stat. 825) passed in 1910 that prohibits taking a person, usually a woman, across state lines for "immoral purposes" such as *prostitution.*

Manpower Development and Training Act of 1962 The federal legislation (P.L. 87-415) that funded state employment agencies and private enterprise for on-the-job training to help workers acquire needed employment skills. In 1973, these programs were incorporated into *CETA.* See also *Economic Opportunity Act of 1964* and *Job Corps.*

manpower planning The systematic process of defining the problems and person-

nel needs of a social organization, such as a *social agency;* establishing a system of objectives relevant to those problems and needs; determining activities required to meet objectives; identifying and analyzing tasks; creating jobs and career ladders; and designing *in-service training.*

manslaughter The unlawful, but unpremeditated, killing of another person. Laws in most jurisdictions distinguish between voluntary and involuntary manslaughter. The involuntary type refers to causing *death* through such criminally negligent acts as reckless driving. The voluntary type is an intentional *homicide* under mitigating but not justifiable circumstances, such as killing someone who has provoked uncontrollable rage or terror.

MAO inhibitors *Psychotropic drugs* prescribed by physicians primarily to relieve the symptoms of *depression* in certain patients. These drugs reduce the metabolism of monoamine oxidase (MAO) after it has been released into the synaptic space, which ultimately eases neural transmission. The process takes up to three weeks before depressive symptoms can be relieved. Some side effects include dry mouth, fatigue, and *impotence* in men. MAO inhibitors are one of the two important types of *antidepressant medication,* the other being the tricyclics (for example, Elavil, Tofranil, Vivactyl, or Sinequan). Trade names of MAO inhibitors include Marplan, Parnate, and Nardil.

marasmus A gradual deterioration and *emaciation* found in some infants and young children, particularly those who are cared for in institutional settings. Often, the child appears to have the symptoms of *malnutrition.* Many investigators believe marasmus is sometimes caused by a child's not being touched, held, fondled, and parented.

marathon group A form of *group psychotherapy* or *sensitivity group* in which participants remain together for extended periods, usually 18 to 24 hours or more.

Marfan's syndrome A hereditary congenital disorder of connective tissue characterized by abnormally long and slender limbs.

marijuana *Cannabis,* a plant whose active ingredient, tetrahydrocannabinol *(THC)*, induces mild *euphoria,* certain intensified sensory impressions, and drowsiness when taken into the system either by smoking or ingestion. Some research indicates that its harmful effects include increased risk of heart and lung diseases, increased likelihood of accidents, loss of motivation, and possibly a greater risk of genetic problems for succeeding generations.

marital contracts 1. The term used by family therapists to indicate the expectations and motives that each partner brings to the marriage. These expectations and motives may be *conscious* or *unconscious* in the person who holds them and may or may not be known to the partner. In healthy marriages, each person's contracts become known to both, and agreements are reached so that the husband's and wife's individual contracts become jointly shared. In those marriages in which the contracts remain concealed and separate, the couple is prone to confusion, suspicion, and disappointment with one another. 2. The term is also used to indicate formal, written, and legally enforced agreements made between marrying couples, usually to specify the financial terms and obligations each partner is to assume. See also *prenuptial agreement* and *postnuptial agreement.*

marital skew A *family therapy* term indicating that a husband or wife dominates the other and controls the relationship or takes the lead in maintaining its healthy or unhealthy aspects.

marital therapy *Intervention* procedures used by social workers, family therapists, and other professionals to help couples resolve their relationship, communications, sexual, economic, and other family problems. There are many theoretical orientations, treatment models, and therapy techniques. The major theoretical approaches currently used by social workers include the psychosocial, behavioral, and systems orientations. Treatment models include *conjoint therapy, concurrent therapy, collaborative therapy,* and *couples group therapy.*

market strategy In *social welfare* policy development, the premise that the nation's free economic institutions can provide needed *social services* without distracting from the work ethic, without the need for extensive public service delivery systems, and without centralized planning. Critics of this strategy contend that this method of delivery of benefits will favor those with the most resources and deprive those who have the greatest disadvantages. See also *social marketing.*

marriage A legally and socially sanctioned union between a man and a woman resulting in mutual obligations and rights. Some societies and subcultural groups sanction unions between members of the same sex or between several people.

marriage counseling A form of *marital therapy.* Many professionals consider the term "marriage counseling" to be synonymous with "marital therapy." Others believe that "counseling" is less intense and more directive and deals with couples who may be less troubled. Existing empirical research has not yet clearly demonstrated significant differences between the two. Nevertheless, many social workers and other professionals who treat couples prefer the term "marital therapy" because they believe it conveys a more technical and sophisticated repertoire of techniques and has a more theoretical and professional orientation.

marriage encounter An *encounter group* comprising several married couples who explore feelings, mutual understandings, and *conflict resolution* to improve their relationships.

Marsh Report The 1943 recommendations by Canadian social workers and others that were a major factor in the development of Canada's present *social welfare* system.

Marxism The sociopolitical ideology, based on the work of Karl Marx (1818–1883) and Frederick Engels (1820–1895), that advocates a classless society so that the efforts of workers (proletariat) are no longer exploited by those who control the means of production (bourgeoisie). In the Marxist scenario, a class struggle and revolution leads to the overthrow of *capitalism,* which is temporarily replaced by a socialistic system of dictatorship of the workers, and finally by the classless society known as *communism.* The scenario has been influential in the political and economic systems of many nations but has never been fully realized, usually stopping at the dictatorship of the proletariat stage.

masochism   1. The *conscious* or *unconscious* tendency to seek opportunities to be physically or emotionally hurt. 2. A *sexual disorder* of the *paraphilia* class, in which the individual becomes sexually excited through being harmed, threatened, or humiliated. See also *sadomasochism* and *self-defeating personality disorder.*

masochistic personality disorder   See *self-defeating personality disorder.*

matching grants   A procedure for raising funds and motivating organizations to allocate funds for certain programs. To raise funds, a contributor promises to give the organization an amount of money that is equal to or a percentage of the amount received from other sources during a specified period. Federal and state governments also use the procedure to motivate localities to develop certain programs by promising to give a specified amount of money for every dollar the locality contributes.

maternity benefits   The provision of cash and social and health services to new mothers. Many nations, not including the United States, provide such benefits to all new mothers regardless of their economic status. See also *demogrant* and *family allowance.*

maternity homes   Temporary residential facilities for unwed mothers that often provide *counseling, social services,* health care, and education as well as shelter away from the expectant mother's usual environment during the *pregnancy.* Some maternity home personnel help facilitate *adoption, abortion,* reintegration into the community, and financial assistance. See also *Florence Crittenden Association.*

maternity leave   Time off from employment during *pregnancy* and the *neonatal* period. Maternity leave policies vary widely. Some employers grant several months off before and after the birth with full pay and restoration of the job on return. Others permit virtually no paid time off or grant only a few days' of "sick leave." Most social workers have long argued for more-generous maternity leave policies, saying that their absence discriminates against women or does not recognize that the nation's future well-being depends on encouraging healthy reproduction. See also *parental leave.*

mathematics disorder   A type of *learning disorder* in which a student is testably below the average in mathematical skills and in understanding numbers concepts that is expected of others of similar ages, intellectual levels, educational levels, and without physical or neurological problems. For the condition to be diagnosable, it must significantly interfere with the student's academic achievement or activities that require math or calculations skills. Many educators call this disorder *dyscalculia.* The other major types of learning disorders are *reading disorder* and *disorder of written expression.*

matriarchy   A social pattern in which mothers or other women are the leaders of the family or group.

MBO   See *management by objectives (MBO).*

McCarran–Walter Act   See *Immigration and Naturalization Service, U.S.*

McKinney Act   A federal homeless assistance program based on legislation passed in 1987 (Stewart B. McKinney Homeless Assistance Act, P.L. 100-77) to provide access to social services, nutrition, housing services, and especially health care for homeless persons. The program was to end in 1989 but was renewed. As funding cutbacks reduced most of its programs, they were supposedly taken over by voluntary and philanthropic organizations.

McNaughten rule   A set of legal principles for the guidance of courts in helping to determine whether or not a defendant may be declared innocent by reason of *insanity*. Based on the 1843 British case of Daniel McNaughten, the accused is considered not responsible for the *crime* if "laboring under such a defect of reason from disease of the mind as not to know the nature or quality of the act; or, if he did know it, that he did not know that what he was doing was wrong." Some jurisdictions use different criteria for judgments in insanity pleas. For example, the American Law Institute's formulation states that "a person is not responsible for criminal conduct if at the time of such conduct as a result of mental disease or defect he lacks substantial capacity either to appreciate the wrongfulness of his conduct or to conform his conduct to the requirements of law." See also *Durham rule*.

MCOs   See *managed care organizations (MCOs)*.

meals-on-wheels   A *home health service*, sponsored by local departments of human services, health care facilities, senior centers, or private organizations, to bring prepared food to the homes of people in need.

mean   A *measure of central tendency*, also known as the arithmetic average, found by adding scores and dividing this sum by the number of scores. For example, if an agency wanted to know the mean, or average, amount of time each client was seen during a week, it would add the total amount of minutes the agency social workers spent with clients that week and divide this sum by the number of clients seen.

means test   Evaluating the client's financial resources and using the result as the criterion to determine *eligibility* to receive a benefit. The client applying for certain economic, social, or health services will be turned down if the investigator determines that the person has the "means" to pay for them. Programs and services that use the means test to determine client eligibility include *Medicaid, Aid to Families with Dependent Children (AFDC),* the *Food Stamp program,* and *general assistance*

(GA). To make means test evaluations, the social worker usually considers the client's income, assets, debts and other obligations, number of dependents, and health factors. See also *income test*.

measure of central tendency   A way of summarizing data about the central portion of frequency distributions in statistics and research. The three types are (1) the *mean,* (2) the *median,* and (3) the *mode*.

media campaigning   A strategy to raise public awareness about a problem or goal and mobilize *social action* toward its elimination or achievement by getting the relevant newspapers and radio and television stations to run stories about it. This is done through such activities as issuing press releases, arranging "photo opportunities" and interviews with reporters, writing letters to the editor, paying for advertising, and preparing free public-service messages.

media event   Activity designed to gain publicity; an event that would not happen if reporters or cameras were not present. Social activists and politicians often stage such events to show graphically the extent of a problem or demonstrate their concern about it.

median   A *measure of central tendency,* the point in a distribution that has the same number of scores above and below it. Its advantage over the *mean* in reporting statistical data is that it is unaffected by a few extreme scores.

mediation   Intervention in disputes between parties to help them reconcile differences, find compromises, or reach mutually satisfactory agreements. Social workers have used their unique skills and value orientations in many forms of mediation between opposing groups (for example, landlord–tenant organizations, neighborhood residents–halfway house personnel; labor–management representatives, or divorcing spouses). See also *conciliation; mediation, divorce;* and *adversarial process*.

mediation, divorce   A procedure used by social workers, lawyers, and other professionals to help settle disputes between divorcing couples outside the courtroom adversarial process. In some states mediation occurs under the auspices of the courts, but in other localities it is done as a private service. The goals include helping the couple make mutually acceptable compromises, understand the nature of their marital difficulties, agree on equitable distribution of possessions, make custody arrangements for the children, and disengage emotionally from the unhealthy parts of the relationship.

mediator role   The activity of the family therapist who sometimes acts as a go-between in getting various members of the family to communicate more clearly and fairly with one another. This role is not the same as in *divorce mediation*. See also *conciliation*.

Medicaid   The means-tested *public assistance* program established in 1965 that provides payment for hospital and medical services to people who cannot afford them. Funding comes from federal and state governments under the auspices of the *Health Care Financing Administration (HCFA)*. In most areas, administration of the program is handled through local public-assistance offices. *Supplemental Security Income (SSI)* recipients may also be helped with Medicaid applications in their local *social security* offices.

medical day care   A community health care service and facility that provides nursing and other health services to chronically ill or disabled people who do not require intense or frequent attention. The facilities are often located in long-term institutions such as state or county hospitals.

Medic Alert   The privately funded national organization that maintains medical records on people who are registered with it and provides emergency medical information about them to health care providers. Medic Alert provides its registrants with special bracelets or other identification so that health care providers are informed about the patient's special needs during crises. For example, a registrant may become unable

to communicate that he or she is allergic to certain medications or has other physical conditions that are not readily evident. A 24-hour-a-day telephone switchboard is maintained and accepts collect calls.

medically assisted suicide   The intentional act by a medical professional of providing someone with the means and information needed to commit *suicide.*

medical model   A social work approach to helping people that is patterned after the orientation used by many physicians. This includes looking at the client as an individual with an illness to be treated, giving relatively less attention to factors in the client's environment, diagnosing the condition with fairly specific labels, and treating the problem through regular clinical appointments.

medical social work   The social work practice that occurs in hospitals and other health care settings to facilitate good health, prevent illness, and aid physically ill patients and their families to resolve the social and psychological problems related to the illness. Medical social work also sensitizes other health care providers about the social–psychological aspects of illness.

medical social workers   Professional social workers employed in health care settings, primarily to provide for the psychosocial needs of patients and alert other health care providers to the social needs of the patients. For example, in a hospital setting the medical social worker might facilitate the doctor's plan for early discharge of the patient by implementing a program of family and volunteer home care.

Medicare   The national *social insurance* health care program for older people, established in 1965 and administered through the *Social Security Administration (SSA);* the *Health Care Financing Administration (HCFA);* and to some extent, in certain localities, with the assistance of some commercial and nonprofit health insurance companies. Funding comes from employer–employee contributions as part of the individual's *social security,* from *earmarked taxes,* and from general federal revenues. Eligibility is not based on need but on reaching age 65.

Medicare/Medicaid Assistance Program (M/MAP)   A volunteer program to help people complete their *Medicare* or *Medicaid* forms, sponsored in most states by the *American Association of Retired Persons (AARP)*.

medication-induced movement disorder Movements, gestures, postures, or muscle rigidity related to the use of medications, usually those prescribed to help the individual with a *mental disorder* or *general medical condition*. Some of these disorders most frequently encountered by staffs in mental hospitals and health care facilities include "neuroleptic-induced Parkinsonism" (medications with dopamine-antagonist properties inducing *Parkinson's disease* tremors) malignant syndrome (severe muscle rigidity), acute *dystonia,* acute *akathisia, tardive dyskinesia (TD),* and *postural tremor.*

medications   The term used in health care facilities for the medicine prescribed for each patient.

Medi-Credit   A proposed health care financing program in which the costs of premiums paid to private health insurance companies could be credited directly against personal income taxes.

medigap   Insurance coverage against health care costs that are not reimbursable by *Medicare.*

medipards   Physicians and other health care providers who accept assignment of *Medicare* payments. Many health care providers consider Medicare payments to be less than their services are worth and the required paperwork to get reimbursed is so great, they decline to accept assignment to serve Medicare-eligible patients. Medicare thus provides a medipard directory listing those providers who will accept assignment; it is available at district *social security* offices or senior citizens centers.

meditation   A state of concentrated relaxation, the systematic practice of which reportedly leads to feelings of heightened well-being and reduced *anxiety.* Meditators typically concentrate on and repeat a word, phrase, or sound (for example, a mantra) for about 20 minutes while remaining in a passive attitude, in one comfortable position, and in an environment free of distractions.

MEDLARS   The Medical Analysis and Retrieval System, a program of the National Library of Medicine, *National Institutes of Health (NIH).* MEDLARS has computer interface with most medical and university libraries so that qualified professionals can have access to the relevant literature and a specific *database.* Such databases include MEDLINE (biomedical journal articles), TOXLINE (information about toxicity, environmental pollution, and adverse drug reactions), and CANCERLIT (the current literature about *cancer* studies). Costs are based primarily on the amount of computer time used.

megalomania   A personality trait characterized by excessive *egocentrism,* grandiose plans for personal influence over many others, and an exaggerated view of self-importance.

melancholic features   Loss of interest or pleasure in all or most activities, or a lack of reaction to usually pleasurable stimuli; *anhedonia.* Clinicians specify melancholic features when it exists in people with major depressive disorders or depressive episodes in bipolar disorders.

melanoma   Tumor composed of cells containing dark pigment. Melanomas are mostly benign, but malignant melanoma is a serious form of skin *cancer.*

meliorism   The belief or ethical doctrine that social conditions are gradually improving or can be made to improve.

melting pot theory   The idea that immigrants to a new nation become socialized and take on the *values, norms,* and personality characteristics of the majority *culture* while losing some of their unique cultural traits.

membership theory in social work   A formal theory of social work that synthesizes physiological functioning, social interaction, *object relations theory*, and symbolization and that views the professional role as rendering aid in the management of human membership. Humanness, according to this theory, does not rest on individualism but is possible only through membership in the community and social structures that are derived from it. The orientation, which was first delineated by Hans S. Falck (*Social Work: The Membership Perspective*, New York: Springer, 1988), emphasizes the common membership of clients and social worker; the mutuality of giving and receiving; the social (rather than individualistic) nature of *self-determination;* and reciprocity among members, institutions, community, and society. Membership theory has spread in recent years to European social work with the translation of the American version into Italian and German.

memory The mental function of recalling or reproducing what has been experienced or learned.

memory recovery therapy A form of *psychotherapy* oriented to retrieving parts of a client's forgotten past experiences that had been concealed from consciousness by *suppression* or *repression*. This type of *intervention* has become controversial because, as a result of it, many clients have accused parents or others of *child molestation* or *sexual abuse*. The person thus accused has often blamed and sued the therapist for inserting false memories into the client. See also *false-memory syndrome.*

menarche The biological process that occurs in young women as menstruation begins.

mendicancy The act of begging. A "mendicant" is one who begs for money or goods.

meningitis Bacterially or virally caused inflammation of the membranes that surround the brain or spinal cord, or both. Antibiotic drugs have greatly reduced mortality and the effects of the disease, such as paralysis, arthritis, deafness, and blindness. Symptoms of meningitis may include fever, headache, vomiting, *delirium,* severe rigidity in the neck and back, and convulsions.

menopause The biological process that occurs in middle-age women as menstruation ceases. In some women, the hormonal changes result temporarily in certain accompanying physiological and psychological symptoms.

"Mensch" 1. A Jewish expression for a person of integrity and character. 2. A Jewish person who has retained the Jewish identity.

men's liberation movement The organized efforts of disparate people and groups to eliminate *sex role stereotyping* and *gender bias* against men and to widen the range of acceptable behaviors identified with masculinity and male roles. See also *women's liberation movement.*

"mens rea" A legal term (literally "criminal mind") pertaining to the guilty intent to commit a *crime.*

mental cruelty A legal ground for *divorce* in many jurisdictions, in which the *behavior* of one spouse imperils the *mental health* of the other to the extent that continuing the relationship is considered unbearable.

mental disorder Impaired psychosocial or cognitive functioning due to disturbances in any one or more of the following processes: biological, chemical, physiological, genetic, psychological, or social. Mental disorders are extremely variable in duration, severity, and prognosis, depending on the type of affliction. The major forms of mental disorder include *mood disorders, psychosis, personality disorders, organic mental disorders,* and *anxiety disorder.*

mental health The relative state of emotional well-being, freedom from incapacitating conflicts, and the consistent ability to make and carry out rational decisions and cope with environmental stresses and internal pressures.

Mental Health Association (MHA) The voluntary citizen's organization, founded in 1909 by *Clifford W. Beers* (1876–1943) and others, whose purpose is to promote social conditions that enhance the potential for good *mental health* and to improve the methods and facilities for treating *mental illness.*

mental health day care A health care service and facility that provides mental health services and a supervised daily environment to mentally ill adults. Patients typically go to the facility for medications, some counseling and sometimes group therapy, recreation and socialization, and educational programs for assistance with coping skills.

mental health professional One who has specialized training and skills in the nature and treatment of mental illness and uses them to provide clinical, preventive, and *social services* for people who have, or may be vulnerable to, a *mental disorder.* Mental health professionals include *psychiatrists, psychologists,* psychiatric *registered nurses, social workers,* and members of some other disciplines that provide special expertise and help for emotionally disturbed people.

mental health team Professionals and ancillary personnel from several disciplines who work together to provide a wide range of services for clients (and the families of clients) who are affected by a *mental disorder.* Members of such teams include *psychiatrists* (who usually head them), *social workers, psychologists,* and *registered nurses.* In some psychiatric facilities the team members may also include physical and occupational therapists, recreation specialists, educators, personnel and guidance counselors, psychiatric aides, *volunteers,* and *indigenous workers.* See also *interdisciplinary teaming.*

mental health workers Mental health professionals, paraprofessionals, volunteers, and aides who work in facilities or organizations concerned with meeting the needs of the mentally ill or those vulnerable to *mental disorder.* Mental health workers are distinguished from *mental health team* members only in that their efforts are not necessarily coordinated with those of other workers to achieve specified, focused goals.

mental hospitals Institutions that specialize in the care and treatment of people suffering from a *mental disorder.* These institutions may be publicly or privately financed and may provide a full range of health care services or be limited in type of care provided. Many of the existing public mental hospitals in the United States were established as a result of the influence of social reformer *Dorothea Dix* (1802–1887).

mental hygiene A synonym for *mental health.* The term often implies efforts to develop facilities and procedures for the treatment of mentally ill people and to educate people to live in ways that foster emotional stability and psychological well-being. See also *Clifford W. Beers.*

mental illness A synonym for *mental disorder.*

mental retardation Significantly below-average intellectual functioning and potential, with onset before age 18, resulting in limitations in communication, self-care and self-direction, home living, social and interpersonal skills, use of community resources, academic skills, work, leisure, health, and safety. It may be the result of genetic factors, embryonic development, pregnancy or perinatal problems, trauma, organ damage, or such environmental influences as social deprivation. One diagnosed with this condition has an *intelligence quotient (IQ)* lower than 70. Degrees of mental retardation are delineated as follows: mild retardation (IQ range of 50–70), moderate (35–50), severe (20–40), and profound (below 20). The IQ scores have a plus or minus 5 points to account for potential measurement error. *DSM-IV* includes mental retardation as an *Axis II disorder.*

mental status exam A systematic evaluation of a patient's level of psychosocial, intellectual, and emotional functioning. The examiner, who is usually a psychiatrist or physician but may be a social worker, observes the patient's *affect,* thought content, perceptive and cognitive functions, and need and motivation for treatment. This may be done, in part, by asking such questions of the patient as, "What day is today?" and "Where are you now?" The patient may also be asked to repeat a series of numbers forward and backward and to interpret several aphorisms, such as "People who live in glass houses shouldn't throw stones."

mercenary   An individual who performs services, which often are distasteful or dangerous, for money. The term is most commonly applied to soldiers employed by countries other than their own.

mercy killing   See *euthanasia*.

Merici, Angela (1474–1540)   Also known as St. Angela, a Catholic religious worker who advocated for the poor and sick, organized programs for their care, and provided educational programs for young girls. She founded the Ursuline Order whose primary mission was to serve ill and destitute people.

meritocracy   Leadership theoretically based on achievements, talent, skill, intelligence, and other relevant virtues rather than based on inheritance (aristocracy), wealth *(plutocracy)*, or the will of the majority (democracy). What is sometimes called "meritocracy" is merely judging candidates for leadership roles based on their performance on some test scores or paper qualifications.

merit system   An organization's set of rules, regulations, and policies used in personnel management to assure employees that their opportunities for promotion and retention on the job will be based fairly on performance. Federal government workers are protected in this system by the *Merit Systems Protection Board*. See also *spoils system*.

Merit Systems Protection Board   An independent organization in the U.S. government designed to protect the integrity of the federal *merit system*. Appeals by federal workers who charge unfair treatment and other violations of federal regulations are evaluated by the board, and violators may be prosecuted.

mescaline   A psychedelic drug that produces *hallucination,* perceptual distortions, and thinking disorders. Although mescaline

is considered one of the *drugs of abuse* in some societies, in others it is used in religious ceremonies. See also *psychedelics*.

mestizo   People from Latin American cultures whose ancestry is mixed native and European.

metaanalysis   The assessment of the outcome of a study by systematically reviewing the findings across similar studies.

metamessage   A person's communication that comments on the verbal statement he or she is making. For example, a client might say, "I'm not angry!" (primary statement) while banging a fist (metamessage). The metamessage may be verbal or nonverbal, *conscious* or *unconscious,* and consistent with or contradictory to the primary statement. See also *paralinguistics* and *communication theory.*

metaphor   A type of analogy or figure of speech used to describe something to which it is not literally applicable. Metaphors are used by social workers and their clients to connote feeling and imagination as well as objective reality. For example, a social worker could describe a client as a "hurricane" to convey a variety of behavioral and personality characteristics. See also *dichos.*

metastasis   The spreading of a disease, such as *cancer,* from one part of the body to others.

methadone   A synthetic pain-relieving drug used primarily in the treatment of *heroin* addiction.

methadone treatment   The use of the synthetic narcotic *methadone* to help wean addicts from *heroin.* However, methadone itself is addictive, even though it has less-severe *withdrawal symptoms.* Methadone clinics give methadone to patients and supervise their use of it. For such treatment to be truly effective, it must be accompanied by *psychosocial therapy.* See also *LAMM* and *naltrexone treatment.*

methodology   The systematic and specified procedures by which a social worker or other investigator develops hypotheses, gathers relevant data, analyzes data acquired, and communicates the conclusions.

methods in social work   The term used by social workers, especially those in education, to identify specific types of *intervention*. Social work activities that have been identified as methods include *social casework, social group work, community organization, administration in social work, research, policy, planning,* direct clinical practice, family and marital treatment, other *micro practice,* and what is called "generic social work practice, combined micro–macro."

Mexican American   A resident of the United States whose parents or ancestors are from Mexico. See also *Chicano.*

mezzo practice   *Social work practice* primarily with families and small groups. Important activities at this level include facilitating *communication, mediation,* and *negotiation*; educating; and bringing people together. This is one of the three levels of social work practice, along with *macro practice* and *micro practice.* All social workers engage, to some extent, in all three, even though they may give major attention to only one or two of the levels.

MHA   See *Mental Health Association (MHA).*

microeconomics   The study of the way individuals and groups produce, distribute, and consume goods, usually on a small scale with simple technology and locally available resources. See also *appropriate technology (AT)* and *macroeconomics.*

micromanagement   Administration of an organization through close supervision of employees who are given little authority or decision-making powers. Social agency administrators sometimes complain that government bureaucrats and lawmakers micromanage by making rules so specific and detailed that there is no room for administrative discretion or innovation.

micro orientation   In social work, an emphasis on the individual client's psychosocial conflicts and on the enhancement of technical skills for use in efficient treatment of these

problems. This perspective is contrasted with social work's *macro orientation.*

micro practice   The term used by social workers to identify professional activities that are designed to help solve the problems faced primarily by individuals, families, and small groups. Usually micro practice focuses on direct *intervention* on a case-by-case basis or in a clinical setting. See also *macro practice* and *mezzo practice.*

midlevel practitioners (MLPs)   Health care practitioners who do not have medical degrees, such as clinical nurse practitioners, nurse midwives, and physician's assistants. Midlevel practitioners provide medical services, generally under the supervision of a physician, at lower cost.

midlife crisis   The inner conflict and, often, the changed behavior patterns that occur in some middle-age individuals who are reassessing the meaning and direction of life, questioning their future goals, examining their relative progress toward achieving their goals, and coping with social demands made on them.

midwife   A nonphysician who assists a mother through the process of childbirth.

Migrant Head Start program   A type of *Head Start* program that serves children whose parents are migrant farm workers. The program coordinates and monitors the educational progress of children who may go from one geographic region to another during the time of eligibility.

migrant laborer   A worker who travels from place to place to take short-term or seasonal jobs, such as those in agriculture and construction. According to Juan Ramos ("Migrant Workers," in Richard L. Edwards [Ed.-in-Chief], *Encyclopedia of Social Work,* 19th ed., Washington, DC: NASW Press, 1995), often such workers travel in groups, typically with their families, and are vulnerable to exploitation by employers. They and their children have limited or minimal opportunities to obtain education, social skills, and health care.

mild neurocognitive disorder   Impaired cognitive functioning with minimal impact on everyday functioning, due to a *general medical condition*. This is a proposed official diagnostic category of the *DSM-IV*.

Milford Conference The study group, comprising social workers, agency executives, and board members, set up to determine whether social work was a disparate group of specialties or a unified profession with integrated knowledge and skills. The group published its conclusions in the book *Social Case Work: Generic and Specific* (New York: American Association of Social Workers, 1929 and republished by the National Association of Social Workers in 1974) and emphasized that *social casework* in all settings used basically the same skills and knowledge. The conference is considered by social workers to be one of the most important milestones in the history of the profession because it led to the still-existing principle that social work, despite its service in a variety of settings, is one profession. See also *generic–specific controversy*.

milieu therapy A form of *treatment* and *rehabilitation* for people with social and mental disorders who usually live in institutional settings. Treatment is not restricted to individual hours with a professional therapist but also occurs in the total environment of this closed setting, which is also referred to as the "therapeutic community." Those being treated attend group sessions for everyone in the facility, elect their own leaders, and provide one another with social and emotional support throughout the day. The entire environment is considered vital to the treatment process.

militant One who seeks *social change* but who is considered less likely to compromise and more inclined to be an *agitator* or *dissident*.

militarism An orientation and sometimes national policy to maintain strong armed forces and being prepared and motivated to use them before all other options are exhausted. See also *pacifism* and *warism*.

military social work Professional social work *intervention* on behalf of active-duty military personnel and their families. This form of practice is accomplished by social work officers in all branches of the U.S. military. Civilian professional social workers also provide services in Navy, Army, and Air Force settings. Military social workers provide such services as evaluating and treating emotionally disturbed military personnel or members of their families, finding and developing social resources, and facilitating communications not only between military personnel but also between individuals in the military and their relatives who live in other locations.

mimesis Imitation of the behaviors of another person, often seen among family members who tend to assume the same verbal and physical gestures, expressions, or postures. Social workers and other therapists sometimes imitate the movements and posture of clients, especially when working with families or groups, to facilitate *joining* or alliance building.

mind The part of a person where intellectual functions occur, including cognitive processing, information accumulation, memories, unconscious material, reasoning, emotional reactions and sensory input, processing, and the personality.

"mind games" A slang expression usually referring to *manipulative behavior*, especially involving attempts to provoke feelings of *guilt, anger*, confusion, or affection.

mind reading The alleged ability of a person to know the thoughts and feelings of another person without direct communication. This term is used by social workers as a figure of speech in *marital therapy* and *family therapy* to describe the tendency of one family member to interpret or describe to the social worker what he or she believes are the views or the feelings of another family member.

"minimal brain dysfunction" An obsolete term for *attention-deficit hyperactivity disorder (ADHD)*.

minimal supervision home Residential facilities for mentally retarded people who can live outside of institutions and apart from families but who benefit from scheduled in-home visits by social workers to help them plan their shopping, money management, recreation, health care, and educational activities. These facilities are overseen by state departments of human services and other agencies and are staffed by professionals, case aides, and volunteers.

minimum market basket A concept used by economists and *social welfare* planners to indicate the least quantity of food required for survival; a form of *minimum-needs estimation*.

minimum-needs estimation The delineation by *social welfare* planners of the least quantities of food, clothing, housing, and goods that an individual requires for survival. This concept is used as a basis in establishing an income *poverty line*.

minimum standard of living The lowest amount of money and quality of essentials that an individual needs to maintain a lifestyle that is tolerable to the society.

minimum wage A payment made to employees that, by law or contract, is the lowest amount the employer is permitted to pay for specified work. U.S. labor policy establishes that employers may not hire workers unless they guarantee to pay at least the amount established by government regulations.

minor The legal designation for a child or adolescent, used to distinguish the different rights, protections, and privileges that exist for adults and for these youths. Each jurisdiction establishes the age at which one legally becomes an adult and specifies any rights available to minors, such as driving, buying property, drinking alcoholic beverages, and marrying.

minorities of color One term for people who have *minority* status because their skin color differs from that of the community's predominant group. In the United States, the term usually refers to *African Americans, Asian Americans, American Indians,* and certain other groups.

minority One term for a group, or a member of a group, of people of a distinct racial, religious, ethnic, or political identity that is smaller or less powerful than the community's controlling group.

Minority Business Development Agency The federal agency, within the U.S. Department of Commerce, designed to help minority groups establish and maintain businesses. The agency administers laws requiring that a percentage of moneys spent on government projects be *set-asides*.

minority report A presentation of dissenting conclusions reached by some members of a committee to give reasons why they did not concur with the majority.

minority set-asides See *set-asides*.

minor tranquilizer *Psychotropic drugs* prescribed by physicians to relieve the symptoms of mild tension, sleeplessness, irritability, and, especially, *anxiety*. Although these medications do not cure the underlying sources of the problems, they do give patients enough respite to work more effectively on those problem sources. Trade names include Valium, Librium, Tranxene, Ativan, Serax, Centrax, Miltown, Equanil, Trancopal, Vistaril, and Atarax

MIPRAs Mentally ill persons in recovery from addictions, a diagnostic term used by social workers and others helping clients who have drug problems and *mental illness*. Many clients have both disorders together, and this designation reminds professionals that treating one disorder without treating the other will likely be ineffective.

Miranda The 1966 U.S. Supreme Court ruling in *Miranda v. Arizona* requiring police to inform suspects of their constitutional rights before questioning them.

misanthropy Hatred or aversion to humanity. The prefix is from the Greek "misos" (to hate) and may be attached to any group to indicate an individual's feelings about them, for example, a misogynist hates women, a misogamist hates marriage, and a misopedic hates children.

miscegenation Marriage or sexual relations between a man and woman of different races in violation of a law. Laws forbidding such marriages were common in the United States but were generally abolished by legislation or court decrees in the 1960s and by the U.S. Supreme Court in 1967.

misdemeanor   A minor criminal offense generally defined by state law in terms of possible jail sentences of fewer than six months. Such acts as breaking street lights, defacing property, and littering are usually misdemeanors. See also *felony.*

misery index   A nation's or society's combined rates of *unemployment* and *inflation.* See also *Index of Social Health.*

misfeasance   Performing a proper act in a way that is harmful or injurious, especially by public officials. See also *malfeasance.*

MISs   See *management information systems (MISs).*

missing person   A designation by law enforcement authorities applied to one whose whereabouts remain unknown to his or her family, *significant other,* or colleagues. If the missing person is a *minor,* the appropriate term is usually *runaway.*

mistrial   In a court of law, a trial that is ended and declared void before a verdict has been reached. This occurs most commonly because of deadlocked jury deliberations (when the jurors cannot achieve necessary consensus) and sometimes because of prejudicial misstatements made by attorneys or illnesses of key participants.

mixed anxiety–depressive disorder   Persistent or recurrent *mood* of *dysphoria* lasting one month or more; it is accompanied by worry, irritability, fatigue or low energy, sleep disturbance, and difficulty concentrating. This is a proposed official diagnostic category of the *DSM-IV.*

mixed economy   A society or environment in which services and transfers of funds occur through the participation of public, non-profit, and proprietary organizations.

mixed receptive–expressive language disorder   A *communication disorder*

characterized by the presence of *expressive language disorder* combined with impaired receptive language development (difficulty understanding words, sentences, or types of words). This disorder may be developmental or acquired (as a result of medical conditions such as head trauma). If mental retardation, motor or sensory deficits, or sociocultural deprivation is present, the language difficulties are greater than usually found in those problems.

MLPs   See *midlevel practitioners (MLPs).*

M/MAP   See *Medicare/Medicaid Assistance Program (M/MAP).*

mobility   The ability to move with relative ease or flexibility. See also *social mobility.*

Mobilization for Youth   A multifaceted social service *demonstration program,* established in New York City in the early 1960s, designed to test the theory that poor urban youths will enter mainstream society if social barriers to opportunities are removed. Funded at first by the Ford Foundation and later by the federal government, the program provided some direct *counseling* services but was more oriented toward training; facilitating communication; providing legal, political, and consumer education; developing purposeful and positive group experiences; and changing the neighborhood social structure. The successful results of the program were largely incorporated on a national scale into the *War on Poverty* programs of the Johnson administration.

mobilizer role   In social work, the responsibility to help people and organizations combine their resources to achieve goals of mutual importance. This is accomplished by bringing clients together, enhancing lines of communication, clarifying goals and steps to achieve them, and devising plans for gaining greater support. Other roles are the *facilitator role,* the *enabler role,* and the *educator role.*

mode   A *measure of central tendency* in statistics and research, it is the number that occurs most often in a given series. For example, an agency wants to know how many clients are seen by most of its workers in a given day. A few of the 20 agency workers typically see about 12 clients daily, and a few others see only about five. But most of the workers see eight clients per day, which is the modal number.

model   A representation of reality. For example, social workers use the *life model* to represent the interplay of forces found in the client's environment that influence and are influenced by the client.

Model Cities program   A federal program established in 1966 to coordinate and integrate the various government efforts in housing; urban renewal; community development of facilities, transportation, and education; and economic opportunities in participating cities. Federal officials would coordinate government programs and resources with local efforts. The federal *block grant* approach, in which funds are supplied to the cities without requiring specific allocations, has largely supplanted the Model Cities program.

modeling   In *behavior therapy* and *social learning theory,* a form of learning in which an individual acquires behaviors by imitating the actions of one or more other people.

Model Licensing Act   Legislative guidelines developed by the *National Association of Social Workers (NASW)* that specify recommended conditions and qualifications for states to use in *licensing* social work practice. Social workers and lobbyists with various state legislatures offer the Model Licensing Act to assist legislators in writing their own laws pertaining to social work licenses. The act specifies what social work practice is and is not, outlines the recommended qualifications for doing it, and indicates the procedures to be taken to enforce compliance.

"mongolism"   An obsolete and inappropriate term for *Down's syndrome.*

monogamy   The state of being married to one person.

mononucleosis   A viral infection that most commonly affects adolescents and

young adults with such symptoms as sore throat, fever, and chills; feelings of weakness and tiredness; and enlarged lymph nodes.

monopolists   The designation given by social group workers or group psychotherapists to those clients who seek to be the constant center of attention.

mood   An emotional state that influences an individual's perceptions, cognitive functions, and actions. To be in a "bad mood" is to be irritable, depressed, anxious, or especially, angry. To be in a "good mood" is to be elated, happy, or especially, cheerful. Social workers and other professionals sometimes describe a client as being in a mood of *dysphoria* or *euphoria.*

mood disorder NOS   A residual category for the classification of *mood disorders* (not otherwise specified) given when the individual presents with enough symptoms to warrant a mood disorder diagnosis but not enough to indicate any one of the specific types.

mood disorders   A group of serious mental disorders involving affective lability (*depression* or persistently elevated moods). The diagnosable mood disorders include *major depressive disorder, dysthymic disorder, bipolar disorder, cyclothymic disorder, substance-induced mood disorder,* mood disorder due to general medical condition, and *mood disorder NOS.* In diagnosing this condition, the term "mood disorder" has replaced the formerly used label *affective disorder.*

mood swings   Going from one general *mood* to another within a fairly short time.

moral development   Acquiring the values, feelings, and thoughts that lead to behaviors that are consistent with standards of right or wrong. Many theorists have proposed models about how this is accomplished, including Gilligan, Kohlberg, Piaget, Mischel, and Erikson. See also *Kohlberg moral development theory* and *values clarification.*

moralizing   Communicating a message about how someone should behave or think, often accompanied by *manipulative behavior* designed to stimulate feelings of *guilt* or obligation. The moralizer implies that the other person has a duty to some vague higher authority such as "the family honor." Social workers who sometimes moralize with their clients tend to cause resentment and diminished receptivity in them.

moral judgment   A choice made about right or wrong *behavior* based on a rational assessment and evaluation of consequences to oneself, to others, and to society.

morbid   Diseased or disordered.

morbidity rate   The proportion of people in a specific population who are known to have a specific disease or disorder during a certain period.

morbidity risk   An individual's lifetime chances of having a specific illness.

mores   Social customs that are accepted as traditional and enforced by others in the social group.

"moron"   An obsolete term, once used to refer to a mildly mentally retarded person with an *intelligence quotient (IQ)* score below 70 and above 50.

morpheme   In *communication theory,* a basic unit of meaningful language. Morphemes include words, prefixes, and suffixes.

morphine   An *opiate,* used medically to induce sleep and relieve pain.

morphogenesis   The concept used in *systems theories* to depict the tendency of a living system to change its structure and to evolve into a system that has a different structure. The tendency of a system toward morphogenesis is balanced by the system's equally powerful tendency toward *morphostasis.*

morphostasis   The concept used in *systems theories* to depict the tendency of a living system to retain its structure and to resist change. The tendency of a system toward morphostasis is balanced by the system's equally powerful tendency toward *morphogenesis.*

mortality rate   The number or proportion of deaths in a specified population during a certain period. The mortality rate is also known as the *death rate.*

Mothers Against Drunk Driving (MADD)   A national organization established in 1980 to influence legislation, police activity, judicial decisions, punishment, prevention, and education pertaining to the operation of motor vehicles while under the influence of alcohol or drugs.

Mothers Without Custody   A national *self-help organization,* with chapters in many larger communities, whose members are mothers living separately from one or more of their minor children because of court decisions, intervention by child protection agencies, or *child snatching* by former spouses. Mothers Without Custody members meet regularly to exchange information and provide mutual support and encouragement.

motivation   A set of physical drives, desires, attitudes, and *values* that arouse and direct *behavior* toward the achievement of some goal.

motivation–capacity–opportunity theory   The assessment model used by social workers to predict the likelihood that a client will make effective use of the help offered. *Charlotte Towle* (1896–1966) first formulated the triad, and social work researchers Lillian Ripple, Ernestina Alexander, and Bernice W. Polemis studied its relevance. Their findings concluded that when clients have adequate motivation and the capacity to partake of services provided in an appropriate manner, they will make use of the services, unless there are restrictive or unmodifiable forces outside the agency or influences on the client.

motor skills disorder   Marked impairment in the development of motor coordination that significantly interferes with academics and daily activities. This disorder is not due to medical conditions such as *cerebral palsy* or *muscular dystrophy.*

motor tension   A symptom of anxiety that results in muscular contractions, stiffness, or uncontrollable movements such as shakiness and trembling.

motor tic disorder   See *tic disorder.*

motor voter law   Popular name for National Voter Registration Act, effective January 1, 1995, giving U.S. citizens the opportunity to register to vote when applying for drivers licenses, welfare assistance, and government services. This legislation was initiated by *human SERVE.*

mourning   The psychological and cultural process of expressing sorrow about *loss* of a loved one; breaking the emotional tie with that loved one; and gradually reinvesting the emotional energy in other people, activities, or things. See also *bereavement* and *grief.*

movement disorders   Unusual and persistent gestures, expressions, postures, and movements believed to be the result of medical conditions, effects of substances, or physiological or mental disorders. A professional can often begin to determine the type of problem by observing such movement patterns. Some of the more notable ones identified include *choreiform movements,* dystonic movements (slow twisting interspersed with prolonged muscle tension), athetoid movements (slow, irregular writhing, mostly in the fingers and toes), myoclonic movements (brief, shocklike muscle contractions), spasms (sterotypic, slower, and more-prolonged movements involving muscle groups), and synkinesis (involuntary movements accompanying voluntary ones). See also *medication-induced movement disorders* and *stereotypic movement disorder.*

movement therapy   A systematic procedure for helping patients with diminished strength, energy, and muscle disorders as well as lethargy, *depression,* and sometimes arthritic conditions, through physical activity. Usually in groups, the patients perform dances and other movements designed for their needs.

MRI   See *magnetic resonance imaging (MRI).*

MSW   The master of social work degree awarded to students who have completed the requirements of accredited schools of social work. Requirements for the MSW typically include successful completion of 60 academic hours, including about 24 hours of field placement, taken over the equivalent of two full-time years. The student is often required to complete a thesis or research project. In some schools, the degree is known as the MSSW (master of science in social work, master of social service work), MSSA (master of social service administration), or MA in social work. All are essentially the same in educational requirements and standards.

muckrakers   The name first used by President Theodore Roosevelt to describe a group of journalists, speakers, agitators, and social activists who sought to make the public aware of abuses, unethical practices, and corrupt business and political activities that exploited and endangered people. The muckraking movement was especially prominent in the United States from 1900 to 1915 and resulted in many of the social reforms of the *Progressive Era.* The term is still used and often applied to social workers, writers, investigative reporters, and other reform-minded people who call attention to current examples of abuse and corruption.

mudslinging   An aspect of *negative campaigning* in which an opponent or opponent's supporters make unflattering public disclosures about a candidate that may be true, partly true, or entirely false.

muina   A *culture-bound syndrome,* found especially among Latino groups, in which the individual experiences nervous tension, trembling, screaming, and various somatic complaints, said to be the result of feeling intense anger or rage. This syndrome is also known as *bilis.*

multiaxial assessment system   The system used in the *DSM-IV* for assessing types of *mental disorder* on five axes, each of which refers to a different domain of information about the client: (1) Axis I, clinical disorders and other conditions that may be a focus of clinical attention; (2) Axis II, personality disorders and mental retardation; (3) Axis III, general medical conditions; (4) Axis IV, psychosocial and environmental problems; and (5) Axis V, global assessment of functioning.

multifactorial inheritance See *genetic disorder*.

multifamily therapy A *family therapy* approach in which several families meet regularly in a *group psychotherapy* format, guided by one or more professional leaders or facilitators, to provide mutual understanding, exchange ideas, make recommendations, role play, and perform psychodramas.

multifinality The systems theory concept in which subsystems have identical beginnings or origins but achieve different outcomes. This term is synonymous with *equipotentiality* and the opposite of *equifinality*.

multi-infarct dementia *Dementia* resulting from *cardiovascular disease*. The dementia is caused by a series of strokes causing a step-by-step deterioration of different mental functions depending on which part of the brain is destroyed. The preferred term for this is *vascular dementia*.

multineeds clients People who seek the social worker's services because of the simultaneous existence of problems. Usually the different problems require the skills and resources of more than one worker or agency. Because multineeds clients constitute a high percentage of the social work clientele, the need for coordination of services and agencies is increasing.

multiple-causation theory The view that a given disorder or social phenomenon is the result of many factors operating simultaneously and in many cases somewhat independently of one another. This is a *holistic* view that is particularly emphasized by those who use *systems theories* as their orientation and by those who question the concept of *linear causality*.

multiple-drug use The simultaneous abuse of two or more drugs, often with a mix of symptoms and contradictory progression in the treatment process. For example, when someone is treated for heroin use, the withdrawal effects may be unusual and unpredictable because the client is also going through barbiturate withdrawal. It is important in assessing for drug abuse to determine all the drugs that are or have been in use because of this increasingly common phenomenon.

multiple etiologies A condition that originated from the combination of several, not necessarily related, factors. For example, a diagnosis due to multiple etiologies could be the result of *head trauma* and *Alzheimer's disease*.

multiple-impact therapy A team form of treatment used by social workers and other professionals, especially with the *multiproblem family*. It is typically intensive and relatively short term, with members of the professional team meeting with various subgroups or individuals from the family. Then different subgroups meet with the professionals, and so on, in a variety of combinations.

multiple intelligences A conception about the different types of *intelligence* made by cognitive researcher Howard Gardner. There are seven distinct types of intelligence: (1) verbal/linguistic, (2) logical/mathematical, (3) visual/spatial, (4) body/kinesthetic, (5) musical/rhythmical, (6) interpersonal, and (7) intrapersonal. In this conception, all people have all these intelligences, but not all of them are developed equally; one or more of these intelligences are more fully developed than the others. Any of them may be developed or diminished through various circumstances and life stages. See also *fluid intelligence* and *crystallized intelligence*.

multiple-personality disorder A form of *dissociative disorder* in which an individual has two or more distinct personalities. The term preferred by professionals is *dissociative identity disorder*. The individual may not be aware of the existence of these other personalities. Nonprofessionals often inappropriately confuse *schizophrenia* for this disorder.

multiple-program participation The involvement by clients in two or more social welfare services simultaneously. For example, in the United States everyone who receives *Aid to Families with Dependent Children (AFDC)* is eligible for *Medicaid,* 90 percent of AFDC recipients receive food stamps, and 25 percent of those receiving AFDC also receive housing assistance. Many other programs also exist and are needed and used by people; yet each program has a different bureaucracy to manage it, has unique rules for becoming eligible, and the agencies are often located far apart. Clients often must go to different locations and go through different workers using different rules to get all the benefits to which they are entitled.

multiple sclerosis A slowly progressive disease of the *central nervous system (CNS)* that usually begins to affect its victims during their twenties. The symptoms may include some of the following: paralysis or numbness of various parts of the body, convulsions, visual and speech disorders, emotional problems, bladder control disturbances, and muscular weakness. The symptoms have a tendency to increase and decrease in severity at varying intervals.

multiple tic disorder See *Tourette's disorder.* See also *tic disorder.*

multiproblem family A kinship group whose members are seen by the social worker and treated for a variety of different social, economic, and personality difficulties at the same time. Viewing some family clients as "multiproblem" enables the social worker to use many intervention techniques to address more than one problem at a time. See also *multiple-impact theory.*

multisystems orientation In social work interventions, the approach that gives special recognition to the client as part of an interrelated–related system, each of which influences and is influenced by other systems and the client. The *intervention* oc-

curs at more than one of these systems and often requires a team of workers and a collaboration of agencies to provide the services needed for effectiveness in this orientation. For example, when the client is a family whose father has been arrested for child molestation, the intervention strategy might include economic and emotional support services for the children and mother, legal and mental health services for the father, and group work with the extended family. An example of the multisystems orientation is the *intensive family preservation services (IFPS)* program.

multivariate analysis In *research,* a group of statistical techniques, including analysis of covariance and factor analysis, that tests the results of two or more variables acting simultaneously.

mumps A contagious viral disease that results in painful swelling of the salivary glands, especially under the jawbone.

Munchausen syndrome An outdated term for *factitious disorder.*

municipal court A local court with jurisdiction over minor offenses (such as traffic violations, curfew violations, and loitering), and over civil disputes (such as landlord–tenant grievances and unpaid debts) where damages claimed are small.

muscle relaxation technique A therapeutic and self-help approach to reducing *stress* and *anxiety;* it is accomplished when the subject first tightens and then relaxes a set of muscles while concentrating on those muscles. The procedure has many variations but basically consists of sitting in a quiet, private place and then flexing, holding for a few seconds, and relaxing different muscle groups in a predetermined sequence (such as right hand, right forearm, right shoulder, and so on) until all the muscle groups have been relaxed. The technique is also used in conjunction with other therapy approaches, such as *systematic desensitization.*

muscular dystrophy A progressive disease of the skeletal muscles that usually begins in early childhood. In some forms, patients are confined to wheelchairs by the time they reach adolescence. Early manifestations of the disease include progressive muscular weakness, waddling gait, coordination problems, and sometimes *learning disorder* and *mental retardation*. Causes are not well established for all types, but in many male victims it is an inherited disease, passed on through the mother.

mutism A refusal or inability to speak.

mutual-aid groups Formal or informal associations of people who share certain problems and may meet regularly in small groups to provide one another with advice, emotional support, information, and other help. Mutual-aid groups are similar to *self-help groups* except they may have professional leaders. See *support system*.

mutual help The efforts of people who face similar problems to provide assistance for one another. Social workers often encourage and facilitate such efforts among client groups. For example, senior citizens in a *network* may provide mutual help by calling one another periodically through-out the day for reassurance. See also *mutual-aid groups* and *support system*.

mutuality The efforts of two or more people to act together in ultimate harmony to achieve benefits for each. In *systems theories* it is the concept of interdependence between various subsystems, such as social worker and client, landlord and tenant, or parents and children. See also *pseudomutuality*.

mutual withdrawal The condition of indifference, boredom, noncommunication, and nonmotivation to resolve problems that sometimes occurs among troubled couples and family members.

myocardial infarction A circulatory system disease in which a blood vessel that carries blood to the heart muscles (for example, a coronary artery) becomes blocked as the result of a blood clot or hemorrhage. Often this occurs because the artery wall has become hardened or narrowed by *arteriosclerosis*. The resulting interruption of blood flow to the heart muscle often results in the *death* of some tissue in the heart and sometimes in heart failure. See also *heart attack*.

N

NA See *needs assessments (NA)*.

NAACP See *National Association for the Advancement of Colored People (NAACP)*.

NAACSW See *North American Association of Christians in Social Work (NAACSW)*.

NABSW See *National Association of Black Social Workers (NABSW)*.

naltrexone treatment A maintenance therapy for those addicted to opiate drugs. Naltrexone, like *methadone,* is an opiate antagonist. It prevents the user of *heroin* and other opium-based substances from "getting high." However, because of this, most addicts do not want to take it. Its usefulness is limited to the highly motivated *"recovering addict"* in conjunction with other therapy.

NAP See *National Academy of Practice (NAP)*.

NAPRSSW See *National Association of Puerto Rican Social Service Workers (NAPRSSW)*.

NARAL See *National Abortion Rights Action League (NARAL)*.

narcissism Excessive self-preoccupation and self-love; an extreme form of *egocentrism.*

narcissistic personality disorder One of the *personality disorders* characterized by excessive *egocentrism, grandiosity,* self-centeredness, preoccupation with feelings of *envy,* fragile *self-esteem,* and behavior that is often seeking approval or admiration. The person usually has little *empathy,* volatile interpersonal relationships, and periodic *depression.*

narcolepsy One of the *sleep disorders* in which the individual is subject to brief attacks of sleepiness resulting in deep sleep, often at inopportune times.

narcotics Natural or synthetic drugs that have a depressant effect on the *central nervous system (CNS),* relieve *pain* and *anxiety,* and alter *mood.* The major narcotic is *opium* (and its constituents *codeine* and *morphine*), from which *heroin is* derived. Narcotics tend to result in *addiction,* and their side effects can often endanger the life of the user.

narrative summary A system of social case *recording* in which the social worker describes and consolidates all the relevant information obtained about the *client system:* the progression of the *intervention,* including procedures used and outcomes, and the interim and concluding *prognosis* and recommendations. The information is written as succinctly as possible and is based on the social worker's ongoing progress notes, findings before the intervention, and overall conclusion about the case. See also *process recording.*

NASSW See *National Association of School Social Workers (NASSW)*.

NASW See *National Association of Social Workers (NASW)*.

NASW Code of Ethics The explication of the *values,* rules, and principles of *ethical conduct* that apply to all *social workers* who are members of the *National Association of Social Workers (NASW).* The original *Code of Ethics* for social workers was implicit in the 1951 Standards for Professional Practice of the *American Association of Social Workers (AASW)*. NASW developed a formal code in 1960 and has made subsequent revisions. See the complete *NASW Code of Ethics* in the appendix of this volume.

National Abortion Rights Action League (NARAL) The organization founded in 1969 to protect and maintain the right to legal *abortion*. The organization was formed as the National Association for Repeal of Abortion Laws and took its present name after the 1973 Supreme Court decision to permit legal abortions. See also *Roe v. Wade* and the *National Right-to-Life Committee (NRLC)*.

National Academy of Practice (NAP) A professional, scientific, and educational organization, established in 1981 and modeled in part on the National Academy of Sciences, that comprises distinguished practitioners from each of the major health professions, including *social work*. NAP's goals are to promote excellence in professional practice for the benefit of all people and to provide a forum to which government and society can direct public policy concerns in *health care*. One of the constituent organizations in NAP is the National Academy of Practice in Social Work.

National Advisory Commission on Civil Disorders See *Kerner Commission*.

National Association for the Advancement of Colored People (NAACP) The largest and oldest of the U.S. *civil rights* organizations. It was established in 1909 when social worker *Mary White Ovington* (1865–1951) and others helped organize *African Americans* and white people who were outraged about a series of lynchings. NAACP now has more than 1,500 local chapters throughout all 50 states and works to achieve its goals primarily through legal actions to protect the rights of black citizens, nonpartisan *political action* to enact civil rights laws, and education and public information.

National Association of Black Social Workers (NABSW) The *professional as-sociation (PA)*, formed in 1968, comprising black social workers and other social workers who are interested in the goals of the organization. These goals are to deal with problems pertinent to the black community on all levels, including working with clients, promoting programs serving *African Americans,* and assisting black social workers. NABSW holds annual conventions, performs research and educational functions, and publishes the journal *Black Caucus*.

National Association of Puerto Rican Social Service Workers (NAPRSSW) The professional association of social workers of Puerto Rican and other *Hispanic* heritages whose members work primarily toward the improvement of social conditions for Puerto Ricans and other Hispanics and for the professional goals of Puerto Rican social workers.

National Association of School Social Workers (NASSW) The professional association composed of social workers in elementary, middle, and high schools. The organization was founded in 1919 as the National Association of Visiting Teachers. In 1955 NASSW merged with six other associations to become the *National Association of Social Workers (NASW)*.

National Association of Social Workers (NASW) The organization of social workers established in 1955 through the consolidation of the *American Association of Social Workers (AASW)*, the *American Association of Psychiatric Social Workers (AAPSW)*, the *American Association of Group Workers (AAGW)*, the *Association for the Study of Community Organization (ASCO)*, the *American Association of Medical Social Workers (AAMSW)*, the *National Association of School Social Workers (NASSW)*, and the *Social Work Research Group (SWRG)*. NASW's primary functions include promoting the professional development of its members, establishing and maintaining professional standards of practice, advancing sound social policies, and providing other services that protect its members and enhance their professional *status*. The organization has developed and adopted the *NASW Code of Ethics* and other generic and specialized practice standards. *Certification* and *quality assurance* are promoted through the *Academy of Certified Social Workers (ACSW)*, the *NASW Register of Clinical Social Workers,* and the *Diplomate in Clinical Social Work.* Among NASW's *political action* programs are *Political Action for Candidate Election (PACE)* and *Educational Legislative Action Network (ELAN).* NASW also sponsors professional conferences and *continuing education* programs and produces journals, books, and major reference works such as the *Encyclopedia of Social Work* and this dictionary. See also *National Center on Social Work Policy and Practice.*

National Center for Health Statistics Research (NCHSR) The agency of the U.S. *Department of Health and Human Services (HHS)* that provides for the collection, interpretation, and dissemination of data pertaining to the nation's health. Data include the *incidence rate* and *prevalence rate* of various diseases and *human resources* for medical and *health care* and *social services.*

National Center for Missing and Exploited Children (NCMEC) A national clearinghouse and resource center to provide assistance in cases of child abduction, parental kidnapping, *child snatching,* lost children, and victims of *child abuse.* Funding comes primarily from the Office of Juvenile Justice and Delinquency Prevention of the U.S. *Department of Justice.* See also *child find organizations.*

National Center on Child Abuse and Neglect (NCCAN) The federal organization, within the *Administration for Children, Youth, and Families (ACYF)* of the U.S. *Department of Health and Human Services (HHS),* whose mission is to mobilize national efforts to prevent, control, and treat the problem of *child abuse* and *child neglect.* The organization, headquartered in Washington, DC, with centers in cities throughout the nation, facilitates research, maintains databases, and accumulates and

disseminates information to health care providers, educators, researchers, practitioners, and others with interests in child abuse. See also *child find organizations.*

National Center on Social Work Policy and Practice The social work organization established by the *National Association of Social Workers (NASW)* in 1986 to collect, analyze, and disseminate information about U.S. health and *social welfare* needs. These data come from the direct experiences of social work practitioners and after analysis are used to inform legislators and the public about *social problems* and proposed solutions. The information also is used to enhance social work practice effectiveness. In 1993, the center was changed from a subsidiary organization to a formal NASW program.

National Conference of Charities and Corrections See *National Conference on Social Welfare (NCSW).*

National Conference on Catholic Charities See *Catholic Charities USA.*

National Conference on Social Welfare (NCSW) A federation of *social welfare* agencies in the public and private sectors, including secular and religious agencies, as well as individuals concerned about the social welfare of Americans. Established in 1879 as the Conference of Charities, it changed its name to the National Conference on Charities and Corrections in 1884, to the National Conference of Social Work in 1917, and to its last name in 1957. NCSW suspended operations gradually in the 1980s.

National Congress of American Indians (NCAI) The *civil rights* and lobbying organization established in 1944 by leaders of the nation's largest tribes. With headquarters in Washington, DC, the congress evaluates government policies pertaining to *American Indians* and promotes programs to enhance economics, educational, and legal rights for its constituents.

National Consumers League (NCL) The *advocacy* and educational organization founded in 1899 to protect those who make and purchase products. In its early years, it was led by social worker–lawyer *Florence Kelley* (1859–1932) and philanthropist *Josephine Shaw Lowell* (1843–1904) and successfully fought for improved working conditions, *child labor* laws, a *minimum wage*, shorter working hours, and safe and effective consumer products.

National Council of Senior Citizens (NCSC) A federation of more than 4,000 senior citizens' clubs around the nation, founded in 1961 to coordinate the activities of older people in educating the public, lobbying, and developing services and programs.

National Council on Aging (NCA) A national organization comprising individuals and agencies that provide services for older people. The council coordinates conferences and procedures for exchanging information between organizations and helps disseminate information to researchers, academicians, health care providers, family members of older people, and others interested in services to older people. Through its *National Institute on Aging, Work, and Retirement (NIAWR)*, it strives to promote opportunities for middle-age or older people to obtain employment or prepare for *retirement*.

National Education Association (NEA) A professional membership association of teachers, school administrators, and related personnel. Its major objectives are improved educational practices, facilities, standards, and conditions for teachers and students.

National Federation of Societies for Clinical Social Work (NFSCSW) The organization, established in 1971, comprising social workers who have at least *MSW* degrees and are interested in *clinical social work practice* in social agencies or *private practice*. NFSCSW publishes the journal *Clinical Social Work* and the newsletter *Managed Care News*. The organization is known informally as the Clinical Society or the Clinical Federation.

national health insurance A proposed program to help every citizen pay for *health care* costs in the existing medical market-place. There are many variations in the proposal, but basically it would use and supplement existing health insurance procedures and extend coverage to everyone. Payrolls would contain *earmarked taxes* for this insurance, and individuals would, if able, pay a percentage of the health care provider's bill, with the remainder to be paid by the government. This proposal is not to be confused with a *national health service*.

national health service Direct government provision of medical personnel and facilities for citizens to receive complete *health care*; also known as "socialized medicine." This system is common in many countries, though not in the United States. However, a form of national health service is provided to certain groups in the United States, including needy veterans, members of the armed forces and their families, *tuberculosis* patients, and *American Indians*. This system is not to be confused with *national health insurance*.

National Incidence-Based Reporting System (NIBRS) A data-gathering and reporting procedure developed in 1986 by the Federal Bureau of Investigation to revise and modernize its *Uniform Crime Reports (UCR)*. NIBRS has added 14 crime categories to the eight in the UCR, including drug violations, weapons offenses, counterfeiting, and other less-serious crimes. NIBRS also includes information about the victims, the amount and type of property lost, information about recovery, and multiple crimes within an incident. As in the UCR, information is obtained from local law enforcement agencies.

National Indian Social Workers Association (NISWA) The national professional association established in 1970 for *social workers* descended from *Native Americans* or *Alaska Natives*. Goals of NISWA include promoting the welfare of *American Indians* through influencing legislation, educating and sensitizing other social workers and social work educators about the needs of American Indians, and conducting research about Indian populations.

National Institute for Clinical Social Work Advancement (NICSWA) This organization was established in 1975 as the National Registry of Health Care Providers in Clinical Social Work with the goal of developing an independent national compendium of social workers, who by education and experience qualified as health care providers in clinical social work. In 1987, in collaboration with the *National Association of Social Workers (NASW)*, the organization established the *American Board of Examiners in Clinical Social Work (ABE)* and its board-certified *diplomate in clinical social work* credential.

National Institute for Occupational Safety and Health (NIOSH) A federal organization within the U.S. *Department of Health and Human Services (HHS)* that conducts studies and surveys relating to health and safety standards in the workplace. NIOSH works closely with and provides scientific support for the *Occupational Safety and Health Administration (OSHA)* in the U.S. *Department of Labor.*

National Institute of Mental Health (NIMH) A federal organization, part of the U.S. *Department of Health and Human Services (HHS)*, that supports research and training, oversees plans for the care and treatment of mentally ill people, and facilitates programs to enhance the nation's *mental health.*

National Institute on Aging, Work and Retirement (NIAWR) A policy development branch of the *National Council on Aging (NCA)* that promotes employment opportunities for middle-age or older workers and helps them prepare for retirement.

National Institutes of Health (NIH) The U.S. *Public Health Service* organization that supports, coordinates, and conducts research into the causes, prevention, treatment, and cure of diseases. NIH has many component institutes, each specializing in a particular disease or health concern. NIH components include the National Cancer Institute; National Institute of Child Health and Human Development; National Institute of Allergy and Infectious Diseases; National Institute of Arthritis, Diabetes,

and Digestive and Kidney Diseases; National Institute of Environmental Health Sciences; National Eye Institute; National Institute on Aging; National Institute of Neurological and Communicative Disorders and Stroke; National Institute of General Medical Sciences; National Institute of Dental Research; National Heart, Lung, and Blood Institute; and National Library of Medicine.

National Insurance Act See *British National Insurance Act.*

nationalization A government's taking over and managing of one or more of its industries. Industries most commonly nationalized include utilities, telephone and postal companies, and mineral production industries formerly under foreign ownership.

National League of Cities (NLC) The public-interest organization, founded in 1924 as the American Municipal Association, whose membership comprises nearly all the towns and cities in the United States, and whose goal is to advocate municipal interests before Congress and other government agencies.

National Network for Social Work Managers (NNSWM) An independent organization established in 1985 comprising social workers who are executive officers and management consultants for public and private social agencies throughout the United States. The organization facilitates communication between social work managers, helps produce the quarterly journal *Administration in Social Work*, publishes the quarterly newsletter *Social Work Executive*, conducts training programs, and sponsors the annual Exemplar Awards for management excellence.

National Organization for Women (NOW) A *volunteer* organization, with local chapters throughout the United States, established in 1966 to enhance the economic and social opportunities for women through educating the public, lobbying, taking legal action against discriminatory procedures, and helping candidates sympathetic to NOW's goals get elected.

National Recovery Administration (NRA) The federal organization established in 1933, early in President Franklin D. Roosevelt's first term, to take immediate action to solve problems arising from the economic crisis. Mostly involved with establishing new codes regulating businesses and labor, NRA was absorbed into other agencies by 1936.

National Right-to-Life Committee (NRLC) The organization founded in 1973 to oppose *abortion, infanticide*, and *euthanasia* and to provide education, counseling, and alternatives such as *adoption*. The committee seeks a constitutional amendment to make abortion illegal. See also *Roe v. Wade* and the *National Abortion Rights Action League (NARAL)*.

National Urban League See *Urban League, National*.

National Welfare Rights Organization (NWRO) An association of public relief clients formed in 1966. The goals of NWRO are to help people fight bureaucratic policies without having to rely on *welfare* workers and to facilitate improvements in welfare legislation and programs.

National Youth Administration (NYA) The *New Deal* federal program that sought to provide part-time jobs for high school and college students so they could complete their educations.

Native Americans Also called *American Indians*, the ethnic–racial–cultural groups of American citizens whose ancestors lived in the Western Hemisphere before its exploration and settlement by Europeans.

nativism The idea that certain personality factors are not learned but are genetically transmitted or present at birth. See also *archetype*.

natural helping network Informal, reliable linkages and relationships between *nonprofessionals* who voluntarily provide important services and supports to people in need and those to whom they provide the services. Most natural helping networks develop among members of the needy person's family or neighbors, fellow employees, members of the person's church, members of associations or social classes to which the person belongs, or altruistic people in the *community*.

naturalization Officially becoming a citizen or national of a country. See also *immigration* and *repatriation*.

natural resources The products and features of the earth that permit it to support life and meet human needs, including land, air, water, climate, minerals, and biological resources such as trees, wildlife, and vegetation. See also *human resources*.

NCA See *National Council on Aging (NCA)*.

NCAI See *National Congress of American Indians (NCAI)*.

NCCAN See *National Center on Child Abuse and Neglect (NCCAN)*.

NCDO See *New Community Development Office (NCDO)*.

NCHSR See *National Center for Health Statistics Research (NCHSR)*.

NCL See *National Consumers League (NCL)*.

NCMEC See *National Center for Missing and Exploited Children (NCMEC)*.

NCSC See *National Council of Senior Citizens (NCSC)*.

NCSW See *National Conference on Social Welfare (NCSW)*.

NEA See *National Education Association (NEA)*.

"near-poor" population Families and individuals who are employed but earn only slightly more than is received by those who benefit from *public assistance* or *social security*.

needle exchange program A program to protect the *IV drug users* from such diseases as *acquired immune deficiency syndrome (AIDS)* by providing new hypodermic syringes to those considered most likely to reuse already infected needles.

needs Physical, psychological, economic, cultural, and social requirements for survival, well-being, and fulfillment. Types of needs include *normative needs, perceived needs, expressed needs,* and *relative needs.*

needs assessments (NA) Systematic appraisals made by social workers and other professionals in evaluating their clients of problems, existing resources, potential solutions, and obstacles to problem solving. In *social agencies,* needs assessments are made on behalf of the clients who receive clinical services and in communities, on behalf of all the residents. The purpose of needs assessments is to document needs and establish priorities for service. The data come from existing records such as U.S. *Bureau of the Census* and local government statistics as well as from interviews and research on the relevant *population.*

needs group People who know a problem through personal experience. In *social policy* development and *community organization,* representative victims of a problem are often included in planning committees to discuss and decide how to assist others who have the problem.

negative campaigning Conducting a political or social-change *campaign,* with less emphasis on extolling the virtues of the candidates or causes and more on disclosing their actual or claimed liabilities. See also *mudslinging.*

negative feedback In *systems theories* and *communication theory,* a signal or message that maintains the system's characteristic or organized state. Many professionals and others also use this term to refer to critical responses to one's efforts or communications.

negative income tax A program designed to standardize procedures for assisting poor families while eliminating a *means test* through use of the federal income tax system. Taxpayers whose incomes fall below a specified minimum are reimbursed up to that amount from the federal treasury. See also *guaranteed annual income.*

negative reinforcement In *behavior modification,* the strengthening of a *response* through escape or avoidance conditioning.

negative transference *Transference* that results in expressions of hostility or distrust or feelings of ill will that a *client* may have for a *psychotherapist* or other person. In *psychoanalytic theory,* it is believed to always exist, whether it is latent or overt.

negativistic personality disorder Also called *passive–aggressive personality disorder,* a pervasive pattern of negativistic attitudes and passive resistance; the individual habitually resents, opposes, and covertly obstructs demands to fulfill obligations and appropriate expectations. This is a proposed diagnosis by the *DSM-IV.*

neglect Failure to meet one's legal and moral obligations or duties, especially to dependent family members. When such conduct results in potential harm to others, legal proceedings may be taken to compel the person to meet the relevant obligations or face punishment.

negligence Failure to exercise reasonable care or caution, resulting in others' being subjected to harm or unwarranted risk of harm; also, failure to fulfill responsibility that is necessary to protect or help another. Contributory negligence may occur when a person's failure to exercise prudent caution, combined with the negligence of another, results in harm to a third individual. For example, if a social worker does not report knowledge about a person's neglect of a child who has been harmed, the social worker could be charged with contributory negligence. Criminal (or culpable) negligence may occur when one is so reckless, careless, or indifferent to others' safety that injury or death results.

negotiation In *community organization* and other forms of *social work,* the process of bringing together those who are opposed on some issues and arranging for them to communicate clearly and fairly, to bargain and compromise, and to arrive at mutually acceptable agreements.

neighborhood   A region or locality whose inhabitants share certain characteristics, values, mutual interests, or styles of living.

neighborhood information center   A social program proposed by Alfred J. Kahn and other *social welfare* planners in which highly accessible and geographically convenient organizations are used as entry points to the total *social services* system. They would provide information, advice, and referrals but would not replace the intake evaluation function of social agencies. The centers could be freestanding or located in post offices, libraries, municipal buildings, and shopping centers.

Neighborhood Youth Corps   The federal program to assure local jobs for unemployed teenagers, established as part of the *Economic Opportunity Act of 1964*. In 1974, it became part of the *CETA* program.

neoconservatism   A revision of certain aspects of traditional conservative philosophies and views that retains most other aspects of these views. Thus, there are many neoconservative philosophies rather than a single one. The term is often applied to an attitude that favors more controls on morality and financial incentives and subsidies to businesses to encourage their growth, rejecting the traditional conservative view that government should be unobtrusive and minimal. See also *conservatism*.

neo-Freudian   A theoretical orientation that basically follows *Freudian theory* but puts greater emphasis on sociocultural factors, interpersonal relationships, and psychosocial development into and through *adulthood*. There is no single neo-Freudian school, because those who have been given this designation also diverge from one another. However, leading neo-Freudians include Harry Stack Sullivan, Karen Horney, Alfred Adler, and Erich Fromm.

neoliberalism   A revision of certain aspects of traditional liberal philosophies and views while retaining most other aspects of these views. Thus, there are many neoliberal philosophies rather than a single one. The term is most commonly applied to those who change their traditional liberal views and espouse fewer direct *welfare* benefits and similar programs.

neonatal   Pertaining to newborn infants.

neo-Nazism   A political *ideology* and movement in which the philosophy of the National Socialist Party of the German Third Reich and its leader, Adolph Hitler, is promoted. Much of the ideology centers around *racism* and the view that only some Aryan peoples should rule and that many other peoples, such as *black people* and Jews, should be exterminated. Because the ideology is so disfavored by most people, at least in public, much of its activity is accomplished through *secret societies*.

nepotism   Favoritism shown to an individual's relatives, especially in appointing them to desirable jobs.

nervios   A *culture-bound syndrome* among Spanish-speaking peoples referring to general "nervousness" and a wide range of emotional distresses, including anxiety, somatic disturbances, headaches, tearfulness, sleep problems, and an inability to concentrate.

nervous breakdown   An imprecise lay term that carries many meanings, usually having to do with any emotional condition that has resulted in hospitalization or severe emotional disability interfering with normal functioning. Social workers or other professionals do not use this term in professional communications.

net present value (NPV) analysis   A method used in program planning and budgeting to help determine what *benefits* are available in relation to costs when measured over time. NPV rates programs according to the difference between the present value of the benefits and the costs required to achieve those benefits. It is an alternative to *cost–benefit analysis*.

network   A formal or informal linkage of people or organizations that may share resources, skills, contacts, and knowledge with one another. Networks may be positive or negative in their effects on individuals and families.

networking 1. The social worker's efforts to enhance and develop the social linkages that might exist between the client and those relevant to the client, such as family members, friends, neighbors, and associates. These efforts include strengthening the supportive quality of existing networks, establishing new ones, creating linkages among the various networks to promote more-competent support, and mobilizing these networks on behalf of the client. Within the *network* are people who can be effective resources in helping to achieve the client's goals. 2. The relationships professionals cultivate with other professionals to expedite action through the social system.

network therapy The family treatment procedure in which a large number of people who are important to an individual or to a *nuclear family* are brought together with that family to discuss how everyone can help resolve the existing problems. Included in such meetings can be members of the *extended family,* neighbors, classmates, fellow employees, other professionals, and clergy members.

neurolinguistic programming (NLP) A communications model of human *behavior* developed by Richard Bandler and John Grinder and others and used by social workers and other psychosocial therapists, educators, and business personnel to assess, build rapport with, and help clients. Major components of the model are "neuro" (the processing of information perceived through the five senses by the nervous system); "linguistic" (the systems of verbal and nonverbal *communication* that organize the neural representations into meaningful data); and "programming" (the ability to organize the neurolinguistic systems to achieve specific outcomes). To assess someone's behavior, the NLP counselor must identify the way the client understands information.

neurological disorder *Dysfunction* of the *central nervous system (CNS)* caused by

injury, disease, or drugs, and resulting in some forms of *organic mental disorders* and diseases of the CNS such as *cerebral palsy, Parkinson's disease,* and *seizure disorders.* The term should not be confused with similar sounding terms such as "neurasthenia," "nervousness," *neurosis,* or "neurotic," which are more closely related to an *anxiety disorder.*

neurologist A physician who specializes in the diagnosis, treatment, and health of the individual's nervous system. The *American Board of Psychiatry and Neurology (ABPN)* is the major credentialing authority for qualified specialists in this field.

neuromuscular disorders A group of neurological diseases that result in progressive weakness or uncontrolled ability of the muscles and in *atrophy.* Major diseases of this type include *muscular dystrophy, Huntington's disease, Tourette's disorder,* and *Parkinson's disease.*

neuron The nerve cell, the basic building block of the *central nervous system (CNS)* on which electrochemical impulses are sent and received. See also *synapse.*

neurosis A term pertaining to a group of *mental disorders* that are characterized by persistent and disturbing symptoms of *anxiety,* such as nervousness, irritability, and *somatic complaints.* The anxiety is said to be a *maladaptive* way of dealing with internal *conflict.* The symptoms can range from mild to severe but are relatively amenable to *psychotherapy.*

neurotransmitters See *catecholamines.*

Newburgh welfare plan The controversial system of providing *public assistance* services in Newburgh, NY, beginning in 1960. Designed primarily to reduce *welfare* costs, the system gave applicants minimal help, often with payments in kind rather than in cash, and subjected them to stringent residency requirements. The program was terminated as state and federal funds became increasingly important in financing welfare costs, but the idea of the Newburgh policy continues to be debated.

New Community Development Office (NCDO) An organization within the U.S. *Department of Housing and Urban Development (HUD)* to assure that the planning and building of new neighborhoods, cities, and housing infrastructures are in compliance with national housing and environmental laws and encourages these communities to provide for the human needs of its residents.

New Deal President Franklin D. Roosevelt's name for the plans, programs, and legislation enacted during his first administration in response to the *Great Depression*. New Deal programs included the *Social Security Act; Federal Emergency Relief Administration (FERA); Civilian Conservation Corps (CCC); Works Progress Administration (WPA);* rural electrification; and legislation that regulated banking and securities practices, farm management, and unemployment exchanges.

new federalism A revision of the traditional federalist *ideology* (a national government sharing power with states and regions over specifically delineated functions, such as *welfare* and education), which generally advocates reduced national spending, federal taxation, and federal responsibility and commensurately more of these at the state level. This term was used by the Reagan administration to describe some of its policies.

new poor People who have recently become impoverished or have had significant reductions in their living standards as a result of job loss or other economic problems. Some sociologists and economists consider these people different from other poor people in that they tend to share the values and backgrounds of middle-class people. New poor could be said to be the opposite of "noveau riche" people who have recently become more affluent but continue to hold the values and backgrounds of less-affluent people.

new property The guaranteed assets, services, and resources that are available to a resident of a jurisdiction. Also known as the "social wage," the "new income," and *entitlement programs,* these assets are seen by social planners and economists as being as important in considering an individual's *standard of living* as income from work or assets from unearned income.

NFSCSW See *National Federation of Societies for Clinical Social Work (NFSCSW).*

NGO See *nongovernment organization (NGO).*

NGRI patients The legal term for people tried but found "not guilty by reason of insanity." Such people are then committed for an indefinite time to mental hospitals.

NIAWR See *National Institute on Aging, Work and Retirement (NIAWR).*

NIBRS See *National Incidence-Based Reporting System (NIBRS).*

niche 1. In the *ecological perspective,* the position a species occupies in the biotic community. 2. In humans, the social position or status occupied in the existing social structure and in those social structures of a community by participating groups, relative to power and oppression. According to Carel B. Germain (*Human Behavior and the Social Environment: An Ecological View,* New York: Columbia University Press, 1991, p. 50), many individuals are required, by discrimination or poverty, to occupy niches that do not support healthy development or opportunities for growth.

nicotine dependence A *psychoactive substance abuse disorder* whose effect occurs primarily through inhaling the smoke of burning tobacco or ingesting chewed tobacco. Even though the disorder has no social impairment or intoxication, it is significantly related to such physical diseases as bronchitis, *emphysema,* coronary artery disease, peripheral vascular disease, and various forms of *cancer.*

nicotine-related disorders The resulting *substance dependence* and *withdrawal symptoms* that commonly occur through the use of nicotine, the psychoactive ingredient in tobacco. These disorders can develop with use of all forms of tobacco, including cigarettes, chewing tobacco, snuff, cigars, and pipes. Symptoms associated with nicotine withdrawal include depression, insomnia, irritability, anxiety, and difficulty concentrating. Craving is another factor leading to continued use of tobacco despite considerable evidence of its contribution to health problems.

NICSWA See *National Institute for Clinical Social Work Advancement (NICSWA).*

nightmare disorder One of the *sleep disorders,* of the *parasomnia* type, characterized by frequent awakenings from sleep due to frightening dreams, resulting in ongoing distress, irritability, anxiety, or occupational and interpersonal problems. The individual usually becomes fully and rapidly awakened after the nightmare, which often involves an elaborate dream sequence of perceived danger. Nightmare disorder was formerly called *dream anxiety disorder;* it is not synonymous with *sleep terror disorder.*

NIH See *National Institutes of Health (NIH).*

nihilism A denial of the worth in all social structures, governments and laws, norms and values, and moral principles. Such an orientation may lead one toward violence or terrorism against the established social system but more often results in passive resistance to everything and with no alternatives in mind.

NIMBY "Not in my back yard!", a slogan attributed to groups and individuals who oppose the location of an undesired facility (such as a *halfway house,* jail, garbage dump, or factory) in their neighborhoods.

NIMH See *National Institute of Mental Health (NIMH).*

Nineline A 24-hour-a-day free national hotline for *runaway* youths. The telephone number, 1-800-999-9999, is posted in areas where runaways tend to go. The hotline is staffed by Covenant House volunteers and professionals who provide support, guidance, information, and access to resources for young people who have left their homes or are contemplating leaving.

NIOSH See *National Institute for Occupational Safety and Health (NIOSH).*

Nisei generation Americans of Japanese ancestry, born mostly between 1910 and World War II, whose parents emigrated from Japan. Members of this generation were subject to problems of *acculturation* and *discrimination,* culminating in their being placed in *internment* camps during World War II. See also *Sansei generation.*

NISWA See *National Indian Social Workers (NISWA).*

NLC See *National League of Cities (NLC).*

NLP See *neurolinguistic programming (NLP).*

NNSWM See *National Network for Social Work Managers (NNSWM).*

"noblesse oblige" Originally a French term pertaining to the obligation of the nobility to help the peasantry, now it refers to the obligation of affluent people to help those less fortunate.

no-fault divorce Legal dissolution of a *marriage* that occurs without the necessity of declaring that one or the other spouse is guilty of marital misconduct. Before the enactment of no-fault *divorce* laws in several states, most marriages could be legally terminated only when one party proved that the other was guilty of behavior that was grounds for divorce. The most common basis for no-fault divorce is voluntary separation for a specified amount of time.

noise pollution An excessive and persistent volume of noise in the environment that may lead to hearing disorders, neurological damage, *stress,* or the inability to rest.

nomadism The regular shifting of habitation by an individual or group, usually in search of a more-suitable environment or better economic opportunities.

nominal group A group whose members work in the presence of one another without verbally interacting, usually to establish goals of common interest. For example, a classroom instructor might use this approach by asking students in a new class to write their goals for the class or their objections to the curriculum so far.

nominal group technique   A tool used by social planners in *organization development (OD)* to assess existing problems, needs, interests, or objectives. Participants in a meeting write these factors on small cards. The leader collects and categorizes the cards and posts them on a board for all to see. Then the group members consider each issue and decide how to proceed. Alternatives are considered as to cost, readiness, motivation, acceptability, and availability of other resources.

nominal measurement   The lowest *level of measurement* used by researchers, consisting simply of classifying observations into categories (for example, gender, race, religion, and so on) that must be mutually exclusive and collectively exhaustive. Appropriate statistics for nominal-level variables include chi-square, phi, lambda, and contingency coefficients.

noncategorical grants   Disbursements of funds from one organization to another without any specified objective or requirement for spending. An example is the federal government's *revenue sharing* with state governments.

nondirective therapy   A term applied to an approach in *counseling* or *therapy* that emphasizes a warm, permissive, accepting atmosphere to encourage the client to discuss problems freely. In the nondirective approach to therapy, called *client-centered therapy* by some professionals, the social worker or therapist asks very few questions and offers few, if any, suggestions or advice. Rather, the social worker prompts and encourages the client to initiate exploration and follow ideas and feelings.

nongovernment organization (NGO)   A *nonprofit agency* that serves some public interest. This term is used in Great Britain and some other English-speaking nations.

nonjudgmental   A fundamental element in the social worker–client *relationship,* in which the social worker demonstrates an attitude of tolerance and an unwillingness to censor the client for any actions. The social worker does not suspend judgment but conveys to the client that the working relationship takes precedence over any possible feelings of disapproval. Although affirming the worth of the client, the social worker does not condone criminal or dangerous behavior and, under certain circumstances, may need to take preventive action. See also *acceptance* and *unconditional positive regard.*

nonprofessional   One who is not a *professional.* Generally, the term is applied to a *paraprofessional,* support staff, ancillary personnel, and *volunteers* who work with professionals in service organizations, such as social agencies and hospitals, and assist the professionals in accomplishing less-technical tasks. Nonprofessionals usually have specific training or experience in the jobs they carry out. The term should not be confused with *unprofessional.*

nonprofit agencies   Organizations established to fulfill some social purpose other than monetary reward to financial backers. Technically the term includes government or tax-supported agencies, but it is usually reserved for private, voluntary social agencies and excludes for-profit *proprietary social agencies.* Nonprofit agencies have explicit policies and established boards of directors. They are funded from a variety of sources, including revenue coming directly from clients, third parties, public contributions, philanthropic contributions, and government *grants-in-aid;* they are usually tax exempt. Most of the traditional *social agencies, professional associations,* and *social change* organizations are nonprofit. Examples include *Family Service America (FSA), Catholic Charities USA,* the *Child Welfare League of America (CWLA),* the *National Association of Social Workers (NASW),* the *National Association for the Advancement of Colored People (NAACP),* the *American Civil Liberties Union (ACLU),* and the *Red Cross.* In Great Britain the term for these groups is *nongovernment organizations (NGO).*

nonsupport 1. In legal terms, the intentional failure to provide food, shelter, and maintenance when legally obliged to do so. 2. Informally, the lack of providing needed emotional encourgement and educational guidance between people in close relationships.

nonverbal communication Exchanges of information between people through gestures, facial expressions, posture, tone of voice, and vocal sounds other than words. See also *communication theory, kinesics, paralinguistics,* and *proxemics.*

nonwhite The U.S. *Bureau of the Census* term for population groups that are not Caucasian, including *African Americans, American Indians, Asian Americans,* and other people of color.

NORD The National Organization for Rare Disorders. See *rare disorders.*

norepinephrine A biochemical of the *central nervous system (CNS)* that in normal amounts facilitates neurotransmission, but in abnormal amounts is related to some forms of *psychosis* and other *mental disorders.*

normal A term denoting a culturally defined concept of behaviors or phenomena that are not markedly different from the average, usual, or expected.

normal distribution An expected frequency distribution of cases or scores that when plotted on a graph is symmetrical and bell shaped. Most scores fall near the *mean,* forming the highest point of the bell, and fewer cases are located on either side of the slope as distance from the mean increases.

normal retirement age (NRA) A *Social Security Administration (SSA)* term for the time when people can begin collecting their full *social security* benefits. The SSA plans that beginning in the year 2000 the NRA will rise gradually over 22 years so that by 2022 it will be age 67.

normative Pertaining to the average or expected *behavior* patterns of a *group* or *community.*

normative needs The requirements for a level of well-being that is comparable to the standards established in the community or culture to which one belongs. Usually, experts or outsiders decide what the standard is. See also *perceived needs, expressed needs,* and *relative needs.*

norms The rules of *behavior,* both formal and informal, and expectations held collectively by a *culture, group, organization,* or society.

North American Association of Christians in Social Work (NAACSW) An organization of professional social workers who profess belief in Christian thought and *values.* The organization began in 1950 at Wheaton College in Illinois with a series of meetings known as the Evangelical Social Work Conference. The conference was incorporated as the National Association of Christians in Social Work in 1953, adopting its present name in 1984.

NOS Not otherwise specified. The NOS abbreviation may appear after use of a general diagnostic label to indicate that the presenting symptoms or available information do not permit further delineation about the disorder. For example, a *mood disorder NOS* diagnosis would suggest affective lability but not indicate whether depression or bipolar episodes predominate.

nosology The science of classification, particularly of diseases and disorders.

nostalgia Longing to return to an earlier time or place. Social workers often see this as a symptom in people who are aged, in crisis or pain, or immigrants from other nations.

NOW See *National Organization for Women (NOW).*

NPV analysis See *net present value (NPV) analysis.*

NRA 1. See *National Recovery Administration (NRA).* 2. See *normal retirement age (NRA).*

NRLC See *National Right-to-Life Committee (NRLC).*

nuclear complex   Freud's original name for the *Oedipus complex.*

nuclear family   The kinship group consisting of a father, a mother, and their children.

nuclear-free zone   A nation or political region that has declared itself to be outside the world's involvement with nuclear weapons. Such zones permit no activities that advance the science of nuclear weaponry or the building, storing, or launching of such weapons.

null hypothesis   A negative statement about proposed relationships in research data. A typical *hypothesis* stated in null fashion would be, "There is no difference between the results of A and B." The null hypothesis permits statistical tests of significance and demands more-rigorous testing procedures than needed to prove an affirmative statement.

nurse practitioner   A professional nurse who completes additional training, such as a master's degree or certificate program, and acquires skills and performs tasks that were traditionally performed only by physicians, including routine physical examinations, taking complete medical histories, providing independent *psychotherapy,* and coordinating health and *social services* resources.

nursing home   A residential facility that provides extended *health care,* skilled-nursing care, and intermediate care for people who are ill or unable to take care of themselves. See also *skilled-nursing facility.*

nurturance   Behaviors and activities that further the growth and development of another person, *family, group,* or *community.*

nutrition   The process by which living organisms assimilate materials that are necessary for sustenance, energy, and growth. Human nutrition involves the use of food substances (nutrients) including the proper balance of proteins, carbohydrates, and fats, as well as vitamins, minerals, and water. Good human nutrition requires a well-balanced diet containing an adequate but not excessive amount of food and calories. Failure to achieve this balance can result in various diseases, dysfunctions, deficiencies, or death. See also *malnutrition.*

nutritional assessment   An evaluation conducted by a dietitian or other professional of the food needed by a client to achieve certain health goals and of the food actually prepared and consumed. The assessment usually includes recommendations about what foods to eat and avoid and how they should be prepared.

NWRO   See *National Welfare Rights Organization (NWRO).*

NYA   See *National Youth Administration (NYA).*

nyctalopia   The inability to see well in dim light or at night. In some people this is caused by a deficiency in Vitamin A.

nyctaphobia   A pathological *fear* of darkness.

nymphomania   Insatiable and uncontrollable desire for sexual intercourse. Usually, the term applies to women, with "Don Juanism" the equivalent term for men; both terms are outdated in professional use.

OAA See *Old Age Assistance (OAA)*.

OAS See *Organization of American States (OAS)*.

OASDHI See *Old Age, Survivors, Disability, and Health Insurance (OASDHI)*.

OASI See *Old Age and Survivors Insurance (OASI)*.

obesity An excessive accumulation of fat in the body, caused by the consumption of too much food, too little exercise, or glandular disorders. Obesity is determined not by a person's height–weight ratio or subjective appearance but by the percentage of fat in body tissue.

objective tree A technique in *social policy* analysis for graphically delineating the various goals of an organization and priorities to be used in their fulfillment. The administrator creates a box at the top of a page with the primary objective of the organization and below that lists in descending order the lesser objectives. The resulting diagram shows an inverted treelike figure that outlines serially the goals and their relative importance, permitting the administrator to establish the dates by which each objective is to be reached.

objectivity The ability to evaluate a situation, social phenomenon, or person without *prejudice* or subjective distortion. Often what is considered to be objective is only *bias* that is widely accepted.

object permanence The understanding that something exists independently of oneself and continues to exist even when it can no longer be seen or otherwise perceived.

object relations theory A psychoanalytic concept about an individual's relationship with others based on early parent–child interactions and internalized self-images that are focused on these interactions. The *neo-Freudian* view is that *libido* and aggressive drives toward self-pleasure are no more important than are the child's object-seeking drives.

OBRA See *Omnibus Budget Reconciliation Act (OBRA)*.

obscenity The production, distribution, or use of materials that are designed to stimulate *prurient interest;* that lack serious artistic, literary, political, or scientific value; and that deviate from the standards of *acceptance* by the average person in the relevant community. See also *pornography*.

obsession A repetitive and persistent thought, action, or ritual that is believed to occur as a mechanism for controlling or relieving *anxiety*.

obsessive–compulsive disorder A type of *anxiety disorder* in which the individual experiences unwanted, recurrent and persistent ideas, impulses, or images (an *obsession*) or engages in seemingly intentional behaviors that are performed ritualistically (a *compulsion*) as a reaction to conflict or other sources of *anxiety*. Obsessive–compulsive disorder is to be distinguished from *obsessive–compulsive personality disorder*.

obsessive–compulsive personality disorder One of the *personality disorders* that is characterized by perfectionistic *behavior,* insistence on having others submit to a certain way of doing things, limited ability to express warm feelings or tenderness, preoccupation with trivial details and rules, stinginess, stiff formality in relationships, and poor ability to prioritize and make decisions. This disorder is also known as *compulsive personality disorder*. It is to be distinguished from the *anxiety disorder* known as *obsessive–compulsive disorder* in that the perfectionistic behaviors are not responses to or attempts to overcome *anxiety*.

obstruction of justice The *crime* of preventing or attempting to prevent officers of the law and court from accomplishing their duties. Specific activities include attempting to bribe or intimidate jurors, witnesses, or officers of the court and interfering with police when they are in pursuit of a criminal suspect.

occupancy rate The number of persons per room, per dwelling, or per household; a figure for determining actual housing density and housing needs.

occupational health The preservation of physical and mental well-being in the *workplace* through the maintenance of sanitary and safe facilities and conditions.

Occupational Safety and Health Administration (OSHA) The organization within the U.S. *Department of Labor* that assures that conditions in the *workplace* are safe. OSHA administers training programs on occupational safety and health standards, conducts inspections, and issues citations to noncomplying employers. See also *National Institute for Occupational Safety and Health (NIOSH)*.

occupational social work The provision of professional *human services* in the *workplace* through such employer-funded programs as *employee assistance programs (EAPs)* and occupational *alcoholism* programs. The goal is to help employees meet their human and social needs by providing services (including *marital therapy* and *family therapy*) and dealing with emotional problems, social relationship conflicts, and other personal problems. Occupational social work can be involved in *macro practice* (such as organizational interventions

on behalf of employee groups) as well as individual clinical activities. Many social workers use the term synonymously with *industrial social work*.

occupational therapy A profession for helping physically disabled people use their bodies more effectively and mentally impaired people overcome emotional problems through specially designed work activity. For example, a recently blinded person may be taught to perform household activities through guided practice in a model kitchen. Most occupational therapists work in hospitals, nursing homes, schools, and rehabilitation centers.

ocholophobia Pathological *fear* of crowds or crowded places.

OD See *organization development (OD)*.

OED See *Office of Economic Development (OED)*.

oedipal personality A descriptive term from *psychoanalytic theory* referring to an individual who seems conflicted about sexuality and sexual identity; guilty about erotic impulses; and as an adult, often regressive into unresolved issues of the *Oedipus complex*.

Oedipus complex In the *Freudian theory* of psychosexual development, the erotic interest and attachment developed by a young child (usually between ages three and seven) for the parent of the opposite sex and the concomitant feelings of rivalry with and envy of the parent of the same sex. The child's feelings are repressed and *unconscious* but are often manifested in flirtatious *behavior* toward one parent and hostile behavior toward the other. See also *Electra complex* and *phallic phase*.

OEO See *Office of Economic Opportunity (OEO)*.

offender registration A legal requirement in many jurisdictions in the United States that requires people convicted of crimes, most often *child molestation* and *rape,* to notify the local law enforcement authorities of their plan to live in the community.

Residents of some of these communities are notified so they may take precautions.

Office of Child Support Enforcement   See *Child Support Enforcement, Office of.*

Office of Economic Development (OED) The federal organization, within the U.S. *Department of Health and Human Services (HHS),* established in 1969 to stimulate the growth of private profit-making businesses in neighborhoods of high unemployment. OED financed the establishment of urban and rural community development corporations. The office has been absorbed into other government agencies, and many of its functions were eliminated in the 1980s.

Office of Economic Opportunity (OEO) The organization created by the *Economic Opportunity Act of 1964* to implement President Lyndon B. Johnson's *War on Poverty.* Various programs originally within the organization included *Head Start, Volunteers in Service to America (VISTA),* and the *Job Corps.* By 1969 much of OEO had been dismantled, and many of its programs were transferred to other federal departments. The remaining part of the office became the *Community Services Block Grant program.*

Office of Fair Housing and Equal Opportunity   See *Fair Housing and Equal Opportunity Office.*

Office of Human Development Service (OHDS)   The organization within the U.S. *Department of Health and Human Services (HHS)* that oversees federally sponsored programs for delivering *personal social services.* Within this office are the *Administration for Children, Youth, and Families (ACYF)*; the *Administration for Native Americans*; and the *Administration on Aging.*

Office of Management and Budget (OMB)   The office within the executive branch of the U.S. government that assists the president in preparing the federal *budget* and formulating the nation's fiscal program. OMB also helps the president administer the budget and determine if allocated funds are sufficient for achieving their goals. OMB

keeps the president informed about how various government agencies' funds are being spent and helps in proposing legislation for congressional action.

Office of Personnel Management (OPM) The federal organization that administers most of the federal employment system. Its functions include recruiting, training, testing, promoting, firing, and laying off federal workers, as well as maintaining criteria for employment, pay grades, and benefits. OPM was established by the Civil Service Reform Act of 1978 (P.L. 95-454), which transferred the functions of the Civil Service Commission to OPM and the *Merit Systems Protection Board.* See also *GS civil service ranks.*

Office of Technology Assessment (OTA) The organization within the legislative branch of the U.S. government that provides Congress with information about the beneficial and adverse effects of technological change and helps Congress anticipate and plan for the uses of technology and policy alternatives. OTA compiles and publishes data on such subjects as the effectiveness of *psychotherapy* and professional interventions.

Office of Volunteer Action   The U.S. government agency in *Volunteers in Service to America (VISTA)* responsible for coordinating the nation's efforts to recruit, train, and efficiently utilize unpaid individuals and groups in local, state, or national public service jobs.

OHDS   See *Office of Human Development Service (OHDS).*

Old Age and Survivors Insurance (OASI) A central part of the *Social Security Act* of 1935 under which certain people older than age 65 or their surviving dependents were covered by the federal insurance program. With subsequent revisions in the Social Security Act, the insurance coverage was expanded to include workers who become disabled and ill *(Old Age, Survivors, Disability, and Health Insurance [OASDHI]).*

Old Age Assistance (OAA)   The *public assistance* program for needy older people.

Once the major form of *outdoor relief* in the United States, OAA was administered and financed by the states, leading to a wide variation in *benefits* and in stringent residency and *relatives' responsibility* requirements. The *Social Security Act* of 1935 and its compulsory insurance program to protect retired workers reduced but did not eliminate the need for OAA. In 1972, the state OAA programs were consolidated, along with the *Aid to the Blind (AB)* and the *Aid to the Permanently and Totally Disabled (APTD)* programs, into the federal *Supplemental Security Income (SSI)* program for needy older, blind, and disabled people.

Old Age, Survivors, Disability, and Health Insurance (OASDHI) The federal government's *social insurance* program under the *Social Security Act* of 1935. Under the provisions of the *Federal Insurance Contributions Act (FICA)*, the government collects payroll and employer taxes from most adult Americans and uses the funds to partially finance the payments made to retired, surviving, and disabled beneficiaries and *Medicare* recipients.

Older Americans Act of 1965 The federal legislation (P.L. 89-73), with several subsequent amendments, that defined U.S. policy toward aging persons and created the *Administration on Aging* to carry it out. The administration oversees state and city agencies that contract with private providers such as *Area Agencies on Aging (AAA)*, as well as directly offers *homemaker services*, transportation, *socialization* programs in senior citizens' centers, and *legal aid* services for older people.

Older Women's League (OWL) A national organization, founded in 1980, that provides a united voice on behalf of middle-age and older women. Of particular concern are such issues as *pension* equity and *social security* provisions and *health care* for women.

old old The *cohort* of people older than age 75, or the *frail elderly*.

olfactory hallucination An imagined perception of smell; smelling something that does not exist outside of subjective experience.

oligarchy A system of *government* or *organization* in which an elite group (such as a wealthy family, a military group, or a religious order) holds the power and rules dictatorially.

OMB See *Office of Management and Budget (OMB)*.

ombudsperson An individual employed by a government or other organization to investigate possible illegal, unethical activities or harmful unforeseen consequences of that organization's actions; a gender neutral term for "ombudsman."

omen formation Belief in one's ability to accurately predict future events.

omnibus bill Legislation that includes several, often unrelated, measures.

Omnibus Budget Reconciliation Act (OBRA) The 1981 federal legislation (P.L. 97-35) that amended *Title XX* of the *Social Security Act* of 1935 and decentralized many *social services* programs, funding activities, and responsibilities from the federal to the state governments, primarily through use of the *block grant*.

oncology The medical specialty that studies and treats *cancer* and tumors.

one-worldism The view that the earth is a single unit and that only through international cooperation rather than nationalistic rivalries can it achieve optimal well-being for all.

on-line A system for communicating with a central computer processor, usually to retrieve or store information. On-line systems permit users with personal computers with modems or library access to retrieve *database* items such as the abstracts of articles published in major social work journals.

on-line public-access catalogs (OPACs) *Computerized databases* that index a library's holdings. OPACs began replacing card catalogs in the 1970s in most libraries and are now being integrated to include what is available in other libraries as well.

ontology   The study of the ultimate nature of existence or reality.

OPACs   See *on-line public-access catalogs (OPACs)*.

open adoption   The legal and *social services* process of *adoption* in which adoptive parents and birth mother or birth parents become known to each other and, in many instances, continue some contact through the child's development. See also *independent adoptions*.

open-door policy   1. The authorization given to employees of an organization to have ready access to supervisors and the department heads and the freedom to discuss any relevant subjects. 2. In international relations, minimal or no restrictions on *immigration*. 3. In *social administration,* the organization understanding that there is free access to supervisors and board members, not necessarily on immediate demand but at times that are regular and convenient. 4. In institutional settings, the permission extended to residents that they are free to leave the facility whenever they desire.

open-ended questions   In the social work *interview,* as well as in systematic opinion research, a form of questioning that permits the respondent to answer any way he or she wants. This is in contrast to *closed-ended questions* (such as yes–no or multiple choice). For example, the social worker asks, "Why do you think it is difficult to get a job?" instead of "Is it difficult for you to get a job?" Both types of question are useful in the social work interview, depending on the goals of the working relationship. See also *questioning*.

open-ended service   A pattern in social work *intervention* procedures in which the *social worker* and *client* maintain the working *relationship* indefinitely. See also *time-limited service*.

open-ended service versus time-limited service   The debate in social work about whether clients are better served with or without time limits on the therapeutic relationships. Arguments for the open model include the following: It is possible to address "deeper" issues; an individual cannot know in advance what will be uncovered in the *intervention*; clients' problems cannot be compartmentalized as is required in the closed model; and social workers, as well as clients, are more familiar and comfortable with the open model because it has been the traditional model of mainstream *clinical social work practice*. Arguments for the time-limited model include the following: Effectiveness and efficacy studies show time-limited work is at least as effective and much less costly—thus, more clients can be served; clients intensify their efforts under time constraints and do not procrastinate as much; even in long-term *treatment*, most of the gains are accomplished within the first six sessions; and most clients drop out of treatment after a few sessions anyway. Practitioners continue to present new arguments on each side. Possibly the "truth" is that some clients and some social workers would do better in one model and others would do better in the other model.

open group   In *social group work* and *group psychotherapy,* the type of *group* that permits the inclusion of new members to replace those who have left the group. Some social workers also use this term for group meetings that have no predetermined ending time. See also *closed group*.

open system   In *systems theories,* a system that accepts input from outside and is amenable to change based on conditions in the environment. For example, an open family system is structured so that its members can become involved with outsiders, bringing them and their ideas into the family unit to effect some changes in the way the family interrelates. The open system concept is generally applied to living systems rather than nonliving or mechanical ones.

operant conditioning   A type of learning defined by B. F. Skinner (1904–1990) in which behaviors are strengthened or weakened by altering the consequences that follow them. Operant conditioning differs from *respondent conditioning,* which has the effect of controlling antecedent rather than consequent conditions. See also *Skinnerian theory.*

operant therapy The use of *operant conditioning* as a form of *treatment.*

operational definition In *research,* the specific delineation of the phenomenon to be studied in terms of how it will be measured.

operational tasks In *task-centered treatment,* one of two types of tasks (the other being general tasks) that calls for the client to undertake a specific action that is spelled out and understood before it is accomplished. For example, the task-oriented social worker asks the client to request a raise from his or her supervisor.

Operation PUSH People United to Serve Humanity, the voluntary *social activist* and *civil rights* organization founded by Jesse Jackson in 1976 as People United to Save Humanity. Among its goals is helping the nation's school children be motivated toward academic excellence and against the use of drugs and nonproductive behaviors.

opiates Drugs containing *opium.*

opinion survey A systematic data-gathering technique used to determine what people at a given time in a given area think about a certain subject. A representative *sample* of the *population* being investigated is interviewed verbally or by means of a structured and sometimes self-administered *questionnaire.* Opinion surveys of certain communities are often made by social activists, planners, and community organizers to understand and later influence the concerns, problems, and goals of the people.

opioid abuse The use of opium-based drugs, such as *heroin* and *morphine,* taken intravenously, orally, by sniffing, or through *"skin popping."*

opioid dependence Addiction to one of the *opiates* as manifested by *opioid abuse, tolerance,* and *withdrawal symptoms.*

opioid intoxication The mental and physical symptoms resulting from recent opioid

depression or *opioid abuse.* The symptoms include *euphoria* or *depression,* sluggishness, *apathy,* dilation or constriction of the pupils, drowsiness, impaired memory or attentiveness, slurred speech, poor judgment, and *impaired social functioning.*

opium A narcotic drug extracted from the juice of the opium poppy. It has been used for centuries as an effective pain killer; however, because of its habit-forming properties, the drug is restricted in most nations. Opium is processed to produce *morphine, codeine, heroin,* and laudanum.

OPM See *Office of Personnel Management (OPM).*

opportunistic infection An attack by microorganisms (that could not normally bring about disease) after the body's immune system has been weakened. The immune system is most commonly weakened by *malnutrition,* organic dysfunction, or other disorder.

opportunity costs A *social planning* concept in which the value of the resources that must be expended to achieve a certain objective is weighed against the cost of alternatives that would have to be forgone to achieve that objective.

opportunity programs *Social welfare* programs and organizations with an orientation toward preparing client groups for greater access to the opportunities that exist for others. The goal of such programs is not necessarily to help clients "adjust" or gain insight but to acquire skills and resources. For example, the *Mobilization for Youth* program was oriented toward helping young people who were vulnerable to *juvenile delinquency* to learn social, economic, and vocational skills so they would have a better chance of entering the economic mainstream.

opportunity theory The hypothesis that deviant *behavior* is more likely to occur among specific groups (for example, youths who are at risk for *juvenile delinquency*) when the opportunities to achieve socially acceptable goals are restricted and opportunities to behave in socially unacceptable ways are more available. The theory has been tested in such programs as New York's *Mobilization for Youth.*

oppositional defiant disorder Persistent negative, defiant, and disobedient *behavior* found in *childhood* and *adolescence,* usually including provocative defiance of authority and resistance to rules. Oppositional defiant disorder is similar to *conduct disorder* (a pattern of *truancy,* theft, physical *aggression, vandalism,* and so forth), except it is not as severe and more typically involves refusal to cooperate rather than destructiveness of others.

oppression The social act of placing severe restrictions on a group or institution. Typically, a government or political organization that is in power places these restrictions formally or covertly on oppressed groups so that they may be exploited and less able to compete with other social groups.

oral personality Also known as "oral character," a descriptive term from *psychoanalytic theory* referring to an individual who tends to be overly dependent or greedy and demands to be "filled up." This individual's satisfactions come largely through such activities as eating, smoking, drinking, and talking. Such a person is thought to be fixed at an early stage of personality development.

oral phase The first stage in the psychosexual development of the personality, which occurs at ages up to two years. During this phase, the infant seeks pleasure by stimulating the mouth and oral cavity and experiences the world through literal or psychic incorporation. According to *Freudian theory,* during this age the zone of sexual pleasure is the oral cavity, which explains the intense satisfaction the infant derives from nursing. Self-concept and feelings of personal worth are usually said to develop during this stage.

ordinal measurement In *research*, a level of measurement that entails classifying observations into mutually exclusive catego-

ries that can also be ordered along some dimension, such as socioeconomic status.

ordinal position See *birth-order theories.*

ordinance A local law that applies and is enforced only within the municipality where it was made. Driving speeds, refuse disposal, loitering, and disturbing the peace are frequently covered by local ordinances.

organic Pertaining to the biological aspects of an individual. The term is used most commonly by social workers and other mental health professionals to distinguish diseases that are caused by physiological disorders from psychosocial problems. See also *functional mental illness.*

organic mental disorders Mental disturbances thought to be caused by permanent or temporary damage to the brain. The disorders may be related to the aging process, to the ingestion of toxic substances such as alcohol and other drugs, or to certain physiological dysfunctions. This term and category have been eliminated as a diagnosis from the *DSM-IV,* because it implies that other disorders do not have an organic basis.

organization In *social work* and *community development (CD),* the process of helping individuals and groups arrange their activities, communication, and structure so that they can work together in a coordinated whole to achieve mutually beneficial goals.

organizational theory Conceptual frameworks about the ways an *organization* fulfills its functions. Several theories or schools have tried to explain this. The classical school emphasizes bureaucratic structure, defined lines of *authority,* specialized functions by employees, and criteria for performance evaluations. The scientific management school emphasizes the use of measurements of human activity and uses time and motion studies and "efficiency experts." The human relations school emphasizes the interrelationship of the work group members, the informal *network* of workers, and the *relationship* between the organization's goals and the workers' social needs. The structuralist or systems orientation sees the organization as an adaptive whole within a changing environment. *Human services* organizations differ from others in that their "raw material" and product are the people being served.

organization development (OD) The administrative technique that draws on *systems theories* and human relations orientations to enhance the group members' ability to solve problems together, communicate more effectively, and achieve greater efficiencies in production by encouraging innovation and coordination. OD is both a long-term process and a management style. It uses a variety of techniques including the *sensitivity group, T-group, feedback* systems, process *consultation*, and team building.

Organization of American States (OAS) The political association of most nations in the Western Hemisphere, founded as the International Conference of American States in 1989 and later called the Pan American Union. In addition to its role in mutual self defense and economic cooperation, OAS is actively engaged in social welfare, human rights, and social justice. Some of its specialized social welfare agencies include the *Inter-American Human Rights Commission, Inter-American Children's Institute, Inter-American Commission on Women, Inter-American Indian Institute,* and the *Inter-American Social Development Center (CIDES).*

organizations Formally structured arrangements of people, tools, and resources brought together to achieve predetermined objectives through institutionalized strategies.

orgasmic disorders The *sexual disorders* characterized by persistent or recurrent delay or absence of orgasm following a normal excitement phase, or *premature ejaculation,* causing marked distress or interpersonal difficulty. These disorders occur in both men and women. Diagnosticians indicate whether the condition is lifelong or acquired, generalized or situational, and due to psychological or combined factors.

In diagnosis the term replaced *inhibited orgasm.*

orphanage A term once used to refer to residential institutions for parentless or poor children. Such facilities have been and are being reduced or dismantled in favor of various foster care programs.

orphan trains Railroad facilities and other modes of transportation used by some eastern child welfare agencies (before 1915) in the United States for *placing out* homeless and family-less children with families in the western United States.

orthopedics The branch of medicine dealing with injuries and diseases of the bones.

orthopsychiatry An interdisciplinary field that emphasizes the development of *mental health* from early *childhood* on, prevention of mental illness, and the early (childhood) treatment of those who have a *mental disorder.*

OSHA See *Occupational Safety and Health Administration (OSHA).*

osteoarthritis *Arthritis,* characterized primarily by wear and tear of the joints, for example, degenerative joint disease. See also *rheumatoid arthritis.*

osteogenesis imperfecta A rare genetic disorder characterized by fragile bones, often resulting in fractures in infants and very young children. When this disorder remains undetected, parents are sometimes wrongfully accused of child abuse.

osteomyelitis An infection of the bone marrow.

osteopath A Doctor of Osteopathy (DO), a physician who is equivalent to an MD in training, licensure, and health care responsibilities but is more oriented to the body's natural ability to defend itself against diseases.

osteoporosis A disorder of the bones associated with calcium deficiency and characterized by increasing porosity and brittleness and decreased density in the bone matter. The major at-risk populations are middle-age and older women. See also *osteogenesis imperfecta*.

OTA See *Office of Technology Assessment (OTA)*.

outcome evaluation A process aimed at determining if a program is achieving its objectives and whether the results are due to the interventions provided. Outcome evaluations range from subjective judgments made by clients and staff to rigorous experimental investigations.

outcome variables In *research,* phenomena that are seen as the consequences of experimental manipulations or interventions.

outdoor relief A historical term referring to a form of *welfare* assistance that occurs outside an *almshouse, orphanage,* and other residential facilities. Most forms of *public assistance* are of this type. See also *indoor relief.*

outing Publicly disclosing a person's *homosexuality* to achieve some political or social objective. The term often refers to the practice by members of the gay community to reveal the sexual orientation of an influential opponent of their goals. See also *"passing"* and *"coming out."*

outpatient One who receives *treatment* at a *health care* facility without being admitted for overnight stays or assigned a bed for continuous care.

outreach The activities of social workers, especially in neighborhood-based agencies, to bring services and information about the availability of services to people in their homes or usual environments. See also *case finding.*

overanxious disorder of childhood A disorder of *childhood* or *adolescence* characterized by persistent *anxiety,* including worry about the future, overconcern about appropriateness of past *behavior,* extreme self-consciousness, inability to relax, and the excessive need for reassurance. *DSM-IV* no longer uses this as a separate diagnostic entity.

overbedding The practice of building more hospital facilities than are needed in a given community. This contributes to increased charges for inpatient care costs, because the full beds have to carry the costs of the empty ones.

overcompensation A *defense mechanism* characterized by an individual's extreme efforts to counterbalance a real or imagined deficiency.

overdetermination The concept used by psychoanalysts to explain a phenomenon such as dreams or neurotic symptoms as being caused by combinations of factors.

overdose The taking in of too much medication or drugs, usually resulting in serious side effects such as unconsciousness, extreme pain, anxiety, confusion, heart or respiratory failure, or even death.

overgeneralization The thought or act of forming broad principles from small or limited details. For example, a client says, "My son stayed out late last night. I know he's always going to do that from now on." When an overgeneralization is an *unconscious* attempt to avoid facing some painful truths, it is considered to be a *defense mechanism.*

overloving Intense emotional investment in another person, including the wish to control that person "for his or her own good." The term was coined by Sophie Freud, who pointed out that it is a feeling or state experienced as *love* but is also narcissistically motivated.

overprotectiveness The tendency of some parents or parent surrogates to shelter their children excessively, through *avoidance* of situations they believe have the potential for psychological or physical harm. The result is that these children often do not learn to become sufficiently independent. Overprotection may also occur between marital partners or other family members.

overseers of the poor People who in 16th- and 17th-century England and Colonial America were appointed as public officials to help collect local taxes and use these funds to provide *relief* for the destitute and, primarily, jobs for the able-bodied unemployed. Overseers of the poor were established in the *Henrician Poor Law* of 1536 and served as local officials for the government and for churches. Some *social welfare* historians trace the evolution of the modern *social work* profession to the overseers of the poor.

oversensitivity   A response pattern of behavior and often a symptom of *depression, paranoia, anorexia nervosa, obsessive–compulsive disorder,* and many other *mental disorders,* characterized by heightened awareness of reactions by others, social fragility, embarrassment, and anxiety about perceived disapproval by others and defensive verbalizations or withdrawal in anticipation of rejection by others.

overt behaviors   An individual's actions that are observable to others. Such actions are now described by behaviorists as "overt" to distinguish them from behaviors that are not observable but that can be recorded or registered by various instruments (electroencephalographs, blood pressure gauges, *lie detectors,* and so forth).

overutilization   See *utilization review.*

Ovington, Mary White (1865–1951)   A principal founder and long-time leader of the *National Association for the Advancement of Colored People (NAACP)*. She began as a settlement house worker where she was exposed to the problems facing *black people* and became active in antilynching campaigns. She was the NAACP Board Chair for 10 years.

ovulation   Release of a female reproductive cell, that is, the ovum or egg, into one of the two fallopian tubes. This takes place in women about 14 days, on the average, after the onset of menstruation.

Owen, Robert (1771–1851)   Welsh philanthropist and social advocate who worked toward elimination of exploitative working conditions for paupers and apprentices, improved *child labor* conditions,

and aided in the establishment of national old-age and sickness insurance programs. He contended that behavior and character were wholly determined by environmental conditions and later established influential utopian communities known as Owenite societies. His son Robert Dale Owen emigrated to the United States, where he became a leader of the antislavery abolitionist movement.

OWL   See *Older Women's League (OWL)*.

OXFAM   See *Oxford Committee for Famine Relief (OXFAM)*.

Oxford Committee for Famine Relief (OXFAM)   An international voluntary organization based in London to raise and distribute funds and emergency supplies to those nations and peoples who lack sufficient food or nutrition to maintain quality life. OXFAM works with international relief organizations such as *United Nations Disaster Relief Organization (UNDRO)* and *Food and Agriculture Organization of the United Nations (FAO)*, and with other private groups. It is a member of the *Steering Committee for International Relief,* the informal group of major relief agencies that coordinates disaster and famine relief.

Ozanum, Antoine Frederic (1813–1853)   Social reformer and founder of the *St. Vincent de Paul Society,* he sought to develop a rational program for helping poor people in France while working as a university educator and lawyer. He established the nonsectarian Conference of Charity to provide financial relief, employment, food, and shelter for poor families. Later he renamed the organization St. Vincent de Paul Society after the 16th-century reformer who helped the poor and freed slaves and helped them establish new lives.

ozone layer   A zone of ozone gas in the atmosphere between 10 and 30 miles above earth, which absorbs much solar ultraviolet rays that would otherwise harm life on the planet. Some scientists believe various manufactured chemicals are depleting this layer.

P

PA 1. See *physician's assistant (PA)*. 2. See *professional association (PA)*. 3. See *Parents Anonymous (PA)*.

PACE See *Political Action for Candidate Election (PACE)*.

Pacific Islanders Indigenous residents of and immigrants from the islands and islets in the Pacific Ocean, including those in the areas known as Polynesia, Melanesia, and Micronesia. In the United States, the term is most often applied to people native to Hawaii and to people from the U.S. Trust Territory of the Pacific Islands, including the Marshall and Marianas Islands, and from Guam and American Samoa.

pacifism The *value orientation* or policy of universal peace and the resolution of all differences between nations by peaceful means. Historically, pacifism movements have been well represented by social workers. The term is sometimes confused with passivism (the passive unwillingness to negotiate differences; appeasement), but "pacifism" implies a much more active effort to find solutions that are alternatives to war. See also *militarism* and *warism*.

PACs See *political action committees (PACs)*.

padrinos In Spanish-speaking cultures, a child's godparents. Usually they are kin or adult friends of the family bonded by a long tradition of friendship *(compadrazgo)* and have an important role in the care and upbringing of the children. See also *hijos de crianze*.

padrone An overseer of farm workers or unskilled laborers. The term originally ap-

plied to employment agents for unskilled Italian immigrants.

pain An unpleasant physical or mental sensation.

pain disorder A medical and psychological condition in which the predominant symptom is continuous, recurrent, or intermittent sensations of *pain*, either localized in specific parts of the body or body systems or generalized throughout. Because pain is usually symptomatic of a medical condition or *mental disorder*, the relevant *diagnosis* is of that disorder. Otherwise, the formal diagnosis would be "pain disorder associated with psychological factors," or "pain disorder associated with both psychological factors and a general medical condition." The former term was *psychogenic pain disorder*.

palimony An award, granted in a court of law, that is similar to *alimony*. Palimony requires support payments to one partner in a couple that formerly lived together in a nonmarital relationship or otherwise maintained an intimate relationship. See also *cohabitation*.

palliative care Providing for the common physical and emotional needs and comfort of a terminally ill patient after efforts to cure are no longer successful. See also *hospice*.

palsy A form of paralysis or diminished ability to move or control motion, often accompanied by *tremor*.

panacea A cure-all; a plan that would solve all problems. Often opponents of a social reform movement deride the plan as "no panacea" because it hopes to solve only part of a problem.

pandemic A term applied to *social problems, disease,* or *mental disorder* that appears on a broad scale throughout a specific large area (such as a city, a nation, a continent, or the entire world).

pandering The *crime* of inducing a person to become a prostitute or procuring customers for a prostitute. An individual who does this is usually called a "pimp."

panhandling Begging for money or food, usually in face-to-face encounters on streets, to sustain the personal needs of the one who is soliciting.

panic attack The sudden onset of intense *fear* and *anxiety,* usually accompanied by such symptoms as sweating; palpitations, *tremor*; nausea; chills; dizziness; *derealization*; and fears or feelings of losing control, going crazy, and dying. The attack occurs suddenly and builds to a peak within a few minutes. It occurs in several types of *anxiety disorders,* including *panic disorder, social phobia, specific phobia, posttraumatic stress disorder,* and *acute stress disorder.* Onset of the attack may be unexpected with no particular *stressor* (uncued), or it may occur almost always when confronted by or in anticipation of a stressor (cued). Panic attacks may also be situationally predisposed, in which the attack is more likely but not invariably going to happen when confronted by or in anticipation of a stressor.

panic disorder An *anxiety disorder* characterized by recurrent *panic attack* or fear of having further panic attacks for more than one month over an extended period in situations in which there is no life-threatening *stressor.* Symptoms include choking and breathing difficulties, palpitations and chest pains, sweating, trembling, dizziness, and faintness. Often the individual anticipates the onset of such attacks and becomes fearful of situations in which such attacks previously occurred. Abnormal avoidance of these places may be diagnosed as "panic disorder with *agoraphobia.*"

paradigm A *model* or pattern containing a set of legitimated assumptions and a design for collecting and interpreting data. For example, the psychosocial paradigm begins with an assumption that behavior is determined largely through learning the experiences of interpersonal relationships.

paradoxical directive In certain types of *family therapy,* an approach in which the social worker or other therapist tells the family members to continue their symptomatic behavior and sometimes to "improve on it." This makes them more aware of the existence of the behavior and the gains they derive from it and finally gives them more control over it.

paralinguistics Nonverbal vocalizations accompanying speech that give additional meaning to communications and convey the speakers' emotions and cultural stances. Paralinguistics include tone of voice, tempo, pauses, loudness, sighs, laughs, clearing the throat, and so on. See also *communication theory* and *metamessage.*

paramedics Health care professionals who provide assistance in emergency situations, more highly trained than *emergency medical technicians (EMTs),* but with less training than emergency room physicians.

paranoia A symptom of *mental disorder* whose most prominent characteristics are permanent and unshakable suspiciousness and persecutory *delusion* but in which the individual is otherwise clear thinking. Paranoia is a prominent feature of *persecutory-type delusional disorder, paranoid schizophrenia,* and *paranoid personality disorder.*

paranoid disorders A general class of *mental disorder* characterized by inappropriate suspiciousness. Diagnosticians tend to use more-specific terms to describe patients with *paranoid ideation,* such as *paranoid personality disorder, paranoid schizophrenia,* and *paranoia.*

paranoid ideation An unfounded suspicion that one is under surveillance or is being followed, talked about, or persecuted. This behavior may be but is not necessarily symptomatic of several mental disorders.

paranoid personality disorder   One of the 11 types of *personality disorders,* characterized by pervasive distrust and suspiciousness of others. These people rarely become close to others or confide in them, often refuse to disclose personal information to anyone, bear grudges, and retain hostile feelings over imagined insults and slights. They devote time to gathering evidence of the malevolence of others and often question the loyalty, fidelity, or intentions of spouses, family members, or others. The condition differs from *paranoid schizophrenia* or *delusional disorder* of the persecutory type in that they include psychotic symptoms such as *delusion* and *hallucination.*

paranoid schizophrenia   Technically known as "schizophrenia, paranoid type," one of the five major subtypes (also including *disorganized, catatonic, undifferentiated,* and *residual*) of *schizophrenia,* characterized by prominent *delusions of persecution* or *delusions of grandeur* and *auditory hallucination.*

paraphilia   A *sexual disorder* in which unusual fantasies, bizarre acts, or the use of nonhuman objects are necessary for sexual arousal. The acts or fantasies may include repeated or fantasized sexual activity involving suffering, humiliation, and nonconsenting partners. Also referred to as "sexual deviations" and "perversions," paraphilias include *fetishism, transvestism, pedophilia, exhibitionism, voyeurism, sexual masochism, frotteurism,* and *sexual sadism.*

paraphilic coercive disorder   A *paraphilia* in which an individual derives erotic gratification primarily from imposing brute force or threats of *violence* on another or from watching them imposed. When the victim is compelled to participate in sexual activity, the term used is *paraphilic rapism.*

paraphilic rapism   A *mental disorder* in men who are aroused only when forcing sexual activity on others. The resulting behavior is *rape.*

paraphrasing   A technique used in a social work *interview* in which the social worker expresses the idea of what the client has just said so that the relevant points are pulled together and emphasized. This helps clients clarify their own thoughts and assures them that the social worker understood the message.

paraphrenia   Late-onset *psychosis,* a disorder whose symptoms begin in older people and resemble those of *paranoid schizophrenia,* except there is a minimum of debilitating *hallucination* and personality disorganization. The term is more commonly used among European psychiatrists and less so in the United States, where for many years it was incorrectly used as a synonym for *delusional (paranoid) disorder* and *schizophrenia.*

paraplegic   One who suffers motor or sensory paralysis of half the body, usually the lower half of the body, usually due to disease or injury to the spinal cord.

parapraxis   Informally known as a Freudian slip; an error in verbalization that, according to Sigmund Freud (1856–1939), reveals what is in the subject's *unconscious.* For example, a client who fears that a social work investigator is going to reduce some *welfare* benefit refers to him or her as the "social worrier."

paraprofessional   An individual with specialized knowledge and technical training who works closely with and is supervised by a *professional* and who performs many tasks formerly carried out by the professional. Such people include paralegals, *physician's assistants (PAs),* and *social work associates.*

parapsychology   A field of study that investigates paranormal behavior and psychic events that are not explained through the *scientific method,* including mental telepathy, extrasensory perception (ESP), *intuition,* precognition, clairvoyance, and memory experiences of being in other worlds or generations.

parasomnia   A primary *sleep disorder* in which psychological or physiological events occur during sleep or during transitions from sleeping and awakening. Cognitive, motor, and *autonomic nervous system (ANS)* processes are activated during sleep stages in these disorders resulting in specific types of parasomnia including *nightmare disorder, sleep terror disorder,* and *sleepwalking disorder.*

parataxic distortion The concept in *psychoanalytic theory* developed by Harry Stack Sullivan (1892–1949) pertaining to the mildly (or sometimes grossly) inaccurate perceptions one has about the behaviors, attitudes, thoughts, and goals of those with whom emotional relationships exist.

pardon A decree to specific people that frees them from being tried or punished for criminal offenses, granted by a state's chief executive. See also *amnesty* and *clemency.*

parens patriae A legal doctrine that refers to the role of the state as *guardian* of people who are unable to care for themselves. The concept is most often used in courts in deciding to intervene in family matters, such as *custody of children, divorce* disputes, and removal of children to *foster care.* Using this authority, the public at large is saying that a child is not the absolute property of a parent but a trust granted to a parent by the state.

parent abuse The recurrent infliction of physical or psychic injury on a parent or guardian, through beating, sexual abuse, degradation, or exploitation. Usually such acts are committed by teenage or adult offspring against older and *frail elderly* parents. See also *elder abuse.*

parental leave An *employment policy* of granting a mother or father time off before, during, or after a child's birth or adoption. This leave may be granted to one or both natural or adoptive parents (partly to facilitate the neonatal *bonding* process). Parental leave policies were established after there was some acceptance of *maternity leave,* when it was recognized that fathers and adoptive parents and their children have essentially the same rights and needs as do new mothers and their infants.

parental liability The amount of financial restitution parents may be compelled to make to compensate for any damages caused by their minor or dependent children. Each jurisdiction specifies the amount of *liability,* if any, that a parent can be compelled to pay. See also *relatives' responsibility.*

parental responsibility The moral, ethical, and often legal obligations of parents (and others who have assumed parental roles) regarding the care and development of their children. These responsibilities include the provision of adequate nutrition, shelter, safety, and protection from physical and emotional harm; exercise; opportunities for education and social development; experience in problem solving; development of social skills; moral and spiritual guidance; and role models for effective social functioning.

Parent Effectiveness Training (PET) An educational program designed by Thomas Gordon to help parents learn to interact with their children more effectively.

parenting style The predominant characteristic manner by which parents or parent surrogates provide the opportunities for their children's psychological and social development. Various family therapists, writers, and commentators have given myriad names for these styles. Some of the better known are laissez-faire, indulgent, strict, domineering, inconsistent, abusive, overprotective, or detached parenting styles.

Parents Anonymous (PA) One of many national *self-help organizations,* with chapters in larger U.S communities, whose members help one another restrain themselves from abusing their children. PA maintains a *hot line* and "buddy systems" and holds regular meetings, patterned partly on the *Alcoholics Anonymous (AA)* program.

Parents Without Partners (PWP) One of many national *self-help organizations,* with chapters in most U.S. communities, most of whose members are divorced or widowed people raising children. PWP provides opportunities for its members to share their mutual concerns about child rearing and maintaining healthy social relationships. It sponsors discussion groups and educational and social activities that are comfortable and useful for the parents and their children.

parent training   Didactic and experiential educational programs to teach parents how to be effective in child rearing and socialization, parent–child communication, and problem solving. The best known of these programs include PET (*Parent Effectiveness Training*), STEP (Systematic Training for Effective Parenting, developed by D. Dinkmeyer and G. McKay on the basis of the recommendations of Rudolph Dreikurs), PIP (Parent Involvement Program, developed by William Glasser on the basis of his *reality therapy* concepts), and *behavior modification* approaches (developed from *social learning theory*).

paresis   Partial or complete paralysis.

paresthesia   The tingling sensation of itching, burning, or *pain* in some part of the body other than the source of the sensation.

Parish Poor Rate   An early system of national taxation to help pay for the needs of eligible poor people, which started in England in 1572. The system included a register of persons needing assistance and made efforts to create jobs and change social conditions to help reduce the incidence of *poverty*. See also *poor law*.

parity   Equivalence or *equality*. In wage parity, a city might be required to pay its firefighters on the same scale as police officers. In international relations, a nation wants military parity with its major rivals. Farmers seek a parity price support from the government so that their spendable income is proportionate to the incomes of previous generations of farmers. In employment parity, an organization's workers at every level are from each racial–ethnic group in the same proportion as that group's percentage of the population.

Parkinson's disease   A disease characterized by progressive motor disability and manifested by *tremor* or shaking, muscle stiffness, poor coordination, and sometimes *dementia*. The initial onset occurs most fre-

quently among people between ages 50 and 65. Some patients become severely incapacitated but live long lives, and others may die within a few years as a result of complications.

parochialism   1. Narrowness of interests, opinions, or knowledge. 2. The policy of delegating social plans and government policies to local interests rather than centralized or national ones.

parole   The release of a prisoner before completion of full sentence because of good conduct in prison, promised good conduct, and continued supervision by an officer of the legal system (often a social worker) once out of prison. See also *probation* and *incarceration*.

partial hospitalization   *Health care* within an inpatient medical setting for a specified period (usually from three to six hours) each day. Such programs give patients needed medical, psychological, or psychosocial treatment in a supervised setting but advance a transition from institutional to community living by encouraging the patient's developing independence and *coping skills*.

partialization   The social work process of temporarily considering a client's interconnected problems as separate entities so that work toward their solution can be more manageable. The process includes developing priorities or distinguishing those problems or needs that demand immediate attention from those that can be postponed for a time.

partial reinforcement   In *social learning theory*, the pattern of providing a reward, not every time a desired response is emitted, but with sufficient frequency to encourage the *behavior*. This increases the likelihood of such behaviors continuing without *extinction*, even when no immediate rewards are forthcoming.

participant modeling   A technique used in *behavior therapy* and *behavior modification* in which the client directly observes the social worker or some other person interacting with a feared *stimulus* without being harmed. The client is then gradually encouraged to interact with the same stimulus without *fear* of harm.

participant observation   A technique in social science *research* in which the investigator systematically becomes as much as possible a member of the group being studied.

participative management   A decision-making strategy used by some *social agency* administrators to involve all those who are likely to be affected by desired organizational change. This strategy includes building voluntary *consensus* and commitment among the organization's personnel, clientele, sponsors, and other interested groups to achieve organizational goals.

"passing"   The process in which homosexuals present themselves to others as being heterosexual. According to Raymond M. Berger ("Passing: Impact on the Quality of Same-Sex Couple Relationships," *Social Work, 35*[July 1990], pp. 328–332), this is a ubiquitous practice among the *gay* and *lesbian* population, commonly done to avoid stigma, hostility, and discrimination. See also *"coming out."*

passive–aggressive   The *behavior* of an individual who uses covert actions to fight another person or organization. The individual may feel angry but powerless in direct confrontations, so he or she becomes obstructionistic, obstinate, and inefficient and tends to pout and procrastinate. Because the *anger* is often *unconscious,* the reaction is also usually unconscious. When this behavior is deeply ingrained and persists through many situations and life phases, it may indicate the presence of a *personality disorder.*

passive–aggressive personality disorder   Also called *negativistic personality disorder,* a pervasive pattern of negativistic attitudes and passive resistance; the individual habitually resents, opposes, and covertly obstructs demands to fulfill obligations and appropriate expectations. This is a proposed diagnosis by the *DSM-IV.*

passive–dependent   The *behavior* of an individual who tries to get others or one other person to assume all the relevant responsibilities in the individual's life. When deeply ingrained and persistent in many situations, the behavior may indicate the presence of *dependent personality disorder.*

passive resistance   A nonviolent form of social activism in which individuals or groups stop using or cooperating with the institutions to which they object. For example, in the late 1950s, when *black people* in the South objected to the rule requiring them to sit in the back of buses, they banded together to *boycott* the buses. Without direct confrontation, the movement passively but effectively resisted the objectionable policy.

passive smoking   Involuntary inhalation of the residue of burned materials, most commonly occurring when one is confined in an enclosed space where tobacco products are being smoked. Several disorders, especially such respiratory diseases as lung cancer and *emphysema,* have been correlated with sustained passive smoking.

passivity   A *behavior* pattern in which the individual seldom initiates action but submissively responds to forces in the environment.

pastoral counselor   Clergy or former clergy who provide *counseling* and *psychotherapy* to clients, either within the auspices of their churches or in autonomous practices. Many of these professionals obtain their training as counselors within theological schools, whereas others obtain additional education in schools of social work and other fields. They tend to specialize in *marital therapy,* premarital guidance, and *spiritual counseling.*

paternalism   A principle of *authority* in which one person or institution manages the affairs of another. The term is often used disparagingly against social workers and *social welfare* organizations that try to help people solve their problems without the direct involvement of those being helped.

paternity establishment   The legal procedure to determine if a man, outside of marriage, is the father of a particular child and to establish his rights and responsibilities to that child. The procedure is relatively easy and accurate through genetic testing and is an important activity in the U.S. *Office of Child Support Enforcement.*

paternity suit   A legal proceeding to determine whether a man is the father of a certain child.

path analysis   In *social research,* a statistical technique for analyzing the direct and indirect relationships between variables and representing them in a diagram.

pathological gambling   An *impulse control disorder* in which the individual continues to make wagers on games of chance despite continuous disruption in life responsibilities, such as financial problems, disrupted family relationships, and nonviolent criminal behavior, to pay for debts. Typically, these individuals believe that money can cause and solve their problems and continue gambling, often secretively, to recoup their losses.

pathology   The study of the nature of physical or mental diseases, including causes, symptoms, effects on the subject, and the circumstances in which the disease occurs. The term is also used more broadly in referring to physical or behavioral deviations from the norm that can or do result in *disease* or *dysfunction.* See also *psychopathology.*

patient government   Participation in the management of a hospital ward by those being treated therein. This system is prevalent in mental hospitals and other residential health care centers and is integral to the therapeutic community or *milieu therapy.*

patients   Those who are receiving care and *treatment* from physicians and *health care* personnel. Social workers generally use the term *client* when referring to the individuals they are serving. However, the term "patient" is more commonly used by social workers who are employed in health care settings (for example, hospital and *medical social workers*).

patients' rights   The legal, moral, and ethical standards that protect *patients* and *clients* from unwarranted *treatment.* Patients' rights also include access to care and opportunities to participate in decisions affecting their care and treatment. The *American Civil Liberties Union (ACLU)* has delineated eight legal rights of patients. They are the right to (1) informed participation in all decisions involving one's health care; (2) privacy respecting the source of payment for treatment and care; (3) prompt attention, especially in emergency situations; (4) clear, concise explanation of all proposed procedures in understandable terms, including the risk of death or serious side effects, and the right not to be subjected to any procedure without voluntary, competent, and understanding consent; (5) clear, complete, and accurate evaluation of one's condition and prognosis before being asked to agree to any test or procedure; (6) access to all information contained in one's medical record while in the health care facility and the ability to examine the record on request; (7) refuse any drug, test, procedure, or treatment; and (8) leave the health care facility at will regardless of physical condition or financial status, although the patient may be requested to sign a release stating that he or she is leaving against the medical judgment of the doctor.

patron   One who supports a charity, social cause, artistic endeavor, or other activity considered socially worthwhile.

patronage   In political terms, the privileges an elected or other government official bestows on others usually in exchange for their past or future support. Often these privileges are government jobs, contracts, or acess to lawmakers.

pauper   A poor person. The term originated in Europe in the early Middle Ages from "pauperes," referring to dependence. Those called paupers were not necessarily in need but could be in their dependent state voluntarily. The "pauperes Christi" were devoted to Jesus Christ and spent all their time near churches, praying, meditating, and depending on donations from the parishioners.

pavement people Those who live in primitive and makeshift shacks on sidewalks or streets, most often near urban areas of *Third World* and *Fourth World* nations. These people technically are not homeless because of their dwellings.

pavor nocturnus See *sleep terror disorder.*

pay equity The principle that people who do the same jobs should receive the same wages or salaries, regardless of sex, age, ethnic or racial backgrounds, or need. See also *comparable worth.*

payroll tax A tax levied on wages or salaries that is paid by employers and employees and usually designated for such programs as *unemployment compensation* and *Old Age, Survivors, Disability, and Health Insurance (OASDHI).* Some economists also refer to this as an income tax. See also *earmarked taxes* and *Federal Insurance Contributions Act (FICA).*

PC 1. See *political correctness (PC).* 2. See *professional corporation (PC).* 3. PC also commonly refers to a type of personal computer.

PCP Phencyclidine hydrochloride, an illegal drug (except as an animal tranquilizer) that in low doses produces *euphoria* and numbness but in higher doses may produce *delirium*, convulsions, violent behavior, and changes in the users' perceptions of their bodies. Also known as *"angel dust,"* "lovely," and "loveboat," the drug can have severe and permanent effects such as *psychosis, coma*, or heart failure.

PCP abuse A *substance-use disorder* involving *PCP* (phencyclidine hydrochloride) or similarly acting arylcyclohexy-lamines, which leads to sensations of *grandiosity, emotional lability, euphoria*, psychomotor agitation, and diminished responsiveness to *pain.* When PCP is used repeatedly, the individual develops *impaired social functioning.*

Peace Corps The federal program, established by President John F. Kennedy in 1961, that sends American volunteers to *underdeveloped nations* for two years to provide training in more than 300 skills, particularly in agriculture, natural resource development, science, and public administration. In 1971, the Peace Corps was placed under the new umbrella agency, *ACTION*, along with *Volunteers in Service to America (VISTA)* and *Foster Grandparents.*

peace dividend Funds that are no longer needed to maintain the *Cold War* military budget that could be allocated for nondefense public purposes such as education, infrastructure, and *social welfare.* At the end of the Cold War in 1990, many political leaders and voters assumed that more of these funds would be available than has proved to be the case.

Pearson's *r* correlation Also known as the Pearson product moment correlation coefficient; a statistical measure of the strength of relationships between two variables (such as weight and height) that are measured at intervals.

PEBES See *Personal Earnings and Benefits Estimate Statement (PEBES).*

pederasty Anal sexual contact with boys.

pediatrics The branch of medicine pertaining to the care and treatment of *children.* The physician who so practices is known as a "pediatrician." See also *physician.*

pediculosis See *head lice.*

pedophilia A *paraphilia* involving the act or *fantasy* of *sexual abuse* of a prepubertal child as the preferred way to achieve sexual excitement or gratification.

"Peeping Tom" Vernacular for one who participates in *voyeurism.*

peer An equal, as in age group, educational level, *ethnic group,* or other classes of people.

peer group An association of people who have the same social *status* (for example, profession, occupation, age group, or gender).

peer pairing A therapeutic technique used especially for socially isolated children and adults who might have difficulty relating to the social worker on a one-to-one basis or who cannot tolerate small groups. The therapist sees the client and another person who has similar characteristics (such as age, gender, or type of personality) together and treats both simultaneously. This model has been used most frequently in schools, residential facilities, hospitals, and clinics.

peer review   A formal evaluation by a relevant *peer group* of an individual's general competence or specific actions. In *social work* and other professions, the term refers to a formal periodic process in which professional standards of *intervention* have been spelled out and practices are monitored by colleagues. For example, if a client or someone making a *third-party payment* (such as an insurance company) suspected some wrongdoing by a social worker and complained to the person's professional association or state licensing authority, a panel of fellow social workers could review the case to determine appropriate action. See also *professional review organizations (PROs)* and *accountability.*

peer review organization (PRO)   A formal and sometimes legally mandated association of people who are members of one profession, brought together to evaluate the work of other members of that profession in accomplishing a specific set of tasks or objectives. The evaluation is commonly done by reviewing the professional's case records to determine if the type of treatment plan, methods, and outcome are commensurate with the organization's objectives and the client's needs. The U.S. government has required the establishment of PROs in hospitals and nursing homes that receive federal funds to oversee the administration of the *diagnosis–related groups (DRGs)* system.

pellagra   A disease of *malnutrition* that results from a dietary deficiency of niacin; its symptoms include inflammation of the skin and mucous membranes and gastrointestinal disturbances.

pelvic inflammatory disease (PID)   Infection of the female pelvic organs. This is commonly caused by *sexually transmitted diseases (STDs)* such as *gonorrhea* and *chlamydia.* PID often causes scarring of the fallopian tubes and *infertility* in 20 percent of the infected women.

penal institution   Penitentiary; a facility for the *incarceration* of convicted criminals that sometimes provides them with education and other resources that might reduce the *recidivism rate.*

penis envy theory   In *psychoanalytic theory,* the idea that women and girls resent the males' possession of penises and sometimes feel inferior because they lack them. Modern psychoanalytic theorists emphasize the symbolic aspect of this resentment, indicating that women and girls are more envious of the opportunities available to males that frequently are lacking for females in most cultures. See also *castration theory.*

Pennsylvania School   The theoretical and practice orientation in social work based on the ideas of University of Pennsylvania School of Social Work educators *Virginia Robinson* (1883–1977) and *Jesse Taft* (1882–1960) and their colleague psychoanalyst Otto Rank (1884–1937). Also known as the *functional school in social work,* or the *Rankian School,* the approach deemphasized diagnostic inquiry, history taking, and *Freudian theory* and stressed a strategy that was time-limited and focused on those issues that came within an agency's function.

penology   The study of prison and reformatory management, *crime* prevention, and the *rehabilitation* of criminals and delinquents. See also *corrections.*

pension   A payment made regularly to an individual because of *retirement,* age, *loss,* or incapacitating injury or to dependents in the event of the beneficiary's *death.* *Social security* benefits as well as retirement income provided by employers are generally considered to be forms of pensions.

penury   *Destitution,* or extreme *poverty.*

People-to-People Committee for the Handicapped   A voluntary organization that provides information to families of disabled people about available services and self-help activities. The committee publishes the *Directory of Organizations Interested in the Handicapped,* which contains an extensive listing of organizations that give information about treatments, training, equipment, and techniques used to help disabled people.

People United to Serve Humanity See *Operation PUSH.*

perceived needs The requirements that people believe they must have to achieve an acceptable level of well-being. See also *normative needs, expressed needs,* and *relative needs.*

perception The psychic impressions made by the five senses (sight, sound, smell, taste, and touch) and the way these impressions are interpreted cognitively and emotionally, based on one's life experiences.

perceptual distortion Incongruity between a physical reality and the way it is perceived, understood, or interpreted cognitively by the individual.

perestroika The Russian term, roughly meaning "restructuring." *Social agency* administrators and other organization officials in many nations increasingly use the term to describe their own organization's intent to change policies and practices.

performance budgeting A plan used by administrators to allocate resources based on predicted or observed results rather than on costs of maintaining existing structures.

perinatal Pertaining to the phase of life that encompasses the several months or so before and after birth.

perinatologist A *physician* who specializes in the care and treatment of the mother and child several months before and after birth.

period prevalence See *epidemiology.*

peripheral nervous system (PNS) That part of the nervous system outside the *central nervous system (CNS),* that is, the entire network of nerve fibers.

peritoneal dialysis See *dialysis.*

perjury The *crime* of making false statements while under legal oath to tell the truth.

Perkins, Frances (1882–1965) The first woman to serve as a U.S. cabinet member, Perkins was President Franklin D. Roosevelt's Secretary of Labor during the *Great Depression* and World War II. Using her social work background, she promoted and helped develop the *social security* system, *child labor* legislation, and *unemployment compensation.*

permanency planning In *child welfare* work, a systematic effort to provide long-term continuity in dependent children's care as an alternative to temporary foster placements. This might be done by facilitating *adoption,* by establishing clear guidelines for remaining in *foster care,* or by helping the children's natural families become capable of meeting the children's needs.

permissiveness A high degree of tolerance by those in control for the *behavior* of an individual or group. Permissiveness is seen in parents who allow their children to behave in ways that others might not find acceptable. It is also seen in *laissez-faire* societies, in which the government authorities exercise relatively little control or enforcement of laws or norms regulating public behavior.

pernicious The term health care workers use for life-threatening.

pernicious anemia A serious form of *anemia* in which the red blood cells decrease as a result of the body's inability to use vitamin B_{12}. Early symptoms include paleness, fatigue, digestive problems, and *anxiety.*

persecutory-type delusional disorder A subtype of *delusional disorder* characterized by nonbizarre delusions, particularly an intense belief that one is being plotted against, harmed, spied on, followed, or obstructed.

The person focuses on an imagined injustice and often seeks remedy through appeals to authorities, legal action, or threatening and violent behavior.

perseveration Preoccupation and intense focus on one thought, word, or act.

personal care services A program, usually under the auspices of local departments of *welfare* or *human services,* that provides basic nonmedical care, such as bathing, grooming, and assistance in dressing, to needy people in their homes.

Personal Earnings and Benefits Estimate Statement (PEBES) A summary of the *Social Security Administration (SSA)* financial record of each beneficiary. SSA recommends that people periodically review their PEBES record while still working to assure that all information is properly recorded. SSA furnishes this statement free of charge to anyone who calls 1-800-772-1213.

personality An individual's entire intellectual and emotional structure including abilities, attitudes, interests, and enduring patterns of understanding and relating to the environment.

personality change A significant deviation from one's previously characteristic pattern of behavior, thinking, and communicating, usually symptomatic of an underlying mental or physical problem. Among the more-common changes are increased *emotional lability,* disinhibition, aggressive or apathetic behaviors, and paranoid behaviors. When used as a formal diagnosis, the clinician must indicate the predominating behavioral change and the general medical condition thought to underlie the change.

personality disorders Patterns of relating to and understanding others that are so *maladaptive,* inflexible, and deeply ingrained that they produce significant social impairment. Personality disorders are usually recognizable in one's *adolescence.* There are 11 major types of personality disorder: (1) *paranoid personality disorder* (2) *schizoid personality disorder,* (3) *schizotypal personality disorder,* (4) *histrionic personality disorder,* (5) *narcissistic personality disorder,* (6) *antisocial personality disorder,* (7) *borderline personality disorder,* (8) *avoidant personality disorder,* (9) *dependent personality disorder,* (10) *obsessive–compulsive personality disorder,* and (11) the atypical personality disorder.

personal response systems (PRS) The use of communications devices, monitors, and on-call personnel to provide emergency assistance to persons who are alone but in need.

personal social services *Social services* with a basic purpose to enhance the relationships between people and between people and their environments and to provide opportunities for social fulfillment. Personal social services are distinguished from institutional services (*income maintenance* programs, *health care,* education, employment, and housing) and include *counseling* and guidance and development of *mutual help* and *self-help groups, family planning,* and services for older people and for children.

personal unconscious In *Jungian theory,* one of two parts of the *unconscious* (the other part being the *collective unconscious*). The personal unconscious is the region of the mind that is not subject to the individual's immediate awareness but that is developed through the individual's unique experiences, drives, and circumstances.

person-in-environment perspective Among social workers and other professionals, an orientation that views the client as part of an environmental system. This perspective encompasses the reciprocal relationships and other influences between an individual, the *relevant other* or others, and the physical and social environment.

Person-In-Environment (PIE) System A tool social workers use to describe and classify problems of *social functioning.* The system is used for the systematic collection and ordering of relevant information that can produce a comprehensive assessment of the social-functioning problems adult clients bring to social workers (James Karls and Karin Wandrei, *Person-In-Environment System*, Washington DC: NASW Press, 1994). The system also helps the worker draw conclusions about the interrelated factors contributing to the client's problem and select interventions that might relieve or solve problems. PIE calls for a description of the client based on four factors: Factor I—Social-functioning problems (including four categories of social role problems: family, other interpersonal, occupational, and special life situation roles); Factor II—Environmental problems (including economic–basic needs, educational, legal, health, safety and social service, voluntary association and affectional support systems); Factor III—Mental disorders, based on parts of the *DSM-IV*, Axes I and II; and Factor IV—Physical health problems based on the *International Classification of Diseases (ICD-10)*. Three indices are also used. The degree to which these problems require social work intervention is rated in a *severity index*. The length and recency of the client's problem is rated in the *duration index*. The *coping index* is a rating of the client's resources for dealing with the problem. A manual detailing the use of the system is available from NASW Press.

personnel standards   A formal delineation of the rules, behaviors, qualifications, and manner of interrelationships that are expected of each employee as a condition of employment. Often these standards are used to fire workers, not hire applicants, or to adjudicate grievances between employer and employee.

person-oriented record   A format used by some social workers and some social agencies to keep specific, accountable, and goal-directed records of the *intervention* process for each client. An adaptation of the physician's *problem-oriented record (POR)*, the person-oriented record contains an initial *database*, treatment plan *assessment*, progress notes, and the progress review (to evaluate a client's progress over a specified time such as every six or 12 weeks).

persons in need of supervision (PINS)   The legal designation used in some states for a *status offender*, such as *runaways*, truants, or juveniles whose parents are unable to manage them properly. In some jurisdictions these same people are known as *CHINS* or *JINS*.

person–situation configuration   The concept used in *social casework* pertaining to the threefold interrelationship consisting of the person with the problem, the situation in which the problem exists, and the interaction between them. The interaction is influenced by internal conflicts or reactions and environmental pressures.

PERT   See *program evaluation review technique (PERT)*.

perturbation   Agitation or distress; the degree to which a person is disturbed about some environmental or internal phenomenon.

pertussis   A highly communicable *infectious disease*, popularly known as whooping cough, occurring predominantly in young children. The person develops respiratory difficulty and eventually begins coughing rapidly. This causes the individual to gasp for air, during which a high-pitched, whooping sound occurs. In the United States, pertussis has been controlled to a great extent by *immunization* during infancy.

pervasive developmental disorders   A classification of physical and mental dysfunctions that appear before the individual reaches maturity and are characterized by severe and inclusive impairment in such areas as communication and social interaction skills or by the presence of stereotyped behavior, interest, and activities. Pervasive development disorders include *autistic disorder, Rett's disorder, childhood disintegrative disorder,* and *Asperger's disorder*.

perversion   See *paraphilia*.

PET   See *Parent Effectiveness Training (PET)*.

petit jury   A group of 12 (sometimes six) citizens selected by the justice system of a jurisdiction to hear evidence and, from that only, decide on the *guilt* or innocence of an accused person. See also *grand jury*.

petit larceny   *Larceny* that involves goods of relatively small value. Each jurisdiction legislates the amount that determines whether a theft is petit (or petty) or *grand larceny*. In most states, that cutoff amount is usually between $50 and $500. The punishment for petit larceny tends to be much less than for grand larceny.

petit mal seizures   See s*eizure disorders*.

PET scan   See *positron emission tomography (PET) scan*.

phallic phase   The third stage in *psychosexual development theory* that occurs approximately between ages three and six. During this phase the child's zone of pleasure centers in the genitalia. The *Oedipus complex* is a culmination of this phase, during which the healthy child works through rivalry with the parent of the opposite sex so that a loving relationship can exist with both parents and *self-esteem* can develop in the child.

pharmacotherapy   The administration of medications to help maximize the physical or mental health potential of a patient. This includes educating the patient about the need for the drug and its proper use, monitoring, and taking efforts to modify the prescription as needed. Counseling and support are also important.

phase-of-life problem   A normative transition in the *life cycle* that requires the individual to use *coping skills* to adapt to unfamiliar but virtually inevitable circumstances. Examples include entering school, getting married, having a first child, and retiring. See *idiosyncratic life-cycle transitions*.

phencyclidine-related disorders   See *PCP abuse*.

phenylketonuria (PKU)   A genetically transmitted metabolic disorder in which the victim's body fails to produce enzymes needed to break down certain natural amino acids. PKU may be characterized by

mental retardation and neurological and skin disturbances.

philanthropy   A term derived from the Greek, meaning "love of humanity"; it has come to refer to practical efforts to promote the *public welfare* by donating funds or resources to worthy causes. Philanthropic activity, especially in the secular community, was rather spontaneous and haphazard until the late 19th century. The field of *social work* was born, in part, as an effort to make these activities more systematic and effective in their raising and distributing funds. Today, philanthropy constitutes a sophisticated and highly complex number of organizations and groups. See also *alms* and *charity*.

phobia   An intense and persistent *fear* of an object or situation. Psychosocial theorists think this is caused by *displacement* of a *conflict* onto an external object, where it will be presumably more tolerable and avoidable. Behavioral theorists think it is a consequence of a chain of associations of various negative stimuli. Phobias are the main symptom of a *phobic disorder*. There are actually an infinite number of identifiable phobias because every potential experience and *stimulus* could result in this fear. Some common ones are *agoraphobia, acrophobia, claustrophobia, nyctaphobia, xenophobia,* and *zoophobia*.

phobic avoidance   A symptom of *phobic disorder* in which the individual attempts to stay away from the feared object or situation *(phobic stimulus)* or even think about such things. This often results in such social and mental constriction that psychosocial functioning is impaired and *activities of daily living (ADL)* are not fulfilled.

phobic disorder   Also called "phobic neurosis," an *anxiety disorder* in which *anxiety* is the predominant disturbance. The essential feature is a persistent and irrational *fear* of a specific object or situation resulting in serious attempts to avoid it. The three types of phobic disorder are *agoraphobia, social phobia,* and *specific phobia*. Specific phobias were once called "simple phobias."

phobic stimulus Clearly discernible, circumscribed objects or situations that produce an immediate *anxiety* response. The stimulus can be an actual object (for example, snakes, high places) or a situation (for example, giving a public speech), or it may be anticipation of an encounter with it. The level of anxiety or *fear* usually varies according to the proximity of the stimulus and the degree to which escape from it seems possible. Types of stimuli in *specific phobia* are animal type (generally with a childhood onset), natural environment type (storms, heights, water), blood-injection type (the sight of blood, needles, medical operations), situational types (entering elevators or tunnels, crossing bridges, flying), and other types (fear of contracting illness, loud noises, falling down). See also *agoraphobia,* and *social phobia.*

phonological disorder A *communication disorder* (formerly known as developmental *articulation disorder*) characterized by one's failure to use developmentally expected speech sounds that are age and dialect appropriate. The individual may have difficulty pronouncing certain sounds clearly or pronouncing such sounds as r, sh, th, f, z, l, or ch, often making substitutions for these sounds. If mental retardation, speech–motor or sensory deficit, or sociocultural deprivation is present, the speech difficulties exceed those associated with such problems. See also *expressive language disorder, mixed receptive–expressive language disorder,* and *stuttering.*

physiatrist A *physician* who specializes in rehabilitation medicine or physical medicine and works primarily with patients who have impairments and disabilities arising from musculoskeletal, neuromuscular, or vascular disorders.

physician A licensed *health care* professional with an educational degree of doctor of medicine (MD) or doctor of osteopathy (DO) and the highest level of responsibility in patient care. Training to be a physician begins after receiving an undergraduate degree. Medical school typically consists of two years largely in classroom and laboratory study and two years emphasizing clinical experience. After an additional year of training (once called the internship) the PGY-1 (first postgraduate year), student takes state exams for medical licensure. The new physician then completes three to six years of in-hospital residency training in an area of specialization. In the United States almost all physicians become board certified in one of 23 specialties: allergy and immunology, anesthesiology, colon and rectal surgery, dermatology, emergency medicine, family practice, internal medicine, neurological surgery, nuclear medicine, obstetrics and gynecology, ophthalmology, orthopedic surgery, otolaryngology, pathology, pediatrics, physical medicine and rehabilitation, plastic surgery, preventive medicine, psychiatry and neurology, radiology, surgery, thoracic surgery, and urology. Physicians known as *general practitioners* are now rare, and primary care is usually filled by physicians who are family practitioners or internists. See also *osteopath.*

physician's assistant (PA) A licensed health care professional qualified to perform physical examinations, provide counseling, and prescribe certain medications under a physician's supervision.

PIA See *Primary Insurance Amount (PIA).*

Piagetian theory A theory of *cognitive development* proposed by the Swiss psychologist Jean Piaget (1896–1980) to explain the processes by which humans come to perceive, organize knowledge, solve problems, and understand the world. According to this theory, human cognitive development is the product of a consistent, reliable pattern or plan of *interaction* with the environment, known as a *scheme.* Schemes are goal-oriented strategies that help the person achieve some intended result. These schemes are sensorimotor (occurring in infancy and early *childhood,* in which reflexes and motor responses are prevalent) and cognitive (based on experience and on mental images, reflecting the person's ability to develop the use of abstract reasoning and symbolism). Two processes in cognitive development are *assimilation* and *accommodation*. Piaget delineated four stages of cognitive development: (1) *sensorimotor stage*, (2) *preoperational stage*, (3) *concrete operations stage*, and (4) *formal operations stage*.

pibloktoq A *culture-bound syndrome* found most commonly among Eskimo and other indigenous peoples of arctic and subarctic regions, in which the individual behaves irrationally for up to 30 minutes and during that time shouts obscenities, tears off clothing, flees outdoors, eats feces, or otherwise acts irrationally and sometimes dangerously. The behavior often follows a period of withdrawal or irritability and frequently ends in convulsive seizures and coma for up to 12 hours. The individual usually remembers nothing about the event.

pica An *eating disorder* involving the frequent consumption of inorganic or nonnutritive substances such as dirt or paper.

picketing A demonstration by an individual or group wishing to call public attention to some *social problem*, political goal, *grievance*, or labor dispute. The demonstrators typically carry signs and march in front of some facility where the grievance occurs or where publicity is most likely.

Pick's disease A degenerative brain disease particularly affecting the frontal and temporal lobes and resulting in such symptoms as *dementia*, deterioration of social skills, behavioral disinhibition, primitive reflexes, and extreme apathy or agitation.

PID See *pelvic inflammatory disease (PID)*.

PIE System See *Person-In-Environment (PIE) System*.

PINS See *persons in need of supervision (PINS)*.

PIRG See *public-interest research group (PIRG)*.

PKU See *phenylketonuria (PKU)*.

placater role A recurrent pattern of *communication* one assumes in relating to others,

characterized by talking in an ingratiating way, apologizing, avoiding disagreements, and attempting repeatedly to gain the approval of the *relevant other*. This role was delineated by *Virginia Satir* (1920–1987) (*Peoplemaking*, Palo Alto, CA: Science and Behavior Books, 1972, p. 63), who described this person as a "yes-man" who feels worthless without the approval of others. Other roles are the *blamer role*, the *computer role*, and the *distracter role*.

placebo An inert preparation that is made to appear identical to or presented to patients as an active drug. When used in research that is *double blind*, the investigator tests the effectiveness of a drug by giving it to half the subjects and the placebo to the others. Sometimes placebos are also given to patients who apparently do not need an active drug but who seek the attention or *secondary gain* that comes from using one. A physical effect based on an individual's belief that the inactive substance is working is called a "placebo effect."

placement The assignment to or location of an individual in a setting that is suitable to achieve a specified purpose. Social workers use the term mostly to indicate the assignment of a child or dependent adult to a facility or person who can provide for their needs. The term also refers to the social work student's assignment to a *social agency* for practice in *field instruction*.

placing out The practice of finding new homes and families in distant areas for institutionalized children or those who could no longer remain with their own families. See *orphan trains*.

plagiarism The act of appropriating the scientific or literary writings of another person and presenting it as one's own work. Plagiarism is a *crime* when such work has been copyrighted or when state laws specify conditions in which such acts are unlawful (as in selling term papers). The act is considered unethical by social workers.

planned parenthood A *social movement* advocating population control and reproductive restraint. The term is also used as a synonym for *contraception* or *birth control*. See also *family planning*.

Planned Parenthood Federation of America
A national organization established by Margaret Sanger (1883–1966) in 1921 to promote planned *birth control* and *contraception*.

planning   The process of specifying future objectives, evaluating the means for achieving them, and making deliberate choices about appropriate courses of action. This process of choice involves two aspects: (1) rational decision making, which seeks to examine all relevant alternatives and select from among them, and (2) incremental decision making, which encompasses a more-limited range of alternatives and practical considerations. See also *social planning* and *social policy*.

platform   A formal public statement by a political party or social cause organization of its guiding principles and goals for the future.

play therapy   A form of *psychotherapy* used by social workers and other professionals to facilitate *communication*. The client uses toys to act out conflicts or to demonstrate situations that cannot be verbalized. Play therapy is most commonly used in work with children but is also effective and useful with adults in certain circumstances.

plea bargaining   *Negotiation* between a prosecuting attorney and a person accused of a *crime* (and his or her defense counsel), resulting in a disposition of the case. Typically, the accused agrees to plead guilty to a lesser charge and forgoes a jury trial. The advantage to the accused person is that the case is resolved sooner and at less risk of serious penalty. The advantages to the public are that court dockets are less backlogged and cases can be resolved with less cost.

pleasure principle   A principle in *Freudian theory* stating that the individual begins life seeking only gratification and pleasure and the avoidance of *pain* and discomfort. The developing child eventually learns that immediate gratification sometimes has to

be subordinated, so the *reality principle* starts to emerge. Thereafter the person faces a lifelong *conflict* between both. The healthy *ego* tries to adhere to the reality principle while allowing some room for the pleasure principle.

plebiscite   A vote by the entire electorate of a nation or other jurisdiction on an issue (rather than on a candidate).

plenary session   A meeting for everyone who attends a conference. Most conference participants spend part of their time at smaller gatherings called workshops or sessions but occasionally meet in the plenary sessions with all the other participants, usually to hear some notable speaker or vote on issues pertaining to the whole group.

Plessy v. Ferguson   The 1896 U.S. Supreme Court decision upholding a state law permitting *segregation* of the races in public transportation. The ruling, which was extended to segregation in other public places, held that segregation was permissible under the Constitution as long as "separate but equal" facilities existed. The ruling was not reversed until the 1954 Supreme Court decision in *Brown v. Board of Education*.

pluralism   Cultural diversity in a society, organization, community, or group, along lines such as *race*, age, gender, ethnic background, educational level, language, or appearance. In an idealistically pluralistic society, each type of group has some *power* or influence. Those who oppose pluralism tend to advocate *assimilation*. See also *melting pot theory*.

pluralistic society   A society comprising people of many different racial, ethnic, religious, and cultural characteristics.

plutocracy   Social or government control by the wealthy.

PMS   See *premenstrual syndrome (PMS)*.

PN   See *practical nurse (PN)*.

PNS   See *peripheral nervous system (PNS)*.

pogrom   An organized attack on or massacre of a group, usually Jews, residing in a nation or *ghetto.*

point prevalence   See *epidemiology.*

polarization   A phenomenon in which two or more objects, individuals, or groups develop opposing or contrasting tendencies. In social activism and *community organization,* the term is used to indicate the process by which an organization's members split into opposing camps over an issue or policy, possibly leading to a stalemate in the organization's decision-making capacity. However, polarization can also lead to the revitalization of an organization. A skilled social worker can point out or emphasize differences among the factions to encourage the formation of more-intense rivalries, greater involvement, and stronger coalitions. Each of the rival groups often achieves better coordination and in-group loyalties and thus is better equipped to achieve the original goals. Using this phenomenon requires intense effort and highly skilled professional *intervention*

police social work   Professional *social work practice* within police precinct houses, courthouses, and jail settings to provide a variety of *social services* to victims of crimes, people accused of crimes, and their families. According to Harvey Treger ("Police Social Work," in Richard L. Edwards [Ed.-in-Chief], *Encyclopedia of Social Work,* 19th ed., Washington, DC: NASW Press, 1995), some of these workers counsel police officers and members of their families under job-related stresses. They sometimes act as advocates and public-relations specialists for police departments and help in *mediation* with various community groups. A major activity is helping resolve domestic troubles for which the police are called. Some police social workers are civilians, and others are police officers as well as professional social workers.

policy   The explicit or implicit standing plan that an organization or government uses as a guide for action.

policy analysis   Systematic evaluations of a *policy* and the process by which it was formulated. Those who conduct such analyses consider whether the process and result were rational, clear, explicit, equitable, legal, politically feasible, compatible with social values, cost-effective, and superior to all the alternatives in the short term and in the long run. According to Neil Gilbert and Harry Specht (*Dimensions of Social Welfare Policy,* Englewood Cliffs, NJ: Prentice Hall, 1986), three approaches to policy analysis are (1) the study of process (sociopolitical variables in the dynamics of policy formulation), (2) the study of product (the values and assumptions that inform policy choices), and (3) the study of performance (cost–benefit outcomes of policy implementation).

policy decision-making theories   Explanations for the sociopolitical influences and considerations that are translated into specific policies and laws. Five models are used to explain how policy decisions are made: (1) "traditional model" (public-spirited citizens form planning groups, hire a planner, make rational decisions, and propose fair plans); (2) "power pyramid model" (a few business leaders influence politicians and impose decisions on those lower in the social structure); (3) "Yale polyarchic power model" (different issues each have different leadership patterns); (4) "qualified diffused-influence model" (influence is spread among many interest groups that change in size and importance over time); and (5) "decision process model" (the systems approach that sees decision making as a flow in which final decisions are the result of a series of interactions between various systems that all have interest in the decision).

policy statement   A formal and accessible explication of the policies that guide an organization or any of its relevant aspects.

poliomyelitis   A contagious viral disease that can cause nerve damage resulting in permanent paralysis of affected muscles; formerly known as "infantile paralysis." Polio, as it is more commonly called, had been controlled in the United States by preventive vaccines administered to young children. A resurgence of the disease is now occuring in some parts of the United States and other countries.

political action   Coordinated efforts to influence legislation, election of candidates, and social causes. Social workers engage in political action by running for elective office, organizing campaigns in support of other candidates or issues, fundraising, and mobilizing voters and public opinion. Political action also includes lobbying, testifying before legislative committees, and monitoring the work of officeholders and government workers.

political action committees (PACs)   Finance groups organized to raise and disburse funds to political candidates. Social workers contribute to several PACs, especially to the *National Association of Social Workers (NASW)*–sponsored *Political Action for Candidate Election (PACE)* group.

Political Action for Candidate Election (PACE)   The *political action committee* of the *National Association of Social Workers (NASW)*. The organization helps coordinate personnel and financial resources of interested members to elect political officials.

political activism   Engaging in activities that influence the decisions and viewpoints of elected officials or their appointees, civil servants, and the electorate. Such activities include *voter registration drives,* social *consciousness-raising,* fundraising to help finance legislators' campaigns, lobbying, running for political office, engaging in *media campaigning,* and helping monitor elections to assure their fairness.

political correctness (PC)   Verbal or written statements to avoid offending any person from a racial, ethnic, religious, or cultural group, any person with a disability, any person with a disease, any person from a geographic region or other entity, and their supporters.

political prisoner   An individual held in confinement by a state for views and actions that its leaders think will jeopardize the continued existence of that state.

poll tax   A tax of a fixed amount that each person in a jurisdiction is obliged to pay; also called a "head tax." It is regressive in that those with lower incomes pay a higher proportion of their income than do those who earn more.

polygamy   Plural marriage; a social custom that permits having more than one wife or husband at the same time. If the marriage involves one man with more than one wife, it is also called "polygyny." If it involves one woman with more than one husband, the term is "polyandry." Polygamy is not synonymous with *bigamy.* Polygamy is legal in some societies. See also *monogamy.*

polysubstance dependence   A *substance-use disorder* in which at least three groups of substances other than caffeine and nicotine are used within the same 12-month period, with no single substance predominating.

poorhouse   1. A form of *indoor relief* funded by government organizations or by private charities in which needy people are provided with temporary or permanent residential care. 2. An *almshouse.*

poor law   A generic term technically referring to any government statute pertaining to the economic and social care of and control of poor people or measures to reduce the extent of *poverty.* However, the term is primarily used to refer to a group of repressive statutes in Colonial America and in England before the 20th century. These laws established the *almshouse, indoor relief,* and concepts about the *"unworthy poor"* and were generally conceived to discourage people from seeking relief. See also *Elizabethan Poor Laws, Henrician Poor Law, Statute of Labourers,* and *Poor Law of 1834.*

Poor Law of 1834   The English legislation enacted to revise the *Elizabethan Poor Laws* of 1601. The new law was punitive and based on the premise that poor people lacked strong or moral character. The laws discontinued *public assistance* for all able-bodied citizens except those in public institutions and imposed the *less-eligibility prin-*

ciple so that no beneficiary would receive as much as the lowest wage earner. The program was taken from local authorities and administered nationally. The principles of the Poor Law of 1834 had a significant influence on *public welfare* policy in the United States for more than a century. See also *Chartist movement* and *Edwin Chadwick.*

"poppers" Slang in the drug subculture for nitrite inhalants, which produce in the abuser *euphoria,* relaxation, erotic feelings, and other symptoms, but which can lead to toxic reactions, irritation of the respiratory system, and impairment of the immune system.

population 1. The total number of people in a nation or other specified geographic region; also, the number of people of a specified class or group (such as women, Roman Catholics, *black people,* and disabled people) in a specified place or geographic region. 2. In *social research,* the term refers to all people or cases that could theoretically be available for an investigation. It is from the population that a *sample* is taken for research. See also *universe.*

populism A political orientation in which the interests of wage earners, farmers, and less-affluent families take precedence over those of business and professional groups.

POR See *problem-oriented record (POR).*

"pork" Political jargon referring to government appropriations for a lawmaker's pet projects in exchange for past or future support of other lawmaker's pet projects. The appropriations are said to come from the "pork barrel" (the government's treasury or national debt).

pornography The depiction of erotic acts, sexual intercourse, sadistic or masochistic activities, and other presentations in writing and pictures designed especially to appeal to one's *prurient interest.*

POS See *purchase-of-service (POS) agreements.*

position paper A written statement declaring one's views on a certain subject and the rationale and documentation for maintaining such views.

positive connotation The family therapy technique in which a *therapist* or family member ascribes virtue to some act that may or may not be beneficial to family functioning. This sometimes causes the person who performed the act to look at it more carefully, reevaluate it from the new perspective, and gain control over when it is performed.

positive reinforcement Strengthening a desired *behavior* or *response* by presenting a reinforcing *stimulus* contingent on performance of the response. The reinforcer may be a desired object, a privilege, verbal approval, or any other stimulus that strengthens the response.

positive transference *Transference* that results in expressions of affection, *love,* erotic desire, or feelings of warmth and closeness that a client may have for a psychotherapist or other person.

positron emission tomography (PET) scan A computerized diagnostic device using radioactive isotopes that are injected intravenously to evaluate cerebral metabolism.

postconcussional disorder Impaired cognitive functioning and neurobehavioral symptoms as a result of closed head injury, a proposed official diagnostic category of the *DSM-IV.*

postconventional morality In *Kohlberg moral development theory,* the last two of the six stages of development. In stage five, moral thought is based on understanding the validity of universal moral principles and the social context in which they must operate. In stage six, the individual understands and becomes committed to universal moral principles. These stages, if they occur at all, usually do not do so until the individual is older than age 20.

postnuptial agreement A written notice by a husband and wife who disclose all their assets and state that, in the event of *death* or *divorce,* they will seek no more of the other's assets than the amount specified. Such agreements usually are validated only when both parties have had separate legal counsel in the preparation of the agreement. See also *prenuptial agreement* and *separation agreement*.

postpartum depression Feelings of sadness experienced by some new mothers in the first few weeks or months after giving birth. The symptoms are thought to be related to hormonal changes and other physiological and psychological adjustments.

postplacement contact Follow-up activity by a *social worker* or *social agency* that has facilitated a new *placement* for a *client* to ensure that the needs of the placed individual and the new *caregiver* are being met. The activity normally includes telephoning or personally visiting the client and the caregiver in the new setting. Usually such contacts are prearranged, but in certain circumstances they take place without prior notice. Postplacement contact is most often done in *foster care* for children, *nursing home* care for older people, and *halfway houses* for people who were incarcerated or institutionalized because of illness, disability, or criminal behavior.

postpsychotic depressive disorder of schizophrenia A major depressive episode occurring during the residual phase of *schizophrenia*. This is a proposed official diagnostic category of the *DSM-IV*.

posttraumatic stress disorder (PTSD) A psychological reaction to experiencing an event that is outside the range of usual human experience. Stressful events of this type include accidents, natural disasters, military combat, *rape*, and *assault*. Stresses that are not unusual to people, such as marital problems, *bereavement*, and illness, are excluded from this class of disorders. Individuals may react to these events by having difficulty concentrating; feeling emotionally blunted or numb; being hyperalert and jumpy; and having painful memories, nightmares, and sleep disturbances.

postural tremor Rapid, regular, and rhythmic oscillation of the hands, fingers, mouth, and limbs that seem most apparent when the individual tries to hold a body part in a sustained posture. This is most commonly a *medication-induced movement disorder*.

poverty The state of being poor or deficient in money or means of subsistence.

poverty cycle A pattern of living in which the children of poor families grow up to become poor and raise their own children to also become poor. An implicit and unproven premise, often used by critics of the U.S. welfare system, says that poverty occurs by choice and that some welfare programs, such as *Aid to Families with Dependent Children (AFDC)*, foster *dependency* and teach the children to live the way their parents live.

poverty line A measure of the amount of money a government or a society believes is necessary for a person to live at a minimum level of subsistence or *standard of living*. The first measure of this type was issued by the United States in 1964. The original poverty line was calculated by a formula that multiplied the cost of a subsistence food budget by a factor of three. Since 1989 the poverty line has meant the previous year's poverty line adjusted for the change in the *Consumer Price Index (CPI)*.

power The possession of resources that enables an individual to do something independently or to exercise influence and control over others.

power-and-control phase The second stage in *group development* in which group members tend to lose their guardedness and ambivalence and begin to establish their respective roles in the group, as leaders, followers, talkers, passive members, and so forth. In this conception about the various stages through which groups progress, this phase follows the *preaffiliation phase* and is followed by the *intimacy phase*, the *differentiation phase,* and the *separation phase*. Many other typologies have also been proposed to describe the phases in the typical life of groupwork or a therapy group.

power group Members of a *community* who, because of their social *status* and positions, influence the decisions made on behalf of the community and who have greatest access to resources. Power group members usually include political leaders, financial and industrial executives, members of the clergy, and local indigenous leaders.

power of attorney   A written and properly witnessed statement in which one person grants another person the *authority* to perform specified acts on behalf of the first. For example, a landowner who wishes to sell property that is far away grants authority to a local realtor to sign the documents needed to complete the sale. See also *durable power of attorney*.

PPBS   See *Program Planning and Budgeting System (PPBS)*.

PPOs   See *preferred provider organizations (PPOs)*.

practical nurse (PN)   A *paraprofessional* specialist in the care of people who are ill and in the maintenance of health and well-being. PNs complete training programs that last one year or more, after which they carry out important but less-technical nursing duties such as administering medication, monitoring tests, and feeding and cleaning patients. See *licensed practical nurse (LPN)* and *registered nurse (RN)*.

practice theory   A grouping of concepts that systematically pulls together what is known about physical and psychological *behavior* and social systems and their interaction, the relevant *values* and goals to be achieved, and the specific techniques and skills available to permit purposeful action. Many practice theories are listed by name in this dictionary.

"practice wisdom"   A term often used by social workers to describe the accumulation of information, assumptions, ideologies, and judgments that have seemed practically useful in fulfilling the expectations of the job. Practice wisdom is often equated with "common sense" and may or may not be validated when subjected to empirical or systematic analysis and may or may not be consistent with prevailing theory.

practicum   Part of the professional education of students in which they apply the knowledge and skills acquired primarily through classroom assignments to direct practice with clients. In *social work education,* this occurs primarily in *field placement* assignments in which students work, under close professional *supervision,* with clients in social agencies or other *social services* settings.

Pray, Kenneth (1882–1948)   Social work scholar who developed *community organization* as a social work method. Pray led the first comprehensive survey of social work education done by the *Council on Social Work Education (CSWE)*.

praxiology   The study of custom and practice in human relationships.

preaffiliation phase   The first stage in *group development* in which group members tend to be ambivalent about belonging, fearful, guarded, distant, and reluctant to engage in self-disclosure and risk taking. In this conception about the various phases through which groups progress, the subsequent stages have been described as the *power-and-control phase, intimacy phase, differentiation phase,* and *separation phase.* Many other typologies have also been proposed to describe the phases in the typical life of groupwork or a therapy group.

precedent   A decision made by a government organization, agency, or court of law that has become the basis for subsequent policies, judgments, or arguments on behalf of some position.

precipitating cause   An event or change that seems to result in an individual's disorder or problem; the "last straw" that leads the person to seek the social worker's help.

precocity   The development of physical or intellectual capabilities at an earlier age than is usual.

preconscious   Thoughts, images, and perceptions that are not in one's immediate awareness but that can be recalled with relative ease.

preconventional morality In *Kohlberg moral development theory,* the first two of the six stages of development. In stage one, moral thought is based on fear of punishment; in stage two, it is based on the desire to obtain rewards. Preconventional morality development usually occurs before age nine.

predelinquency A pattern of behaviors and social circumstances that, when found in some youths, significantly increases their chances of *juvenile delinquency.* Such behaviors include attending school erratically, disrupting class, fighting, "borrowing" things from peers, associating with older delinquents, and being unmanageable by parents. Circumstances include living in a crime-plagued neighborhood, having little or no supervision or guidance, and having role models who glamorize antisocial behavior.

predictor variable In *social research,* a systematically measured performance, rating, or score that is used to estimate the likelihood that a subsequent objective is accomplished. For example, many schools of social work require student applicants to take academic aptitude tests. The resulting scores are predictor variables to indicate the likelihood of a student's success in the program.

predisposition A tendency to develop a trait or attribute under the right circumstances. For example, an obese child who has obese parents could have a predisposition toward adult obesity.

pre-elderly A diagnostic term applied to people who show some of the physical, mental, and behavioral characteristics of old age but whose chronological age is below that of the older person. The specific age depends on the function being evaluated.

preexisting condition A disorder or incipient health condition that occurred before the patient signed on for coverage by an insurance company or third-party organization. Many insurance companies refuse to enroll people with preexisting conditions or to reimburse for any health problems related to that condition.

preferred provider organizations (PPOs) Affiliations of professionals, often in *private practice,* who fulfill contracts to receive *third-party payments.* PPO members agree to provide professional services to members of a designated group at a favorable fee-for-service rate, and the *third party* agrees to channel members of its group to the PPO. See also *independent practice associations (IPAs)* and *managed health care program.*

pregenital In *psychoanalytic theory,* the *oral phase* and *anal phase* of personality development and the manifestations of those stages that recur in later life.

pregnancy The reproductive state of carrying a *fetus* within the body; that is, the time between *conception* and birth. Human pregnancy normally lasts about 280 days, during which time rapid changes in the development of the fetus occur in the mother's uterus. Determining the existence of pregnancy may be based on observation of certain symptoms. Physicians use three categories of pregnancy criteria: (1) presumptive symptoms include failure to experience the anticipated menstrual period, nausea or vomiting ("morning sickness"), fatigue and need for excessive sleep, frequent urination, alteration of skin pigmentation around the nipples, and softening of the cervix; (2) probable symptoms include positive results of laboratory tests for pregnancy (urine sampling for the presence of a specific level of the hormone chorionic gonadotropin), abdominal enlargement, and uterine changes; (3) positive signs include fetal heartbeat, fetal movements within the uterus, and the presence of a fetal skeleton as shown by X-ray. It is important to determine the existence of pregnancy fairly soon after conception and to determine the relative health of the fetus. See also *amniocentesis* and *chorionic villa sampling (CVS).*

prejudice An opinion about an individual, group, or phenomenon that is developed without proof or systematic evidence. This prejudgment may be favorable but is more often unfavorable and may become institutionalized in the form of a society's laws or customs. See also *bias, discrimination, separatism, individual racism,* and *institutional racism.*

preliminary examination An evaluation of an individual or situation made in advance of acquiring all the relevant information that eventually will become available. Such examinations are made to evaluate emergency medical situations, to begin some *intervention* processes, to determine if sufficient evidence exists to hold a person for trial, or to determine if an individual seems ready to proceed to the next stage of evaluation. The slang term for this is "prelim." Social workers make preliminary examinations primarily during *intake* and initial client contacts. The social worker always tries to determine at least four facts in the prelim: (1) Is the client suicidal? (2) Should the client also seek medical care? (3) Does the client constitute a danger to others? and (4) Does the client need any emergency social services to maintain health, safety, and security?

premature birth The birth of a baby significantly before completion of the normal *gestation* period or of a baby with very low body weight (usually less than four pounds).

premature ejaculation A *sexual disorder* in which the man recurrently reaches orgasm before he wishes to, resulting in unsatisfactory *coitus*.

premature termination Discontinuing services to clients who are still in need. This is considered unethical, and many *malpractice* suits have been made over this action. See also *"client dumping."*

premenstrual dysphoric disorder A markedly depressed *mood*, *anxiety*, affective lability, and decreased interest in activities that regularly occur during the last week of the luteal phase of the menstrual cycle (the period between ovulation and the onset of menses), which significantly interfere with usual social activities and relationships. This disorder is considered far less common than *premenstrual syndrome (PMS)* but may be more discomforting or impairing. This is a proposed official diagnostic category of the *DSM-IV.*

premenstrual syndrome (PMS) Feelings of discomfort and related personality fluctuations that affect some women during the several days of their menstrual cycles immediately before menstruation. Some medical researchers indicate that hormone secretions peak during these days and hypothesize that this may influence the feelings and behaviors of some, but not all, women. Other professionals discount this hypothesis, and some discount the existence of PMS entirely.

prenatal Before birth.

prenuptial agreement A contract entered into by two people who plan to marry, delineating ownership of property and rights and obligations of each. See also *postnuptial agreement* and *separation agreement.*

preoccupation Conscious and prolonged attention to a worrisome event or general mental self-absorption so that the individual's contact with current responsibilities or relationships is hindered. Preoccupation is often symptomatic of mental disorders, especially *depression, schizophrenia,* and *narcissism.* However, it is also common in healthy, but concerned or absent-minded, people.

preoperational stage The second stage of development described in *Piagetian theory,* lasting from about age two to seven. During this time, the child begins to use symbols and some reasoning ability but still cannot group objects and must deal with each item individually.

prescribing the symptom A technique, used by social workers and other professionals engaged in *family therapy,* in which the therapist uses *paradoxical directive* to tell one or more members of a family to continue their symptomatic *behavior* under specified circumstances. For example, the therapist might tell certain family members to pout every Tuesday. This helps them realize the existence of the symptom and that it is under their voluntary control.

prescription, medical A physician's written order to a pharmacist or patient describing the type and amount of drug or other *treatment* to be used, the duration of use, and other special directions. Physicians often use some of the following abbreviations in writing prescriptions: ad lib. (as needed), a.c. (before meals), b.i.d. (twice a day), dieb. alt. (every other day), o.d. (every day), p.c. (after meals), q.h. (every hour), q.2h (every two hours), q.3h (every three hours), t.i.d. (three times a day), q.i.d. (four times a day), q.s. (as much as needed), stat. (immediately), and p.r.n. (when needed).

pre-senile The mental and physical characteristics of a person immediately before old age. The term "pre-senile dementia" once was used to describe mental deterioration in people who had symptoms of *senility* but who were not of advanced years; however, this term now is rarely used because of its lack of precision.

presenium Just before old age.

presenting problem The perceived symptoms, overt issues, or difficulties the *client* believes to constitute the problem and for which help is sought. The one who presents the problem may be the person for whom help is sought or others who recognize the need for helping that person. Because the social worker recognizes that the problem may be the result of underlying causes or that there can be inaccuracies in the way the problem is understood by the client, consideration of the presenting problem is only the beginning of the *assessment* phase.

pressure group An organization or collective of like-minded individuals that seeks to influence the policies of governments, political candidates, agencies, or the general public. Such groups present their views through the use of a *media event, legislative advocacy tactics, lobbyists, political action committees (PACs), fundraising,* and voter campaigns. Two types of pressure groups are the *public-interest group* and the special-interest group. See also *interest group.*

pretest A preliminary test, such as a *questionnaire,* administered to a small group of people who have relevant traits that are similar to those who will be evaluated. A *research* procedure, the pretest's purpose is to identify any problems, confusing questions, or other errors before going through the entire research process.

pretrial detention Confinement of a person who is accused of a *crime* before a conviction has been reached in a court of law. This happens when a defendant cannot raise the amount of *bail* or is held without bail.

prevalence rate A measure of the number of cases of some problem or disease that exists in a given *population* during a specified period. See also *incidence rate* and *epidemiology.*

preventative detention A form of *pretrial detention* applied to a person who is considered likely to be found guilty at the trial and who poses an immediate threat to the public if released.

prevention Actions taken by social workers and others to minimize and eliminate those social, psychological, or other conditions known to cause or contribute to physical and emotional illness and sometimes socioeconomic problems. Prevention includes establishing those conditions in society that enhance the opportunities for individuals, families, and communities to achieve positive fulfillment. See also *primary prevention, secondary prevention,* and *tertiary prevention.*

preventive health programs Activities in the public and private sectors to ensure that people remain in good health and are protected from disease. The U.S. *Public Health Service,* state and local health departments, private health and *welfare* organizations, and *foundations* are the primary coordinators of these programs in the United States. The activities include vaccinating against disease, providing instruction in hygiene, enforcing standards of sanitation, and researching the causes and cures of diseases.

preventive social work Professional *social work* practiced to achieve the goal of enhancing human potential, maintaining and protecting the individual's psychosocial resources, and promoting competencies that enable people to avoid or overcome the predictable and unexpected problems of living. This approach emphasizes *habilitation* rather than *rehabilitation* and uses proactive rather than reactive measures in helping healthy clients remain that way.

price controls Government regulations that limit the amount of increase or decrease in the prices consumers are charged for goods and services. The purpose is to control inflation and increase employment. This policy is often accompanied by *wage controls.*

price discrimination Charging different people different prices for the same goods or services. See also *means test* and *sliding fee scale.*

price supports *Price controls* in which a government maintains prices at a specified level regardless of the costs of production or the amount people would pay on the open market. Governments usually do this by giving direct financial assistance to producers of the goods or services or by purchasing them at a set price. See also *subsidy* and *Commodity Credit Corporation (CCC).*

prima facie evidence Information that can be used in a court of law that requires no further support to establish its credibility or validity.

primal therapy A form of *psychotherapy* based on intense *catharsis*. The therapist may encourage *regression* in clients by focusing on early *childhood* experiences to the extent that the client expresses primitive (primal) emotions through such dramatic means as loud, prolonged screaming.

primary alcoholism One of the three major types of *alcoholism* (the other two being *secondary alcoholism* and *reactive alcoholism*) in which the individual has high tolerance for alcohol, drinks in response to physiological withdrawal symptoms, and puts drinking ahead of all other activities. This appears to be a genetically influenced disease and begins, in most people, between ages 25 and 35.

primary care In the system for delivery of *health care,* the first contact type of *intervention* that occurs in hospital emergency rooms, outpatient clinics, and doctor's offices. Primary care usually includes monitoring symptoms, screening for diseases, treating minor injuries, and managing chronic diseases. See also *secondary care* and *tertiary care.*

primary degenerative dementia A *mental disorder* in which *dementia* begins gradually with steady deterioration thereafter. Symptoms begin for most people in their mid-60s and are rare before age 50. *Alzheimer's disease* is the most common of the primary degenerative dementias.

primary gain Direct relief from *anxiety* achieved by using a *defense mechanism.* See also *secondary gain.*

primary group People who are in intimate and frequent face-to-face contact with one another, have norms in common, and share mutually enduring and extensive influences.

Primary Insurance Amount (PIA) The term used by the *Social Security Administration (SSA)* for the full monthly amount of money one receives when beginning to collect social security benefits at age 65. If the beneficiary retires earlier than 65, the PIA is lower; if retirement is delayed past 65, the benefits are more than 100 percent of the PIA.

primary prevention Actions taken to keep conditions known to result in *disease* or *social problems* from occurring. For example, a community's development of sanitation facilities, recreation centers, and parks helps prevent diseases and stress-related disorders. Social welfare efforts in primary prevention include the development of *social insurance* programs and *settlement house* activities that help socialize and educate people so they can avoid problems and enhance their opportunities. See also *prevention, secondary prevention,* and *tertiary prevention.*

primary process thinking Disorganized and irrational thoughts expressed without reference to the individual's external world.

Psychoanalytic theorists believe that such expressions represent thoughts from the deepest parts of the *psyche* and include *unconscious* thoughts that have not been screened or "processed" by the *ego.* Such expressions are sometimes seen in psychotic patients and in some people who speak while asleep.

private adoption   *Adoption* that occurs outside of legally regulated agencies. Also known as *independent adoptions,* the process is often facilitated by a physician, lawyer, or broker who, usually for a fee, places a child with the adoptive parents. See also *gray-market adoption.*

private case management   The employment of autonomous organizations or professionals to help clients negotiate and use a wide range of needed health and social services. Private case managers may serve in nonprofit or for-profit organizations and work independently or for industrial organizations. Fees may be paid by the client, the employing company, or insurance companies. Private case managers are most typically engaged in helping older clients or their families obtain appropriate services from the existing array of agencies. For example, these managers might be employed by the family of a senior citizen to help with preparing *Medicare* documentation and obtaining homemaker and chore services, day care and health care. Nurses and social workers are the two professionals most involved in such activities.

private practice   In *social work,* the process in which the *values,* knowledge, and skills of social work, acquired through sufficient education and experience, are used to deliver social services autonomously to clients in exchange for mutually agreed payment. According to Robert L. Barker (*Social Work in Private Practice,* 2nd ed., Washington, DC: NASW Press, 1993), 10 norms apply to private social work practitioners. The private practitioner (1) has the *client* (rather than an agency or organization) as the primary obligation, (2) determines who the client will be, (3) determines the techniques to be used, (4) determines practice professionally rather than bureau-cratically, (5) receives a fee for service directly from or on behalf of the client, (6) has sufficient education as a social worker, (7) is sufficiently experienced, (8) adheres to social work *values* and standards, (9) is licensed or certified to engage in private practice if the jurisdiction has such regulations, and (10) is professionally responsible.

private social agencies   *Nonprofit agencies* that provide *personal social services,* mostly to members of targeted *population* groups (such as residents of a certain neighborhood or those of a certain religious affiliation, *ethnic group,* age category, or *interest group*). These agencies are funded by voluntary and philanthropic contributions and money from government grants. They are generally incorporated and have elected board members who represent the *community* and establish *policy.* Organizations that provide such services for profit are called *proprietary social agencies.*

privatization   The tendency in some societies to rely on or encourage the private sector to meet the social needs of the people. In the United States, this tendency is seen in the reliance on private health, educational, and social institutions and entrepreneurs to provide services. In social work, this tendency is seen in the growth of *social services* provision through private for-profit corporations, partnerships, *private practice,* and *proprietary social services.*

privileged communication   The premise and understanding between a *professional* and *client* that the information revealed by the client will not be divulged to others without expressed permission. In fact, the laws and judicial interpretations in each state are not always consistent or clear about this premise. Courts in many states have honored privileged communication for social workers and other professional groups, except when there is a risk of public danger or a threat to the public good. See also *confidentiality, absolute confidentiality,* and *relative confidentiality.*

PRO   1. See *peer review organization (PRO).* 2. See *professional review organizations (PROs).*

probability sampling In *social research,* the systematic selection of cases in a way that allows the researcher to calculate the likelihood, or level of probability, that any given case would be selected from the *population.* This makes it possible to estimate the degree to which the sample is likely to represent the population. See also *random sample.*

probation 1. A specified time during which an individual is to demonstrate possession of certain abilities or qualifications. 2. In the *corrections* field, probation is a status in which *incarceration* is suspended on the condition that the subject fulfills certain requirements. These requirements often include periodic visits to a court-designated probation officer, who may be a social worker.

problem An unanswered question or unresolved circumstance involving deficiency from a norm or ideal. Social problems pertain to any deficiency from an ideal social structure or *social institution.* A client's *presenting problem* is a perceived deficit between the existing situation and the norm or ideal.

problem-oriented record (POR) A format used by physicians, social workers, nurses, and other professionals to develop and maintain efficient case records. Developed by Lawrence Weed, originally as the problem-oriented medical record, it has been applied in multidisciplinary contexts and adapted for the needs of many professions. The record contains four components: (1) the database (*face sheet* information; *presenting problem;* relevant demographic, cultural, and medical data; addresses and mailing lists; and so on); (2) the problem list (each problem is numbered, so that when it is resolved it is convenient to identify and check off); (3) the plan (possible steps to take in resolving each numbered problem); and (4) the follow-up action (what has actually been done to implement the plan). POR is highly focused on specific problems and their progress and resolution and thus makes the professional more easily accountable than do less-focused, chronological summaries.

See also *process recording, SOAP charting method,* and *person-oriented record.*

problem-pregnancy counseling Therapeutic *intervention* with women who have psychosocial conflict about their pregnancies. The process is most often applied to young unmarried women and is oriented to educating them about available options. This occurs after determining, as early as possible, whether there actually is a *pregnancy.* If tests are positive, then the options discussed include *abortion, marriage, adoption,* and rearing the baby alone. The father and family members are included in these discussions whenever possible and helpful, but the pregnant woman makes the ultimate decision.

problem-solving casework A form of *social casework,* developed primarily by Helen Harris Perlman (*Casework: A Problem-Solving Process,* Chicago: University of Chicago Press, 1957), that draws on concepts in *ego psychology, role theory,* and, implicitly, on a consolidation of the *diagnostic school in social work* and the *functional school in social work.* Among the most important practice methods this *model* stresses are clear delineations of the goals of the casework *intervention,* focused and time-limited intervention, and concern for the environmental and social forces that influence and are influenced by the client.

pro bono publico "For the good of the public," the Latin phrase used primarily by lawyers in reference to providing professional services at no charge to a needy recipient, especially one whose case has broader social implications.

Procedural Terminology for Psychiatrists **(PTP)** A systematic listing and coding of procedures and services performed by psychiatrists on behalf of their patients. PTP is a part of the physician's *Current Procedural Terminology (CPT).* Services of nonphysicians are not included in the PTP codes, and nonphysicians should not use them to report services.

process-and-content issue See *content-and-process issue.*

process recording A method of writing about the social worker–client interactions during the *intervention* process. The *case record* using this format begins with *face sheet* of factual data about the client and relevant social, environmental economic, and physical factors. Then it briefly describes the *presenting problem* and includes documenting data about the problem. The social worker then includes a statement of goals, obstacles to reaching the goals, means to reaching them, and—where applicable—a written contract signed by social worker and client. The record then contains entries for each contact the client makes with the social worker or agency, including telephone calls and messages from other family members. The entry is headed by the date and time of the visit or contact and a summary of the factual information obtained as well as any subjective impressions the social worker has developed. These entries are not as elaborate as those in *verbatim recording* but are more chronologically stated than in the *problem-oriented record (POR)* or *person-oriented record*. Because of recent legislation, court rulings, and ethical principles, social workers are often advised to prepare their records so they are accessible to other social workers, clients, peer reviewers, or providers of *third-party payments*. This is to protect the client's rights during emergencies, when the social worker is inaccessible, or in cases of *quality assurance* evaluations and *peer review*. See also *narrative summary*.

prochoice movement Organized efforts to influence public opinion, legislation, judicial interpretations, and legal enforcement and to gain financial support and medical access that are considered necessary for maximizing reproductive choices, especially keeping the option of *abortion* legal and accessible. The name of this movement came about primarily as a response to the name used by those who were fighting against abortion, known as the "prolife movement." The prochoice movement advocates education, *family planning,* and opportunities for pregnant women to choose abortion, *adoption,* or to keep their babies. See *National Abortion Rights Action League (NARAL)* and *Planned Parenthood Federation of America.*

prodromal phase The early stages of a *disease.* See also *schizophrenia.*

profession A group of people who use in common a system of *values,* skills, techniques, knowledge, and beliefs to meet a specific social need. The public comes to identify this group as being suited to fulfill the specific need and often gives it formal and legal recognition through *licensing* or other sanctions as the legitimate source for providing the relevant service. The group enhances its public credibility by expanding its body of knowledge, making the knowledge accessible to its members, refining its skills and values, ensuring that its members comply with its established standards, and making public the actions it takes to reach these goals.

professional An individual who qualifies for membership in a specific *profession* and uses its practices, knowledge, and skills to provide services to client systems, and in so doing, always adheres to its *values* and *code of ethics.*

professional association (PA) The designation used by some individuals and groups who provide professional services to indicate their *status* as corporations or other group entities. PA is placed after the professional's name (for example, Jane Doe, MSW, PA). PA can also refer to a group of professionals who are unincorporated. See also *professional corporation (PC).*

professional certification The public assurance by a recognized professional association, consisting of a significant part of a profession's membership, that a member of that profession has attained a specified level of knowledge, experience, and skill. The *National Association of Social Workers (NASW)* offers five professional certificates: (1) The *Academy of Certified Baccalaureate Social Workers (ACBSW)*, (2) the *Academy of Certified Social Workers (ACSW)*, (3) the *School Social Work Specialist cre-*

dential, (4) the *Qualified Clinical Social Worker (QCSW),* and (5) the *Diplomate in Clinical Social Work.*

professional corporation (PC) A corporation or legal association formed to practice a *profession.* The *professional* or professional group that is incorporated has the letters PC or PA after the names and degrees. Members of the corporation are shareholders, and all are members of the profession being practiced. Individuals as well as groups can incorporate. Professional corporations allow professionals certain tax advantages unavailable to individuals and permit professionals to join together without assuming personal *liability* for the practices of other members. See also *professional association (PA).*

professionalism The degree to which an individual possesses and uses the knowledge, skills, and qualifications of a profession and adheres to its values and ethics when serving the client.

professional review organizations (PROs) A federally sponsored system established in 1984 in the U.S. *Department of Health and Human Services (HHS)* to evaluate the social and *health care* services provided by professionals in hospitals and nursing homes that receive federal funds. The program established regional PRO offices that oversee the standing review groups within each facility to help contain costs. The PRO system has taken over the functions of the *professional standards review organizations (PSROs)* system.

professional sanctions Punishments levied against a *professional* for violation of that profession's *code of ethics.* The most-common punishments levied against social workers belonging to the *National Association of Social Workers (NASW)* include the requirement of retraining and professional counseling for a specified length of time, public notification of the violation, probation of membership status, and expulsion from membership.

professional standards review organizations (PSROs) A federally mandated program based on the 1972 amendments to the *Social Security Act* of 1935 that requires those professions and service-providing organizations such as hospitals, nursing homes, and residential care facilities, which receive *third-party payments* from federal and state treasuries, to have their work evaluated by objective overseers. The program permits local review organizations to be set up by professional groups and associations of provider organizations if they follow specified federal guidelines. These organizations periodically review case records, medical charts, and other documents to determine if procedures are necessary and if they are implemented competently, efficiently, and cost effectively. These programs were reorganized in the Peer Review Improvement Act of 1982 (P. L. 97-248), and *professional review organizations (PROs)* is now the preferred term.

profoundly handicapped Individuals who have been diagnosed as severely mentally retarded, autistic, or mentally disturbed such that minimal *social functioning* is expected.

progeria Premature aging.

prognosis The social worker's or other professional's prediction of the likely course, direction, and outcome of the problem that is being addressed.

program 1. A plan and guideline about what is to be done. 2. A relatively permanent organization and procedure designed to meet ongoing client needs (as opposed to a "project," which is more flexible and short-term in scope).

Program Evaluation and Review Technique (PERT) A procedure commonly used in organizational management to relate goals to means in a rational and systematic way. PERT looks at program objectives and indicates all the activities that need to be performed, the time required for each, the sequence in which they should take place, and the resources required. This may be charted and posted so that all personnel are informed.

Program Planning and Budgeting System (PPBS)   An administrative analysis procedure used in federal government agencies and departments as well as other large organizations. PPBS relates costs to outputs (goods, services, and other products) rather than to inputs (labor, capital, and interest on debt). The procedure specifies objectives and measures progress in achieved end products, including amounts and distributions.

progression   Forward movement. *Social workers* and other *professionals* often use this term in reference to the client's changes in symptoms or results of the therapeutic *intervention*.

Progressive Era   The name given by historians to the period (roughly 1890–1915) in the United States when social reformers and advocates for socioeconomic justice were effectively demanding changes. The reformers and *muckrakers* sought and achieved changes in corrupt political practices at the local and national levels; established *settlement houses* in many poor neighborhoods; enacted laws for occupational and consumer safety; and influenced enactment of *social welfare* laws and programs for children, women, and disadvantaged people.

progressive tax   A government's revenue-collecting system in which those in a higher-income bracket pay a higher percentage (as well as a higher amount of money) in taxes than do those in lower-income brackets. For example, a person with a taxable income of $20,000 would pay 10 percent of that amount in taxes, and a person with a taxable income of $100,000 would pay 30 percent of that amount in taxes. See also *regressive tax*.

Project Follow Through   A *Great Society* program established in 1967 to help children from low-income families receive additional compensatory education through the elementary years. The program was primarily for children in the *Head Start* program.

projection   A *defense mechanism* in which unacceptable aspects of one's own personality are rejected or attributed to another person or entity, such as a parent, a colleague, or the government.

projective identification   A process whereby an individual uses *projection* onto another member of his or her family, group, or organization and then induces that person or the others to behave in accordance with the projected attitudes. This process also may occur when the individual comes to perceive that others are behaving accordingly, whether or not they actually are doing so.

projective test   A procedure that uses systematic but unstructured *stimulus* objects or situations designed to elicit the subject's way of perceiving and understanding the world. The premise is that the subject will project *unconscious* thoughts onto the stimulus object and reveal possible *psychopathology*. Major projective tests are the *Rorschach test* and the Thematic Apperception Test (in which the subject is shown a series of vague pictures and tells a story for each). Certain forms of *play therapy* are also considered to be types of projective tests.

prolife movement   See *right-to-life movement*.

promiscuity   Casual, frequent, and indiscriminate sexual encounters.

propaganda   Planned efforts to convince segments of the public about certain opinions or beliefs. Usually this is done with powerful slogans, testimonials, attractive images, and promises of better circumstances and the ending of problems. Propaganda is usually an important part of any political or social movement.

property-tax-relief programs   State and local laws that reduce, defer, or cancel property taxes on the homes of needy older people. These programs are designed for people whose houses have escalated in value during their residency to the point that the taxes are more than they can afford. Three such programs are *circuit-breaker tax relief, homestead exemptions,* and *homeowner tax deferrals.*

proprietary practice   In *social work,* the delivery of *social services* for profit, generally in nonclinical settings by self-employed professionals. The term "proprietary practice" is essentially synonymous with *private practice,* except that "private practice" is usually used to refer to clinical practice. Proprietary practice social workers typically provide their own facilities and offer these facilities and their own professional skills in such capacities as private consultants, organizers of special-interest groups, and caretakers for specific client groups. Some develop private profit-making institutions for clients who require physical care along with special social services (for example, a private facility for adolescent substance abusers).

proprietary social agencies Organizations or facilities that are usually owned or staffed by social workers and other professionals and that are intended to make a profit by providing a specified social service. These agencies provide essentially the same services as traditional nonprofit agencies, except that the charges to the recipient or recipient's agent may be higher. Examples of such organizations are private *halfway houses,* residential and educational facilities, camps, inpatient mental health facilities, training centers, research institutes, consultation services, and *social action* and *community organization* programs.

proprietary social services The use of the knowledge, training, skills, *values, ethics,* and methods of professional social work to make a profit for providing *social services.* See also *privatization* and *private practice.*

prosocial behavior Actions an individual, organization, or society takes to benefit society without the anticipation of external reward. What is considered to be of social benefit is relative and based on one's cultural *values.*

prosthesis The replacement of a missing body part with an artificial one. The part, such as a leg, tooth, or hand, is a "prosthetic device," and the professional who administers such treatment is a "prosthetic surgeon" or "prosthodontist."

prostitution The illegal act of offering oneself for sexual contact with another in exchange for money or other benefits.

protective custody The *placement* of an individual by the legal authorities in a facility to keep him or her from the danger of harm by others or from self-inflicted injury.

protective services Interventions by social workers and other professionals on behalf of individuals—such as children, disabled people, older people, and mentally retarded people—who may be in danger of harm from others or who are unable to take care of their own physical needs. The social workers are usually employed by the local *Department of Social Services (DSS)* or a similar agency, or they may work with the courts or law enforcement agencies. The primary job is to investigate situations in which a person may be at risk (as in *child abuse* or neglect of a disabled person), to help ameliorate the situation, to minimize further risk, and to find and facilitate alternative placements and resources for the person at risk.

Protestant ethic A value and behavioral orientation that is generally associated with hard work, self-discipline, deferred gratification, and the belief that such efforts will result in rewards, possibly including more money, higher social status, greater freedom, and eventual entry into heaven. This orientation derives its name from the moral teachings of such Protestant leaders as John Calvin, Martin Luther, and Charles and John Wesley and has guided the conduct of many middle-class U.S. families since colonial times. See also *Puritanism.*

protest movement An organized effort by a part of the public to show dissatisfaction and possible noncompliance with a new law, policy, or situation. Those involved in the movement use a variety of tactics to inform their political leaders, policymakers, or people in positions of authority over them of their dissatisfaction. The tactics include strikes, *propaganda*, marches, and *political action.*

provider The term used by *third-party payment* organizations in referring to the professionals and institutions that have served the client and to which reimbursement is made. See also *vendor.*

provision systems   The interacting social organizations that supply the products and services that people need, want, and demand; also, the *network* of social relationships that, together or individually, identify products and services needed and demanded, develop the necessary natural and social resources, distribute those resources, and evaluate the effects. In different societies, these systems may have a competitive, self-interested orientation or an egalitarian, cooperative orientation.

proxemics   Spatial behavior; the study of the way humans influence one another through the use of space. This includes such factors as the distance people need between one another for various types of *communication* and the arrangement of their furniture, homes, and streets to facilitate certain kinds of communications. See also *communication theory, sociofugal arrangements,* and *sociopetal arrangements.*

PRS   See *personal response systems (PRS).*

prurient interest   Attention devoted to erotic materials or situations that stimulate erotic interests. See also *pornography.*

PSA victims   Children harmed by pediatric *sexual abuse.*

pseudocyesis   False *pregnancy;* a woman's sensation of being pregnant or showing some of the symptoms of pregnancy when she is not. Symptoms might be due to psychogenic factors, physiological changes, or both.

pseudomutuality   A facade of harmony among members of a family, group, or organization when the members are actually antagonistic. According to the *family therapy* approach, pseudomutuality may result in serious internal conflict within individual members.

PSROs   See *professional standards review organizations (PSROs).*

psyche   The mind and soul, including the totality of one's conscious and unconscious mental processes. See also *ego* and *spirituality.*

psychedelics   *Drugs of abuse* that produce intensified and distorted sights and sounds, *hallucination, delusion, euphoria,* and other symptoms. *LSD, mescaline,* psilocybin, and peyote are psychedelics.

psychiatric emergency   Sudden or unexpected behavior in a person that indicates symptoms of *mental disorder* requiring immediate action by a *psychiatrist* or members of a *mental health team.* The most common behaviors that result in psychiatric emergencies include *suicide* attempts or threats, active *hallucination* that seems threatening, *fugue* states, drug-induced harmful behavior, and precipitous deterioration of the mental faculties. Sometimes this deterioration is related to the misuse or discontinuance of prescribed *psychotropic drugs.*

psychiatric labels   Descriptive or diagnostic terms applied to people by *psychiatrists, physicians,* or *mental health* professionals to characterize a person's psychiatric processes. They may be formal diagnostic terms (such as *bipolar disorder* or *borderline personality disorder*) or less-formal characterizations (such as "phobic" or "drug addict"). Critics of psychiatric labels say their use is inaccurate and dehumanizes people, precludes the principle of *individualization,* oversimplifies problems, and minimizes the impact of the psychosocial and environmental systems in which they occur. Proponents of psychiatric labeling say it is necessary for efficient *communication* among helping professionals and important for the conduct of research. Formal diagnostic terms apply to illnesses and should not be used as descriptive nouns to characterize people (such as "a schizophrenic").

psychiatric social work   *Social work* in a *mental health* setting. The psychiatric social worker provides *psychotherapy* and other social services for those with a *mental disorder* and, in collaboration with the *psychiatrist* and other members of the *mental health team,* works with the patient's family members. The worker usually has an *MSW* or higher degree and additional experience in working with psychiatric problems. Because the social work profession emphasizes the common element of its various specialties, psychiatric social work is not so distinct an entity as it formerly was. This team has largely been replaced by the term *clinical social work* practice. See also *American Association of Psychiatric Social Workers (AAPSW)*.

psychiatrist A *physician* who specializes in the treatment of mental disorders. The psychiatrist makes specific diagnoses of the *mental disorder* and prescribes, supervises, or directly provides the necessary *treatment,* which may include *psychotherapy, psychotropic drugs,* and hospitalization with *milieu therapy.* Qualifications to be a psychiatrist include four years of medical school and four or more years of approved residency training, usually in mental hospitals or hospital psychiatric wards.

psychic energy An individual's mental and physical drives and forces that lead to the processes of the mind, including thinking, remembering, storing and retrieving information, providing *ego* defense mechanisms, acting willfully with determination, and many other functions.

psychoactive drugs Drugs that induce changes in the user's *mood,* cognitive ability, or perceptions. They include both *psychotropic drugs* and many *illicit drugs* or *controlled substances.*

psychoactive substance abuse disorder Any one of a group of disorders involving a continuing pattern of *maladaptive* behavior resulting from the chronic ingestion of a *psychoactive substance.*

psychoactive substances Compounds or chemicals that produce an alteration of the mental or affective processes of the user. These chemicals may be illegal, as in *drugs of abuse,* or medically prescribed, as in *psychotropic drugs.*

psychoanalysis A method for diagnosing and treating *mental illness* and achieving better self-awareness using the principles of *psychoanalytic theory* originated by Austrian physician Sigmund Freud (1856–1939).

psychoanalyst A *professional* who uses the theories of *psychosexual development* and personality structure as well as the special *psychotherapy* techniques originated by Sigmund Freud (1856–1939) and his followers. Most psychoanalysts in the United States are *psychiatrists,* but the specialty also includes *social workers* and other *mental health* professionals who have qualified through advanced psychoanalytic training and personal psychoanalysis. Typically, psychoanalysts see their patients for 45 or 50 minutes, four or five times weekly, for an indefinite period, sometimes lasting several years. The client often reclines on a couch and verbalizes through *free association.* The psychoanalyst interprets the patient's dreams and the expressions of emotions related to *drive, unconscious* motives, and unhealthy use of *defense mechanisms.*

psychoanalytic enactment Symbolic and reciprocal interactions between the client and the analyst that have *unconscious* meaning to both. Typically the enactment occurs when the client's transference reactions provoke unconscious responses in the analyst, although theoretically the opposite interaction can also occur.

psychoanalytic theory The hypotheses and *treatment* applications about human personality and its development as proposed by Sigmund Freud (1856–1939), with later elaborations and modifications by many theorists and analysts such as Carl Jung (1875–1961), Alfred Adler (1870–1937), Otto Rank (1884–1937), Wilhelm Stekl, Melanie Klein, and Ernest Jones (1879–1958). Most of the concepts now recognized as psychoanalytical are from *Freudian theory* (that is, the *pleasure principle,* the *reality principle,* the *libido,* the *unconscious,* the *id,* the *ego,* the *superego,* and *psychosexual development theory*). Concepts that were emphasized by other analysts include *defense mechanisms* (Anna Freud, 1895–1982); *object relations theory* (H. V. Dicks), *inferiority complex* (Adler); *collective unconscious* and *archetypes* (Jung); *psychosocial development theory* (Erik Erikson, 1902–1994); *separation–individuation* (Margaret Mahler); and *parataxic distortion* (Harry Stack Sullivan, 1892–1949). Psychoanalytic theory and especially its progenies *ego psychology* and *neo-Freudian* theory have been influential in the theories of *clinical social work* practice and *social casework,* particularly in the *diagnostic school in social work,* and especially between 1940 and 1965.

psychobiology The science that studies the interrelationships between mental and biological functions, especially as they influence personality.

psychodrama A technique used primarily in certain forms of *group therapy* in which clients perform roles, often playing the parts of themselves in various socially stressful situations and sometimes playing the parts of their antagonists. This gives them the opportunity to act out their inner feelings to relieve *anxiety,* to practice handling situations better, and to experience the situation from another person's viewpoint. The other group members or psychodrama participants play roles, too, which gives everyone a chance to relate to one another from different perspectives.

psychodynamic Pertaining to the cognitive, emotional, and volitional mental processes that consciously and unconsciously motivate one's *behavior.* These processes are the product of the interplay between one's genetic and biological heritage, the sociocultural milieu, past and current realities, perceptual abilities and distortions, and one's unique experiences and memories.

psychoeducation The process of training mentally ill clients and their family members about the nature of their illness, including its *etiology, progression,* consequences, *prognosis, treatment,* and alternatives.

psychogenic A disorder or condition that originates in an individual's *mind* or *psyche* rather than in the body's physiological mechanisms. The term is generally used as the antonym for *organic.*

psychogenic amnesia An obsolete term for the sudden onset of *amnesia* that was thought not to be the result of organic dis-

orders. The current diagnostic term is *dissociative amnesia.*

psychogenic fugue A *dissociative disorder* characterized by an individual's sudden travel away from familiar places, inability to recall past events, and sometimes by the assumption of a new identity. The condition is not the result of *organic mental disorders* or *malingering,* although it is difficult for professionals to determine if the individual is feigning or actually unable to remember previous life experiences and location of home.

psychogenic pain disorder Recurrent symptoms of severe *pain* not resulting from physical disturbances. Often the symptoms are associated with some environmental *stressors* or the wish to avoid some responsibility *(secondary gain)*; however, the individual is apparently not pretending to have pain symptoms, as in *malingering.* In current clinical use the preferred terminology is "*pain disorder* associated with psychological factors."

psychogeriatric clients Older people who are cognitively impaired.

psychographics A depiction of the psychosocial characteristics of a given *population,* including such things as lifestyle, value orientations, and ideological commitments. In *social planning* and *social marketing,* psychographics often are as important as *demographics.*

psycholinguistics The study of language, *communication,* and metacommunication as they are affected by psychosocial factors. See also *communication theory.*

psychological morbidity A rarely used term for *mental illness* or *mental disorder.*

psychologist One who studies *behavior* and mental processes and may apply that knowledge to the evaluation and treatment of a *mental disorder.* Psychologists have many specialties, including experimental, educational, *counseling,* industrial, and clinical orientations. Clinical psychologists are those who apply the knowledge about human behavior to the treatment of various psychosocial disorders, usually in offices, hospitals, or mental health settings. To become a clinical psychologist, a person must obtain an academic degree in psychology, either a master's degree or a PhD or PsyD degree from an accredited academic institution. This is usually followed by a requirement of two years supervised work experience.

psychomotor Muscular activity coming from or directly related to mental processes.

psychoneurosis A synonym now rarely used for *neurosis* or *anxiety disorder*. In the 19th century, Sigmund Freud (1856–1939) and other neurological researchers needed to distinguish between disorders that were apparently caused by physical problems and those that seemed to come from the *psyche*. The term "psychoneurosis" was coined to refer to nervous symptoms of a psychological origin, whereas "neurosis" was used for somatic neurological problems. See also *neurosis*.

psychopath An imprecise lay term for one who has a serious *mental disorder*. The word is derived from the word "psychopathology," the study of psychological pathology or disease, and was once used by *mental health professionals* to refer to a person with a diagnosis of *antisocial personality disorder*.

psychopathic personality See *antisocial personality disorder*.

psychopathology The study of the nature of mental, cognitive, or behavioral disorders, including causes, symptoms, effects on the subject, and the psychosocial circumstances in which the *dysfunction* occurs. The term is also used in referring to personality or behavioral traits that may lead to problems or underachievement for the individual or for those in contact with the individual. Virtually every mental or behavioral disorder or any social relationship problem that prevents an individual from reaching his or her potential for well-being can be considered pathological.

psychopharmacological violence A type of *crime* identified by the U.S. *Department of Justice* that occurs when the perpetrator or victim ingests specific substances that lead to excitability or irrationality that results in the commission of a violent criminal act. This category of crime also includes people who ingest substances purposefully to reduce anxiety or boost courage and thus facilitate the previously planned crime.

psychopharmacology The study and use of drugs to bring about changes in behavior and personality. See also *psychotropic drugs*.

psychosexual development theory The concepts derived from *psychoanalytic theory*, which describe the process by which much of the individual's personality is formed. According to this theory, the individual is motivated by innate drives and instincts toward pleasure and immediate gratification. As the individual matures, there is a transformation through various stages of development. These stages are the *oral phase* (up to age two), *anal phase* (ages two to three), and the *phallic phase* or oedipal stage (ages three to seven). These are followed by a *latency stage* (from age seven to *puberty)* and the *genital stage* (*adolescence*). If the individual resolves the conflicts inherent in each of these stages, the mature *adult* is relatively free of psychic pathology. If not, then adult *intrapsychic* conflict, *fixation*, and potentially serious emotional problems may result.

psychosexual disorder Disturbances of human *sexuality* that are considered primarily *psychogenic*. The degree to which these disorders are psychogenic or *biogenic (organic)* is still being debated. For this reason the preferred term is *sexual disorder*.

psychosis A group of serious and frequently incapacitating mental disorders that may be of *organic* or psychological origin. These disorders are characterized by some or all of the following symptoms: impaired thinking and reasoning ability, perceptual distortions, inappropriate emotional responses, inappropriate *affect,* regressive behavior, reduced impulse control, impaired reality testing, *ideas of reference, hallucination,* and *delusion*. See also *schizophrenia* and *organic mental disorders*.

psychosocial assessment The social worker's summary judgment as to the problem to be solved; also referred to as the "psychosocial diagnosis." This description may include diagnostic labels (such as *DSM-IV* terms and codes, *International Classification of Diseases* terms, descriptors from the *Person-In-Environment [PIE] System*), results derived from psychological tests and legal status, brief descriptive expressions of the problem configuration, a description of existing assets and resources, the prognosis or prediction of the outcome, and the plan designed to resolve the problem. Throughout the *intervention* process the psychosocial assessment is a "work in progress," in that it is revised continually as new information is acquired, as circumstances and goals change, and as progress toward goals is made.

psychosocial crisis An important turning point or role change in one's life for which the individual has had little previous coping experience. The concept is that individuals go through predictable phases or stages of development mentally and socially throughout their lives and that each stage presents unique circumstances and challenges that the person must meet to make healthy developmental progress. The crisis occurs when the individual has not yet learned how to meet the demands of the new stage and may become conflicted and less effective until the necessary social and psychological adjustments are made.

psychosocial development theory The concepts delineated by Erik Erikson (1902–1994) and others to describe the various stages, life tasks, and challenges that every person experiences throughout the *life cycle*. The phases and life tasks are *trust versus mistrust, autonomy versus shame and doubt, initiative versus guilt, industry versus inferiority, identity-versus-role confusion, intimacy versus isolation, generativity versus stagnation,* and *integrity versus despair.* Some other psychosocial theorists describe different ages and life tasks.

psychosocial diagnosis See *diagnosis* and *psychosocial assessment.*

psychosocial study The social worker's process of acquiring the relevant information needed to decide on and develop a rational plan for helping the *client* (an individual, family, group, or community). This information may include the client's description of the problem; corroboration from other sources (such as medical records, school and personnel files, letters, telephone communication, and direct meetings with the client's family members and others who know the client), psychosocial history taking; information about the client's cultural and subcultural groups; information about the environment in which the client lives; and information about resources that might be used to help the client. The information obtained in the psychosocial study is used in arriving at the *psychosocial assessment.*

psychosocial therapy A *relationship* that occurs between a *professional* and an individual, *family, group,* or *community* for the purpose of helping the *client* overcome specific emotional or *social problems* and achieve specified goals for well-being. Psychosocial therapy is a form of *psychotherapy* that emphasizes the *interface* between the client and the client's environment. The psychosocial therapist tends to focus on interpersonal and social *relationship* problems in addition to intrapsychic concerns. Psychosocial therapy also seeks to mobilize available resources or create needed ones and combine them with individual, group, and familial relationships to help people modify their behaviors, personalities, or situations. This is done to help attain satisfying, fulfilling functioning within the framework of one's *values* and goals and the available resources of society.

psychosomatic The interrelationship of the mind and body; usually the term refers to an individual's symptoms that appear to be physical but are partly or fully the result of psychological factors.

psychotherapist A *mental health* professional who practices *psychotherapy.* The major disciplines whose members practice psychotherapy include *social work, psychiatry,* and clinical psychology. Some members of other professions are also psychotherapists, including *nurse practitioners, physicians, family therapy* specialists, clergy, guidance counselors, and educators. The legal qualifications for use of this title vary from state to state.

psychotherapy A specialized, formal interaction between a *social worker* or other *mental health* professional and a *client* (an individual, couple, family, or group) in which a therapeutic relationship is established to help resolve symptoms of *mental disorder,* psychosocial *stress, relationship* problems, and difficulties in coping in the social environment. Some specific types of psychotherapy are *psychoanalysis, family therapy, group psychotherapy, supportive treatment, gestalt therapy, experiential therapy, primal therapy, transactional analysis (TA), psychosocial therapy, psychodrama,* and *cognitive therapy.* Recent surveys show more than 200 identifiable and distinct types of intervention and theoretical schools in mental health.

psychotic Characteristic of a *psychosis.*

psychotropic drugs Drugs used by psychiatrists and other physicians to help their patients achieve psychological or emotional changes. These drugs include *antidepressant medications* (such as Elavil, Norpramin, Pertofrane, Sinequan, Aventl, and Vivactil), *antianxiety drugs* (such as Valium, Librium, Tranxene, Ativan, Serax, and various barbiturates), *antipsychotic medication* (such as Thorazine, Haldol, Compazine, Selazine, Navane, Mellaril, Serentil, Trilafon, and Prolixin), and *antimanic medication* (lithium carbonate—that is, Eskalith, Lithane, or Lithonate).

PTP See *Procedural Terminology for Psychiatrists (PTP).*

PTSD See *posttraumatic stress disorders (PTSD).*

puberty The period of biological development in which the reproductive capacity of the male or female is established.

puberty rites Formal or informal socially institutionalized behaviors applied to or required of youngsters to mark their newly established biological reproductive capability. In some cultures, these behaviors are formal and ceremonial, such as requiring the youngster to start wearing "adult" clothing or to spend the night alone in the forest. Many puberty rites exist in the United States today, but they are informal and vary greatly among subcultural groups. Examples include beginning to wear makeup, smoke, drink, drive, or have sexual intercourse.

public assistance Also known as *social assistance,* a government's provision of minimum financial aid to people who have no other means of supporting themselves. Funds come from the general revenues of the federal and state governments and not from any social insurance funds such as *Old Age, Survivors, Disability, and Health Insurance (OASDHI).* Some public assistance programs are administered at the federal level, including *Supplemental Security Income (SSI)* payments, which cover the *Old Age Assistance (OAA), Aid to the Blind (AB),* and *Aid to the Permanently and Totally Disabled (APTD)* programs. Other public assistance programs are administered by states and localities with the help of federal funding. These include *Aid to Families with Dependent Children (AFDC)* and *general assistance (GA)* for those ineligible for any other *categorical assistance* programs.

public defender An attorney for people who are accused of crimes or require legal services but are unable to pay for their own counsel. Public defender systems exist in most states largely as a result of the U.S. Supreme Court's ruling in *Gideon v. Wainwright* that indigent defendants must be furnished with legal representation.

public domain Property of the society at large, and within specified limits, legally available to all. Uncopyrighted software, books, and some national park lands are examples.

public health A system of programs, policies, and *health care* personnel whose goal is to prevent disease, prolong life, and promote better health. Efforts to achieve these goals are made through such public health measures as improving sanitation, controlling communicable diseases, educating people about personal hygiene, organizing medical and nursing services for early diagnosis and prevention of disease, and developing health care facilities and access to these facilities. Public health programs are administered by many federal, state, and local agencies.

Public Health Service, U.S.   The federal organization established in 1870 and now within the U.S. *Department of Health and Human Services (HHS)* to initiate and coordinate the nation's effort to maintain and improve the health and *health care* of its people. The service is involved in improving sanitation and health education, facilitating *primary prevention,* setting and enforcing standards for food and drug processing and handling, investigating imported organic products, controlling epidemics, and overseeing and conducting health research. Within the U.S. Public Health Service are the *Centers for Disease Control and Prevention (CDCP),* the *Food and Drug Administration (FDA),* the *Health Resources Administration (HRA),* the *Health Services Administration (HSA),* the *National Institutes of Health (NIH),* and the Alcohol, Drug Abuse, and Mental Health Administration (ADAMHA).

public housing   Residential facilities that are built, maintained, and administered by a local or federal government to provide low-rent or no-rent homes for needy people. Most of these programs are under the *authority* of the U.S. *Department of Housing and Urban Development (HUD)* and local housing authorities. "Public housing" is a term that could theoretically apply to many additional federally subsidized programs designed to help people obtain residences, such as the Rent Supplement Program, Lower Income Housing Assistance, Rural Housing Loans, Farm Labor Housing Loans and Grants, and the Indian Housing Improvement Program, as well as the *Federal Housing Administration (FHA)* homeowners' loans and the home loan programs of the U.S. Department of Veterans Affairs.

public-interest group   An organization or collective of like-minded individuals seeking to influence the policies of governments, political candidates, agencies, or the general public toward changes that are believed to benefit the whole society rather than one special-interest group. Such groups often employ *lobbyists* to present their views through the use of a *media event, legislative advocacy tactics,* lobbying, *political action committees (PACs), fundraising,* and voter campaigns. See also *pressure group* and *interest group.*

public-interest research group (PIRG)   Organizations funded by private and philanthropic contributions to identify the existence of particular *social problems,* determine their causes, evaluate proposed solutions, and present findings to the public and those institutions that can address the problems.

public welfare   The relative well-being of a society and its people as manifested by a nation's policy of providing for the protection and fulfillment of its citizens. To most people this term is now also a synonym for *social welfare* and *public assistance.*

public works   The existing and ongoing construction, under government auspices, of that part of the infrastructure that is built for public use, such as highways, parks, irrigation projects, power plants, and canals.

Public Works Administration (PWA)   The *New Deal* program established in 1935 to stimulate depressed industries and cope with the unemployment of their former workers by contracting with private organizations to build public facilities such as parks, recreation centers, post offices, and government buildings.

pulmonary disorders   A group of diseases associated with decreased ability to inhale oxygen into the lungs and expel carbon dioxide. Such disorders include bronchial *asthma, emphysema,* pneumonia, chronic obstructive pulmonary disease (COPD), and acute respiratory distress syndrome. These conditions have varying causes, including smoking, injury to the respiratory system, and obstructions of the airways.

punishment   1. A penalty imposed for misbehavior (for example, a parent spanking, isolating, or withdrawing privileges from a child) or illegal acts (for example, *incarceration*). 2. In *behavior modification,* the presentation of an unpleasant or undesired event following a *behavior,* the consequence of which is that there is decreased probability that the behavior will be repeated.

punitive damages   A legal judgment requiring a person who has harmed another to compensate the other for the actual harm caused, plus an additional sum as a punishment for intentional and malicious misconduct that led to the harm.

purchase-of-service (POS) agreements   A fiscal arrangement between two or more social agencies or between an agency and a government body, usually involving a contract between an agency with funds and another that can provide needed services. Purchaser agencies are thus able to extend services to their clientele, and provider agencies can increase their budgets, extend their services, and in some cases increase their profits.

Puritanism   The system of *values* and beliefs that was prominent in the 17th century, characterized by severe penalties for nonconforming behavior, strict discipline, and controls on what was considered immoral. Much of the Puritan philosophy was implicit in the English *poor laws* and was imported into Colonial America. See also *Protestant ethic.*

purposeful expression of feelings   One of the fundamental elements of the social worker–client *relationship,* in which the social worker encourages the client to communicate certain emotions. The client is helped to express those emotions that may be debilitating when not communicated. The worker encourages purposeful expression of feelings by listening, asking relevant questions, listening intently to answers, and avoiding any behavior that seems intolerant or judgmental.

PWA   See *Public Works Administration (PWA).*

PWP   See *Parents Without Partners (PWP).*

pyromania   An *impulse control disorder* in which the person frequently has compelling urges to start or watch fires.

Q

QCs Quarterly credits, the name used by the *Social Security Administration (SSA)* for the work credit units that a future beneficiary pays into the *Federal Insurance Contributions Act (FICA)* system for coverage eligibility. One QC is obtained by paying into the FICA system one quarter of a year. Workers born after 1929 must earn 40 QCs to be fully and permanently insured for retirement, survivors, and disability benefits. A worker born before 1929 needs slightly fewer QCs for full benefits.

QCSW See *Qualified Clinical Social Worker (QCSW)*.

qi-gong psychotic reaction A *culture-bound syndrome,* found mostly in China, in which the individual experiences an acute psychotic episode or nonpsychotic dissociative or paranoid reaction, often after intensive involvement in the "exercise of vital energy" practice known as qi-gong.

"quack" A term of disparagement, applied to medical professionals and to unqualified persons who fraudulently provide medical care.

quadriplegic A person with paralysis of all four limbs or paralysis from the neck down.

Qualified Clinical Social Worker (QCSW) A professional credential sponsored by the *National Association of Social Workers (NASW)* certifying that the holder has acquired specified levels of education and experience and is qualified to perform the functions required in *clinical social work* practice.

qualitative research Systematic investigations that include inductive, in-depth, nonquantitative studies of individuals, *groups, organizations,* or communities. Examples include *field study,* ethnography, and historiography.

quality assurance The processes and measures an organization takes to determine that its products or services measure up to the standards established for them. This determination may be accomplished by having supervisors, peers, consumer advocates, or legally designated overseers inspect the work, review the description of the work, or evaluate the system for producing the work. Products or services that fail to meet standards may be rejected, procedures for their completion may be revised, and sanctions can be brought against the provider. According to Alma T. Young ("Quality Assurance," in Richard L. Edwards [Ed.-in-Chief], *Encyclopedia of Social Work,* 19th ed., Washington, DC: NASW Press, 1995), the quality assurance measures used for social workers include the following: sufficient education from accredited schools of social work; entry-level work experience under qualified *supervision; licensing* and *certification*; competency examinations; and *continuing education* requirements. For the profession, measures include a professional *code of ethics* that is accessible to the public, *peer review, utilization review,* program evaluations, professional *sanctions,* civil *malpractice* suits, and criminal *negligence* charges. Quality assurance programs tend to be more concerned with compliance than with client outcome. This term is synonymous with quality control.

quality assurance programs in social work
Those measures taken by the social work profession to determine and demonstrate that its practitioners meet the standards that have been made explicit. These programs contain one or more of the following components: a patient or client information system (which tends to record physical and social characteristics of the client, problems or goals, and services received and outcomes), a *peer review* system (which evaluates the social worker's initial contact, *assessment,* formulation of goals, actual *intervention,* and *termination* and outcomes), and various systems for assuring that social work coverage is available. In the process, reviewers outline the standards of care, evaluate cases to determine if standards are being met, make recommendations for improvements, and have a follow-up review to see if improvements were achieved.

quality circles   In organizational management, a procedure in which a small number of employee volunteers, usually six to 12 people from the same work area, meet regularly to discuss positive ways to solve problems. The organization usually provides advance training in decision making for these volunteers, but they have no direct decision-making power. Quality circles are considered effective alternatives to the anonymous "suggestion box" method of gaining new insights from the employees' perspective. This approach has been developed and used more in Japan and other nations than in the United States and in commercial industries more than in human services agencies.

quality control   See *quality assurance.*

quantitative research   Systematic investigations that include descriptive or inferential statistical analysis. Examples are experiments, survey research, and investigations that make use of numerical comparisons.

quarantine   Isolation of a person or persons who may have or carry a *communicable disease.*

quarterly credits   See *QCs.*

quarterway houses   Transitional residences for individuals who require more *supervision,* support, or protection than is available in *halfway houses* but less than full-time institutionalization.

"queer"   A vernacular term for *homosexual.* Once a pejorative name used only by intolerant and homophobic individuals, "queer" is being reclaimed and used as a positive self-identifying term, especially by younger homosexual men and women involved in civil rights activities (for example, the "Queer Nation").

questioning   A primary tool in the social work *interview,* the procedure in which the worker systematically requests from the client information, *feedback*, and emotional expression. The social worker's questioning process gives focus and direction to the client and to the working *relationship* and is a medium through which the client develops self-understanding and learns new skills and insights. Questioning takes many forms, depending on the immediate and long-term goals of the interview.

questionnaire   A set of written questions seeking specific facts or subjective opinions on a given subject, used by social work interviewers and researchers to guide and systematize the information being gathered. Questionnaires may be so highly structured that they can be self-administered by the client, who merely gives yes–no responses. Or they can be relatively unstructured, consisting of a list of subjects that remind the investigator to ask relevant questions.

questions, closed-ended   See *closed-ended questions.*

questions, direct   *Questioning* that compels the client to address a certain topic, often one that the client may wish to avoid or minimize. Direct questions may be closed-ended ("Did you drink any liquor this week?") or open-ended ("How do you think you are affected by alcohol?").

questions, indirect   *Questioning* that helps the client feel less pressured and bombarded and permits him or her not to respond if desired and to have more flexibility about how to respond. An example is when a social worker comments to a client, "It must be difficult to have to work all day and then take care of the kids all night."

questions, open-ended   See *open-ended questions*.

quorum   The minimum number of members required to be at a meeting before it can conduct its official business.

quota system   An organizational plan, *social policy*, or legal doctrine that specifies how many, or what proportion of, people of an identified status will be included in an identi-

fied group. The system may be designed to exclude people (as in some past U.S. immigration laws that permitted a higher number of Europeans than Africans or Asians to enter the country) or include people (as in some *affirmative action* programs). For example, a city may decide that half its police officers should be black to reflect the population and overcome past discriminatory policies, so it mandates that efforts will be made to reach the 50–50 quota.

q-sort technique   A tool used in *social research* in which subjects are given a series of statements—each written on a separate card—and asked to sort them into various piles to indicate the degree to which they apply to the subject.

R

race The major subdivisions of the human species whose distinguishing characteristics are genetically transmitted. Races are divided in myriad ways, including the three traditional groups (Negroid, Mongoloid, and Caucasian); the "geographical races" (African, American Indian, Asian, Australian Aborigine, European, Indian, Melanesian, Micronesian, and Polynesian); and the groupings of various national ancestries, tribes, and even families. Many characteristics by which people seek to distinguish racial groups are not genetically transmitted but culturally learned. The U.S. government through various entities has recognized specific groups of people as composing a racial group, at least for purposes of legal protection. For example, the U.S. Supreme Court has held that people of Arabian ancestry and Jewish ancestry are to be protected from racial *discrimination*. For reporting purposes, the *Equal Employment Opportunity Commission (EEOC)* delineates many race categories including white, not of Hispanic origin; Hispanic (people of Latin and South American and Spanish culture origin, regardless of race), African, *American Indian* or *Alaska Native*, Asian, and *Pacific Islander*. ·

race relations See *intergroup relations.*

racism Stereotyping and generalizing about people, usually negatively, because of their race; commonly a basis of *discrimination* against members of racial groups. It is an ideology that a group's unchangeable (racial) physical characteristics are linked in a direct causal way to psychological, intellectual, or behavioral traits and, on that basis, that distinguishes superior and inferior groups. See also *institutional racism, individual racism,* and *able-ism.*

racketeering Organized *crime*. The process by which a group of people conspires to acquire property of others unlawfully through various crimes, especially *extortion,* smuggling, and sales of illicit goods and services, often facilitated by *bribery,* murder, intimidation, and the influencing of corrupt officials.

radical environmentalism Social *activist* movements advocating militant measures to protect the natural world. Activities include *demonstration, boycott,* obstruction of developments, and highly confrontative actions against those considered to be engaged in ecologically harmful activities. See also *Greenpeace* and *ecotage.*

radical social work The ideology among some social workers that the most effective way to achieve goals of *equality* and solutions to social problems is to eliminate or make major changes in existing institutions. Radical social work includes techniques for peaceably bringing about these changes, including *passive resistance, demonstration,* strikes, and political and social activism.

Ragged School Movement The educational and social development program started by *Lord Shaftesbury* in England in the 1850s to help educate poor children, who previously had little access to any schooling. The Ragged Schools provided schooling, social services, vocational development, and health care and were originally staffed by volunteers. Later, as education became more accessible to all British children, the role of these schools changed to focus on providing social services and assistance for handicapped children and poor families. The Ragged School organization was renamed Shaftesbury Society in 1944.

rainbow coalition   A group of people from different racial backgrounds working together to achieve specific political or social goals.

randomization   In *social research*, the assignment of subjects to experimental and control groups in such a way that each subject has an equally likely chance of being assigned to either of the groups.

random sample   A group of subjects or cases systematically taken from a *population* so that each one is as likely to have been selected as every other one. In this way the resulting sample is likely to be a valid representation of the population from which the cases were selected. See also *stratified sample*.

rank and file   The masses, or that group of people who are outside leadership roles.

Rankian School   See *functional school in social work*.

Rapaport, Lydia (1923–1971)   Psychiatric social worker who helped integrate *psychodynamic* theory with social work theory; later she developed the theoretical underpinnings for *crisis intervention* and *short-term therapy*.

rape   The *crime* of forcing a nonconsenting person to engage in some form of sexual contact usually involving penetration. The force may take the form of violent assault or real or implied threat. The victim most frequently is a woman or girl but may be a man or a boy, and the perpetrator is almost always a man. See also *acquaintance rape* and *statutory rape*.

rapid-cycling specifier   The indication, in a formal diagnosis of *bipolar disorder* I or II, of frequent changes of *mood*, occurring four or more times during the previous year.

rapport   In the social work *interview*, the state of harmony, compatibility, and *em-*

pathy that permits mutual understanding and a working *relationship* between the client and the social worker.

rapprochement   The fourth subphase in the *separation–individuation* process of human development proposed by Margaret Mahler, which lasts from about the age of one month to two years. If *fixation* or deviation occurs during this phase, according to Mahler, it is likely to lead to *borderline* or narcissistic disturbances in later life.

rare disorders   Diseases that are found in few people and thus receive little attention, research funding, or awareness of their existence. More than 5,000 of these diseases have been identified, and more than 20 million Americans are affected by them. Some may be fatal or severely disabling, incurable, or untreatable. Because they are rare, some physicians and other health care providers, as well as the victims themselves, do not recognize them. A coalition of agencies, researchers, and health care providers have formed the National Organization for Rare Disorders (NORD) to coordinate efforts to deal with these diseases.

rate review   A procedure in which *third-party* funding organizations such as government or insurance companies attempt to contain the costs of *health care* and social services by periodically evaluating the charges and procedures made by providers. The third parties and providers agree in advance about how much to charge for each specified service, and this is reconsidered usually every year. See also *fourth party*.

ratio   A mathematical relationship of one number to another, found by dividing one of the numbers into the other. For example, if an agency has 10 social workers and 500 clients, there are 50 clients for every social worker, and the ratio is 50 to 1. In social agency management, ratios are frequently used for the ratio of assets to liabilities, of revenue to expenses, and of salaries to total budget. When the base number (for example, the total agency budget) is expressed as 100, the ratio is expressed as a percentage (for example, 80 percent of the total agency budget goes for salaries).

rational casework   A type of clinical social work intervention, based on the concepts of *cognitive theory* and delineated especially by Harold D. Werner. This approach concentrates on the client's rational thinking processes.

rational–emotive therapy   A psychotherapeutic method based on *cognitive theory* and the ideas of psychologist Albert Ellis, in which the client is encouraged to make distinctions between what is objective fact in the environment and the inaccurate, negative, and self-limiting interpretations made of one's own behavior and life.

rationalization   1. Presenting in logical terms, or interpreting the reasons for, some action or event. 2. A *defense mechanism* in which a person explains or justifies an action or thought to make it acceptable when it is unacceptable at a deeper psychological level.

rationing   A process of allocating goods and services from limited available supplies. Rationing has been used when famine, war, disasters, or unexpected shortages of needed goods disrupt normal marketing price and distribution systems.

raw score   In *research,* the original and unprocessed quantitative result of a test. For example, a student's raw score on a test of 25 items would be the number of items answered correctly.

RDS   See *respiratory distress syndrome (RDS).*

reaching out   Activities by the social worker to gain the trust or motivation of fearful, unmotivated, or *hard-to-reach clients.* Such activities might include tangible gifts (a cup of coffee or a piece of candy), *concrete services* (cutting through some *red tape* with another agency), or special favors (extending the length of a session, telephoning the client between meetings, and so on). Reaching out also includes making services known and more accessible to people in need.

"reactionary"   A term of derision applied to an *activist* or an *ideologue* who opposes all forms of *social change* except those that go back to some former, idealized system.

reaction formation   A *defense mechanism* in which the person behaves or thinks in ways or assumes values that are the opposite of the original *unconscious* trait. Thus, a social worker who has an unconscious dislike for children might specialize in working with them, advocating more-stringent legal measures against *child abuse.*

reactive alcoholism   One of the three major types of *alcoholism* (the other two being *primary alcoholism* and *secondary alcoholism*) characterized by heavy or excessive drinking that starts soon after experiencing a perceived crisis such as the death of a loved one, surviving an accident, or crime victimization. No prior indication of a drinking problem is noted, but after the traumatic event, the individual may or may not become and remain addicted to alcohol. See also *posttraumatic stress disorder (PTSD).*

reactive attachment disorder   A disorder of infancy or early childhood characterized by the age-appropriate failure to initiate or respond to social interaction, thought to be related to pathogenic care (that is, persistent disregard of the child's emotional or physical needs or repeated changes of primary caregiver that prevent formation of stable attachments). The child may manifest this disorder through excessively inhibited responses or by indiscriminate sociability.

reading disorder   A type of *learning disorder* in which there is a deficiency in reading skills not resulting from limited education or cultural deprivation. The person may lack these skills because of visual or hearing impairment, cognitive or intellectual functions, or *organic mental disorders.* If the individual has been unable to develop reading skills, the condition is known as developmental reading disorder. See also *dyslexia.*

reality principle   An idea in *Freudian theory* stating that the young child soon learns that the satisfaction of immediate impulses must be reconciled with the often competing demands of the environment. Thus, the *ego* finds ways to compromise between the demands of the environment and the internal drives that are related to the *pleasure principle.*

reality testing   One's relative ability to judge and evaluate objectively the external world and to distinguish between it and the ideas and values that exist in one's mind.

reality therapy   A form of psychosocial and behavioral *intervention,* developed by William Glasser, in which the client is helped to develop a success identity based on love and worth. Reality therapists focus on the client's behavior rather than feelings and on the present and future rather than the past. They encourage responsible behavior and the working out of alternative solutions to problems. They do not accept client excuses, rarely ask "why," and place little emphasis on taking case histories. Positive results have been reported with the use of reality therapy in institutional settings in particular, and it has also been used extensively in individual and group work with people who have *schizophrenia* and with *delinquents.*

realpolitik   Practical *social planning* that is acceptable to enough voters that it has a chance of being legislated.

reapportionment   The political process of changing the boundaries of a legislative district or the number of representatives to which a district is entitled. See also *gerrymandering.*

reassurance   In the social work *interview,* the expression by the social worker of positive belief in the client and in the client's activities and motivations to improve the situation.

recertification   The *quality assurance* measure in which experienced professionals are required to demonstrate that they have maintained their ability to provide competent services. Once the professional shows that the ability remains, a formal declaration that the requirements have been fulfilled is made. This is often done by compelling professionals to pass examinations at designated times during their careers, to take a specified number of qualified training and retraining programs or units of continuing education, or to demonstrate continued practice competence to peers. See also *continuing education, CEUs,* and *grandparenting clause.*

recession   A socioeconomic condition characterized by lowered business activity, higher unemployment, and reduced purchasing power. Recession is considered a milder or shorter version of economic *depression.* See also *stagflation.*

recidivism rate   The number of people in a specified period who return to an institution relative to the population of that institution. For example, a mental hospital with a 50 percent annual recidivism rate would see half of its discharged patients return within a year.

recidivist   1. An individual who relapses or returns to a former condition or tendency. 2. One who returns to an institution because of a recurrence of the *behavior* or condition that led to the original *incarceration.*

reciprocal causality   A concept emphasized in the *ecological perspective* that views social interrelationships and transactions as occurring, not in a simple linear cause–effect outcome, but with circular *feedback* so that cause becomes effect and effect becomes cause all around the circular loop. In this view, the individual's problems are the consequence of people–environmental exchanges rather than the sole result of personality or environmental factors.

reciprocal goals model   In *group work* and therapy group conceptions, the group is seen as an integral element in the social system, and all its members and leaders influence and are influenced by the system, including one another. The leader's role is to mediate between the group and society. The group process is as important as any of its outcomes. See also *remedial goals model* and *social goals model.*

reciprocal inhibition A technique used in *behavior modification* in which suppression of an undesired *response* or *behavior* is accomplished by associating it with a dominant antagonistic response. For example, in *systematic desensitization*, relaxation responses are paired with anxiety responses until the *anxiety* is inhibited. The technique was developed by Joseph Wolpe.

reciprocal interactions Mutual responsiveness. For example, the *behavior* of one person to another leads to a behavior by the other, leading to a behavior of the first, and so on.

reclassification Formal and official changes made by an employer organization in the job descriptions, educational requirements, and personnel standards of its current and potential employees. Social workers in public agencies have been particularly affected by such actions, which have included reducing educational requirements for entry-level jobs, equating formal education with experience, and using non-BSWs and non-MSWs to perform tasks once reserved for them. Organization leaders sometimes say they use reclassification to streamline their operations and reduce expenditures. See also *declassification.*

reconstituted family A family unit comprising a legally married husband and wife, one or both of whom have children from a previous marriage or relationship who live with them. See also *stepfamily* and *blended family.*

recording In social work, the process of putting in writing and keeping on file relevant information about the *client;* the problem; the *prognosis;* the *intervention* plan; the progress of treatment; the social, economic, and health factors that contribute to the situation; and the procedures for *termination* or *referral.* There are many types of recording, depending on the agency's requirements, the social worker's social style, and the type of intervention. These may include the *narrative summary,* the *psychosocial assessment,* the *behavioral assessment, verbatim recording,* the *problem-oriented record (POR),* and the *SOAP charting method.*

recovered memory Retrieving parts of a client's forgotten past experiences that had been concealed from consciousness due to *suppression* or *repression.* See also *memory recovery therapy, false-memory syndrome,* and *implanted memory.*

"recovering addict" The preferred term for one who has been addicted to alcohol or other substances but who has maintained long-time sobriety. Because of the chronic relapsing tendency in addictions, the person is never referred to as "recovered."

Recovery, Inc. The national *self-help organization,* with chapters in most larger communities, whose members meet regularly to help one another recover from emotional problems or the effects of mental illness.

recurrent expenditures The amount an organization, such as a social agency, must pay out on a regular basis, including salaries, costs of expendable supplies, interest on loans, and so on.

recycle Preparing disposable items for reuse.

Red Crescent *Disaster relief* and humanitarian organizations in Muslim nations, affiliated with the International *Red Cross.*

Red Cross The international organization and federation of more than 100 autonomous national societies concerned with the alleviation of human suffering and the promotion of public health and civil rights. The organization was founded in Switzerland in 1863 by Jean Henri Dunant, and its emblem is based on the Swiss flag. The International Red Cross often acts as a neutral intermediary between nations at war or in conflict and works to ensure humane treatment of prisoners of war. The American Red Cross, founded in 1881 by *Clara Barton* (1821–1912), emphasizes *disaster relief, social services* to military personnel and veterans, health and safety programs, and the coordination of blood and organ donations to hospitals.

red-light district In many cities, an area where there is a concentration of *prostitution,* sexually oriented shops and clubs, and drug-related *crime.*

redlining The practice by certain financial institutions of designating an area of a city as being too risky and unprofitable to lend money to those who want to rebuild or refurbish buildings there. The term came from the red line that various institutions drew on maps around *ghetto* areas to identify those locales that would not be funded. The practice was made illegal with passage of the *Community Reinvestment Act of 1977*. See also *greenlining*.

"redneck" A disparaging term originally used to describe unsophisticated, dogmatic, racially prejudiced, and often hostile people with rural or small-town orientations. The term has more recently been applied to people who strongly advocate law and order, social control, and conservative ideologies.

red tape Bureaucratic procedures and rules.

reductionism A method of explaining a theory, a methodology, or data by reducing the more-complex aspects to less-complex ones. Often, the effect of doing this is to oversimplify the phenomenon and give it an inaccurate interpretation

referee A peer reviewer of a social worker's or other professional's written material to help publishers determine its suitability for publication. Publishers of serious scholarly journals, textbooks, and other professional documents usually ask several of the author's professional colleagues, usually those with some expertise in the topic discussed in the proposal or submitted manuscript, to evaluate the material. The publisher commonly uses the *double blind* process to help ensure that the decision to publish or not to publish is based only on the merits of the writing.

reference group A social *status, culture,* subculture, or association of any type whose behaviors, values, and lifestyles are emulated by an individual. The person may or may not be a member of the *group* with which he or she is identifying.

referendum A direct vote by the citizens on a proposed law, constitutional amendment, or funding measure.

referral The social work process of directing a *client* to an agency, *resources,* or a *professional* known to be able to provide a needed service. This process may include knowing what the available resources are, knowing what the client's *needs* are, facilitating the client's opportunity to partake of the service, and following up to be certain that the contact was fulfilled.

"referral fatigue therapy" A facetious term for the practice of sending clients to other helpers so often or with so many complications that the client eventually becomes discouraged and discontinues the search for help or obtains it from other sources. This reduces the social worker's caseload and appears in records as a success in providing service.

reflection of feeling The technique used in a social work *interview* in which the social worker clarifies and shows the client what his or her feelings are at the moment and encourages further expression and understanding of those feelings. Often the social worker reflects the client's feelings by *paraphrasing,* pointing out revealing *parapraxis,* and *paralinguistic* expressions of concealed feelings.

reflex An involuntary response to some *stimulus.*

reformatory An institution where young people who have been found to have committed delinquent or criminal activity are confined and given special training, therapy, and education to help them overcome *antisocial behavior* tendencies; also known as "reform school."

reformer A *social activist* who seeks to bring about changes in institutional structures or human behavior.

reform movement A coordinated social or political activity to bring about changes in existing institutions or government structure. Usually such movements are formed to eliminate *corruption* or unethical business practices.

reform school See *reformatory.*

reframing A technique used by family therapists to help families understand a symptom or pattern of behavior by seeing it in a different context. For example, a family might see a child diagnosed as depressed as being disrespectful and detached from them. Reframing changes the understanding of the problem from an individual's illness to a family problem.

refugee One who seeks safety or protection from previously experienced dangers, such as immigrants to the United States who have sought to escape religious, ethnic, or political persecution in their native lands. Such people often become the clients of social workers, and the workers are often called on to find the resources to help in their protection. See also *United Nations High Commissioner for Refugees (UNHCR)*.

Refugee Assistance program The federal program administered by the *Family Services Administration (FSA)* of the U.S. *Department of Health and Human Services (HHS)* to provide funds and assistance to immigrants to the United States.

regional planning The process, usually sponsored by a group of local or adjacent state governments, by which goals for a geographic area are specified and the means and timetables for achieving them are delineated.

registered nurse (RN) A *professional* who practices the science of providing continuous care for people who are ill and facilitates the health and well-being of individuals, groups, and communities. Nurses have successfully completed extensive training in professional schools of nursing and are registered as being skilled in the performance of specific *health care* services. Many nurses become specialists, working with psychiatric patients, newborn infants, and maternity patients; specializing in emergency room care; or providing skilled assistance to surgeons. There are several routes to becoming a registered nurse: a four-year baccalaureate program in a university; a two-year associate degree program in a community college; and a two- or three-year diploma from a degree-granting hospital program. Increasingly, as the need for

greater knowledge and skills becomes essential, more RNs come from the four-year baccalaureate route. See also *practical nurse (PN)* and *nurse practitioner.*

registration of social workers An organization's or government's listing (or registry) of people who identify themselves or are identified as *social workers*. This is a form of *quality assurance* and sometimes public regulation that has a minimal degree of regulatory power (compared to *licensing* and *certification*). The organization usually specifies some qualification criteria to permit a worker to be included in the registration. For example, in the *NASW Registry of Clinical Social Workers* the applicant for registration must pay a fee, have a master's or doctoral degree from an accredited school of social work, have two years or 1,500 hours of post-master's professionally supervised *clinical social work* practice, and be a member of the *Academy of Certified Social Workers (ACSW)* or be licensed or certified in a state that requires an examination.

regression Behaviors and thought patterns that indicate a return to earlier or more-primitive levels of development. This phenomenon is often seen in people who are exposed to severe stress, trauma, or conflicts that go unresolved.

regression analysis In *social research,* a statistical technique for assessing the contribution of one or more independent variables in predicting the outcome of a *dependent variable.* See also *independent variable.*

regressive tax A government's revenue-collecting system in which less-affluent people pay an equal or higher percentage of their taxable incomes than do more-affluent people. For example, a person with a taxable income of $20,000 pays 20 percent of that amount for taxes, and someone earning $100,000 pays 15 percent tax on his or her income. See also *progressive tax.*

rehabilitation Restoring to a healthy condition or useful capacity to the extent possible. Social workers usually use this term in the context of helping people who have been impaired through injury, *disease*, or *dysfunction*. This process of helping occurs in hospitals, social agencies, clinics, schools, prisons, and many other settings and may include physical therapy, *psychotherapy*, exercise, training, and lifestyle changes. See also *habilitation*.

reinforcement In *behavior modification*, a procedure that strengthens the tendency of a *response* to recur. If a reinforcer is arranged to follow a *behavior*, there is increased probability that the behavior will be repeated. Similarly, if performance of a response removes an aversive event, there is increased probability that the behavior will be repeated.

rejection Refusal to grant, acknowledge, or recognize something or someone. Individuals may experience rejection when their ideas, presence, or requests are not accepted by a *relevant other*. Social workers find that some of their clients with low *self-esteem* or poor self-confidence believe they are experiencing rejection when being ignored or not being given what they want.

relabeling A technique used by family therapists to make a family problem more amenable to treatment by defining a *symptom*. By considering the problem from an alternative perspective, the family members may change the way they understand the symptom or *behavior* and begin to respond to it in a different, often healthier way.

relapse The recurrence of symptoms that had been removed in the course of *therapy* or some other helping *intervention*.

relationship In social work, the mutual emotional exchange; dynamic interaction; and affective, cognitive, and behavioral connection that exist between the social worker and the client to create the working and helping atmosphere. Social workers such as Felix Biestek (*The Casework Relationship*, Chicago: Loyola University Press, 1957) have found that it is created through adherence to certain ethical behaviors, including *acceptance, confidentiality, individualization*, and *nonjudgmental* view of the client, as well as permitting the client

ultimate *self-determination, purposeful expression of feelings*, and controlled emotional involvement. The term "relationship" was first described for social workers by *Virginia Robinson* (*A Changing Psychology in Social Casework*, Chapel Hill: University of North Carolina Press, 1930).

relative confidentiality A position held by some social workers and other professionals that, under certain circumstances, they may ethically disclose information about a client. The circumstances include putting the information in records and computers for review, but only by colleagues who are involved in the case; audio or video taping of sessions, but letting tapes be reviewed by others only with client consent; providing information to legal and law enforcement officials in conformity with relevant regulations; or when *privileged communication* has been waived by the client. See also *absolute confidentiality* and *Tarasoff*.

relative needs The requirements for an acceptable level of well-being as compared to the resources available to enable people to achieve these requirements. This term is often used in reference to apparent gaps between needs and services or between equity of services available to different groups of people in need. See also *normative needs, expressed needs*, and *perceived needs*.

relative poverty Assets and income that are so little the person or group cannot maintain a *standard of living* in accordance with the standards of the mainstream community. For example a family living in *public housing* on *Aid to Families with Dependent Children (AFDC)* may be considered poor in relation to other U.S. citizens, but not so poor in comparison with malnourished, homeless people in a *Fourth World* nation. See also *absolute poverty*.

relatives' responsibility Laws and moral codes that compel specified members of the *family* to care for or pay for the care of another family member who is in need. The legal requirements in this area vary widely from state to state. All states have such laws pertaining to the care of minor children. Most states have eliminated or relaxed their laws requiring a person to care for parents, siblings, or more distant relatives, although a few have recently activated or enforced them. See also *parental liability.*

relevant other In *role theory,* the individual who makes the expectation that defines the role. For example, the relevant other of a wife is the husband; of a mother, the child; of a client, the social worker. This term is often incorrectly confused with *significant other.* Although it can include others who are emotionally significant, it also includes others who are generally insignificant but important in a single context (such as a grocery store cashier when one is in a checkout line).

reliability 1. In *psychosocial assessment,* the individual's degree of dependability and consistency. 2. In *social research,* the dependability and consistency of scores on a test that is repeated over time with the same group. Researchers use three types of reliability: (1) *test–retest reliability, (2)* split-half reliability (the correlation between the scores achieved by a group of subjects in one part of a test and the group's scores on another similar part of the same test), and (3) *interrater reliability.*

relief A historical term referring to money, goods, or services provided to needy people by government or private philanthropic agencies.

relocation camps Temporary living facilities for groups of people who are compelled to or choose to move. Such camps usually are established by governments, with the assistance of private organizations and volunteers, to help people become reestablished in a new area. These people often are displaced from their previous homes by war, famine, natural disaster, or political and economic conditions. Some are involuntarily held in such facilities because they are considered too dangerous to be assimilated into the new country. See also *internment* and *sociocultural dislocation.*

remarried family See *reconstituted family.*

remedial goals model In *group work* and therapy group conceptions, the group objective of bringing about change within individual members who experience problems. Also known as the "treatment goals model," the group goal in this case is to help each member achieve more-effective social functioning and to help at-risk members prevent problems. This group goal is most commonly seen in *group psychotherapy* programs. See also *reciprocal goals model* and *social goals model.*

remediation The elimination or reduction of an existing problem or its effects.

reminiscence therapy A treatment procedure used primarily for older people, especially in *existential social work* therapy and *logotherapy,* in which the client remembers and describes life events to the professional and sometimes to others in a group setting. Presenting this material enables the client to achieve greater insight and recognize the meaningfulness of life.

remission Cessation or abatement of the symptoms of a physical or mental disease.

renal disease Malfunction of the kidneys.

rental vouchers A part of the *Section 8 Housing* program, enacted permanently in 1988, to help needy and eligible people get into private housing. The vouchers help the client pay part or all the costs of renting a private apartment or house.

rent control A government's regulation of the amount of money tenants are required to pay landlords and of the conditions under which evictions may occur, and the general overseeing of relationships between landlords and tenants.

Renticare A provision in the Housing Act of 1964 (P.L. 88-560) authorizing rent subsidies for poor people. Even though the legislation passed, Congress never granted the funds. Renticare was replaced by the *rental vouchers* part of the *Section 8 Housing* program.

rent strike A strategy, often used in *community organization,* in which tenants withhold rent payments to pressure their landlords into improving the conditions of their housing.

reparation 1. Compensation by a country or political entity defeated in war for the damages caused. 2. The legal procedure whereby money, property, or services are given by one person to another for damages in a crime or civil action (for example, *restitution*).

repatriation The act of voluntarily returning or being sent back to one's country of birth or citizenship. This is the preferred outcome in most *refugee* situations because the person returns to a familiar *culture* and *social networks,* but often repatriation is impossible because of potential persecution by the country's government.

repetitive checking behaviors A pattern of self-reassurance activity in which one frequently returns to a former setting to be sure all is well. The behavior is only considered a symptom of *anxiety* or *obsessive–compulsive disorder* when it is particularly time-consuming or interfering with *activities of daily living (ADL).*

replacement cost The amount of money, work, or services that must be provided to maintain the status quo if and when some loss occurs. In management and budgeting, it is often less important to calculate the current value of something that has been lost than to calculate the amount needed to get back its equivalent.

replication In *research,* the process of duplicating an experiment—in which the same *hypothesis,* variables, sampling procedure, testing instruments, and techniques for analysis are used—with a different *sample* of the same *population.*

repossession The legal process of seizing a debtor's property and holding it or selling it to recover the funds owed. To repossess, the creditor files a complaint with the legal authorities, and fair hearings and opportunities are given to the debtor to make *restitution* and recover the property. Otherwise, the creditor may proceed with a sale after informing the debtor and potential buyers about the sale.

representativeness A concept in *social research* pertaining to the extent to which the information gathered is unbiased and typical of the entity from which the information was extracted.

repression A *defense mechanism,* derived from *psychodynamic* theory, in which the individual unconsciously pushes out of the consciousness certain memories, ideas, or desires that are unacceptable or cause a high level of *anxiety.* Once these ideas or desires are contained in the *unconscious,* they cannot be recalled directly. However, they may emerge in one's *behavior* in disguised forms, and their effects are sometimes seen in slips of the tongue *(parapraxis)* or dreams. Because repression is, by definition, a mechanism of the unconscious, it should not be confused with the *conscious* act of *suppression.*

reproductive technology Medically supervised systems of artificially facilitating a fetus's *conception* and development through to birth. These technologies include *artificial insemination, surrogacy, in vitro fertilization,* and embryo freezing.

rescission Cancellation of the funds and budget authorizations that had previously been allocated.

research Systematic procedures used in seeking facts or principles.

resettlement The act of moving and establishing a new, permanent residence in another area.

residency laws Statutes that specify what qualifications must be fulfilled before an individual can be considered eligible for the privileges and obligations of that jurisdiction. For example, a person must live in a state for a specified time before becoming eligible to receive lower public college tuition rates or being able to obtain a divorce in that state. Residency laws that restricted eligibility for certain types of social services have been relaxed in recent years. For example, the U.S. Supreme Court ruled in 1969 (in *Shapiro v. Thompson*) that under usual circumstances, residency laws eliminating *public assistance* were unconstitutional.

residential care facilities Structures that house people who are without homes or who, for a variety of reasons, cannot stay in their homes. These facilities include boarding schools, *shelters* for abused women, *orphanages,* homes for juvenile delinquents, and centers where *residential treatment* occurs.

residential treatment   Therapeutic intervention processes for people who cannot or do not function satisfactorily in their own homes. Such treatment typically occurs in certain environments such as private schools, medical centers, penal institutions, and *shelters*. It usually includes a variety of professionally led assistance, such as individual or group psychotherapy, formal schooling, social skills training, recreation, and fulfillment of the needs usually met in one's home.

residual phase   The stage often found in the *progression* of various mental illnesses when the symptoms have ceased or diminished considerably.

residual schizophrenia   One of the five subtypes of *schizophrenia* (also including *paranoid, disorganized, catatonic,* and *undifferentiated*), in which there has been at least one episode of schizophrenia but the current clinical picture is without prominent psychotic symptoms. There is an absence of prominent delusions, hallucinations, and disorganized or catatonic behaviors found in the other subtypes, but the other major symptoms of schizophrenia such as thought disorder and flat or inappropriate affect are present. If these symptoms have occurred for less than six months the diagnosis would be *schizophreniform disorder.*

residual versus institutional model   The dichotomy described by H. L. Wilensky and C. N. Lebeaux (*Industrial Society and Social Welfare,* New York: Free Press, 1958) comprising two concepts of *social welfare.* The residual model views social welfare as being primarily a *safety net* function in which programs are temporary substitutes for the failures of individuals and institutions. The institutional model views social welfare as having a "main line" function (equal to the other social institutions, such

as family, religion, economics, and politics) in which programs are permanent and provide for the overall security and emotional support of humans.

residual welfare provision   The idea that the public should provide *social services* and *public assistance* only to those people who, because of unusual circumstances, are unable to receive needed help through the family or the normal social structure and marketplace. See also *safety net.*

resilience   The ability to recover, spring back, or return to previous circumstances after encountering problems or stresses. This is a factor that social workers consider in assessing their clients and in developing prognoses and treatment plans.

resistance   1. *Avoidance* behavior used by a client to defend against the influences of the social worker. 2. In *psychoanalytic theory,* the mental process of preventing one's *unconscious* thoughts from being brought into the consciousness. Resistance may be *conscious* or unconscious, and the client uses it for protection against self-realization. It is an inevitable facet of therapy.

resistant attachment   A form of *insecure attachment* seen in children who seem angry at their *caregivers* after any separation but obstruct the caregivers' efforts to provide reassurance and comfort. See also *attachment, secure attachment,* and *avoidant attachment.*

resocialization   Preparing someone to enter and live in a *culture* and environment that is or has become unfamiliar because of crises, trauma, or life-stage transition. For example, an immigrant becomes resocialized into a new culture partly by learning the new language, or a recently divorced woman reenters the job market after learning the new *norms.*

resocialization group   A type of *group therapy* or *self-help group* that helps people adapt to unfamiliar roles and statuses. Such groups exist for people like *displaced homemakers,* recently widowed or divorced people, people who become physically disabled, and adults who must care for their elderly parents.

resolution 1. A formal statement made by the members of an organization, usually after a vote, to express their sentiments, goals, or intentions to the public or to office holders. 2. The outcome or conclusion of an event, as in the solving of a client's problem.

resource allocation The distribution of goods and services based on systematic decision making and predetermined criteria.

resource mobilization In *social agency* administration, the process of bringing together and making available the organization's assets including existing funds, funds to be raised from the constituency and other sources, information base, personnel and volunteers, and the knowledge and talents of board members and others who can be called on for assistance. This process depends on the organization's making clear its needs and mission, identifying the population to be served, and communicating this information to the public.

resources Any existing service or commodity that can be called on to help take care of a need. A primary skill of social workers is their ability to know of and use the existing resources of a *community* that can help their clients. Resources used by social workers typically include other social agencies, government programs, other *professional* or *volunteer* personnel, *self-help groups,* natural helpers, and individuals in the community who possess the qualities and motivations that can help the client.

resource systems The biopsychosocial and environmental sources of the material, emotional, and spiritual *needs* required for a person to survive, to realize aspirations, and to cope with life tasks. The three types of resource systems are (1) the informal type (family, friends, and neighbors), (2) the formal type (membership organizations, such as the *National Association of Social Workers [NASW],* and *labor unions*), and (3) the societal type (social security programs and educational and health care systems). A basic purpose of *social work practice* is to enhance the functioning of these resource systems and their linkages with people. See also *networking.*

respiratory distress syndrome (RDS) A common, sometimes fatal, disease mostly affecting newborns (especially premature infants). Treatment includes concentrations of oxygen, intravenous fluids, and sometimes mechanical breathing apparatus to keep lungs from collapsing.

respite care The temporary assumption of responsibilities of a person who provides for the *home care* of another. For example, the parents of an adult child with mental retardation are relieved every few weeks by someone who comes to their home to help, or the child goes to a facility for a few days. The goal is to give the caretaker a break from the responsibility so that tensions are minimized, so the caretaker can have some other interests or take care of personal crises, and so the client can stay out of institutional care.

"respondeat superior" doctrine The legal *liability* of employers or supervisors for the job-related actions of the employees. The term is Latin for "let the superior answer" and has the effect of requiring supervisors to monitor their workers. Social work supervisors have been held liable, along with their supervisees, for practices found to be damaging to clients.

respondent behavior *Behavior* that is elicited by specific stimuli and subject to the principles of *respondent conditioning.*

respondent conditioning The procedure in *behavior modification* in which a *stimulus* (such as food) that automatically results in a *response* (such as salivation) is presented repeatedly along with a neutral stimulus (such as a ringing bell) to elicit essentially the same response from the previously neutral stimulus. This term is a synonym for *classical conditioning* (or Pavlovian conditioning).

response A *behavior.* Usually the term is used to indicate a discrete form of behavior such as a knee jerk, salivation, or a pressing of a key, but the term also applies to broadly defined behaviors such as bringing home flowers for one's spouse or expressing anger to the social worker after being turned down in a request for assistance.

response prevention A procedure commonly used in *behavior therapy* to eliminate a *maladaptive* behavior by distraction, persuasion, or redirection of activity whenever the behavior is anticipated. Often the procedure requires hospitalization or a controlled environment and participation by family members to be effective.

response repertoire The accumulation of knowledge and skills that a person has learned and can perform effectively, comfortably, and without trial-and-error behavior.

restitution The restoration of property or rights that had previously been taken away. People who have committed theft or property destruction are sometimes compelled to provide restitution to those they victimized. See also *victim compensation.*

restitution center A small residential facility where convicted felons live while engaged in community service work or other employment. The residents' incomes are budgeted and allocated in such a way that living expenses are met and remaining funds are withheld to help compensate the victims.

restraining order A temporary decree, made by a judge or other legal authority without a prior hearing, prohibiting an individual or organization from performing some action pending an outcome of a trial or hearing. See also *injunction.*

restricted funds Monetary or other gifts or grants and the income generated by them, which may be expended only for purposes specified by the donor or grantor.

restricted affect Diminished variability and intensity with which emotions are expressed.

retardation 1. The slowing of an individual's physical or mental development or social progress. 2. A significantly lower-than-average capacity for intellectual functioning *(mental retardation)* or a slowing of physical and emotional reactions *(psychomotor* retardation).

Retired Senior Volunteer Program (RSVP) A national organization that uses the talents and knowledge of retired people by placing volunteers in a variety of settings such as hospitals, schools, and senior centers, often on a short-term basis. See also *Senior Companion Program* and *Foster Grandparents.*

retirement A state of withdrawal from regular employment or certain forms of work activity. Some employers encourage older or disabled workers to retire by providing a *pension* or lump-sum retirement compensation if they leave by a certain time. Many workers who have inadequate retirement benefits find they cannot retire or, if required to do so, find they need financial assistance. See also *social security.*

retrenchment Cutting back, as in reducing the agency's expenditures or services to a previous and reduced level. See also *cutback strategies.*

retribution The dispensing of *punishment* for wrongdoing. The term can also refer to future rewards for good works.

retrograde amnesia The inability to recall experiences that have occurred only before a certain time, usually before some physical injury or psychic stress. See also *amnesia.*

retrospective data Information collected through indirect means such as rekindling subjects' memories, reviewing records, comparing the study findings from previous eras with contemporary results, and reevaluating current information from different perspectives.

Rett's disorder One of the *pervasive developmental disorders* in which, following a few months of normal development and functioning after birth, the child (usually female) declines. There is deceleration of head growth, loss of previously acquired motor skills, and severely impaired language development. The disorder begins before age four and in most cases recovery is limited. See also *autistic disorder.*

reunification service Interventions by social workers and others in *foster care* to help children and their *birth parents* develop mutual relationships to facilitate being able to live together again. After the problems that led to the separations are resolved or improved, the workers often act as go-betweens to restore lines of communication. Then they may act as facilitators of face-to-face communication and finally as monitors and consultants in followup after the reunion has taken place.

revenue sharing   The government process of dividing a proportion of its income, which comes from taxes, and contributing those funds to another level or sector of government that provides needed services to the people. For example, the federal government contributes money to state governments so that they can provide *Aid to Families with Dependent Children (AFDC)* benefits. See also *apportioned tax.*

"reverse discrimination"   The term sometimes used to describe the preferential treatment of a previously victimized *minority* group or person to the disadvantage of the majority. Generally, the practice has been used to withhold opportunities from white people and men to give more opportunities to people of color and women. See also *affirmative action.*

revolution   A sweeping change in the established order of things, usually after those who preferred the status quo are forced to relinquish their authority to those who sought change. Major types of revolution include political (in which a civil war or protest movement results in a new government structure), industrial (in which technology and invention change the way economic institutions are administered), and cultural (in which changes occur in *values, norms, mores,* and tastes).

revolving credit system   A capital acquisition system funded through the savings of individuals and groups from the same ethnic or kinship group and dispersed to those in the group for use in starting businesses, getting education, or overcoming emergencies. Once the borrower has started the business or used the funds in the way specified, the money is repaid to the system for use by another member of the group

for a similar purpose. This system has been most effective in those close-knit groups where failure to reimburse would be unthinkable.

rheumatic fever   An *infectious disease* whose symptoms often include inflammation of the joints, fever, nosebleeds, and skin rash. In its more serious forms, there is inflammation of the heart valves, which may become scarred and deformed (rheumatic heart disease). Penicillin and extended rest are used in treating rheumatic fever. Maintenance doses of penicillin, often for several years, are sometimes given to children to prevent a recurrence of the fever, especially to prevent rheumatic heart disease.

rheumatoid arthritis   A form of *arthritis* that affects the joints and sometimes the lungs, nervous system, and other parts of the body. This disorder can affect the young as well as older people and is often extremely painful.

Ribicoff children   People younger than 21 who meet *Aid to Families with Dependent Children (AFDC)* income and resource requirements but who are not considered dependent children. Such children can be considered *categorically needy* and thus eligible for some *Medicaid, Supplemental Security Income (SSI)*, AFDC, or other benefits. The name refers to Senator Abraham Ribicoff, who initiated legislation that made these young people eligible.

Richmond, Mary E. (1861–1928)   Considered one of the principal founders of professional social work, Richmond led the *Charity Organization Societies (COS)* movement to develop schools to train social caseworkers. She taught volunteers and paid employees in various settings and developed some of the first teaching programs for social work. Her books were among the first to be used in training for social work. They included *Friendly Visiting Among the Poor* (1899), *Social Diagnosis* (1917), and *What is Social Case Work?* (1922).

rickets   A bone disease caused by vitamin D deficiency. In children, the disease's symptoms include softening of the bones, enlargement of the cartilage, bowleggedness, and deformities in the chest and pelvis. With the addition of vitamin D to milk and the use of vitamin supplements, prevention of rickets has been effective in the United States.

rights 1. The obligations of society to each of its members. 2. That which is legally or morally due to an individual by just claim. These are more specifically identified as *civil rights, equal rights,* and *human rights.*

Rights of the Child Convention The proposed United Nations resolution that calls for worldwide protections against child labor exploitation, opportunities for educational and social development, freedom from discrimination, inadequate nutrition and standard of living, and the right to live with one's family.

right-to-die Opposition to artificial life-support and extreme treatment measures to prolong the life of one who is incurably ill.

right-to-life movement A loosely coordinated body of groups, institutions, and individuals working to change laws and norms that permit and facilitate *abortion.* The movement is also referred to as the "prolife movement." Supporters of this movement emphasize the rights of the unborn embryo/fetus and encourage *adoption* and other alternatives to abortion for unwanted pregnancies. Religious and philosophical beliefs about the point at which human life begins are important in this movement. The movement is opposed by the *prochoice movement.* See also *National Right-to-Life Committee (NRLC).*

right to refuse treatment The legal principle, upheld in numerous court cases or contained in explicit statutes in several states, that an individual may not be compelled to undergo any form of *treatment,* including social work *intervention,* unless there is a life-threatening emergency or the person exhibits seriously destructive behavior. This principle has been applied to people who are involuntarily committed to men-

tal hospitals, prisons, and other institutions. It has also influenced the way social work services are integrated with *income maintenance* programs in *public assistance* programs. Thus, a public assistance recipient is no longer compelled to receive counseling to obtain financial aid.

right to treatment The legal principle, established in the *Wyatt v. Stickney* decision, that an individual who is confined in an institution has the right to receive the *treatment* necessary to offer a reasonable chance for improvement so that the person can function independently and be released from that institution. This right has led many facilities that lack the resources for individual treatment to discharge their clients. See also *deinstitutionalization.*

right-to-work laws Statutes in various jurisdictions that make it illegal for membership in a *labor union* to be a condition of *employment.*

"right wing" A slang expression for a conservative sociopolitical orientation. The term originated in the British Parliament where liberals sat on the left of the aisle and the conservatives sat on the right.

Riis, Jacob (1848–1914) Writer and social reformer, whose descriptions of slum conditions awakened America to the need for economic reforms and better assistance for poor people. His most influential book, *How the Other Half Lives* (1890), led to widespread support for the *Charity Organization Societies (COS)* movement, which in turn helped develop social work as a profession.

risk pool All the individuals and families an insurance company is obligated to cover against the financial consequences of a specified problem. In the climate of competition among insurance companies, the tendency is to make these pools highly restrictive, limited only to the youngest, most healthy people. This eliminates coverage for those most likely in need and ultimately places the financial burden on the general taxpayer population. When risk pools are larger and more inclusive, the cost burden for those at greater risk is reduced but it is usually increased for those less at risk.

rite of passage A formal or informal activity, ceremony, or *behavior* that a group uses to recognize the movement of one of its members into another *role* or set of expectations. Examples include graduation ceremonies, bar mitzvahs, retirement parties, and mothers helping their daughters apply makeup for the first time. See also *puberty rites.*

robbery The *crime* of forceable stealing. Robbery differs from theft in that it occurs through direct *violence* or intimidation.

Robinson, Virginia (1883–1977) Social work theoretician and educator at the University of Pennsylvania, Robinson wrote the influential textbook *A Changing Psychology in Social Casework* in 1930 and developed important texts on supervision and training. With her long time partner *Jessie Taft,* she developed the *functional school in social work* and influenced social work's movement toward a more *intrapsychic* orientation.

Robison, Sophie Moses (1888–1969) Social work researcher and activist, whose studies in *juvenile delinquency* led to redefinitions about how the problems can be addressed. Her works became models for social work research.

Roe v. Wade The 1973 decision by the U.S. Supreme Court that state laws forbidding *abortion* were unconstitutional under specified circumstances. The Court held that, in the first *trimester,* abortion must be left to medical judgment. In the second trimester, the state may, if it chooses, regulate abortion to protect maternal health but may not prohibit abortion. In the third trimester, the state may regulate or prohibit abortion except when necessary to preserve the mother's life. The decision has been the source of considerable controversy, and there have been numerous challenges in the courts. *Political action* in support of the decision is led by the *prochoice movement* and the opposition is led by the *right-to-life movement.*

role 1. A culturally determined pattern of *behavior* that is prescribed for an individual who occupies a specific *status.* 2. A social *norm* that is attached to a given social position that dictates reciprocal action. For example, a person who occupies the status of "social worker" is expected by others— that is, clients, supervisors, the profession, the general public, and so on—to behave in the manner generally prescribed for all social workers.

role ambiguity A situation in which the expectations of a *role* are unclear or diffuse either to the person enacting it or to the *relevant other.* For example, a new client goes to a social worker but is not sure what social workers do to help and thus does not know quite what to expect from the meeting.

role boundary The dividing line that distinguishes one's *role* from all other roles. For example, there are specific and normative expectations of one who occupies the status of social worker, and the worker who meets those expectations but does not go beyond them is behaving within the boundary. But workers who develop *dual relationships* with clients go beyond the professional boundary. Role boundaries are most commonly violated in situations of *role ambiguity,* often resulting in problems of *role conflict* or *role discomplementarity.* See also *enmeshed family.*

role complementarity See *complementarity.*

role conflict The experience of one who occupies two or more social positions that carry incompatible expectations. For example, a social worker may be expected by the client to be immediately available during times of crisis but is expected by the supervisor to see clients only according to a predetermined schedule.

role discomplementarity The condition that exists when an individual's various *roles* are inconsistent with one another or with the expectations held by a *relevant other.* For example, the client and the supervisor have certain expectations of the social worker but have not made clear what those expectations are, so they cannot be fulfilled. Social scientists identify five conditions in which role discomplementarity occurs: (1) cognitive discrepancy, which is based on a lack of knowledge of what the appropriate expectations are (for example, the social worker or client does not know what the other expects and thus cannot fulfill those expectations); (2) status discrepancy, in which one person expects another to fulfill expectations that are inappropriate to that person's social position (for example, the client expects the social worker to provide medical information); (3) allocative discrepancy, in which one person does not choose to accept responsibility for fulfilling the other's expectations even though he or she is capable of doing so (for example, the client wants the social worker to treat the whole family, and the worker wants to work only with the individual); (4) discrepancy of value orientations, in which those who have expectations of one another have incompatible values (for example, the client expects the social worker to help her end her marriage, and the worker expects to help save the marriage); and (5) absence of instrumental means, in which the reciprocal expectations are compatible but the people lack the tools necessary to carry them out (for example, the client and social worker both want the welfare department to increase the financial supports to the family, but there is not enough money to do this).

role model One whose conduct, accomplishments, personality, or social position serves as a standard for emulation by others. The standard may be socially beneficial (for example, a basketball star who shows young people how to avoid drugs) or not (for example, a wealthy and charismatic figure who is a crime boss).

role modeling Purposeful demonstration of behaviors that one wants others to emulate. This demonstration is often done in *social group work, group psychotherapy, counseling,* and various educational programs to assist a client in learning more-effective ways to achieve desirable goals.

role playing 1. A rehearsal of behaviors that can be useful in a subsequent situa-

tion to fulfill some expectation or achieve some goal. 2. A reexperiencing of the past as one imagines being another person (a parent, a sibling, and so on); a technique to elicit self-awareness and understanding of others. Social workers often help their clients rehearse for real situations. For example, a social worker asks a client to pretend she is going to ask her boss for a raise to make it easier for the client to actually confront her boss. Role playing is a technique developed in the 1920s by J. L. Moreno in his *psychodrama* method of therapy and is now used in various *group work, social group work,* teaching, *group therapy* systems, game analysis, and leadership training programs to help individuals test certain behaviors and receive immediate feedback about approaches to the situation.

role reequilibration The process that takes place between two or more people to end *role conflict* or *role discomplementarity.* Usually this is achieved by clarifying mutual expectations.

role reversal A situation in which one person changes behaviors and begins to act in a way that is expected of another person. For example, a father might begin to act childishly around his son, who in turn acts with more maturity around his father.

role strain Any form of *role conflict, role discomplementarity,* or social relationship difficulty that prohibits or limits the enacting of a *role* in a stress-free manner. This can arise from *role ambiguity,* role conflict, role discomplementarity, or lack of access to information necessary for the role.

role theory A group of concepts, based on sociocultural and anthropological investigations, which pertain to the way people are influenced in their behaviors by the variety of social positions they hold and the expectations that accompany those positions. See also the related terms used in this dictionary, including all those beginning with *role,* as well as the terms *status, norms,* and *sanctions.*

role vigor The relative degree of deviation from a role's expectations permitted by the culture. For example, more role vigor is permitted for women in large, pluralistic urban areas than in small towns.

rootwork A *culture-bound syndrome* found most commonly among Caribbean societies and people of the southern United States of European and African ancestry in which the individual is believed to be placed under a spell or hex. This results in the individual experiencing anxiety, fears, dizziness, and various somatic complaints until the "root doctor" removes the hex or root.

Rorschach test A *projective test,* designed in 1921 by Swiss psychiatrist Hermann Rorschach (1884–1922), in which clients are given a series of 10 standardized inkblots and asked to report what they see. Responses can indicate personality traits, interests, thought processes, and so forth.

RSVP See *Retired Senior Volunteer Program (RSVP).*

rubber-fence concept A *metaphor* used in *family therapy* to describe how some families maintain *boundaries* between themselves and others. A boundary may seem to stretch to incorporate what is seen as positive and to contract when apparently threatened. For example, if a social worker makes suggestions to such a family, the members might appear to expand in incorporating the new ideas into the family dynamics but would later contract to their original configuration.

rubella A short-term, mild form of measles, also called German measles or three-day measles. Although rarely fatal to children or adults, this disease is particularly dangerous to the *fetus* of an infected pregnant woman and can result in miscarriage or a variety of *congenital* conditions.

Rubinow, Isaac Max (1875–1936) Economist and social work educator who helped draft legislation leading to the *Social Security Act* of 1935. He helped found the *Anti-Defamation League of B'nai B'rith* and was editor of the *Jewish Social Service Quarterly.*

rugged individualism The *ideology* espoused by certain economists, politicians, and others that people should be left to their own initiative in providing for their needs. According to this view, even though difficulties might be experienced, it strengthens peoples' character and capacity to cope more effectively with any other problems that might be faced in the future.

rumination disorder One of the *eating disorders* in some infants and young children, characterized by repeated regurgitation, in which the infant loses weight or fails to gain weight and may develop nutritional deficiencies. The cause of this condition is not understood, but it is not the result of gastrointestinal illness or nausea.

runaway A minor who has departed the home of his or her parents or legal guardians contrary to their wishes and who intends to remain independent of their control. The federal government maintains a national runaway *hotline* to help these youngsters and possibly reunite them with their parents. See also *Nineline.*

ruralite A person who resides in a nonmetropolitan area, often the client of *rural social work.*

rural social movement Efforts and organizations that raise the consciousness of citizens and professionals about the problems of rural areas and advocate legislation to correct rural social problems. The movement grew in the 1970s and is now active in forging coalitions with the grass-roots community. Some of the rural advocacy organizations include Rural America, the Rural Social Work Caucus, and the National Association for Rural Mental Health.

rural social work Social work practice oriented to helping people who have unique problems and needs arising out of living in agricultural nonmetropolitan or sparsely populated areas or small towns. These people face many of the same problems and needs as do urban clients; in addition, however, they often encounter difficulties because of limited services and *resource systems,* less acceptance of any variations from the social norms prevalent in the area, and fewer educational and economic opportunities.

rural social workers Professional social workers whose predominant clientele and practice activities are in sparsely populated regions. The most successful workers in these settings are well-trained, creative professionals who can work in relative isolation with limited additional resources.

Russell Sage Foundation A philanthropic organization, founded in 1907 by *Margaret Slocum Sage* (1816–1918), the widow of entrepreneur Russell Sage, for the improvement of social and living conditions in the United States. The foundation's financing of systematic research in social service programs and of the development of social agencies contributed significantly to the professionalization of social work. Information made available through the foundation was used in the training of *friendly visitors.*

Ryan White Comprehensive AIDS Resources Emergency Act of 1990 Legislation (P.L. 101-381) named for the young AIDS victim that provides federal funds to cities and states for planning, implementing, and evaluating programs to prevent transmission of *human immunodeficiency virus (HIV)* and to improve the quality and availability of health care social services for people affected by HIV and *acquired immune deficiency syndrome (AIDS).*

S

sabotage Purposefully causing damage to institutions, manufacturing facilities, or social procedures to achieve a sociopolitical objective. See also *insurgency* and *ecotage*.

SAD See *seasonal affective disorder (SAD)*.

sadistic Deriving pleasure from inflicting or causing pain to others.

sadistic personality disorder A diagnostic term used by some mental health professionals to describe a type of *personality disorder* in which a person frequently seeks opportunities to impose mental or physical cruelty on one or more other persons.

sadomasochism The presence, within an individual or between couples, of cruel, punishing behavior and behavior that is self-destructive. For example, in a sadomasochistic relationship, one person would persist in cruel behavior to the other, and the other would remain in the relationship and encourage more of the cruelty. See also *masochism, masochistic personality disorder,* and *folie à deux*.

safety net The idea that if some social service programs are eliminated through economic cutbacks, benefits and programs of last resort will remain in case individuals or families cannot find needed *resources* on their own. See also *residual welfare provision*.

Sage, Margaret Slocum (1816–1918) Philanthropist and creator of the *Russell Sage Foundation* to improve the social and living conditions in the United States. Widow of Russell Sage, her creation helped to fund the early organizations, conferences, and publications that became the knowledge base of the new field of social work.

Salvation Army An international religious service organization involved in philanthropic and evangelical work. Founded in England in 1878 by William Booth, it is patterned after military structures, including uniforms and military rank, because its goal is to wage war against evil and human suffering. It has programs in nearly 100 nations, with its international headquarters in London. It operates hospitals, community centers, social work agencies, alcohol and drug *rehabilitation* centers, emergency care facilities, *disaster relief* services, and the well-known *soup kitchen*.

sample In *research,* a part of a *universe* from which a representative selection is made. Researchers want to use the largest sample possible because the larger the sample, the smaller the likelihood of error or deviation from the universe or *population*. Larger samples give the principle of randomness a better chance to work. See also *random sample* and *stratified sample*.

sampling error Generalizing about the characteristics of a population from a *sample* that is not totally representative.

sanction 1. Permission to carry out or official ratification of some plan granted by the established authority. 2. A provision in law or a response by a *reference group* that penalizes an individual for not conforming. For example, social workers who are found to have violated their professional *code of ethics* may be subject to sanctions in the form of suspension from the organization or of the license to practice. See *professional association (PA)*.

sanctuary   A place of refuge or protection.

sandwich generation   Men and especially women in their middle years who have the major caregiving responsibilities for their children and parents. This generation is growing dramatically because of the prolonged life spans of older people who tend to need increasing care and because of the trend among younger people to stay with their parents longer.

sangue dormido   A *culture-bound syndrome* most commonly found in people of Portuguese ancestry in which the individual experiences pain, convulsions, *tremor, stroke,* blindness, heart attack, infection, and miscarriage. The term means "sleeping blood."

Sanitary Commission, U.S.   The health and welfare agency set up during the U.S. Civil War to manage the welfare of Union soldiers and their families. Managed almost entirely by volunteer women, the agency established and maintained hospitals, supplied food, and raised money for destitute family members.

Sansei generation   Third-generation Americans of Japanese ancestry, born primarily after World War II, the offspring of the *Nisei generation.* Members of the Sansei generation are integrated into American society and tend to adopt cultural values of mainstream America more than those of their Japanese ancestors.

sarcoma   One of the four major types of *cancer* (including *carcinoma, leukemia,* and *lymphoma)* characterized by spread of the disease into the bones, fat, or cartilage.)

SASG   See *sexual assault survivor group (SASG).*

Satir, Virginia (1920–1987)   A major theoretician and educator in *family therapy,* she developed many of the innovative communications concepts of the field. She wrote the highly influential books *Conjoint Family Therapy* (Palo Alto, CA: Science and Behavior Books, 1964) and *Peoplemaking* (Palo Alto, CA: Science and Behavior Books, 1972) and led countless workshops to instruct social workers and others in the theory and practice of family therapy.

satisficing   A term used by social planners and *community organizers* to describe decision making among disparate groups in which the option chosen is a "good enough" compromise rather than the best possible choice. The compromise is made to keep the group progressing and moving incrementally toward the optimal goals.

Save the Children Federation   The voluntary agency founded in 1932 to provide social services and community development and financial assistance to communities, families, and especially children who live in impoverished nations or areas that have suffered disasters or are undergoing economic problems. Programs exist in many *Third World* nations as well as in such areas in the United States as Appalachia, *American Indian* reservations, poor neighborhoods in inner cities, and *Chicano* areas.

scapegoat   A member of a family or group who has become the object of displaced conflict or unfair criticism.

scarlet fever   A contagious disease whose symptoms include a red rash, sore throat, and high temperature.

schedule of reinforcement   In *behavior modification,* a plan determining when the subject will be reinforced. This may occur at regular intervals or according to the number and type of responses the subject makes. See also *reinforcement.*

scheme   The mental structure, described in *Piagetian theory,* that allows information to be understood and processed if it fits the individual's cognitive processes.

"schizoid"   A term applied to personality traits that include aloofness, social withdrawal, and indifference to others. If such traits seem deeply ingrained and relatively permanent, the individual might be diagnosed as having *schizoid personality disorder.* If the person has these traits and is younger than 18, the diagnosis might be schizoid disorder of childhood or adolescence.

schizoid personality disorder   One of the 11 types of *personality disorder,* characterized by an ingrained pattern of aloofness, social withdrawal, indifference to the feelings of others, and a restricted range of emotions. Often described as "loners," people with this disorder usually have no close friends and choose solitary interests and occupations.

schizophrenia   A *psychosis,* not apparently the result of *organic mental disorder* or *mood disorder,* that has lasted more than six months and whose active phase has begun before the subject is 45 years old. Its typical features include thought disturbances (often including misinterpretation of reality, misperceptions, *loose association, delusion,* or *hallucination*); mood changes (*inappropriate affect,* blunted emotions, inability to empathize, and *ambivalence*); communication problems (incoherence or poverty of speech content); and behavior patterns that may be bizarre, regressive, or withdrawn. Many subtypes of schizophrenia have been identified, including *disorganized schizophrenia, catatonic schizophrenia, paranoid schizophrenia,* and *undifferentiated schizophrenia* according to the symptoms. The prognosis for complete recovery is extremely rare, although *psychotropic drugs, psychotherapy,* and help with *social functioning* enable most people to live fairly comfortable and somewhat independent lives. Many researchers believe schizophrenia is not a single disease but a group of disorders with similar overt features but differing etiologies. Lay people often confuse schizophrenia with the rare and unrelated *dissociative disorder* known as *multiple-personality disorder.*

schizophreniform disorder   A disorder whose symptoms are identical to those of *schizophrenia* except that its duration is more than two weeks but less than six months.

schizophrenogenic parent   A concept used by some family therapists and psychoanalysts to describe a mother who is domineering and inconsistent or a father who is submissive and inconsistent in such ways as to precipitate *schizophrenia* in their offspring. There is little, if any, scientific evidence verifying this theory, and most experts discount it.

schizotypal personality disorder   One of the *personality disorders* in which the client shows many of the symptoms of *schizophrenia,* including disturbances of thought, perception, and speech, but the symptoms are not as severe. Typical but not inevitable traits are *ideas of reference, paranoid ideation, magical thinking,* strange fantasies, eccentric or peculiar behavior, and social isolation.

school leaver   An individual who discontinues formal education before high school graduation. This term is now preferred by many school social workers and educators over the pejorative word "dropout."

School Lunch program   A national food program administered by the U.S. *Department of Agriculture (USDA),* with input from the U.S. *Department of Education* and the U.S. *Department of Health and Human Services (HHS),* in which federal funds and farm commodities are given to states and local administrations to provide nutritious lunches for school children, including free lunches for eligible children from poor families.

school phobia   A young child's irrational *fear* of going to school, thought by some psychodynamically oriented therapists to be related to unresolved *dependency* needs or strong *separation anxiety.*

school social work   The specialty in social work oriented toward helping students make satisfactory school adjustments and coordinating and influencing the efforts of the school, the *family,* and the *community* to help achieve this goal. School social workers are often called on to help students, families, and teachers deal with such problems as *truancy*; social withdrawal; over-aggressive behavior; rebelliousness; and the effects of special physical, emotional, or economic problems. They also interpret the methods and philosophy of the school to the parents and community. See also *visit-*

ing teacher service and *School Social Work Specialist credential.*

School Social Work Specialist credential A program established by the *National Association of Social Workers (NASW)* to identify school social workers who have met rigorous national standards for education and experience in *school social work* practice. Social workers are eligible for the School Social Work Specialist credential if they obtain an *MSW* from a program accredited by the *Council on Social Work Education (CSWE),* have at least two years or 3,000 hours of supervised school social work experience (one year of a school social work practicum as part of the graduate training may be substituted for one year of supervised work experience), submit supervisory evaluations and professional references, and take the School Social Work section of the National Teachers Examination. It is not necessary to be a member of NASW to apply for the credential.

Schwartz, William (1916–1982) Social work educator who developed many of the theories and principles of *social group work.* He wrote the influential textbook *The Practice of Social Group Work* (New York: Columbia University Press) in 1971.

scientific method A set of rigorous procedures used in social and physical *research* to obtain and interpret facts. The procedures include defining the problem, operationally stating in advance the method for measuring the problem, defining in advance the criteria to be used to reject hypotheses, using measuring instruments that have *validity* and *reliability,* observing and measuring all the cases or a representative *sample* of those cases, presenting for public scrutiny the findings and the methods used in accumulating them in such detail as to permit *replication,* and limiting any conclusions to those elements that are supported by the findings.

scientific philanthropy A movement and social orientation that emerged in Europe and the United States between 1870–1900 to use systematic procedures for determin-

ing who was in need, raising private funds, coordinating the efforts of organizations and individuals who provide help, and providing the specific type of help that would be most effective and efficient. The movement eventually helped replace the haphazard method of raising and dispersing funds and became an integral part of the creation of a social work profession from helpful volunteers and *friendly visitors.*

SCLC See *Southern Christian Leadership Conference (SCLC).*

scoliosis A disease of the musculoskeletal system characterized by lateral curvature of the spine.

SCORE/ACE See *Service Corps of Retired Executives/Active Corps of Executives (SCORE/ACE).*

scripts Characteristic patterns of *behavior* that tend to accompany specific social situations or relationships and that are often followed despite the fact that they can lead to outcomes that are inconsistent with the individual's overt objectives. The term was popularized through *transactional analysis (TA)* theory, which is partly built around an examination and analysis of these patterns, the circumstances in which they occur, and their consequences.

sculpting An experiential technique, used especially by group and family therapists, in which one member of a *group* or *family* is asked to depict his or her understanding of the relationship with others. This is done by moving the people into certain positions and asking them to hold certain gestures.

scurvy A disease caused by vitamin C deficiency resulting in such symptoms as *anemia,* weakness, bleeding in the mucous membranes, and spongy gums. See also *nutrition* and *malnutrition.*

SD See *standard deviation (SD).*

search warrant An order by a judge authorizing specified law officers to examine a subject's premises or possessions and to bring any evidence found to the court.

Search warrants can be issued only if there is probable cause to believe a *crime* has been committed and must explicitly describe the place to be searched and the items or persons to be seized.

seasonal affective disorder (SAD) A *mood disorder,* characterized by many symptoms of *depression,* which affects some individuals during the colder, darker months of the year. Some researchers attribute SAD in some people to deficiencies in needed exposure to light for an extended period of time each day. Treatment for these people may involve moving to sunnier climates or providing regular exposure to special light-emitting equipment.

seasonal pattern specifier Onset and remission of major depressive episodes or bipolar I or II disorders at specific times of the year, with onset most commonly in fall–winter and remission in spring–summer.

seasonal unemployment One of the four types of *unemployment* (including *structural unemployment, cyclical unemployment,* and *frictional unemployment*). This type is related to regular changes in the weather or season. For example, farm workers, lifeguards, snow removal workers, and some construction workers cannot work at their jobs during certain predictable times of the year in certain localities.

seasonal worker One who seeks or obtains *employment* for only specified periods of each year. Examples include a ski lodge employee, a spring and fall agricultural worker, and a department store Santa Claus.

SECA See *Self-Employment Contributions Act (SECA) of 1954.*

secondary alcoholism One of the three major types of *alcoholism* (the other two being *primary alcoholism* and *reactive alcoholism*) in which the individual has a major psychiatric disorder before the onset of drinking problems. The most common of these mental illnesses are *affective disorder* and *antisocial personality disorder.*

secondary care In the system for delivery of health care, the type of *intervention* provided by specialists, usually in community hospitals, including obstetrics and gynecology, dermatology, and cardiology. See also *primary care* and *tertiary care.*

secondary gain The advantages or benefits one derives from a physical or mental illness, such as attention, freedom from responsibility, and disability benefits. See also *primary gain, tertiary gain, malingering,* and *factitious disorder.*

secondary prevention Efforts to limit the extent or severity of a problem through early identification of its existence, early case finding, isolation of the problem so that its effects on other people or situations are minimized, and early treatment. See also *primary prevention* and *tertiary prevention.*

secondary process thinking In *psychoanalytic theory,* the type of thinking that occurs in the *conscious* part of the *ego.* It is the refined, culturally influenced, environmentally responsive pattern of thought.

second opinion 1. Consultation about a client by a professional with one or more colleagues and specialists to enhance the assessment and intervention process. 2. The process by which a client or patient seeks information from one or more other professionals. Clients and patients have the right to ask for second-opinion referrals. In health care, according to the American Medical Association, second opinions should be sought whenever surgery is proposed, the diagnosis is of a potentially fatal or disabling disease, symptoms persist unrelieved without explanation, risks and benefits of proposed procedures are not satisfactorily explained, diagnostic procedures seem unnecessarily complex or expensive, or the patient lacks confidence in the doctor. Clients of social workers could use similar criteria in deciding whether to seek second opinions about social work services.

second-order change In *systems theories,* a fundamental and relatively permanent change in the structure of a system and the way it functions. See also *first-order change.*

secret societies   Organizations whose goals and procedures are kept from the general public. Some of these groups operate secretively as forms of elitism or social exclusivity. Others are secretive because they emphasize political ideologies or tactics deemed by the public to be threatening to society. Such groups include the Communist Party, the *Ku Klux Klan (KKK),* the American Nazi Party, the Posse Comitatus, and The Order.

sectarian services   Social welfare programs that began their existence under the auspices of or with the financial support of religious organizations or that are oriented toward providing social services primarily to members of a specified religious group. Examples are *Catholic Charities USA, Jewish social agencies, LDS Social Services, Lutheran Social Services,* and the *Salvation Army.*

Section 8 Housing   A program administered by the U.S. *Department of Housing and Urban Development (HUD)* to help poor people live in homes in the private sector. One Section 8 program helps low-income renters by paying the difference between what they can afford and the fair-market rent for a living unit. Some Section 8 units are in new or rehabilitated housing but most are in existing structures.

sectoral planning   *Social planning* within a special problem area, usually involving the interests of a specified target population or geographic area (for example, older people, undernourished mothers, delinquent youths, unemployed Hispanics, inner-city residents, or all residents of Baltimore County, Maryland). See also *intersectoral planning.*

secure attachment   In *attachment theory,* one of the three general patterns of attachment (with *avoidant attachment* and *resistant attachment*) in which children are able to explore their environments and interact fairly comfortably with strangers while in the presence of their primary caregivers.

sedatives   Drugs or procedures used to reduce *anxiety* or *psychomotor* activity. See also *tranquilizer.*

sedative-use disorders   A class of substance-related disorders involving the use of sleeping pills, tranquilizers, anti-anxiety drugs, barbiturates, and other brain depressants. Symptoms from *intoxication* by these chemicals may include *delirium, amnesia, psychosis, mood disorder, anxiety disorder, sexual dysfunction, sleep disorder,* and significantly reduced social effectiveness. *Withdrawal symptoms,* resulting from cessation or reduction of use, may include *hyperactivity, insomnia,* hand *tremor,* nausea, *hallucination,* anxiety, or seizures.

Seebohm Report   The 1968 study conducted for the British Home Office by Frederic Seebohm (leader of the British National Institute for Social Work Training). Officially titled *The Report of the Committee on Local Authority and Allied Personnel Social Services,* the document analyzed the structures of local social services departments and recommended ways to improve their efficiency. The report led to a unification of the social services in Great Britain.

segregation   The separation or isolation of a group through social *sanctions,* laws, peer pressure, or personal preference. Voluntary segregation occurs when people choose to associate with others like them. Involuntary segregation occurs when legal, political, or normative requirements, usually established by a dominant group, are imposed on the members of a less-powerful group. See also *Plessy v. Ferguson, apartheid, separatism,* and *discrimination.*

seizure disorders   Disorders associated with abnormal electrical activity in the brain, often resulting in distressing *psychomotor* activity. The causes of these disorders, once commonly called *epilepsy,* are thought to include lesions in the brain, endocrine abnormality, or neurological deficits. According to the manifestations that occur during attacks, the disorders may be classified into four major groups. Grand mal seizures usually begin with an "aura," which may include feelings of numbness and dizziness, then loss of consciousness and jerking movements of the limbs, followed by a period of deep sleep and, just after awakening, muscular stiffness, fatigue, and headache. The attacks may last from less than a minute to more than 30 minutes, and their frequency can vary from several per day to one in several years. *Petit mal seizures* are transient losses of contact with the environment. They may last only a second or up to two minutes, occurring infrequently or as often as 30 times per hour. Petit mal seizures usually occur in childhood and may disappear in adulthood. Psychomotor seizures, more commonly known as "partial seizures" or "temporal lobe seizures," are usually not characterized by loss of consciousness, but by stereotyped movements and dramatic affective changes. Jacksonian seizures tend to begin with convulsive twitching in one part of the body that may spread to others. For most victims of seizure disorders, medication can control or significantly reduce the symptoms.

selective amnesia   See *psychogenic amnesia.*

selective attention   Concentration focused on information, situations, or the like while ignoring other stimuli. Skilled social work interviewers use selective attention so they can attend to only the most significant information out of all the material that a client presents. See also *centration* and *decenter.*

selective eligibility   A policy by which *social services* are provided only to those people who meet predetermined criteria, and the amount of benefit is related to the recipient's specific circumstances, economic status, or special needs, often determined by a *means test.* This policy may be contrasted with *universal eligibility* and *exceptional eligibility.*

selective mutism   A childhood disorder, formerly called *elective mutism,* characterized by the refusal to talk in social situations where talking is expected, for at least one month and to the extent that it inter-

feres with educational or occupational achievement. An individual with selective mutism does not lack knowledge of the language or have another *communication disorder.*

selective programs   *Social welfare* programs based on individualized assessments to determine *eligibility.* This occurs in programs using the *means test,* including *Aid to Families with Dependent Children (AFDC), Medicaid,* and the *Food Stamp program.* Selective programs are so named to distinguish them from *universal programs.*

self   An individual's identity as a unique being; that part of the personality or character that distinguishes the person or entity from all others.

self-actualization   A term referring to the full development of one's potential. According to Abraham Maslow, this is a basic human motivation toward which one strives, especially after fulfilling the *basic needs,* including physiological needs (food, air, water, and rest), safety needs (security, stability, and freedom from fear), needs of belonging (family, friends, affection, and intimacy), and esteem needs (self-respect and recognition of worth from others).

self-assertion   One's expression of thoughts and feelings that are direct rather than manipulative.

self-control   An individual's relative ability to restrict impulses or behaviors to appropriate circumstances in the environment.

self-defeating personality disorder   A pervasive pattern of behavior characterized by avoidance or subversion of pleasurable experiences and attraction to situations where suffering is a likely result. The term is synonymous with *masochistic personality disorder.*

self-determination   An ethical principle in social work, which recognizes the rights and needs of clients to be free to make their own choices and decisions. Inherent in the principle is the requirement for the social worker to help the client know what the resources and choices are and what the consequences of selecting any one of them will be. Usually self-determination also includes helping the client implement the decision made. Self-determination is one of the major factors in the helping *relationship*.

self-disclosure In the social work *interview,* the social worker's revelation of personal information, values, and behaviors to the client. The profession does not declare that such revelation should or should not be made, and in certain limited circumstances it may be considered useful. However, there is some consensus that self-disclosure should not occur unless it serves a therapeutic purpose or is designed to help achieve the client's goal. There is also a consensus that the social worker's personal self should be synthesized with the social worker's professional function.

self-efficacy A client's expectation and belief in his or her ability to accomplish specified tasks that are needed to reach therapeutic goals. The social worker seeks to enhance the client's belief by offering direct assistance, pointing out client strengths, breaking down the tasks into doable elements, and using all available resources.

Self-Employment Assistance Program A *social welfare* program in the Philippines that provides loans without collateral or interest to needy families to help them develop businesses or income-producing projects and thus enhances their self-sufficiency.

Self-Employment Contributions Act (SECA) of 1954 The annual tax a self-employed person pays to the Internal Revenue Service, which is then used for that person's *Old Age, Survivors, Disability, and Health Insurance (OASDHI),* better known as *social security.* It is the equivalent of a worker's *Federal Insurance Contributions Act (FICA)* payroll tax, except that with SECA the person pays the entire tax, whereas in FICA the employer pays part.

self-esteem An individual's sense of personal worth that is derived more from inner thoughts and values than from praise and recognition from others.

self-fulfilling prophecy An expectation one has of another person, group, or social phenomenon that influences the way that person, group, or phenomenon is subsequently perceived. For example, a social worker may view all *Aid to Families with Dependent Children (AFDC)* recipients as too lazy to get jobs and ignore an AFDC client's request for advice about getting employment.

self-help groups Voluntary associations of *nonprofessionals* who share common needs or problems and meet together for extended periods of time for the purpose of mutual support and exchange of information about activities and resources that have been found useful in problem solving. These groups usually meet without the direction of a *professional*.

self-help organizations Formally structured organizations that provide mutual assistance for participants who share a common problem with which one or more of the participants have coped successfully. Some of the organizations of this type that have chapters throughout the United States include *Alcoholics Anonymous (AA), Al-Anon, Batterers Anonymous,* Depressives Anonymous, *Gamblers Anonymous, Mothers Without Custody,* Narcotics Anonymous, Neurotics Anonymous, Overeaters Anonymous, Parents of Premature and High-Risk Infants, *Parents Without Partners (PWP), Recovery, Inc.,* Stroke Club International, and *Women for Sobriety.*

self-hypnosis The act of placing oneself in a mental state of aroused concentration that everything else in the subject's consciousness is ignored. Social workers and other psychotherapy providers sometimes use *hypnotherapy* and also instruct their clients in ways to self-administer hypnotic suggestion for therapeutic purposes outside the formal sessions.

self-incrimination Providing information directly to law authorities that can be used as evidence for one's own criminal conviction. The U.S. *Fifth Amendment rights* protect individuals from being compelled to provide such information. However, the individual may offer such information by voluntarily waiving these rights after being informed about them (see *Miranda*).

self-psychology A psychodynamically oriented theory and therapy based on the work of Heinz Kohut and others who delineated two forms of *narcissism,* one toward the self and the other toward the object. Self–objects are entities in the world that we experience as part of ourselves. Individual growth can occur when the client transforms positive healthy objects into an internalized self-structure, a process called "transmuting internalization." In therapy, through empathic attunement, the patient transforms the self–object functions of the therapist into an internalized self-structure.

semantics The study and analysis of the meanings of words and the varying ideas conveyed by the words over time. The term is often used to suggest the twisting of words to confuse or mislead.

semicomatose Not fully conscious. An individual in this state usually drifts in and out of conscious awareness of the environment or has only partial awareness.

semiotics Aspects of *communication theory* pertaining to signs and gestures used in language to clarify or obscure what is being communicated.

semiprofession Occupations that meet some but not all of the criteria the public and social scientists use to distinguish *professions* from other entities. These criteria include the group's own theoretical *knowledge base,* autonomy from other professions, unique skills, and a *code of ethics.* Some scholars once described social work, along with nursing, librarianship, engineering, occupational therapy, and various technical fields, as semiprofessions. Most now consider social work to be a profession.

Seneca Falls Convention The 1848 feminist meeting in Seneca Falls, New York, that outlined the right to *equality* for women. This delineation of feminist positions helped lead to the passage in 1920 of the 19th amendment to the Constitution, giving women the right to vote and became a major part of the *platform* of the *women's liberation movement.* See also *suffrage.*

senescence The normal biological process of human aging as evidenced by the decline in functioning of various organs and senses. This term, which should be distinguished from *senile dementia,* implies frailty, vulnerability to illness, and awareness of *death* but does not necessarily imply disease or death.

senile dementia A syndrome of old age that is associated with deterioration of brain tissues, often leading to such symptoms as loss of memory, confusion, stubbornness, perceptual distortions, and *thought disorders.* It is a syndrome characterized by generalized irreversible disturbance of the higher cortical functions. Senile dementia is not a disease itself but a syndrome associated with several diseases. The most common types of senile dementia are *Alzheimer's disease* and *multi-infarct dementia.* Senile dementia is also referred to as *senility,* "senile psychosis," "primary degenerative dementia, senile onset," and *organic mental disorder.*

senility The condition of old age. Although this term originally was simply a synonym for "old," it has become a pejorative and lay term implying deterioration of physical and mental faculties. Social workers, gerontologists, and other professionals prefer not to use this term. See also *age-related cognitive decline.*

Senior Companion Program A program of the *ACTION* service comprising volunteers who visit homebound older persons. See also *Retired Senior Volunteer Program (RSVP).*

seniority The achievement of a certain rank or *status* through length of time on the job.

senium The time of old age.

sensitivity group A training and *consciousness-raising* group rather than one that meets to resolve psychosocial or mental disorders. Such groups typically consist of 10 to 20 members and a leader, called a trainer or facilitator. The members participate in discussions and experiential activities to demonstrate how groups function, to show how each member tends to affect others, and to help them become more aware of their own and other people's feelings and behaviors.

sensorimotor stage   The first phase of human development, according to *Piagetian theory,* which occurs from birth to about 18 months and is characterized by the formation of increasingly complex sensory refinements and motor skills that permit the child to better understand and control its environment.

sensorium   The consciousness; that part of the *psyche* that organizes the input from the senses into a fairly coherent understanding of the immediate environment. When a psychiatric report describes a patient as having a "clear sensorium," it indicates that the individual is oriented accurately as to time, place, person, and memory.

sentiment group   Individuals and groups that possess and express the predominant *values, norms,* and goals of the community. Sentiment groups often include fraternal and *civic associations, labor unions,* and ad hoc groups that have been brought together because of some problem or social cause.

separation   The breaking off of a tie or relationship. Social workers use this term in several contexts, including marital separation (a husband and wife living in different residences), *legal separation, separation anxiety,* and *separation–individuation.*

separation agreement   An informal understanding or, more commonly, a written and witnessed agreement between spouses who intend to live apart, specifying the future conditions of their relationship. Usually the agreement describes how property is to be divided and covers *custody of children* and support payments. Formal agreements may be entered in official records and become legally enforceable and not subject to modification unless both parties want a change. The terms of a separation agreement are frequently incorporated into a *divorce* decree. See also *legal separation.*

separation anxiety   The fear that a young child experiences when threatened by the loss of the primary *caregiver.* This fear decreases or ends as the child gets older but often returns during acute *stress, crisis,* or life-stage transitions. Older children and adults sometimes suffer separation anxiety, especially during times of acute stress, crisis, or life-stage transitions.

separation anxiety disorder of childhood   A childhood *mental disorder* characterized by excessive *anxiety* and *fear* when the major attachment figure goes away. The child becomes afraid that the *caregiver* will not return and will be harmed. The child also fears being lost, kidnapped, or victimized. Many children with this disorder develop somatic symptoms such as stomachache and nausea and are afraid of the dark and of sleep. These children will stay very close to the attachment figure and become tense when anticipating separation. The disturbance begins before age 18 and lasts more than four weeks.

separation–individuation   According to Margaret Mahler, a psychosocial stage in human development in which the young child develops a sense of self-identity and a recognition that he or she is distinct from the mother. See also *individuation.*

separation phase   The fifth and final stage in *group development* in which group members tend to regain their sense of individuality and autonomy from other members and become more oriented to life without the group. This phase occurs as preparation for termination and comes after the *preaffiliation phase,* the *power-and-control phase,* the *intimacy phase,* and the *differentiation phase.* Many other typologies have also been proposed to describe the phases in the typical life of groupwork or a therapy group.

separatism An ideology that espouses voluntary or compulsory *segregation* between peoples based on such differences as race, ethnic background, religion, age, or other statuses. See also *apartheid, ghetto,* and *gray ghettos.*

sequela The consequences or after-effects of a disease.

Service Corps of Retired Executives/Active Corps of Executives (SCORE/ACE) A volunteer program sponsored by the U.S. Small Business Organization. Its members use their skills and experience to help people start and develop their own businesses.

service strategy A *social welfare* policy designed to help clients obtain needed goods and services (such as food, housing, transportation, health care, or counseling) rather than direct monetary aid. For example, a service strategy would be to provide public housing for a needy client rather than providing the client with money for housing. This strategy is sometimes described as providing benefits in-kind rather than in cash. See also *income strategy.*

set-asides The allocation of a certain percentage of business for companies owned by members of racial and ethnic groups.

settlement houses Neighborhood-based facilities established in most urban centers to bring together people of different socioeconomic and cultural backgrounds to share knowledge, skills, and values for their mutual benefit. These centers are financed primarily through voluntary contributions and grants and are staffed primarily by people indigenous to the neighborhood, educators, recreation specialists, and social workers whose primary orientation is *social group work, community organization,* and *social planning.* The social settlement movement began in London in 1884 at *Toynbee Hall,* where university students lived and met with their neighbors to exchange ideas. Soon hundreds of settlement houses were established in the United States with the same goals. Many of them have

discontinued the residential aspect of the program, but many remain active in establishing neighborhood self-help programs and *crime* and *delinquency* abatement efforts and are involved in *political activism.*

severity index A rating system used by social workers to indicate the degree of seriousness of a client's problem. One of the several indexes of this type was developed for the *Person-in-Environment (PIE) System* which delineates six levels on its severity index: catastrophic, very high severity, high severity, moderate severity, low severity, and no problem.

sex discrimination Treating people differently based on their sex. Usually the term refers to favorable treatment of males and relegation of females to subordinate positions. Sex discrimination is manifested in such activities as promoting men over equally capable women and paying male employees more than female employees for comparable work. See also *gender bias.*

sex education Providing knowledge about the human reproductive system, often including information about the anatomy and physiology of the male and female reproductive organs, fertilization, fetal development, childbirth, *contraception, family planning, reproductive technology,* protection from *sexually transmitted diseases (STDs),* responsible sexual behavior, and concepts of eroticism and *love.*

sexism Individual attitudes and institutional arrangements that discriminate against people, usually women and girls, because of *sex role stereotyping* and generalizations. An example is assuming that female social workers will prefer direct service over administrative roles and thus advising them to emphasize their clinical education.

sexist language The use of written or spoken words that implies or conveys the idea that one of the sexes is more important than the other. This use may occur intentionally or unintentionally and exists whether or not the producer of the words or the receiver of the words consciously recognizes that such an idea is being communicated. Sexist language is found most commonly in using males to represent humanity (for example, "Man is the most intelligent creature on earth") or applying generic masculine pronouns for both sexes (for example, "If a client is motivated, he will find a way to get help"). See also *unbiased writing*.

sex roles   Culturally defined expectations for "male behavior" and "female behavior."

sex role stereotyping   Preconceived and relatively fixed ideas about all males or all females and the attribution of negative characteristics to people because of their gender. When these ideas are overtly acted on, the result is *sex discrimination*.

sex therapy   Professional clinical treatment of the psychological and physiological dysfunctions of human sexuality. Such treatment is now typically provided to couples in *cotherapy* situations and provided by male–female teams of therapists. There are four levels of such therapy: (1) providing permission—conveying to the couple that their behaviors and desires are normal; (2) providing general information—helping the couple know how to get the most out of sexual relationships; (3) providing specific information—advising the couple about how to correct some sexual disorders or improve some unsatisfactory behaviors; and (4) providing intensive sex therapy. Intensive sex therapy begins with thorough physical examinations to rule out or correct physiological problems. This examination is followed by intensive psychosocial and sexual history taking. If the sex therapists use *psychodynamic* perspectives, the subsequent treatment is likely to be more insight-oriented work toward resolving underlying conflicts that lead to the problem. If the sex therapists use behavioral perspectives, the subsequent treatment involves teaching the couple techniques for greater success and using *systematic desensitization* and other methods to achieve specified goals.

sexual abuse   The exploitation and mistreatment of children and adults in ways that provide erotic gratification for the abuser. Abusers tend to have serious psychological problems such as a *personality disorder, paraphilia* or another *sexual disorder,* or *psychosis*. Victims often cannot or are unwilling to understand or resist the advances of the abuser. Sexual abuse can include sexual intercourse without consent (or when the victim is younger than the age of consent), fondling genitalia, *frotteurism,* taking or showing pornographic pictures, and other forms of sexual *acting out*. Some social workers also include *rape*, seduction, *sexual harassment,* and sexual coercion as other forms of sexual abuse.

sexual arousal disorder   The *sexual disorders* characterized by the recurrent and persistent inability to complete satisfactorily all phases of the sexual response cycle, causing marked distress or interpersonal difficulty. See *female sexual arousal disorder* and *male erectile disorder.*

sexual assault survivor group (SASG)   A form of time-limited group therapy for women who have been victims of sexual assault. SASGs typically consist of six to eight women led by two female *clinicians*. The group meetings last 90 minutes per week for 12 weeks and focus on themes related specifically to sexual assault issues.

sexual aversion disorder   A *sexual disorder* characterized by active avoidance of and aversion to genital sexual contact with a sexual partner, causing marked distress or interpersonal difficulty. Individuals experience varying degrees of fear, disgust, or anxiety when in sexual situations, ranging from lack of pleasure to severe distress.

sexual desire disorders   Absence of fantasy or desire for sexual activity leading to marked distress or interpersonal difficulty. The major types of sexual desire disorders include *hypoactive sexual desire disorder* and *sexual aversion disorder*. See also *sexual arousal disorder.*

sexual development   Anatomical, hormonal, physiological, cognitive, emotional, and social changes in an individual that are related to the reproductive function of life. Sexual development begins at *conception,* when the egg is fertilized by a sperm cell that carries either an XX (female) or an XY (male) sex chromosome. Sexual development continues through puberty and menopause and ends only at death. See also *psychosexual development theory.*

sexual deviation   See *paraphilia.*

sexual disorder   Disturbances of human sexuality, including the type of problem known as *paraphilia,* and *sexual dysfunction.* This type of disorder was once labeled as a *psychosexual disorder;* however, because the degree to which it is *psychogenic* or *biogenic (organic)* has not yet been determined, the preferred term is "sexual disorder."

sexual dysfunction   The inability of an individual or couple to experience sexual intercourse in a satisfactory way. The cause of the dysfunction may be psychological or physiological or a combination of both. The most prevalent types include *orgasmic disorders, vaginismus, dyspareunia, erectile disorder, premature ejaculation, ejaculatory inhibition, sexual aversion disorder,* and *paraphilia.*

sexual equality   Opportunities, benefits, and rights that are uniformly available to people, regardless of gender.

sexual foreplay   Erotic or amorous stimulation before *coitus.*

sexual harassment   Abusive and unfavorable treatment or *sex discrimination* of a person because of his or her sex. Such treatment typically includes making lewd gestures and propositions, touching someone who does not want to be touched, or seeking to exchange sexual favors for employment opportunities. According to Terry L. Singer ("Sexual Harassment," in Richard L. Edwards [Ed.-in-Chief], *Encyclopedia of Social Work,* 19th ed., Washington, DC: NASW Press, 1995), in the United States, sexual harassment is against the law, and employers have the responsibility to provide workplaces that are free from it.

sexual identity   The degree to which an individual takes on the behaviors, personality patterns, and attitudes that are usually associated with male or female *sex roles.* This is a synonym for *gender identity.*

sexuality   Characteristics of an individual that essentially pertain to the reproductive function, including anatomy and physiology, primary and secondary sexual traits, sex role patterns, and behavioral characteristics.

sexually transmitted diseases (STDs) *Venereal diseases*—infectious illnesses passed from one person to another through *coitus* or other intimate contact. They occur by the exchange of bodily fluids and contact with mucous membranes such as in the mouth, rectum, eyes, penis, and vagina. STDs include *gonorrhea, chlamydia,* genital *herpes, syphilis,* and *acquired immune deficiency syndrome (AIDS).* See also *condom.*

sexual masochism   The act of deriving erotic excitement or arousal by being subjected to *pain,* humiliation, or suffering. Excitement occurs by the actual, not fantasized, experience of being bound, tortured, or beaten.

sexual orientation   Inclination toward or preference for sexual activity with members of one's own sex (homosexual orientation), the opposite sex (heterosexual orientation), or both (bisexual orientation).

sexual pain disorder   A *sexual disorder* in which the individual experiences unpleasantness or *pain* during some or all phases of the sexual response cycle. The major disorders of this type are *dyspareunia* and *vaginismus.*

sexual predator   A person who has been convicted of sexual assaults on children or women and, after release from incarceration, is still considered dangerous to children or women. Some communities and jurisdictions have brought about laws and judgments designating the person as a "sexual predator" as long as that individual remains in the neighborhood.

sexual sadism The act of deriving erotic excitement or arousal by inflicting *pain* on others. Excitement occurs by subjecting a consenting or nonconsenting partner to humiliation and simulated or actual injury and suffering.

sexual trauma A shocking experience involving sexuality that has a lasting effect on an individual's personality and mental health. The experience is usually *rape, incest, sexual abuse,* or exposure to a *psychosexual disorder* of others. The resulting symptoms of these experiences include inability to forget, *flashback, anxiety, shame, posttraumatic stress disorder (PTSD),* and subsequent difficulties in having intimate relationships.

Shaftesbury, Lord (Anthony Ashley Cooper, 1801–1885) Founder of the *Ragged School Movement* and England's foremost social reformer in the 19th century. Through his work as a member of Parliament, he guided legislation that improved conditions in housing, physical and mental illness care, slums, and education for poor children. He also helped found the Society for Improving the Conditions of the Laboring Classes and the *Young Men's Christian Association (YMCA).*

shame A painful feeling of having disgraced or dishonored oneself or those one cares about because of an intentional act, involuntary behavior, or circumstance.

shame versus autonomy According to the *psychosocial development theory* of Erik Erikson (1902–1994), the basic conflict found in the second stage of human psychosocial development, occurring between ages two and four. During this time, the toddler experiences social controls and discipline and is helped by the *socialization* process to achieve recognition of his or her uniqueness.

shantytowns Densely populated settlements of impoverished people who have built homes out of scrap materials on land they do not own. Because these people usually occupy the land illegally, they cannot demand public services and have little fire and police protection, water and sanitary facilities, or schools. Shantytowns are growing rapidly, especially in *Third World* nations, and are also found in more-affluent nations that do not provide adequately for their poor populations. See also *slum* and *ghetto.*

shaping Procedures used in *behavior modification* in which new patterns of behavior are fashioned by reinforcing progressively closer approximations of the desired behaviors and not reinforcing other behaviors.

shared psychotic disorder A psychotic disorder in which two or more people experience in common *delusions of persecution* or other delusions. The disorder is exacerbated because each participant fuels the delusions of the other. See also *codependency, folie à deux, conjugal paranoia, jealousy,* and *induced psychotic disorder.*

sheltered-care facility A program and agency that provides a protected and monitored environment for those unable to function independently. These facilities are similar to nursing homes except their residents usually do not require such intensive health care services. Most are 24-hour residential centers, but others provide only *day care.* Many facility residents are mentally ill or physically handicapped or are relatively healthy frail elderly persons. According to Steven P. Segal and Sung-Dong Hwang ("Licensure of Sheltered-Care Facilities—Does It Assure Quality?" *Social Work,* 39 [January 1994], pp. 124–131) the decentralization of such facilities makes it difficult to evaluate the quality of their programs.

sheltered employment A *vocational rehabilitation* and training service that provides a protected and monitored work environment, additional testing, guidance, vocational training, and *social rehabilitation* for people who are otherwise difficult to employ. Most clients of these programs include people with disabilities, older people, former convicts, people with substance abuse problems, and others who need work while readjusting to societal demands.

shelters Facilities that provide and maintain temporary residences and protection for people or animals in need. Shelters exist in most communities for battered and abused women, homeless men and women, abandoned or abused children, victims of crimes and natural disasters, and people experiencing a variety of other circumstances.

shenjing shuairuo A *culture-bound syndrome* found most commonly in China in which the individual experiences anxiety and moodiness and various somatic complaints.

shenkui A *culture-bound syndrome* found most commonly among people of Chinese and Taiwanese ancestry in which the individual experiences *sexual disorders* such as *impotence* and *premature ejaculation,* dream disturbances and *insomnia,* and fatigue and weakness, said to be the result of excessive loss of semen through frequent intercourse, masturbation, and nocturnal emissions. See also *dhat.*

Sheppard–Towner Act The U.S. federal child welfare and maternity health legislation (Maternity Act, ch. 135, 42 Stat. 224) enacted in 1921 and discontinued in 1929. Administered by the *Children's Bureau* under the leadership of social worker *Grace Abbott* (1878–1939), the act established almost 3,000 child and maternity health centers across the nation, mostly in rural areas. Despite great improvements in the nation's infant and maternal *mortality rates,* political pressure led to the act's abolition. See also *WIC program.*

Sherman Anti-Trust Act The federal law (ch. 647, 26 Stat 209) enacted in 1890 to eliminate business monopolies and conspiracies in the restraint of trade or commerce.

shin-byung A *culture-bound syndrome* found most commonly among Koreans in which the individual experiences *anxiety* and various somatic complaints, including dizziness, *insomnia,* and weakness, said to be the result of possession by ancestral spirits.

shingles A painful viral infection, formally called herpes zoster, resulting in blisters and inflammation along the path of a nerve. The virus can remain latent in the body for years before becoming active again.

shock 1. A physical condition, often following a traumatic injury, in which the victim's blood circulation is impaired. Symptoms often include weak pulse, chills, nausea, irregular breathing, faintness, and weakness. 2. Sudden surprise, fright, and the feeling that one's bodily systems have temporarily come to a halt.

shock therapy See *electroshock therapy (EST).*

shoplifting The *crime* of stealing goods from a store during its business hours.

short-term long-term care (STLTC) The health and social services program that provides *long-term care (LTC)* for fewer than 90 days.

short-term therapy *Psychotherapy* or other forms of helping *intervention* that the professional and the client agree in advance to end within a set time, usually less than three months, and within 12–15 sessions. In this form of intervention, the goals and the issues addressed in the sessions are limited. See also *long-term therapy.*

sibling abuse The physical, emotional, or sexual mistreatment of a child by a brother or sister. Usually, the abuser is older and stronger and has more influence with parents or other authorities. See also *child abuse.*

sibling rivalry Competition between *siblings,* basically to gain parental favor or attention.

siblings Brothers and sisters.

sibling therapy The use of *family therapy* and other forms of helping interventions with a *multiproblem family,* working only with children. This model is sometimes used when parents are uncooperative, resistant, or so inconsistent that their presence is more disruptive than productive. The children are helped to develop and strengthen the bonds that exist between them so they can be more effective in providing one another with needed supports.

sickle-cell anemia A genetically transmitted blood disorder in which a large proportion of red cells assume sicklelike shapes. The disorder affects primarily *black people* of West African descent. In the United States, government grants have led to the establishment of free testing for the sickle-cell trait in health centers around the nation. See also *genetic counseling* and *genetic disorder.*

side-taking A technique used especially in *family therapy* in which the social worker actively and deliberately advocates for one family member over others to unbalance a dysfunctional system or break up a pattern in which both sides are stalemated.

sidetracking In the social work *interview,* the client's or worker's intentional or unintentional shifts in focus of attention. Frequently getting away from the relevant subject impedes the helping process. The effective interviewer sometimes prevents this by intervening, reminding the client of the subject, and labeling the digression for what it is.

SIDS See *sudden infant death syndrome (SIDS).*

significance level The degree to which a value that has been obtained through systematic data collection will not occur by chance. In *research* reporting, this level is expressed numerically to indicate the number of times out of a specified number of samplings that the result would probably occur by chance. In the social sciences, the significance levels are most often .01, .05, or .001, even though any other figure could be used as well. For example, if the .05 level is used, a specified outcome would occur by chance five times among 100 samplings.

significant other A generic lay term referring to one who, because of affection, proximity, family relationship, or *codependency* need, is considered more important than others. See also *relevant other.*

simple deteriorative disorder Also referred to as "simple schizophrenia," a pro-

gressive development within the past year of the following symptoms: marked decline in academic or occupational functioning, increasingly flattened affect, reduced quantity and quality of speech and activity, poor interpersonal rapport, and social withdrawal. This is a proposed official diagnostic category of the *DSM-IV.*

simple phobia See *specific phobia.*

simple schizophrenia See *schizotypal personality disorder.*

single-focus group An orientation in *social group work* or *group psychotherapy* in which all the group members share the same or closely related problems and, in single or ongoing sessions, work only on those problems. These groups, also called *homogeneous groups,* are becoming more common in mental health settings and predominate in *self-help groups.*

single-parent family A family unit and household comprising the children and the mother or father but not the other spouse. This family unit is not to be confused with the *reconstituted family,* in which the children and one parent are joined by a stepparent and perhaps that person's children.

single-session group A form of *group therapy* or *social group work* in which the members meet only once. Usually such groups are highly structured and focused on one type of problem. Some groups of this type are scheduled to last only an hour or two, but others may be scheduled for many hours, as in a *marathon group.*

single-subject design A *research* procedure, often used in clinical situations to evaluate the effectiveness of an *intervention.* Behavior of a single subject, such as an individual client, is used as a comparison and a control. Typically, the results of progress or change are plotted graphically. Single-subject design is also known as $N = 1$ design.

"sin tax" An informal term referring to a tax to be paid on those particular goods and services that some citizens consider ignoble, such as cigarettes, alcoholic beverages, gambling winnings, and legal *prostitution* services.

sitdown strike Tactics used by labor unions and activists to interfere with the normal operation of some social organization by encouraging participants to passively occupy an important space to obstruct activities there. See also *passive resistance*.

sit-ins A method of *passive resistance* in which demonstrators occupy a public place and refuse to leave until action is taken to redress their grievances. Sit-ins were used extensively during the Civil Rights movement of the 1960s, especially in segregated restaurants, legislators' offices, and bus stations.

situational tests A procedure social workers in *direct practice* and *research* use to measure client *behavior* and behavioral changes by having the *client* perform some contrived tasks while under observation. The social worker describes a problem–situation and shows how a person might respond. Then, using such tools as videotape simulations, role plays, or written descriptions of problems, the client demonstrates probable responses when confronted with the actual situation.

skew A concept in *research* indicating that a distribution curve is not symmetrical.

"skid road" A term once commonly used to describe areas, usually found in larger cities, frequented by homeless people and alcoholics and containing many tenement houses, cramped and deteriorating buildings, pawnshops, religious missions, and shelters. This term is also known as "skid row."

skill Proficiency in the use of one's hands, knowledge, talents, personality, or resources. A social worker's skills include being proficient in communication, assessing problems and client workability, matching *needs* with *resources*, developing resources, and changing social structures. See also *social work skills, direct practice skills*, and *social skill*.

skilled-nursing facility *Health care* structures and programs for patients who need relatively intensive and often long-term care, staffed primarily by more highly trained and experienced professional *nurses* and *nurse practitioners* who may be specialists in certain types of health care. These facilities are sometimes described as hybrids between nursing homes and hospitals. The designation "skilled-nursing home" has also been used in federal legislation, especially in the *Medicaid* provisions of the *Social Security Act*. These provisions required Medicaid patients in need of nursing home care to be placed in skilled-nursing homes, which were defined as being headed by a nonwaivered practical nurse. Facilities that Medicaid calls "skilled-nursing homes" range from active treatment and rehabilitation programs to limited health care. See also *extended-care facilities (ECF)*.

skim The illegal practice of concealing receipts or income from legitimate sources to avoid paying taxes or sharing the proceeds with others entitled to it.

Skinnerian theory The learning theories developed by American psychologist B. F. Skinner (1904–1990). His concepts, especially that of *operant conditioning*, have greatly influenced the development of modern *behaviorism* and its use in treatment.

"skin popping" An activity of drug abusers who make small cuts in their flesh and place the substance under the skin.

slander Spoken false statements that damage the reputation of another person. See also *libel*.

slave labor Work an individual is compelled to do with no choice or opportunity to select an alternative.

sleep disorders A group of disorders involving chronic and persistent disturbances in sleep patterns, including abnormalties in the amount, quality or timing of sleep, abnormal behavioral or physiological events in association with sleep, or sleep disturbance patterns due to a variety of specified conditions. Among these disorders are primary sleep disorders (including *dyssomnia* and *parasomnia*), sleep disorders due to other mental disorders (*insomnia* and *hypersomnia*), and sleep disorders related to another mental disorder or substance abuse.

sleep terror disorder   A *sleep disorder* characterized by repeated awakenings in a state of fright. The individual often cannot remember the source of the fear but awakens with a scream or with panicky escape movements. This condition, once known as "pavor nocturnus," differs from *nightmare disorder* in that the individual does not awaken as easily or remember the stimulus dream clearly.

sleep–wake schedule disorder   A *sleep disorder* in which the individual's opportunity for sleeping and ability to sleep at that time are mismatched. Clinicians use the term *circadian rythmn sleep disorder*.

sleepwalking disorder   A *sleep disorder*, *parasomnia* type, in which the individual arises from bed during sleep and moves about. The individual has reduced alertness and responsiveness and limited recall of the episode, which usually lasts for several minutes to a half hour. The pattern is most common among children and ends in most people by age 15.

sliding fee scale   The practice, found among many social agencies and workers, in which clients are charged fees for service based on their ability to pay rather than on a fixed rate established in advance for everyone who receives the same service. See also *flat-rate fee*.

"slow learner"   A descriptive term for students whose below-average academic achievements are not attributable to mental illness, retardation, physical problems, or special needs. Most students who are so described have been intelligence tested in the *intelligence quotient (IQ)* range of 75 to 90 (above those who are considered educably mentally retarded but below average). However, many of these students begin to make progress after successful help with emotional or social relationship problems.

slum   A concentration of deteriorating buildings, many of which are inhabited by people who are economically and socially deprived.

"slumlord"   An owner of houses and buildings, usually in deteriorated or deteriorating neighborhoods, who realizes excessive profits by charging high rents and withholding repairs.

small-group therapy   Group therapy with fewer than 10 members.

"snorting"   The ingestion of powdered forms of a drug of abuse, such as *cocaine*, by rapid inhalation into a nostril. Some users prefer this over other ways of ingesting the drug, such as smoking, chewing, swallowing, intravenous injecting, or *"skin popping,"* believing it produces more rapid or more intense effects.

SOAP charting method   A system used by social workers, physicians, nurses, and other professionals, especially in health and mental health care settings, to organize their notes on the medical charts. Part of the *problem-oriented record (POR)* originated by Lawrence Weed in 1968, such charting involves classifying information according to the acronym SOAP, which arranges records in four elements: (1) subjective information (such as symptoms reported by the client or family members), (2) objective information (such as sociodemographic information or data obtained from medical tests), (3) assessments and conclusions that the professional draws from the data, and (4) the plan (what the professional or agency is doing to resolve the problem).

social action   A coordinated effort to achieve institutional change to meet a need, solve a social problem, correct an injustice, or enhance the quality of human life. This effort may occur at the initiative and direction of professionals in social welfare, economics, politics, religion, or the military, or it may occur through the efforts of the people who are directly affected by the problem or change.

social activist   A professional organizer or indigenous layperson skilled at raising the public consciousness about a social problem or injustice and mobilizing available resources to change the conditions leading to these problems.

social adult day care Community programs and facilities for adults whose social functioning has become impaired and who can no longer function independently. Many such facilities provide transportation to and from the client's home, a midday meal, and a variety of recreational and social programs five days weekly while family members are at work. Most funding comes from the *Title XX* provision of the *Social Security Act, Medicaid,* or *third-party* private insurance.

social agency An organization or facility that delivers *social services* under the auspices of a board of directors and is usually staffed by human services personnel (including professional social workers, members of other professions, *paraprofessionals*, clerical personnel, and sometimes *indigenous workers*). It provides a specified range of social services for members of a population group that has or is vulnerable to a specific social problem. The agency may be funded by combinations of philanthropic contributions and privately solicited donations, by governments, by fees paid by those served, or by *third-party payment*. Social agencies are accountable to their boards through accessible financial records, statements of purpose, and representatives from the community who serve on the boards of directors. The board members set overall policy, and administrators coordinate activities to carry out those policies. The organization has explicit bylaws that determine which clients to serve, what problems to combat, and what methods to use in providing service. Public organizations, such as social security offices, hospitals, and community mental health offices, are considered social agencies, as are private organizations such as *Family Service America (FSA)* offices, *Lutheran Social Services,* and *Catholic Charities USA.*

Social and Occupational Functioning Assessment Scale (SOFAS) A 100-point scale in development by the American Psychiatric Association to assist in the clinician's evaluation of the degree to which an individual maintains job-related and social functions not directly related to existing psychological symptoms. Individuals who function most effectively score highest (81–100), whereas those unable to function independently and maintain minimal standards of personal hygiene score lowest (1–20). See also *severity index*.

social assistance A synonym for *public assistance;* the provision of benefits financed from a nation's general revenues and usually subject to a test of the recipient's need and means. This is a *residual welfare provision* in most nations, such as the United States, because the funds do not come from *social insurance* programs. In countries that do not use the social insurance funding system, this is a primary welfare program.

Socialbidrag The means-tested *income maintenance* program used in Sweden as a supplement to its *social security* program. It is administered and primarily funded at the local level; the rates and types of assistance are determined on a case-by-case basis. Usually cash payments are made as part of a package of social and educational services.

social care The provision of concrete and especially relationship-based *social services* for those people with normal developmental needs as well as extraordinary dependency and deprivation problems. The social care concept emphasizes that all people, at least some times, have needs for some social services and that many of these services can be provided by a *volunteer, paraprofessional,* or *indigenous worker*. This system is more prominent in *international social work* than in the United States.

social casework The orientation, value system, and type of practice used by professional social workers in which psychosocial, behavioral, and systems concepts are translated into skills designed to help individuals and families solve intrapsychic, interpersonal, socioeconomic, and environmental problems through direct face-to-face relationships. Many social workers consider social casework to be synonymous with *clinical social work* practice.

social causation theory   The idea that insecure and stressful economic and social conditions strongly increase the probability that a given individual experiencing them will develop social problems or mental disorders. This theory is often advanced to explain why there is a higher *incidence rate* and *prevalence rate* of mental illnesses *poverty, divorce, spouse abuse,* and so on among people of certain socioeconomic classes, ethnic and racial backgrounds, and geographic areas of residence.

social change   Variations over time in a society's laws, *norms, values,* and institutional arrangements.

social class   A category of people in a society, ranked according to such criteria as relative wealth, power, prestige, educational level, or family background.

social consciousness   Awareness of the *needs* and *values* of other people and of society in general, often accompanied by actions to meet those needs and enhance those values.

social control   1. The organized effort of a society or some of its members to maintain a stable social order and to manage the process of *social change.* 2. Efforts to constrain people, requiring them to adhere to established *norms* and laws.

social cost   1. The expenditures for certain programs or activities that are borne by society as a whole. For example, the rising *unemployment* rate among black youths is considered a social cost of racial *discrimination* and social and educational inequalities. 2. Societal problems that do not easily lend themselves to financial calculations. An example is the social and emotional investment required for young couples to care for their disabled parents at home.

social Darwinism   The philosophy first articulated by English sociologist Herbert Spencer (1820–1903), who coined the phrase "survival of the fittest" and applied Darwin's theories of evolution to human economic conditions. The philosophy suggested that competition was normal and inevitable, that those who could not compete would be eliminated through natural selection, that only those who were inferior or inadequate to survive in society would be poor, and that the laissez-faire economic system was best because self-help was the only way out of *poverty.* This philosophy has had great influence in the development of *social welfare* policy in the United States.

social distance   The relative degrees of isolation, aloofness, intimacy, and *social mobility* among people that occur or are permitted within a society or part of that society (such as a *family,* a *group* of workers, or a *socioeconomic class*). For example, one culture might discourage and another encourage physical embraces between men.

social ecology   The study of the reciprocal and adaptive relationship between the natural environment and human society.

social engineering   A term, often used disparagingly, for *social planning* and for efforts to change the *law, norms, mores,* and *social institution.*

social functioning   Fulfilling one's roles in society in general to those in the immediate environment and to oneself. These functions include meeting one's own *basic needs* and those of one's dependents and making positive contributions to society. Human needs include physical aspects (food, shelter, safety, *health care,* and protection), personal fulfillment (education, recreation, *values,* esthetics, religion, and accomplishment), emotional needs (a sense of belonging, mutual caring, and companionship), and an adequate self-concept (self-confidence, *self-esteem,* and identity). Social workers consider one of their major roles to be that of helping individuals, groups, or communities enhance or restore their capacity for social functioning.

social gerontology   The scientific study of the societal and psychological aspects of aging.

social goals model In *social group work* and therapy group conceptions, the group objective of bringing about *social change* in those institutions, norms, and structures that affect the group's members. The goal in this case is to help each member become more effective in recognizing and bringing about desired social changes than would be possible through individual efforts. See also *reciprocal goals model* and *remedial goals model*.

Social Gospel The reform movement that occurred in the United States beginning in the 1870s under the sponsorship of Protestant Church leaders to advocate for improved conditions among workers, abolition of child labor, occupational protections for women, and the right to living wages. The movement declined when its goals were taken over by organized labor, and the goals were later accomplished in the 1930s.

social group work An orientation and method of social work *intervention* in which small numbers of people who share similar interests or common problems convene regularly and engage in activities designed to achieve certain objectives. In contrast to *group psychotherapy*, the goals of group work are not necessarily the treatment of emotional problems. The objectives also include exchanging information, developing social and manual skills, changing value orientations, and diverting antisocial behaviors into productive channels. Intervention techniques include but are not limited to controlled therapeutic discussions. Some groups also include education and tutoring; sports; arts and crafts; recreational activities; and discussion about such topics as politics, religion, sexuality, values, and goals. Whereas social group work draws on the theoretical perspectives of existential theory, *learning theory, psychoanalytic theory,* and social exchange theory, its major theoretical perspective is social systems theory to describe group functioning. This orientation provides workers with a way to conceptualize about the effect of group dynamics and interrelationships outside the group. Social group work theorists delineate three major conceptions of group

work: (1) the *social goals model,* (2) the *reciprocal goals model,* and (3) the *remedial goals model.* See also *group development, phases of.*

Social Health Index See *Index of Social Health.*

social history An in-depth description and *assessment* of the current and past client situation, often included in the *case records* and medical records of clients. It is a document that describes the person's family and socioeconomic background and relevant developmental experiences. Typically, this document is prepared by social workers and social work assistants based on interviews with the client and members of the client's family, reviews of records and reports, consultation with other professionals and agencies, and direct observation of the client and the client's environment. The social history often precedes and forms the basis for social work assessment and service planning. It may also be used by other professionals, such as physicians, lawyers, and teachers, in their own decision making to serve the client. Many social histories are written in a narrative, chronological fashion. Others are organized topically. They frequently include the information under specific headings similar to the following nine headings: (1) *presenting problem,* (2) symptoms of the problem, (3) history of the problem (including recurring situations or repetitive psychological events), (4) current situation (including family; job; economic status; and relevant environmental, social, and health factors), (5) family background (including parents, grandparents, and other close relatives and relevant health and psychological factors about them), (6) educational and vocational background, (7) client goals (including relevant goals of immediate members of the client's family), (8) social worker's assessment, and (9) social worker's recommendations (including social work treatment plans). The history may also include other information the social worker deems to be relevant to the presenting problem, goal, or agency function.

social indicators Quantitative measures about demographic, environmental, and societal conditions that are used in establishing comprehensive and balanced planning.

social inequality A condition in which some members of a society receive fewer opportunities or benefits than other members.

social institution A formal organization of relationships whose purpose is to serve a specific and unique sociocultural function. Examples of social institutions include religion, the *family*, military structures, *government*, and the *social welfare* system.

social insurance Government programs to protect citizens against statutorily stipulated risks, such as old age, disability, death of a breadwinner, unemployment, and work-related injury and sickness. Social insurance programs are characterized by compulsory contributions and participation, presumptive needs, clearly defined benefit formulas, and the absence of the *means test*. Unlike private insurance programs, benefits under social insurance programs are not necessarily proportional to contributions. Major social insurance programs in the United States are *Old Age, Survivors, Disability, and Health Insurance (OASDHI), Unemployment Insurance, workers' compensation,* and state temporary disability insurance.

socialism A system of economic organization in which all or most of the planning is centralized, and most of the means of production are controlled by the government or a collective institution.

Socialist Workers Party A national political organization founded in 1938 by a *splinter group* from other leftist organizations, it generally advocates abolition of capitalism and more rights for racial and ethnic groups, women, and workers. Because of the similarity of names, some people confuse the party with the social work profession. There is no connection between the two.

socialization The process by which the *roles, values,* skills, knowledge, and *norms* of a *culture* are transmitted to individual members in the society.

socialized conduct disorder See *conduct disorder*.

socialized medicine A *health care* system in which a national government directly employs health care providers, builds and maintains health care facilities, and pays for this care through public taxation and international trade revenues. This system is more commonly known as *national health service* and is the system used by many nations. It is not synonymous with *national health insurance*. The term "socialized medicine," rather than "national health service," is often used derisively by its opponents to convince the public that it is inefficient, lowers standards, increases government control and spending, and reduces accessibility.

social justice An ideal condition in which all members of a society have the same basic rights, protection, opportunities, obligations, and social benefits.

social learning theory The conceptual orientation and treatment application that builds on and modifies principles of *behaviorism*, taking into account some internal cognitive processes. The major developer of this theory, which emphasizes reciprocal relationships and the ability to learn new responses through observing and imitating others, has been psychologist Albert Bandura.

social legislation Laws and resource allocations providing for human welfare needs, income security, education and cultural progress, civil rights, consumer protection, and programs that address *social problems*.

social marketing Activities designed to generate interest and demand by consumers, resource suppliers, licensing and credentialing organizations, and the general public for the services of social agencies. The social marketer's role, unlike that of the traditional social planner, is to help the public find ways and *resources* to use those services as well as to facilitate their existence. See also *market strategy*.

social minded Having an active concern for the welfare of a society and its institutional services that enhance the well-being of people.

social ministry Activities and *sectarian services* carried out by clergy, religious workers, and volunteers to help poor and disadvantaged people and to combat social injustice.

social mobility The degree to which a society permits, encourages, or forces people to change statuses, geographic residence, socioeconomic level, or cultural value orientations.

social movement An organized effort usually involving many people representing a wide spectrum of the population to change a law, public policy, or social norm. Examples of social movements include the *temperance movements,* the *Townsend Plan,* and various *equal rights* movements.

social networks Individuals or groups linked by some common bond, shared social status, similar or shared functions, or geographic or cultural connection. Social networks form and discontinue on an ad hoc basis depending on specific need and interest. Included as some of the many types of social networks are the *support system,* the natural *helping network, self-help groups,* and groups of formal organizations that address a common problem.

social phobia An intense, continuous, and unreasonable *fear* of being observed or evaluated. Victims of this *anxiety disorder* are most commonly afraid of public speaking or performing before audiences, using public lavatories or bathing facilities, or eating in restaurants. Typically, they fear they will show *anxiety* and be humiliated, a condition that often leads to the outcome they fear (a *self-fulfilling prophecy*). See also *specific phobia.*

social planning Systematic procedures to achieve predetermined types of socioeconomic structures and to manage *social change* rationally. These procedures usually include designating some individual or organization to collect the facts, delineate alternative courses of action, and make recommendations to those empowered to implement

them. Social planning is one of the methods of *social work practice.*

social policy The activities and principles of a society that guide the way it intervenes in and regulates relationships between individuals, groups, communities, and social institutions. These principles and activities are the result of the society's values and customs and largely determine the distribution of *resources* and level of well-being of its people. Thus, social policy includes plans and programs in education, *health care, crime* and corrections, economic security, and *social welfare* made by governments, voluntary organizations, and the people in general. It also includes social perspectives that result in society's rewards and constraints.

social problems Conditions among people leading to social responses that violate some people's *values* and *norms* and cause emotional or economic suffering. Examples of social problems include *crime, social inequality, poverty, racism, drug abuse,* family problems, and maldistribution of limited resources.

social reform Activity designed to rearrange *social institutions* or the way they are managed to achieve greater *social justice* or other desired change. The term is most often applied to efforts to eliminate corruption in government or structural inequities such as *institutional racism.*

social rehabilitation Programs and activities that facilitate an individual's entry into a relatively unfamiliar society or cultural system. For example, former prison inmates are sometimes reacquainted with the *norms* and circumstances of society after long periods of *incarceration.* See also *deinstitutionalization.*

social research A systematic investigation, using the principles of the *scientific method,* to test hypotheses, acquire information, and solve problems pertaining to human interrelationships.

social security The provisions a society makes to provide income support for citizens whose incomes are lost because of encountering statutorily defined hazards, such as being old, sick, young, or unemployed. In the United States the term "social security" refers to cash payments provided by *Old Age, Survivors, Disability, and Health Insurance (OASDHI)* and health benefits provided in the *Medicare* program. In other countries it also includes health benefits for all residents regardless of need or circumstances and cash benefits to children regardless of their parents' income level.

Social Security Act The federal legislation (ch. 531, 49 stat. 620) enacted in 1935, with several subsequent amendments, designed to meet many of the economic needs of older people, dependent survivors, disabled people, and needy families. In its original form the act contained two major provisions—a compulsory insurance program for workers and a public assistance program financed jointly from the federal and state treasuries. The insurance program collected payroll taxes from certain groups of workers and matching contributions from their employers and, with those funds, established specific funds used to pay benefits to retired workers. Surviving dependents could also receive benefits. Benefits varied according to how much the worker had earned and contributed. Through grants to the states, the act also established an *Unemployment Insurance* program and awarded funds to states to develop uniform programs to care for poor children (Aid to Dependent Children), needy older people (*Old Age Assistance [OAA]*), and blind people (*Aid to the Blind [AB]*). The Social Security Act has been used as the framework for much of the subsequent national legislation that provides for people's economic and *social welfare* needs. See also *Old Age, Survivors, Disability, and Health Insurance (OASDHI), Medicare, Social Security Administration (SSA), Federal Insurance Contributions Act (FICA), and Title XX.*

Social Security Administration (SSA) The federal organization created to implement the provisions of the *Social Security Act*. It has more than 1,200 local service offices in nearly every county in the United States, and its central records are maintained in

its Baltimore headquarters. The local offices are primarily oriented to helping people with its largest programs, *Old Age, Survivors, Disability, and Health Insurance (OASDHI)* and *Supplemental Security Income (SSI)*. SSA was created in 1946, superseding the Social Security Board.

Social Security Number The nine-digit number given to almost all people in the United States to identify them for future *social insurance* benefits. Because of its near-universality, the number is being used as an identifier for other official documents, including taxes, licenses, passport applications, and other records. As of 1993 all children who are claimed as dependents on Internal Revenue Service (IRS) tax returns must have such a number. Certain working and nonworking aliens who need to report income to the IRS must also have these numbers.

social services The activities of social workers and others in promoting the health and well-being of people and in helping people become more self-sufficient; preventing dependency; strengthening family relationships; and restoring individuals, families, groups, or communities to successful *social functioning*. Specific kinds of social services include helping people obtain adequate financial resources for their needs, evaluating the capabilities of people to care for children or other dependents, *counseling* and *psychotherapy, referral* and *channeling, mediation*, advocating for social causes, informing organizations of their obligations to individuals, facilitating health care provisions, and linking clients to *resources*.

social services vouchers A system in which clients eligible for public *social services* are given authorizations for service providers to remit bills to the welfare or human services department for the care they provided to the client. Providers are reimbursed if they meet specified standards. The rates are negotiated in advance between the service providers and the department. This system is thought to give clients greater choice, cut costs, foster innovative service delivery procedures, and provide more-efficient delivery of welfare services.

social skill   The ability to relate to and work with others in achieving specific social goals. Examples include speaking understandably, writing clearly, managing time and finances adequately, and empathizing with and influencing people.

social status   See *status.*

social stratification   The division of society into classes (for example, upper class, middle class, working class, lower class, and underclass) according to such criteria as economic level, educational level, or cultural value orientation

social study   In earlier social work delineations, one of the three major working processes, including *diagnosis* and *treatment.* The study phase of the process consisted of the systematic collection and organization of the information relevant to serving the client, which is then analyzed in the diagnostic phase.

social support   Formal and informal activities and relationships that provide for the *needs* of humans in their efforts to live in society. These needs include education; income security; *health care;* and especially a network of other individuals and groups who offer encouragement, access, empathy, role models, and social identity.

social therapy   A term often applied to the activities of social workers. In contrast to *psychotherapy,* it refers to providing concrete services, facilitating environmental supports for clients, and helping people deal with social problems and conflicts.

social utility   A way of looking at social services as part of the normal system of needs most people may use at some time in their lives. This construct sees social services as inherently the same as any other public utility and part of the *infrastructure,* including the transportation system, the educational system, the postal system, the water and sewer systems, libraries, and museums. People who use social utilities, and thus rely on others in society, are not considered deviant or helpless. In the social utility concept, the user of social services is seen as a citizen, not a patient or client.

social value   The relative worth to society of a service or commodity. The term is used to differentiate between the cash or dollar value of some items that are measured objectively and the value of other items that enhance the social good but cannot be measured in dollars. For example, a library building and its contents may have the same dollar value as a liquor store and its contents, but their social values differ.

social wage   See *new property.*

social welfare   1. A nation's system of programs, benefits, and services that help people meet those social, economic, educational, and health needs that are fundamental to the maintenance of society. 2. The state of collective well-being of a community or society.

Social Welfare History Archives   The repository for the significant records, documents, and memorabilia of the social work profession and epochal events in the history of *social welfare* in the United States. The archives are located at the University of Minnesota in Minneapolis and include taped oral histories by some leading figures in the development of social welfare as well as important written materials.

social work   1. The applied science of helping people achieve an effective level of psychosocial functioning and effecting societal changes to enhance the well-being of all people. 2. According to the *National Association of Social Workers (NASW),* "Social work is the professional activity of helping individuals, groups, or communities enhance or restore their capacity for social functioning and creating societal conditions favorable to this goal. *Social work practice* consists of the professional application of social work values, principles, and techniques to one or more of the following ends: helping people obtain tangible services; providing counseling and psychotherapy with individuals, families, and groups; helping communities or groups provide or improve social and health services; and participating in relevant legislative processes. The practice of social work requires knowledge of human development and behavior; of social, economic, and cultural institutions; and of the interaction of all these factors" (*Standards for Social Service Manpower,* Washington, DC: National Association of Social Workers, 1973, pp. 4–5).

social work associates   Members of the *social work team* who perform a specific task or *episode of service (EOS)* when so assigned by the professional social worker–team leader. Social work associates are similar to *case aides,* although the range of their activities can go beyond work on a specific case.

Social Work Curriculum Study   The landmark report published in 1959 by the *Council on Social Work Education (CSWE),* under the direction of Werner Boehm, which delineated the components of graduate-level social work education. The 13-volume study was used as a guide by CSWE in establishing criteria for accrediting schools of social work and by the schools as a means of developing effective educational programs. See also *Hollis–Taylor Report.*

social work education   The formal training and subsequent experience that prepare social workers for their professional roles. The formal training takes place primarily in accredited colleges and universities at the undergraduate *(BSW)* level and in accredited professional schools of social work in *MSW, DSW,* PhD, and other *doctoral programs.* Social work education includes extensive classroom activity as well as direct supervised work with clients *(field placement).* Social workers do not consider their education to be completed only because they have acquired their degrees. On graduation, most social workers provide services under the *supervision* of more-experienced colleagues and then take additional formal courses *(continuing education).* See also *Council on Social Work Education (CSWE), curriculum policy statement, Group for the Advancement of Doctoral Education in Social Work (GADE), Hollis–Taylor Report,* and *Social Work Curriculum Study.*

social worker cooperatives   A form of *proprietary practice* in social work in which an organization is formed, staffed, and owned by a group of professionals and sometimes paraprofessionals who provide for-profit or nonprofit social services. The cooperatives' owner–workers participate equitably in decision making and direct practice. Income is often derived from grants or capitation fees from third parties or governments to provide specified social services.

social workers   Graduates of schools of social work (with either bachelor's or master's degrees) who use their knowledge and skills to provide social services for clients (who may be individuals, families, groups, communities, organizations, or society in general). Social workers help people increase their capacities for problem solving and coping, and they help them obtain needed resources, facilitate interactions between individuals and between people and their environments, make organizations responsible to people, and influence social policies.

social work knowledge   According to the *Standards for the Classification of Social Work Practice* (Silver Spring, MD: National Association of Social Workers, 1982, p. 17), social work requires knowledge in some or all of the following areas: *social casework* and *group work* theory and techniques; community resources and services; federal and state *social services* programs and their purposes; *community organization* theory and the development of health and welfare services; basic socioeconomic and political theory; racial, ethnic, and other cultural groups in society—their *values* and lifestyles and the resultant issues in contemporary life; sources of professional and scientific *research* appropriate to practice; concepts and techniques of *social planning;* theories and concepts of *supervision* and the professional supervision of *social work practice;* theories and concepts of personnel management; common social, psychological, statistical, and other research methods and techniques; theories and concepts of *social welfare* administration; social and environmental factors affecting clients to be served; theories and methods of *psychosocial* *assessment* and *intervention* and of *differential diagnosis;* theory and behavior of organizational and social systems and of methods for encouraging change; community organization theory and techniques; *advocacy* theory and techniques; ethical standards and practices of professional social work; teaching and instructional theories and techniques; social welfare trends and policies; and local, state, and federal *laws* and regulations affecting social and health services.

social work practice The use of *social work knowledge* and *social work skills* to implement society's mandate to provide *social services* in ways that are consistent with social work *values.* Practice includes *remediation;* restoration (rehabilitating those whose *social functioning* has been impaired); and *prevention.* Some of the most important social work practice roles are clinician, administrator, advocate, broker, caregiver, case manager, communicator, consultant, data manager, evaluator, mobilizer, outreacher, planner, protector, researcher, socializer, supervisor, teacher, and upholder of equitable social values. Social work practice may occur in *micro practice, mezzo practice,* or *macro practice.*

social work purpose The *Working Statement on the Purpose of Social Work,* developed by the *National Association of Social Workers (NASW)* in 1981, states that social work is to promote or restore a mutually beneficial interaction between individuals and society to improve the quality of life for everyone.

Social Work Research Group (SWRG) The professional association founded in 1949 to facilitate the development of the research specialty in social work. In 1955 SWRG merged with six other associations to become the *National Association of Social Workers (NASW).*

social work skills The *Standards for the Classification of Social Work Practice* (Silver Spring, MD: National Association of Social Workers, 1982, pp. 17–18) identifies 12 essential skills in social work. They are

being able to (1) listen to others with understanding and purpose; (2) elicit information and assemble relevant facts to prepare a *social history, assessment,* and report; (3) create and maintain professional helping relationships; (4) observe and interpret verbal and nonverbal behavior and use knowledge of personality theory and diagnostic methods; (5) engage clients (including individuals, families, groups, and communities) in efforts to resolve their own problems and to gain trust; (6) discuss sensitive emotional subjects supportively and without being threatening; (7) create innovative solutions to clients' needs; (8) determine the need to terminate the therapeutic *relationship;* (9) conduct *research* or interpret the findings of research and professional literature; (10) mediate and negotiate between conflicting parties; (11) provide interorganizational liaison services; and (12) interpret and communicate social needs to funding sources, the public, or legislators. The same policy statement identified the abilities necessary for social work practice. Social workers should be able to speak and write clearly, teach others, respond supportively to emotion-laden or crisis situations, serve as role models in professional relationships, interpret complex psychosocial phenomena, organize a workload to meet designated responsibilities, identify and obtain resources needed to assist others, assess their own performances and feelings and use help or consultation, participate in and lead group activities, function under stress, deal with conflict situations or contentious personalities, relate social and psychological theory to practice situations, identify the information necessary to solve a problem, and conduct research studies of agency services or their own practices. See also *direct practice skills.*

social work team A system for delivering *social services* in which several professional social workers, *social work associates, case aides, indigenous workers, volunteers,* and various ad hoc specialists work in an integrated and coordinated way to achieve a specified goal or *episode of service (EOS).* The team members discuss in advance all the activities that can be accomplished to achieve the goal efficiently, and then various assignments toward that end are made by the social worker–team leader. Social workers also participate in interdisciplinary teams in such fields as *mental health, health care,* and developmental care.

Societies for the Prevention of Cruelty to Children (SPCCs) Independent organizations in many larger communities that advocate for the rights and protection of children. The first SPCC was established in 1874 in New York after it was found that there were more legal protections against the abuse of animals than children. The well-established Societies for the Prevention of Cruelty to Animals began taking child abuse cases to court, holding that children were animals and deserved at least as much protection. Soon thereafter, SPCCs were developed in more than 250 communities. They were instrumental in early efforts to provide legal protections for children and in developing *child welfare* legislation.

Society for Hospital Social Work Directors See *Society for Social Work Administrators in Health Care (SSWAHC)*.

Society for Social Work Administrators in Health Care (SSWAHC) A professional membership organization, established as the Society for Hospital Social Work Directors in 1966 and affiliated with the *American Hospital Association (AHA)*. Members include social workers who manage social services departments of *health care* facilities. In 1993, the society adopted its current name.

Society for the Right to Die A national organization formed in 1975 as an outgrowth from the Euthanasia Society, with the purpose of enhancing individuals' rights to control medical decisions at the end of their lives. The organization merged with *Concern for the Dying (CFD)* in 1991 to become *Choice In Dying*.

sociobiology The science of social behavior in humans and other animals and the genetic basis for that behavior.

sociocultural dislocation The movement of an individual or group into a sociocultural system that has unfamiliar or unacceptable *norms.* The move may be permanent and inclusive, as in migrating from a *Third World* nation to an economically developed one, or it may be temporary and partial, as experienced by some racial and ethnic groups who live in ghetto areas and have jobs in affluent offices dominated by white people. See also *relocation camps.*

socioeconomic class Categorization of groups of people according to specified demographic variables, such as level of income or education, location of residence, and value orientation. Sociologists often categorize the classes as "upper," "middle," "lower," and *working class*. Other observers make further distinctions, such as "upper middle class" and *underclass*.

sociofugal arrangements The physical design, setting, and decor of offices and facilities that tend to keep people apart and inhibit their interaction. For example, a social worker's sociofugal office and waiting room might contain stiff chairs lined straight against walls that are too far apart for easy communication; long, dark hallways in which clients must wait before seeing the social worker; and metal desks and filing cabinets that act as barricades and further isolate the social worker from the client. See also *sociopetal arrangements*.

sociogram A diagram or graphic presentation used by group workers and other professionals to display how members of the group feel about one another and how they tend to align themselves with some and against other members of the *group* or *organization*.

sociolinguistics The study of language in relation to the social context in which it is expressed. The social work interviewer can understand the context of the transaction much more fully through a microanalysis of such sociolinguistic concerns as repetitions, interruptions, silences, pause placements, words emphasized, and hesitations.

sociopath   See *dyssocial.*

sociopetal arrangements   The physical design, setting, and decor of offices and facilities that tend to draw people together and encourage interaction. For example, a social worker's sociopetal office might have comfortable chairs close to one another at attractive angles, have good lighting and music in the waiting area, and use file cabinets to form conversation nooks rather than barricades. See also *sociofugal arrangements.*

SOFAS   See *Social and Occupational Functioning Assessment Scale (SOFAS).*

"soft sciences"   The name sometimes attached to less empirically based bodies of knowledge, including such social sciences as economics, psychology, and sociology. This is contrasted to what are called the *"hard sciences,"* including such natural sciences as biology, chemistry, and physics. Social work is usually placed in the "soft science" category as an applied social science.

software   In computers, the programs (or instructions) that make the physical equipment *(hardware)* execute the desired operations.

solidarity movement   The labor movement that began in Gdansk, Poland, in the late 1970s to advocate for better working conditions and more-efficient means of productivity. Many historians consider this movement to be the precipitator of the downfall of the Communist system of governing Eastern European (Iron Curtain–Warsaw Pact) nations and the end of the *Cold War.*

solitary aggressive-conduct disorder   That type of *conduct disorder* in which the person's pattern of *antisocial behavior* is harmful or threatening to others and does not take place within the context of a group or *gang.* This is considered usually more pathological than the *group-type conduct disorder.*

solvency   The ability of an individual or organization to pay debts.

somatic complaints   The description by a client or patient of physical symptoms or dis-comforts, such as headaches, dizzy spells, cramps, fatigue, or apparent injury or illness.

somatic-type delusional disorder   A subtype of *delusional disorder* characterized by nonbizarre delusions, particularly an intense concern about bodily functions or sensations. The delusion takes different forms, for example, the conviction that one is emitting a foul odor, is infested with internal parasites or insects, possesses ugly or misshapen body parts, or is afflicted with an undiscovered disease. See also *taijin kyofusho.*

somatization disorder   One of the *somatoform disorders,* characterized by a subject's long history of complaints about symptoms that are not caused by physical disease, injury, or drugs. Symptoms include being sickly for much of one's life, gastrointestinal symptoms (such as abdominal pain, nausea, vomiting, or diarrhea), pseudoneurological symptoms (such as fainting, muscle weakness, blurred or double vision, or memory loss), psychosexual symptoms (indifference to or pain during intercourse), pain, palpitations, shortness of breath, and reproductive disorders.

somatoform disorders   Mental disorders that have the appearance of physical illness but, lacking any known organic basis, are generally thought to be *psychogenic.* The specific disorders in this category are *somatization disorder, body dysmorphic disorder, hypochondriasis, conversion disorder,* and *psychogenic pain disorder.* When the individual experiences only a few of these symptoms of a shorter duration the diagnosis is "undifferentiated somatoform disorder."

somatoform pain disorder   One of the *somatoform disorders,* in which the person is overly concerned about hurt or the potential for being hurt. The preoccupation with *pain* occurs in the absence of any physical findings that would account for the pain or the intensity with which it is experienced. This condition is currently called *psychogenic pain disorder.*

somnambulism   See *sleepwalking disorder.*

soporific   A drug or procedure designed to induce sleep.

soup kitchen   A facility, usually operated by a private charitable or religious organization, that prepares and serves food to poor people at little or no cost to the recipients. See also *bread line*.

Southern Christian Leadership Conference (SCLC)   The *civil rights* organization founded in 1956 by Martin Luther King, Jr., and others whose goal is the peaceful combat of racially motivated injustice.

Sozialhilfe   The means-tested *income maintenance* program used in Germany as a supplement to its *social security* program. Sozialhilfe is funded primarily from local government taxes and is not related to the amount of contributions made by the recipient, as in the case of the German Social Security program. The amounts paid are consistent with the German policy to ensure a "dignified existence," and the rates to achieve this are determined by the German Association for Public and Private Relief (comprising volunteer representatives from religious organizations, trade unions, and some private social service groups such as the *Red Cross*).

"Spanglish"   A term describing the combination of the English and Spanish languages used by some Spanish-speaking immigrants to the United States and Canada. "Poncho" and "Tex-Mex" are other names for this language.

span of control   In administration, the number of people or activities under one person's supervision, including the amount of time the manager takes to supervise them effectively.

SPCCs   See *Societies for the Prevention of Cruelty to Children (SPCCs)*.

special education   Any form of schooling, training, tutoring, or other educational formats to meet the needs of exceptional children and adults. The term has been most commonly applied to educational programs for people with visual impairments, hearing impairments, physical disabilities, cognitive disturbances, mental retardation, advanced talents, or intellectual giftedness.

special-interest group   See *interest group*.

specialist   A social work practitioner whose orientation and knowledge are focused on a specific problem or goal or whose technical expertise and skill in specific activities are highly developed and refined. See also *generalist*.

specialization   A profession's focus of knowledge and skill on a specific type of problem, target population, or objective.

special-needs clients   People who, by reason of some mental or physical disability, require additional or different kinds of assistance to achieve their goals in seeking social services. For example, a couple seeks marital therapy and the wife has multiple sclerosis, or a child entering the adoption system is quadriplegic.

special populations   People and groups classified together because they share some distinguishing attributes, traits, talents, problems, disorders, obstacles, orientations, or other unique characteristics.

speciesism   The ideology that the human species is the only one with rights and that all other species and their habitats exist only to meet the needs and desires of humans.

specific development disorders   See *developmental disorder*.

specific phobia   An *anxiety disorder* characterized by marked and persistent *fear* of a clearly identifiable object or situation. Formerly called "simple phobia," this condition is one of three major types of phobias, including *social phobias* and *agoraphobia*. Some of the more common specific phobias are *acrophobia, algophobia, aquaphobia, claustrophobia, hematophobia, nyctaphobia, ocholophobia, thanatophobia,* and *zoophobia*. Other specific phobias are also defined in this dictionary.

"speed"   A slang term for *amphetamine*. When used illicitly, as in taking excessive dosages over extended periods or in intravenous injections, these drugs are dangerous and physiologically and psychologically addictive.

Speenhamland   An income subsidy system that originated in the Speenhamland district of England in 1795 and was later widely imitated. Workers who earned less than a predetermined amount had the difference made up from public funds.

spell   A *culture-bound syndrome* found most commonly among European Americans and African Americans in which the individual enters a trance-like state while seeking to communicate with spirits or deceased significant others.

spending down   An individual's intentional attempt to reduce total assets and income to be eligible for certain means-tested *social insurance* benefits. For example, a person who has a substantial amount of money in the bank would be ineligible for Medicaid; therefore, he or she would dispose of the funds to become eligible for Medicaid.

spina bifida   Failure of the spinal column to close properly during early fetal development. The disorder is frequently associated with other problems such as mental retardation and hydrocephalus and its complications. People afflicted with this disorder often require orthopedic, neurological, hospital, and other medical care and social services throughout their lives.

spin control   A public relations effort to change the way the public understands some news event.

spiritual counseling   Professional clinical *intervention* with an orientation to the client's moral, emotional, and religious perspective. Psychologist Carl Jung (1875–1961) integrated the spiritual perspective with clinical treatment, hypothesizing that *spirituality* is the essence of human nature. *Pastoral counselors* have led the helping professions in this orientation, and many social workers consider a rejection of a client's spiritual and religious values to be as harmful as racism or sexism. See also *transpersonal social work*.

spirituality   Devotion to the immaterial part of humanity and nature rather than worldly things such as possessions; an orientation to people's religious, moral, or emotional nature. According to Patricia Sermabeikian ("Our Clients, Ourselves: The Spiritual Perspective and Social Work Practice," *Social Work*, 39[March 1994], 178–183), social workers recognize that many of their clients use spirituality as an important component in coping, and this practice is consistent with the social work goal of helping clients meet their basic needs and mental health.

splinter group   Those who dissent on one or more issues from a larger organization, break away, and form their own group.

split-half reliability   See *reliability*.

splitting   In *psychoanalytic theory,* a primitive defensive process in which the individual is thought to repress, dissociate, or disconnect important feelings that have become dangerous to his or her psychic well-being. This may cause the person to get out of touch with his or her feelings and to develop a "fragmented self."

spoils system   A political and economic procedure in which those loyal to a winning candidate or organization leader receive more benefits than nonsupporters regardless of merit. See also *merit system*.

spontaneous remission   The disappearance of symptoms of mental or physical disorders that often occur among clients but is not attributable to outside help. Many critics of psychotherapy claim this accounts for many of the gains made by clients rather than the therapy itself.

spouse abuse   The infliction of physical or emotional harm on one's wife, or less frequently, on one's husband.

spurious correlation   A pattern of variation between two phenomena that seems to indicate causality or mutual reciprocity but results instead from other factors.

squatter   One who settles on rural or urban land belonging to another without title or right.

squatter's rights   The presumed entitlement of a person to own land or buildings merely by occupying them for a specified length of time. Such "rights" no longer have legal validation as they once did in some jurisdictions. However, in various forms of *urban homesteading,* people who occupied and restored abandoned buildings have claimed legal title and received it, but not on the basis of squatter's rights.

SSA See *Social Security Administration (SSA).*

SSI See *Supplemental Security Income (SSI).*

SSWAHC See *Society for Social Work Administrators in Health Care (SSWAHC).*

staff development Activities and programs within an organization designed to enhance the abilities of personnel to fulfill the existing and changing requirements of their jobs. These activities often include short-term in-service training classes, distribution of relevant information, group conferences, use of outside consultants and speakers to meet with personnel, and funding of certain employees to participate in meetings or training programs outside the organization. Staff development, although usually related to the specific job requirements of the employing organization, has broader functions as well. It also seeks to help personnel improve their overall career objectives and opportunities. A latent function of staff development is for the organization to attract and keep competent personnel and clarify and "humanize" the organization. Staff development is distinguished from professional education in that it does not grant academic credit, and its participants may have different degree levels. See also *in-service training.*

staffing In *social welfare* administration, an organization's activities designed to maintain and improve personnel effectiveness. This activity includes recruiting and interviewing prospective employees and volunteers; assigning, promoting, transferring, and firing employees; and providing for *in-service training* and *staff development.*

stage theories The concept that every period of life is characterized by some underlying challenges and orientations that modify one's behavior and priorities. Each stage has characteristics that make it unique, and each higher stage incorporates many of the gains made in earlier ones. The degree to which one reconciles the conflicts inherent in each stage largely determines the likelihood of coping successfully in subsequent life stages. Among the best known of these concepts are Erik Erikson's *psychosocial development theory;* Sigmund Freud's *psychosexual development theory; Kohlberg moral development theory;* Piaget's theory of *cognitive development;* and the concepts delineated by Roger Gould, Daniel Levinson, Bernice Neugarten, Talcott Parsons, and Robert Bales.

stagflation A nation's economic condition in which there is *inflation* without accompanying economic growth. This is often an indicator of economic *recession* or *depression.*

stammering See *stuttering.*

standard deviation (SD) A statistical measure to indicate the degree of dispersion of a distribution. It is the average difference between individual scores and the mean score in a distribution, obtained by squaring the deviation scores, adding them together, dividing by one less than the number of scores, and taking the square root of the result. In a normal (symmetrical or bell-shaped) distribution, 6.2 percent of the cases will fall between +1 or −1 standard deviation from the *mean;* 95.4 percent will fall between +2 or −2 standard deviations; and 99.7 percent of the cases will fall between +3 or −3 standard deviations.

standardized tests Measurement tools used by social researchers, educators, and clinicians. The tests have already been used on many subjects, permitting a high degree of confidence in their *validity* and *reliability.* Standardized tests provide instructions, scoring procedures and standards, time limits, norms, and statistical data to make possible comparisons of the sample group with a much larger segment of society.

standard of living A concept comprising the necessities, luxuries, and comforts an individual, group, class, or society needs or uses to live in a particular circumstance. The concept is often confused with "standards of consumption." Consumption involves the availability of consumer goods to the individual or the society. "Standard of living" includes available consumer goods but adds choices and variety of these goods, normal working conditions, amount of leisure time, and opportunities for using that time.

"stare decisis" doctrine The judicial system premise that decisions formerly made in courts of law stay in effect unless there is good cause for overturning them.

Starr, Ellen Gates (1859–1940) Cofounder, with *Jane Addams*, of *Hull House* in Chicago in 1889, Starr later worked as an advocate in the trade union movement and for improved conditions for workers. She also worked closely with *Florence Kelley* to improve *child labor* conditions.

state's attorney A prosecutor in a court of law who represents the interests of the state and its people. The state's attorney may also be known as an attorney general or a district attorney or an assistant to one with that title.

statistical inference Systematic analysis of a *sample* and drawing conclusions about the *population* from which it was drawn.

statistical significance See *significance level.*

statistics 1. In *research,* quantitative procedures (which may be descriptive or inferential) that are used to describe or assess *variables* or relationships between variables. 2. Characteristics of a *sample* or subset of a larger *population.*

status 1. A social position that carries culturally defined expectations or *roles.* Statuses may be "achieved" (such as social worker, Aid to Families with Dependent Children [AFDC] recipient, or government bureaucrat) or "ascribed" (such as woman, Hispanic, or child). 2. Lay people use this term as a synonym for "prestige."

status offender One whose actions would not be considered a violation of criminal law if they were committed by someone with a different *status.* For example, children who run away from home are truant, or they are defined as unmanageable by their parents and are considered status offenders.

Statute of Labourers One of the world's earliest *public welfare* programs, initiated in England in 1349, it forbade giving charity to able-bodied people, compelled unemployed people to work for anyone who would hire them, forbade unemployed people to leave their hometowns or villages (or allowed them to go only to areas where there was work), and fixed the maximum wages that could be paid to workers.

statute of limitations A law that specifies the amount of time within which a person must be charged with a *crime* or sued for damages. Courts do not hear cases involving acts that occurred beyond this time limit. The major exception is *homicide*; a person can be charged with this crime no matter how long after the event.

statutory rape A consenting sexual relationship with someone who is under the legal age of consent in a given jurisdiction.

STDs See *sexually transmitted diseases (STDs).*

Steering Committee for International Relief An informal association of the five major private organizations for international relief—*Oxford Committee for Famine Relief (OXFAM), Catholic Relief Services (CRS),* the World Council of Churches, the *Lutheran World Federation (LWF),* and the *League of Red Cross Societies.* Headquartered in Geneva, the Steering Committee coordinates efforts of the private organizations with one another and with such groups as *United Nations Disaster Relief Organization (UNDRO)* and provides information and instruction to *disaster relief* workers.

stepfamily A primary *kinship* group whose members are joined as a result of second or subsequent marriages. Such a family may include a stepfather (the husband of one's mother); a stepmother (the wife of one's father); a stepchild (the offspring of one's spouse by a previous marriage or relationship); and stepbrothers and stepsisters (the children of one's stepparent). Owing to the increased divorce and remarriage rates, stepfamilies constitute a major type of family constellation. See also *reconstituted family* and *blended family*.

stepsibling An individual whose family role is that of a brother or sister even though there is no biological connection. The stepsibling relationship occurs primarily when a mother of one child marries the father of another child. Stepsiblings may or may not live in the same home and may or may not be children.

stereotypes Preconceived and relatively fixed ideas about an individual, group, or social status. These ideas are usually based on superficial characteristics or overgeneralizations of traits observed in some members of the group.

stereotypic movement disorder A disorder of infancy, childhood, and adolescence characterized by intentional and repetitive gestures or activities that have no socially acceptable purpose. Some of these behaviors include teeth grinding, body rocking, head banging, hitting oneself, skin picking, or repetitive vocalizations, often performed in a rhythmic fashion. This condition was formerly known as "stereotypic habit disorder." See also *Tourette's disorder* and *tic disorder*.

sterilization A medical procedure that ends a person's ability to reproduce. This method of permanent *birth control* or *reproductive technology* usually involves *tubal ligation* or vasectomy (tying off a man's vas deferens). Attempts to reverse sterilizations have limited success rates.

steroids Drugs based on natural hormones or synthetics intended for use in treating inflammations, *arthritis*, *asthma*, and other disorders. Steroids are rapidly becoming a drug of abuse, especially by athletes, body builders, and others wanting to look more muscular but who risk serious long-term physical and social consequences of using them improperly. In prolonged misuse, the initial sense of enhanced well-being, strength, and energy is replaced by depression, irritability, low energy, and general medical conditions, especially liver disease.

stillborn A baby born dead after the twentieth week of pregnancy.

stimulants *Psychoactive substances* that produce in the user mild to intense feelings of *euphoria* and states of alertness, heightened awareness, and relief from feelings of sleepiness or tiredness. These substances tend to be habituating and addictive and often have serious side effects. Drug abusers know forms of such substances as "*uppers*" and "*speed.*"

stimulus Any event in the environment that is perceived by the individual. A stimulus may be discriminative, eliciting, reinforcing, punishing, or neutral. See also *response*.

stimulus discrimination In *social learning theory*, the phenomenon in which the subject does not respond to a *stimulus* even though it is similar to one that had previously evoked a *response*.

stimulus generalization The ability of a subject to respond to one *stimulus* in the same way he or she responded to another, similar stimulus; the opposite of *stimulus discrimination*.

sting operation 1. A method police officials use in apprehending felons by posing as business people who buy stolen or illicit goods. 2. *Confidence crimes* in which victims pay for services to phony businesses.

STLTC See *short-term long-term care (STLTC)*.

stolen children Youths who have been abducted from the legal custodial parent, usually by the other parent after a *divorce* and loss of *custody*. See also *child snatching*.

stonewall To stubbornly refuse to give information or negotiate about debatable issues. An example is a client who remains noncommunicative or rigid about new ideas.

stranger anxiety Fear or apprehension in the presence of unfamiliar people, most common among very young children. See also *separation anxiety.*

strategic family therapy The orientation and procedure used by some family therapists to help families and their members discontinue reciprocal interactions in which recurring patterns of *symptomatic* behavior occur. The therapist designs an *intervention* to resolve specific problems, the resolution of which will require the family system to modify all other interactions.

strategic marketing The development of a product or service that serves the interests of specific publics. These publics include input (resource suppliers and funders), output (clients and other beneficiaries), and throughput (paid staff and volunteers who are charged with turning resources, funds, and concepts into products or services). Strategic marketing uses technical means to segment the public geographically, demographically, functionally, and psychologically to define an agency's or program's *niche* or market. It also involves pricing, placing, and promotions to regulate demand for a specific product or service.

strategic planning The process of formally or implicitly defining long-term goals and the alternative means toward their accomplishment. The goals are defined by specifying the target of *intervention,* auspices, value implications, feasibility, and interrelationships among various components of the social system. The goals thus established provide guidelines for looking at alternative means of achieving desired ends, which can often result in major modifications of existing programs and services.

strategies Carefully designed and implemented procedures an individual or group uses to bring about long-term changes in another individual or group. Strategies refers to long-range approaches and ultimate goals, and *tactics* refers to short-term or day-to-day maneuvers.

stratified sample In *research,* the division of a *population* into strata, randomly selecting from each of the strata, and pooling the result. This stratification assures that a certain proportion of representation oc-

curs from each component. For example, a stratified sample might consist of a random selection except that an equal number of people were born in each decade.

"street kids" Adolescents who live on or near the streets of urban areas. Younger boys and girls are usually referred to as *runaways* or abandoned or lost children. Adolescents on the streets who have families are usually described as runaways or kidnapped. Street kids constitute a large subpopulation that is officially not recognized to exist; they are not counted among homeless people in the United States. (The U.S. *Bureau of the Census* counts only people older than 21 as homeless.)

"street people" A popular name for urban adults who congregate near centers of business activity and spend much of their time socializing, wandering about, seeking employment or assistance, or *"hustling."*

streetwise Possessing survival and *coping skills*, descriptive of some youths and adults who spend most of their time in public places. Their skills include being able to avoid exploitation by others, finding sources of money or goods whenever needed, avoiding unwanted contacts with authorities, and being able to live outside the established social system. This is a relative term, and everyone possesses or lacks some of these *social skills* or *coping skills* at times. The term is synonymous with "streetsmart."

stress Any influence that interferes with the normal functioning of an organism and produces some internal strain or tension. "Human psychological stress" refers to environmental demands or internal conflicts that produce *anxiety.* People tend to seek an escape from the source of these influences—*stressors*—through such means as a *defense mechanism, avoidance* of certain situations, *phobia,* somatization, rituals, or constructive physical activity.

stress–diathesis theory The hypothesis that some mental disorders, including *schizophrenia,* are the result of genetic predisposition combined with some stressful situations in the environment.

stressful life events *Crisis* occurrences experienced by an individual that require coping responses but at a time when familiar sources of support or resources are no longer available. Major stressful life events include the *death* of a spouse or child, loss of a job, *divorce, disease* of a family member, and moving to a new neighborhood.

stressor A *stimulus* that leads to *anxiety* or other mental disorders unless the individual's *coping skills* are used effectively.

stroke A sudden interruption or blockage of the flow of blood to the brain, usually caused by the formation of a blood clot in the blood vessel. The resulting manifestations may include paralysis of certain parts of the body, speech and language deficits, sensory loss, cognitive and communicative disturbances, convulsions, and coma. Stroke survivors vary in their recovery progress; approximately 50 percent retain some permanent disability, such as speech or motor coordination problems. Recurrence is frequent and often fatal. The term is also known as *cerebrovascular accident (CVA)*.

structural approach A social work model developed by Gale G. Wood and Ruth R. Middleman (*The Structural Approach to Direct Practice in Social Work*, New York: Columbia University Press, 1989) in which the social environment is the primary target of change, and the intervention is to improve the quality of the relationship between people and their social environment by changing, creating, or using existing social structures.

structural family therapy An orientation and procedure in *family therapy* based on identifying and changing maladaptive arrangements, interactions, and the internal organization of subsystems and boundaries of a family. Structural family therapy was developed in the 1970s primarily by Salvador Minuchin and emphasizes helping families understand how they have developed rules and roles for their members and between themselves as a unit and outsiders.

structural social change Basic and relatively rapid changes in social institutions and social values, often brought about by revolution, great political upheaval, or natural disaster. This is the opposite of *incremental social change*.

structural social work A practice model that assumes that inadequate social arrangements are mainly responsible for many clients' problems. The model aims to help people modify the social situations that limit their functioning—for example, by connecting them with needed *resources*, negotiating difficult situations, and changing certain existing limiting social structures.

structural unemployment One of the four types of *unemployment* (including *cyclical unemployment, seasonal unemployment*, and *frictional unemployment*), caused by poor economic conditions in one industry or geographic area when *employment* elsewhere is good.

structured group See *group, structured*.

structured observation In social work *research*, the practice of systematically witnessing those aspects of a social phenomenon that fit a predetermined plan. It may take place in a clinical setting, laboratory experiment, or in the field, and the observer usually has a checklist of categories to note. The categories were developed by the investigator based on hypotheses or findings from previous research.

student aid programs Financial assistance to people attending colleges or other educational institutions, mostly through grants or loans. Sources of funds are privately funded scholarships, foundation grants, and state and federal grant and loan programs. The major federal programs include Pell Grants (based on a formula of student need and expected family contribution); National Direct Student Loans (low-interest loans to needy students); Supplemental Educational Opportunity Grants (based on need); Guaranteed Student Loans (the government guarantees repayment to banks that lend money to students); and the College Work Study Program, which provides matching funds to colleges to hire students on campus.

stupor A state of numbness and dazed confusion, often symptomatic of people with *organic mental disorders, schizophrenia,* and *intoxication.*

stuttering One of the *communication disorders* characterized by disturbance of speech function, usually involving frequent repetitions of words or parts of words, disruptions in the flow of speech, and hesitations or prolongations of sounds. Stuttering, which also is known as "stammering," tends to be more intense when the individual is under scrutiny or feels under pressure to communicate. See also *cluttering* and *expressive language disorder.*

St. Vincent de Paul Society An international Catholic lay group established in France in 1833 by *Antoine Frederic Ozanum* to provide financial relief, *counseling,* and *social services* for poor people. The organization has local centers in most nations with significant Catholic populations, including the United States.

subemployment The condition of having a job that pays below *subsistence level* or a job that does not use much of the worker's education or previous experience. Social workers describe many people who are *working poor* as being subemployed.

subject An individual, group, organization, or entity that is being evaluated in the *research* design.

subjugated knowledge The range of information and understanding that is acquired outside the established (scientific method) knowledge-building procedures and possessed indigenously by people who are not considered "experts." Because this type of knowledge comes from and is maintained outside the academic or professional establishment, it is given little serious attention, that is, it is subjugated. According to Ann Hartman ("In Search of Subjugated Knowledge," *Social Work, 37*[November 1992], pp. 483–484), when the privileged hypotheses of the experts are challenged by grassroots movements of people who have learned other truths, there is a valuable "insurrection of subjugated knowledge."

sublimation In *psychodynamic* theory, a *defense mechanism* in which those desires

and instinctive drives that are consciously intolerable and cannot be directly realized are diverted into creative activities that are acceptable to the individual and society.

subpoena A legal document ordering an individual to appear in court at a certain time. Failure to comply may result in some penalty.

subpoena duces tecum A type of *subpoena* requiring the witness who is called to bring to the court or deposition any relevant documents possessed. See also *case record* and *relative confidentiality.*

subsidized adoption The provision of public financial assistance to families who adopt dependent children. Recent federal and state legislation has established criteria for subsidizing *adoption.* The two prominent criteria are that the child is unlikely to be returning to the natural parents or should not be returning to them and that adoptive placement without a subsidy has already been attempted for a specified amount of time by the proper authorities but has been unsuccessful because of the child's physical or emotional condition or racial or ethnic background.

subsidized employment Work that is paid for partly by the employer and partly by another organization. For example, a government reduces its welfare expenditures and provides work and training opportunities and reimburses an employer who has hired an *Aid to Families with Dependent Children (AFDC)* recipient for part of that employee's wages.

subsidy Money or commodities granted by a government or other organization to another level of government, organization, industry, or individual. See also *grants-in-aid* and *block grant.*

subsistence economy The economic system of a country or group that produces only the minimum amount of goods and services needed for survival, with few *resources* available for education, cultural advancement, or savings.

subsistence level The lowest amount of money or *resources* one needs to survive.

substance abuse   A maladaptive pattern of using certain drugs, alcohol, medications, and toxins despite their adverse consequences. Substance abuse is considered less problematic than *substance dependence* in that *tolerance* and *withdrawal symptoms* have not yet occurred.

substance dependence   Continued use; craving; and other cognitive, behavioral, and physiological symptoms that occur through the use of certain drugs, alcohol, medications, and toxins. Some of the symptoms include preoccupation about the substance; taking greater amounts than intended; persistent efforts to control its use; reducing occupational or social activities; and continued use despite recognizing that it is causing recurrent physical, psychological, or social problems. If *tolerance* or *withdrawal symptoms* have not yet occurred, the condition is known as *substance abuse.*

substance-induced anxiety disorder   Excessive apprehension, tension, fear, restlessness, sleep disturbance, difficulty concentrating, and other symptoms of *anxiety* that are judged to be due to the direct physiological effects of a drug of abuse, medication, or toxin.

substance intoxication   Specific behavioral patterns and symptoms (including cognitive impairment, *emotional lability,* belligerence, impaired judgment, and poor social or occupational functioning) due to recent use of a drug, alcohol, medication, or toxin.

substance intoxication delirium   A *delirium* that occurs within minutes to hours after taking relatively high doses of medication or other substances. The delirium usually ends as the *intoxication* ends or within a few hours to days. A formal diagnosis of this condition would specify the type of substance, as in "alcohol intoxication delirium." See also *substance-use disorders.*

substance-use disorders   A classification of disorders related to the taking in of a drug of abuse, alcohol, medication, or toxin resulting in undesirable symptoms and side effects. In the *DSM-IV* classification the substances used or induced are alcohol, *amphetamine,* caffeine, *cannabis, cocaine, hallucinogen,* inhalant, nicotine, *opium,* phencyclidine, *sedatives,* polysubstances, and other or unknown substances. Disorders that result from this include substance-induced psychotic disorder, *mood disorders, anxiety disorder,* sexual dysfunction, and *sleep disorders.*

substance withdrawal   Significant patterns of physical discomfort and emotional distress, cognitive impairment, *emotional lability,* belligerence, impaired judgment, and poor social or occupational functioning due to reduced or discontinued use of a specific drug, alcohol, medication, or toxin.

substance withdrawal delirium   A *delirium* that occurs after termination or reduction of relatively high doses of certain medications or substances. Duration ranges from minutes after withdrawal begins to two to four weeks. When alcohol is the substance, the condition is also known as *delirium tremens (DTs).*

substitution   In *psychodynamic* theory, the *defense mechanism* in which the individual replaces an unattainable or unacceptable goal with one that is attainable and acceptable.

subsystem   A part of a *system* that itself comprises interacting and reciprocally influencing elements. For example, in the family system such subsystems are the parents, the children, the females, the males, the *nuclear family* system, and the *extended family* system.

successive approximation   A technique commonly used in *behavior therapy* in which each small, incremental step toward the goal behavior is reinforced. See also *shaping.*

sudden infant death syndrome (SIDS)   The unexplained death of a young child, most frequently occurring between ages two and five months, sometimes referred to as "crib death." The cause is not yet well understood, but speculation centers around the possibility that some babies have not established adequate defense responses to respiratory problems. See also *apnea*.

sudden unexplained death syndrome (SUDS) Fatalities, not in infants, whose causes cannot be determined. SUDS was identified first by the U.S. *Centers for Disease Control and Prevention (CDCP)* in young Southeast Asian males who emigrated to the United States, appeared healthy with no warning signs, and died in their sleep.

SUDS See *sudden unexplained death syndrome (SUDS)*.

suffrage The legal right to vote. Many of the early social workers were women who advocated for this right and were called "suffragettes." See also *Seneca Falls Convention*.

suicidal ideation Serious contemplation of *suicide*, or thought patterns that lead to killing oneself. According to André Ivanoff and Marion Riedel ("Suicide," in Richard L. Edwards [Ed.-in-Chief], *Encyclopedia of Social Work*, 19th ed., Washington, DC: NASW Press, 1995), social workers note specific clues and circumstances to judge the probability that a client is going to attempt suicide. Among those that suggest higher probability are *depression,* especially when accompanied by a sense of hopelessness or unconnectedness with others in the present or past; major changes in sleep patterns; clear or implied statements indicating a wish to die or an intention to commit suicide; *substance abuse;* a recent experience of irrevocable *loss;* absence of a support system; easy access to lethal means (weapons, drugs, and so on); previous suicide attempts; suicide or suicide attempts by role models; and strong feelings of failure and rejection.

suicide The act of intentionally killing oneself.

sunk costs In social agency administration and *social planning,* the investment of time and effort made by an organization's personnel to develop, maintain, and facilitate their relationship patterns, status and power arrangements, and traditional ways of doing things.

sunset laws Statutes that require an organization to demonstrate periodically that it is achieving the goals it was established to achieve. If the organization cannot do this, according to these laws, it is automatically discontinued. For example, some states have required certain professions that sought licensing to show after several years that the granting of licenses provided some benefit to the public.

sunshine laws Federal requirements, based on a law enacted in 1976 (Government in the Sunshine Act, P.L. 94-409), stating that the meetings and hearings of most federal agencies—especially those that directly affect people's economic, legal, and welfare rights—must be conducted in public. This term now applies to the requirements that other organizations and levels of government conduct their business open to the scrutiny of those affected.

superego In *psychodynamic* theories, that part of the *psyche* or personality that regulates the individual's ethical standards, *conscience,* and sense of right and wrong. The superego is said to begin its development by identifying with the apparent *values* and rules established by parent figures. See also *ego* and *id*.

Superfund The Resource Conservation and Recovery Act of 1976 (P.L. 94-580), a federal program that allocates resources to be used in the cleanup of *toxic waste sites* and other environmentally hazardous conditions.

superstition Beliefs and practices founded on nonrational expectations, *culture-bound syndromes,* folk tales, and fears of or answers for unexplained phenomena. Clinicians do not consider superstitious ideas or practices to be indicative of mental disorder unless they become so constricting or time-consuming that they interefere with *activities of daily living (ADL)*.

supervised community living The social structure of a group residential facility in which residents are monitored and assisted as needed to fulfill their *activities of daily living (ADL)*.

supervision An administrative and educational process used extensively in social agencies to help social workers further develop and refine their skills and to provide *quality assurance* for the clients. Administratively, supervisors often assign cases to the most appropriate social worker, discuss the assessment and intervention plan, and review the social worker's ongoing contact with the client. Educationally, supervision is geared toward helping the social worker better understand social work philosophy and agency policy, become more self-aware, know the agency's and community's resources, establish activity priorities, and refine knowledge and skills. Another function of supervision is to enhance the morale of the staff while maintaining the system. Less-experienced workers tend to be supervised according to a tutorial model, whereas those with more experience achieve similar purposes through case consultation, peer-group interactions, *staff development* programs, or *social work teams*. Educational supervision (oriented toward professional concerns and related to specific cases) is distinguished from administrative supervision (oriented toward agency policy and public *accountability*).

Supplemental Security Income (SSI) The federal *public assistance* program, established in 1972, that provides a minimum cash income for poor people who are old, disabled, or blind. Funding comes from the federal treasury and is usually supplemented by state funds. It is administered primarily by the *Social Security Administration (SSA)*, although its funds do not come from the funds earmarked for financing *Old Age, Survivors, Disability, and Health Insurance (OASDHI)*. According to Daniel R. Meyer ("Supplemental Security Income," in Richard L. Edwards [Ed.-in-Chief], *Encyclopedia of Social Work*, 19th ed., Washington, DC: NASW Press, 1995), *eligibility* for SSI is determined by a *means test* and not related to one's previous work record.

suppleness The degree to which the body's muscles and joints permit ease of movement.

supply-side economics The thesis in economic theory, popular during the Reagan administration, that lower taxes permit more money to flow into the economy, and therefore results in more jobs and growth.

supply subsidy The concept of providing funds to organizations or allocating funds to establish new organizations so that they can provide services. This is in contrast to the *demand subsidy* concept, in which funds or vouchers are provided to individuals and families so that they can purchase goods and services in the existing service-providing market. Public housing is an example of the supply subsidy concept, and food stamps are an example of demand subsidy.

support group A structured ongoing series of meetings between people who share a common problem and who give advice, encouragement, information, and emotional sustenance. The group may be led by a professional social worker but more often comprises only the members themselves, and the degree of structure varies considerably.

supportive feedback In social work administration and *supervision*, the communication of approval when observing the fulfillment of desired behaviors. See also *corrective feedback*.

supportive treatment The helping interventions used by social workers and other professionals, designed primarily to help individuals maintain adaptive patterns. This is done in the *interview* through *reassurance*, advice giving, information providing, and pointing out client strengths and *resources*. Supportive treatment supposedly does not seek to reach *unconscious* material. However, the boundaries between supportive therapy and "deeper" *insight therapies* are unclear and overlapping.

support system An interrelated group of people, *resources,* and organizations that provide individuals with emotional, informational, material, and affectional sustenance. Members of a support system may include an individual's closest friends, family members, key members of the peer group, fellow employees, membership organizations, and institutions that can be called on for help in times of need.

suppression 1. In psychosocial theory, the conscious psychic mechanism of putting unpleasant thoughts out of one's mind. Suppression is similar to *repression,* except that the latter is a *defense mechanism* operating unconsciously to remove threatening ideas from one's awareness. 2. In social conflict theories, actions taken by one group or organization to prevent other groups or individuals from expressing their ideas, from assembling, or from developing political power.

surrogacy A form of *reproductive technology* in which a man donates his sperm or a woman donates her egg or use of her body so that a *fetus* can be conceived and developed through to birth. A male surrogate donates sperm to a "bank," which, through *artificial insemination,* is used in conceiving a fetus in the biological mother. Male surrogacy generally is used when a man is sterile so that the couple can have a baby that is 50 percent biologically related. A female surrogate donates an egg to a couple; the egg then is artificially inseminated with the husband's sperm in a petri dish. The fertilized egg is then placed in the wife's uterus or in the uterus of the egg donor (or sometimes the uterus of another woman). Female surrogacy generally is used when a woman's anatomy or physiology precludes development of a healthy fetus. Usually the surrogate mother who carries the fetus to delivery is paid and is contracted to relinquish the baby soon after birth. Legal debates have challenged whether these contracts are irrevocable.

surrogate parent 1. In the justice system, an individual who is not a child's biological parent but who voluntarily or through court appointment assumes the parent's rights and obligations. 2. A man who donates his sperm or a woman who donates an egg or temporary use of her uterus to a couple so that they can become parents.

survey A systematic fact-gathering procedure in which a specific series of questions is asked, through written or oral *questionnaires,* of a representative *sample* of the *group* being studied or of the entire *population.*

survival bonding The pairing of social workers in agencies with high rates of employee stress to provide them with the *mutual help* and collaborative opportunities needed to reduce the likelihood of *burnout.* According to Kathleen Wade and Ellen Perlman Simon ("Survival Bonding: A Response to Stress and Work with AIDS," *Health & Social Work*), the pairing gives both workers a degree of shared responsibility, mutual respect and dependence, stress reduction through mutual ventilation, elimination of isolation, and opportunities for the exchange of information. This shared responsibility is particularly useful in working with terminally ill clients such as those with *acquired immune deficiency syndrome (AIDS).*

survivor guilt A strong sense of *shame, depression,* and regret that often follows escape from some danger that harmed others. Survivors of war, earthquakes, group hostage-taking, and similar experiences are particularly vulnerable. When this feeling persists and interferes with adequate social functioning, it is known as *survivor syndrome.*

survivor syndrome The behavior patterns, traits, and symptoms that tend to occur in people who have experienced dangerous, life-threatening events or *trauma.* Such people often have prolonged periodic *anxiety,* guilt feelings, anger, and fears, especially in situations that seem similar to the traumatic event. The syndrome has been experienced especially by *Vietnam veterans,* former prisoners of war, *Holocaust* survivors, sexual assault victims, *crime* victims, and people who have lived through serious natural disasters. See also *posttraumatic stress disorder (PTSD).*

suspended sentence The deferral of a legally prescribed punishment, such as incarceration or payment of damages, until a probationary period is over. The sentence may be set aside if the conditions of the probation have been met.

suspicion The belief that someone has done or intends to do something wrong or harmful, often with little evidence. This is a major symptom of *paranoia* and the paranoid type of *schizophrenia.*

sustaining procedures Relationship-building activities used by the social worker to help the client feel more self-confident and confident of the worker's competence and good will, including listening with sincere interest and sympathy and conveying a sense of mutual respect rather than superiority over the client. *Acceptance, reassurance,* encouragement, and *reaching out* are other sustaining procedures.

susto A *culture-bound syndrome* most common to Latinos and Spanish-speaking peoples in which the individual experiences sickness and unhappiness, which is said to be caused by the soul leaving the body after a frightening event. Symptoms include *sleep disorders,* appetite disturbances, and various somatic ailments, sometimes days to years after the onset event. Ritual healings to call the soul back to the body sometimes reduce or eliminate the symptoms.

SWAP program Social workers assistance program, a volunteer group of colleagues attached to various *National Association of Social Workers (NASW)* chapters, who provide confidential consultation and referral services to other social workers who are experiencing personal problems.

SWRG See *Social Work Research Group (SWRG).*

symbiosis A relationship between two organisms in which there is mutual biological or psychological dependence. This may occur between different species (flowers depend on insects for cross-pollination and provide food necessary for the insects' survival) or within a species (termites help one another to survive). Symbiosis occurs between a parent and a child and to some extent between mature adults in certain mutually beneficial social relationships. The term also refers to a person's identification with others to such an extent that it blocks his or her differentiated identity. See also *codependency.*

SYMLOG See *Systematic Multiple-Level Observation of Groups (SYMLOG).*

sympathetic nervous system The part of the nervous system that controls the invol-untary responses to perceived danger, such as increasing the rate of heartbeat and dilation of the pupils.

symptom An indicator of the possible presence of an underlying psychological or physical disorder or of a psychosocial problem. For example, *flat affect* is symptomatic of *schizophrenia; depression* and *ideas of reference* are symptomatic of *paranoia;* abnormally high fever is symptomatic of an infection, dramatic weight loss is symptomatic of *anorexia nervosa,* and *inflation* is symptomatic of a supply–demand imbalance.

symptomatic Indicators within an individual, family, group, society, or system of an underlying disorder, disease, or problem.

synapse The space between adjacent *neuron* fibers through which neurotransmitters travel.

syndicalism The political ideology advocating better conditions and wages for workers and the elimination of state authority over economic organizations. It also advocated anarchy and revolution. The ideology developed in France in 1890 and spread throughout Europe and South America primarily in the trade union movement but lost influence at the beginning of World War I.

syndrome A cluster of behavior patterns, personality traits, or physical symptoms that occur together to form a specific disorder or condition.

synergism 1. Cooperative effort by discrete organizations, social agencies, or subsystems that produces a more-effective result than the sum of the output that could be achieved if the organizations acted independently. 2. The combined effect of two or more drugs that is greater than the total effect of each drug working alone. See also *systems theories.*

synoptic planning A model of *social planning* for economic, health, physical, and social needs that is comprehensive and rational. This is the planning "ideal," but many suggest that it can never be realized because of the limits of human rationality and the complexities of fully comprehensive planning.

syphilis A contagious *venereal disease* transmitted primarily by sexual contact and rarely by contact with an open wound or transmission of infected blood or plasma. Untreated, the disease causes lesions in subcutaneous tissue and internal organs and degeneration of the nerves, often causing blindness and psychosis. Treatment with penicillin in the early stages is very effective.

system A combination of elements with mutual reciprocity and identifiable *boundaries* that form a complex or unitary whole. Systems may be physical and mechanical, living and social, or combinations of these. Examples of social systems include individual families, groups, a specific social welfare agency, or a nation's entire organizational process of education.

systematic desensitization A *behavior modification* technique, designed by Joseph Wolpe in the 1950s, that gradually alleviates the *fear* and *anxiety* associated with an object or event. Using relaxation exercises and *imagery relaxation technique,* the client is exposed to stimuli from a gradation of anxiety-provoking situations. For example, if a client is afraid of heights of more than six feet, the social worker might encourage the client to stand on the lowest rung of a stepladder while thinking of some pleasant experiences long enough for anxiety to end at that level. This process would be repeated slowly until the client is comfortable at levels higher than six feet.

Systematic Multiple-Level Observation of Groups (SYMLOG) A method developed by social psychologist Robert F. Bales to assess client behavior graphically and to quantify systematically actions in the social worker–client system.

systemic requisites In *community organization* and social policy development, the identification of existing as well as potential *resources* and programs and the collaborative effort to link and coordinate these resources so that duplication and competition are avoided and the range and quality of service are expanded. See also *functional requisites.*

systems analysis The process of evaluating through the *scientific method* data about any set of dynamically interconnected elements and the environment in which they function.

systems theories Those concepts that emphasize reciprocal relationships between the elements that constitute a whole. These concepts also emphasize the relationships among individuals, groups, organizations, or communities and mutually influencing factors in the environment. Systems theories focus on the interrelationships of elements in nature, encompassing physics, chemistry, biology, and social relationships. See also *general systems theory, ecological perspective, life model,* and *ecosystems perspective.*

T

TA See *transactional analysis (TA)*.

tachycardia Excessively rapid heartbeat.

tactics Carefully designed and implemented procedures an individual or, more usually, a group uses to bring about short-term changes in another group or individual. Tactics refers to short-term or day-to-day maneuvers, whereas *strategies* refers to the long-range approaches and ultimate goals. See also *legislative advocacy tactics*.

tactics of influence Activities of *community organizers, social activists,* and other social workers to encourage adoption of one policy over another. Some actions include holding case conferences with individuals and organizations to determine needs and needs provision, gathering facts, taking advocacy positions, convening and participating in committees, petitioning, *media campaigning,* providing expert testimony, working as *lobbyists, bargaining,* organizing a *demonstration,* initiating or coordinating a *class action suit,* and engaging in *disruptive tactics.* See also *tactics, strategies,* and *legislative advocacy tactics.*

Taft, Jessie (1882–1960) Social work educator and casework practitioner who developed the *functional school in social work* with her colleague *Virginia Robinson* and integrated the theories of psychoanalyst Otto Rank (1884–1937) into the social work curriculum. Her best known book is *A Functional Approach to Social Casework* (1944).

taijin kyofusho A *culture-bound syndrome* found most commonly in Japan in which an individual experiences intense fear of being offensive to others through physical appearance, body odors, or gestures. See also *somatic-type delusional disorder.*

take-turns format A procedure in which each member of a *social group work* or *group psychotherapy* session sequentially discusses an issue. This procedure is considered less effective because it discourages free interaction, forces premature self-disclosures, and produces undue anxiety in those waiting.

"taking the fifth" Refusing to answer questions asked by law authorities by exercising the U.S. Constitution's *Fifth Amendment rights* against self-incrimination. See also *Miranda.*

Tarasoff The 1976 ruling by the Supreme Court of California *(Tarasoff* v. *Regents of the University of California)* stating that, under certain circumstances, psychotherapists whose clients tell them that they intend to harm someone are obliged to warn the intended victim. Subsequently, this decision has been upheld in many other states. Some social workers have argued that the effect of the ruling is to make it more difficult for therapists to assure their clients of *confidentiality* and for clients to express certain hostile feelings to their therapists. Others argue that the effect of the ruling is to save the lives of innocent people. See also *confidentiality, relative confidentiality,* and *code of ethics.*

tardive dyskinesia (TD) A *medication-induced movement disorder* including abnormal and uncontrollable physical movements, especially of the mouth, lips, and tongue, and sometimes repetitive movements of the head, hands, and feet. This is seen in many clients who have used antipsychotic drugs over time.

target behavior In *behavior modification,* the behavior or behaviors selected for analysis or modification. Identifying the target behaviors is the first step in the therapist's *behavioral assessment.* This includes delineating the specific behaviors and the time and conditions in which they occur. For example, a social worker would list a target behavior for a youngster who frequently skips school as follows: "Student was absent from school an average of two times per week during the past two months." See also *unit of attention.*

target of intervention In social work practice, that which is to be changed so that the problems presented or recognized by the *client,* the *client system,* or the *social worker* can be solved or mitigated.

target segments of society In *social planning* and policy development, a category of people who are deemed most vulnerable to a given social problem or who are given special attention in efforts to find solutions or enhanced well-being. For example, a target segment might be all American mothers, everyone who is functionally illiterate, or all residents of Tacoma, Washington. See also *unit of attention.*

target system The individual, group, or community to be changed or influenced to achieve the social work goals. This is one of the four basic systems in social work practice (the others being the *change agent system,* the *client system,* and the *action system*). Target systems and client systems are sometimes but not always identical. They are different when the client is not to be changed. For example, a client may be a poor family that is being evicted, and the social worker's target system might be the landlord. Target systems and client systems may be the same when the client wants to achieve some self-change, such as relief from symptoms of emotional distress. See also *unit of attention.*

task-centered treatment A model of short-term social work *intervention* in which the social worker and client identify problems and the tasks needed to change them, develop a contract in which various activities are to occur at specified times, establish incentives and a rationale for their accomplishment, and analyze and resolve obstacles as they are identified. The client may also be helped to accomplish tasks by simulation and guided practice in the social worker's office before performing them independently during the week. The social worker also facilitates a contextual analysis by helping the client identify, locate, and use *resources* and modify distorted perceptions or unrealistic expectations.

task force A temporary *group,* usually within an *organization,* brought together to achieve some previously specified function or goal. An effective task force or task group knows why it is meeting, what jobs must be accomplished, who has responsibility for carrying out its decisions, and when the work is completed.

task implementation sequence (TIS) A systematic procedure for helping clients accomplish general tasks and *operational tasks* by enhancing the client's commitment to carrying out a specific task; planning the details for carrying it out; analyzing and resolving the anticipated obstacles; having clients rehearse the behaviors in carrying out the task; and summarizing the plan for task implementation, conveying encouragement and expectation that the client will carry out the task. TIS should be applied systematically but with flexibility to fit different client circumstances and models of *intervention.*

Tavistock group A type of psychoanalytically oriented *group psychotherapy,* originated in 1944 by Wilfred Bion at the Tavistock Clinic in Great Britain, in which the group therapist assumes an apparently passive, almost bystander, role and makes interpretations only to the whole group. A major goal is for members to attain insight into the transference reactions that emerge.

tax A mandatory charge, usually of money, imposed by a *government* to help pay for its operating costs. See also *regressive tax, progressive tax,* and *"sin tax."*

tax incentives   Government programs designed to encourage certain behaviors through policies of taxation. For example, a government may reduce or forgive taxes on a business that agrees to establish labor-intensive factories in its jurisdiction. A government may also attempt, through heavy taxation, to discourage actions such as smoking tobacco products or driving automobiles that consume great amounts of fuel, which is also known as a tax disincentive.

Taylor, Graham (1851–1938)   Settlement house founder and early developer of *social work education,* he developed training courses for volunteers and *friendly visitors* that were incorporated into the first social work curriculum. He also founded and edited one of the first social work journals, *The Survey.*

Tay–Sachs disease   A genetically transmitted metabolic disorder that results in fatal brain damage. It occurs mostly in infants of East European Jewish ancestry. See also *genetic disorder* and *genetic counseling.*

TD   See *tardive dyskinesia (TD).*

teams in social work   See *social work team.*

technique   The knowledge-based skills, methods, and procedures purposefully used to achieve explicit goals.

technocrat   An official of a government or private organization whose decisions are based on scientific and technological findings rather than sociopolitical ones. See also *apparatchik.*

technological disaster   A *disaster* caused by accidents within manufacturing plants or conveyances that causes mass destruction to people, property, or the environment in a widespread area. The designation is used by disaster experts to distinguish these kinds of problems from the natural disasters such as earthquakes, drought, famine, floods, and hurricanes, and from war or civil conflict. Technological disasters in-

clude such events as massive oil spills, nuclear power generator breakdown and contamination of an area, or dams bursting and flooding populated areas downriver.

teleological   1. Purposeful; goal directed. 2. Clinical social workers and other psychotherapists sometimes use this term to refer to the client's ultimate goal directedness and the worker's effort to help sort out goals and move purposefully. Workers influenced by Alfred Adler's (1870–1937) form of psychoanalysis emphasize the need to understand and modify goals.

telephone reassurance   A program to provide daily contact for people who live alone and have concerns about their health and security. Local senior centers, social services departments, and city and state agencies on aging sponsor such programs, which are usually staffed by volunteers.

telephone scatologia   A *sexual disorder (paraphilia)* involving the making of obscene telephone calls.

temperament   The affective component of a person's personality.

temperance movements   Organized efforts to influence people to abstain from or modify their consumption of alcohol. These movements were especially strong in the United States, Canada, and European nations in the years 1850 to 1930. The major groups in the United States were the Women's Christian Temperance Union, the Prohibition Party, and the Anti-Saloon League, which helped influence passage of many antiliquor laws, culminating in the 18th Amendment to the U.S. Constitution in 1919, or Prohibition. The influence of these groups declined when Prohibition was repealed by the 21st Amendment in 1933.

temporary disability insurance   State-run *social insurance* programs to protect workers from some of the financial consequences of being out of work due to injuries or disabilities that are not expected to last indefinitely. When the disability is expected to be permanent, federal disability insurance programs such as *Supplemental Security*

Insurance (SSI) or *Disability Insurance (DI)* are used.

tenant management   A program in *public housing* projects whereby residents participate in making and implementing decisions affecting their homes.

tenant organization   A formal or informal association of people, most of whom live in the same apartment building or housing complex and share an interest in maintaining or improving the conditions of their residence. Tenant organizations often present unity in confrontations with landlords or public housing authorities.

tenement house   A multifamily residential structure, usually old, run down, and rented to poor people.

terminal illness   A disease that is expected to result in a person's death.

termination   The conclusion of the social worker–client *intervention* process; a systematic procedure for disengaging the working *relationship*. It occurs when goals are reached, when the specified time for working has ended, or when the client is no longer interested in continuing. Termination often includes evaluating the progress toward goal achievement, *working through, resistance, denial,* and *flight into illness.* The termination phase also includes discussions about how to anticipate and resolve future problems and how to find additional *resources* to call on as future needs indicate. See also *premature termination* and *"client dumping."*

terrorism   The systematic use of fear, intimidation, and disruption of social systems, usually by politically motivated or criminal groups, to gain publicity or concessions. This is a violent form of social activism. See also *social activist.*

tertiary care   In the system for delivery of health care, the type of *intervention* provided by highly specialized professionals, usually taking place in large health care centers and university-based hospitals where sophisticated diagnostic and treatment equipment is found. Patients are referred to this level of care by primary or secondary-level physicians. See also *primary care* and *secondary care.*

tertiary gain   The advantages and benefits a person with a physical or mental illness brings to others as a result of the illness. For example, a patient's sickness requires that the spouse remain home to provide care and avoid working at an unpleasant job.

tertiary prevention   Rehabilitative efforts by the social worker or other professional to assist a client who has already experienced a problem to recuperate from its effects and develop sufficient strengths to preclude its return. Most forms of clinical *intervention* can be considered forms of tertiary prevention. See also *primary prevention* and *secondary prevention.*

test bias   A tendency built into a test causing its results to be inaccurate. For example, some aptitude tests are said to be culturally biased against some racial and ethnic groups when those groups tend to score lower than do other test takers.

test case   A lawsuit to determine whether a law or legal practice is valid. Often the case is brought intentionally by a cause-oriented group to test the validity of a newly passed law. For example, a state enacts a law stating that psychotherapy may be provided only by psychiatrists. A social work group might designate one of its members to provide psychotherapy and therefore be arrested. The resulting court case could test whether the law could be upheld.

test–retest reliability   In *research,* the degree to which a test or procedure achieves a similar outcome the second time it is administered to a group of subjects. For example, a group of social work students might be asked to take an aptitude test and after a period of time to retake it. *Reliability* is considered low if the second set of scores is very different from the first set.

tetanus   A disease characterized by violent *tremor,* spasms, muscle contraction and stiffness, and sometimes death, caused by certain bacilli entering the body through wounds. The disease is preventable by *inoculation*.

tetrogens Factors that are potentially harmful to a developing fetus or embryo, sometimes resulting in miscarriage, neonatal death, congenital deformities, mental retardation, learning disabilities, and growth retardation. Tetrogens include drugs and chemicals (alcohol, cocaine, tobacco, some antibiotics), infections (*rubella*, some *sexually transmitted diseases [STDs]*, *acquired immune deficiency syndrome [AIDS]*), and radiation. Tetrogenic effects vary with type of agent, duration and frequency of exposure, and stage of fetal development; some fetuses are more vulnerable than others to the same tetrogens. Fetal exposure to alcohol is a major cause of mental retardation.

T-group A training group, often made up of people who work together in one organization, that emphasizes communication, self-development, and cooperative problem solving. Some T-groups are structured, whereas others are unstructured to encourage the members to learn by experience how to be more effective in interpersonal relationships.

thanatophobia Pathological *fear* of death.

THC Tetrahydrocannibinol, the active ingredient in *marijuana*.

theme group A type of *group therapy* or *social group work* for which the range of discussion is highly focused around a single subject or theme that is of concern to all participants.

theory A group of related hypotheses, concepts, and constructs, based on facts and observations, that attempts to explain a particular phenomenon.

therapeutic community See *milieu therapy*.

therapist One who helps individuals to overcome or abate disease, disability, or problems. Usually a therapist has had extensive training and supervised experience and often uses specialized techniques, tools, medications, and *resources* to accomplish goals. So-cial workers often use this term as a synonym for *psychotherapist* and are more specific when discussing other kinds of therapists, such as physical therapists, marital therapists, and occupational therapists.

therapy A systematic process and activity designed to remedy, cure, or abate some disease, disability, or problem. Social workers often use this term as a synonym for *psychotherapy, psychosocial therapy,* or *group therapy.* When social workers discuss other types of therapy, such as *occupational therapy,* physical therapy, recreational therapy, medication therapy, or *chemotherapy,* they use these more specific terms.

think tanks Organizations funded largely by federal government and foundation moneys to conduct research and systematic inquiries, primarily into existing sociopolitical and environmental conditions and future trends. Such organizations include the Rand Corporation, the Hudson Institute, the Brookings Institution, and the Institutes for the Study of Poverty.

third party A government funding agency or private insurance company that reimburses a social worker or other service provider (first party) for helping a client (second party). See also *fourth party* and *managed health care program*.

third-party evaluations A professional determination about some aspect of a client, such as mental or emotional state; preexisting health condition; or capacity to undertake some new status such as marriage, a job, or a clearance. The information is obtained by the social worker from interviews and tests with the client and provided to a third party. This could be an insurance company, a potential employer, a prospective spouse, an attorney, or others. The information is given only with the client's *informed consent*.

third-party payment Financial reimbursement made to the social worker, social agency, or other provider of services to a client by an insurance company or government funding agency. See also *fiscal intermediaries* and *fourth party*.

Third World The nations of the world that are economically underdeveloped but growing. The term derives from these nations' expressed nonalignment with the Western and Eastern-bloc nations (first and second worlds). Third World countries are distinguished from *Fourth World* countries (which have few resources and little hope of development) by regular increases in literacy rates, per capita income, financial reserves, and use of natural resources. Examples of Third World countries are India, Brazil, Nigeria, and Egypt. See also *developing countries* and *underdeveloped nations*.

Thomas, Jesse O. (1883–1972) Leader in the *National Urban League* and social work educator, he led the movement to encourage more *black people* to enter social work and helped found various training programs for black social workers, including the Atlanta University School of Social Work.

thought disorders Disturbances in the process and content of one's thinking, including such patterns as *hallucination, delusion, loose association, paranoid ideation, flight of ideas,* and *ideas of reference.* Thought disorders may be symptomatic of *organic mental disorders* or of *schizophrenia.*

thought insertion The *delusion* sometimes found in certain forms of *schizophrenia* and other mental conditions that others are placing alien thoughts in one's mind.

thought stopping A technique used in *behavior therapy* in which obsessive thoughts are ended when the therapist or others says the word "stop."

thought switching A procedure commonly used in *behavior therapy* and *cognitive therapy* designed to eliminate fear-inducing anticipatory thoughts, such as speaking before large groups. The client is taught to stop the fearful thought, sometimes by saying "stop" and then concentrating on achieving relaxation, or by replacing the negative thoughts with positive ones until they predominate. Behavioral therapists also call the technique *thought stopping.*

thought withdrawal The *delusion* sometimes found in certain forms of *schizophrenia* and other mental conditions that one's mental processes and ideas are being extracted by outside forces.

thrombosis Clogging of a blood vessel as a result of a blood clot. In a coronary thrombosis, the coronary arteries that supply blood to the heart are clogged, resulting in damage to the heart muscle.

thrownaway children Children who no longer live in the homes of their parents or legal guardians, or usually any other suitable residential facility, because of the wishes or indifference of the parents or guardians. Otherwise, the circumstances of these children are similar to or identical with those of *runaways.*

tic A recurrent, uncontrollable, and inappropriate muscle movement of a part of the body.

tic disorder A disorder characterized by involuntary rapid muscle movements or vocalizations. This disorder includes the *transient tic disorder, chronic motor or vocal tic disorder,* and *Tourette's disorder.*

TIE framework A conceptualization about the transactions between individuals and environments. Developed by Marjorie M. Monkman ("Outcome Objectives in Social Work Practice: Person and Environment," *Social Work,* 36[May 1991], pp. 260–266), TIE deals with the action taken by social workers to change the simultaneous transactions between people and environment (the *independent variable*). The action seeks to match the coping behavior with the qualities of the impinging environment.

time-limited eligibility In *public assistance* programs, the discontinuance of benefits after a certain point, regardless of whether the client needs further assistance or not. Many states and jurisdictions have put time limits on clients using their *general assistance (GA)* programs. GA is not federally regulated, and the states argue that the program was never intended as a permanent aid system.

time-limited hot line A *hot line* or *help line* system set up to exist for only short duration, during which intense, focused community attention can be given. For example, they can be set up for a few days after television specials or telethons dealing with certain problems, political events that seek new supporters, and holiday season programs to attract year-round volunteers.

time-limited service A relatively short-term *intervention* model in which the date of termination or number of meetings is specified in advance. See also *open-ended service* and *open-ended service versus time-limited service*.

TIS See *task implementation sequence (TIS)*.

Title IX Part of the Education Amendments Act of 1972 (P.L. 92-318) that prohibits most forms of *sex discrimination* in educational programs that receive federal funds. The legislation has influenced school systems to increase their athletic programs for girls and women, although it has not resulted in equal expenditures for athletics for both sexes.

Title XX The 1975 provision (P.L. 93-647) added to the *Social Security Act* of 1935 to separate *income transfer payments* from *personal social services* programs and to encourage the states to take a larger part in developing funding for these programs and to put a ceiling on federal funding for social services. Funding comes through *block grants* from federal to state governments. The states then have greater discretion in deciding where to put those funds. The ultimate goal is to help low-income families achieve greater self-sufficiency and to provide for needy people in an economical way. Title XX encourages such programs as *day care* for low- to moderate-income mothers who work and services for abused children and homebound older people. It is the nation's largest single source of funds for personal social services.

Titmuss, Richard (1907–1973) British scholar, administrator, and developer of many *social welfare* programs and *social work education* programs. He had international influence on the development of social welfare theory and practice and wrote many of the field's most important works, including *Problems of Social Policy* (1950), and *Income Distribution and Social Change* (1962).

toddler A young child, about one to three years old, who is just developing walking and other *gross motor skills*.

token economy The therapeutic procedure, used in *behavior modification, milieu therapy*, and various institutional settings, in which the clients are given tokens, slips of paper, or coupons whenever they fulfill specified tasks or behave according to some specified standard. These tokens may then be redeemed for the client's choice of certain goods or privileges.

tokenism Pretending to meet public pressure or legal requirements for nondiscrimination by hiring, promoting, or including for membership one or a few people of color or women.

tolerance An individual's capacity to endure or resist the effects of certain drugs. Because drug response tends to decrease with repeated doses, the user increases the amount taken to get the same effect.

tort A wrongful act that harms someone and for which the injured party has the right to sue for damages in civil courts. Examples include *malpractice, libel,* and *slander. Crime* and breach of contract are not considered torts.

total disability As used in *workers' compensation* and insurance contracts, the term refers to an individual's inability—usually caused by work-related injury or health problems—to perform the occupational requirements of the job category once held.

total quality management (TQM) An orientation to management of organizations, including social services agencies, in which quality, as defined by clients and consumers, is the overriding goal, and client satisfaction, employee empowerment, and long-term relationships determine procedures. According to Lawrence L. Martin (*Total Quality Management in Human Service Organizations*, Newbury Park, CA: Sage Publications, 1993), TQM change is continuous and accomplished by teamwork, with organizational communication going in all ways, and long-term relationships with providers are developed (rather than encouraging them to compete with one another solely on the basis of price).

tough-love parenting   The parenting style based on the premise that some children and adolescents need firm discipline as well as love and forgiveness. Tough-love programs help parents establish minimum acceptable standards for their children's behavior and show them techniques for enforcing those standards. Tough-love emphasizes controls on children by providing and depriving them of privileges based on their conformity with explicit rules. Many communities have tough-love *self-help groups* comprising parents who provide mutual support to reinforce their goals and techniques with their children.

Tourette's disorder   A *tic disorder* manifested in the victim by facial grimacing, abrupt and jerky movements of the limbs, hyperactive behavior, explosive temper, and foul language. Although the disorder is usually lifelong, its symptoms tend to begin in children from ages two to 13, worsen through childhood, and decline in later years. The symptoms may spontaneously remit or cease during adulthood or be controlled successfully with certain drugs. The disorder is also known as "Gilles de la Tourette's disease."

Towle, Charlotte (1896–1966)   Social work educator and scholar who created an influential generic casework curriculum used in many schools of social work and developed concepts for integrating *public assistance* programs with human behavior and *needs*. She wrote the social work classic *Common Human Needs* in 1945 (Silver Spring, MD: National Association of Social Workers, revised 1987).

Townsend Plan   A proposal, made by Francis Townsend in the early 1930s, advocating federal payments of $200 monthly to all people older than age 60 who agree to retire from work and spend the money within a month. The plan spurred a strong *social movement,* especially among older people in the United States, and contributed in part to the development of the *Social Security Act* of 1935.

toxic shock syndrome (TSS)   An acute and sometimes fatal disease with symptoms including high fever, vomiting, diarrhea, and a sharp drop in blood pressure. The symptoms are caused by bacterial infection, often stimulated by the use of vaginal tampons.

toxic waste disposal   Elimination of the poisonous chemicals that had been the residue of manufactured products. The enormous costs of cleaning up *toxic waste sites* have led environmentalists and scientists to seek better alternatives. So far the alternatives are to build better dumps, break down the poisons to eliminate their toxicity, and find manufacturing procedures that do not produce the toxins. Building better dumps (by developing landfills with secure liners or systems that recapture any leaked liquids or gasses) is the most economical response in the short term, but it only postpones the problem. Breaking down the poisons, mostly by neutralizing them with heat or other chemicals, is another alternative, but it is proving to be expensive and still wasteful. The best solution, changing the manufacturing process, is underway in many industries, but it is costly and meets with resistance from many groups.

toxic waste sites   Disposal grounds and dumps where hazardous materials such as nuclear and chemical pollutants have been placed. Often these materials are poorly contained and escape into the atmosphere, soil, or water table and contaminate the environment. See also *Superfund.*

toxin   A poison.

TOXLINE   A *database* maintained by the National Library of Medicine, *National In-*

stitutes of Health (NIH), to provide access to information about environmental pollutants, adverse drug reactions, and toxicity. Charges for this service are based on computer time used.

toxoids The poisonous waste products of disease-causing microorganisms that are used to make certain vaccines to protect against specific diseases.

Toynbee Hall The British settlement house that was established in 1884 by *Samuel A. Barnett* and became the prototype for the 400 American *settlement houses* that developed during the next 20 years. It was located in a poor section of London and served as something of a "missionary outpost," bringing the ideas, *values,* and *social skills* of affluent people to those who were less fortunate.

TQM See *total quality management (TQM).*

tranquilizer A *psychotropic drug* used by physicians in the treatment of mental disorders and emotional discomfort. Major tranquilizers such as Thorazine, Stelazine, and Mellaril are frequently used to help with *psychotic* symptoms. Minor tranquilizers such as Valium, Librium, and Tranxene are frequently used to help with symptoms of *anxiety.*

transactional analysis (TA) A form of group and individual *psychotherapy* that explores the way clients tend to interact with others; play games; perform roles as though scripted to do so; and are influenced by the three parts of the mental–cultural apparatus known as the "parent," "adult," and "child."

transactions Reciprocal exchanges between two entities, influencing or changing both. See also *circular causality.*

transference A concept, originating in *psychoanalytic theory,* that refers to emotional reactions that are assigned to current relationships but originated in earlier, often unresolved and *unconscious* experiences. For example, a client who as a child felt extremely hostile to a parent and never resolved the feeling develops extremely hos-

tile feelings toward the social worker even though no overt reason exists for such feelings. Transference is used by psychodynamically oriented social workers and other therapists as a tool for understanding and *working through* past conflicts. The transfer of affectionate feelings to the worker is known as *positive transference* and that of hostile feelings as *negative transference.* See also *countertransference.*

transfer payments Cash benefits, theoretically taken from one population group and redirected to another. Typically, this is done indirectly with money withheld from one group and placed into the government treasury, which then disburses funds to the eligible other party. For example, money is transferred from young to older people in *social security,* from employed to unemployed people in *unemployment compensation,* and from more-affluent to poor people in *Aid to Families with Dependent Children (AFDC).* In the United States, some of the other major income transfer programs are *Supplemental Security Income (SSI), Medicare,* and *Medicaid.*

transfer summary The social worker's final notes made about a client and placed in the relevant *case record* before the case is turned over to another professional. Included in this summary are the following (not necessarily in this order): the client's *prognosis;* probable service needs in the near future; a description of any anticipated or possible special health, emotional, or situational crises; unfinished tasks, goals, or commitments; an overall description of the entire *intervention* process; and a summary of the worker's final impressions, concerns, and recommendations.

transients People who change places of residence frequently or maintain no fixed address. Although such people are often the most in need of health and social services and financial assistance, because they have no permanent homes they are frequently not eligible for existing welfare assistance, which tends to be contingent on fulfillment of certain residency requirements.

transient tic disorder A disorder characterized by rapid repetitive muscle movements that have existed with varying intensity for less than one year. These movements are basically involuntary but can be suppressed for several minutes at a time, usually for no longer than a few hours. The movements tend to increase under stress and diminish during sleep or relaxed times. In diagnosing this disorder, it is necessary to specify whether the symptoms are recurrent or are a single episode. See also *tic disorder.*

transitional group This term is used several ways by social workers: 1. People brought together in a living situation or as a support group for mutual support while they move from one life stage or life crisis to another. 2. Residents of a *transitional living facility.* 3. A form of *group psychotherapy* or *social group work* involving preadolescent and pubescent children (latency–age children) who do not need the intensive experience of group treatment but benefit from mutual support that they cannot get in home situations or with peers.

transitional living facility A residential program for people returning from some form of institutional living to a relatively independent home in a community. Typically, these are short-term group facilities that provide some guidance and monitoring of the residents. See also *halfway houses* and *quarterway houses.*

transpersonal psychology An orientation in the philosophies and therapies related to psychology that emphasizes *spirituality, moral development,* and human connectedness with the cosmos. Its focus is on the next level beyond *self-actualization* to the relationship between humans and all the natural and spiritual components of the universe. The transpersonal orientation draws on Eastern philosophies that recognize intuitive and mystical experiences and other sources of "transrational" wisdom. This orientation is considered the *fourth force* in psychology after the psychoanalytic, behavioral, and humanistic orientations.

transpersonal social work A holistic and multidimensional approach to providing social services that emphasizes *spirituality, moral development,* and other aspects of *transpersonal psychology.* According to Au-Dean S. Cowley, "Transpersonal Social Work: A Theory for the 1990s," *Social Work, 38* [September 1993] pp. 527–534), reductionistic, linear models of social and psychological problem solving are insufficient for today's models of intervention, and transpersonal social work also values the positive, healthy expansion of human consciousness to the realm of the cosmos.

transpersonal therapist A *psychotherapist* or *pastoral counselor* who provides a full range of *holistic* mental health services but who emphasizes issues of *spirituality, moral development,* and access to one's higher levels of consciousness including the soul. The therapist does not focus exclusively on pathology or social problems and goes beyond *self-actualization* toward higher states of consciousness and a cosmic connection between humanity and the universe.

transracial adoption *Adoption* of a child of one racial background by a family of another racial background (for example, a black child and white adoptive parents). This is the opposite of *inracial adoption.*

transsexualism 1. The changing of one's sex through surgery, hormone injections, *psychotherapy,* and special training. 2. A *gender identity disorder* in which an individual has a strong and persistent desire to be a member of the opposite sex.

transvestic fetishism See *transvestism.*

transvestism The *sexual disorder* in which erotic pleasure is derived from wearing clothing designed for members of the opposite sex. Mental health professionals refer to this disorder as "transvestic fetishism." See also *cisvestism.*

trauma An injury to the body or *psyche* by some type of *shock,* violence, or unanticipated situation. Symptoms of psychological trauma include numbness of feeling, withdrawal, helplessness, *depression, anxiety,* and *fear.* See also *posttraumatic stress disorder (PTSD).*

Traveler's Aid Services and programs, located especially in airports, train stations, and bus terminals, to help people who are traveling. Services emphasize helping people find needed facilities in strange cities, locate emergency accommodations and health care, and provide counseling with people who have developed emotional problems related to the stress of travel.

treatment Correcting or alleviating a disorder, disease, or problem. This term was once commonly used, in addition to "study" and "diagnosis," in social work; however, the preferred term now is *intervention* because it does not have the medical connotation and implies an orientation toward resolving a wider range of problems. See also *therapy* and *typology of casework treatment.*

treatment matrix In *family group therapy* or *marital therapy,* the specific worker–client combination used—for example, one therapist for each family member, one therapist of the same gender for each marital partner, one therapist seeing both spouses either together or individually, or any other possible combination.

tremor Shaking or trembling, a symptom often seen in *anxiety, palsy, delirium tremens (DTs),* and some *organic mental disorders.*

triage A *crisis intervention* technique for prioritizing the help that will be available to disaster victims. For example, physically injured earthquake victims may be organized or placed in such a way that medical personnel can first provide help to those in the most critical condition rather than on a first-come, first-served basis. The term originated as a military battlefield procedure of dividing casualties into three categories—those who will die regardless of help, those who will live whether they get help or not, and those who will live only if they receive immediate care. Help is given to this last group first.

triangulation The process in which one individual who feels pressured, distressed, or powerless in relating to another individual brings into the relationship a third person to act as an ally or a distracter. For example, a mother who feels she has too little control over her children brings the father or a grandparent onto the scene. Or, a social worker will sometimes find that an individual client will bring in a spouse or call attention to another family member who is present whenever there is pressure or confrontation.

trichotillomania An *impulse control disorder* involving the obsessive pulling of one's hair, often seen in anxious toddlers and children and sometimes in adults with *anxiety,* masochistic tendencies, or another *mental disorder.* The pattern results in noticeable hair loss in those sites where it occurs (mostly the scalp, eyebrows, and eyelashes).

trickle-down theory The view that federal funds flowing into corporations and private sectors of the economy will stimulate more job opportunities and economic growth than would direct federal payments and programs for unemployed and poor people.

trimester A three-month period during *pregnancy,* usually identified as first, second, and third trimesters.

truancy Failure to fulfill one's duty. This term especially applies to a child who stays away from school without permission.

trust versus mistrust The basic conflict found in the first stage of human development, according to the *psychosocial development theory* of Erik Erikson (1902–1994), occurring from birth to about age two. The infant may develop feelings of security and confidence in those who provide care, or, possibly, because of inconsistent nurturing, may come to doubt that others are reliable.

Truth in Lending Act The 1968 federal law (P.L. 90-321) requiring full and clear disclosure of the terms of loans for which individuals apply. Commercial lenders, including banks, credit card companies, retailers, and real estate organizations, are required to reveal the amount of interest charged, both as an annual percentage and a dollar amount. See also *usury*.

TSS See *toxic shock syndrome (TSS)*.

tubal ligation A surgical method of *birth control* in which the fallopian tubes are severed and tied off. See also *sterilization*.

tuberculosis An *infectious disease* that most commonly affects the lungs and is caused by the tubercle bacillus, which may enter the human body through contact with infected people, through inhalation, or through ingestion (contaminated food or dishes). The incidence of tuberculosis has been dramatically reduced by better sanitary conditions, pasteurization of milk, early case findings through sputum examinations and skin tests, and vaccines.

Tuckerman, Joseph (1778–1840) A Unitarian minister who was influenced by the work of *Thomas Chalmers* in Scotland and organized the Boston Society for the Prevention of Pauperism in 1835, using many of Chalmers's principles of individualized work with poor families, volunteer visitors, coordinated fundraising, and *social action*. His work influenced the subsequent development of the *Charity Organization Societies (COS)*.

Tufts Report A 1923 study on social work education by James H. Tufts formally delineating the components necessary to provide adequate education for social workers. The report was influential in developing the social work education system toward social cause and macro perspectives. See also *social work education, Hollis–Taylor Report,* and *Social Work Curriculum Study.*

"turf issues" Conflicts, usually between members of an organization or between different professional groups, about the allocation of responsibilities and benefits. For example, social workers are sometimes involved in such conflicts with psychologists, psychiatrists, or pastoral counselors in deciding who should be authorized to provide psychotherapy.

two-provider family One in which both parents are wage earners, usually in such a way that there is little time to meet all the family demands and needs.

Type A personality A pattern of thinking and behaving characterized by impatience, competitiveness, and excessive concern about time. People who have Type A personalities are said to be at high risk for heart disease and other disorders, even though this is not substantiated by most research. See also *Type B personality.*

Type B personality A pattern of thinking and behaving characterized by patience, noncompetitiveness, and a relaxed attitude about time. People who have Type B personalities are said to be at low risk for heart disease and other disorders, although most research does not substantiate this assertion. See also *Type A personality.*

typhoid fever An *infectious disease*, spread primarily through contaminated water or food. Symptoms include high fever, diarrhea or constipation, red spots on the body, enlargement of the spleen, and damage to various organs. Its incidence has been dramatically reduced through vaccination, sanitary laws pertaining especially to food handlers, and laws promoting a cleaner and safer environment.

typhus An acute *infectious disease* with symptoms of high fever, dark red spots on the skin, delirium, and extreme weakness. The disease is transmitted by fleas, ticks, mites, and lice.

typologies Classification systems used by social workers and others to delineate the components of an entity under scrutiny. For example, many social workers use the *typology of casework treatment*, developed by Florence Hollis in the 1960s to classify the various activities used in social work intervention.

typology of casework treatment The classification of techniques used by social workers in direct work with individual clients, formulated by Florence Hollis in the 1960s and later with Mary E. Woods (*Casework: A Psychosocial Therapy,* 4th ed., New York: McGraw-Hill, 1989, pp. 114–123). The techniques consist of *sustaining procedures, direct influence, ventilation,* reflective consideration of the person–situation configuration, reflection about the dynamics of patterns or tendencies, and thinking about the historical development of those patterns. The typology permits examination of environmental as well as internal influences.

U

UCR 1. See *Uniform Crime Reports (UCR)*. 2. See *usual, customary, or reasonable (UCR)*.

UJA See *United Jewish Appeal (UJA)*.

ulcer An open sore in the wall of the stomach or intestine or other internal organs, in the mucous membrane, or on the skin.

unbiased writing The use of language in the professional literature that avoids the promotion of stereotyped or discriminatory attitudes or assumptions about people. Editors of virtually all social work publications maintain explicit policies against biased writing. The *National Association of Social Workers (NASW)* offers suggestions (Linda Beebe, *Professional Writing for the Human Services*, Washington, DC: NASW Press, 1993 p. 252) for helping to achieve this goal. They include avoiding male pronouns by using plural pronouns to avoid specific gender references, using nongender designations for occupations (police officer instead of policeman), and, when referring to an ethnic group, using the name that group itself prefers.

UNCA See *United Neighborhood Centers of America (UNCA)*.

"Uncle Tom" A term of contempt, based on the character in Harriet Beecher Stowe's antislavery novel, *Uncle Tom's Cabin* (New York: National Era, 1851), referring to a black person whose behavior toward white people is considered servile or whose behavior is seen as antithetical to the interests of *black people* as a group.

unconditional positive regard An element in the social work ethical principles of *acceptance* and *nonjudgmentality* in which the *professional* considers the *client* to be a person of worth, whose rights and dignity are to be respected without reservation if the effective working *relationship* is to be viable. This position is maintained by the ethical professional even if the social worker personally does not approve of or condone the client's actions.

unconditioned response (UR) A response that occurs without the necessity of prior conditioning. In Ivan Pavlov's (1849–1936) experiments, the dog's salivation when given food was the UR. Then food was presented after a bell was rung; eventually the dog began to salivate at the sound of the bell, whether or not food was given. Salivation at the sound of the bell was the *conditioned response (CR)*.

unconditioned stimulus (US) A *stimulus* that elicits a response without the necessity of conditioning or learning. For example, in Ivan Pavlov's (1849–1936) experiments, the food was the US because it elicited salivation with no prior conditioning. When a bell was rung before the presentation of food, the bell became the *conditioned stimulus* (CS) when it began to elicit salivation from the dog even when no food was near.

unconscious In *psychoanalytic theory*, that region of the mind or psychic structure that is not subject to an individual's immediate awareness and is the seat of all forgotten memories and thoughts, *primary process thinking*, repressed impulses, biological drives, and the *id*.

unconscious motivation A compelling wish or drive that is out of an individual's immediate awareness but that influences him or her to act in a way that would seem contrary to his or her rational objectives. For example, a client who has had a difficult session with a social worker "forgets" to attend the next scheduled session.

U.N. Convention on Rights of the Child See *Rights of the Child Convention*.

underachiever One whose overt performance is not as accomplished as would be expected from the person's past activities, school or work record, or scores on aptitude tests.

underclass A term used by some journalists and economists in referring to people and families who have been long-term poor, unemployed, and lacking in the resources or opportunities to improve their situations in the future. See also *culture of poverty*.

underdeveloped nations Those countries of the world that have extremely low rates of literacy and income and few natural resources. They are also called *Fourth World* countries to distinguish them from *Third World* or *developing countries* that have resources and socioeconomic growth.

underemployment 1. For individuals, the condition of working fewer than full-time hours or working in jobs that are beneath their levels of education or previous salary, usually because there are no more-suitable jobs available. 2. For societies, the economic condition in which workers have to limit their work hours or incomes so that others can also work and have some income. See also *seasonal unemployment*.

underground economy The unregulated system of financial transactions, exchange of goods and services outside regular accounting procedures, and bartering, especially to avoid taxes.

underprivileged A term pertaining to people who are deprived of the social, cultural, and economic benefits that are available to most others in their society.

undersocialized conduct disorder An outdated term referring to a type of *con-duct disorder* in which a person has not been able or willing to establish relationships with others that include affection, empathy, or bonding. This person seeks to harm or manipulate others for personal advantage but has no feelings of remorse or guilt.

understimulating environment The condition in which an individual is confined, physically, intellectually, socially, or emotionally, in such a way that precludes sufficient access to the resources needed for healthy development. Examples include classrooms in which intelligent children are not challenged, drab mental hospitals devoid of opportunity for interaction, and high-rise slums where most residents feel compelled to stay inside.

underutilization See *utilization review*.

underworld Organized *crime*, or the criminal element of society.

undifferentiated ego mass A *family therapy* concept describing the members of a *family* as lacking much separate identity or differentiation of self and being "stuck together."

undifferentiated schizophrenia A diagnostic category for *schizophrenia* in which the patient has *hallucinations, delusions,* incoherence, and disorganized behavior but does not meet the specific criteria for the other types of schizophrenia. See *catatonic schizophrenia, disorganized schizophrenia,* and *paranoid schizophrenia*.

undifferentiated somatoform disorder One of the *somatoform disorders* in which the individual experiences only one or a few symptoms longer than six months. It is differentiated from *somatization disorder,* which has many symptoms over several years and begins before age 30.

undocumented alien 1. In the United States, an individual from another nation who has entered this country without legal status and is subject to deportation. 2. In certain circumstances, a person who enters the country legally but who remains after expiration of his or her visa.

undoing A *defense mechanism* in which an individual engages in a repetitious ritual to abolish the results of an action previously taken and found to be unacceptable. For example, an individual who injures a youngster through reckless driving begins driving slowly and carefully every day through the area where the accident occurred.

UNDP See *United Nations Development Program (UNDP)*.

UNDRO See *United Nations Disaster Relief Organization (UNDRO)*.

unearned income Money received from sources unrelated to employment, such as interest on savings, dividends on investments, and capital gains.

unemployable Being considered unable to work because of disability, age, insufficient education, or lack of job openings. This term often is used to describe people who are not in the potential workforce and thus are not counted as part of the *unemployment rate*.

Unemployed Parent Program of AFDC (AFDC–UP) The 1961 revision of *Aid to Families with Dependent Children (AFDC)* regulations, which in many states extended eligibility to families that included unemployed fathers. Before AFDC–UP, eligibility in most states was restricted to poor families that had no male *head of household*. See also *"man in the house" rule*.

unemployment The condition of being without a job and the resulting income that is necessary to meet economic needs independently. The term is usually applied by economists and government statisticians only to those people without jobs who want to and are able to work. See also *cyclical unemployment, seasonal unemployment, frictional unemployment,* and *structural unemployment.*

unemployment compensation Financial assistance for eligible persons who have temporary loss of income as a result of *unemployment*. In the United States, this assistance is provided primarily through the *Unemployment Insurance* program.

Unemployment Insurance The program established as part of the *Social Security Act* to protect workers temporarily from economic hardship caused by involuntary job loss. The federal government levies a payroll tax on nearly all employers and credits most of these funds to each state's unemployment insurance fund. When an eligible worker becomes unemployed, compensation is paid for a specified time. Applications, eligibility determination, and processing of funds are, for the most part, handled through the states' public employment offices. The amount and duration of benefits vary from state to state.

unemployment rate The economic and statistical measure of the proportion of people without jobs who are willing and able to work, relative to the number of people in the labor force. The figure is often used by social and economic planners to help determine actual and potential economic circumstances of specific population groups, such as teenagers, black people, college graduates, people older than age 50, women, and blue-collar workers.

UNEP See *United Nations Environmental Program (UNEP)*.

UNESCO See *United Nations Educational, Scientific, and Cultural Organization (UNESCO)*.

unfreezing An element in *psychotherapy*, especially *group therapy* and *social group work*, in which clients are helped to reexamine rigidly held assumptions about themselves and others (that is, status symbols and familiar social conventions) to achieve motivation for change.

UNHCR See *United Nations High Commissioner for Refugees (UNHCR)*.

UNICEF See *United Nations Children's Fund (UNICEF)*.

Uniform Crime Reports (UCR) Data about the number of crimes committed in specified categories during identified time periods, published by the Federal Bureau of Investigation. The information has been published since 1937 and is based on input from most of the nation's police departments. Although the UCR is useful to researchers, especially in determining long-term crime trends, it has been criticized as deemphasizing *white-collar crime* and *racketeering* and for relying too much on police reports that have public relations motivations. See also *National Incident-Based Reporting System (NIBRS)*.

unilateral family therapy Psychosocial treatment of a *family* even though only one family member is present or directly involved in the therapeutic *intervention*. This is sometimes necessary when *pathology* exists within the family, affecting all its members, but key participants in the pathology refuse therapeutic intervention. A basic premise of *family therapy* is that a change in one member will result in a change in all members, so it is possible to help the whole family without seeing each member.

unipolar disorder A rarely used term referring to a *mood disorder* in which only one side of the emotional continuum is present. Almost invariably this side is *depression*. See also *affective disorder* and *bipolar disorder*.

United Jewish Appeal (UJA) The organization founded in 1939 to systematize and coordinate fundraising efforts for programs in behalf of needy Jews. Contributions to the organization help support domestic Jewish social service agencies and educational facilities and needy Jews worldwide. Funds are also designated for helping immigrants become established in Israel. See also *Zionism*.

United Nations Children's Fund (UNICEF) An agency of the United Nations established in 1946 as the U.N. International Children's Emergency Fund. Its primary goal is to provide health, education, and social services to children, especially in *underdeveloped nations*. It is financed by voluntary contributions from nations and individuals.

United Nations Development Program (UNDP) Established by the United Na-

tions in 1965 to help nations maximize their natural and other resources by providing expertise and resources, the UNDP also works with other U.N. organizations to provide emergency relief services; upgrade educational levels of population groups; and, in cooperation with the *World Bank,* provide funding for development projects.

United Nations Disaster Relief Organization (UNDRO) An office established in 1971 by the United Nations to coordinate the efforts of nations, groups, volunteers, and individuals in assisting populations experiencing disasters. UNDRO classes disasters according to three general types: (1) sudden disasters, such as floods, hurricanes, earthquakes, and volcanic eruptions; (2) slow-developing disasters, such as droughts and epidemics; and (3) human-caused disasters, such as international wars and genocide. UNDRO does not participate in relief in human-caused disasters.

United Nations Economic and Social Council (ECOSOC) The primary U.N. body for promoting the member nations' social and human services policies and economic and social development. ECOSOC's major goals are to promote higher standards of living, full employment, social health, human rights and freedoms, and cultural and educational development.

United Nations Educational, Scientific, and Cultural Organization (UNESCO) An agency of the United Nations established in 1945 with headquarters in Paris. Its primary objectives include promoting the free interchange of ideas and cultural and scientific accomplishments, fundamental education for all people, and preserving the cultural heritage of humanity.

United Nations Environmental Program (UNEP) Founded in 1972 with headquarters in Nairobi, Kenya, to coordinate intergovernmental measures to protect the environment, UNEP monitors environmental trends through *Earthwatch*.

United Nations High Commissioner for Refugees (UNHCR) The organization formed in 1951 by the U.N. General Assembly to provide economic assistance for refugees, social services, international protection, voluntary repatriation, and resettlement in other countries.

United Nations Relief and Works Agency for Palestine Refugees in the Near East (UNRWA) A program of the United Nations that was formed in 1950 primarily to help Palestinians who lived in what became Israel. It is funded by voluntary contributions from individuals and countries.

United Nations Research Institute for Social Development The Geneva-based U.N. organization to conduct research about the conditions in which humans live and especially to study the effects of development policies in developing nations.

United Neighborhood Centers of America (UNCA) The organization whose aim is to improve the quality of life at the *neighborhood* level. Founded by *Jane Addams* and other social workers and pioneer leaders of the *settlement houses* movement, the organization was formerly known as the National Federation of Settlements. In 1959 it became known as the National Federation of Settlement and Neighborhood Centers; it took its present name in 1979.

United Service Organizations (USO) The program established in 1941 to coordinate the recreational, social, and welfare services given by six private voluntary agencies (*Young Men's Christian Association [YMCA], Young Women's Christian Association [YWCA], Traveler's Aid,* the *Salvation Army, Catholic Community Service,* and *Jewish social agencies*) to members of the U.S. armed services.

United Way The national federation of local organizations established to systematize and coordinate voluntary fundraising efforts. The money raised through the United Way is used to fund social agencies; nonprofit human services organizations; and some health, education, and recreation programs in local communities. The organization was established in 1918 and has been known in some localities as the United Campaign, the United Fund, the Community Chest, and the Red Feather Organization.

unit of attention The focal point of *intervention* to which the social worker or other professional directs efforts to provide help or effect change. For example, the unit of attention for the clinical social worker with a psychoanalytic orientation would be the *intrapsychic* processes of the individual, and that of a community organizer would be the interacting social forces that exist in a given community. Units of attention for group workers are the group process and for psychosocially oriented workers, the person–situation configuration. Specific behaviors may be considered the unit of attention for behaviorally oriented workers, and a proposed bill in Congress could be the unit of attention for a social activist. See also *target behavior, target segments of society,* and *target system.*

universal eligibility A *social services* policy in which services or benefits are provided at the same rate to all citizens or residents of a nation without regard to their specific needs, economic status, or circumstances. When applied, this policy can take the form of such *universal programs* as the family allowance system in some nations. This concept is contrasted with the policy of *selective eligibility.* See also *demogrant.*

universality In *social group work* and *group psychotherapy,* the exposure of people to others in the group who have similar problems, followed by the growing realization that the problems are not unique nor incomprehensible to others and that they need not be faced alone.

universal programs *Social welfare* programs that are open to everyone in a nation who falls into a certain category. These programs do not subject people to individualized tests of income or need. *Social security* and *Medicare* are examples of universal programs in the United States (*public assistance* and *Medicaid* are *selective programs*).

universe A term used in *research* to designate a group of people or objects that are identified as the whole from which a *sample* is taken. In voter preference polls, for example, this universe consists of all potential voters. See also *population.*

unlawful entry The *crime* of using force or fraud to come into the home or office of people without their permission. This crime is similar to *burglary* except that it need not entail breaking in or the intention to steal property.

unprofessional A term applied to behavior engaged in by a *professional* during the course of practice that does not measure up to the standards of the *profession*. Usually it is conduct in violation of the profession's *code of ethics* or misuse of knowledge or the laws pertaining to the licensing of the profession in the relevant jurisdiction. The term is not to be confused with *nonprofessional*.

UNRWA See *United Nations Relief and Works Agency for Palestine Refugees in the Near East (UNRWA)*.

unsocialized delinquent A youngster whose periodic trouble with the authorities and whose *antisocial behavior* stem from insufficient guidance, role models, or exposure to people who have more acceptable standards of behavior.

unstable Not firmly fixed or secure. Social workers often apply this term to phenomena in their clients' personalities, health, environment, or social relationships to indicate that the existing situation is likely to change.

"unworthy poor" A pejorative term applied to poor people who were considered too lazy to work or too dishonest to be acceptable in polite society. This designation was used primarily before the 20th century to distinguish people who did not "deserve" public assistance from the *"worthy poor"* (such as widows and disabled people) who did. The term is no longer used officially, but its underlying philosophy is still held by many. See also *victim blaming*.

unwritten law 1. Social *norms, mores,* and customs that regulate the conduct of people rather than written statutes and formal laws. 2. An erroneous belief that certain crimes can be committed and the law authorities will not prosecute or will be lenient. Such crimes are thought to include killing or beating a person who raped a family member, attacking the man who engaged in coitus with one's wife, or taking revenge on a person who has disgraced the family honor. In fact, such laws are written and do not indicate special leniency.

"uppers" Slang for *amphetamines*, the *controlled substances* that have been used to control weight and to keep people awake and alert. When abused they are psychologically and physiologically addictive.

Upstream Head Start program An educational program within the *Head Start* program for children of migrants, especially in farm labor. Local programs over a vast geographic area are linked and coordinated so that children are not deprived of Head Start benefits even though they must move frequently.

Upward Bound The *War on Poverty* program, established in 1964, designed to provide special education and incentives to encourage students not to drop out of school.

upward mobility Socioeconomic advances by individuals, groups, or nations. In nations this is due to good and productive economic conditions that result in high employment and increased wages, stable prices, better use of natural resources, political changes, and enhanced opportunities for education and cultural development. In individuals it is also a common result of getting better education and jobs and exploiting opportunities. See also *downward mobility*.

UR See *unconditioned response (UR)*.

urban homesteading The process of occupying a formerly empty house, usually in a run-down city neighborhood, and living in it while restoring it. Often this is made possible by government laws, grants, and tax incentives to encourage community improvements. See also *gentrification*.

urbanization 1. A social trend in which people adopt the lifestyles, residential patterns, and cultural values of those who live in or near cities. 2. The physical development of a rural area so that it includes features found in cities.

Urban League, National The community service and *civil rights group* established in 1910 by social workers *George E. Haynes* (1880–1960) and Ruth Standish Baldwin to help end racial *discrimination* and help socially disadvantaged people. Largely staffed by social workers and professionals from related fields, it provides direct services in such areas as unemployment, housing, education, social welfare, family counseling and planning, legal affairs, and business development.

urbanology The scientific study of cities and their problems.

urban renewal A social philosophy and a set of programs designed to prevent urban blight in those areas where satisfactory housing exists, to tear down slums and replace them with new buildings where suitable housing no longer exists, and to rehabilitate neighborhoods that are beginning to decay. The Housing Act of 1949 (ch. 338, 63 stat. 413) and subsequent legislation provided for procedures by which cities could apply for federal urban renewal aid. In 1970 the act (P.L. 91-609) was revised to include new *community development (CD)*, which can result in new additions to cities and freestanding new communities. Most federal urban renewal funding now comes through *block grants*. See also *gentrification*.

urinalysis Chemical testing of the urine to help determine the existence of certain diseases, potential diseases, or drug use. Urinalysis is the most convenient and common method of *drug testing*.

US See *unconditioned stimulus (US)*.

USDA See *Department of Agriculture, U.S. (USDA)*.

user charges The *social services* policy of requiring the client or recipient of a service to pay for part or all of the cost of provid-ing the service. This policy is in contrast to programs that are provided at no cost or low cost to the recipient, with the funds coming from general government revenues, through public or privately supported agencies, or from private insurance payments.

USO See *United Service Organizations (USO)*.

usual, customary, or reasonable (UCR) A method of reimbursing health care providers. Generally, the third party paying the fees develops a profile of prevailing fees in a geographic area and uses it to determine what the company will pay for any service. One method is to average fees and set the UCR at 80 percent or 90 percent of the average.

usury The act of charging excessive or unlawfully high rates of interest on loaned money. See also *Truth in Lending Act*.

utilitarianism The ethical philosophy that holds that the rightness or wrongness of an action is determined by whether its consequences are useful or not.

utility programs In the use of computers, the programs that help in the general running of the system for such things as transferring data from one storage site to another, making copies of files, locating and eliminating viruses, and saving data.

utility theory In economics, the concept that a person obtains satisfaction (utility) through the consumption of goods and that the individual will attempt to establish priorities of consumption to achieve the highest possible level of satisfaction. The theory suggests that the higher the level of satisfaction for a given cost and unit of time, the more desirable a particular item.

utilization review A formal process of evaluating the type and amount of service offered and delivered to organizations to determine if those services are justified. Organizations that receive funds from government bodies or other third-party groups are most likely to be subject to such evaluations, because the funders want to know if they are getting proper value for their costs. The review might determine the existence of overutilization (too many services delivered or too many demands made on available services) or underutilization (insufficient demand or delivery to justify the costs spent on services). See also *quality assurance.*

V

vaccine   A preparation used to increase the body's resistance to a specific disease.

vaginismus   A *sexual disorder* in women in which continuing involuntary spasms of the musculature of the outer third of the vaginal wall interfere with satisfactory coitus. See also *dyspareunia*.

vaginitis   An inflammation of the vagina, caused primarily by the presence of an excessive number of otherwise harmless microorganisms.

vagrancy   Wandering from place to place with no permanent home or job.

validator role   One of the major functions of social work *intervention* with clients: that of confirming and legitimizing the clients' own ideas, values, and emotions. According to Mark Tobias ("Validator: A Key Role in Empowering the Chronically Mentally Ill," *Social Work*, 35 [July 1990], pp. 357–359), when the social worker provides validation for the client's thoughts and feelings, the client is empowered to work more effectively toward problem resolution.

validity   In *social research*, the concept concerned with the extent to which a procedure is able to measure the quality it is intended to measure.

value-added tax (VAT)   An indirect sales tax that is levied on products at each stage of production in proportion to their increase in worth. These add-ons are finally passed on to the consumer. VAT is a *regressive tax* rather than a *progressive tax*. This form of taxation is common in many European nations.

value judgment   An assumption made about the worth of some person, group, place, or event.

value orientation   The characteristic way individuals or groups look at their own and others' standards of conduct, moral principles, and social customs.

values   The customs, standards of conduct, and principles considered desirable by a culture, a group of people, or an individual. Social workers, as one group, specified 10 of their overall values in the *NASW Standards for the Classification of Social Work Practice* (Silver Spring, MD: National Association of Social Workers, 1981) as follows: (1) commitment to the primary importance of the individual in society; (2) respect for the confidentiality of relationships with clients; (3) commitment to social change to meet socially recognized needs; (4) willingness to keep personal feelings and needs separate from professional relationships; (5) willingness to transmit knowledge and skills to others; (6) respect and appreciation for individual and group differences; (7) commitment to develop clients' ability to help themselves; (8) willingness to persist in efforts on behalf of clients despite frustration; (9) commitment to social justice and the economic, physical, and mental well-being of all members of society; and (10) commitment to a high standard of personal and professional conduct.

values clarification   A method of education in morality and ethical principles that occurs by bringing together people to share their opinions and value perspectives. This exposes the participants to different ideals and permits them to appreciate the relative nature of values.

vandalism Intentional and illegal destruction of public or private property.

variable In *social research,* a characteristic that may vary or assume different quantified values. See also *dependent variable* and *independent variable.*

variable interval schedule In *behavior modification,* a planned procedure for reinforcing behaviors at varying times after they occur. Often the times are varied around some average.

variable ratio schedule In *behavior modification,* a planned procedure of *intermittent reinforcement* in which the *reinforcement* is given on a varying basis, around some average. The reinforcement is given only after several of the behaviors are emitted on one occasion and then given after a different number of behaviors are emitted on a different occasion.

variance 1. In *research,* a measure of dispersion within the distribution of events. 2. In statistics, the square of the *standard deviation.* 3. In social administration, the difference between budgeted expectations and actual results. 4. In urban development, a legal exemption from *zoning* and building codes.

vascular dementia Multiple cognitive deficits, including memory impairment, that persists over several months, causing significant impairment in social or occupational functioning. This dementia results from cerebrovascular disturbances such as strokes. This disorder was formerly known as *multi-infarct dementia.*

VAT See *value-added tax (VAT).*

V Codes A list of conditions that are not specific mental disorders but are included in the American Psychiatric Association's *DSM-IV* because they are frequent reasons for which individuals seek the services of mental health professionals. The V Code conditions and their numbers include the following: relational problems, including those with siblings (V61.8), partners (V61.1), parent–child (V61.20), and those relational problems related to a *mental disorder* or *general medical condition* (V61.9); problems related to *abuse* or *neglect,* including physical or *sexual abuse* or neglect of a child (V61.21) or physical or sexual abuse of an adult (V61.1); noncompliance with treatment (V15.81); *malingering* (V65.2); adult *antisocial behavior* (V71.01); child or adolescent antisocial behavior (V71.02); *borderline intellectual functioning* (V62.89); *age-related cognitive decline* (780.9); *bereavement* (V62.82); academic problem (V62.3); occupational problem (V62.2); identity problem (313.82); religious or spiritual problem (V62.89); *acculturation* problem (V62.4); and *phase-of-life problem* (V62.89). Organizations that make a *third-party payment* tend to reject treatment reimbursement claims if these are the sole reasons for treatment.

vegetative signs Behavior in which there is little indication of mental activity. The person is passive, mute, unresponsive to the environment, and not inclined to move. This behavior is often symptomatic of *organic mental disorders* and some types of *schizophrenia.*

vendor One who sells a product or service. Because they are paid to provide social services, social workers and their agencies are referred to as vendors by insurance companies and other third-party funding organizations.

vendor payments Money a government agency or insurance company pays to a social agency, institution, or independent professional to provide services. The U.S. government uses the term primarily to apply to payments made to professionals or agencies on behalf of people who cannot afford to pay for the services themselves. The largest vendor payment system of this type in the United States is *Medicaid.*

vendorship 1. The practice of providing goods and services for specific fees that are charged either to the consumer or to a *third party.* 2. In social work, the vendorship model is practiced primarily by private social work practitioners, proprietary workers, and even traditional social agencies selling specific professional services to individuals and groups and being reimbursed for each unit of service by the consumer or by such third parties as health insurance companies, government agencies, or business organizations.

venereal diseases Infections acquired through sexual contact and the exchange of body fluids; these may include *gonorrhea*, *syphilis*, genital *herpes*, and *acquired immune deficiency syndrome (AIDS)*. See also *sexually transmitted diseases (STDs)*.

ventilation In the social worker–client therapeutic *relationship*, the process of permitting the client to express feelings during the description of the problem situation. According to psychosocial theorists, this releases or discharges emotions that have built up and caused the individual to have internal *stress* and conflict. It is also referred to as *catharsis*. See also *purposeful expression of feelings*.

verbal following responses See *following responses*.

verbatim recording In the social work *case record*, the process of writing down every word said in the *interview*, and, to the extent possible, every gesture, expression, and tonal inflection so that the meaning is accurately conveyed. This process is used primarily for social worker training purposes or for legal issues in the interview and generally only in a single session or parts of sessions. It has become rarely used because it is distracting to the interview process and has been supplanted by the use of audio or video recording.

verbigeration A series of verbalizations that are continuous, repetitive, and pressured and that extend over a significant time period or frequently recur. This is often seen in certain types of *schizophrenia*.

vertical career move Taking a new job in which the pay, benefits, responsibilities, and prestige are higher or, less typically, lower. See also *horizontal career move*.

vertical disclosure The revelation by a member of a *social group work* or therapy

group of some significant information and the group's analysis of that information and how it will affect the one who disclosed it. This is the opposite of *horizontal disclosure*.

vested interest A special concern an individual has about some cause, property, commitment, or institution that, if lost or changed, will be perceived as personally harmful. For example, social workers in private practice have vested interests in third-party recognition of their capabilities.

Veterans Administration, U.S. See *Veterans Affairs, U.S. Department of*.

Veterans Affairs, U.S. Department of The federal organization, formerly known as the U.S. Veterans Administration, responsible for providing health, education, and welfare services for former military service personnel in need. The Department of Veterans Affairs was established in 1920 as the U.S. Veterans Bureau and renamed in 1930 as the Veterans Administration. The department administers hospitals for physically and mentally ill patients, maintains programs of financial assistance and personal social services, establishes loans and insurance services, and offers training and rehabilitation programs and many other services. According to Rosina M. Becerra and JoAnn Damron-Rodriguez ("Veterans and Veterans Services," in Richard L. Edwards [Ed.-in-Chief], *Encyclopedia of Social Work*, 19th ed., Washington, DC: NASW Press, 1995), social workers, who are a large and integral part of the department's professional staffs, face significant challenges in serving veterans given reduced budgets, increased demands, and rapid changes in health care delivery systems.

vicarious The feelings derived from sharing the experience of another person. This phenomenon is often observed in *family therapy*, when a parent experiences the child's achievements or pains, and in *codependency* situations.

vicarious learning In *behavior modification*, the premise that a client's desired *behavior* is strengthened through observing someone else being rewarded for that behavior; a form of imitation or *modeling*.

vice Criminal activity including *prostitution, pornography,* gambling, sales of illegal drugs or contraband, and other behaviors that are made illegal because they offend the community's moral standards.

victim blaming A philosophy or orientation that attributes complicity to the person who is harmed by some social phenomenon. For example, a woman who is raped or sexually harassed is accused of seducing the attacker; an abused spouse is accused of being masochistic and encouraging the abusive action; or a poor person is accused of being too lazy to work.

victim compensation Public payment in cash or services to people who are judged to have been harmed as a result of another person's negligence or criminal activity.

victim–offender mediation programs A conflict resolution process sponsored primarily by social service agencies that work closely with the courts to develop mutually acceptable restitution plans and meet informational and emotional needs. The offenders are most often people convicted of theft or *burglary* who are referred to the mediator, who meets separately with offender and victim. Joint meetings may be held if both agree, and victims are given the rare opportunity to express their feelings directly to the offender. *Restitution* usually involves repayment, working for the victim, or working for a charity of the victim's choice.

victimology The study of people who are harmed, usually by sociocultural phenomena, and the conditions in which the harm occurs.

"victim precipitation" A term used by law enforcement officials referring to violent acts on a person who originated the situation that resulted in the crime. The term is most often used in situations in which wives kill or injure their husbands after they have been assaulted or abused.

video feedback A *intervention* procedure by social workers and other professionals to show clients how they appear to others, by showing videotape replays of the client's past behavior and systematically analyzing the results. The procedure has been used with effectiveness in working with clients who have substance abuse problems, emotional self-control problems, communications problems with family members or peers, or other behavioral problems. See also *audio feedback.*

Vietnam veterans Military personnel who served in Vietnam during the protracted war that ended in 1975. Many American veterans of this war have experienced considerable difficulties in readjusting to life in the United States and thus have needed help from social workers, vocational counselors, physicians, and other professionals. These difficulties have been attributed or related to such factors as the lack of popular support for the war and its participants; "losing" the war; poor postwar economic conditions supposedly resulting in reduced veterans' services; the widespread use of drugs; and the use of defoliants such as *Agent Orange,* which may be *carcinogenic.* See also *posttraumatic stress disorder (PTSD).*

vigilante One who engages in crime fighting and carries out judicial rulings without legal authority, because of the perception that the duly constituted legal system is inadequate.

violence Severe and intense exercise of force and power, usually resulting in injury or destruction. The term "crimes of violence" pertains to those crimes in which physical harm occurs or is threatened, such as *homicide, rape, assault,* and *battery.*

viruses Tiny, simple, spherical- or rod-shaped organisms (or bits of nucleid acid wrapped in coats of protein) that cause mild and serious diseases in plants, animals, and humans, including *acquired immune deficiency syndrome (AIDS),* some forms of *cancer,* colds, flu, *poliomyelitis,* and *hepatitis.* Viruses reproduce only within the cells of other organisms. Antibiotics that are effective in fighting bacterial diseases have little use in the fight against viral diseases.

visitation rights A court-ordered legal right of parents or other relatives who no longer have *custody of children* to be in contact with them during the times agreed to and specified.

visiting teacher service   Programs within the educational system in which professionals in *school social work* provide personal social services to students and their families and help acquaint the schools with the special needs of these families. Originally these services were provided by educators, but eventually professional social workers assumed these duties in many school districts. The National Association of Visiting Teachers, which was established in 1916, was absorbed into the *American Association of Social Workers (AASW)* as the School Social Work Section in 1921.

VISTA   See *Volunteers in Service to America (VISTA)*.

visual hallucination   An imagined perception of seeing something that does not exist outside subjective experience.

VITA   See *Volunteers in Technical Assistance (VITA)*.

vital signs   Indicators (such as pulse, respiration, temperature, and movement) that the body is alive and functioning.

vital statistics   Official demographic data pertaining to the incidence of marriages, divorces, births, deaths, health statuses, diseases, causes of death, and so on.

Vivas, Juan Luis (1492–1540)   Spanish humanist who advocated for poor people and in 1525 published the influential treatise on poor relief, *De Subventione Pauperum*. He recommended the centralization of relief funds, forced labor, schools for poor children, and the prohibition of begging.

vivisection   Experimentation on living animals to study biological and behavioral responses to various conditions.

vocational education   A program of studies, often including supervised hands-on experiences, designed to prepare students for employment in one or more technical, semiskilled, or skilled occupations.

vocational guidance   Assisting people in the systematic process of locating suitable *employment*. The activities inherent in such assistance include delineating qualifications and possible job opportunities and helping individuals determine if they have the aptitude and qualifications for a specific job, helping them find the training necessary to do a job, and counseling them on how to apply for a position.

vocational rehabilitation   Training people who are physically or mentally disabled so they can do useful work, become more self-sufficient, and be less reliant on public financial assistance. *Block grants* and other funding through the U.S. *Department of Health and Human Services (HHS)* go to states to facilitate specific vocational rehabilitation programs. The U.S. *Department of Veterans Affairs* also works with state agencies for the training of disabled veterans.

Vocational Rehabilitation, Office of   Federally mandated, locally administered programs in every state to provide free vocational counseling and referral to training programs or job placement services for people with disabilities. In some states the programs are administered by the Department of Social Services, while in others the Department of Labor is in charge.

volition   Free will, the act of deciding or choosing without being compelled to do so. Problems of volition are often seen in *schizophrenia, organic mental disorders,* and *drug intoxication.*

Voluntary Action Centers   See *volunteerism.*

voluntary associations   Organizations whose funding comes from private contributions and whose goals are to provide health, social, and other services to the disadvantaged outside government auspices. Voluntary associations tend to specialize in particular needs and services. These include health and hospital support (for example, the American Cancer Society, the American Heart Association, and the National Kidney Foundation), help for specific groups (for example, *Big Brothers/Big Sisters of America* and the National Shut-in

Society), church-related organizations (for example, *Catholic Charities USA* and *Lutheran Social Services*), and community fund-raising groups (for example, the *United Way*).

volunteer One who offers to serve, of his or her own free will, usually without financial compensation. See also *volunteerism*.

volunteerism The mobilization and use of unpaid individuals and groups to provide human services outside the auspices of government agencies. This term, or "voluntarism," according to Eleanor Brilliant ("Voluntarism," in Richard L. Edwards [Ed.-in-Chief], *Encyclopedia of Social Work*, 19th ed., Washington, DC: NASW Press, 1995) also pertains to the ideologies of *self-help groups, mutual-aid groups, self-help organizations,* and *philanthropy*. The U.S. government maintains, in its *ACTION* programs, the Office of Volunteer Action to help coordinate some of these efforts throughout the nation. Other organizations that serve the same purpose include the National Self-Help Clearinghouse, the National Self-Help Resource Center, and the National Center for Voluntary Action, which promoted the national network of local Voluntary Action Centers.

Volunteers in Service to America (VISTA) The program established as part of the *Economic Opportunity Act of 1964* and designed to bring volunteers into those urban and rural areas of the United States that are experiencing economic and cultural deprivation. Often called the "Domestic Peace Corps," the workers help with training, socialization, and development of resources. VISTA is now part of the federal government's *ACTION* program.

Volunteers in Technical Assistance (VITA) A volunteer organization comprising primarily engineers, architects, scientists, computer experts, and others who provide technical assistance, advice, and information to businesses and organizations in developing countries through the use of mail, computer interfaces, telephone, and E-mail.

voter registration drives A strategy used by social activists, community organizers, and other social workers to strengthen the power and influence of a community or segment of the population by encouraging and facilitating the enrollment of eligible citizens to permit them to vote in subsequent elections. See also *human SERVE* and *motor voter law*.

voucher system A method of subsidizing a person's social service, health care, and other needs on the open market. Typically, in this system a poor person is given vouchers, often in the form of redeemable stamps or coupons, worth a certain amount of money as long as they are spent on a specified service or product. Among the most common of these systems are food stamps, tuition grants, and housing subsidy checks.

voyeurism A *sexual disorder* characterized by repetitive looking at unsuspecting people who are undressed or engaged in sexual activity. Popularly referred to as "peeping tomism," this activity is the preferred source of sexual excitement for voyeurs. People who enjoy watching or observing others in everyday situations are sometimes informally referred to as voyeurs.

vulnerable populations Those individuals or groups who have a greater probability of being harmed by specific social, environmental, or health problems than the population as a whole. For example, black men are a vulnerable population at risk for *hypertension*, and citizens of *underdeveloped nations* are more vulnerable to *malnutrition*. This is a synonym for *at-risk population*.

vulnerability factors Conditions within people's bodies, groups, or environments that make them open to harm or disease. These factors are not, by themselves, the cause of the harm or disease but they increase the chances when occurring in conjunction with other risk factors.

W

wage controls Government regulations that limit the amount of increase or decrease in money that employers can pay to their workers. The stated purpose is usually to control *inflation* and increase *employment*. This policy is often accompanied by *price controls*.

WAIS test See *intelligence quotient (IQ)*.

Wald, Lillian (1867–1940) Advocate for *public health* and *child welfare* programs, she founded one of the most influential of the *settlement houses*, the Henry Street Settlement in New York and, with *Florence Kelley*, founded the U.S. *Children's Bureau*. In 1970 she was named the second social worker, after *Jane Addams*, to be included in the Hall of Fame for Great Americans.

warism The orientation that military conflict is morally justified and promises unique advantages for the nation that cannot be achieved in any other way. See also *militarism* and *pacifism*.

Warner, Amos G. (1861–1900) Social planner and welfare administrator, he wrote the influential text *American Charities* in 1894, the first attempt to find a scientific approach to the problems of *poverty*.

War on Poverty President Lyndon B. Johnson's plans and programs established during his administration to encourage economic well-being, equal opportunity for all, and realize the *Great Society*. The "war" was to be fought primarily through the programs of the *Economic Opportunity Act of 1964*. This included a major revision of the *Social Security Act* of 1935, including greatly extended coverage; *Volunteers in Service to America (VISTA)*; the *Job Corps*; *Head Start*; the *Legal Services Corporation*; and the *Community Action Program (CAP)*.

"WASP" A term used sometimes disparagingly in referring to white Anglo-Saxon Protestants, virtually the only population group whose male members are not considered "minorities" or socially disadvantaged. Actually, the term also is frequently applied to white people who are Catholics and to people of non-English European ancestry—that is, white nonethnics. The "WASP" label often is used to imply that there is a single lifestyle (bland and comfortably affluent), political orientation *(conservatism)*, and economic value orientation *(social Darwinism)* among these people, even though they are highly disparate in these characteristics. See also *ethnic group* and *white ethnic groups*.

watchdog group An ad hoc or formal *coalition* established to scrutinize the actions of political leaders, government officials, or institutions that influence the public. Watchdog groups usually comprise concerned citizens, paid or volunteer lobbyists, professional and trade associations, and business groups whose interests might be affected by the actions of those being observed.

waxy flexibility A symptom seen especially in *catatonia* in which the person's facial expressions, limbs, and body posture remain relatively fixed or will move only gradually.

WCTU Women's Christian Temperance Union. See *temperance movements*.

Webb, Bernice (1858–1943) and **Webb, Sidney** (1859–1947)   British social reformers, leaders of the Fabian Society, advocates for better conditions for laborers and poor people, and founders of London School of Economics. While Bernice worked to change existing poor laws and advocated for guaranteed minimum standards of living, Sidney engaged in politics and helped develop the Labour Party. They worked toward improved education and wrote influential books about the trade union movement.

welfare   1. A condition of physical health, emotional comfort, and economic security. 2. The efforts of a society to help its citizens achieve that condition. The term is also used popularly as a synonym for *public assistance* or other programs that provide for the economic and social services needs of poor people.

welfare backlash   Resistance and opposition by some citizens and groups to public expenditures for the poor people, often manifested in such social movements as "taxpayer revolts" and in political pressure to eliminate funding for some welfare programs.

"welfare queen"   A pejorative term applied to people, especially mothers receiving *Aid to Families with Dependent Children (AFDC)* payments, who defraud the public assistance and social security systems. The fraud is accomplished by using many aliases; different addresses; and exaggerating the need to obtain more money, goods, and services. The term is often a code to suggest that many recipients would live in luxury if not scrutinized.

welfare reform   Various efforts to change the way social welfare programs are administered, funded, and used. Some reformers seek more-stringent rules to discourage people from obtaining assistance. Others advocate elimination of bureaucratic obstacles and any *means tests*. Some advocate replacing the entire welfare system with a *guaranteed annual income* for all people that would meet each person's minimal requirements. The welfare reform proposals listed in this dictionary include the *Family Assistance Plan (FAP)*, the *guaranteed annual income*, the *negative income tax*, the *Newburgh welfare plan*, and *workfare*.

welfare rights   The view that public assistance and other social services are entitlements available to any of a nation's citizens. Welfare rights organizations say that among the rights of welfare recipients are confidentiality of personal information from welfare investigators, greater availability of information about the benefits for people who are eligible, increased accessibility of welfare offices (nearer to transportation routes, open longer hours, and shorter waiting lines), and more-equitable distribution of services and funds.

welfare state   A nation or society that considers itself responsible for meeting the basic educational, health care, economic, and social security needs of its people.

whistle blowing   Informing those people in positions of influence or authority outside an organization about the existence of an organization's practices that are illegal, wasteful, dangerous, or otherwise contrary to its stated policies. The informant is compelled to notify outsiders (investigative commissions, the media, *ombudspersons,* congresspersons, and others) because authorities within the organization ignore complaints. Some organizations, such as the U.S. government, encourage whistle blowing by maintaining toll-free *hot lines* for anonymous tipsters and by protecting employees from subsequent retribution from their employers. Organizations such as the *National Association of Social Workers (NASW)* give awards to whistle-blowers whose information has led to significant improvements. NASW bestows a biennial prize, the Jack Otis Whistleblower Award, to social workers who take steps to prevent unethical practices by employing organizations.

white backlash   See *backlash*.

white-collar crime   Nonviolent illegal acts typically committed by corporations or individuals, usually in the course of the offender's occupation. Such offenses include *embezzlement, fraud, forgery*, tax evasion, fraudulent use of credit cards, stock manipulation, *bribery*, and computer crime.

white ethnic groups   People of the Caucasian race who, because of their orientation toward a shared national origin, religion, or language other than that of the *"WASP"* mainstream, have as much or more in common with other racial and cultural groups. Such people include first- or second-generation Italian Americans, Greek Americans, and Jews. According to Charles Guzzetta ("White Ethnic Groups," in Richard L. Edwards [Ed.-in-Chief], *Encyclopedia of Social Work*, 19th ed., Washington, DC: NASW Press, 1995), it is important in *research* when comparing these groups with people of color to take into account the variability and cultural variations of different groups of white people.

"white flight"   A lay term used to describe demographic patterns of racial resegregation in residential neighborhoods. The pattern is said to begin in some neighborhoods when one or more black families establish residence. Some white families who fear the possibility of negative economic or social conditions or who are racist move away precipitously. Many homes thus become vacant and then become occupied by more black families. The pattern continues as more white families "flee."

White House conferences   Formal meetings, convened by the U.S. president, of the nation's leaders in various social welfare and health fields to discuss specified social problems and potential solutions. The prototype conference was President Theodore Roosevelt's 1909 White House Conference on Child Welfare, which led to the development of the *Children's Bureau*. Subsequent conferences have focused on problems of older Americans, *health care*, and families, and most have culminated in new laws and programs designed to resolve some of the problems addressed.

white supremacist groups   Organizations in the United States whose members seek to suppress people of color or religions other than Christianity or the speaking of languages other than English, often through *ethnoviolence* and *hate crimes, propaganda,* and intimidation. The groups maintain *Ku Klux Klan (KKK)* or *neo-Nazism* ideologies and methods and include such organizations as Aryan Nations, Posse Comitatus, the National Alliance, the White Aryan Resistance, The Order, and the Skinheads.

WHO   See *World Health Organization (WHO)*.

whole-family foster care   An *intervention* system in which social workers provide therapy and other social services not only to children removed from their homes into foster placements, but also to the children's family members, to prepare all of them for their eventual reunion and improved family relationship.

whooping cough   See *pertussis*.

WIC program   The Special Supplemental Food Program for Women, Infants, and Children, which provides assistance services under the auspices of the U.S. *Department of Agriculture (USDA)*. The program is designed to protect women, infants, and children, who are identified as being at risk of nutritional deficiency as a result of inadequate income, primarily by subsidizing certain food purchases.

widowhood   The stage of life following the death of one's spouse.

Wilberforce, William (1759–1833)   British humanitarian and political leader who led the fight for prison reform and especially for abolition of slavery, which he achieved in Great Britain in 1807 and in the entire British Empire in 1833.

"wild analysis"   The expression used primarily by psychotherapists with a Freudian orientation to describe a therapist's poorly planned verbalizations and idiosyncratic approaches to *therapy*.

Wiley, George (1931–1973)   Community organizer and advocate for poor people, he helped found a chapter of the *Congress of Racial Equality (CORE)* and became a founder and first director in 1966 of the *National Welfare Rights Organization (NWRO)* to organize poor people as a political force.

willfulness   Determination, stubbornness, or purposeful intention. This quality is seen as having good and bad characteristics depending on its use. It exists in various degrees in leaders of social causes, activists, rebellious adolescents, obsessive–compulsive people, people with personality disorders, and other people said to have "strong personalities."

"window period"   A term used by researchers of *acquired immune deficiency syndrome (AIDS)* for the time just after infection with the *human immunodeficiency virus (HIV)*, during which the individual is infectious but antibody tests do not detect it. See also *incubation*.

WIN program   See *Work Incentive (WIN) program*.

witchhunt   The identification and persecution of people suspected of some activity thought to be detrimental to the existing political or social order. The term derives from the efforts to protect society in the 1600s by attempting to locate and kill actual witches.

withdrawal   A pattern of removing oneself physically or psychologically from other people or circumstances that are disturbing. See also *withdrawal symptoms*.

withdrawal delirium   A state of consciousness that is manifested by cloudy and unfocused thought, unclear awareness of the environment, and inconsistent attention to sensory stimuli, all associated with the cessation of alcohol or drug use. See *delirium tremens (DTs)*.

withdrawal symptoms   The physical and emotional reactions of a person who has discontinued the use of certain drugs or alcohol to which he or she has become dependent, addicted, or habituated. The individual may experience such reactions as *tremor, pain* in the digestive system, *delirium tremens (DTs)*, convulsions, *fear* and *panic disorder*, acute *anxiety*, and *mood swings*.

Wittman, Milton (1915–1994)   A social worker who greatly expanded federal education and employment opportunities for social workers and guided the social work training program in the *National Institute of Mental Health (NIMH)* for three decades. He was social work's first professional liaison officer in the U.S. *Public Health Service*, a position that gave social work greater influence in federal health care administration.

"Wobblies"   Slang for supporters of the Industrial Workers of the World (IWW), a federation of labor unions prominent before World War I that sought to improve working conditions and unite workers from all nations. IWW often was accused of trying to supplant U.S. government and social structures with a world government and order.

Wollstonecraft, Mary (1759–1797)   English writer, reformer, and one of the earliest feminists, she advocated especially for the opportunity for girls to receive educations.

Women for Sobriety   The national *self-help organization*, with chapters in many localities, whose members are mostly women with drinking problems. The members believe that women who have *alcoholism* have different needs and problems than do their male counterparts and thus need their own organization for combating the problem. They meet regularly to provide mutual support, inspiration, and information about dealing with specific problems of alcoholism.

Women's Bureau, U.S.   The organization within the U.S. *Department of Labor* whose primary concern is the working conditions of women. It administers a variety of programs to see that these conditions are favorable. Other programs of the Women's Bureau include helping *displaced home-*

makers, teenage mothers, and women of color and providing child care services.

Women's Christian Temperance Union (WCTU) See *temperance movements.*

women's liberation movement The organized efforts of disparate people and groups to eliminate *sex role stereotyping* and *sex discrimination* against women, achieve equality of opportunity with men, and widen the range of acceptable behaviors identified with female roles and femininity. See also *men's liberation movement.*

women's suffrage movement The organized political and social campaign to establish civil and social rights for women, especially the right to vote. In the United States this movement was strongest from the time of the *Seneca Falls Convention* in 1848, which outlined the equal rights for women goals, to the passage in 1920 of the 19th Amendment to the Constitution giving women the right to vote. The movement continues in several nations where the rights of women to participate in the political process are limited.

worker performance The productivity, efficiency, effectiveness, and quality of service by which an employee fulfills the requirements of the job.

worker satisfaction The degree to which an employee feels positive attitudes about the employer, the working conditions, relationships with other workers and those served, and future opportunities. The traditional view among social welfare administrators that increased job satisfaction leads to better work performance may not always be valid. Some evidence indicates that the two are not correlated.

workers' compensation Programs—funded by employers, insurance companies, and government—to pay employees for some part of the cost of occupational diseases and injury. Most industrial countries have uniform national programs for such reimbursement. However, in the United States the programs are primarily established under state law and thus vary widely as to the amount of compensation and the conditions under which it is to be awarded. In most states, the benefits are underwritten through private insurance companies whose premiums are paid by employers. The specific awards are usually under the scrutiny of state boards and U.S. *Department of Labor* supervision.

work ethic An ideology and a behavior found in many individuals and sociocultural groups that emphasize purposeful activity, productivity, and accomplishment. People so oriented are considered to be socially responsible and deserving of the advancements they tend to receive. However, they often are considered, by those who do not share this ideology, to be dull, unimaginative, and spiritless.

work experience programs Social service and labor programs designed to help clients become more employable by placing them in subsidized jobs in *nonprofit agencies,* usually for short periods. The goal gives less emphasis to training for specific marketable skills and more to improving workplace *coping skills.* This includes enhancing the clients' self-confidence, sense of responsibility, and self-discipline; stressing the importance of timely reporting for work; and teaching clients to relate cooperatively with co-workers. See also *Community Work Experience Program (CWEP).*

workfare The proposal by various economists, social planners, and politicians to discourage able-bodied people from receiving welfare benefits. It would establish programs and facilities in the public and private sectors so that these people could earn some of their benefits through work. It is a generic term rather than any specific program. See also *workhouse.*

work force 1. Those individuals who are employed in a given organization or industry. 2. All individuals who are working or looking for jobs.

workhouse An *indoor relief* form of "assistance," common in various countries in the 18th century, in which poor people who received help had to live and work in special facilities. The government contracted with private individuals to feed and house these people in exchange for the work they could do. The programs, which housed infants, children, older and disabled people, and diseased as well as able-bodied adults, were phased out in the late 18th century in favor of slightly more humane *almshouses* and *outdoor relief* programs.

Work Incentive (WIN) program The 1967 revisions in the *Aid to Families with Dependent Children (AFDC)* program that permitted and encouraged mothers receiving AFDC payments to work. Since 1986 the program has been within the *Family Services Administration (FSA)* of the U.S. *Department of Health and Human Services (HHS)*. Formerly, in the AFDC program, all of an employed mother's earnings were subtracted from the amount she could receive in AFDC benefits. WIN permitted these mothers to retain part of the money they earned without losing their AFDC money. The legislation also encouraged development of *day care* centers and job-training programs. Some critics say the program coerces some AFDC families by ending assistance to those who refuse job or training opportunities. Subsequent legislation has modified the WIN program significantly.

work incentives Benefits, requirements, or special aid to encourage people to seek and remain in suitable *employment* and to encourage employer organizations to hire and keep people on the job. Work incentives for individuals include such programs as *day care*, higher wages (made possible by government subsidy), reduction or termination of welfare payments for those who refuse to work, and improvements in the work environment. Work incentives for employer organizations include tax breaks for hiring and retaining specified numbers or categories of people (as in *experience ratings*), direct payments to subsidize wages paid, and stimulation of the general economy to allow the organization to employ more workers.

working class The *socioeconomic class,* according to many sociologists, whose family members tend to hold steady *employment* in industry and blue-collar jobs and who have relatively modest incomes, limited education, and aspirations and values that tend to be oriented toward maintaining security and preserving their existing lifestyles.

working poor Employed people whose assets and incomes from their jobs are so low that they fall below the *poverty line.* Although working poor people may be eligible for food stamps and some other means-tested programs, they often have limited access to housing, health care, or other necessities.

working through 1. In the social worker–client *relationship,* the process of mutually exploring a problem until there is agreement about the solution and the means to achieve it. 2. In *psychoanalytic theory,* the term refers to those processes that enable infantile and repressed *unconscious* material to be made *conscious* so it can be analyzed in therapy.

workplace The setting in which one's employment or other work activity occurs.

work release program A system whereby an inmate of a correctional or other institution is permitted to leave the facility regularly to maintain his or her paid employment. Often this program is used in conjunction with a *halfway house* so that the inmate has greater local access to the job and greater opportunity to reenter society when the required period of *incarceration* is concluded. See also *community service sentence.*

Works Progress Administration (WPA) A *New Deal* employment program established in 1935 under the leadership of social worker *Harry Hopkins (1890–1946)*, WPA provided jobs for more than 8 million people during its existence. Federal funds were used to build parks, bridges, roads, and airports and to sponsor the work of artists, musicians, writers, and scholars. The program was renamed the Work Projects Administration in 1939; it was disbanded in 1943 when employment conditions changed as a result of World War II.

World Bank   The informal name for the International Bank for Reconstruction and Development, headquartered in Washington, DC, with offices in every part of the world, to lend money and economic advice to *developing countries*. The World Bank was founded in 1944 to help the economies of war-torn nations.

World Food Programme   A subsidiary of the United Nations *Food and Agriculture Organization (FAO)* that obtains and provides emergency supplies of food for populations suffering famine or disaster; it also helps nations where such populations exist to receive and distribute food.

World Health Organization (WHO)   The United Nations agency established in its present form in 1948, with headquarters in Geneva, whose purpose is the "attainment by all peoples of the highest possible level of health." WHO sponsors medical research, health education, disease prevention programs, and the standardization of health and mental health statistics throughout the world.

"worthy poor"   The term once used to describe people who were poor because they were widowed, disabled, or had experienced unexpected economic reversals. They were considered to be honest, motivated to contribute, and basically hardworking. This term was used, mostly before the 20th century, to distinguish those people who "deserved" assistance from those who did not (the *"unworthy poor"*). Although the term is no longer officially used, many people still believe the concept. See also *victim blaming*.

WPA   See *Works Progress Administration (WPA)*.

Wright, Frances (Fanny) (1795–1852)   A social reformer, Wright came to the United States from Scotland and spent her life working for *human rights*, the gradual abolition of slavery, free public education, and *birth control*. A movement known as the "Fanny Wrighters" worked for these principles and gained political influence in the 1840s and 1850s.

Wyatt v. Stickney   The 1971 legal ruling in Alabama declaring that mental patients who had been committed on civil grounds have the constitutional right to receive such individual treatment as will give them a realistic opportunity to be cured or to improve their mental condition. See also *right to treatment* and *deinstitutionalization*.

X Y Z

xanthines A group of drugs, related to *amphetamines* and *cocaine,* that act as *central nervous system (CNS)* stimulants; caffeine is a common example.

X chromosome One of the two human sex chromosomes, whose pairing (XX for females, XY for males) determines an individual's sex. See also *Y chromosome.*

xenophobia Persistent, intense, and unreasonable *fear* of strangers or foreign people.

"YAVIS client" A term, including the acronym for "young, attractive, verbal, intelligent, and sexy," which refers to the type of person some psychotherapists seem to prefer treating, even though other clients may be in greater need.

Y chromosome One of the two human sex chromosomes, whose pairing (XX for females, XY for males) determines one's sex. See also *X chromosome.*

yellow fever An *infectious disease* caused by a virus transmitted by the bites of infected mosquitoes, found mostly in warm, damp climates. Symptoms include high fever, chills, jaundice, and often hemorrhaging and death. Prevention occurs through the control of mosquito habitats and inoculations.

YMCA See *Young Men's Christian Association (YMCA).*

YM–YWHA See *Young Men's and Young Women's Hebrew Associations (YM–YWHA).*

Young Men's and Young Women's Hebrew Associations (YM–YWHA) Organizations in communities with significant Jewish populations designed to provide young people with education, recreation, and social and spiritual opportunities.

Young Men's Christian Association (YMCA) The worldwide group of organizations devoted to the physical, intellectual, social, and spiritual well-being of young men. No longer limited to young people, Christians, or even men in some localities, the YMCA was first established in London in 1844 and in the United States in 1851.

"young Turks" A popular designation for ambitious, newer members of a political or industrial organization who seek to change the status quo.

Young, Whitney M. (1921–1971) Social worker and *civil rights* leader who led the *National Urban League* through the civil rights movement in the early 1960s, while serving as president of several social work organizations.

Young Women's Christian Associations (YWCA) The worldwide group of organizations devoted to educating young women spiritually, socially, and physically. These organizations originated in boarding houses for young women in London in 1855, and in 1877 several of them formed the YWCA.

youth service organizations Privately funded and administered federated organizations, usually with chapters or recreational facilities in most communities in the United States, whose purpose is to help young people achieve their developmental potentials. They focus on educationally oriented recreation, handicrafts, and sports activities designed to help youngsters keep physically fit and emotionally healthy while learning social skills, practical coping strategies, and moral conduct. Among the many groups of this type are the Boy Scouts of America, the Boys Clubs of America, the Girls Clubs of America, the Girl Scouts of the United States of America, the *Young Men's Christian Associations (YMCA)*, the *Young Women's Christian Association (YWCA)*, the *Young Men's and Young Women's Hebrew Associations (YM-YWHA)*, and the Campfire Girls.

YWCA   *See Young Women's Christian Associations (YWCA).*

zakat   Giving charitable donations, a requirement of those faithful to Islam; that portion of a Muslim's income that must be allocated for *alms* to poor people.

zar   A *culture-bound syndrome,* found more commonly in North African and Middle Eastern nations, in which an individual seems to experience possession by spirits and engages in such behavior as detachment, refusal to carry out daily tasks and functions, shouting, singing, laughing, and crying.

zeitgeist   From the German for "spirit of the time," the characteristic feelings or thoughts of a people in a given period.

zero-based budgeting   In social administration, the process of evaluating the entire future plan for the financial operation of the organization without reference to past expenditures. Each new financial plan starts from zero. Thus, the organization does not simply study whether to increase or decrease funds for each of its units but considers the objectives of the organization and means of achieving them.

zero population growth   A state of stability in the population in which the number of births and deaths are equal. Advocates suggest that this is to be achieved through improved *sex education, contraception, family planning,* and sometimes tax penalties for those who have more children than prescribed. Population stability is a policy goal for some nations and an international movement supported by those concerned about the social, economic, and environmental costs of the expanding world population. A formal organization, also known as Zero Population Growth, was established in 1968 and promotes these goals.

zero sum orientation   In *social planning,* budgeting, and management, the perspective that the available resources are relatively fixed so that an increased expenditure of funds or resources in one sector must be accompanied by a commensurate decrease of funds or resources in another.

Zionism   The worldwide social movement whose goal is to help maintain and develop the nation of Israel, primarily through fundraising, political advocacy in nations having relations with Israel, the facilitation of immigration to Israel, and public relations campaigns. The movement officially started in 1897. The World Zionist Congress, the principal organization, has no official connection with the government of Israel.

zoning   Municipal rules about the use of land and the types of structures permitted on the land.

zoophobia   Pathological *fear* of animals.

Zwingli, Huldreich (1484–1531)   Reformation clergyman who established and developed a public welfare plan for the poor people of Zurich and later the rest of Switzerland. The model was emulated by many other cities and states. The system provided work, education, and nutrition; some protections for children, older people, and disabled people; and a system of fundraising to pay for the program.

MILESTONES IN THE DEVELOPMENT OF SOCIAL WORK AND SOCIAL WELFARE

B.C. 1750   In Babylonia, King Hammurabi issues his code of justice, which includes a requirement that the people help one another during times of hardship.

B.C. 1200   In Israel, the Jewish people are told that God expects them to help poor and disadvantaged people.

B.C. 500   Philanthropy, from the Greek word for "acts of love for humanity," is institutionalized in the Greek city–states. Citizens are encouraged to donate money, which is used for the public good. Parks are built, and food, clothing, and other goods are kept in public facilities to be used for people in need.

B.C. 300   In China, the *Analects* of Confucius declare humans to be social beings bound to one another by *Jen*, a form of sympathy that is often expressed through helping those in need.

B.C. 100   In Rome, the *annona civica* tradition—in which patrician families distribute free or low-cost grain to all Roman citizens in need—is well established.

A.D. 30   Jesus Christ teaches that people's love for one another is God's will. He emphasizes the importance of giving to those who are less fortunate ("Inasmuch as ye have done it unto one of the least of these my brethren, ye have done it unto me").

313   Christianity is legalized by the Roman emperor Constantine. The more affluent converts can donate funds openly, and the church is able to use these funds to care for poor people.

400   "Hospitals" are developed and extended throughout India. These facilities provide shelter for poor and disabled homeless people and resemble almshouses rather than modern hospitals.

542   Hospitals similar to those in India have spread to China and the Middle East and now make their first appearance in Europe. The first of these, the Hôtel Dieu ("house of God") is established in Lyons, France, and is staffed primarily by religious workers and volunteers.

600   With the fall of the Roman Empire, Pope Gregory organizes programs to help poor people; the church replaces the state as the "safety net."

650   The followers of the Prophet Muhammad are told they have an obligation to poor people and that paying a *zakat* ("purification tax") to care for poor people is one of the Five Pillars (obligatory duties) of Islam.

787   Clergy establish the first modern foundling hospital (orphanage) for abandoned children in Milan, Italy.

1084   Almshouses for poor and disabled people, similar to the hospitals in France, are established in Canterbury, England.

1100   The Roman Church issues the *Decretum*, a compilation of its canon law, which includes an elaborate discussion of the theory and practice of charity. It states that rich people have a legal and moral obligation to support poor people.

1140 Norman King Roger II decrees that only physicians with licenses issued by the government may practice medicine.

1215 King John of England signs the Magna Carta, which establishes some human rights (for the nobility).

1348 The social system of feudalism begins to break down, partly because of bubonic plague, which kills nearly one-third of the population of Europe. Without the protection of the barons and lords, the serfs and peasants are at the mercy of economic and military threats.

1349 The Statute of Labourers is issued in England, requiring people to remain on their home manors and work for whatever the lords want to pay. Begging and almsgiving are outlawed except for older people and those unable to work. For the first time, a distinction is made between the "worthy poor" (older people, disabled people, widows, and dependent children), and the "unworthy poor" (able-bodied but unemployed adults).

1452 The first professional association is formed in Regensburg, Germany, for midwives.

1526 Juan Luis Vives, a Spaniard living in northern Europe, develops a plan for organized relief. The plan includes registering poor people, raising private funds to help them, and creating employment for able-bodied poor people. Many of his ideas were later used in European cities and influenced the Poor Laws in England and colonial America in the next century.

1529 The city–state of Venice enacts a poor law requiring licensing for people seeking alms and some public service work in order to get the license.

1531 England's first statute dealing with poor relief is issued. The statute empowers local justices to license certain people (older and disabled people) to beg in their own neighborhoods and to give harsh punishment to any unlicensed beggars. To implement this law, the justices developed criteria and procedures for deciding which persons to license. Thus, each applicant was evaluated by representatives of the justices.

1536 The Henrician Poor Law, also known as the Act for the Punishment of Sturdy Vagabonds and Beggars, is established. The government of Henry VIII classifies types of poor people and establishes procedures for collecting voluntary donations and disbursing funds. The law requires that these procedures be carried out at the local rather than the national level. It also acknowledges that the state rather than the church or volunteers must play some role in caring for poor people.

1572 England can no longer depend on voluntary contributions to care for its poor people. A national tax, the Parish Poor Rate, is levied to cover these costs. This is accompanied by a register of people needing relief. Funds left over from poor relief are used to create jobs for able-bodied people.

1601 The Elizabethan Poor Law is established. Built on the experiments of the earlier Henrician Poor Law (1536) and the Parish Poor Rate (1572), this legislation becomes the major codification of dealing with poor and disadvantaged people for more than 200 years. It also becomes the basis for dealing with poor people in colonial America. The Poor Law keeps the administration of poor relief at the local level, taxes people in each parish to pay for their own poor parishioners, establishes apprentice programs for poor children, develops workhouses for dependent people, and deals harshly and punitively with able-bodied poor people.

1625 Father Vincent de Paul (canonized as St. Vincent de Paul in 1737) establishes seminaries, religious orders, and charitable organizations to care for the poor people of France and is the founder of organized charity in Europe. In many of those nations that do not become Protestant during the Reformation, the church rather than the state retains more responsibility for the care of poor people.

1642 Plymouth Colony enacts the first poor law in the New World, based on the Elizabethan Poor Law of 1601.

1650 The influence of Luther, Calvin, and others has become established and manifested as the Protestant ethic, a philosophy that becomes influential in England, parts of Europe, and the American colonies. It emphasizes self-discipline, frugality, and hard work and leads many of its adherents to frown on those who are dependent or unemployed.

1657 The first private welfare organization in America, the Scots' Charitable Society, is established in Boston.

1662 The Law of Settlement and Removal is established in England as one of the world's first "residency requirements" in determining eligibility to receive help. Municipal authorities are authorized to help only poor local citizens and to expel from their jurisdictions anyone else who might become dependent for assistance. This law causes authorities to evaluate people as to the likelihood of their becoming poor. Thus, although the law is basically harsh and punitive, some efforts to look at the causes of poverty are codified.

1679 Writ of habeus corpus is instituted in England.

1690 John Locke's *Essay Concerning Human Understanding* is published, arguing that all human knowledge comes exclusively from experiences and perceptions.

1697 The workhouse system is developed in Bristol and soon spreads throughout England and parts of Europe. The system is designed to keep down poor taxes by denying aid to anyone who refuses to enter a workhouse. These institutions are usually managed by private entrepreneurs who contract with the legal authorities to care for the residents in exchange for using their work. Residents—including very young children, disabled people, and very old people—are often given minimal care and are worked long hours as virtual slaves.

1711 David Hume's *Treatise of Human Nature* uses the experimental method in problems of mental functioning and human nature.

1729 Ursuline Sisters of New Orleans establishes America's first residential institution for orphaned children.

1773 The colonies' first hospital for mentally ill people is established in Williamsburg, Virginia.

1782 The Gilbert Act is passed in England, enabling humanitarians, appalled by the exploitation of workhouse residents, to institute reforms in many English jurisdictions. Many workhouses are closed, assistance to poor people in their own homes is established, and children younger than six are placed with families. Many private entrepreneurs are replaced by municipal employees as managers of the remaining workhouses.

1790 The first publicly funded orphanage in the United States is established in Charleston, South Carolina.

1795 The Speenhamland system is inaugurated. In the English district of Speenhamland, a "poverty line" is developed, and some workers are made eligible for subsidization whenever their wages are below this amount. The amount is based on the price of bread and the worker's number of dependents. As prices increase or wages decline, the public treasury makes up the difference.

1798 The U.S. Public Health Service is established.

1798 Thomas Malthus publishes his *Essay on the Principle of Population as It Affects the Improvement of Society.*

1819 Scottish preacher and mathematician Thomas Chalmers assumes responsibility for Glasgow's poor. He develops private philanthropies to help meet the economic needs of poor people and organizes a system of volunteers to meet individually and regularly with disadvantaged people to give them encouragement and training.

1824 The Bureau of Indian Affairs (BIA) is established. It is the first federal organization to attempt to provide direct assistance in the welfare of some Americans.

1833 Antoine Frédéric Ozanum establishes the St. Vincent de Paul Society in Paris, using lay volunteers to provide emergency economic and spiritual assistance to poor people.

Slavery is abolished in the British Empire.

1834 The new Poor Law is established in England to reform the Elizabethan Poor Law (1601). The underlying emphasis of the new law is on self-reliance. Public assistance is not considered a right, and government is not seen as responsible for unemployed people. The principle of "less eligibility" (a recipient of aid can never receive as much as does the lowest-paid worker) is enforced.

1835 The Reverend Joseph Tuckerman, a Unitarian minister who is influenced by the reports of Thomas Chalmers's work in Scotland, organizes the Boston Society for the Prevention of Pauperism. This organization uses many of Chalmers's principles of individualized work with poor families, volunteer visitors, coordinated fundraising, and social action. Tuckerman's organization is influential in the subsequent development of the Charity Organization Societies (COS).

1836 Laws offering some protection for child laborers are enacted in Boston.

1843 Robert Hartley, using the teachings of Thomas Chalmers, Joseph Tuckerman, and French philanthropist Baron de Gerando, establishes the New York Association for Improving the Condition of the Poor. Soon imitated in many other American cities, the association stresses character building as a way to end poverty. Volunteers, usually middle-class Protestant laypersons, work to get poor people to abstain from alcohol, become more self-disciplined, and acquire the work ethic.

1844 The Young Men's Christian Association (YMCA) is founded in London.

Parisian nuns establish the first "day care" facility for infants of mothers working away from home.

1845 As a result of the social movement led by Dorothea Dix, the first state asylum for mentally ill people is established in Trenton, New Jersey. Soon Dix's efforts convince many other states to build mental hospitals.

1847 The British Factory Act restricts the working day for women and children to 10 hours, down from 13 to 18 hours a day.

1848 Feminists from throughout the United States convene at Seneca Falls, New York, to declare the goal of equal rights for women and to establish the philosophy and objectives of the women's movement, including suffrage, equal opportunities in education and jobs, and legal rights.

1850 Old Age Insurance is established in France.

1851 Mary Carpenter establishes reformatory schools for juvenile offenders.

1853 The Reverend Charles Loring Brace, concerned about the plight of New York's street children and children living in almshouses, organizes the Children's Aid Society. The society transports thousands of children every year to the West to live with rural families.

1854 Congress, pressured by Dorothea Dix's movement on behalf of mentally ill people, allocates funds and land to build mental hospitals. President Franklin Pierce vetoes the legislation, saying that charity is the province of the states and localities.

1860 The Food and Drug Act is established in Great Britain.

1862 Congress establishes the U.S. Department of Agriculture (USDA).

The Homestead Act (Ch. 75, 12 Stat. 392) is passed, giving 160 acres of unoccupied public land to any American citizen who agrees to live on it for five years.

Freedmen's Aid Societies are established in the northern states to assist former slaves with education and supplies.

1863 Massachusetts establishes a state board of charities to investigate and supervise its almshouses, prisons, and mental institutions. Other states soon follow suit.

The Red Cross is established in Switzerland by writer Jean Henri Dunant, and soon there are Red Cross and Red Crescent organizations in many other nations.

1864 French sociologist and engineer P. G. Frédéric Le Play completes the first scientific study of poverty—its extent, causes, consequences, and possible solutions.

1865 At the end of the Civil War, the United States establishes its first federal welfare agency, the Freedmen's Bureau, as part of the War Department, to provide temporary relief, education, employment, and health care for the newly released slaves.

Octavia Hill begins London tenement dwelling reforms.

1866 The Young Women's Christian Association (YWCA) establishes its first group in Boston.

1868 Orphans are boarded in private family homes in Massachusetts using public funds.

1869 In London the first Charity Organization Society (COS) is established. Formally named the "Society for Organising Charitable Relief and Repressing Mendicity," the society works to coordinate efforts at fundraising and to disburse funds in a systematic fashion. Volunteers are recruited to befriend applicants for assistance, make individual assessments of the reasons for their poverty, and help correct those reasons.

1870 Social Darwinism gains influence. Herbert Spencer's thesis was that "survival of the fittest" should apply to human society and that poverty was merely an aspect of natural selection. Helping poor people, it was believed, would make them lazy and nonindustrious.

The 15th Amendment to the U.S. Constitution is ratified, guaranteeing each citizen (not including women) the right to vote, regardless of race, color, or previous condition of servitude.

1872 The Freedmen's Bureau is abolished. Charles Loring Brace publishes *The Dangerous Classes of New York and Twenty Years' Work Among Them*, which raises U.S. consciousness about the plight of urban poor people.

The American Public Health Association (APHA) is established.

1874 Members of private charity organizations, religious agencies, and public officials from several northeastern states begin meetings to discuss their mutual concerns. These meetings lead to the establishment of the National Conference of Charities and Corrections (which evolved into the National Council on Social Welfare).

1877 The Society for Prevention of Cruelty to Children is formed in New York by E. T. Gerry.

Using the London organization as his model, the Reverend S. Humphreys Gurteen establishes America's first Charity Organization Society (COS) in

Buffalo, New York. Volunteer workers dispense advice rather than money to poor people and information about them to philanthropists and private relief agencies. A sign at the doorway of the Buffalo COS reads "No relief here!" Within a decade, COSs are established in most larger cities, and many are giving direct financial relief to needy people.

1878 The Reverend William Booth reorganizes his East London Revival Society as the Salvation Army.

1881 Clara Barton establishes the American Red Cross.

1883 In newly united Germany, Chancellor Otto von Bismarck establishes a national health insurance system and, shortly thereafter, accident insurance and old age and invalid insurance programs. This system becomes a model for social security programs in many other nations, excluding Great Britain and the United States.

1884 Toynbee Hall, the first settlement house, is established in London by Vicar Samuel A. Barnett. The settlement movement spreads quickly, and facilities are developed in most larger British and American cities. Their philosophy is to eliminate the distance between socioeconomic classes by locating settlements in working-class neighborhoods where ideas and information can be exchanged.

1886 Stanton Coit, who had resided in Toynbee Hall, opens America's first settlement house, the Neighborhood Guild, in New York. Eventually more than 400 houses are established. Their residents are involved in social advocacy, group work, and community development.

1889 In Chicago, Jane Addams and Ellen Gates Starr open Hull House, which becomes one of the most influential social settlement houses in the United States.

1890 The Consumer's League is established in England and, later, in the United States. Its purpose is to fight for better conditions in the work environment and safer products for the public. In the United States, the National Consumers League (NCL), under the leadership of social worker–lawyer Florence Kelley, establishes local chapters in most larger communities and leads successful campaigns to abolish child labor practices and to achieve minimum wages and shorter working hours as well as safe and effective consumer products.

1894 Amos G. Warner's *American Charities*—the first U.S. social welfare textbook—is published.

Japan's first social welfare law, the Indigent Person Relief Regulation, is enacted, requiring families to care for disabled, ill, and frail elderly people and children.

1896 In *Plessy v. Ferguson*, the U.S. Supreme Court upholds the "separate but equal" doctrine, which gives legal sanction to segregated schools and other facilities.

1898 The first school for social workers is established. The New York School of Philanthropy (later to become the Columbia University School of Social Work) grows out of a series of summer workshops and training programs for volunteers and friendly visitors and offers a one-year educational program.

1899 Faculty member and COS administrator Mary E. Richmond publishes *Friendly Visiting Among the Poor*.

The Institute for Social Welfare Training, a two-year course in social services, is established in Amsterdam.

The American Hospital Association (AHA) is established to develop and maintain standards in the nation's health care facilities.

Chicago establishes the nation's first juvenile court.

1900 Educator Simon N. Patten coins the term "social workers" and applies it to friendly visitors and settlement house residents. He and Mary Richmond dispute whether the major role of social workers should be advocacy or delivering individualized social services.

1902   Homer Folks, founder and head of the New York State Charities Aid Association, publishes *Care of Destitute, Neglected and Delinquent Children.* His philosophy becomes influential in subsequent child welfare goals and methods.

1903   Graham Taylor and others establish the Chicago School of Civics and Philanthropy, which eventually becomes the University of Chicago School of Social Service Administration.

1905   A social services department is established in Massachusetts General Hospital in Boston to help patients deal with the social problems of their illnesses. Within the next decade, more than 100 hospitals hire hospital social workers.

1906   School social work programs are introduced in New York and other cities.

Upton Sinclair's novel *The Jungle* leads to the U.S. Pure Food and Drugs Act (Ch. 3915, 34 Stat. 768).

1907   Psychiatric social work begins at Massachusetts General Hospital when social workers are hired to work with mentally ill patients.

The United States passes laws governing immigration.

1908   Pittsburgh Associated Charities is founded as the first community welfare council in the nation.

1909   The National Association for the Advancement of Colored People (NAACP) is founded. Social workers Mary White Ovington and Henry Moskowitz and others help organize black and white people to establish this voluntary organization oriented toward the protection of the legal and social rights of black people and other groups.

President Theodore Roosevelt convenes the first White House Conference, bringing together social workers and other leaders to discuss the problems of America's children.

1910   Several states pass "workmen's compensation laws" to protect wage earners from the economic risks of injury or unemployment. By 1920, all but six states have some form of workers' compensation program.

Boy Scouts of America is founded, based on the British Boy Scouts established in 1907.

Social workers and others found the National Urban League.

1911   Great Britain passes the National Insurance Act, which organizes a health and compensation program paid for by contributions from workers, employers, and the public.

The Charity Organization Societies (COS) become oriented increasingly toward helping families. Many local societies change their names to Family Welfare Agency. The National Alliance for Organizing Charity is renamed the American Association for Organizing Family Social Work. By 1946, this organization is known as the Family Service Association of America, renamed Family Service America (FSA) in 1983.

1912   The U.S. Children's Bureau is created, headed by social worker and former Hull House resident Julia Lathrop.

Girl Scouts of America is founded as part of the Girl Guides/Girl Scouts movement.

1913   The U.S. Department of Labor is created, primarily to promote the welfare of American workers.

The U.S. Department of Commerce is established.

1914   The Harrison Narcotics Acts (Ch. 1, 38 Stat. 785) becomes U.S. law, establishing the government organization later known as the Bureau of Narcotics; the act makes the sale and use of certain drugs a criminal offense.

The Boston Psychopathic Hospital establishes a social services department and uses the title "psychiatric social worker" for the first time.

1915 In an address to the National Conference of Charities and Corrections (NCCC), Abraham Flexner declares that social work has not yet qualified as a profession, especially because its members do not have a great deal of individual responsibility and because it still lacks a written body of knowledge and educationally communicable techniques.

Margaret Sanger publishes *Family Limitation*, the first book on birth control.

1917 Mary Richmond publishes *Social Diagnosis* (New York: Russell Sage Foundation). Social workers use her book as a primary text and as an answer to Abraham Flexner's 1915 report.

The first organization for social workers is established. The National Social Workers Exchange exists primarily to process applicants for social work jobs. Later the group becomes the American Association of Social Workers (AASW).

1918 The American Association of Hospital Social Workers (AAHSW) is formed as the first specialty within the new field. The organization is renamed the American Association of Medical Social Workers (AAMSW) in 1934.

Ida M. Cannon, director of medical social work at Massachusetts General Hospital, delineates the principles of medical social work.

Smith College, Northampton, Massachusetts, establishes the first training program for psychiatric social workers.

1919 The 17 schools of social work that exist in the United States and Canada form the Association of Training Schools for Professional Social Work to develop uni-

form standards of training and professional education. This group is later renamed the American Association of Schools of Social Work (AASSW), which later merges with the National Association of Schools of Social Administration (NASSA) to become the Council on Social Work Education (CSWE).

Social workers employed in schools organize as the National Association of Visiting Teachers.

1920 The Child Welfare League of America (CWLA) is formed.

The National Conference of Catholic Charities is established.

The 19th Amendment to the U.S. Constitution gives women the right to vote.

Unemployment insurance is established in Great Britain and Austria.

1921 The American Association of Social Workers (AASW) is created.

The U.S. Sheppard–Towner Act (Maternity Act, Ch. 135, 42 Stat. 224) goes into effect. Federal funds are granted to state health departments to provide for the pre- and postnatal health care of needy mothers and infants. Nearly 3,000 child and maternal health centers are established nationwide, and the nation's infant and maternal mortality rates drop significantly. Nevertheless, the program is dropped in 1929.

Social work educator Edward C. Lindeman publishes *The Community* (New York: Republic Press), in which the basic concepts of community organization are delineated.

Japan's Women's College establishes that nation's first school of social welfare.

1923 Clara Kaiser begins teaching the first social work course in social group work at Western Reserve University in Cleveland.

The Tufts Report on social work education is completed (*Education and Training for Social Work*, by James H. Tufts), formally delineating the components necessary to provide adequate education for social workers. The report recommends training students in bringing about improvements in society as well as in individuals.

1926 The American Association of Psychiatric Social Workers (AAPSW) is founded, as social work increasingly comprises caseworkers and clinical practitioners.

The U.S. Veterans Bureau (now U.S. Department of Veterans Affairs) begins employing social workers in its hospitals.

The Canadian Association of Social Workers (CASW) is founded.

1928 The Milford Conference convenes to discuss whether social work is a disparate group of technical specialties or a unified profession with integrated knowledge and skills. The conclusion is that social work is one profession with more similarities than differences among its specialties. In 1929, the report of the conference is published as *Social Case Work: Generic and Specific* (New York: American Association of Social Workers).

The International Council of Social Work (ICSW) is founded in Paris.

1929 The stock market crashes, heralding the Great Depression.

The International Association of Schools of Social Work (IASSW) is founded.

1930 The American Public Welfare Association (APWA) is established.

Virginia Robinson, who with Julia Jessie Taft developed the "functional school" of social casework, publishes the first comprehensive text to integrate social and psychodynamic concepts, *A Changing Psychology in Social Casework* (Chapel Hill: University of North Carolina Press).

Grace Coyle publishes the first comprehensive text on social group work, *Social Process in Organized Groups* (New York: Richard R. Smith).

1931 Social worker Jane Addams becomes co-recipient of the Nobel Peace Prize.

1933 President Franklin D. Roosevelt proclaims a "New Deal" for Americans and establishes major social welfare programs to combat poverty and unemployment. Programs include the Civilian Conservation Corps (CCC), the Civil Works Administration (CWA), the Federal Emergency Relief Administration (FERA), and later the Works Progress Administration (WPA). Social workers Harry Hopkins and Frances Perkins are appointed to the highest relevant positions, Hopkins as head of FERA and Perkins as U.S. Secretary of Labor (the first woman to head a cabinet department).

Through FERA, Harry Hopkins begins a federal grant program establishing public assistance offices in the states. Each office has to have at least one trained social worker on its staff.

1934 Puerto Rico passes a law regulating social work practice. This is the first time social work is legally regulated in any U.S. state or territory.

1935 The U.S. Social Security Act (Ch. 531, 49 Stat. 620) is signed into law. It includes a workers' retirement insurance program and coverage for dependent survivors and disabled workers. The act also establishes a federal welfare program that helps states pay for and administer programs in Old Age Assistance (OAA), Aid to the Blind (AB), Aid to Dependent Children, and General Assistance (GA) for needy people who do not qualify for other forms of help.

The National Conference on Social Work recognizes social group work as a major function of social work.

Social worker Jane Hoey is appointed head of the U.S. Bureau of Public Assistance. She influences the state departments of public assistance so that qualified applicants for help receive counseling as well as income maintenance. She sees to it that professional social work education is a requirement for public assistance administrators.

Alcoholics Anonymous (AA), the nation's first self-help organization, is established in Akron, Ohio, and becomes the prototype for many other self-help groups such as Gamblers Anonymous, Narcotics Anonymous, and Parents Anonymous (for those who abuse their children).

1936   Group workers begin regular meetings and form the American Association for the Study of Group Work, an association that in 1946 becomes the American Association of Group Workers (AAGW).

The National Association of Schools of Social Administration (NASSA) is established. In 1952 it merges with the American Association of Schools of Social Work (AASSW) to become the Council on Social Work Education (CSWE).

1937   The American Association of Schools of Social Work (AASSW) declares that beginning in 1939 the requirement for social work accreditation will be a two-year master's degree program. The master of social work (MSW) degree becomes a requirement to be considered a professional social worker.

1938   The Federal Housing Administration (FHA) begins its home-loan guarantee program to encourage home ownership.

Japan establishes its Ministry of Health and Welfare.

1939   The Lane Report (*The Field of Community Organization*, by Robert P. Lane) presents a systematic and comprehensive description of the roles, activities, and methods in the field of community organization. The work built on previous studies by Edward C. Lindeman in his 1921 book, *The Community*, and Jesse F. Steiner's 1930 book, *Community Organization*.

1940   Mary Parker Follett's posthumous book *Dynamic Administration* is pub-

lished; it becomes an influence in the field of social welfare administration.

1941   The Fair Employment Practices Committee (FEPC) is established to monitor and correct discrimination practices in the U.S. labor market. FEPC is abolished in 1945.

1942   The Beveridge Report is issued in Great Britain, recommending an integrated social security system that attempts to ensure cradle-to-grave economic protections for its citizens. Many of the report's recommendations go into effect after World War II.

The Lanham Act (Ch. 14, 56 Stat. 11) is passed in the United States for the first federal funding for day care for children of working mothers.

1943   Social agencies begin charging modest fees for clients who can afford them.

The Marsh Report is issued in Canada. Based partly on Britain's Beveridge Report, it establishes the guidelines for the Canadian social welfare system.

1945   World War II ends. On October 24, the United Nations is established, with many agencies for dealing with world social welfare problems, including the United Nations Children's Fund (UNICEF); the World Health Organization (WHO); the United Nations Educational, Scientific, and Cultural Organization (UNESCO); and the United Nations High Commission for Refugees (UNHCR).

The GI Bill is implemented. The program is designed primarily to provide educational and vocational training opportunities for returning veterans of World War II.

California becomes the first state to pass a social work regulatory act, a registration law.

1946   Great Britain establishes its National Health Service.

After meeting in special study groups since 1936, group workers formally organize as the American Association of Group Workers (AAGW).

The Association for the Study of Community Organization (ASCO) is established.

The National Mental Health Act (Ch. 538, 60 Stat. 423) is passed, establishing the National Institute of Mental Health (NIMH) and encouraging states, through grants, to develop and upgrade community and institutional mental health services. The Hill–Burton Act (Hospital Survey and Construction Act, Ch. 958, 60 Stat. 1040) is passed, providing federal funds to develop new hospital facilities.

The School Lunch program is established. Cash and commodities are supplied to the states, municipalities, and schools to ensure that poor children have adequate midday nutrition.

Emily Green Balch, social reformer and social work educator, receives the Nobel Peace Prize.

1947 More than 1 million war veterans enroll in colleges under the U.S. G.I. Bill.

1949 The Social Work Research Group (SWRG) is formally established.

1950 The first licensing for independent social work practice goes into effect in San Diego, California.

Japan's first MSW program is established at Doshisha University in Kyoto.

1951 The Hollis–Taylor Report is published as *Social Work Education in the United States* (New York: Council on Social Work Education) and recommends a more generic orientation. Many of its recommendations are adopted.

1952 The Council on Social Work Education (CSWE) is formed through a merger of the American Association of Schools of Social Work (AASSW) and the National Association of Schools of Social Administration (NASSA)—the two competing organizations that had been setting standards for schools of social work. CSWE is soon granted the authority to accredit graduate (master of social work) schools of social work.

The McCarran–Walter Act (Immigration and Nationality Act, Ch. 477, 66 Stat. 163) is enacted to codify the requirements for immigration and naturalization into the United States. The law includes a quota system that permits many more people from northern European nations to come to the United States than people from Asia, Africa, or Latin America.

1953 The U.S. Department of Health, Education, and Welfare (HEW) is established.

1954 The U.S. Housing Act of 1954 (Ch. 649, 68 Stat. 590) becomes law, establishing a massive urban renewal program in most American communities.

In social casework, the so-called "diagnostic" and "functional" schools begin to merge and lose their separate identities. The functional school had been oriented toward a highly focused, goal-oriented approach to casework intervention. The diagnostic school had been influenced by Freudian theory, but adherents of this approach develop more of a psychosocial orientation in the 1950s.

In *Brown v. Board of Education of Topeka, Kansas*, the U.S. Supreme Court rules that racial segregation in public schools is unconstitutional.

1955 On October 1, the National Association of Social Workers (NASW) is created through the merger of seven organizations—the American Association of Social Workers (AASW), the American Association of Medical Social Workers (AAMSW), the American Association of Psychiatric Social Workers (AAPSW), the National Association of School Social Workers (NASSW), the American Association of Group Workers (AAGW), the Association for the Study of Community Organization (ASCO), and the Social

Work Research Group (SWRG). Membership is limited to members of the seven associations and to master's degree–level workers graduating from accredited schools of social work.

1956 The International Federation of Social Workers (IFSW) is established and comprises national social work professional associations. The Council of International Programs (CIP) is founded in Cleveland to facilitate an exchange program in social work education between the United States and 110 other nations.

1957 The U.S. Civil Rights Act of 1957 (P.L. 85-315) is passed.

1958 The National Defense Education Act of 1958 (P.L. 85-864) is passed, providing federal aid to all levels of public and private education in the United States. The act stressed education in math, sciences, and foreign languages and gave extensive funding for low-interest student loans.

1959 The first professional school of social work to focus exclusively on social policy and planning is established in Waltham, Massachusetts. It is the Florence Heller Graduate School for Advanced Studies in Social Welfare at Brandeis University.

Social Work Curriculum Study, a 13-volume evaluation and recommendation for improved social work education, edited by Werner Boehm, is published (New York: Council on Social Work Education).

1961 Unemployed parents may be included in Aid to Families with Dependent Children (AFDC) payments in states that elect to include them.

Rhode Island becomes the third jurisdiction to pass a regulatory law for social workers.

The White House Conference on Aging develops plans for effective care for the nation's older people. Its work leads to the Older Americans Act of 1965 (P.L. 89-73).

The National Association of Social Workers (NASW) organizes the Academy of Certified Social Workers (ACSW), restricted to NASW members with accredited master of social work (MSW) degrees, two years' agency experience under certified social work supervision, and adherence to the *NASW Code of Ethics*. ACSW membership requirements are subsequently revised to include testing and professional recommendations.

1962 The Council on Social Work Education (CSWE) recognizes community organization as a legitimate specialization for social work education.

Congress passes the Manpower Development and Training Act of 1962 (P.L. 87-415), a full-scale government training program to return displaced and unemployed workers to new fields.

President John F. Kennedy signs into law the social security amendments, which provide greatly increased federal support for states to employ social workers and others. The workers would provide counseling and training to help people get off the welfare rolls.

1963 In *Gideon v. Wainwright*, the U.S. Supreme Court rules that all needy defendants in criminal cases have the right to free legal counsel.

The Joint Commission on Mental Illness and Health issues its findings. President Kennedy signs into law the Community Mental Health Centers Act (P.L. 88-164), which funds development of mental health centers, training programs, and outpatient treatment programs.

1964 President Lyndon B. Johnson launches the Great Society programs. With legislation in the Economic Opportunity Act of 1964 (P.L. 88-452) and the Civil Rights Act of 1964 (P.L. 88-352), the resulting programs include the Job Corps, Operation Head Start, Volunteers in Service to America (VISTA), the Neighborhood Youth Corps, and the Community Action program. Federal funding is also used to train thousands of social workers and end the social work personnel shortages.

Racial discrimination in public places is made illegal.

The Food Stamp program (Food Stamp Act of 1964, P.L. 88-525) is enacted. Recipients are required to purchase coupons that are redeemable in food stores. A family of four with a monthly income of $140 could buy $166 worth of coupons for $37.

1965 More Great Society programs and organizations are enacted and implemented, including Medicare, Medicaid, the Older Americans Act of 1965 (P.L. 89-73), and the Elementary and Secondary Education Act of 1965 (P.L. 89-10).

The U.S. Department of Housing and Urban Development (HUD) is established.

The Voting Rights Act of 1965 (P.L. 89-110) becomes law.

Wilbur Cohen, a social worker and economist who helped found the National Association of Social Workers (NASW) and served on the committee to create the Social Security Act, is appointed Secretary of the U.S. Department of Health, Education, and Welfare (HEW), which is to administer most of the Great Society programs.

1966 The U.S. Supreme Court issues the *Miranda* decision, requiring that police inform a suspect of his or her constitutional rights before questioning.

1967 The Social Security Act is amended to include a Work Incentive (WIN) program designed to encourage recipients of Aid to Families with Dependent Children (AFDC) to work without losing most of their benefits.

Amendments (P.L. 90-36) to the Social Security Act separate the welfare system's income maintenance features from personal social services. Clerks can replace professionals in administering the income maintenance program. Social workers are needed only to provide personal social services; thus, their role in public welfare is greatly diminished.

The *In re Gault* decision by the U.S. Supreme Court determines that juveniles have the same constitutional rights as adults. The juvenile court system, which had minimized the adversary process and used social workers as advocates and probation officers, is greatly curtailed.

1968 The Kerner Commission (National Advisory Commission on Civil Disorders) issues its report, blaming white racism and limited opportunities for black people as major causes of the strife and rioting in urban ghettos. The Omnibus Crime Control and Safe Streets Act of 1968 (P.L. 90-351) is passed and establishes the Law Enforcement Assistance Administration (LEAA) to help state and municipal governments control crime, rehabilitate offenders, recruit and train corrections officers and police, and improve correctional facilities.

The Office of Economic Opportunity (OEO) and War on Poverty programs start to dismantle. Within the next three years, many programs are abolished and others are downgraded and placed within other federal agencies, especially the Community Service Administration.

The National Association of Black Social Workers (NABSW) is established; the National Association of Puerto Rican Social Service Workers (NAPRSSW) is founded; and the Asian American Social Workers (AASW) is formed.

1969 Membership in the National Association of Social Workers (NASW), once restricted to people with master of social work (MSW) degrees, is opened to social workers with qualified bachelor's degrees. The NASW Delegate Assembly approves the resolution to pursue licensing of social work practice within each state.

President Richard M. Nixon proposes the Family Assistance Plan (FAP) to reorganize the nation's welfare program. The plan, which proposes a minimum guaranteed annual income and incentives to encourage people to work, is not enacted.

1970 The National Indian Social Workers Association (NISWA) is created.

1971 The National Federation of Societies for Clinical Social Work (NFSCSW) is established.

The National Association of Social Workers (NASW) establishes the Educational Legislative Action Network (ELAN). Its political action functions are later assumed by local NASW chapters and by other NASW bodies at the national level.

ACTION is established as an independent federal umbrella agency that includes the Peace Corps, Volunteers in Service to America (VISTA), and the Foster Grandparent program.

1972 The Supplemental Security Income program (P.L. 92-603) is enacted, which combines and federalizes public assistance for adult poor, aged, blind, and disabled people. Sex discrimination in federally assisted educational programs is abolished.

1974 CETA (the Comprehensive Employment and Training Act, P.L. 93-203) provides job opportunities and education for disadvantaged people. Section 8 of the Housing and Community Development Act of 1974 (P.L. 93-383) helps low-income people live in housing provided by the private sector at fair market value. The Equal Credit Opportunity Act (P.L. 93-495) prohibits discrimination in credit based on gender or marital status, among other criteria.

The Child Abuse Prevention and Treatment Act (P.L. 93-247) is signed. The National Center on Child Abuse and Neglect (NCCAN) is established. In 1978, this law is expanded to cover improvements in the nation's adoption system.

1975 Personal social services, work training, housing and community development, and juvenile justice and delinquency programs become law. The amendment to the Social Security Act known as Title XX (P.L. 93-647) becomes the major source of funds for personal social services. Each state is reimbursed by the federal government for helping individuals achieve economic self-support and independence, preventing and remedying neglect and abuse, and reducing and preventing improper institutional care.

The Education for All Handicapped Children Act of 1975 (P.L. 94-142) becomes law, requiring that the nation's public schools will provide equal educational opportunities for handicapped and learning-disabled youngsters.

The American Psychiatric Association (APA) removes "homosexuality" from its diagnosable mental disorders.

1976 The National Association of Social Workers (NASW) establishes Political Action for Candidate Election (PACE).

The Rural Social Work Caucus is formed (at the first national Institute on Social Work in Rural Areas) to coordinate the activities of social workers who serve nonmetropolitan people.

1977 President Jimmy Carter proposes a thorough revision of the nation's social welfare system with a Jobs and Income Security program, which fails to gain approval in Congress and is abandoned when he is not reelected.

The Group for the Advancement of Doctoral Education in Social Work (GADE) is formed.

1979 The U.S. Supreme Court rules that welfare benefits must be paid to families left needy by the mother's loss of her job, just as to families in which the father becomes unemployed.

The American Association of State Social Work Boards (AASSWB) is incorporated to coordinate the procedures and activities of state licensing for social workers.

The National Association of Social Workers (NASW) Delegate Assembly approves the profession's new *Code of Ethics*.

1980 The U.S. Department of Health and Human Services (HHS) is established when the Department of Health, Education, and Welfare is divided. The U.S. Department of Education is established as an independent cabinet-level department.

The British government's Barclay Report is completed, defining the roles and tasks of social workers in public assistance and personal social services. It states that social workers should be more involved in social care planning and counseling, promoting community networks, negotiating, and social advocacy.

The Adoption Assistance and Child Welfare Act of 1980 (P.L. 96-272), which provides programs for children, including subsidized adoptions, changes in foster home care, and day care facilities, is passed.

The Parental Kidnapping Prevention Act of 1980 (P.L. 96-611) clarifies laws pertaining to parental custody rights and obligations and helps state and local law enforcement agencies coordinate their efforts to reunite children with their custodial parents.

1981 The Omnibus Budget Reconciliation Act of 1981 (P.L. 97-35) and the social services block grants are established to fund social services programs at the state level with reduced federal scrutiny and funding and to decentralize social services programs to states.

1982 The proposed Equal Rights Amendment (ERA) for sexual equality fails to be ratified by two-thirds of the states by the deadline required by law.

The Job Training Partnership Act (P.L. 97-300) and the Emergency Job Bill (P.L. 97-404) are enacted. This legislation replaces many CETA public service job-training programs and seeks to encourage state governments and private industry to train needy people for suitable employment.

The Tax Equity and Fiscal Responsibility Act of 1982 (P.L. 97-248) is enacted, cutting back social services funding as well as Medicare, Medicaid, Aid to Families with Dependent Children (AFDC), Supplemental Security Income (SSI), and unemployment compensation.

The Association for the Advancement of Social Work with Groups (AASWG) is formally established.

1983 The National Association of Social Workers (NASW) establishes the National Peer Review Advisory Committee and trains social workers to evaluate the work of other social workers to promote accountability and to meet quality control requirements of government and third-party funding organizations.

The Council on Social Work Education (CSWE) issues a Curriculum Policy Statement for baccalaureate as well as master's degree programs in social work education. Bachelor of Social Work education is recognized as the first level of professional social work education.

1985 The Canadian Health Act is established to provide universal comprehensive health care.

1986 The Family Services Administration (FSA) is created as a unit within the U.S. Department of Health and Human Services (HHS). It consolidates the six major federal low-income programs (Aid to Families with Dependent Children [AFDC], Work Incentive [WIN] program, Community Services Block Grants, Low-Income Home Energy Assistance, Refugee Assistance, and the Child Support Enforcement program).

The Immigration Reform and Control Act of 1986 (P.L. 99-603) establishes new criteria for immigration and opportunities for U.S. residents of illegal alien status to become citizens.

The National Association of Social Workers (NASW) establishes the Center for Social Policy and Practice to coordinate the exchange of information, education, and policy formulation pertaining to social work and social welfare in the United States.

1990 The Americans with Disabilities Act of 1990 (P.L. 101-336) makes it illegal to discriminate against disabled people in terms of employment opportunity in businesses with more than 15 employees.

The *NASW Code of Ethics* is revised.

1991 The Academy of Certified Baccalaureate Social Workers (ACBSW) is established.

1993 The Brady Bill (Brady Handgun Violence Prevention Act, P.L. 103-159), to limit access to handguns in the United States, is passed.

The Family and Medical Leave Act of 1993 (P.L. 103-3) becomes law, requiring larger U.S. companies to permit employees job-protected unpaid leave to care for family members.

1994 Americorps is established to facilitate volunteer human services efforts in American communities.

The *Person-in-Environment (PIE) System* is published by the NASW Press to enable social workers to classify and code problems of psychosocial, health, and environmental functioning.

1995 The U.S. National Voter Registration Act goes into effect, giving U.S. citizens easier access to registering to vote while applying for government services.

NASW CODE OF ETHICS

Preamble

This code is intended to serve as a guide to the everyday conduct of members of the social work profession and as a basis for the adjudication of issues in ethics when the conduct of social workers is alleged to deviate from the standards expressed or implied in this code. It represents standards of ethical behavior for social workers in professional relationships with those served, with colleagues, with employers, with other individuals and professions, and with the community and society as a whole. It also embodies standards of ethical behavior governing individual conduct to the extent that such conduct is associated with an individual's status and identity as a social worker.

This code is based on the fundamental values of the social work profession that include the worth, dignity, and uniqueness of all persons as well as their rights and opportunities. It is also based on the nature of social work, which fosters conditions that promote these values.

In subscribing to and abiding by this code, the social worker is expected to view ethical responsibility in as inclusive a context as each situation demands and within which ethical judgment is required. The social worker is expected to take into consideration all the principles in this code that have a bearing upon any situation in which ethical judgment is to be exercised and professional intervention or conduct is planned. The course of action that the social worker chooses is expected to be consistent with the spirit as well as the letter of this code.

In itself, this code does not represent a set of rules that will prescribe all the behaviors of social workers in all the complexities of professional life. Rather, it offers general principles to guide conduct, and the judicious appraisal of conduct, in situations that have ethical implications. It provides the basis for making judgments about ethical actions before or after they occur. Frequently, the particular situation determines the ethical principles that apply and the manner of their application. In such cases, not only the particular ethical principles are taken into immediate consideration, but also the entire code and its spirit. Specific applications of ethical principles must be judged within the context in which they are being considered. Ethical behavior in a given situation must satisfy not only the judgment of the individual social worker, but also the judgment of an unbiased jury of professional peers.

This code should not be used as an instrument to deprive any social worker of the opportunity or freedom to practice with complete professional integrity; nor should any disciplinary action be taken on the basis of this code without maximum provision for safeguarding the rights of the social worker affected.

The ethical behavior of social workers results not from edict, but from a personal commitment of the individual. This code is offered to affirm the will and zeal of all social workers to be ethical and to act ethically in all that they do as social workers.

The following codified ethical principles should guide social workers in the various roles and relationships and at the various levels of responsibility in which they function professionally. These principles also serve as a basis for the adjudication by the National Association of Social Workers of issues in ethics.

In subscribing to this code, social workers are required to cooperate in its implementation and abide by any disciplinary rulings based on it. They should also take adequate measures to discourage, prevent, expose, and correct the unethical conduct of colleagues. Finally, social workers should be equally ready to defend and assist colleagues unjustly charged with unethical conduct.

NASW Code of Ethics

I. THE SOCIAL WORKER'S CONDUCT AND COMPORTMENT AS A SOCIAL WORKER
   A. *Propriety*—The social worker should maintain high standards of personal conduct in the capacity or identity as social worker.
      1. The private conduct of the social worker is a personal matter to the same degree as is any other person's, except when such conduct compromises the fulfillment of professional responsibilities.
      2. The social worker should not participate in, condone, or be associated with dishonesty, fraud, deceit, or misrepresentation.
      3. The social worker should distinguish clearly between statements and actions made as a private individual and as a representative of the social work profession or an organization or group.
   B. *Competence and Professional Development*—The social worker should strive to become and remain proficient in professional practice and the performance of professional functions.
      1. The social worker should accept responsibility or employment only on the basis of existing competence or the intention to acquire the necessary competence.
      2. The social worker should not misrepresent professional qualifications, education, experience, or affiliations.
      3. The social worker should not allow his or her own personal problems, psychosocial distress, substance abuse, or mental health difficulties to interfere with professional judgment and performance or jeopardize the best interests of those for whom the social worker has a professional responsibility.
      4. The social worker whose personal problems, psychosocial distress, substance abuse, or mental health difficulties interfere with professional judgment and performance should immediately seek consultation and

take appropriate remedial action by seeking professional help, making adjustments in workload, terminating practice, or taking any other steps necessary to protect clients an others.

C. *Service*—The social worker should regard as primary the service obligation of the social work profession.

1. The social worker should retain ultimate responsibility for the quality and extent of the service that individual assumes, assigns, or performs.

2. The social worker should act to prevent practices that are inhumane or discriminatory against any person or group of persons.

D. *Integrity*—The social worker should act in accordance with the highest standards of professional integrity and impartiality.

1. The social worker should be alert to and resist the influences and pressures that interfere with the exercise of professional discretion and impartial judgment required for the performance of professional functions.

2. The social worker should not exploit professional relationships for personal gain.

E. *Scholarship and Research*—The social worker engaged in study and research should be guided by the conventions of scholarly inquiry.

1. The social worker engaged in research should consider carefully its possible consequences for human beings.

2. The social worker engaged in research should ascertain that the consent of the participants in the research is voluntary and informed, without any implied deprivation or penalty for refusal to participate, and with due regard for the participants' privacy and dignity.

3. The social worker engaged in research should protect participants from unwarranted physical or mental discomfort, distress, harm, danger, or deprivation.

4. The social worker who engages in the evaluation of services or cases should discuss them only for professional purposes and only with persons directly and professionally concerned with them.

5. Information obtained about participants in research should be treated as confidential.

6. The social worker should take credit only for work actually done in connection with scholarly and research endeavors and credit contributions made by others.

II. The Social Worker's Ethical Responsibility to Clients

F. *Primacy of Clients' Interests*—The social worker's primary responsibility is to clients.

1. The social worker should serve clients with devotion, loyalty, determination, and the maximum application of professional skill and competence.

2. The social worker should not exploit relationships with clients for personal advantage.

3. The social worker should not practice, condone, facilitate, or collaborate with any form of discrimination on the basis of race, color, sex, sexual orientation, age, religion, national origin, marital status, political belief, mental or physical handicap, or any other preference or personal characteristic, condition, or status.

4. The social worker should not condone or engage in any dual or multiple relationships with clients or former clients in which there is a risk of exploitation of or potential harm to the client. The social worker is responsible for setting clear, appropriate, and culturally sensitive boundaries.

5. The social worker should under no circumstances engage in sexual activities with clients.

6. The social worker should provide clients with accurate and complete information regarding the extent and nature of the services available to them.

7. The social worker should apprise clients of their risks, rights, opportunities, and obligations associated with social service to them.

8. The social worker should seek advice and counsel of colleagues and supervisors whenever such consultation is in the best interest of clients.

9. The social worker should terminate service to clients, and professional relationships with them, when such service and relationships are no longer required or no longer serve the clients' needs or interests.

10. The social worker should withdraw services precipitously only under unusual circumstances, giving careful consideration to all factors in the situation and taking care to minimize possible adverse effects.

11. The social worker who anticipates the termination or interruption of service to clients should notify clients promptly and seek the transfer, referral, or continuation of service in relation to the clients' needs and preferences.

G. *Rights and Prerogatives of Clients*—The social worker should make every effort to foster maximum self-determination on the part of clients.

1. When the social worker must act on behalf of a client who has been adjudged legally incompetent, the social worker should safeguard the interests and rights of that client.

2. When another individual has been legally authorized to act on behalf of a client, the social worker should deal with that person always with the client's best interest in mind.

3. The social worker should not engage in any action that violates or diminishes the civil or legal rights of clients.

H. *Confidentiality and Privacy*—The social worker should respect the privacy of clients and hold in confidence all information obtained in the course of professional service.

1. The social worker should share with others confidences revealed by clients, without their consent, only for compelling professional reasons.

2. The social worker should inform clients fully about the limits of confidenti-

ality in a given situation, the purposes for which information is obtained, and how it may be used.

3. The social worker should afford clients reasonable access to any official social work records concerning them.

4. When providing clients with access to records, the social worker should take due care to protect the confidences of others contained in those records.

5. The social worker should obtain informed consent of clients before taping, recording, or permitting third-party observation of their activities.

I. *Fees*—When setting fees, the social worker should ensure that they are fair, reasonable, considerate, and commensurate with the service performed and with due regard for the clients' ability to pay.

1. The social worker should not accept anything of value for making a referral.

III. THE SOCIAL WORKER'S ETHICAL RESPONSIBILITY TO COLLEAGUES

J. *Respect, Fairness, and Courtesy*—The social worker should treat colleagues with respect, courtesy, fairness, and good faith.

1. The social worker should cooperate with colleagues to promote professional interests and concerns.

2. The social worker should respect confidences shared by colleagues in the course of their professional relationships and transactions.

3. The social worker should create and maintain conditions of practice that facilitate ethical and competent professional performance by colleagues.

4. The social worker should treat with respect, and represent accurately and fairly, the qualifications, views, and findings of colleagues and use appropriate channels to express judgments on these matters.

5. The social worker who replaces or is replaced by a colleague in professional practice should act with consideration for the interest, character, and reputation of that colleague.

6. The social worker should not exploit a dispute between a colleague and employers to obtain a position or otherwise advance the social worker's interest.

7. The social worker should seek arbitration or mediation when conflicts with colleagues require resolution for compelling professional reasons.

8. The social worker should extend to colleagues of other professions the same respect and cooperation that is extended to social work colleagues.

9. The social worker who serves as an employer, supervisor, or mentor to colleagues should make orderly and explicit arrangements regarding the conditions of their continuing professional relationship.

10. The social worker who has the responsibility for employing and evaluating the performance of other staff members should fulfill such responsibility in a fair, considerate, and equitable manner, on the basis of clearly enunciated criteria.

11. The social worker who has the responsibility for evaluating the performance of employees, supervisees, or students should share evaluations with them.

12. The social worker should not use a professional position vested with power, such as that of employer, supervisor, teacher, or consultant, to his or her advantage or to exploit others.

13. The social worker who has direct knowledge of a social work colleague's impairment due to personal problems, psychosocial distress, substance abuse, or mental health difficulties should consult with that colleague and assist the colleague in taking remedial action.

K. *Dealing with Colleagues' Clients*—The social worker has the responsibility to relate to the clients of colleagues with full professional consideration.

1. The social worker should not assume professional responsibility for the clients of another agency or a colleague without appropriate communication with that agency or colleague.

2. The social worker who serves the clients of colleagues, during a temporary absence or emergency, should serve those clients with the same consideration as that afforded any client.

IV. THE SOCIAL WORKER'S RESPONSIBILITY TO EMPLOYERS AND EMPLOYING ORGANIZATIONS

L. *Commitments to Employing Organization*—The social worker should adhere to commitments made to the employing organization.

1. The social worker should work to improve the employing agency's policies and procedures, and the efficiency and effectiveness of its services.

2. The social worker should not accept employment or arrange student field placements in an organization which is currently under public sanction by NASW for violating personnel standards, or imposing limitations on or penalties for professional actions on behalf of clients.

3. The social worker should act to prevent and eliminate discrimination in the employing organization's work assignments and in its employment policies and practices.

4. The social worker should use with scrupulous regard, and only for the purpose for which they are intended, the resources of the employing organization.

V. THE SOCIAL WORKER'S ETHICAL RESPONSIBILITY TO THE SOCIAL WORK PROFESSION

M. *Maintaining the Integrity of the Profession*—The social worker should uphold and advance the values, ethics, knowledge, and mission of the profession.

1. The social worker should protect and enhance the dignity and integrity of the profession and should be responsible and vigorous in discussion and criticism of the profession.

2. The social worker should take action through appropriate channels against unethical conduct by any other member of the profession.

3. The social worker should act to prevent the unauthorized and unqualified practice of social work.

4. The social worker should make no misrepresentations in advertising as to qualifications, competence, service, or results to be achieved.

N. *Community Service*—The social worker should assist the profession in making social services available to the general public.

1. The social worker should contribute time and professional expertise to activities that promote respect for the utility, the integrity, and the competence of the social work profession.

2. The social worker should support the formulation, development, enactment, and implementation of social policies of concern to the profession.

O. *Development of Knowledge*—The social worker should take responsibility for identifying, developing, and fully utilizing knowledge for professional practice.

1. The social worker should base practice upon recognized knowledge relevant to social work.

2. The social worker should critically examine and keep current with emerging knowledge relevant to social work.

3. The social worker should contribute to the knowledge base of social work and share research knowledge and practice wisdom with colleagues.

VI. THE SOCIAL WORKER'S ETHICAL RESPONSIBILITY TO SOCIETY

P. *Promoting the General Welfare*—The social worker should promote the general welfare of society.

1. The social worker should act to prevent and eliminate discrimination against any person or group on the basis of race, color, sex, sexual orientation, age, religion, national origin, marital status, political belief, mental or physical handicap, or any other preference or personal characteristic, condition, or status.

2. The social worker should act to ensure that all persons have access to the resources, services, and opportunities which they require.

3. The social worker should act to expand choice and opportunity for all persons, with special regard for disadvantaged or oppressed groups and persons.

4. The social worker should promote conditions that encourage respect for the diversity of cultures which constitute American society.

5. The social worker should provide appropriate professional services in public emergencies.

6. The social worker should advocate changes in policy and legislation to improve social conditions and to promote social justice.

7. The social worker should encourage informed participation by the public in shaping social policies and institutions.

STATE BOARDS REGULATING SOCIAL WORK

ALABAMA
Alabama State Board of Social Work Examiners
64 N. Union St., Suite 129
Montgomery, AL 36130
Alice W. King, Administrator   James Dupree, Jr., Chairperson

ALASKA
Board of Clinical Social Work Examiners
Division of Occupational Licensing
Department of Commerce and Economic Development
P.O. Box D-LIC
Juneau, AK 99811
Wanda Fleming, Administrator   Colleen Patrick-Riley, Chairperson

ARIZONA
Board of Behavioral Health Examiners
1645 W. Jefferson, 4th Floor
Phoenix, AZ 85007
David Oake, Administrator   Aliki Coudroglou, Chairperson

ARKANSAS
Social Work Licensing Board
P.O. Box 250381
Hillcrest Station
Little Rock, AR 72225
Troylene Jones, Administrator   Walter Darnell, Chairperson

CALIFORNIA
Board of Behavioral Science Examiners
Department of Consumer Affairs
400 R St., Suite 3150
Sacramento, CA 95814
Karen Walton, Chairperson

COLORADO
Colorado State Board of Social Work Examiners
1560 Broadway, Suite 1340
Denver, CO 80202
Amos Martinez, Administrator   Walter Simon, Chairperson

CONNECTICUT
Department of Health Services
Division of Medical Quality Assurance
Social Work Certification
150 Washington St.
Hartford, CT 06106
Joe Gillen, Administrator   Stanley Peck, Chairperson

DELAWARE
Board of Social Work Examiners
Cannon Bldg.
861 Silver Lake Bldg., Suite 203
Dover, DE 19901
Sean Hebbel, Chairperson

DISTRICT OF COLUMBIA
DC Board of Social Work
Department of Consumer and Regulatory Affairs

Occupational and Professional Licensing Administration
614 H St., NW, Room 904
Washington, DC 20001
Patsy Lockett, Administrator   Vivian L. C. Smith, Chairperson

FLORIDA — Board of Clinical Social Work
Marriage and Family Therapy, Mental Health Counseling
1940 N. Monroe St.
Tallahassee, FL 32399
Lucy Gee, Administrator   Larry Shyers, Chairperson

GEORGIA — Georgia Composite Board of Professional Counselors, Social Workers, and
Marriage and Family Therapists
166 Pryor St., SW
Atlanta, GA 30303
Lori Gold, Administrator   Alan Yorker, Chairperson

IDAHO — Bureau of Occupational Licensing
Board of Social Work Examiners
Owyhee Plaza
1109 Main St., Suite 220
Boise, ID 83702
Carmen Westburg, Administrator   Ginny Dickman, Chairperson

ILLINOIS — Social Workers Examining and Disciplinary Board
Department of Professional Regulation
320 W. Washington St.
Springfield, IL 62786
Dan Harden, Administrator   Jay Morgerman, Chairperson

INDIANA — Health Professions Bureau
402 W. Washington St., Suite 41
Indianapolis, IN 46204
Barbara J. Powers, Administrator   Madelaine Pinkus-Rohn, Chairperson

IOWA — Board of Social Work Examiners
Department of Public Health
Lucas State Office Bldg.
Des Moines, IA 50319
Harriett Miller, Administrator   Bruce Buchanan, Chairperson

KANSAS — Behavioral Sciences Regulatory Board
712 S. Kansas Ave.
Topeka, KS 66612
Mary Ann Gabel, Administrator   Joseph Robb, Chairperson

KENTUCKY — State Board of Examiners of Social Work
P.O. Box 456
Frankfort, KY 40602
Wendy Satterly, Administrator

LOUISIANA — Louisiana State Board of Certified Social Work Examiners
P.O. Box 345
Prairieville, LA 70769
Suzanne Pevey, Administrator   Peggy Salley, Chairperson

MAINE	State Board of Social Work Licensing Department of Business and Financial Regulation State House Station, Suite 35 Augusta, ME 04333 *Patricia Beaudoin, Administrator Virginia Vaitones, Chairperson*
MARYLAND	State Board of Social Work Examiners 4201 Patterson Ave. Baltimore, MD 21215 *Harold Gordon, Administrator Richard Stanzione, Chairperson*
MASSACHUSETTS	Board of Registration of Social Workers 100 Cambridge St. Boston, MA 02202 *Dale L. Van Meter, Chairperson*
MICHIGAN	Board of Examiners of Social Workers P.O. Box 30018 Lansing, MI 48909 *Suzanne Jolicoeur, Administrator Daniel Klimaszewski, Chairperson*
MINNESOTA	Board of Social Work 2700 University Ave., West Suite 225 St. Paul, MN 55114 *Tom McSteen, Administrator William A. Anderson, Chairperson*
MISSISSIPPI	State Board of Health Social Work Advisory Council P.O. Box 1700 Jackson, MS 39215 *Kae Covington, Administrator Gwendolyn Prater, Chairperson*
MISSOURI	Advisory Committee for Licensed Clinical Social Workers Division of Professional Registration P.O. Box 85 3605 Missouri Blvd. Jefferson City, MO 65102 *Patricia Handly, Administrator Mark Klein, Chairperson*
MONTANA	Board of Social Work Examiners and Professional Counselors 111 N. Jackson, Arcade Bldg. Helena, MT 59620 *Mary Hainlin, Administrator Richard A. Simonton, Chairperson*
NEBRASKA	Board of Examiners in Social Work Bureau of Examining Boards P.O. Box 95007 Lincoln, NE 68509 *Kris Chiles, Administrator Sunny Andrews, Chairperson*
NEVADA	Board of Examiners of Social Workers 4600 Kietzke Lane, Suite A101 Reno, NV 89502 *Lisa Adams, Administrator Jane Lamb Nichols, Chairperson*

NEW HAMPSHIRE	Board of Examiners of Psychologists Box 457 105 Pleasant St. Concord, NH 03301 *Peggy Lynch, Administrator Deborah Dillingham Hartz, Chairperson*
NEW JERSEY	Board of Social Work Examiners P.O. Box 45033 Newark, NJ 07101 *Leslie Aronsen, Administrator*
NEW MEXICO	Board of Social Work Examiners P.O. Box 25101 Santa Fe, NM 87504 *Bonnie Jones, Administrator Jose Eli Fresquez, Chairperson*
NEW YORK	State Board for Social Work State Education Department Cultural Education Center Room 3041 Albany, NY 12230 *Norman Cohen, Administrator Winston Ross, Chairperson*
NORTH CAROLINA	Social Work Board P.O. Box 1043 Asheboro, NC 27204 *Carl Mumpower, Chairperson*
NORTH DAKOTA	Board of Social Work Examiners P.O. Box 6145 Bismarck, ND 58502 *Tom Tupa, Administrator Keith Fernsler, Chairperson*
OHIO	Counselor and Social Worker Board 77 S. High St., 16th Floor Columbus, OH 43266 *Beth Farnsworth, Administrator H. Breneman Blaine, Chairperson*
OKLAHOMA	State Board of Licensed Social Workers 4145 NW 61st Terrace Oklahoma City, OK 73112 *Mary Sue Counts, Administrator Judy Leaver, Chairperson*
OREGON	State Board of Clinical Social Workers 895 Summer St., NE Salem, OR 97310 *Elizabeth A. Buys, Administrator Carol Ormiston, Chairperson*
PENNSYLVANIA	State Board of Social Work Examiners P.O. Box 2649 Harrisburg, PA 17105 *Deborah Orwan, Administrator Reginald Bethel, Chairperson*
PUERTO RICO	Board of Examiners of Social Work Box 22039 San Juan, PR 00931 *Illia Ivette Amador, Administrator*

RHODE ISLAND Department of Human Services
Board of Registration of Social Workers
600 New London Ave.
Cranston, RI 02920
Christine Marshall, Administrator   Daniel Wheelan, Chairperson

SOUTH CAROLINA Board of Social Work Examiners
P.O. Box 11329
Columbia, SC 29211
Judy Weesner, Administrator   David Jeffreys, Chairperson

SOUTH DAKOTA Department of Commerce and Consumer Affairs
Board of Social Work Examiners
P.O. Box 654
Spearfish, SD 57783
Carol Tellinghuisen, Administrator   Walter Schaefer, Chairperson

TENNESSEE Board of Social Worker Certification and Licensing
Department of Health and Environment
283 Plus Park Blvd.
Nashville, TN 37247
Janet Floyd, Administrator   Margaret Kellogg, Chairperson

TEXAS State Board of Social Work Examiners
Texas Department of Human Services
1100 W. 49th St.
Austin, TX 78756
Michael Doughty, Administrator   Carolyn Starkey, Chairperson

UTAH Division of Occupational and Professional Licensing
160 East 300 South
Salt Lake City, UT 84145
David Fairhurst, Administrator   Pat Gamble-Hovey, Chairperson

VERMONT State of Vermont
Secretary of State's Office
109 State St.
Montpelier, VT 05609
Diane W. Lafaille, Administrator   Charles Gottlieb, Chairperson

VIRGINIA Virginia Board of Social Work
Department of Health Professions
6606 W. Broad St., 4th Floor
Richmond, VA 23230
Evelyn B. Brown, Administrator   Joseph Lynch, Chairperson

VIRGIN ISLANDS Board of Social Work Licensure
Department of Licensing and Consumer Affairs
Property and Procurement Bldg.
1 Subbase, 2nd Floor, Room 205
St. Thomas VI 00802
Marylyn A. Stapelton, Administrator   Jane Christiansen, Chairperson

WASHINGTON Social Work Certification Advisory Committee
Department of Health
Professional Licensing Service

1300 SE Quince St., EY-22
Olympia, WA 98504
Barbara Hayes, Administrator   Jan Ottenfeld, Chairperson

WEST VIRGINIA Board of Social Work Examiners
P.O. Box 5477
Charleston, WV 25311
Judith Williams, Administrator

WISCONSIN Department of Regulation and Licensing
1400 E. Washington Ave., Room 166
Madison, WI 53708
Alfred Hall, Administrator

WYOMING Mental Health Professions Licensing Board
2301 Central Ave.
Barrett Bldg., Room 347
Cheyenne, WY 82002
Veronica Skoranski, Administrator   Lela Ladd, Chairperson

Addresses are valid as of January 1995.

NASW Chapter Offices

ALABAMA
Governors Park II
2921 Marti Lane, Suite G
Montgomery, AL 36116

ALASKA
1727 Wickersham Dr.
Anchorage, AK 99507

ARIZONA
610 W. Broadway, Suite 218
Tempe, AZ 85281

ARKANSAS
1123 S. University, Suite 1010
Little Rock, AR 72204

CALIFORNIA
1016 23rd St.
Sacramento, CA 95816

CALIFORNIA—L.A. BRANCH OFFICE
6030 Wilshire Blvd., Suite 202
Los Angeles, CA 90036-3617

COLORADO
6000 E. Evans, Bldg. 1, Suite 121
Denver, CO 80222

CONNECTICUT
2139 Silas Deane Hwy., Suite 205
Rocky Hill, CT 06067

DELAWARE
3301 Green St.
Claymont, DE 19703

DISTRICT OF COLUMBIA
(Metropolitan Area)
2025 Eye St., NW, Suite 105
Washington, DC 20006

FLORIDA
345 South Magnolia Dr., Suite 14-B
Tallahassee, FL 32301

GEORGIA
300 W. Wievca Rd., Suite 220
Atlanta, GA 30342

HAWAII
245 N. Kukui St., Suite 206
Honolulu, HI 96817

IDAHO
200 N. Fourth St.
Boise, ID 83702

ILLINOIS
180 N. Michigan Ave., Suite 400
Chicago, IL 60601

INDIANA
1100 W. 42nd St., Suite 316
Indianapolis, IN 46208

INTERNATIONAL
CMR 419
APO, AE 09102

IOWA
4211 Grand Ave., Level 3
Des Moines, IA 50312

KANSAS
Jayhawk Towers
700 S.W. Jackson St., Suite 901
Topeka, KS 66603

KENTUCKY
230 W. Main
Frankfort, KY 40601

LOUISIANA
700 N. 10th St., Suite 200
Baton Rouge, LA 70802

MAINE
181 State St.
Augusta, ME 04332

MARYLAND
5710 Executive Dr., Suite 105
Baltimore, MD 21228

MASSACHUSETTS
14 Beacon St., Suite 409
Boston, MA 02108

MICHIGAN
230 N. Washington Sq., Suite 212
Lansing, MI 48933

MINNESOTA
480 Concordia Ave.
St. Paul, MN 55103

MISSISSIPPI
P.O. Box 4228
Jackson, MS 39216

MISSOURI
Parkade Center, Suite 138
601 Business Loop 70 West
Columbia, MO 65203

MONTANA
555 Fuller Avenue
Helena, MT 59601

NEBRASKA
P.O. Box 83732
Lincoln, NE 68501

NEVADA
1651 E. Flamingo Rd.
Las Vegas, NV 89119

NEW HAMPSHIRE
c/o New Hampshire
   Association for the Blind
25 Walker St.
Concord, NH 03301

NEW JERSEY
110 W. State St.
Trenton, NJ 08608

NEW MEXICO
1503 University Blvd., NE
Albuquerque, NM 87102

NEW YORK CITY
545 8th Ave., 6th Floor
New York, NY 10018

NEW YORK STATE
225 Lark St.
Albany, NY 12210

NORTH CAROLINA
P.O. Box 27582
Raleigh, NC 27611

NORTH DAKOTA
P.O. Box 1775
Bismarck, ND 58502

OHIO
42 E. Gay St., Suite 700
Columbus, OH 43215

OKLAHOMA
116 E. Sheridan, Suite 210
Oklahoma City, OK 73104

OREGON
7688 S.W. Capitol Hwy.
Portland, OR 97219

PENNSYLVANIA
1007 N. Front St., Suite 2 North
Harrisburg, PA 17102

PUERTO RICO
271 Ramon Ramos
Casellas St.
Urb. Roosevelt
Hato Rey, PR 00918

RHODE ISLAND
341A Broadway
Providence, RI 02909

SOUTH CAROLINA
P.O. Box 5008
Columbia, SC 29250

SOUTH DAKOTA
830 State Street
Spearfish, SD 57783

TENNESSEE
1720 W. End Ave., Suite 607
Nashville, TN 37204

TEXAS
810 W. 11th St.
Austin, TX 78701

UTAH
University of Utah
Graduate School of Social Work
Salt Lake City, UT 84112

VERMONT
P.O. Box 147
Woodstock, VT 05091

VIRGINIA
The Virginia Building
1 N. Fifth St., Suite 410
Richmond, VA 23219

VIRGIN ISLANDS
Havensight Secretarial Services
2 Buccaneer Mall
St. Thomas, VI 00802

WASHINGTON
2601 Elliott Ave., Suite 4175
Seattle, WA 98121

WEST VIRGINIA
1608 Virginia St., East
Charleston, WV 25311

WISCONSIN
14 Mifflin St., Suite 104
Madison, WI 53703

WYOMING
P.O. Box 701, A-2003
Cheyenne, WY 82003

Addresses are valid as of January 1995.

Cover and interior design by G. Quinn Information Design, Cabin John, MD
Text composed by Harlowe Typography, Inc., Cottage City, MD
Type set in Sabon and printed on Windsor
Printed and bound by Boyd Printing Company, Albany, NY

Order These Fine Reference Works from the NASW Press

The Social Work Dictionary, 3rd Edition, *by Robert L. Barker.* The new, updated edition surpasses its predecessor with 60 percent more content. It presents a concise, alphabetized listing of 5,000 social work definitions, organizations, concepts, values, and historical events. One of the most valuable tools ever written for the human services professional—from the beginning student to the seasoned expert. *ISBN: 0-87101-253-7. Item #2537.* **$34.95**

Social Work Almanac, 2nd Edition, *by Leon Ginsberg.* The latest facts and figures have been rigorously researched and compiled to update this practical compendium of statistical data related to social welfare. The second edition is over 61 percent larger, with 69 percent more tables and 73 percent more figures. *ISBN: 0-87101-248-0. Item #2480.* **$34.95**

Encyclopedia of Social Work, 19th Edition, *Richard L. Edwards, Editor-in-Chief.* Nearly 300 comprehensive entries—over 3,000 pages—inform the reader on virtually every aspect of social work with a depth and breadth that are unmatched in any other social work volume. Features include 142 biographies; 80 Reader's Guides; charts, graphs, and tables; free-standing cross-references; and key words for every entry. Your choice of casebound, softcover, and CD-ROM* formats. *Casebound (Item #2553)—* **$150.00,** *softbound (Item #2561)—* **$120.00,** *CD-ROM (Item D01)—* **$275.00.** Package discounts are also available. Call for information.

* CD-ROM disk includes *The Social Work Dictionary, 3rd Edition,* and *Social Work Almanac, 2nd Edition.*

(order form on reverse side)

ORDER FORM

Title	Item #	Price	Total
__ The Social Work Dictionary, 3rd Edition	Item 2537	$ 34.95	_____
__ Social Work Almanac, 2nd Edition	Item 2480	$ 34.95	_____
Encyclopedia of Social Work, 19th Edition			
__ Casebound version	Item 2553	$150.00	_____
__ Softcover version	Item 2561	$120.00	_____
__ CD-ROM version	Item D01	$275.00	_____
	add 10% postage and handling		_____
		Total	_____

☐ I've enclosed my check or money order for $_____.

☐ Please charge my   ☐ NASW Visa*   ☐ Other Visa   ☐ MasterCard

Credit Card No. _____ Exp. Date _____

Signature _____
*Use of this card generates funds in support of the social work profession.

Name _____

Address _____

City _____ State/Province _____

Country _____ Zip _____

Phone _____ NASW Member # (if applicable) _____
(Make checks payable to NASW Press. Prices are subject to change.)

NASW Press
P.O. Box 431
Annapolis JCT, MD 20701
USA

NASW PRESS

Credit card orders call
1-800-227-3590
(In Metro Wash., DC, call 301-317-8688)
Or fax your order to
301-206-7989

*SWDz 1/95